SOJOURNER TRUTH'S AMERICA

Sojourner Truth's America

MARGARET WASHINGTON

UNIVERSITY OF ILLINOIS PRESS
URBANA AND CHICAGO

Library of Congress Cataloging-in-Publication Data
Washington, Margaret.
Sojourner Truth's America / Margaret Washington.
p.   cm.
Includes bibliographical references and index.
ISBN 978-0-252-03419-0 (cloth : alk. paper)
1. Truth, Sojourner, d. 1883.
2. Truth, Sojourner, d. 1883—Political and social views.
3. Truth, Sojourner, d. 1883—Friends and associates.
4. African American abolitionists—Biography.
5. African American women—Biography.
6. Social reformers—United States—Biography.
7. Social problems—United States—History—19th century.
8. Progressivism (United States politics—History—19th century.
9. United States—Social conditions—19th century.
10. United States—Race relations—History—19th century.
I. Title.
E185.97.T8W37   2009
306.3'62092—dc22 [B]   2008041147

FOR MY CHILDREN

Celeste Beatrice Creel
Her charm strikes the sight;
her merit wins the soul.

AND

James Bryant Creel (Ras Kebo),
September 2, 1975 to June 18, 1994
Buffalo Soldier

Contents

Illustrations follow pages 8, 50, 128.

A WORD ON LANGUAGE

In this book, I use the term "race" as it was employed contemporarily. Race was a means of defining and marginalizing people on the basis of their phenotype, and was an almost totalizing concept in the historical period under study. Reform is a subtheme of this work; for emphasis, I have capitalized reforms that are most significant to the aims of this book. I sometimes refer to womanist consciousness. By that I mean that women knowingly, often collectively, focused on issues and embraced perspectives that were covertly and overtly political, communal, and gendered. I reject the term "fugitive," and use it only in quotations or as an allegation. I prefer to represent black people fleeing bondage as self-emancipated freedom seekers, rather than criminals. I reject the term "illiterate" when referring to Sojourner Truth; "illiterate" suggests "ignorant," as indeed some writers have labeled Sojourner because she could not read and write. I view literacy as but one form of learning, not the only means of knowledge, wisdom, or understanding.

ACKNOWLEDGMENTS

This book was such a long time in the making, I am sure some people believed that I, like the main character in Stanley Kubrick's movie *The Shining*, was sitting at my desk writing "All work and no play makes Jack a dull boy." Yet scholarly biographies take longer than other books, especially when a Southern historian takes on a Northern project. Nonetheless, other factors contributed to the long gestation. Besides unforeseen personal issues, the book, like Sojourner herself, had several migrations. I began the project with a generous contract with an eastern trade press. When the first draft was almost complete, we parted company for various reasons. I submitted the finished manuscript to Cornell University Press and undertook revisions on the basis of a very useful reader's report. When my collaborating editor resigned, that arrangement fell through, and *Sojourner* was again homeless. In searching out several other academic publishers, I decided to work with the University of Illinois Press. Its excellent African American list and its being in the land of Lincoln seemed appropriate for a book about Sojourner Truth, freedom, and equality. A very special thanks to Laurie Matheson at the University of Illinois Press for believing in the manuscript, working with me in trimming it down, and her assistance throughout the publication process. I warmly thank Paul Johnson, one of the Press's two readers, for his careful scrutiny of the manuscript, his perceptive comments, and especially for his understanding of what I wanted to convey about Sojourner Truth and her times.

The staffs at many libraries, historical societies, and other repositories made this book possible. In England: the Rylands Library at the University of Manchester, the Manchester Public Library, and the Rhodes House Library at Oxford. In Ottawa: the National Archives of Canada. In Pennsylvania: the Friends' Library at Swarthmore College, and the Historical Society of Pennsylvania. In New York State: the Cayuga County Historical Society in Auburn, the History Center in Ithaca, the Huguenot Society in New Paltz, the Old Senate House, the Public Library, and the Ulster County Hall of Records in Kingston, the Roslyn Public Library, the Staten Island Historical Society, the State Library in Albany, the Syracuse University Research Library, the Schaffer Library of Union College in Schenectady, and the University of Rochester Rush Rhees Research Library. In New York City: the City Municipal Archives and Records, Columbia University Special Collections, the New-York Historical Society, the New York Public Library, and the Surrogate's Court. In New Jersey: Special Collections at Rutgers University, and the Reformed Church Archives at New Brunswick Seminary. In Connecticut: the Beinecke Rare Book and Manuscript Library at Yale University, Special Collections at Wesleyan University, the Prudence Crandall Museum in Canterbury, the Harriet Beecher Stowe Center and the State Library in Hartford, and the Hall of Records and Public Library in Brooklyn. In Massachusetts: the American Antiquarian Society in Worcester, rare Books and Manuscripts at the Boston Public Library, the Massachusetts Historical Society in Boston, the Houghton Library at Harvard University, the Forbes Public Library in Northampton, the Historic Northampton Society, the Sophia Smith Collection at Smith College, the Martha's Vineyard Historical Society, the Nantucket Historical Association, and the Public Library in New Bedford. In Michigan: the Burton Collection at the Detroit Public Library, the Willard Public Library, and the Community Archives of Heritage Battle Creek, in Battle Creek, the Calhoun County Hall of Records in Marshall, the Clements Library, the Bentley Historical Library and the Michigan Historical Collection at the University of Michigan in Ann Arbor, and the State Library and Archives of Michigan in Lansing. In Ohio: Ashtabula Public Library and Ashtabula County Historical Society in Austinberg, the Historical Society in Jefferson, and Special Collections and Archives at Kent State University. My thanks to the Manuscript and Photo Divisions of the Library of Congress, to the Huntington Library in San Marino, California, and the Interlibrary Loan Department at California State University in Sacramento.

I owe a special acknowledgment to the Cornell University Libraries. The John M. Olin Graduate Library was my second home, and so was the Kroch Library, where the Division of Rare and Manuscripts Collections houses delicious nineteenth-century treasures. I thank all the wonderful folks there, and especially Laura Linke, who could find anything, and Patrina Jackson, whose expert knowledge of African American archival resources greatly enhanced my research. While I worked on this book, Sarah Thomas, now Bodley's librarian and director at Oxford University, was head of the Cornell Library System. I appreciate and thank her for her open-door accessibility, innovative vision, willingness to listen to my "information" frustrations, and many favors. Julie Copenhagen in Cornell's Interlibrary Loan Services warrants more gratitude than I can convey. Over the years, Julie and the staff located and borrowed books, obscure newspapers and journals, and privately published materials for me. In addition, their searches revealed a plethora of uncomputerized, little known, priceless nineteenth-century books and journals hidden away in Cornell's dusty library annex. I thank Elaine Westbrooks of the Metadata Services at Olin Library and Suzanne Schwartz in Microfilms. I thank Fiona Patrick for copyright information. Peter Hirtle was also helpful with copyright issues, and revealed intriguing ways to get historical information on Sojourner through the digital process. At Cornell's Africana Library, Eric Acree and his staff were a mainstay in my quest to locate old books and bibliographies about African Americans, and in identifying new search engines that daily make the history of black Americans more accessible. I am especially grateful to Robin Messing for his invaluable, generous assistance with the time-consuming job of working on images. I also thank Cornell Photography.

This was a costly project, which my pockets were not deep enough to cover fully in money or time. Cornell University's Society for the Humanities provided a crucial reduced-teaching fellowship as I began the project. A fellowship from the National Endowment for the Humanities permitted a year of full-time research. Wesleyan University, in Middletown, Connecticut, awarded me a one-year position as Senior Fellow at their Humanities Center. That opportunity allowed me to familiarize myself with Sojourner's western Massachusetts and southeastern Connecticut haunts, and introduced me to some great people. Two one-semester sabbaticals and a study leave from the Cornell History Department provided time to write. The Dean's Research Account and the Alexander Meigs Research Fund through the Cornell History Department helped bankroll a number of research trips. At California State University, in Sacramento, where I took my sabbatical, Henry Chambers, the chair of the History Department, graciously gave me office space, photocopying access, computer services, and—most important of all—library and parking privileges. J. Victor Koschman, chair of the History Department at Cornell, was most supportive and generous as I finished the final copy of the book. And Katie Kristof deserves my thanks for coordinating all those little pieces of paper called receipts, for her patience, and her mitigation.

I received warm hospitality during some of my research trips. In Ulster County, I had frequent access to Joan Voss Greenwood's beautiful historic summer home in the Catskills. I also thank Neil Greenwood, Joan's son and my former student at the University of California at Los Angeles. In Northampton, Daniel and Helen Horowitz generously offered their lovely guest quarters. In Battle Creek, my hosts were Dorothy and Michael Martich, two local historians who continue to keep Sojourner's memory alive. Finally, they will see the fruits of my research. In Ashtabula County, Ohio, my hosts were the descendants of Betsy Mix Cowles, a founder of the legendary Ashtabula Female Anti-Slavery Society. I thank Ginny Siefert, her mother, and sisters for sharing letters, pictures, and time in Betsy's lovely historic house, with its rockers (including a "mammy" rocker left by an underground passenger) and straight-back chairs where I am sure the Sojourner rested.

I first discussed my ideas about Sojourner Truth in the Black Women's Research Collective—a group of academics from diverse disciplines teaching at nearby campuses. Our monthly gatherings provided an important professional nurturing ambiance and a relaxing social and cultural venue, mitigating our sense of isolation in upstate New York. Founding members included Anne Adams, Josephine Allen, Rae Banks, Thelma Crivens, Carol Boyce Davies, N'Dri Assie Lumumba, Marcia Magnus, and Janis Mayes. I am grateful to my sisters for their comments, good cheer, and the crucial sense of community we provided one another.

A number of people offered advice on particular events, sent me historical information, wrote letters of recommendation, listened more times than I had a right to expect, and contributed in other ways. I thank Lisa Baskin, Aimee Lee and William Cheek, Michael J. Cuddy, Rena Down, Norman Dann, Lisa Farrar-Frazer, Ellen Fladger, Charles Gablehouse, Brad Griffin, Henry Hoff, Patricia Holland, Joyce Horan, Alice Kessler-Harris, Charles Joyner, Gerda Lerner, Brad Mitchell, Harryette Mullen, Willie F. Page, Richard Polenberg, Kathryn Kish Sklar, Claire Reed, David Vorhees, and Martijna Aarts Briggs for her translation skills. My special thanks to R. Laurence Moore for his friendship, encouraging collegiality, and confidence in this book. The late Erskine Peters, literary scholar and poet, was a special friend who early on offered significant suggestions about my research and interpretive approach, and asked of me thoughtful probing questions about Sojourner's place in history. He was a steadfast source of encouragement for what he called my "noble pursuit." I am honored by the dedication in his beautiful poem, written before his shocking midcareer death: "Homage to Battle Creek: Sojourner Truth."

I received editorial assistance from Jayne Dieckmann and Laura Van de Mark. A special thanks to Christopher DiCicco for editing the final full draft with an eagle eye and with a sense of humor that gave me permission to laugh at my own gaffes.

Friends and colleagues in the profession took time out of busy schedules to read chapters, make suggestions, and share information that, I hope, improved the book. I thank Mary Beth Norton for organizational suggestions about part I and for investigating sources about Sojourner's son Peter. Lisa Norling was also very helpful to my efforts to unravel Peter's fate. I thank Michael Gomez and John Thornton for their comments on my attempts in chapter 1 to connect Sojourner to her African heritage. Early in the project, C. Peter Ripley, editor of *The Black Abolitionist Papers,* provided me with newspaper notations that mentioned Sojourner Truth. Although by no means complete, these notations alerted me to Sojourner's impact in the press. Kerry Buckley and Christopher Clark were kind enough to share with me their unpublished manuscript of the James and Dolly Stetson letters from the Northampton Community. I have also benefited from Christopher's excellent knowledge of western Massachusetts and southeastern Connecticut, and from his insightful reading and comments on my Northampton chapters. I thank Mary White for reading my chapters on the 1850s and the Civil War. Mary also shared with me many tidbits from the Samuel J. May Diaries, which she indexed for the Kroch Library at Cornell. Mary was also a main source of information on the intricate local workings of the Underground Railroad in "North Star Country." Feminist scholars Victoria Sullivan, Rosalyn Terborg-Penn, and Judith Wellman read chapters and offered suggestions about my perspective on nineteenth-century women's issues. My thanks to Louis DeCaro Jr., biographer of John Brown, for reading an early chapter of the manuscript, for sharing his research, and for offering fascinating insights on how the prophetic Christianity and spirituality of "Old Brown" impacted pacifist Abolitionists such as Sojourner Truth. There is no way to sufficiently thank Sarah Elbert, biographer of Louisa May Alcott. Sarah read two full drafts of the entire manuscript, offered encouragement as well as criticism, and was never too busy to be a sounding board. Her acute perspicacity, sharp historical eye, and understanding of American reform are amazing. During many lively conversations and friendly disputes about race, class, gender, and culture in nineteenth-century America, I learned much from her wondrous range of knowledge. Whatever this book's shortcomings, they all are mine, perhaps because I am too inclined to go my own way.

My undergraduate history students—dedicated, enthusiastic, and smart—gave me another set of eyes. Liz Botein of Wesleyan University was a helpful assistant. At Cornell, my thanks to Francois Baldwin, Jung Kyu Koh, Nikki Kalbing, Maison Rippeteau, Rachel Teck, and Maisie Wright. Andrea Rakow, Caty Cavanaugh, and Un Mi Chong, worked for me through Cornell's student research program, in exchange for course credit. They were fine detectives. Andrea was very helpful in locating sources on Sojourner's Washington, D.C., years. Caty devoted one year to painstaking research in Ulster County and New York City sources, tenaciously following scores of productive and unproductive leads, and creating her own investigative methods. Un Mi and I worked together for two and a half years. She exhausted hundreds of leads in newspapers, indices, books, articles, and periodicals. She followed up on hundreds of names, scores of events, and expertly gauged what was important to Sojourner's story. With nothing to gain except goodwill, my former student Nick Hollander took time from the demands of law school to do research for me at the Library of Congress. All of these Cornellians will recognize some of their zealous research in this book.

The graduate students in history and Africana studies provided me with immeasurable inspiration. I thank them all for their wonderful intellectual curiosity, refreshing wit, insights, and commitment to the discipline. Our probing, often uncomfortable, sometimes unanswerable questions stirred inquiry, stimulated reflection, and invariably led us back to the archives. Our seminars and other gatherings helped me shape and refashion the biography's chapter topics, themes, and structure. Special thanks to Marie Johnson, Moon-Ho Jung, Winston Willis, Moon Hoo Yung, Michael Boston, Michelle Scott, Kate Haulman, Scott Brown, and David Nieves. My thanks to Suzie Lee, for researching the Long Island Quakers, and to Peter Shaw, for important research in the New Jersey archives so long ago that he has probably forgotten. I thank Peter also for *Z* and *Nation*. Leslie M. Alexander spent a summer as an undergraduate Mellon fellow from Stanford University acting as my research assistant when I edited Sojourner's *Narrative*. Besides combing the archives, Leslie and I had great fun doing hands-on field study. We trekked through the ruins of Gerrit Smith's burned-out Peterboro mansion, gathered pieces of pottery as memorabilia, and listened to local history aficionados. During Leslie's graduate study at Cornell, we continued our collaborations on exciting discoveries about nineteenth-century black life in the North. Leslie endured my hard-line pedagogical mentoring with characteristic grace, forbearance, and respect, while holding fast to her own perception of what a scholar-activist should be. She and most of the other students are now practicing historians and part of a generation that is admirably creating a new vision for the profession.

Friends and associates in the documentary film world gave me the honor and privilege of advising and consulting on historical documentaries, which kept me thinking about history creatively during some difficult personal times. Documentary film work also gave me an opportunity to view the historian's craft through another lens. I have enjoyed collaborating with talented, fascinating, dedicated people who create popular historical culture. Above all, this work took me out of the sometimes confining ivory tower, so that I could have a small part in bringing history to the public. I am particularly grateful to the folks at WGBH in Boston, which produces the highly acclaimed program *American Experience*. And my very warmest thanks to Llewellen Smith, David Grubin, Judy Creighton, Lisa Jones, and Orlando Bagwell.

In a significant nonprofessional category, I am beholden to a thoughtful group of people: Michelle Allard; Joan and David Brumberg; Judy and Nelson Burkhard; Mary Buckley; Sherm and the late Jan Cochran; Vanja Gacnik; Sarah, Kebbeh and Michael Gold; Robert L. Harris; Nancy Koschmann; Dominick

LaCapra; Walter and Sandra LaFeber; Lauris McKee; Judy and Daryl Rippeteau; the late Don Ohadike; Sandra Ohadike; the late Elsie Russell; the late Wanda Stambaugh; Heather Tallman; and Andrea Soto de Valdés, *mi hija chilena*. I could not ever express what I owe to Faye Dudden and Marshall Blake for their consistent kindness, understanding, and generosity.

Among close friends, a heartfelt thanks to Reverend Rebecca Dolch and my spiritual family at St. Paul's United Methodist Church. Rebecca is in a class by herself, whether dealing with things of the spirit, of the heart, or of the mind. For years, Thomas Schneider was a patient counselor, helping me to again embrace the beauty in life. Libby Ritch has remained my steadfast friend over many years, even after I dropped out of zydeco dancing. Josephine Allen and I have stood side by side on many very happy and very sad occasions. Through our years at Cornell, we have drawn strength from each other—juggling careers, children, home life, and activism and trying to remember what is really important. I thank many other unnamed friends who have been supportive, helpful, and giving.

My family has been my foundation. My late sister, Janie Louise Washington Gray, was my loyal champion for as long as I can remember. Since her untimely death, I miss her every day. I thank my brothers Clifford and Minor Jr. for their love and support. My brother John is a tower of strength, and was there with me when most needed. I will always remember the late Dr. George W. Creel as a doting grandfather, whether making chocolate chip cookies or teaching about hunting mushrooms. I thank him posthumously for helping me to create the humanitarian award at Sacramento State College, in honor of his grandson. My mother, the late Beatrice Washington, was the soul force in my life. She died when this project was merely an idea, but she would have identified with Sojourner Truth. My father, Minor Washington Sr., the venerable old Baptist deacon, was my Scripture teacher for this book. Whenever Sojourner mentioned a biblical passage unknown to me, he knew exactly where to find it and the cross-references. He helped me put Scripture in contexts and has influenced this book more than he knows. Watching him rise above life's challenges and vicissitudes and observing his bold dignity in the face of crisis has inspired me at my most difficult moments. His long life has afforded our extended family the continued blessings of his wisdom, counsel, and leadership. I must acknowledge my late nephew, Rawland M. Crawford Jr. His sudden death can only be seen as an inexplicable tragedy. He was in the prime of life and at the height of his much-needed, much-appreciated usefulness—father, math teacher, track coach, and counselor to at-risk children. I will miss his keen intellect, warmheartedness, quiet manner, and beautiful smile. He will be eternally loved and always remembered.

My children have been the sunshine of my life. I dedicate this book to them. Celeste (Tess) came of age hearing almost daily about Sojourner Truth.

She gave history reports on Sojourner and rode shotgun with me in Ulster County and New York City. At an early age, Celeste bore tragedy with amazing grace and fortitude, believing that love should have the last word. My greatest joy has been watching Celeste grow into an intelligent, "whole-souled" young woman of beauty and unique style and very much in touch with her mental and spiritual self.

My son James (Jimmy), my peaceful warrior, who was suddenly stricken with brain cancer at seventeen, endured great suffering for months before his spirit was released. He never complained or showed a trace of self-pity. Far wiser than his chronological years, his articulate precociousness was perhaps a harbinger of what we could not know. He possessed a quiet spirituality, an intuitive sense of principle, and concern for the human condition. And at fifteen, he was able to see something of the world by spending a year in Ecuador through the wonderful Rotary International Scholarship program. He loved unity, and he brought us all together. No tribute is worthy of him. His spirit pervades all I do, and his strength and philosophical courage sustain me. He will always be my hero.

ABBREVIATIONS

AAS	American Antiquarian Society, Worcester, Massachusetts.
AIPFP	Amy and Isaac Post Family Papers, Rush Rees Library, University of Rochester.
AMA	American Missionary Association Archives, The Amistad Research Center, Tulane University, New Orleans.
ASB	*Anti-Slavery Bugle.*
BAP	*The Black Abolitionist Papers.* Edited by C. Peter Ripley. 5 vols. Chapel Hill, N.C.: 1985–92.
BPL	Boston Public Library.
CA	*Colored American.*
CAJZH	*Christian Advocate and Journal and Zion's Herald.*
CDI	*Chicago Daily Inter-Ocean.*
CSL	Connecticut State Library, Hartford, Connecticut.
DPL	Burton Collection, Detroit Public Library.
DRMCCU	Division of Rare and Manuscript Collections, Cornell University.
Ecc.Rec.	*Ecclesiastical Records of the State of New York.* 6 vols. Albany, 1901.
FP	Papers of Charles G. Finney, Oberlin College Archives.
HSNBH	*Historical Society of Newburgh Bay and the Highlands,* Newburgh, New York.
IN	Gilbert Vale, *Fanaticism; It's Source and Influence, Illustrated by the Simple Narrative of Isabella, in the Case of Matthias, Mr. and Mrs. Folger, Mr. Pierson, Mr. Mills, Catherine, Isabella, &c. &c.* 2 vols. New York, 1835.
JNH	*Journal of Negro History.*

KSU	Kent State University Libraries and Media Services, Department of Special Collections and Archives.
MM	*Methodist Magazine and Quarterly Review.*
MHC	Michigan Historical Collection, Bentley Historical Library, University of Michigan, Ann Arbor.
NAEI	Northampton Association of Education and Industry Records, American Antiquarian Society, Worcester, Massachusetts.
NASS	*National Anti-Slavery Standard.*
NGSQ	*National Genealogical Society Quarterly.*
NST	*Narrative of Sojourner Truth, A Bondswoman of Olden Time.* Originally dictated to Olive Gilbert, Boston, 1850. Edited by Margaret Washington. New York, 1993.
NSTBL	*Narrative of Sojourner Truth.* Compiled by Olive Gilbert and Frances W. Titus. With a History of Her Labors and Correspondence Drawn from Her "Book of Life." Also a Memorial Chapter, Giving the Particulars of Her Last Illness and Death. Battle Creek, Mich., 1884.
NYFQ	*New York Folklore Quarterly.*
NYGBR	*New York Genealogical and Biographical Record.*
NYCMAR	New York City Municipal Archives and Records.
NYT	*New York Tribune.*
PF	*Pennsylvania Freeman.*
REAS	Raymond English Anti-Slavery Collection, Rylands Library, University of Manchester, England.
SSC	Sophia Smith Collection, Smith College, Northampton, Massachusetts.
STC	Sojourner Truth Collection, Manuscript Division, Library of Congress.

SOJOURNER TRUTH'S AMERICA

Introduction

On June 1, 1843, the Sojourner boarded the Brooklyn Ferry in Lower Manhattan and headed for Long Island. A thrifty woman with a savings account, she carried only a few coins to "pay Caesar." Once "vain in her clothes," she carried only a few belongings in a knapsack. After disembarking on Long Island and walking along the sandy road, she met a Quaker woman. "I can see her now," Sojourner Truth told a Chicago newspaper reporter, as she recalled that conversation from long ago.

The Sojourner asked the woman for a drink of water.

"What is thy name?" said she.
Said I, "Sojourner."
"Where does thee get such a name as that?"
Said I, "the Lord has given it to me."
"Thee gave it to thyself, didn't thee?" said she, "and not the Lord. Has that been thy name long?"
Said I "No."
"What was thy name?"

"Belle."

"Belle what?"

"Whatever my master's name was."

"Well, thee says thy name is Sojourner?"

"Yes."

"Sojourner what?"

Sojourner confessed that she hadn't thought of that, whereupon the Quaker woman "picked that name to pieces" so much that it looked different, and "didn't seem to be such a name after all." Crestfallen, and hastily excusing herself, Sojourner "plodded on over the sandy road and was very hot and miserable." In her frustration she cried, "Oh God, give me a name with a handle to it." After all, since God's voice had led her out of the city into an unknown region, she now needed God to give her a last name. At that moment of despair, it came to her "as true as God is true, Sojourner *Truth.*" She "leapt for joy" and thanked God for the name. "Thou art my master, and Thy name is Truth, and Truth shall be my abiding name till I die." Finally, after five masters and five children, and over forty years on the earth, Sojourner recalled, "I was liberated."[1]

Thus began the sojourn of perhaps the most remarkable black woman in the nineteenth century. Sojourner Truth waged a forty-year battle as a champion of the downtrodden, and as a spokeswoman for social justice. Convinced that she was an anointed messenger, she followed God's "voice" wherever it led. That voice guided her to take up religious radicalism, Abolition, temperance, health reform, Spiritualism, women's rights, anti-Sabbatarianism, and other causes. Sojourner Truth traveled through twenty-one states and the District of Columbia. She attributed her verbal power to divine dispensation; few people who knew or heard Sojourner Truth questioned her calling. Her riveting speeches, narrations, pronouncements, and labors stirred many listeners. "No one can have the least idea of the powerful woman by any written or any description of her," Sojourner's Detroit friend Eliza Leggett wrote. "Her presence was so powerful, her magnetism so great, her personal appearance so majestic—her eye keen." Sojourner's Abolitionist compatriot Parker Pillsbury noted that like the New Testament apostles, a few honorable women upheld the antislavery banner. Their Acts "could register great numbers of such, who went everywhere preaching the anti-slavery word." In recounting these women's bold heroism, and recognizing them by name, Pillsbury added, "but the most wondrous of all was the Ethiopian . . . Sojourner Truth."[2]

"There was both power and sweetness in that great, warm soul and that vigorous frame," the minister Samuel Rogers recalled. Her "withering sarcasm" was matched with a gentle and kind nature. Before and after the Civil War, Sojourner Truth was part of the Lyceum speakers' movement, which included vice presidents, senators, poets, clergy, scientists, suffragists, and foreign dignitaries. The American public at that time was "never more in earnest" or more "intellectual in their demands" for able speakers. Sojourner Truth, Lyceum organizer F. P. Powell said, "carried the people by storm." Of all the "strong characters I met on the platform," he observed, "there were none stronger than Sojourner Truth," whose "eloquence was only equaled by her wit." She was extemporaneous, tense, vigorous, and "a great smoker." She would swing out one long arm, walking back and forth and gesticulating as she "struck out the straightforward logic of intuitive nature."[3]

Sojourner Truth was exceptional by any standards, but her achievements are so notable because she overcame so much: crucibles of race, gender, poverty, lack of education, and enslavement. She bridged cultural, intellectual, and religious differences between herself and progressive, middle-class whites. Middle-class African American activists could not dismiss the bold perspicuity, insights, biblical knowledge, commitment, and courage of this dark-skinned former slave. Sojourner Truth's rural roots created solidarity with common folk of both races who were interested in change. Her homespun humor, parables from country life and Scripture, even her labor skills endeared her to humble people throughout the North and to many freed people from the South. Possessing "a heart of love" and "a tongue of fire," she always stood on principle, thereby provoking notoriety as well as commendation. She was the subject of correspondences and was quoted in newspapers, invoked at the speaker's podium, and praised and denounced from the pulpit. On the public stage, enveloped in a sense of divine dispensation, Sojourner Truth merged two cultural antecedents: the gift of African oral expression and the pragmatism of rural nineteenth-century America.

Truth's friends, across the Mid-Atlantic, New England, the West, and the Upper South, warmly anticipated her visits and her public appearances and worried about her lameness, the result of long, cold rides and walks. "Give my love to Isaac Post," she said, speaking of her Rochester Spiritualist "trance" companion. "Tell him I have a warm corner here. . . . And I want him when he sits where Sojourner used to sit, to think of her." Tell him, she said, that Sojourner "sleeps between two fires." Hosts saved the best bed, the most comfortable chair near the fire, and the head of the dinner table for "the Sojourner." They sat rapt with attention when she recounted her travels and experiences. Children in the households climbed into her lap, read to her, wrote for her, ran errands; and she in return told them stories, nursed them during illnesses, and offered advice. She was a fountain of wisdom and humor, even when ill and in old age.[4]

The exploits of Sojourner Truth, Parker Pillsbury said, could fill an entire library.[5] She was a quintessential representative of antebellum progressive America, speaking out against injustice wherever she found it. As an Abolitionist, she confronted racist, proslavery Northern mobs and raised the level of consciousness among lethargic blacks and whites. Calling herself a "woman's rights," the name given to the woman's movement, Sojourner championed gender equality. She spoke against alcoholism as a cause of degeneracy and domestic abuse. She chastised the churches for their cold, status quo religiosity that claimed to love God but did not love the world. Although a pacifist, Truth welcomed the Civil War as a necessary spiritual and national purge. Afterward, she worked on behalf of freed people around Washington, D.C. She supported universal suffrage, but settled for black men obtaining the vote before women. As postwar conditions worsened, Sojourner urged her people to speak with their feet and leave the South. In the course of her activism, Sojourner Truth met three American presidents—Abraham Lincoln, Andrew Johnson, and Ulysses S. Grant.

Her words come to us mostly from newspaper accounts, letters written by others, and some diary entries, as well as dictated narratives and her autobiographical *Book of Life*. Yet since so few women took the public stage, the records of her movements encompass a fairly large body of literature. The press favored this colorful black woman with the odd accent. Questions of historical accuracy and interpretation regarding Sojourner Truth do surface. This has prodded me to make careful assessments of the reliability of sources, to compare evidence, and in some cases to make judgments about the usefulness of certain material. Sojourner's words were transcribed differently by different writers and for different readers—especially, for example, her famous "A'rn't I a Woman?" speech. While historians excavate and investigate to find the most trustworthy accounts, ultimately, Sojourner's deeds remain the central "truths" of her life and influence.

This book attempts to unravel Sojourner Truth's world within the broader panorama of African American slavery and the nation's most significant reform era. The book offers a contemporary perspective on nineteenth-century American progressivism that places a black woman at the center of those stormy times. Truth and her associates were unyielding women and men, hoping to change the world through adherence to a beloved community, faith in primitive Christianity, and faith in American republicanism. As advocates of immediate emancipation, they maintained that human bondage was not only brutal and inhumane but that it thwarted individual free will, was *the* national sin, and mocked the concept of American democracy. Struggling on these premises, radical Abolitionists also embraced other reforms. Although radical reformers came from all walks of life, most were largely unknown people inhabiting small towns, hamlets, villages, and farms of America. They worked secretly underground, attended conventions, read antislavery newspapers, hosted traveling lecturers, and judged politicians on the stump by their commitment to black freedom. This book tells their story vicariously, through the lens of Sojourner Truth and other well-known women and men of their number.

Recovering Sojourner Truth's voice requires reconstructing her material circumstances, her cultural geography, and her friendships and linking her words to her deeds. The quest for Sojourner's voice has also inspired me to frame the narrative around the concepts she considered most important. This book is a spiritual biography, because nonsectarian faith gave meaning and cohesion to Sojourner's vision and to American reform, and sustained an unshakable movement that gained the force and magnitude to foment a revolution. A sacred ethos guided Sojourner's secular life and molded her crusades. Her cultural background was African, Dutch, and American. How that heritage coalesced within her consciousness helps explain her commitment, prophetic sense, and appeal.

A womanist perspective also pervades this book. Sojourner Truth was nurtured on female authority, but within patriarchal, male-centered African, Dutch, and American traditions. This broadened her concepts of womanhood to include political, economic, spiritual, and secular influence. Even Sojourner's unusual physical prowess outside a woman's sphere added to her confidence that "no man could head me." Her sense of community also framed her life and activism. Her concepts of community went beyond her nuclear and extended family to embrace utopian collective spiritual living. Slavery, the problem of the age, obliterated families and communities. Because her search for community arose from a longing fed by the ravages of bondage, Sojourner's hue and cry on behalf of her people was an extension of her communitarian impulse.

This book's three parts correspond to the three significant phases of Truth's life, involving slavery, race, and reform. Part I begins before her birth, offering an analysis of her heritage and the Hudson Valley milieu into which she was born as Isabella Hardenbergh. Patriarchal Dutch slavery, the female household, and its religious ambiance shaped her formative years. Part II centers on Isabella's physical and spiritual maturation, which included self-emancipation, tests of faith, and triumphant confrontations with the legal system in the Hudson Valley and New York City. Despite many pitfalls, her move to the city reinforced her faith in her summons by the Spirit of Pentecost, and in her gift of prophecy. Under subpoena from God as a messenger to the people, she joined a host of women and men under the same charge. In part III, the heart of the book, the narrative follows the footsteps of Sojourner Truth and her closest associates, analyzing and interpreting their activism. The times were a complexity of ebbs and flows. In addition to internal splits in movements and new causes that were emerging, there was societal ostracism, sectionalism, violence, and a war that produced victory over slavery but left much undone. After that war, Sojourner Truth continued making her mark among the freed people and for women's suffrage. By then, her lived experience was already competing with myth. Yet even this mythmaking illuminates the magnitude of Sojourner Truth's place in national history, and reveals the extent to which she transcends the era.

Sojourner Truth's experiences identify her as a leading radical reformer. For many years, the public called these activists fanatics. In the words of nineteenth-century radical Frances Wright, it was the spirit of the age to be a little fanatical.

PART I

Bell Hardenbergh and Slavery Times in the Hudson River Valley

Thus saith the Lord: A voice was heard in Ra'mah, lamentation, and bitter weeping; Ra'hel weeping for her children refused to be comforted for her children, because they were not.

—JER. 31:15

Sojourner Truth in Detroit. Sojourner's Detroit Quaker friends promoted a refined domestic image. Burton Collection, Detroit Pubic Library.

Laura Haviland, Sojourner's Michigan coworker, with slave irons. Haviland Papers, Michigan Historical Collection, University of Michigan, Ann Arbor.

SOJOURNER TRUTH.

A Picture taken in the days of her Physical Strength.

Sojourner Truth in 1850. Author's personal collection.

I Sell the Shadow to Support the Substance.

SOJOURNER TRUTH.

Sojourner Truth, seated—wearing black dress and shawl: "I Sell the Shadow . . ." Chicago History Museum.

Sojourner Truth in
patriotic red, white,
and blue, with copies of
documents in her lap.
Community Archives of
Heritage Battle Creek.

Diana Corbin,
Sojourner's eldest
daughter. Community
Archives of Heritage
Battle Creek.

Frances Titus,
Sojourner's Battle Creek
biographer and friend.
Community Archives of
Heritage Battle Creek.

Last photo taken of
Sojourner Truth, March
1883. Photographs
and Prints Division,
Schomburg Center for
Research and Black
Culture, New York
Public Library.

F. C. Courter, *Abraham Lincoln and Sojourner Truth*. Painted from their photographs (Diana Corbin modeled for Sojourner's hand). Burton Collection, Detroit Public Library.

Mary Ann Shadd, activist, editor, friend of Sojourner Truth. National Library and Archives of Canada, Ottawa.

Gilbert Haven, Methodist bishop, radical Abolitionist, Sojourner's friend and Northampton neighbor. Special Collections Library, Drew University.

Sojourner Truth wearing the attire from her Indiana Civil War campaign. Sojourner signed the back of this image. Chicago History Museum.

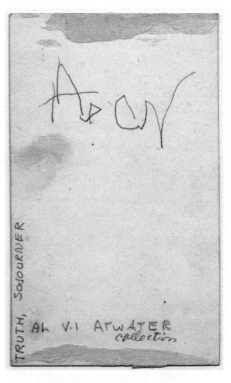

Sojourner's first known signature (around 1863), written on the back of her carte de visite. Chicago History Museum.

I have been sent from God to your head to preach
to the people. — BEATRIZ KIMPA VITA

As Oliver Cromwell put it, the Dutch preferred
"gain to godliness." — SECRETARY THURLOE

CHAPTER I

African and Dutch Religious Heritage

I

"I am African," Sojourner Truth told an audience. "You can see that plain enough." Traveling the antislavery circuit, facing detractors as well as supporters, Sojourner acknowledged ties to the Motherland even as some whites declared her race to be descended from "monkeys and baboons." She was not born in Africa. However, her maternal grandparents were first-generation "salt water" people who experienced the brutal Middle Passage, "seasoning" into a new culture, and another world. Truth's mother-in-law always spoke broken English. On the Abolitionist platform, Sojourner sometimes shared with her audience stories of Africa told by her husband's mother.[1]

When Sojourner was born, in 1797, slavery flourished among the rural Dutch who owned her family. Her mother named her Isabella, and she was nicknamed Bell. Isabella's unusually tall father, James, was nicknamed "Bomefree," merging the Dutch word for tree (*bome*) with the English word "free." Africans from the inland Gold Coast (present-day Ghana) were very tall, and this region was the second major European trading station. The tallest Gold Coast Africans were mainly of esteemed, militaristic Denkyira or Ashanti ethnicity. Sojourner's father was known as an honest, dependable, and hardworking bondman who possessed the proud spirit that Europeans insisted Gold Coast Africans (called Coromanti) exhibited in great measure. They were "intrepid to the last degree," one slaveholder said. "No man," he insisted, "deserved a Coromanti unless he treated him like a brother."[2] Isabella, nearly six feet tall as an adult, inherited her father's impressive physical stature, strength, and height. Bomefree also reportedly was half Mohawk Indian. Ohio Abolitionists first mentioned this in 1851, and the story persisted from then on. In 1880, Eliza Seaman Leggett of Detroit wrote about Sojourner Truth in a letter to Walt Whitman, her former Long Island neighbor. According to Leggett, Sojourner "greatly admired" Whitman's *Leaves of Grass,* and her "father's mother was a squaw."[3]

Sojourner's mother, Elizabeth, was "Betsy" to white adults and "Mau-mau Bet" to black and white children in the household. Elizabeth's heritage was most likely that of West Central Africa—the region of Kongo, north of Angola. The Dutch purchased Africans from that area from the Portuguese, who controlled commerce with Kongolese traders. In the seventeenth century, Africans serving the Dutch in America (New Netherlands) learned Indian languages, and became traders and interpreters. After the British conquest (in 1664) changed New Netherlands to New York and New Jersey, Kongo peoples still dominated the North American enslaved population. By the mid-eighteenth century, civil wars had transformed a once strong Kongo monarchy into groups of politically autonomous, rural-based city-states. Around the same time, New York experienced a surge in economic growth, demand for labor, and carrying trade directly from Africa. African elites and traders were the middle men in the African domestic trade. Merchant caravans, "fairs," and systems of regional markets and coastal entrepôts filled Portuguese traders' coffers with ethnic people generically called BaKongo, whose main language group was KiKongo. Sojourner's grandparents fell victim at this time to the slave trade.[4]

Colonial New York contained the North's largest enslaved population; it grew by 70 percent between 1750 and 1770. By then, merchants imported captives directly from Africa to discourage entry of "refuse and sickly Negroes" and because colonial vessels coming from Africa paid lower duties. American "sloops"—small, swift, seaworthy vessels—conducted a triangular trade. They transported Hudson Valley foodstuffs to Caribbean and Carolina markets, then carried furs and lumber to England, and then returned to America with Holland duck, housewares, rum, sugar, and Africans. Some New York City families traded with Africa directly and had mercantile collaboration with Ulster County elites. Traders maneuvered their sloops up the Hudson, trading black captives for Ulster's renowned agricultural products, destined for urban markets or West Indian plantations. Isabella's owners were local merchants, gentlemen farmers, and customers of these traders.[5]

The work Africans performed in America—the gendered divisions of labor and the structures of household economy—was not completely unfamiliar. African village life centered on agriculture and herding. Men and boys performed the heavy arboricultural tasks, tended herds, built homes, hunted, and fished. Men also conducted long-distance commerce and monopolized artisan skills. Women and girls tended to household animals, did domestic chores, and oversaw the land's agrarian gifts. Women had more independence on the coastal littoral. Some produced luxury items, including salt derived from seawater. Others dove for seashells, the most valuable of which (*nzimbu*) were thin, brilliantly black, and the currency mainstay of the slave trade. Both sexes frequented local markets to sell goods and exchange regional specialties. Dutch New Yorkers wanted women for domestic labor, and children they could train; a large proportion of women figured into the British trade, and West Central Africa exported the largest number of youth. "For this market they must be young," a New York merchant cautioned; "the younger the better if not quite children."[6]

Sojourner Truth's African-born grandparents provided a connection to the spirituality and cultural provenance of the Motherland, most likely BaKongo, and a crude exposure to Catholicism. Throughout Kongo, the Portuguese set up chapels, where Africans catechized their own people. However, only whites administered the sacraments, baptizing captives with a pinch of salt and bestowing Christian names before shipment. Dutch Calvinists, who hated anything Catholic, would not use the name Isabella. Yet Isabella was the name of a female saint revered in Kongo, and the name of the militant sister of the Kongo king Pedro IV. Africans generally named their children after ancestors, grandparents, and even living parents. Thus, Isabella may have been the name of Sojourner Truth's grandmother. It is also intriguing that the naming practices of Sojourner's mother, Elizabeth, differed from less numerous West African ethnic groups in New York, who recycled Akan names such as Cuffee, Kofi, Mingo, and Quashee. Both naming practices reveal autonomous ethnic socialization, but only Isabella's suggests a West Central African heritage and Catholic influence.[7]

Young Isabella may not have known her African grandparents. But they made the Middle Passage like countless millions, in a state of bone-chilling emotional shock that was mitigated only by reforging new cultural bonds. Isabella certainly heard stories of the homeland from her mother and later from her mother-in-law. Memory and oral history were major links with the past for nonliterate folk, facilitating adjustment to new environments, community formation, identity grounding, and construction of new lifestyles. Geography separated Africans from their Motherland, but the routes to American slavery during the Atlantic trade era operated as "a series of cultural highways" that connected the enslaved in America to transatlantic societies of Africa.[8]

Isabella's verbal gifts and remarkable recall were reminiscent of an African griot (an oral historian and storyteller) and symbolic of her leadership. She also embraced spirituality long before embracing Protestantism; even after her Christian conversion, she claimed clairvoyance and a "second sense." African Americans called it being "born with a caul"—the fetal membrane or a special body mark or imaginary veil representing supernatural insight. Historians' recorded evidence of African female leadership enriches our understanding of the non-American contextual heritage that may have impacted Isabella. Her African homeland produced priestesses, prophetesses, queens, and female warriors. Some cultures were matrilineal and celebrated earth mothers; in others, women engaged in civic and commercial enterprise. In Kongo, prior to Catholicism, female authority was recognized through powerful matrilineal descent groups and cults of social formation called *kanda*. They represented a central source of collective female influence, symbolized by controlling land use, labor, and production distribution. *Kanda* political authority included selecting chiefs and cochiefs.[9]

Even after the Portuguese introduced Catholicism, women in Kongo were *ngangas*—diviners and priestesses with special access to God, called Nzambi. As Other World mediums and channels to supernatural knowledge, *ngangas* dispensed positive sacred medicine (called *nkisi*) and had the power to invoke harm, or *kindoki*. After Catholic priests outlawed as heretics all *ngangas* except themselves, women continued to assert their power through revitalization movements. Beatriz Kimpa Vita, a revered *nganga,* challenged the Catholic Church and Kongo elites by opposing the slave trade, leading a massive reunification movement, and embedding Kongo cosmology within Catholicism. Beatriz's influence was so unassailable that even after she was burned at the stake twice, to deter followers from retrieving her bones for amulets, her movement continued.[10]

Beliefs, memories, stories, and legends that traveled with Africans on the Middle Passage were repeated and reinvented in Dutch New York and elsewhere. These chronicles endowed the people's spirits and enriched their survival impulses. Such remembrances would have included narratives about powerful women. Given Sojourner Truth's African heritage, the sacred authority and strength of the Motherland's women should not be separated from the substance of Sojourner's character and social justice mission.

II

"I was bred and born," Sojourner Truth said, "if I was born at all, in the State of New York, among the Low Dutch people." The large stone house in Ulster County where she began life still exists, as does the little hamlet of Hurley, with its quaint, bucolic architecture from another time. Hurley is nestled in the valley of the Esopus, where rushing local waterways wind into the majestic Hudson River. "There were no railroads, or steamboats, or telegraphs when I was born," she added. "There were only horses, wagons, oxen and sloops."[11]

Ulster County, a rural backwater 50 miles north of New York City, could not claim the ethnic diversity of the latter, where even in the colonial era some eighteen languages were reportedly spoken. However, Palatine Germans, French Huguenots, and Walloons settled in Ulster early on and melted into the numerically dominant Dutch via language, religion, and marriage. Nor did the British conquest alter the mid–Hudson Valley's Dutchness, although some place names changed from Dutch to English. Only after the American Revolution did an influx of New England settlers and war veterans produce a more Anglo-American character.[12]

People of color added greatly to Ulster County's pluralism. Towns called Wawarsing, Shawangunk, and Shandaken hark back to the Algonquin and Iroquois confederations. As for blacks, however, only an occasional etching, painting, or literary piece reminds us of their former presence as a labor force instrumental in cultivating and milling grain, loading sloops, tending livestock, nursing children, and keeping homes. Moreover, their numbers increased with settlement and cultivation. During the seventeenth-century Esopus Indian wars, some enslaved Africans fought and died with Dutch owners, others were taken prisoner, and still more fled to Indian villages. In Ulster, one colonial traveler observed, every other house was a barn, and "every other white a Negro."[13] Little labor was done among the Dutch without the strong backs and nimble hands of Africans.

Isabella's birthplace was unmatched in haunting geophysical beauty. The distant, towering Catskill and Shawangunk mountains and the imposing Hudson River created magnificent landscapes. Ancient rivulets and creeks ("kills" in Dutch) and year-round moisture fed the rich soil and created bountiful forests. Unpretentious, stately stone houses, small austere churches, farms, windmills, great barns, and silo granaries dotted the lush countryside, while livestock grazed on meadows and rolling hills. Ulster was especially remarkable in late summer and autumn, when tree foliage was brilliant and its fields ripe with wheat, corn, oats, and barley. It was this region's natural beauty that inspired the Hudson Valley school of painters and deeply impressed Washington Irving, man of letters and author of *Rip Van Winkle* and *The Legend of Sleepy Hollow*, who called Ulster an unforgettable land of "wonder and romance."[14]

In Isabella's day, blacks and whites lived and worked in close proximity. Dutch women did "genteel" work alongside enslaved African Dutch women engaged in arduous labor, while white farmers often worked in the fields with black men. "Even the poorest family" in Ulster County "has one or two negroes or negresses," French observer La Rochefoucauld-Liancourt noted. And both races generally resided in the white household. Washington Irving also noted a sense of independence among some enslaved African Dutch men. Traveling by boat up the Hudson in 1800, Irving observed the black Dutch-speaking crew, who doubled as boatmen and farmhands. Before obeying any of the white captain's orders, they discussed them among themselves, and then decided to heed an older enslaved man's more experienced advice. He had sailed with the young captain's father. Armed with superior knowledge, the savvy old salt "usually had his own way and did as he pleased." Another traveler told of coming to a Dutch farm and asking for directions. Neither the farmer nor his wife knew the way, but the Boer's "slave," who did business for his owner and traveled to see compatriots, gave perfect directions.[15]

Isabella's owners were Hardenberghs—a name once almost as common in Ulster County as Jones became in Middle America. The Hardenberghs were Knickerbockers—a sobriquet, made famous by Washington Irving, for affluent Dutch New Yorkers tied to Old World customs. The first Hardenbergh, Holland-born Gerrit, was appointed commander of Albany (in 1690) during Governor Jacob Leister's ill-fated struggle with the English. Gerrit's son, Johannes, escaped English wrath by moving to Kingston. At the time of Isabella's birth, Johannes "Hans" Hardenbergh Jr. was the family patriarch, the third of his line born in America. His grandfather, Johannes Hardenbergh, who first settled in Kingston, married Catherine Rutsen, whose father, Jacob Rutsen, was a wealthy Holland-born merchant-proprietor. Hardenbergh I inherited his father-in-law's business enterprises and a country estate called Roosendall (today the town of Rosendale). In addition, he joined noted land baron Robert Livingston and others in purchasing 2 million acres of choice Hudson Valley lands, including the Catskill Mountains, from Esopus Indian leaders for 200 pounds. Hardenbergh I, derisively called Lord of the Catskills, controlled perhaps the largest land grant in New York. When he died, in 1748, the patentees divided the hotly contested "Great Hardenbergh Patent," and his heir, Johannes II, retained the lion's share. The family's most prosperous years began with the ascendancy of this imposing patriarch, who reportedly spoke several Native American languages and was a welcome guest in Indian settlements. Even after splitting his lands with his adult sons, Johannes II was still the third highest taxpayer in Hurley, which was where the family lived but was only one of their domains. When conflict with England arose, Johannes II quickly pledged allegiance to America. As a seventy-year-old colonel, he served in the Provincial Congress and the New York General Assembly and hosted the Continental Army's commander-in-chief, George Washington.[16]

The colonial Knickerbockers' lifestyle resembled that of slaveholding Southerners. Roosendall, the Rutsen-Hardenbergh ancestral home, was a large stone structure without exterior ostentation; inside, it was a showplace and "among the great houses in its part of the world." It had "numerous rooms, fireplaces, and handsome paneled woodwork and recesses for beds enclosed by paneled doors." The estate also had slave quarters and a jail for "delinquent slaves." Most Hardenbergh children and grandchildren were born and baptized at Roosendall. All colonial Hardenberghs owned enslaved people, and the 1750 Census of Slaves lists Johannes II among the largest slaveholders in the county.[17]

As noted, Isabella's religious heritage, in addition to her African roots, was also Dutch Reformed. The Hardenberghs were Dutch Pietists—Calvinists who practiced evangelical religion. Oliver Cromwell's assertion that the Dutch preferred gain to godliness was not exactly true of the Hardenberghs, who esteemed both pursuits equally. They helped found the first Ulster County church in Kingston and actively supported Dutch Reformed revitalization movements. In the middle colonies, Theodorus Jacobus Frelinghuysen, a Westphalia-born, classically trained Hardenbergh kinsman, began the spiritual revival that led to the Great Awakening. Only the dearth of Dutch *dominies* (ministers) prompted Holland's conservative supervising ecclesiastical board (the Classis of Amsterdam) to appoint the insubordinate young Frelinghuysen. In 1720, he was simultaneously the pastor of three New Jersey churches in different Raritan Valley counties—covering a 250-square-mile radius of mostly wild, uncultivated lands. He was the first to bring the "New Light" to the Dutch churches in America, preaching that faith came from an inner identification and oneness with God, the direct influence of the Spirit, the efficacy of prayer, and the striving for perfection. He preached that conversion and regeneration, not baptism, determined salvation, and these required heartfelt reformation in daily life. He promoted evangelistic and missionary outreach, and purification of the Mother Church through personal faith and strict morality; he favored experience with the Holy Ghost over rigid orthodoxy and doctrinal knowledge.[18]

Isabella's owners embraced Frelinghuysen's Pietism, and this would impact her spiritual ethos. This passionate *dominie* was the forerunner and colleague of British Anglican (Methodist) George Whitefield, Northampton Puritan (Congregationalist) Jonathan Edwards, and Pennsylvania's fiery young Presbyterian Gilbert Tennant. These New Light Awakening divines shared preaching grounds despite the language difference. Their insistence that "the largest portion of the faithful have been poor and of little account in the world" attracted thousands of rural whites and blacks (if their owners allowed it). But affluent orthodox Dutch men complained to the governing body of Holland's Reformed Church about Frelinghuysen's doctrines, charismatic leadership, loud "howling" prayers, extemporaneous outdoor preaching, and inviting of English-speaking ministers into his pulpits. The elders also locked Frelinghuysen out of his churches, but the multitudes followed him into barns. As one historian noted, Frelinghuysen attracted "an economically deprived, embittered underclass." Thus the wealthy

Hardenberghs complicated notions of Pietism from a solely class perspective while creating interesting spiritual links for Isabella as someone born into such a household.[19]

If blacks such as Isabella's African-born grandparents attended a massive open-air religious meeting, they would have understood little of the New Light messages. Yet the Awakenings lasted long past Frelinghuysen's untimely death in 1748, and Isabella's American-born mother, Elizabeth, identified with the Pietists' simple faith, expressive spirituality, and teachings of universal salvation. The Dutch versions of the Awakenings did not emphasize spiritual egalitarianism for blacks, but the enslaved certainly took that meaning, just as nonprivileged whites took a message of social leveling. Thus, Isabella was born into a household where ecstatic religion had been practiced for three generations. Elizabeth taught her daughter that God was the ultimate authority figure—a notion of patriarchal Protestantism that also connected to African Catholic and BaKongo concepts of hierarchy. Yet Elizabeth's teachings also included traditional African cosmology—God was a kind being, and the sun, moon, and stars were part of the godhead.[20]

Isabella's first owner, whom she called "the Old Colonel" and whites called Hans Junior, listed himself on tax records as a farmer and miller, and reportedly produced the best "super fine" wheat flour in the county. However, he was no ordinary Boer "farmer." He controlled and managed his father's massive enterprises—lands, sawmills, and flour mills—and before the Revolution was a prosperous Indian trader. During the Revolution, he was a colonel under General Washington and commanded the levees during the unsuccessful battle for New York City. Hans Junior's younger brother, Jacob Rutsen Hardenbergh, became rural New York and New Jersey's most notable *dominie*. He married Dina Van Bergh, the widow of Frelinghuysen's son. This Hardenbergh couple frequently entertained the Washingtons when they were headquartered in New Jersey, and the friendship continued after the war. Jacob was the architect of the post-Revolution Reformed Dutch Church movement that achieved an amicable separation from Amsterdam's supervision and put the rural American Dutch church on the road to a more liberal polity. Jacob and his father also spearheaded the founding of Rutgers University in New Jersey, and Jacob became its first president. He raised the only two surviving Frelinghuysen heirs, thereby heading a dynamic American political family. Dina Frelinghuysen Hardenbergh, as discussed in the next chapter, was a leading religious zealot among her kinswomen who provided Isabella and her mother's access to Pietism.[21] Thus, Isabella was born into a white family with extensive secular and religious power.

Isabella's birth among rural Dutch Pietists connected her with a Protestant religious legacy, particularly through female culture, as I will show. However, Isabella's mother passed on a lasting spiritual heritage to her daughter through a "hidden church," fusing African and Catholic beliefs with Protestantism. "There is a God," Elizabeth counseled. "He lives in the sky, and when you are beaten or cruelly treated, you must ask help of him and he will always hear you." Elizabeth's God was more the African Nzambi than the distant, possessive Protestant Jehovah. And unlike the Catholic God, Elizabeth's God required no go-between; Nzambi was as close as the ancestors. Elizabeth spoke personally to God, through direct, divine dialogue via prayer and meditation.[22] While neither Jehovah nor Nzambi condemned human hierarchy, Elizabeth taught Isabella that no one was beyond the purview of *her* God, who protected the lowly as well as the highborn, and whose wrath, or *kindoki,* rained down on all classes. Self-worth and dignity in the eyes of God—whether called Jehovah or Nzambi—humanized enslaved people.

"When a Negro-woman's child attained the age of three years, the first new year's day after, it was solemnly presented to a son or daughter, or other young relative of the same family, who was of the same sex with the child so presented.
— ANNE GRANT, *MEMOIRS OF AN AMERICAN LADY*

How sweet a thing is Liberty. — "PINKSTER ODE"

CHAPTER 2

"Home Is Like a Grave"

DOMESTICITY, SPIRITUALITY, AND PATRIARCHY

I

"The Low Dutch," Sojourner Truth recalled, "were very close and igno-rant, and so, naturally, to this day, I can neither read nor write." Nor did she go to church. "I knew God," she added, "but I didn't know Jesus Christ."[1] Nurtured in this narrow, Dutch-speaking insular world, it is a wonder that Sojourner Truth developed into such a spiritual woman and a gifted orator in the English language. How was Bell, as a youngster, exposed to religion? Why did the very religious Dutch, unlike other denominations, deny church affiliation to their black domestics?

The linchpin connecting Dutch Pietism with black exclusion from Dutch Reformed churches was baptism. Like Catholics, Dutch Calvinists rigorously practiced infant baptism, but unlike Catholics, did not baptize the enslaved. Among the Dutch, baptism represented civic, social, and legal privileges, includ-ing the rights to inherit, marry, be buried in a Christian cemetery, and to bear witness. In Ulster County, whites recorded the baptismal date more often than the birth date of an infant.[2] Given the poignant spiritual meanings of water in West African cultures and the Catholic Christian heritage, African Dutch women probably initially chafed at this exclusion. Denial of baptism—offering a child to the Creator for blessing, protection, and a calling—reveals how thoroughly the Dutch racialized religion and society.

Reformation clerics dodged the issue of Christianizing nonwhites by giving that responsibility to each head of household. But the 1618 Council of Dordt decreed that all baptized persons "should enjoy equal right of liberty with all other Christians." Colonial laws and clerical edicts overrode that provision, stipulating that "heathens" (Africans and Indians) could not strike, assault, curse, swear, or "speak impudently to any [white] Christian." Observer Anne Grant recalled that Dutch slaveholders "sought their code of morality in the Bible," using Abraham as a hierarchical model. But unlike the biblical patriarch, the colonial Dutch provided no religious education. After the Revolution, when Jacob Rutsen Hardenbergh took the lead in severing formal religious ties with Holland, a 1788 statement proclaimed that baptized "slaves or black people" should "be admitted to equal privileges with all other [church] members of the same standing." Although official Dutch American policy had shifted by Isabella's birth, another generation passed before even a few African Dutch joined the rural Hardenbergh Patent churches.[3]

The contours of Dutch female authority, rather than formal instruction, helped shape Bell's early sacred and secular orientation. Dutch women were custodians of culture, had economic position, and exercised spiritual influence. This status for affluent rural Dutch women prevailed long after English policy eroded women's position legally, urban Dutch women lost their customary economic opportunities, and urban Dutch men adopted English primogeniture. Rural Dutch women continued to make contracts, hold property, and conduct business. Hardenbergh men willed property to their wives, made them executors, and provided liberally for their daughters. The first Johannes Hardenbergh bequeathed most of his extensive property to his wife, who divided it among their heirs. Johannes II disinherited his wayward son Geradus and willed the son's inheritance to Geradus's wife. Jacob Rutsen Hardenbergh bequeathed his property to his wife Dina, "so long as she remained a widow." Rural Dutch women who were capable only of signing documents with an X had the business acumen and authority to make binding contracts. Their lives were generally more free than their English and urban Dutch counterparts. Rural middle-class Dutch women smoked pipes, drank ale, kept taverns, and commonly married while pregnant. When married, women still asserted an identity separate from their husbands' and used their maiden names.[4]

Dutch women in America were often outspoken, independent, and thrifty, had a sense of entitlement, and were efficient in business. Sojourner Truth later demonstrated this confidence by bringing lawsuits, buying and selling property, holding bank accounts, handling financial negotiations of her publications, and willing property—all by signing with her X. Nonetheless, Dutch women adhered to the patriarchy: they did not generally seek religious institutional positions, preach, or challenge clerical leadership. Yet, while women appeared to have internalized the Pauline doctrine to "keep silent" in the churches, their economic significance, control of ethnic identity, and numerical majority all suggest a feminization of rural Dutch social structure and religion. Bell observed a strong Dutch female culture in which women asserted more spiritual authority than anywhere else in America. She herself clung to old ways in matters of language, economy, and mystical religion; and she transposed this female assertiveness into civic and social prerogatives.[5]

Dutch women, as the souls of the family and the church, facilitated rudimentary home religious observance. Sojourner Truth's characterization of Dutch households as "close" suggests a number of meanings, all related to conservative routines. Pietist gentlewomen avoided balls, card playing, or other frivolities in favor of church activities, kinship events, and socioreligious commemorations. Their world of labor consisted of refined domestic work—supervising meals, quilting, embroidering, spinning, and weaving—performed side by side with enslaved women. Hardenbergh homes at Roosendall, Raritan, Kingston, and Hurley rivaled the churches as spiritual centers and sacred circles. Dutch women kept the old ways alive through childbirth practices, baptisms, child rearing, weddings, funerals, feast days, and holidays, all tied to a sense of the sacred. Most elite women who were literate in Dutch mainly read the Bible and Calvinist tracts. Bell's first owner bequeathed his "Old Dutch Bible" to his daughter Cornelia, illustrating women's importance as keepers of the spiritual flame and family name. Only Dutch was spoken in homes, and many rural gentlewomen never learned English. Those who did, Anne Grant noted, spoke it "imperfectly and few were taught writing." Grant further notes that women's restricted education "precluded elegance; yet, though there was no polish, there was no vulgarity."[6]

Dina Hardenbergh, always addressed as Jufvrouw (Madam), was the most exemplary white female spiritual teacher and a ubiquitous presence in Ulster County. Dina's bourgeois European birth set her apart; her cosmopolitan education in the classics and Calvinist doctrine surpassed her husband Jacob's. She was wealthy, schooled by renowned Pietists in Holland, and favored by her iron-willed father-in-law, Johannes II. Dina's rustic, unpolished teenaged suitor reportedly could "hardly read" when they married. Although Jacob later studied at Kings College (later Columbia University), Jufvrouw Hardenbergh was reportedly the human agent behind his intellectual growth and rise to clerical prominence and a college presidency. After his untimely death, *dominies* confidentially consulted Dina about church polity. Her behind-the-scenes influence epitomized the subtle power of women in the Dutch church.[7]

The cornerstone of Dutch Pietist home life was family worship, largely a female sphere. Elite women greatly indulged their children, but also taught strict obedience to God through holiday observance, scriptural recitation, Bible stories, family prayers, and psalm singing. This environment comprised young Bell and her mother's spiritual and temporal training. For it was in Dutch women's interests to impart elementary biblical knowledge to the enslaved domestics influencing and tending white children. Stories and recitations were most likely guides for Elizabeth and Bell's religious instruction, while prayers and singing were special forms of spiritual manifestation. Singing grounded the spirit and prepared the heart for sacred messages. Swedish traveler Peter Kalm observed the Dutch cantor singing David's psalms rendered into verse. Pietists also supplemented psalm singing with "spiritual songs" as expressions of personal feelings. Dutch women sat at spinning wheels, weaving and singing along with their enslaved women, who were long accustomed to combining monotonous work with creative impulses and spiritual impulses. The entreating prayers that made Bell a popular preacher in New York City originated in the Dutch cultural ambiance. Later, as Sojourner Truth, she always began lectures with singing to awaken her audience's higher emotions. Her rich, powerful voice, though nurtured among the Methodists, began with the African and Dutch penchant for song.[8]

Bell's mother apparently attended Dutch services on occasion, if only to serve her owners. In the eighteenth and early nineteenth centuries, "it was not uncommon" to see, "on a Sunday, from fifty to seventy-five colored servants or slaves, at the church door, awaiting the arrival of master or mistress." Carrying "two or more foot-stoves in hand, filled with live hickory coals taken from Dutch fire-places," the domestics supplied heat for slaveholders, who sat, segregated by gender, on the main floor of the cold stone churches. Bond people might remain, sitting in the galleries, adding more coals when the hickory cinders cooled. Tenants and other poor white communicants also squeezed into the tiny galleries. With heat traveling upward, the lower stratum of society listened to sermons in relative comfort. Little changed after the Revolution, but during Bell's youth, Ulster County's Shawangunk church added a separate entrance and section on the second floor. There is historical controversy about whether the gallery housed poor whites or enslaved people. Yet the fact that Johannes Hardenbergh Jr. founded both the Shawangunk and Bloomingdale churches suggests that Elizabeth attended. By the early nineteenth century, a few black baptisms occurred in some rural Dutch churches. Yet since neither black nor white children attended worship, we can believe that as she stated, young Bell never went to church.[9]

Whether in church service or home teaching, Elizabeth heard value-laden instruction. Both the heavenly and earthly father figures required obedience on pain of displeasure, disinheritance, and, if one was enslaved, punishment or banishment. Pietists tempered conservative doctrine with mysticism, and Bell's mother taught her about "praying from the spirit" and the powers of "special illumination." Pietism's stress on spontaneity, an inner voice, and spiritual personality helped Elizabeth create a sacred space for herself and Bell.[10]

The Dutch practice of reproductive exploitation had a profoundly debilitating effect on enslaved families. It involved using black mothers as nurses and giving weaned enslaved toddlers to white progeny—as gifts on special occasions, as childhood companions, when a couple set up independent housekeeping, or as bequests in wills. Bell's siblings were parceled out to Hardenbergh offspring by these methods. Wet-nursing was also an important aspect of reproductive exploitation. Sojourner Truth insisted that she nursed white babies to the exclusion of her own. Enslaved African Dutch Sylvia DuBois said of her young master: "I remember that while we were small children . . . my mother . . . used to tell me that we both nursed the same breast, alternately, the same day." Most Dutch American women married between the ages of nineteen and twenty-two, gave birth every one to one and a half years, and bore children past age forty. The high fertility rate among prominent rural Dutch American women and the longer spacing between pregnancies for enslaved women suggests that black women were wet nurses, as they maintained. Production of the hormone prolactin interferes with ovulation, and the record suggests that Elizabeth gave birth every two and a half to three years. The last white birth in the Hardenbergh household occurred on March 30, 1798, while Elizabeth was nursing Bell, born sometime in 1797. African Dutch women's extended periods of childbearing and nursing white as well as black infants created a relentless cycle that domestic labor made even more draining.[11] The contradiction of Dutch women's piety and reverence for their families with their simultaneous disregard for the same connection among the African Dutch was certainly not lost on Elizabeth.

Bell was born into a crowded household—a "stem family" arrangement, in which one married son lived with the parents and inherited the homestead. Hans Jr.'s stone house had five front and two back bedrooms, or "dormers," and a separate "shed" dormer in back, probably for hired white help. Upstairs rooms included separate space for spinning, weaving, and sewing. The house had a number of large fireplaces, including "one cellar fireplace in the slave quarters." This was where Bell, her family, and other slaves lived and where her mother did the cooking. They were more fortunate than many enslaved African Dutch who inhabited musty attics, odd corners near kitchen fireplaces, narrow garrets, even barns, gardens, and cow pastures. Black living arrangements were indiscriminate rather than family-based; biracial overcrowding and close living conditions prompted one traveler to label Dutch households "over stacked hives." Rural elite households resembled the Roman patriarchal concept of *familia* more than those of the biblical Abraham. As a metaphor for church and state, and the bedrock of civil society, the family was a center for womb-like, private nurturing and collectivity. "The home is like a grave wherein we always dwell," a Dutch writer observed. But the enslaved African Dutch "kitchen family," occupying cellars designed for storage and cooking "but not for living," had more reason to think of the household as "like a grave." It was hardly a "home."[12]

Elizabeth's and Bell's domestic chores included washing, sewing, knitting, starching, ironing, cooking, milking, brewing, poultry tending, gardening, and making cheese, butter, soap, and candles. Bell's youth was no deterrent, and she soon joined Elizabeth as a laborer. Enslaved girls everywhere began laboring as young as four or five. With three white generations in the household, Bell and Elizabeth worked constantly, and under continuous white female surveillance, had little opportunity for regular interaction with other black women, and endured a cultural isolation rarely experienced in the American South. And in the South, Elizabeth would have been valued and perhaps rewarded for her fertility, but among the Dutch, reproduction interfered with labor output and exacerbated overcrowding. The Hardenberghs apparently anticipated that Bell and her younger brother Peter would replace their parents as the "kitchen family." Hence Bell remained with Elizabeth longer than her older children, who were removed one by one.[13]

II

Enslaved parents could not protect their children against white physical or psychological abuse, but parents tried to help children negotiate bondage. And while often only a thin line existed between a cruel master and a more tolerant one, there was a difference. Despite the ways in which master and slave were natural enemies, Bell's parents taught her that a bond person's honesty and good character might be a form of defense. Bomefree had more skills and geographical mobility than most enslaved men, yet he remained "faithful." Likewise, Elizabeth had endured the removal of many children but instructed Bell to be submissive. But other African Dutch preferred to challenge rather than accommodate slavery in the face of broken promises, family separation, physical mistreatment, or wanton disregard of customary expectations. Laws passed to regulate the black community reflect not only white fear and paranoia but also black resistance.

Proximity to Canada, liaisons with Indians, and sometimes white collusion with blacks provided tempting liberation prospects. The prosecution of the Ulster County bond people who were implicated in the New York Negro Plot of 1741 prompted laws forbidding any travel 40 miles beyond Albany. In 1775, African

Dutch rebels in Ulster plotted to burn Kingston and unite with Indians. Enlisting blacks from Hurley, Marbletown, and Kingston and amassing substantial powder and shot, the rebels were thwarted only because a slaveholder overheard their plan. Also that year, Johannes Hardenbergh II presided over a freeholders' meeting that excluded "small tenant farmers, the poor, Negroes and Indians" because the British had promised freedom to enslaved blacks and patroon lands to all loyal landless Hudson Valley whites.[14]

It is noteworthy that Bell's parents, especially her father, remained loyal to their owners during the turbulent revolutionary times. Perhaps they took solace in the measure of status associated with the prestigious Hardenberghs rather than "dull, torpid Hollanders." Bomefree and Johannes Jr.'s relationship may illustrate what traveler and slavery apologist Anne Grant called the "strongest attachment" and loyalty, when an enslaved child was "given" to a white one; "some piece of money or a pair of shoes" also enhanced youthful black fealty. The connection matured through working, eating, sleeping, drinking, hunting, and sometimes fighting side by side. During the battle for New York City, the patriot officers' favorite gathering place was Black Sam's, named for the free West Indian whose daughter had reportedly saved General Washington from eating poisonous peas. Enslaved men served in Ulster County regiments as drivers, orderlies, and soldiers; they saw combat in New York City, Fort Ticonderoga, and Canada. Men such as Bomefree, though not promised liberty, remained with white owners nevertheless. Others, finding the contradictions between white freedom and black bondage too obvious, fled to the British, preferring to trust the devil they did not know.[15]

The American Revolution weakened but did not destroy Northern slavery. At the time of Bell's birth, no provision existed for New York manumission, and Dutch patriots remained vehemently proslavery. Nonetheless, New York Quakers spearheaded debate on slavery before independence, and later, republican ideology and black military service, resistance, and political agitation helped force the issue. By 1785, the Quaker-dominated New York Manumission Society and the Northern industrial economic vision inspired antislavery discussions in many venues. Private manumissions also increased in urban regions, but the issue made little significant progress in the state legislature. Reporting from Ulster County, traveler La Rochefoucaut-Liancourld insisted that slavery was "as strictly maintained in the state of New York as in that of Virginia."[16]

Nonetheless, New York finally passed its first emancipation law in 1799, amid heavy Dutch opposition. It freed no one immediately, but emancipated all males at age twenty-eight and females at twenty-five if born after July 4, 1799.[17] This law did not affect Isabella.

Also in 1799, Johannes Hardenbergh Jr. died. "Faithful Bomefree" and Maumau Bet were integral to the Hardenbergh household, and to patriarchal Dutch concepts of duty, lifestyle, and entitlement. While the Old Colonel displayed a distorted affection for the couple, as though they were favorite pets, he had not emancipated them or their two remaining children. It took about three years to liquidate his property, call in his debts, and divide his estate. He left the milling enterprise to his grandson John E. Hardenbergh, and bequeathed to his son Charles a sizeable amount of property, the homestead, and the slaves. Bell's earliest recollection, from around age five, was "the removal of her master Charles Ardinburgh, into his new house, which he had built for a hotel." Since Charles had inherited land on the turnpike road leading from Esopus, near Delaware County, this was a logical place for his inn. Here Bell's life centered on tavern culture: a world of conviviality, debate, loose conversation, and free-flowing information. Controlled by licensing and excise taxes, public houses were as important to colonial and early national life and landscape as churches. Taverns were rooming houses, assembly halls, eating establishments, and transportation centers. Women and men were both customers and proprietors. The sale of alcohol and the presence of women dictated that the landlords at the better inns be sober, well-respected, and even prominent in the church, which was often nearby.[18]

At the Hardenbergh hotel, Bell's family was at the hub of rural Dutch culture. Few establishments reflected the sentiments, life, and activities of the community like taverns and inns, through the exchange of gossip, goods, and news and the mingling of patroons with freeholders, artisans, and tenants. During the volatile days of debate over the church separation, conservatives opposing the American ordination of Jacob Rutsen Hardenbergh faced his father's fisticuffs at a Dutch tavern. In 1783, George Washington bid his officers an emotional farewell at Black Sam's. When encroaching English cultural mores threatened the rural Dutch, they gathered at taverns to debate the issues of using English in Dutch churches, sending children to English-speaking schools, and establishing a theology college in New Brunswick, New Jersey. Court business conducted at taverns sometimes became a backdrop for real estate, political, and religious controversy, which could degenerate into brawls, and in one case ended in a murder—over the Hardenbergh Patent.[19]

Inns and taverns affected enslaved people directly. The first slave market in New York City was erected in 1709 at a tavern called the Meal Market. In 1750, an advertisement reported the arrival of "a parcel of likely negroes to be sold at public vendue to-morrow at ten o-clock at Merchants Coffee House"—where, ironically, the New York Manumission Society would be formed thirty-five years later. Large crowds of paying and drinking customers negotiated private or sheriff sales, individual trades, and larger slave auctions. Newly arrived sloops often auctioned their wares—Africans, horses, sheep, and other "livestock"—directly from the taverns. Ignoring propriety, decorum, and ceremony, men enjoying their alcohol and tobacco inspected, fondled, and humiliated Africans of both sexes. In addition, the subject of black emancipation generated spirited arguments in public houses.[20]

Elizabeth and Bell's work at Hardenbergh's public house was decidedly more unpleasant than general domestic labor. Individual attention to each guest room included the distasteful tasks of cleaning and emptying privies, changing bedding, and doing laundry for complete strangers. At inns, mealtime labors were the most time consuming. The Hudson Valley had abundant local produce, and African women used spices, seasonings, broths, and sweetening to transform bland Dutch fare into delectable meals. Breakfast, prepared by sunrise, consisted of corn mush with milk, sometimes molasses, and the previous day's leftovers. While guests ate, Elizabeth and Bell completed other chores and baked breads. The simple midday meal of milk and bread gave Elizabeth and Bell time to prepare a substantial supper—generally "stampot," a famous dish of meat and vegetables creatively cooked together and well seasoned. Sometimes fish, potatoes, and fruit served with flat cakes baked in oven ashes might constitute the last daily meal. Various pastries and yeast breads served at teatime included doughnut-like honey cakes, spicy gingerbreads, buttery pound cakes, various cutout cookies, fruit tarts, and pies. Before making these dishes, Elizabeth and Bell laboriously dried flour and washed the salt (used as a preservative) out of the butter. Setting out the tablewares and cleaning them after mealtimes added to the daily chores. Bell's dark cellar home also housed the white family's meat, dairy, preserved supplies, and at least one oven. Preparing the simplest food began before dawn, though little natural light reached the cellar even on bright sunny days. An old African Dutch custom involved taking a rooster to the cellar at night, and its "lusty crow" alerted the inhabitants when dawn was streaking the eastern sky.[21]

In her formative years, Bell learned a range of domestic and hospitality skills under the careful supervision of her mother. Like many enslaved girls, she did a full day's work before age ten. Although Dutch enslavement seemingly retarded and thwarted Bell's sense of the larger world, tavern life provided a thorough household education, while exposure to the sociopolitical interactions planted seeds of inquisitiveness, skepticism, and reasoning.

III

Most important of all, Bell was given early parental nurturing and a sense of responsibility and kinship. The family cultivated a plot of land, raising foodstuffs to embellish their own diet, flax for clothing, and tobacco to consume and sell. Bell's family was better off than most enslaved African Dutch and many poor whites. Although black men outnumbered women and slavery kept most couples apart, Bomefree and Mau-mau Bet lived monogamously. Bell recalled her parents' many stories of blacks suffering physical cruelty, but they reported no personal instances of it. The Hardenberghs' kitchen family was popular with local whites and blacks; at the tavern they were also probably the eyes and ears of the geographically dispersed African Dutch. Although enslaved blacks everywhere depended on a grapevine, it was even more essential in the rural North. Talk of legal emancipation, individual manumissions, escapes, deaths of owners, sales, transfers, and brutalities overheard at the Hardenbergh hotel certainly informed the larger African Dutch community.[22]

African Dutch parents sometimes kept track of their offspring, despite crushing separations at tender ages. Obedient women such as Elizabeth might even have a say in who obtained their children. Elizabeth's instructive guidance of Bell supports Anne Grant's observations: African Dutch women not only practiced "dexterity, diligence, and obedience," they "piqued themselves on teaching their children to be excellent servants." Bondage might "be sweetened by making themselves particularly useful, and excelling in their deportment." Bell later reunited with two of her siblings. Later, Sojourner Truth also spoke of her grandparents, mother-in-law, and an extended family in Ulster County. When she was in New York City her son Peter wrote from sea inquiring about his "cousins."[23]

The situation of Bell's absent siblings differed from what it would have been in the South, where enslaved relatives usually disappeared forever. Nonetheless, an estimated one-half of New York's enslaved population were denied family cohabitation. Hence Bell's parents seized all opportunities to retain family identity, memory, and connection. Kitchen slaves on hand for large white family gatherings got to see their own scattered kin and briefly reunite. Holidays were especially joyful occasions, even for ascetic Dutch Pietists. Sanct Herr Nikolaas Avond (Santa Claus Eve) and Sanct Herr Nikolaas Dag (Santa Claus Day) became national celebrations in America. Both reveal the significance of race in the patriarchal *familia*. Both are based on the story of a generous canonized Spanish Catholic: the bishop of Myra, protector of children and patron of fertility, family, and parenthood. Sanct Herr Nikolaas Dag, celebrated on December 6 (the day the bishop died), spread throughout Europe despite the Reformation. As the patron saint of New Amsterdam, the bishop symbolized trade and the importance of sailors. In anticipation of his visit, children were on their best behavior. On the appointed night, they put out food for the kindly old saint and filled shoes with hay for his horse. Dressed in his red bishop's robes, he placed goodies in the shoes of obedient children. But his black servant—Pedro Negro to Catholics and Zwart Piet (Black Pete) in Dutch lore—was terrifying, complete with black face, horns, a red tongue, fiery eyes, and a clanking chain. He threw bad children into a bag and dragged them off to hell. Men actually dressed up as this character and appeared at Dutch homes. This frightening little black devil instilled in white children a loathing and foreboding of blackness, supposedly synonymous with evil.[24] By the time Christmas became a holiday in the North, reportedly because of Washington Irving stories, American folklore had transformed Black Pete into a harmless little white gnome or "elf."

African Dutch children—including Bell and her brother Peter—certainly viewed Sanct Her Nikolaas Dag with the same warmth and eagerness as white children. Yet Sojourner Truth recalled that psychological confusion and racial shame about blackness was baggage from slavery. Parental love lessened her sense of unworthiness and degradation, but children outside of kin-related households or communal settings had trouble counterbalancing this negativity about blackness. For the African Dutch, unlike the enslaved people of the American South, December 25 was little known, and "New Year" was the dreaded time when black children were sold or given away as presents.[25]

New York blacks considered Pinkster (Whitsuntide to the English and Pentecost to Catholics) their favorite holiday, and combined African hierarchical and authoritarian customs with European traditions. In Africa, agricultural harvest festivals gave thanks to God for first fruits and paid homage to secular leadership. Pageantry lasting for at least three days, and sometimes up to a week, celebrated gifts from the earth, a popular king, past military triumphs, rites of passage for youth, sealing bonds of courtship, and marriage. On Pentecost Sunday in seventeenth-century Kongo, newly baptized Africans, to the horror of the priest, "fell a playing upon several instruments, a Dancing and a Shouting so Loud that they might be heard half a league off." In America, the occurrence of Pinkster in the spring coincided with the Kongo-Christian St. James's (or Alfonso's) Day and with harvest time. For Catholics and Dutch Reformed whites, Pinkster recognized the Holy Spirit's descent on Christ's apostles. Hollanders secularized Pinkster before their American settlement, and the African Dutch further refashioned it in continuity with old customs, cultures, and circumstances of enslavement. Pinkster briefly reunited families and provided opportunities for courting, ceremonial dancing, competition in oral abilities, sports, and games. It reminded blacks that despite geographical fragmentation and separate living arrangements, they were a people sharing a common oppression, displacement, and heritage.[26]

During long New York winters, pious white families exchanged church worship for domestic religious observance corresponding to the ecclesiastical year (all holy days, Sundays, days of fasting and penance). The highlights of such worship centered on Christ, particularly the weeks of his anticipatory suffering, redemptive death, and resurrection, which was commemorated on the Dutch Paas (Easter). Paas bears intricately on the significance of Pinkster. Occurring fifty days later, it represents new beginnings. By then, the weather was temperate and the Dutch churches were full again. Commemorating the coming of the Holy Ghost after Resurrection provided the ultimate acknowledgment of the power of salvation for those with the grace of God. This annual event was also testament of spiritual unity—believers speaking in different languages, filled with the power of the Holy Ghost, understood each other. [27]

Pinkster was also another rudimentary element of Christianity that Elizabeth could pass on to Bell. Catholics baptized Africans with salt instead of water, and Pietists maintained that water baptism was damnation if it occurred without repentance and inward transformation; but through the celebration of Pinkster, blacks could experience regeneration and salvation without sacraments or church membership. Pinkster emphasized individual possession by the Holy Spirit, telepathic revelation, and works of grace open to all. The key to Christian salvation was the infusion of the Holy Spirit (Pneuma Hagion), the fundamental purifying element of conversion viewed as breath, wind, or air in movement. Pneuma was the soul giving life to the body, yet was not of the body. It was the spiritual "Comforter" Jesus sent, probably to complete the concept of the Trinity (Father, Son, and Holy Ghost).[28]

Bell's mother may have understood little about the Trinity, but she embraced the concept of God's soothing, sacred breath. Like Africa's children all over the Diaspora, rural New York blacks were a spiritual people. They inherited a tradition in which social life and sacred ontology abided together harmoniously.[29] This informed their understanding of Christianity.

In whatever way whites wanted Pinkster to both reinforce social control and create a subservient type of religious instruction, the message of promise and hope in the workings of divine authority was stronger than the intended hegemony. That message anticipated an extraordinary, individual, sacred, unseen gift—a power not born of the Christian sacraments such as baptism or the Reformed Church, both of which excluded blacks. Despite Pinkster's popularity as a carnival, it also asserted spiritual connection through the simple story of Jesus and his sacrifice for all believers. Pinkster was not black-white communion or spiritual egalitarianism; nonetheless, it was as close as the Dutch ever came to "democratization" of Christianity among blacks.[30]

While spiritually Pinkster offered a sense of the sacred without compromising the conflicting secular interests, most bond people, Bell included, looked forward to Pinkster for temporal reasons. A British traveler describing Albany's "King Charles" sheds light on Pinkster's relationship to black leadership and the "talking-up" of freedom. Although past his prime, agile Charles was, "like Israel's Saul, nobly born, well made and tall." The holiday began when Charles entered the Pinkster grounds:

You'll know him by his graceful mien;
You'll know him on the dancing ground,
For where he is folks gather round;
You'll know him by his royal pose;
You'll know him by his Pinkster clothes
And when you know him, then you'll see,
A slave whose soul was always free.

Charles was a commanding leader; when he "harangues, a hundred fiddles cease their twangs." He urged his "subjects" to enjoy but not abuse their temporary freedom and to endure the ills they could not cure. But Charles also spoke of longings for liberty in the souls of all the enslaved:

Tho' torn from friends beyond the waves,
Tho' fate has doom'd us to be slaves,
Yet on this day, let's taste and see
How sweet a thing is Liberty.[31]

Not only were Bell and her family denied true liberty, but her parents' ostensible privilege as the Hardenbergh's kitchen family ended with Charles Hardenbergh's untimely death in May 1808. After that, Bell often found Elizabeth crying. Taking the corner of her mother's apron and wiping away her tears, Bell asked, "Mau-mau, what makes you cry?" Her mother answered, "Oh, my child, I am thinking of your brothers and sisters that have been sold away from me." She recounted details about Bell's siblings: how an older brother had hidden under the bed, and a three-year-old sister had been spirited away, locked in a sleigh box. Actually, Mau-mau Bet was lamenting the "impending fate of her only remaining children." She tried to prepare Bell and Peter for their separation. At night, sitting "under the sparkling vault of heaven," she spoke to them of God. She taught them the universal Christian prayer—a tribute to the Almighty and submission to his will, but also a plea for deliverance. "Thus, in her humble way," Mau-mau Bet imparted two fundamental lessons: "to show them their Heavenly Father, as the only being who could protect them in their perilous condition; at the same time, she would strengthen and brighten the chain of family affection, which she trusted extended itself sufficient to connect the widely scattered members of her precious flock." Bell treasured her mother's instructions as "sacred."[32] Though Bell was separated from her parents at a crucial time in the earliest formation of her personal identity, their socialization had already grounded her character and framed her values. Bomefree's independence and boldness and Mau-mau Bet's examples of motherhood and mystical religiosity fashioned their daughter's future. They also taught her that obedience was not necessarily unqualified docility, and that good work habits generated trust, goodwill, and white protection. Bell's Hudson Valley birth also influenced her formative development; Pietist women taught spirituality, men asserted secular patriarchal power, and African Dutch people struggled to create a separate cultural space.

Life certainly held the tribulations associated with black bondage and white cultural chauvinism. Overcoming this domination required challenging the Dutch ethos, selectively gleaning substance from older traditions, and constructing one's own sacred orientation. Like many enslaved people, Bell's mother was spiritually independent enough to weave Christianity and African mysticism into an individual faith. If an omnipotent "God the Father" conformed to patriarchal Catholic and Protestant beliefs, this deity also had attributes of an African Supreme Being—a warm, personable, and approachable Nzambi. This instructive merger was an armor and shield for Bell as she faced the dreaded day of separation.

I have as much muscle as any man, and can do
as much work as any man.
I have plowed and reaped and husked and chopped
and mowed, and can any man do more than that?
— SOJOURNER TRUTH

With black sheep's wool is my head crowned
I am a Devil for the Dutch women
My nose, a flat beak, exhibits a horrible beauty,
Such are suspicious in squeamish eyes.
— FLIP DE DUYVEL

CHAPTER 3

"Better to Me Than a Man"

FEMALE LIFE, LABOR, AND SLAVERY IN RURAL NEW YORK

I

Bell's family remained together for two years after Charles Harden-bergh's death in 1808, while his estate was settled. Advertisements appearing repeatedly in the 1808 *Plebeian* might have been for Elizabeth, "a middle aged Negro wench, brought up on a farm, for sale for life." The deceased Old Colonel's instructions that his kin care for "old Negro James" led to a contentious debate that was finally resolved by emancipating both of Bell's parents. Elizabeth would care for James, now nearly blind. Another *Plebeian* sale notice beginning January 16, 1810, sounds like Charles Hardenbergh's real estate. It offered property "on the turnpike road leading from Esopus," consisting of a "tavern and store," as well as "a large, convenient new dwelling house, with a ball chamber, and other convenient rooms for a store and tavern." Livestock, Bell, Peter, and a man named Sam were listed in Hardenbergh's inventory but were not advertised for sale. The Dutch commonly held private tavern sales, especially as slavery became unpopular. "My mother, when I was sold from her," recalled Sojourner Truth, "set down and wept as though her heart would break." In what had been their home, early in 1810, Elizabeth and James watched Charles Hardenbergh's "slaves, horses, and other cattle" go under the hammer.[1]

The man who purchased Bell, John Neely Jr., was a yeoman whose family came from Rye, in Westchester County. Like many of the English in Ulster, the Neelys were not previous slave owners. But they were a roguish family. John Neely Sr. and other family members appeared in court for felonious assault in 1729, and in 1739 the two John Neelys were charged with passing "counterfeit dollars." In 1762, a John Neely was charged with "breach of the peace and grand larceny." And unlike other yeomen and freeholders, Neelys never appear on grand jury or petit jury duty lists.[2]

Bell's work at the Neelys's was simple enough—household, garden, and yard chores. She was strong, obedient, and disciplined—what Southerners called a "sound slave." But the Neelys treated Bell cruelly. They clothed her scantily, and she went barefoot all winter, causing extreme frostbite. The Neelys also beat her mercilessly. Completely unfamiliar with English American language and culture, Bell constantly misunderstood her instructions. "If they sent me for a frying-pan, I carried them the pot-hooks and trammels. Then, oh! How angry mistress would be with me!" Floggings at the hands of John Neely scarred Bell for life. The most torturous whipping happened one Sunday morning, when Mrs. Neely directed the unsuspecting child to the barn, where John Neely had prepared a bundle of rods bound with cords. He tied her hands, stripped her to the waist, and beat her until "the flesh was deeply lacerated and the blood streamed from her wounds" onto the ground. Besides her physical anguish, this treatment bespoke Bell's isolation from sympathetic influences. No female healing hands rubbed salve into Bell's wounds after the whippings; no soothing poultices treated her numbed, frostbitten feet; no spiritual leader offered emotional comfort.[3]

Bell's suffering, confusion, and fear had to have been mixed with shame. She was at the age of menarche. Laboring girls had no childhood to speak of and experienced physical maturation earlier than their middle-class counterparts. In particular, enslaved girls such as Bell had womanly bodies before their mental, emotional, and chronological progression occurred. If Bell's mother did not alert her tall, well-developed daughter about the wiles of men and the pitfalls of black womanhood, this was not unusual. Enslaved mothers rarely taught their daughters about sexuality, even as their bodies changed. The disrobing and flagellation of enslaved people involved a perverse eroticism and homoeroticism. One slaveholder admitted that he would rather flog a black woman than eat when hungry. "When I go before the throne of God," Sojourner Truth told an audience, "and God says, 'Sojourner, what made you hate the white people?' I have got my answer ready." Having made this statement, she turned, pulled down her dress to the shoulder, and revealed the mosaic pattern of healed-over ridges and stretched and broken lumps of skin engraved on her back. On the antislavery circuit, those enduring stripes were authentic, irrevocable symbols that could silence any doubter. "I hated them," Sojourner said of whites. "I had cause."[4]

Besides Bell's experience of enslavement's worst sides—separation, brutality, and loneliness—the Neelys's intolerance of her linguistic difficulties exemplified bigotry toward blacks and disdain for the Dutch, whom the English considered ignorant, boorish, and backward. The increasing English presence in Ulster County created a culture clash. "No Dutchman need apply," read one English newspaper ad in a Catskill community seeking turnpike workers, "unless he is pretty well Yankeyfied."[5]

Bell was resilient, however, even in this compassionless household. Recalling her mother's counsel about a Divine Heart, Bell implored God to "protect and shield her from her persecutors." Mau-mau Bet had also taught Bell that human agency was linked to spiritual trust and divine will. Hence she counted on God's earthly mediation. It came when her beloved father appeared, making the approximately 15-mile trip to Kingston. The Neelys did not allow father and daughter a private visit, but Bomefree saw Bell's shoeless, frostbitten feet. And as he left, during their brief walk together to the gate, Bell "unburdened her heart to him." Could he not do something for her? Could he not "get her a new and better place?" He promised he would, and she was confident that "God would help her father" do so. Each day, shoeless, Bell traced Bomefree's footprints in the snow and prayed, trusting that soon, her father would return with good news.[6]

The Dutch customarily allowed a dissatisfied bond person to solicit a new owner. "Faithful Bomefree," the Old Colonel's lifelong companion and top man, pursued this option for his daughter. Traversing the countryside doing odd jobs, Bomefree took these opportunities to approach Dutch men known for kindness.[7] He and Mau-mau Bet could also accost trusted families after Sunday church services, to seek a new owner for hardworking, well-trained Bell. The black couple certainly would have emphasized the English owner's cruelty toward their daughter.

Bell's next owner, Martimus Schryver, was a Dutch Boer, fisherman, and tavern keeper who knew her family. The Schryvers were longtime Ulster County residents, former Hardenbergh tenants, and pewless members of Dutch churches, which their landlords established. During colonial times, the Schryvers were impoverished and were often admonished for inadequate contributions to the *dominie*'s salary. But in the 1790s, Martimus Schryver became a freeholder who used the powerful Hardenbergh family's mills and communed with Charles Hardenbergh at the Klyne Esopus Church. Although he had never owned slaves, at Bomefree's bidding, Schryver purchased Bell.[8]

The Schryvers' establishment, unlike Charles Hardenbergh's, was a grog shop for lower-class Dutch; the family was crude, uneducated, and their farm was wholly unimproved. Their biggest crop, corn, was cultivated for whiskey. Bell's jobs included helping make beer and cider, carrying the daily fish catch, hoeing corn, bringing roots and herbs from the woods for beer, and carrying molasses from "the Strand" for rum. Although she was completely unaccustomed to this "wild, out-of-door kind of life," the work was not hard, and the family was Dutch. Most of all, the Schryvers were "kind, honest, well-disposed people."[9]

However, Bell could "ill describe the life she led" among these earthy Dutch folk. She was accustomed to alcohol; everyone drank, and fathers such as Bomefree customarily "treated" their children from tankards. Yet she had never lived and worked amid constant drinking, dancing, gaming, and vulgarity. "Morally, she retrograded," according to the *Narrative*, in this world of bawdy and coarse farmers, tenants, laborers, and Schryver's three unmarried adult sons. Dutch painter Jan Steen, also an innkeeper, depicted risqué tavern behavior in Holland, including the unabashed, saucy interplay between a "common" woman (prostitute, barmaid, or housemaid) and her "seducer," as his compatriots eyeball them and guffaw shamelessly.[10] Although Bell did not remain with the Schryvers for long, it is unlikely that she remained chaste.

Bell may have been sold because of Martimus Schryver's declining circumstances. In November 1810, he defaulted on his payments for a large parcel of farmland he had purchased nine years earlier. The land was seized the following May and "sold at public vandue [sic]." By then, Schryver had sold Bell, in "a private sale," to John Dumont of New Paltz for 70 pounds (over $200). Bell was just approaching her prime, and Schryver doubled his money. And so within a year of leaving her parents, Bell had three different owners.[11]

John Dumont was a prosperous, thirty-six-year-old landowner in 1810. His French Huguenot forebears had migrated to New Netherlands and quickly embraced Dutch language, religion, and customs through marriage and a combination of economic interests. Dumont's father, Johannes Ignacias Dumont Sr., was a Kingston merchant, was a New Paltz landowner, was one of the largest Ulster County slaveholders, and married among the Dutch. John Dumont Jr., his only son, inherited the family estate, anglicized his name, and married two half-English sisters successively—Sarah (Sally) and Elizabeth Waring. The sisters' Dutch mother had raised them amid Dutch customs, including baptism in churches where *dominies* still preached in Dutch. While Dumont's wives were the only two of Solomon Waring's six daughters who married Dutch, all of John Dumont's six sisters had Dutch husbands. The old ethnicity was certainly waning, but even as late as 1824, travelers observed that Ulster's culture and the inhabitants remained principally Dutch—descended from early settlers. And so at the Dumonts' Bell was still in a Dutch-speaking familiar world.[12]

John Dumont's eight-year-old daughter Gertrude (Getty) remembered Bell as "a young slip of a girl" when she was first purchased. Getty and her younger brother Solomon were Dumont's children by his first wife, Sally. When she died after Solomon's 1805 birth, Dumont, following a common Dutch American custom, had married Sally's older sister Elizabeth. When Dumont came home with Bell, Elizabeth was pregnant with a son, born in 1811.[13]

Bell was well worth her purchase price. African Dutch women possessed a wide range of household expertise, as newspaper ads reveal: "For Sale: A Negro wench about 19 years of age, healthy and strong, understands sewing, spinning, knitting, washing, ironing, & c. was brought up with a good Dutch farmer, and is handy at all kinds of housework." Bell's responsibilities were even more diverse. She began work at daybreak, warming the house before the whites stirred. When the fires were roaring, she gathered water and peeled vegetables for breakfast. While the meal cooked, she gathered eggs and milked cows. Household chores began after breakfast. While black and white women sometimes labored together, Bell did the dirtiest, most arduous domestic tasks, as well as working in the yard and garden. Getty and Solomon Dumont probably joined Bell in picking fruit and berries for the local truck market. Dumont had large apple orchards, and Bell also made hard cider, a skill learned at the Schryvers's. Another responsibility was gathering manure, potash, and pearl ash, all popular fertilizers in the Hudson Valley.[14]

Bell was not only "a good, faithful servant" and "uncommonly smart," Getty Dumont recalled; she was "an excellent cook." She had been educated to the kitchen by Mau-mau Bet, and her culinary skills increased as she matured. The Dutch loved an abundance of meats, cheeses, vegetables rich in butter and sour cream, simple breads, and intricate pastries. The dinner table in a large, prosperous farm family, including all the help, was well laden. Favorite old Dutch dishes undoubtedly endeared Bell to the children at holiday times: drop biscuits with caraway seeds, *oly-koeks* (honey cakes), sugar gingerbread, puddings, and various fruit tarts. Bell could be extra creative with *stampot*, the famous staple, and used secret seasonings in the *rolletjes*—beef stomach stuffed with spiced meat, fried and sliced—and the *snip-raapjes*, thinly sliced salt pork and turnips.[15]

Despite Bell's skills, life in the Dumont household was a trial. Elizabeth Dumont hated Bell and insisted she was incompetent. She became the domestic scapegoat and recipient of jibes exchanged in English between Elizabeth and her Irish help. Even Olive Gilbert, the sympathetic amanuensis who wrote down Sojourner's *Narrative,* suggested that Bell was a poor worker. "Naturally," wrote Gilbert in an aside, Mrs. Dumont had no patience with Bell's "creeping gait, the dull understanding, or see any cause for the listless manners and careless, slovenly habits of the poor down-trodden outcasts. The slave would find little ground for aught but hopeless despondency."[16] This description not only contrasts markedly with everything Bell narrated about her skills and work habits, it differs from what we know about Sojourner Truth.

In any case, Bell understood where the real source of power lay. Unsuccessful at rapprochement with Mrs. Dumont, she cultivated and won over John Dumont as well as his two eldest, motherless children. This created further resentment. At every turn, Mrs. Dumont and her white household minions sought Bell's downfall, plotting to discredit and "grind her down." Getty Dumont stood ready to mitigate these stings and to bolster her father's confidence in Bell. Events came to a head when Bell was about fifteen and Elizabeth Dumont engaged Kate, a white servant, in a plot involving the breakfast potatoes. Bell's potatoes had had a dingy color of late, which resulted in a foul-tasting meal. This, Elizabeth Dumont told her husband, was a "fine specimen of Bell's work," and the "way all her work is done." The Dumonts and Kate scolded Bell harshly in front of the household. Crestfallen, humiliated, and puzzled, Bell peeled the potatoes carefully as usual, set them to boil, and went out to milk. However, each morning on her return, they had the same gritty color and bad taste. Getty volunteered to arise extra early and guard the boiling potatoes while Bell did her milking. When Kate attempted to send Getty out on some errand, she refused to go and continued her vigil by the fireplace. Along came stealthy Kate, who, "sweeping about the fire, caught up a chip, lifted some ashes with it, and dashed them into the kettle."[17]

The mystery was solved, and Bell was vindicated, thanks to her admiring young friend. Once again in Dumont's good graces, Bell "became more ambitious than ever to please him." As John Dumont professed Bell's indispensability, and her confidence in her position increased, so, too, did Elizabeth's rancor. Whether by design or force, Bell began working in the fields as well as the house and yard.

The crops, which mid–Hudson Valley farmers produced for noncommercial markets, give some idea of Bell's field labors. Although wheat was the primary crop, farmers also produced other marketable grains such as rye, barley, and corn; buckwheat for feeding poultry and swine; oats as both a grain and as hay; and timothy to feed horses. Truck crops—tomatoes, squash, peas, beans, peppers, peas, garden pumpkins, potatoes, and watermelons—were especially important for local exchange and households, as was tobacco. Flax was central to the home economy through midcentury, before the manufacturing of ready-made clothing. As a substantial farmer, John Dumont had access to a wider market through proximity to New York, the Hudson waterway, and merchants who owned sloops. Completion of the Erie Canal in 1825 coincided with the expansion of apple cultivation, and yeomen such as Dumont could reach even farther beyond regional markets and the lineal family unit for production exchange.[18]

Bell was as indispensable in the fields as in the house. While most serious fieldwork began in springtime, farmers planted wheat in both fall and spring, making farming a year-round activity. First, workers prepared the ground with fertilizer and plowed. During Bell's working years, laborers used the heavy, wooden-wheeled, one-handled Dutch plow, pulled by two or three horses, instead of the more balanced, wheel-less, and coultered but also wooden English plow, or the newly invented cast-iron plow. Workers then manually and painstakingly harrowed the soil with a spike-like implement. Plowing continued along with planting. By April, the fields were also ready for potatoes and flax, which were sown in together. After planting, Bell may have helped the men castrate ram lambs and wash sheep.[19]

The heaviest fieldwork occurred in summertime: planting corn, pumpkins, and other crops; dressing corn; preparing the ground for planting buckwheat; pulling flax from the potato fields; and harvesting grains. Reaping wheat and mowing grass were especially arduous. Although methods and implements had advanced beyond the colonial era's clumsy, backbreaking sickle and scythe, Dutch farmers eschewed new techniques and new instruments, preferring old ways of mowing grass, and harvesting grain with a cradle, an implement with rods like fingers attached to a scythe, which allowed the grain to be laid in bunches as it was cut. Sickles and scythes appear in mid–nineteenth century inventories as important farming implements. Besides frostbitten feet and a lacerated back, from her time with John Neely, Bell had another lifelong physical reminder of bondage. In 1825, her industrious fieldwork, either with a scythe while cutting grass, or with a cradle while reaping wheat, cost her an index finger.[20]

According to Getty Dumont, when Sojourner Truth later asserted her prowess in the fields, she did not exaggerate. She was so quick at binding wheat, Getty recalled, that "she could bind a sheaf, throw it up in the air, and have another one bound before the other fell." If this was merely a tale, it was a familiar one among tenants and small farmers in the early national period, when binding was woman's work. Sojourner Truth recalled that poor German women could bind just as fast as she, and one historian wrote about a farm woman working with her husband. "In the strength and suppleness of her young wifehood, there were very few men who could equal her in binding grain; and, more specifically . . . she would bind behind a cradler all day long, pressing close at his heels, and at the end of the day in a spirit of mockery would catch in her waiting arms the last clip off the cradle and bind it without allowing it to touch the ground."[21]

Bell performed other field labor such as cradling wheat and mowing grass, generally men's work, since the "all-day use of the cradle called for mighty biceps and an unbreakable back." While men "prided themselves on their ability to cradle all day long with the tireless swing of a steel mechanism," Getty Dumont also remembered Bell as a champion cradler. Aged farmers insisted that a good man could cut four acres of grain a day, and some did seven. In comparison, using the lighter scythe to mow grass required more power but a much slower pace, because the worker took a narrower swath, and could not reach as far forward at each swing. Mowing was clumsy and grueling, while cradling was rhythmic, measured, and graceful. In any case, Getty recalled that Bell could do more work than any man. She was "exceedingly strong and healthy, tall, thin and bony," and "tough as a whip."[22]

Although Bell inherited a tall, erect build from her father, certainly hard labor also contributed to her willowy, straight stature. Hours of wielding the heavy cradle and standing upright to mow with a long stubble made Bell's already striking physique more impressive, as did spinning the family's flax and wool. A busy spinner paced back and forth at least four miles in one day, and Bell probably did more. Reportedly, no occupation equaled spinning for "developing grace and supple poise in a woman." Bell's carriage and bearing were the same conspicuous traits that Sojourner Truth possessed even as a middle-aged and elderly woman. She was indeed Dumont's most valued human asset. "That wench," he boasted, "is better to me than a man—for she will do a good family's washing in the night, and be ready in the morning to go into the field, where she will do as much raking and binding as my best hands."[23]

Fieldwork was strenuous and grungy and in summer lasted until dark— about 8:30 p.m. The ambiance was rough and racially offensive. Bell drove a horse-drawn threshing machine called the "wooden nigger." As its name implies, this device duplicated and eventually replaced black labor. Yet among rural Mid-Atlantic blacks, work, like recreation, reinforced collectivity and sustained culture through seasonal and communal chores, corn husking, barn raisings, and other labor-driven activities. Because their folkways developed in a more acculturated setting, this richness is sometimes overlooked. African Dutch people spoke their own "Negro Dutch," although Bell's diverse enslavement also exposed her to the language of the Boers, called *de Tawl*, and Dutch spoken by the higher classes. Stories about witches, black tricksters outsmarting whites, and racial relations were part of African Dutch lore. Nineteenth-century sculptures, possibly African-influenced, have also been discovered in the Mid-Atlantic region. Moreover, Bell's method of transporting objects on her head reinforced African heritage. The African Dutch, like Southern black Americans, created work songs such as the following:

> Cold, frosty morning,
> Nigger berry good.
> Wid his axe on his shoulder,
> And way to the wood.
> Wid a piece of cold pancake,
> And a little hog's fat,
> And de grumble like de debble,
> If you get too much of dat.[24]

However unequal the social status between blacks and whites, and however harsh the bondage, laboring together in the fields could foster a certain camaraderie. Traditionally, Dutch slavery encouraged loyalty from certain blacks through concessions and special privileges. For Bell, fieldwork was not only a respite from Elizabeth Dumont: the socialization, the mobility, John Dumont's praise, even the hard labor afforded Bell a kind of independence that also enhanced her skills and range of knowledge. She was at ease in the fields and forests; familiar with weather patterns; could tell time by the sun's place in the sky; could test properties of roots and herbs; knew the attributes of plants and insects; and knew the habits of local nondomesticated animals. She also was a horsewoman, drove a buggy, and guided skiffs, and thereby learned local water and roadways. Groomed for service by devoted parents, she doggedly put her training into action. Her obedience and industry created the avenues for developing mother wit and homespun knowledge—future assets to Sojourner Truth when traveling and working alone. Abolitionist friends called her a child of nature.[25]

Growing into womanhood on John Dumont's farm, Bell looked on her owner as "a God" and basked in self-serving flattery.[26] She may have been a better worker than a man, but she was very much a woman.

II

It is no quantum leap to maintain, as some writers do, that adolescent Bell and John Dumont were sexually intimate.[27] Certainly antebellum history is replete with accounts of white male sexual license toward enslaved and free black women.[28] Yet in Bell's case, historians have not elaborated on their insinuations or contextualized the possible circumstances surrounding the relationship. Sexual indiscretions are a far cry from the famous Sojourner Truth—whom we have transfixed as an asexual icon of aged black female virtue. While we cannot know with certainty if Bell and Dumont were sexual partners, my discussion will posit the overwhelming likelihood that the two were lovers at least during Bell's teens. This perspective takes into account Bell's isolation and vulnerability; her youthful appeal; her mistresses' jealousy; her place in a sexually charged rural culture; and the Victorian-era gender conventions under which Sojourner Truth dictated her *Narrative*.

Bell's mother had a practical game plan for her unprotected daughter that depended on amenable coexistence in the biracial female household and support from the disparate black network. Instead, Dumont, young Bell's white master, was her refuge, and afforded her "many small favors." This angered not only her mistress but her black associates. During her early years on Dumont's farm, she was taunted and disdained by her own people, who labeled her a "white folks' nigger."[29] Being ostracized no doubt enhanced her attachment to Dumont.

Her mother's sudden death added to Bell's isolation. After her parents' emancipation, they remained in the stone house cellar, where Bet worked for the new owners. But one "early autumn" day, Mau-mau Bet had a fatal attack of "palsy." This apparently happened in 1810, because Lewis Hardenbergh, the Old Colonel's son, began deducting money from his father's estate for "finding old Negro James vittles & wood at the house of Charles." So long as Bet lived, such expenditures were unnecessary. When she died, the Hardenberghs honored her with a funeral, which Bell and her brother Peter attended. Bell was bereft of feminine or practical guidance in her life. "There was no body to tell me anything," Sojourner Truth recalled.[30]

Reflecting on young Bell's enthrallment with John Dumont challenges our comfortable image of Sojourner Truth. Associates who saw her as "Old Sojourner" and historians deconstructing the larger-than-life "Truth" both lose sight of her womanliness and humanness.[31] This seems especially relevant in exploring Sojourner's physiognomy and young Bell's attractiveness. Toni Morrison has posited that one of the most destructive ideas in the Western world is its concept of beauty. If one suspends this modern, media-nurtured construction, one can envision Bell's comeliness and gaiety and how her very black-skin presence might have incited Elizabeth Dumont's hatred while attracting John Dumont and other men. Conceptualizing Bell in the bloom of life expands Sojourner Truth from an aged symbol to a passionate woman. Sojourner Truth's beauty and charm are best appreciated in African rather than Western terms.

On encountering Sojourner Truth, most people not blinded by race or class prejudice thought she was someone special. Yet her charisma was evident even before that. New York City editor Gilbert Vale met Isabella in 1835; she was thirty-eight years old, a poor domestic and a victim of scurrilous slander, and she had no worthy prospects in life. Physically, Vale wrote, she was "not exactly bad looking" but simply "not handsome" and had "nothing prepossessing or very observant or intelligent in her looks." Her African features revealed "no apparent mixture of blood," and nature had not "furnished her with a beautiful . . . body." Nonetheless, she impressed him. "This middle age . . . coloured female," he added, "is not what she seems." She was powerful and energetic, was naturally gay, and possessed a strong mind, he noted. She had a reflective, observant nature, a sharp eye for detail, a keen memory, a deep sense of moral rectitude, and unusual mental acuity. The black domestic thoroughly won him over, and he became her champion.[32]

Vale's description says more about his ethnocentrism than about the future Sojourner Truth's physical appearance. She was definitely African-featured. Yet even the crude photographs taken thirty years later reveal her regal bearing, her well-formed features, and the luminous glow on her face. She sat straight, with shoulders evenly squared, and head erect. Her broad countenance was impressively symmetrical: forehead wide and prominent; eyes large, level, deeply set, and piercing; lips full and shapely; cheekbones prominent; chin ample, firm, and square. Her head was that of a trim woman—taut and highlighted by the curvature of a long neck partly covered by a Quaker collar. While slavery's scars pierced Sojourner's back, and she spent eighteen years as Dumont's field hand and domestic, her face, a deep, rich, chocolate brown, appeared flawless—youthfully smooth and blemish- and wrinkle-free. Yet—perhaps because she did not have the effete, cosmetic, delicate dazzle of some mixed-race women—Vale saw nothing "soft" in Isabella's appearance.[33]

The late Sylvia Boone's study of women in Sierra Leone and other African cultures presents provocative insights into the beauty of Sojourner Truth. Africans placed the head as supreme over the body. A broad forehead, casting no shadows over the eyes or face, was highly desirable. The eyes, the window to the soul, which "command the head," were the single most important facial feature. In Mende culture, the most beautiful eyes were large, round, and widely placed; a beautiful neck, though not "like a giraffe's," informants said, was long, firm, and flexible nevertheless. Africans, naturally a dark-skinned people, also possess various skin-tone gradations from brown, dark copper, chocolate, black, and very black. Racially mixed copper-colored Mende women were "beautiful and desirable" for prestige purposes among Europeanized paramount chiefs. However, Boone's African informants stated: "very black skin, completely black, is the most desired and adored"; "The blacker the better"; "black people are *the people*"; and "jet black is the most beautiful." Deep blackness was an extremely provocative contrast, highlighting the visibility of white teeth and whites of the eyes. Above all, a beautiful woman's skin was smooth and free of blemishes.[34]

Aesthetic and practical beauty were even more important than physical beauty. Aesthetic beauty was refinement, fastidiousness, cleanliness, and gracefulness. Practical beauty was knowledge in child care, home craft, healing arts, ethics, and morality—what American female culture called "domesticity." In addition, singing and dancing were part of artistic beauty. "No bird is as beautiful as its song," the Mende said, and "no being is as beautiful as its essence." According to Ivorian ethnographer and historian Harris Memel-Fote, artistic movement and serenading sounds captured this essence and symbolized the beauty of a woman's soul.[35]

African concepts of beauty—physical, innate, artistic, cosmic, and relative—characterize Sojourner Truth, who confidently presented her likeness to posterity through the new medium of photography. Gazing past the camera in earnest, straight-faced solemnity, reflecting the perilous times and enormity of her mission, she also smiled slightly in some photos, exuding warmth, sagacity, strength, and intelligence. Her face, her bearing, and her powers of communication gave this African woman a certain star quality and appeal that, years earlier, Gilbert Vale sensed but neither understood nor characterized adequately. On the other hand, by 1844, white progressives recognized that middle-aged Sojourner Truth had magnetism, vibrancy, and her own style of beauty. Nearly forty years later, immediately after her death, cleric Samuel Rogers drew on Milton to write a remembrance of Sojourner Truth:

> Black, but such as in esteem
> Prince Mammon's sister might beseem
> Or that starred Ethiop queen that strove
> To set her beauty's praise above
> The Sea-nymph's[36]

How much more striking Sojourner must have been in her youth, when she was just Bell.

Long after Bell's physical attraction faded, her aesthetic and practical beauty remained. Fastidiousness and cleanliness were African beauty traits, but also Dutch cultural norms, and for patriarchal Calvinists were metaphors of purity, distinctiveness, patriotism, and morality. Nor was cleanliness separated from sexuality. Since home was a little commonwealth and a bulwark against the material world, its pristine state, ostensibly under the mistresses' domestic reign, was the antithesis of indolence, lust, and vileness. Since domesticity represented chastity, an immaculate home signified piety of soul, purity of heart, peace, and harmony. The Dutch were praised and sometimes ridiculed for obsessive order and cleanliness. In America, the Dutch brushed their country homes with lime and whitewash and scrubbed floors several times a week. In Holland, manuals instructed women on cleaning regimens as a "holy rite," and with strict military precision. In both cultures, each day was fully devoted to some particular task, while other chores were daily rituals. Camphor, turpentine, and chalk repellents kept cobwebs and insects at bay. Domesticated dogs, used for security, were cherished and sanitized, while cats were considered useless and disgusting. (Dumont once beat Bell for "being cruel to a cat.") Guests removed their shoes for slippers at front doors, even though the stoop and front pavements were washed daily. It was all too much for many visitors.[37]

Although Bell excelled in the domestic arts, Elizabeth Dumont viewed her as the antithesis of domesticity—a defiler and despoiler of Elizabeth's household. Moreover, as Bell matured and became more indispensable, her natural assertiveness emerged; rather than cower before Elizabeth Dumont, she probably "gave as good as she got." She may have emulated a small number of enslaved women who, having the master's ear and protection, became defiant in the face of their mistresses' injustice. Despite their stormy relationship, Mistress Dumont apparently never struck Bell.[38]

But the power dynamics engulfing adolescent Bell also blurred her practical vision. In describing Dumont as a "humane master" who "sometimes whipped me soundly, though never cruelly" and who ultimately proclaimed slavery a wicked sin, Bell excused his egregious acts during her bondage. Her demonizing of Elizabeth while rationalizing John Dumont's behavior further suggests the likelihood that a sexual involvement was the source of Elizabeth Dumont's hatred. Devoid of female companionship in the Dumont household, Bell nonetheless had a measured sense of power. And in the fields, she equaled, if not surpassed, everyone in efficiency, energy, strength, and skill. Asserting physical prowess with men muted her gender as a worker, but blackness, enslavement, and womanhood reinforced her vulnerability.

By the time Bell began working in the fields, mostly poor white and black women did this labor. White men did not want "respectable" white women in the fields, because they were considered fragile and the "indispensable" prevalence of alcohol made women sexual prey. Any farmer "who refused each hay or harvest hand a daily portion of one pint of rum was considered a mean man." In addition, "when bond people, white workers, and neighbors assembled to aid in raising a barn, shearing sheep, or to draw and stack the minister's winter supply of wood, the bottle was deemed requisite to give strength to arm and will, and to restore flagging energies." In fact, liquor was central to rural life, "from the cradle to the grave." Even before family prayers, white patriarchs often called together "wife, children, and servants" for a drink. Public drinking was exclusively a masculine prerogative, and "a tippling woman was regarded as far outside the pale of respectability." Hence, "gentle women-folk imbibed secretly, under medicinal auspices," or privately at quilting bees, barn raisings, and other gatherings. "Common" women without reputations to protect drank openly. The fields were likely places of sexual resort for intoxicated workers and managers. Bell, Getty Dumont recalled, "was fond of liquor and tobacco, and used both when she could get them."[39]

Bell came of age during the era of the great "communal binge": public drinking and overconsumption resulting in aggressive, rowdy, violent behavior. The drinks of choice—whiskey and cider—were important to the rural economy, cheaply produced, plentiful, and home-processed. They also contained the most alcohol, at least 20 percent. New York and Pennsylvania produced three-fourths of the nation's beer, and Ulster brewed its own especially potent "famous Esopus beer." By 1810, rural New York was a whiskey-distilling center, and apple cultivation made hard cider a household beverage, much preferred to water, coffee, or tea. Dutch men and women in America and Holland were such lusty drinkers, feasters, and smokers that even Pietist elders and *dominies* turned a blind eye to these manifestations of ethnic culture.[40]

As Dumont's "man" and his "wench," Bell certainly traveled the Ulster countryside for marketing and purchasing purposes. Carding and fulling (two important processes in manufacturing woolen cloth) were no longer performed on farms, and Bell probably traveled to the mills alone and with Dumont. She knew the roads to Esopus, Kingston, New Paltz, and Marbletown and to the Quakers in Poppletown. She also visited her aged father.[41] While her field labors and mobility gave her freedom of movement, they also placed her in a man's world of sexual license.

If field labor culture created interracial situations perilous to black women, recreations such as Pinkster extended it further. Bell loved Pinkster, and Getty Dumont remembered her as "an excellent dancer and a good singer." As a Pinkster reveler, she engaged in European folk dancing as well as rhythmic, muscular, erotic African performances. "Original Congo dances" included a "double-shuffle, heel-and-toe-breakdown"; the "jug"; and the sexually provocative "Totau" or "Toto Dance," accompanied by drum, tabor, fiddles, lyres, and fifes. One eyewitness described the Totau as "the most indecent dance that can well be imagined." When dancers "from time to time imbibed," movements became more intense, and their dresses developed an enticing décolletage. The *Pinkster Ode* highlights the scene, including an erotic female presence:

> Now they strike the lyre again,
> With louder and louder strain,
> The fiddles touch their sweetest strings,
> While the ebon lassie sings.
> And the pipe and tabor plays,
> Brisk and merry rounde lays.
> Again the fife and hollow drum
> Calls you—come together come . . .
> Afric's daughters full of glee,
> Join the jolly jubilee.[42]

Bell had romantic relationships with black men—Robert, her first "husband," and Thomas, her second, who reportedly characterized their connection as a "frolic." She was undoubtedly a "belle"—tall, attractive, agile, provocative in the dance, and competitive in the games. Pinkster ground, also a convenient environment for white men seeking black women, provided another setting for intimacies between Bell and her Dutch master.

Since matrons such as Elizabeth Dumont considered Pinkster below their dignity, their sons and husbands had free rein: "Men of every grade you'll see, from lowest born to high degree." Mariners, politicians, "sons of Herman . . . an honest German," the "Burgomaster in place . . . with sober pace," the "Yankee, deep in trade," the "French Monsieurs," the "solemn Scot," "Saint Patrick's sons," and "Saint Davy's sons," from high Welsh mountains, all enjoyed the Pinkster fete. White children and young gentlewomen with escorts also attended Pinkster. While "respectable females" avoided the interracial drinking booths (reportedly no more than brothels), they witnessed the seductive Totau Dance "as a matter of course."[43]

When conventional white society labeled black women promiscuous, knavish, unclean, and base, they inverted the sex quest and the conquest from male to female. Yet runaway ads for "molatto" slaves attest to the relative frequency of biracial sex in the Mid-Atlantic. Notices also advertise sales of black women with a "mulatto child." Moreover, Ulster coroner records cite cases of black women brought to court for murdering "mulatto" children. Nevertheless, Dutch art, literature, and poetry depict black women as sexual predators:

> My skin is like a mole's
> My hair is black as jet
> My teeth like ivory
> My curled lips
> My round breasts are hidden reefs
> And as for my lap,
> It challenges the whitest wife:
> Thus many a man seeks
> To spend his time with me.[44]

Such stereotypical representations should not obfuscate Bell's attempt to turn an exploitative intimacy to her advantage. Portions of her life, Sojourner Truth told Olive Gilbert, were too intimate for publication; other experiences were so base that if revealed, people would "call me a liar! . . . and I do not wish to say any thing to destroy my own character for veracity, though what I say is strictly true."[45] In camouflaging the true source of dissonance between Bell and Elizabeth Dumont in the *Narrative*, Sojourner was not only protecting her former owner, his children, and her children but also her own reputation as an Abolitionist speaker, preacher, and reformer. A sexually passionate Bell involved with a white master threatened Sojourner Truth's virtuous image. Although Olive Gilbert was herself a radical reformer, she nonetheless accepted the conventional sexual standard of woman as pure at best and victim as next best, which placed "good" women on a moral and spiritual pedestal. Only later was an enslaved black woman (Harriet Jacobs) encouraged to publicly expose her sexual transgressions.

Sojourner Truth embraced not only the ideal of the virtuous woman being supposedly devoid of passion but also that of perfectibility.[46] As Perfectionist movements swept the North in the late 1820s, some churches criticized revivals as conducive to eroticism and female spirituality as another channel for woman's depravity. Hence sexual indiscretions became a special concern to woman reformers. Even after the Perfectionist-evangelist movement waned and splintered, an intensely spiritual worldview remained central to the radical Abolitionist wing headed by William Lloyd Garrison. Revealing sexual relations in the *Narrative*, even in 1850, might have destroyed Sojourner Truth's authority as a reformer spreading the Gospel of Christ through the gospel of human rights. If she had admitted "sinning" with her former master, her credentials would have been suspect.

Masking sexuality in favor of a moral, upright, and passionless image was politically advantageous for Sojourner Truth, though it has confounded historians. She has also consistently and mistakenly been given a matronly persona, depicted as perennially old and asexual. Yet it is more than idle musing to assert that Bell and Dumont were lovers—and as I will discuss in the next chapter, he fathered one of her children.

Although Bell possessed a strong sense of the possible, after separation from her family, she groped her way through early life much the way her blind father did after Mau-mau Bet's death. During much of this time, her religious faith was dormant, manifested mainly through mechanical recitation of the Lord's Prayer, mystical lamentations, and supplications in needy times. As she matured and revisited her early training, she became more spiritually reflective, approaching God as Mau-mau Bet had taught: openly, directly, and personally. But for years, Bell channeled her spiritual inclinations through faith in Dumont, the patriarch who ruled everything in her small world. Adulation and elevation of a male figure to godhead is not a distortion peculiar to an enslaved, unlettered, female adolescent. Middle-class evangelical white women paid similar homage to men of the cloth.[47] For Bell, seeking shelter, praise, and comfort and accustomed to male authority, it was a small step to imagine that John Dumont was her fixed point. Nonetheless, like her parents before her, she discovered that trusting a white slave owner was a high-stakes gamble.

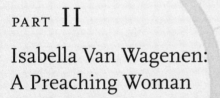

PART II

Isabella Van Wagenen:
A Preaching Woman

> The Spirit of the Lord is upon me, because he hath
> anointed me to preach the gospel to the poor.
> — LUKE 4:18

Engraved by J C Buttre

William Wells Brown,
Abolitionist, novelist,
friend of Sojourner Truth.
Collection of the New-York
Historical Society.

Statue of Sojourner Truth
in Northampton. Historic
Northampton Museum.

Sojourner Truth's grandson, probably James Caldwell, before joining the Fifty-fourth Massachusetts Regiment. Manuscript Division, Library of Congress.

I Sell the Shadow to Support the Substance.

SOJOURNER TRUTH.

Sojourner Truth (Detroit) seated in black dress with knitting. Berenice Lowe Papers, Michigan Historical Collection, University of Michigan, Ann Arbor.

Sojourner Truth, Abolitionist, in polka-dot dress and leather apron, with picture of grandson in her lap. Chicago History Museum.

Abby Kelley Foster, first woman Abolitionist traveling agent, Sojourner Truth's friend and eastern traveling companion. American Antiquarian Society.

Parker Pillsbury, radical reformer, Sojourner's friend and traveling companion on western campaigns. New Hampshire Historical Society.

Eliza Seaman Leggett, Abolitionist, Underground Railroad worker and Sojourner's Detroit confidant. Burton Historical Collection, Detroit Public Library.

Young Frederick Douglass in 1845, around the time he met Sojourner Truth in Northampton. Author's personal collection.

Frances Ellen Watkins Harper, Abolitionist poet, joined Sojourner Truth on the lecture circuit. From H. F. Kletzing and W. H. Crogman, *Progress of the Negro Race, or the Remarkable Advancement of the Afro-American from the Bondage of Slavery . . . to the Freedom of Citizenship, Intelligence, . . . and Trust* (Atlanta, 1897) (only known photo).

Frederick Douglass during the Civil War era, when he and Sojourner championed black male suffrage. Courtesy of the Department of Rare Books and Special Collections, University of Rochester Library.

Sojourner Truth speaking to the people. Drawing from Associated Publishers (*Journal of Negro History*), Photographs and Prints Division, Schomburg Center for Black Research and Culture, New York Public Library.

No, I did not *run* away; I walked away by day-light.
— ISABELLA

And ye shall know the truth, and the truth shall make
you free.
— JOHN 1:31

If any person shall . . . seize and forcibly confine, inveigle, or
kidnap, any negro, mulatto, or mustee, or other person of color
with intent to send or carry him out of state against his will . . .
or shall conspire with any other person to commit said offense
shall be fined or imprisoned, or both. . . . And further, that
every slave or servant so exported or attempted to be exported,
or sent sea, shall be free. — LAWS OF NEW YORK, 1816

CHAPTER 4

Like Hagar and Her Children

LONG WALKS TO FREEDOM

I

In 1817, New York State passed a law emancipating all enslaved adults
on July 4, 1827, if they were born before 1799. Individuals born after 1799 remained enslaved until the age of twenty-five if female and until twenty-eight if
male.[1] Free blacks and antislavery whites spread the news quickly. At first, this
law may have meant little to twenty-year-old Bell. But as time passed, the hope
of liberty gradually dampened her slavish devotion to John Dumont.

So much had happened to Bell after Charles Hardenbergh's death thrust her
away from her parents and a false sense of security. But her training included the
importance of family connection. Getty Dumont recalled that Bell and Thomas
got together in 1820 and "had five children, four living to grow up." However,
two of those children were born before Thomas came along—James, Bell's first-
born, died in childhood; her daughter, Diana, was born around 1815. The children
born after Bell and Thomas's union were Peter, born about 1821; Elizabeth, born
about 1824; and Sophia in 1826. The *Narrative* is silent on paternity. Instead,
a separate section notes that in due course, Bell "found herself the mother of
five children."[2] Bell named all the children after her beloved parents and the

siblings Bomefree and Mau-mau Bet had etched in her memory. Bell wanted freedom for herself, and to prepare a dwelling place for her children.

As she anticipated 1827, what memories haunted her thoughts of a free family and home? Over time, her bondage experiences had created within her a festering sense of rage. Prior to Thomas, Bell had "truly loved" Robert, an enslaved man owned by Charles Catton Jr., a Hudson Valley landscape painter. An established English artist, Catton moved to Ulster in 1804. Although whites described him as "intelligent and pleasant," he was cruel. Unions between enslaved couples living at different locations (called "abroad marriages" in the South) were generally accepted. However, Catton wanted Robert to choose a woman on his own farm. Once Catton and his son followed Robert on a secret visit to Bell. Using "the heavy ends of their canes," the Cattons beat Robert so mercilessly around the face and head that John Dumont finally intervened. The Cattons dragged Robert away, and Dumont, fearing they would kill him, followed; his "blood flowed till it could be traced for a mile in the snow." The clubbing broke his spirit, terminated his relationship with Bell, and shortened his life. Such brutality was the focal point of condemnation as slavery lost its hold on New York. Robert's tragedy haunted Bell. As an activist reformer, speaking of this love of her youth with tears, anguish, and affection, she often recounted this brutal beating.[3]

Bell and Robert may have had a child together, or at least he thought one of Bell's children was his. She was almost certainly "ill" from childbirth when he visited her against his owner's orders. Since Bell had two children before 1820, she might have been impregnated at the Schryvers' at age thirteen, and lost that child, who could have been James. She might also have conceived James later, with Dumont, or even with Robert. But Diana, Bell's second child, was probably fathered by Dumont. Olive Gilbert admits that Bell was not virtuous, and that many incidents in her life were too "delicate" to print; some events even revealed that sometimes she was devoid of "every high and efficient motive."[4]

What makes Dumont's fatherhood likely is that Diana remained with him after her legal emancipation around 1840, kept his name, united with his church, and even briefly attended school while in his household. Diana knew that she and her siblings had different fathers. A 1904 obituary states that her father was a slave named "Thomas," owned by an Englishman. Obviously, the press or Diana herself, who was very old, muddied the waters. Diana was the only one of Bell's children who left surviving photographs. Taken late in life, they show an attractive woman past her prime with the height, bearing, and dignified poise of her mother. However, Bell's face was broad, her features were African, and her skin tone was brownish black. Diana's face was narrower, her features sharper and somewhat chiseled, and her skin lighter, even in old age, when skin tends to darken. In the photographs the elderly Diana appears as racially mixed as

Frederick Douglass or Booker T. Washington, both of whom claimed white paternity, which their mothers never acknowledged. Either Robert was fair-skinned and mixed-race himself or Diana's father was the white Dumont. Such factors point to a hidden text in the *Narrative* and support the logic of a colonial saying, "Motherhood is a matter of fact, but fatherhood is a matter of opinion."[5]

Biracial enslaved children in households exposed white male infidelity, white female helplessness, and a black woman's shame. Such children's presence also mitigated white women's sense of superiority over black women. Like Hagar in the patriarchal narratives of Genesis, the enslaved Egyptian who bore a child with the patriarch Abraham and had contempt for his wife, Sarah, Bell had contempt for Elizabeth Dumont. Also like Hagar, Bell represented rivalry. Whether Bell was pregnant when Dumont purchased her or he impregnated her, Bell's biracial infant would have confirmed Mrs. Dumont's prejudices about "wanton" black women. Yet Elizabeth had brought little property into her marriage, and Bell was valuable. Like many "wronged" white mistresses, and like the biblical Sarah, Mrs. Dumont endured her husband's adultery but harassed Bell and her children.[6]

Bell survived in this triangle of discord and claimed a privileged position from Dumont. If, for example, Dumont entered the house and witnessed Bell being forced to neglect her (and possibly his) infant, he intervened and even reproved his wife. "'I will not hear this crying,' he would exclaim. 'I can't bear it. . . . Here, Bell, take care of this child, if no more work is done for a week.'" Because of Elizabeth Dumont, Bell endured "a long series of trials," the nature of which, Olive Gilbert said, "we must pass over in silence . . . from motives of delicacy." Nineteenth-century readers understood this titillating comment as a code name for sexual intimacy. Such language, and Gilbert's admission that her "tame" presentation of Bell's "thrilling" life involved a conscious suppression, implies that Bell and John Dumont's intimacy was the source of Elizabeth Dumont's hatred.[7]

Elizabeth Dumont clearly forced Bell to neglect her children, which may have led to her son James's death. Though she was nineteen years younger than Elizabeth, Bell's childbearing coincided with her mistress's. Between 1809 and 1824, Mrs. Dumont baptized eight children, the last at age forty-five. Hence thirteen infants (including Bell's five) had to be nursed; these were the white babies Sojourner Truth later said she had nursed to the exclusion of her own. Bell's children also sometimes went hungry because she refused to engage in what enslaved people called "taking" and whites called stealing. Most enslaved mothers pilfered food at great personal risk, and challenged draconian mistresses, notorious as the cruelest dispensers of punishment. Bell reasoned that taking food without permission bred distrust. Later, she felt guilty about not having taken a more protective stance on her children's behalf and pleaded ignorance: "Oh . . . how little did I know myself of the best way to instruct and counsel them! Yet I did the best I then knew, when with them."[8]

Getty Dumont remembered that Bell and Thomas "agreed to live as husband and wife" after a night of carousing. Getty's brother Solomon said that Bell and Tom "lived unhappily together." Reportedly much older than Bell, Tom had had two previous wives. As a young man, he had fled slavery, lived free in New York City for some time, and then returned to slavery in Ulster. Not only was the union apparently unhappy, Tom, perhaps worn out, possessed little ambition.[9]

Of all the losses embedded in Bell's memory, none was more painful than that of her father, Old Bomefree, the most important man in her life. His strength and stature, his protective attitude toward her, and his exemplary service to three generations of Hardenberghs made him a hero to his daughter. Having outlived his usefulness to whites, unable to care for himself, Bomefree was destitute and abandoned. When Bell visited with him after Mau-mau Bet's funeral, Bomefree cried aloud like a child—"*Oh, how he* DID *cry*! I HEAR it *now*—and remember it as well as if it were but yesterday—*poor old man*!!! . . . and my heart bled within me at the sight of his misery." Local blacks helped Bomefree for a time, and "when all had left him," some Hardenberghs cared for their "favorite slave." Though blind and crippled, Bomefree grasped his last measure of independence, by walking, staff in hand, sometimes twenty miles from one sprawling Hardenbergh homestead to another. Bell searched out Bomefree when she could, once to show him a new grandchild. On their last visit together, around 1817, he bewailed his condition and lamented about his many children: "all taken away from me! I have now not one to give me a cup of cold water." Why, he wondered, "should I live and not die?" Freedom was coming in ten years, so "the white folks say," Bell assured, begging him to be strong and live a while longer. "Do live, and I will take such *good* care of you."[10]

He could not live ten more years, he told his daughter, and he was probably near eighty then. Yet his strong constitution outlasted Hardenbergh generosity and probably the Old Colonel's purse. His grandson, John E. Hardenbergh, freed Bell's Uncle Caesar and Aunt Betty, on condition that they care for Bomefree, who was no longer welcome at white homesteads. Hardenbergh built a crude, isolated cabin for the infirm threesome. Neither Caesar nor Betty outlived Bomefree, however, and he was soon alone again. Hardenbergh goodwill had run its course.[11]

Unable to obtain or prepare food, wash himself, collect wood, or build fires, and having no assistance, Bomefree froze to death. However long his body lay undiscovered, his death was newsworthy. John E. Hardenbergh financed Bomefree's funeral and buried him in a painted coffin, a symbol of his status. Since Dutch funerals were traditionally festive occasions, the Hardenberghs supplied

Bomefree's mourners with abundant spirits and tobacco. In the Dutch style, he received a better send-off than the poorer class of Boers.[12]

This last earthly rite of passage had special significance to African Dutch people. Rather than black—the Christian mourning color, which expressed darkness in the afterworld—the African afterlife was bright, transparent, and a spiritual continuum. There, ancestors communicated with and directed some activities of the living. Such beliefs alleviated Bell's piercing sadness over Bomefree's suffering. She did not and would not believe his death was the end. Bell's African spirituality would later nudge her toward American Spiritualism. Both persuasions viewed loved ones as crossing the river into the land of brilliance, where, in the BaKongo tradition, the fourth moment of life never ceased. "Nothing that is good is dead," Sojourner Truth later insisted. "Only the bad stuff rots, don't you know." Good spirits lived on. "Everything that is true is seed," she believed, and "grows like a flower." This faith provided some measure of peace regarding an unspeakable loss, and a demonic past of bondage and oppression.[13]

Nonetheless, Bomefree's death nurtured Bell's hatred of whites and her desire for freedom. After the funeral, black mourners gathered, and Old Soan, an emancipated woman, explained herself to Bell. When Soan last saw Bomefree, her heart had ached with pity for he was filthy and covered with vermin. But she was weak and barely able to survive herself; she left Bomefree in his deplorable condition. Instead of censuring the old woman, Bell said blame for Bomefree's neglect and disgraceful death lay at the feet of white people. Hardenberghs *took* and gave nothing back, even for her exemplary father. What had her people done to be treated so? It was simply because they were black, Bell surmised, an accident of nature. Whites drew "blood, sweat and tears" from black people, whose sacrifice was "sufficient to cover the earth all over the United States." Bell had lost her mother, her husband, her first-born son, and the father after whom she named him. In 1826, Dumont sold her son Peter, at the age of five, to his nephew by marriage and neighbor Solomon Gidney. White people were responsible for all the tragedies in Bell's life. What could they say on Judgment Day? Bell prayed that God would "kill all the white people and not leave one for seed."[14] She would not give her entire life to white service as her parents had done.

As the time of adult emancipation drew near, John Dumont promised Bell that if she worked hard, he would liberate her and Thomas a year early, and even build them a little family cabin. These pledges inspired Bell to step up her labor so much that, as mentioned earlier, one day in the fields she cut off an index finger. Still, she claimed the promise of early "free papers." But Dumont insisted that she had lost too much time because of her injury. She pleaded, reminding Dumont of her service; he would not "give up the profits of his faithful Bell."[15] Bell considered her options. If she remained, she would bear more children with aging Thomas, who himself was a dependent; she would be a free domestic working like a slave, and sinking deeper into the awful poverty that plagued most Northern blacks. Bell wanted a life for herself, away from the scenes of her enslavement.

Bell had an isolated spiritual sanctuary, concealed among weeping willows beside a noisy, rushing stream that muffled her voice. Stealing away to this clandestine bush-arbor retreat, she prayed as her mother had taught. Speaking in Dutch, she began with the Lord's Prayer, then recounted a litany of suffering and iniquities. She poured out her heart about Dumont's duplicity and reasoned that God also disapproved. The Spirit and the servant together decided that Bell should flee and seek freedom independently. Divine guidance also inspired the time of her flight. It should be just before the day dawned. "Yes," Bell said. "That's a good thought! Thank you, God for *that* thought!"[16]

II

The spectacular array of color and light in a rural eastern New York autumn dawn is best enjoyed inside by a cozy fire. Until the sunshine's brilliance mitigated the frosty chill in the air and dried the dew from the grasses, only the domestics, the field-workers, and the most conscientious yeomen preparing for the day's labor stirred in the semidarkness. Normally, by sunrise, before the household arose, Bell lit the fires, had the morning meal in progress, and was busily engaged in other domestic work. But one autumn morning in 1826, probably a Sunday when there was less bustle in the household, the Dumonts awoke to find Bell gone.

Slipping out the back door, she had crept past the poultry she would no longer feed, past cows she had milked for the last time, and sheep in the meadow whose wool she never again expected to spin. She carried a knapsack with provisions, meager clothing, and shoes, since bare feet were essential to her silent escape. She had a secure grasp on Sophia, her nursing baby. Faithful, accommodating, cheerful Bell Hardenbergh was fleeing the House of Bondage.

She had told Thomas that she was leaving. And she gave Diana the responsibility of looking after her little sister Elizabeth. Bell was not exactly sure where to go, but some people in Ulster abhorred slavery, and God would direct her to them.

Even as the cold air chilled her legs and feet, she walked on, leaving the immediate vicinity where neighbors, such as Elizabeth Dumont's relatives or the cruel Cattons, would betray her. By sunrise, Bell was a considerable distance from the farm. After reaching the summit of a high hill, she stopped to rest, feed Sophia, and contemplate her next move. She was like the enslaved man Ned whose story she had heard so often. Ned had worked "early and late" to get the harvest in, and his master had promised he could make the thirty-mile trip to see his wife. His master reneged, but Ned calmly prepared to go anyway. This "impudence" led to one powerful blow on the skull, killing Ned instantly. But Bell did not expect such a fate. She had allies, and she had rights. The numbers of enslaved people were decreasing all around her. By 1800, 43.9 percent of New York's black population was free, and by 1820, 85 percent. Yet in 1825, Ulster County had 597 free and 1,523 enslaved blacks. Farmers such as Dumont, in rural, traditionally Dutch counties, held out. Bell finally understood why her brothers and sisters in bondage were resistant and recalcitrant. She looked back on her own behavior as a "fitful dream." White people cared only for each other. Even when a slave was "good," the goodness was all on one side. "How could slaves be good while masters and mistresses were so bad?" Bell resolved to use her faith as a resource to control her circumstances.[17]

Moving on in daylight, past neighboring farms where life was astir, had special dangers. If someone saw her, they would inquire where she was going so early in the morning, with her baby and knapsack. Lying would compromise her righteous indignation. Honesty would send her back into slavery. Such thoughts probably took Bell off the main road, over a less familiar, less traveled landscape, involving some danger from wild animals out for their early morning feed. She headed for the vicinity of her birth.

On that fateful morning, Bell did not consider herself a runaway, and did not intend to go far. Yet she needed to be in a safe haven among white folk when Dumont appeared and challenged her. She headed for the Quaker settlement near Marbletown and a man named Levi Roe.

Roe's story goes back to the 1790s, when Elias Hicks established a liberal wing of the Society of Friends. Born in 1748 in Jericho, Long Island, Hicks spread the message of the sect's founder, George Fox, that an "Inner Light," revealed through the promise of Jesus, made redemption available to all. During the Revolution, Hicks manumitted his enslaved people and educated their children, living his beliefs about morality, relief to the poor, temperance, and antislavery. By 1799, Quakers, Federalist politicians, and Methodists had secured a gradual abolition law, despite fierce opposition from Dutch slave owners. In 1817, the Quakers led the effort to persuade Governor Daniel Tompkins to call for a final adult abolition law, which went into effect ten years later.[18]

As Quaker influence spread to Ulster, so did the antislavery movement. Rural African Dutch such as Bell watched anxiously, noting which whites emancipated and to whom the enslaved could appeal. Hicksite Quakers were not only the most outspoken opponents of bondage, they were educated, knew the law, and eagerly informed blacks of their rights. The Marlborough Meeting, the oldest in Ulster, had a strong Hicksite group, including Levi Roe, which forced out the orthodox Friends. Quakers were tradespeople as well as farmers, and Bell knew who was "likely to befriend her." She could have met Roe through two free black families who lived next to him, had the same surname, and included women around her age.[19]

The walk from Dumont's farm to Levi Roe's was approximately 12 miles, a long day's journey for a woman carrying a baby and knapsack. In some ways, Bell's walk had begun unconsciously years earlier. Less diligent workers, less loyal and less honest women were freed almost daily, while Dumont sapped Bell's youth and strength. Hence, Bell *took* her freedom openly and defiantly in daylight. Her hard-won practicality grounded her future political activism. she knew that the man who called himself her owner would pursue his *property.* She also knew that she would make their next meeting a moral confrontation.

She reached her destination tired, hungry, and anxious. She made herself understood in English, perhaps soliciting assistance from her black friends. The sympathetic Roes insisted that she refresh herself first and care for Sophia. But Levi Roe was gravely ill, and could not help her directly. Moreover, Bell's situation was thorny, because she and her baby were legally enslaved. The dying man suggested two safe havens, and the Quakers took Bell to Esopus, her old home ground. She immediately recognized the farm of the first family she was taken to. They were not Quakers but Dutch. Nonetheless, she said, "That's the place for me; I shall stop there."[20]

She had childhood ties to this family. Isaac D. Van Wagenen and his wife, Maria Schoonmacher, had ancestral roots in Ulster as deep as the Harden- berghs'. Some Van Wagenens owned large colonial land tracts, but most were modest farmers. Isaac, of the sixth generation, inherited a farm in Esopus at Wagondahl (later called Bloomingdale, and then Bloomington). For genera- tions, Hardenberghs and Van Wagenens had worshipped and founded Dutch churches together. Later, in a letter of recommendation for Bell, Isaac wrote that he had "been acquainted with her from her infancy." He and his brother Benjamin, born in 1796 and 1798, respectively, were childhood playmates to Bell. Benjamin, who lived until 1887, recalled making frequent visits as a little boy to "Col. Hans" Hardenbergh's home even after his death. Benjamin Van Wagenen fondly remembered Bell's parents, Mau-mau Bet and Bomefree. Both John E. Hardenbergh and Isaac D. Van Wagenen were elders at the Bloomingdale (Bloomington) church, and Isaac milled his flour at the Hardenbergh mill. The two families also had marriage ties, and minor joint economic interests.[21]

Some Van Wagenens owned as many as ten enslaved people, even after the Revolution. Isaac D. Van Wagenen's grandfather owned one in 1790, but in 1800, Isaac's father had none. Thus the Van Wagenen brothers had no slave inheritance from their father or their wives. Unlike other Dutch men, the Van

Wagenens joined Quakers and Methodists in supporting black emancipation. Clearly, then, Bell had reason to believe that Isaac D. Van Wagenen would help her. He and Maria were not home when she arrived. Bell explained her plight to Isaac's elderly widowed mother, a Dutch woman who probably avoided speaking English as much as Bell did. She invited Bell to wait for Isaac.[22]

Knowing this family, relying on the Dutch custom of changing owners, and confident in Levi Roe's advice, Bell bargained with Isaac for a quasi-free status. No doubt she explained Dumont's broken promise, Peter's removal, and the disadvantages of being in Dumont's household after the July 4, 1827, emancipation date. If the Dutch elder would agree to pay Dumont for the remainder of her time, Bell could work for Van Wagenen until emancipation. Van Wagenen encouraged Bell to remain, and her moment of truth dawned.

> Dumont appeared that same day:
> "Well, Bell, so you've run away from me."
> "No, I did not *run away*; I walked away by day-light,
> and all because you promised me a year of my time."
> "You must come back with me."
> "No, I *won't* go back with you."
> "Well, I shall take the *child*."[23]

Dumont also threatened that Bell could go to jail for breaking the law. "I can do that," she said, "but I won't go back."[24]

Both Bell and Dumont were unyielding. He would not believe that she, who had never previously questioned his authority, could now defy him so adamantly. Standing her ground, Bell refused to return or to relinquish her child; Dumont refused to leave without her. Finally, Van Wagenen broke the stalemate, and the two Dutch men negotiated. Van Wagenen purchased Bell and Sophia, hence recognizing Dumont's existing property rights, but nevertheless emancipating the future Sojourner Truth.[25]

Historians have never found the document that transferred the ownership of Isabella and Sophia from John I. Dumont to Isaac D. Van Wagenen. But Bell was free, Van Wagenen explained, and she could work off the $25 he paid for her and Sophia. John Dumont left Wagondahl without his bond woman. Bell thanked Van Wagenen profusely and called him "master." The Reformed Dutch elder's response surely rang in Dumont's ears. "There is but *one* master, and he who is *your* master is *my* master," Van Wagenen said. "And didn't I grow tall [all] of a sudden," she recalled.[26]

Bell claimed a new name in her transition from slavery to freedom. To white folks in Ulster County, she was still Bell, from the old Hardenbergh kitchen family, late of the Dumonts. But emancipation, the milestone of her life thus far, was a new beginning. Following the fashion of many formerly enslaved blacks, she took the family name of the man who made freedom possible for her and her baby. The white family held a ceremony in honor of the emancipation of Isabella and Sophia Van Wagenen.

III

Soon after she obtained her freedom, Isaac Van Wagenen informed Isabella that her son Peter was gone from the neighborhood. Under the Manumission Act, children had to remain in the state, although in "virtual slavery," until reaching adulthood. This significant wrinkle disrupted and fragmented black families. Children such as Peter were placed in white households away from parents and other kin networks. The service obligation rendered manumission so "gradual" that children whose parents were freed in 1827 were not themselves emancipated until 1848. Only in the mid-1870s did an entire generation exist with no firsthand ties to New York slavery. Thus, it was not illegal for Dumont to sell Peter, but Solomon and his brother Eleazer Gidney could not take the boy out of the state.[27]

Northern blacks feared the interstate black market that kidnapped bond people destined for freedom, and especially sought young children. Blacks sold at premium prices during this slave-buying boom; Northern slaveholders lied, judges were corrupted, and purchasers asked no questions. Threats, bribes, and skulduggery victimized northeastern African Americans. The 1817 law was silent about rescuing and returning a kidnap victim to New York. Nonetheless, freedom was granted ipso facto to such a victim, and the perpetrator of the deed faced a fine and imprisonment.[28]

For Isabella, Peter's removal was a traumatic déjà vu. As a girl, she had shared her mother's despair and agony over her lost children. Devastating trauma and fear impaired both mother and child: the child felt deserted, and the powerless mother understood the impossibility of again seeing her offspring. Adults often relived the memories of wrenching sales, displacements, and a "stolen childhood." Peter was spirited, mischievous, inquisitive, and a bit of a rascal, according to Getty Dumont. On one occasion, while living with the Gidneys, Peter "yoked up a pair of young colts with an ox-yoke!" No one could do anything with him, she said, and everybody expected he "would land in State Prison."[29]

After Isabella left the Dumonts, Solomon and Eleazer Gidney left New Paltz for New York City with Peter in tow. Eleazer, a London dentist, went back to England. He supposedly had intended to use Peter as an apprentice, but said the boy was "too small" and left him with Solomon. Two other possible scenarios seem more likely: Eleazer could not explain Peter's presence on the ship or his status to the captain, who faced a $500 fine and prison sentence for "exporting, or attempting to export" bonded New York children. Or, given the "alarming extent" to which bonded children were disappearing, the brothers had intended to sell Peter all along. Despite stiff penalties for these actions, in order to be punished, buyers and sellers had to be caught, brought before the courts, and prosecuted. New York State remained a mecca for slave traders. The state Manumission Society and urban black activists helped black city dwellers defend themselves, but rural blacks bore the brunt of kidnapping and knew little about legal procedures or how to use the system.[30] These factors made Isabella's monumental task of recovering Peter all the more daunting and unlikely to succeed.

According to the *Narrative*, Solomon Gidney took Peter to Alabama, where the brothers had a sister, Eliza, who had married Dr. John Fowler, formerly of Newburgh, New York. The Fowler family were not previously slaveholders, but by 1827 John Fowler had apparently become one. Eliza Gidney Fowler, a twenty-four-year-old mother of two children, was also devoid of a slaveholding background and adjusted poorly to her assigned role as a slave mistress. She tried to protect the enslaved people in her household from her sadistic, ill-tempered, often inebriated husband, who purchased Peter from her brother. Even at his young age, five or six, Peter was a "quarter hand," expected to do one-fourth the work of an adult male. Black children worked "soon's us could toddle," one former bond man recalled. "First us gather firewood. Iffen its freezin' or hot us have to go to toughen us up." Other children claimed they had "little hoes" and they "walked many a mile . . . up and down de rows, followin' de grownfolks" and chopping weeds.[31] Isabella considered Peter's sale a death sentence. In the South, "menstealers" could buy and sell Peter as if he had not been born in New York.

She was shocked, angry, fearful, and anxious for her son; but she was also mobilized. She trekked the dusty road from Wagondahl to New Paltz, stubbornly pursuing Peter's trail and spreading the news as she went. She defiantly confronted Elizabeth Dumont, who may have orchestrated the sale of Peter to the Gidneys, who were her nephews. Elizabeth despised black people, and especially Isabella. Her former mistress drew a battle line, believing "Bell" would not cross it:

"*Ugh!* a *fine* fuss to make about a little *nigger*! Why, haven't you as many of 'em left as you can see to, and take care of? A pity 'tis, the niggers are not all in Guinea! Making such a halloo-balloo about the neighborhood, and all for a paltry nigger!!!"[32]

But the formerly enslaved woman's retort was like an incision. After a moment's hesitation, Isabella proclaimed, perhaps as much to herself as to Elizabeth Dumont: "*I'll have my child again.*"

Elizabeth Dumont was unmoved: "Have *your child* again! . . . How can you get him? And what have you to support him with, if you could? Have you any money?"

"No . . . I have no money," Isabella answered defiantly, "but God has enough, or what's better! And I'll have my child again."[33]

Sojourner Truth related her pronouncement in 1849, "in the most slow, solemn, and determined measure and manner." Olive Gilbert, her chronicler, was deeply moved, and lamented her own pitiful attempts to capture in print "the look, the gesture, the tones of voice" that Sojourner evinced "when moved by lofty or deep feeling." She possessed, Gilbert wrote, a "spirit-stirring animation that, at such a time, pervades all she says." It was a triumphant moment, as Isabella's inspired confidence dwarfed the mere human will of Elizabeth Dumont and the power of man stealers. Her former mistress's degrading words no longer touched or wounded Isabella. *"Oh my God! I know'd I'd have him again. I was sure God would help me to get him. Why, I felt so tall within—I felt as if the power of a nation was with me!"*[34]

Isabella invoked a black Jeremiad: implicit and explicit warnings and a prophecy of judgment against whites. The secular rule of law, heretofore favoring slavery, would become a sacred weapon, making "men" instruments of divine law. While dictating the *Narrative*, Sojourner articulated slavery as the national sin that made America a Babylon instead of a New Israel. She embodied the seething presence of enslaved black masses, whose suffering, in the image of Jesus, moved the righteous to champion their cause. This power was destined to wreak vengeance on America in bloodshed. In articulating her sentiments to Elizabeth Dumont, Isabella was connected to a messianic tradition older than Christianity, reaching back to traditional African antecedents. Voicing a black Jeremiad, she proclaimed her right to her own child, and *claimed* a promise: that through the redemptive power of her "Friend," and on behalf of a grieving black nation, her boy would return.[35]

Next, Isabella, as one mother to another, sought out Mary Waring Gidney, who emulated her sister in mocking the black woman. "Dear Me! What a disturbance to make about your child! What is *your* child better, than *my* child? My child is gone out there, and yours is gone to live with her, to have enough of everything, and be treated like a gentleman." "Your child," countered Isabella, "is married, and my boy has gone as a slave! And he is too little to go so far from his mother. Oh, I must have my child." Mary Gidney laughed.[36]

After walking to New Paltz, Isabella was no closer to getting Peter. Dark thoughts passed through her mind, particularly about the boy's treatment. In late fall, 1826, as the chilly autumn air turned frigid, Isabella walked and talked to everyone. Though confused and crestfallen, she was steadfast in her faith. She approached God earnestly—entreating, cajoling, and negotiating with the "miracle worker." Her talks with God were meditations and conversations between supplicant and provider. She explained her circumstances as a faithful if sometimes errant servant. Though God might not answer as she desired, an answer would come. Reaching deep into her heart, where God and she conversed, Isabella pleaded "with constancy and fervor" for Peter's life. "Oh, God, you know how much I am distressed, for I have told you again and again. Now, God, help me get my son. If you were in trouble, as I am, and I could help you, as you can me, think I wouldn't do it? Yes, God, you *know* I would do it." "Oh, God, . . . you can make the people do for me, and you must make the people do for me. I will never give you peace till you do, God." She pleaded with God to intervene, and "make the people hear me—don't let them turn me off, without hearing and helping me."[37]

The depth and intensity of Isabella's faith inspired her human action and optimism. As she broadcast her son's deplorable fate, a nameless, sympathetic man suggested she go to the Poppletown Quakers, who had helped her before. This time she went to the home of activist Edward Young, a fifty-two-year-old antislavery Hicksite Quaker who had recently been removed as elder in the bitterly divided Marlborough Meeting. Young had close ties to the New York Manumission Society, and informed Isabella of Peter's rights. She did not grasp all he said, but understood that she had legal recourse and the boy, if returned, would be free. Young invited her to spend the night in his home and said he would take her to court in Kingston the next morning.[38]

Isabella was so surprised when given a room with such a "nice, high, clean, white, *beautiful* bed" that she recoiled at the thought of sleeping in it. In her experience, blacks made pallets on Dutch floors. Moreover, she was unwashed and unkempt after trotting around the country roads. Unaccustomed to this luxury, astonished that the Quakers offered her *such* a bed, she lay on the floor most of the night. Toward morning, however, not wanting to offend the kind family, she slept in a bed apparently for the first time in her life.[39] One day, she would become as comfortable sleeping in fancy beds as she was sleeping under the stars and on pallets. Moreover, her Ulster County association with the Quakers would blossom into a lifelong connection with this white sect in the vanguard of the black liberation struggle.

Kingston had a population of three thousand, three "commodious hotels," at least fifteen stores, and several independent artisans, and received daily public mail from Albany and New York. The town was proudly attempting to become more urbane, and looking forward to dedicating a small stretch of water—where Rondout Creek joined the Hudson River—that would become the tidewater lock of the 108-mile, 110-lock Delaware and Hudson Canal—the route to the Pennsylvania anthracite mines. St. James Methodist Episcopal Church, though hardly a rival to the Old Dutch Church, was another example of change. But old Kingston residents still preferred a village atmosphere, and the Board of Directors, for example, failed in prohibiting "swine, cows, bulls, oxen" from running loose.[40] Isabella probably dodged the domestic animals in the streets.

The Quakers pointed out the courthouse, and told Isabella to go and file suit with the "grand jury," which had the power to return and free her son. The naïve African Dutch woman went inside, approached the "*grandest* looking man," and entered her complaint verbally, to the amusement and laughter of jury members, clerks, and lawyers. But they stopped laughing when they realized the enormity of her suit, and that the Quakers were involved. John Chipp, called "Squire Chipp" in the *Narrative,* the longtime justice of the peace—active in public and legal affairs and concerned about Kingston's image—gave Isabella immediate attention, ushering her into a private room.[41]

This black woman's suing for the return of her kidnapped child presented the court with a case complicated by white family ties, ethnicity, law, race, and patriarchal slavery. The jurors for the circuit court were members of the tangled network of Isabella's former enslavers and their kinfolk, as well as English residents. Some were Hardenberghs, including three of the Old Colonel's grandsons; one had buried Bomefree. The Gidneys also had connections. Originally from Westchester County, most Gidneys had been British Loyalists who had fled after the Revolution. However, Solomon Gidney's father, Joseph, was a patriot whose service under Colonel "Hans" Hardenbergh (Isabella's first owner) had earned him 500 acres next to John Dumont's farm. He had married Mary Waring, Elizabeth Dumont's sister. Their nine children included Solomon, Eleazer, and Eliza. The Gidney-Warings had influential connections through John Dumont, who was himself educated for the law. Dumont's Dutch niece married Charles Ruggles, a rising star and Ulster district attorney. And Dumont's wealthy Dutch brother-in-law was magistrate and clerk of the court.[42]

However kindly disposed some Dutch men were toward Bomefree's daughter, Isabella was a black woman and a former slave. Yet her persistent agitation and Quaker backing created an unsettling, embarrassing situation for many people of privilege. John Dumont, who had sold Peter in the first place, was not the least among them. His nephew, as district attorney, was responsible for prosecuting Solomon Gidney, also Dumont's nephew. And Isabella, by Dumont's admission and by reputation, was an exemplary servant. On the other hand, she was now boldly challenging servitude as a foundation of stable society. Kingston, eager to become a "bustling," business-oriented trading center, was hardly sympathetic to a public kidnapping case.

After listening to Isabella's story, John Chipp brought her back into the courtroom, handed her a Bible, and instructed her to swear that Peter was her son. Not understanding the significance of taking an oath and, in her own words, "as ignorant as a horse in those days," Isabella relied on her senses. In the African tradition of her forebears desiring to "talk" to books, Isabella addressed the Bible by putting it to her lips and literally speaking to it. Once again the clerks erupted into raucous guffaws. Enduring their ridicule, with Chipp's help, she comprehended the meaning of oath taking. Chipp then gave her a notice for the New Paltz constable, ordering Solomon Gidney to appear in court. She quickly delivered the writ. But the constable, purposely no doubt, served notice on the wrong Gidney.[43] Rather than gaining her son's return, Isabella had won only a piece of paper. She watched Solomon Gidney sail safely across the Hudson River.

The New York Manumission Society received word of the case of a "col'd Boy vs. S. Gidney," in January 1827. William C. White and John C. Merritt read a letter Edward Young had sent them, and entered in the record that Solomon Gidney had "sold a coloured boy to a brother-in-law who has taken him away as it is supposed to Indiana."[44] The notation adds a new wrinkle to the story about Peter's destination. The Quakers may have simply misunderstood Isabella's English. However, slavery was indeed practiced in Indiana at this time, despite its prohibition under article 6 of the Northwest Ordinance. Indiana Quakers were vigilant but were unsuccessful in stemming slavery and slave trading in Indiana. Whether Peter was in Alabama or Indiana, thanks to Hicksite Quakers and Isabella's persistence, Solomon Gidney returned with the child under a court order in the spring of 1827, slyly missing the April circuit court deadline. He claimed Peter as his property and posted bond. Isabella, Chipp said, would have to wait for the fall court date. "What! wait another court! Wait *months?*" This made no sense. "Why," she complained, "long before that time, he can go clear off, and take my child with him—no one knows where. I *cannot* wait, I *must* have him *now*, whilst he is to be had." Even if Gidney put the boy out of the way, Chipp remarked, Isabella was entitled to half of the $600 bond. That money, he noted, would buy her a "heap of children."[45]

Squire Chipp did not understand that Isabella had a mother's heart. She wanted her son safely with her—aware that he was frightened, bewildered, and possibly abused. This was not about money, Isabella argued to the magistrate. She would never sacrifice her boy for material gain. No, she insisted, "it was her son alone she wanted, and her son she must have." Nor would she wait for the next court. She wanted Peter now.[46]

The Englishman was now truly irritated. Where, he must have wondered, did this uncouth black woman just out of bondage get her intrepid boldness? She was ungrateful for what the law had already done for one such as her, he admonished. She must wait, and do so "patiently."[47]

Isabella waited busily rather than patiently—speaking out while maintaining "unwavering confidence" in an all-powerful "arm." Sometimes the dismissive looks of Kingston whites "fell on her like a heavy weight." And, she told

Olive Gilbert, "Neither would you wonder, if you could have seen me, in my ignorance and destitution, trotting about the streets, meanly clad, bare-headed, and bare-footed!" [48]

Powerful, respectable families sometimes prided themselves on their paternalist compassion for hardworking, faithful members of a "kitchen family." According to the *Narrative,* while Isabella was walking barefoot around the countryside, talking to herself and to God, a total stranger accosted her and suggested she seek out a Kingston lawyer whom she called "Demain" in the *Narrative.* This was actually Herman M. Romeyn, and his involvement was probably not a mere happenstance or initiated by a stranger. Born in 1792 in Livingston, Columbia County, New York, Romeyn's father, Jeremiah, was a *dominie* at Linlithgow Reformed Dutch Church. Young Romeyn studied law, inherited land in the Hardenbergh Patent, and settled in Ulster County. By 1820, he was practicing law in Kingston and had married into a wealthy old Catskill family. By the time of Peter's sale, Herman M. Romeyn had a thriving practice, and "a great reputation as an advocate." He knew of the case and knew Isabella's family; he was a grandson of patriarch Johannes II, a grandnephew of Isabella's first owner, Hans Hardenbergh Jr., and a blood kinsman of the Frelinghuysens. Like that of the Quakers and the New York Manumission Society, Herman M. Romeyn's assistance and involvement were crucial to the fate of Isabella's son.[49] Well-connected squires stood on both sides of Peter's case. The rule of law in Ulster County was at stake.

On one level, Peter's case represented Dutch and English rivalry. The Dutch were proslavery, while the English had advocated emancipation at the expense of Dutch slaveholders. Now an Englishman had defied the antislavery laws that rendered Peter's sale illegal. "Bell Hardenbergh," once owned by the largest landowning family in Ulster, had continued a tradition of loyalty and service with Dumont. Bomefree's daughter demanded justice from man's laws and God's law. Isabella and Romeyn certainly spoke in Dutch, her language of choice. He agreed to take the case at cost, which was $5. He might just as well have said $500. It was another stumbling block for Isabella, who had never had a dollar in her life. "If you will go to those Quakers in Poppletown, who carried you to court, they will help you to five dollars in cash," Romeyn advised, "and you shall have your son in twenty-four hours." The sequence of events indicates that it certainly took longer than that, and Romeyn arranged employment in Kingston for Isabella with John Rutzer, another wealthy Knickerbocker. So she and Sophia had left the Van Wagenens' by the summer of 1827.[50]

Searches for Circuit Court documentation of Isabella's case against the Gidneys have heretofore been fruitless. Because the *Narrative* was dictated, the story about Peter might be viewed as a mere rhetorical literary invention to promote antislavery. However, the bond that Solomon Gidney had to post is

reportedly extant. In any case, the verifiable records of the New York Manumission Society clearly prove the *Narrative*'s veracity—that Peter was sold away and
returned. Moreover, rather than use the untrustworthy New Paltz constable, the
court ordered one of Kingston's constables, Matthew Styles (referred to in the
Narrative as "the famous Matty Styles"), to bring in the child and the defendant.
Finally, the Dutch employers for whom Isabella worked in Ulster all wrote reference letters attesting to her good character and to her story regarding Peter.
No circuit court records have been found because the court was not in session
when Peter's case was argued.[51]

As Romeyn had promised, he secured a special writ for Solomon Gidney's
appearance with Peter. The boy's physical condition shocked even the justice of
the peace. Peter's face was scarred from "Fowler's horse hove" and by "running
against the carriage." Having been threatened, the frightened child denied knowing Isabella and begged for his "dear master." It must have been quite a scene.
Romeyn pleaded Isabella's case on the basis of the Emancipation Statutes of 1817.
The Gidneys and Warings protested, making harsh accusations against Isabella
and calling her claims fraudulent. Dumont was there, and apparently supported
Isabella. Politically speaking, Isabella's advocates—Romeyn, Charles Ruggles,
A. Bruyn Hasbrouck, and John Dumont—were of Federalist-Whig persuasion
and/or were ethnically Dutch through blood or marriage. Her detractors were
English farmers and Democrats. The two sides argued the boy's fate while his
mother remained silent, "scarcely daring to breathe," thinking of the enemies
she was making. Romeyn claimed Peter for Isabella and demanded that the
culprit pay the fine for taking the child out of the state. Isabella insisted that she
did not want money, only her son. Finally, the judge's order came: Peter was to
be "delivered into the hands of the mother—having no other master, no other
controller, no other conductor, but his mother."[52]

Still under the sway of fear, threats, and violence, and separated from his
mother for well over a year, Peter initially refused to acknowledge Isabella. Ultimately quieted and assured by "kind words and *bon-bons*," he gave in. "Well,"
he told her, "you *do* look like my mother *used* to."[53]

Isabella's struggle to extricate Peter from near tragedy exposed conflicts
among whites. As slaveholders, the Dutch might appear more antiblack and
the English more liberal. Yet the circumstances surrounding Peter's kidnapping
and its ultimate resolution illustrate the complexity of relationships and the
difficulty in attributing specific mind-sets to either group. Isabella embraced
the progressive Quaker rationale and political sense yet took advantage of the
historic Dutch-English antipathy and competitiveness, as well as the traditional
patriarchal associations of her childhood. Moreover, her assertiveness was a
direct challenge to the white women who refused to recognize her motherhood
or personhood.

"God only could have made such people hear me," Isabella asserted. Bound by a testament of faith, within one year she secured freedom for herself, her infant daughter, and her son and rescued him from the bowels of slavery. Despite her reliance on God's intervention, she was herself a shrewd manipulator of circumstances in an audacious battle of wills, and a sharp judge of character. On January 15, 1828, the New York Manumission Society held its annual meeting. One case the Society "resolved to discharge . . . from the minutes" was that of "Col'd Boy vs. Solomon Gidney." Peter was now "Enjoying Freedom."[54]

If the Son therefore shall make you free, ye shall be free indeed. — JOHN 8:36

She "looked back into Egypt," . . . she saw . . . all her former companions enjoying . . . their wonted convivialities, and in her heart she longed to be with them. — *NARRATIVE OF SOJOURNER TRUTH*

CHAPTER 5

"A Rushing Mighty Wind"

ISABELLA'S BAPTISM OF THE SPIRIT

I

On March 1, 1832, Isabella dictated a record of her religious conversion. She carried this note in her carpetbag throughout her life, and it was preserved in a museum in Lansing, Michigan. The heading, dated 1827, is followed by a testament: "Isabella Van Wagner . . . experience . . . It is now five years this winter since I knew there was a risen Savior."[1] At the time Isabella dictated her note, she was a popular camp meeting exhorter, recognized for her calling and access to the highest sacred authority. The spiritual liberation attested to in the 1832 record completed Isabella's emancipation—a journey that began with her physical walk to freedom in 1826.

She "never went to meeting" during slavery. And "to tell the truth," she said, whites who went "didn't know much themselves." Before attending Methodist meetings at the Van Wagenens', Isabella, like many enslaved people, had vague notions of the Creed; the Ten Commandments; and stories of the life, death, and Resurrection of Christ. Her mother planted Isabella's belief in God through practical faith, not salvation; Isabella knew Jesus was a great man but had no awareness of him as Savior and interceder. Only personalized religious instruction familiarized blacks with the meaning of Christ's life in relation to their own.[2] At the time she was introduced to Methodism, Isabella's belief system was based on strong spiritual roots: Mau-mau Bet, Hardenbergh home instruction, Pentecost, and occasional local black preachers.

God was always Isabella's special friend; she prayed in times of trouble but then ignored God after her difficulties subsided. She later recalled "with very dread," how she had once considered God under obligation to her, and "bound to do her bidding." She tried to be good, but "could never get through a day" without some wickedness. "Never mind, God," Isabella negotiated, "throw this day away, and I will try another." As expressed to Olive Gilbert, Isabella "demanded, with little expenditure of reverence or fear, a supply of all her more pressing wants." Thus, Isabella's God was like Nzambi, the benevolent BaKongo deity, detached from the world unless called on. She made promises in exchange for mediation, *intending* to fulfill them. But either she forgot, or some unforeseen, overwhelming temptation interfered. Nonetheless, Isabella felt close to God, and was convinced that they had a special relationship. Yet she retained the old habits of slave life: smoking, drinking, carousing, indulging in anger and profanity. Surrounded by good influences at the Van Wagenens', Isabella convinced herself that God was pleased because she remained honest and obedient. But guilt sometimes nudged her when she reflected on her broken pledges to God. She knowingly transgressed on many occasions but "did not lay it deeply to heart."[3]

Thus emancipation brought a change of circumstances and of name, but not an immediate change of heart. At Wagondahl, the God-fearing Van Wagenens included Isabella in their domestic religious observances. Although they were Reformed Dutch, the Van Wagenen family went to Methodist camp meetings. According to Methodist Benjamin Van Wagenen, so did Isabella while living at his brother Isaac's house. Ulster County had no campgrounds, but a small band of Newburgh Methodists was active nearby. Isabella's sister Sophia lived in Newburgh, and most likely Isabella attended the camp meetings on her visits.[4]

Methodist doctrines of individual free will and unconditional election and Methodist support of black preaching attracted black converts. Moreover, the British Methodists who formally organized the American church—Francis Asbury, Thomas Coke, and Richard Whatcoat—were antislavery. A generation after George Whitefield's mercurial tours, American Methodism reemerged simultaneously in two places in New York. In 1766, when pious Barbara Heck shamed her male cousin into organizing a Methodist "band" in New York City in the loft of the rigging shop, a black woman was there. The same year in the heavily Dutch village of Albany, a British Army officer, Captain Thomas Webb, converted a few British residents and enslaved people. Following the American Revolution, the Methodist Episcopal Church was born in New York City as Wesley Chapel, later the John Street Methodist Church. However, Methodism languished in the Hudson Valley, until 1788, when Maryland preacher Freeborn Garrettson arrived. The dedicated preacher converted Catherine Livingston, daughter of founding father Judge Robert R. Livingston. "Catherine, enjoy your religion here at home," her dismayed family implored. "But for heaven's sake don't join those Methodists; why . . . no body belongs to them, only three fishermen and a negro!" Catherine married Garrettson over parental objections, but her father eventually converted to Methodism, as did several aristocratic families in the region. Dutch Pietism and Methodism enjoyed some spiritual coexistence. Despite the Dutch clergy's hostility, Dutch common folk flocked to camp meetings—but avoided uniting with Methodists.[5]

Besides sectarianism, the inclusion of blacks made early Methodism unpopular. Francis Asbury and Freeborn Garrettson's favorite traveling companion, "Black Harry" Hosier, was so impressive that many whites and blacks preferred his preaching. Such racial leveling offended High Church Christians. Garrettson characterized Albany's Dutch and English residents as "hard as rocks," and accused the *dominies* of "informing the people that we were deceivers and robbers." In 1799, Asbury wrote from Isabella's neighborhood of a little Methodist center near Phoenicia on Esopus Creek: "here I gave a small exhortation to a small congregation. It was a day of small things." Likewise from Marbletown, Asbury wrote, "A marble-headed congregation as well as a Marbletown, and probably will remain so." Poughkeepsie was also "no place for Methodism," Asbury lamented in 1800. But Garrettson's persistence, his fortuitous marriage, and Yankee migration into the Hudson Valley gradually shifted the tide. "We have had a hope here many years," Asbury wrote in 1812 from Ulster, although there were no signs of a church.[6]

The hope bore fruit in the 1820s among blacks and whites. A black itinerant Methodist reportedly married Isabella and Thomas. Black preachers, often without white sanction, built on an African tradition of gifted "good talkers" who traversed their coastal homeland in search of spiritual experiences to impart to their people. Early national advertisements from Dutch regions note that some fleeing bond people were self-proclaimed preachers. Yet belief in God, deep spirituality, and a life of general integrity were not sufficient for attaining Christian grace. Isabella's sacred sense apparently involved no concepts of salvation and rebirth before she went among the Methodists.[7]

Kingston's St. James Methodist Episcopal Church, Isabella's first church home, emerged from Ulster County preaching stations. "Our people have built a very handsome church in this place," Garrettson wrote in 1824, although the membership remained very small. Dutch residents considered it "a crime" to forsake the religion of their ancestors and hear a Methodist. Yet a time was coming, Garrettson predicted, "when there will be shaking among the dry bones of this place. Unbelief must give way to the sacred truths of the gospel."[8]

One of the dry bones soon to be shaken was Isabella, who certainly heard Methodist exhortation at least occasionally before her emancipation. By 1825, the New York Methodist Conference had a Hudson River District that included Kingston, New Paltz, Newburgh, and ten preaching stations. Isabella could hear Freeborn Garrettson at a preaching station, at the camp meetings held near his Rhinebeck home, in Bern outside Albany, or in Newburgh. In 1824, indefatigable at seventy-two, Garrettson drew six thousand people to the Newburgh camp meeting. In 1826, the year before his death and the year of Isabella's freedom, Garrettson was still New York's "conference missionary."[9] Methodism ultimately benefited from the seeds planted by the early Dutch Pietists. Isabella learned from both traditions

Isabella came to love camp meetings, with their teeming humanity, collectivity, warmth, and spiritual energy. Some generous farmer allowed families to put up well-stocked tents. Traveling preachers, visiting ministers, appointed clergy, the converted, and the unconverted all gathered. Intermediate hours, between preaching at 10 P.M., 2 P.M., 5 P.M., and 8 P.M., "were filled up . . . with prayer, praise, and exhortation." There were "singing, some praying, some jumping, some clapping and wringing their hands," and worshippers falling everywhere. Old men lay transfixed in mud. At the 1825 Newburgh camp meeting, "there were fifty persons observed to be crying for mercy," while in another tent, twenty persons were converted. Garrettson delivered "a very solemn and weighty discourse, which was heard by listening thousands," on "Christian perfection," perhaps the most significant doctrine in Isabella's spiritual development. The meeting, an observer said, represented a new high for religious revival in the region.[10]

Camp meetings had a mixed reputation even among Methodists. Thomas Coke abhorred and suppressed them. Asbury said camp meetings were like fishing with a large net. Some people ridiculed camp meetings because of their carnival-like ambiance, interracial mingling, and belief that spiritual ecstasy ignited sexual misconduct. "For beauties were there, both of brown and of fair, and some were as black as a coal," one poetic commentator stated. In Bern, New York, innocent "possessed" women were fair game for lecherous men, while other young women invitingly extended their arms, threw back their heads, and fell on their backs. One young woman remained comatose for several hours and was eventually "hauled off by six or seven men, followed by two or three hundred spectators . . . exclaiming 'D . . n her, she can walk.'" Mockers and disrupters also flocked to meetings, crashing prayer circles and harassing converts. While many people bore witness during love feasts, others were in grog tents drinking, playing cards, and fighting. On the evening of the last day, "under the sable wings of night, the forest in almost every direction was filled with people of both sexes, and many of them indulged themselves in obscene conduct."[11] Isabella's attraction to camp meetings put her on the fringe of religious respectability.

Certainly in that late winter or early spring of 1827, even as she awaited news of her son, her mind was not on religion. She was lonely. She wanted to see her daughters and her friends, and share her new experiences with them. She was free, working independently, and living with a good family, and she was courageously challenging the slaveholders on Peter's behalf. Her friends were preparing for the Dutch holiday of the Pentecost. She wanted to join them in the gaiety of that coming saturnalia, the last Pinkster celebration before emancipation. Thinking also of the "impression her fine clothes would make among her old companions," sure that John Dumont was coming for her, she prepared herself and Sophia for an extended stay in New Paltz.[12]

It was not coincidental that she expected John Dumont to appear at the Van Wagenens'. Undoubtedly they had once enjoyed this recreation together, and the event was ideal for luring Isabella back to work. Sometimes, Sojourner Truth said, her people's minds were no longer than their little finger. She was describing herself in 1827, when individual appetites and selfish wishes and desires were foremost in her mind. As she predicted, or probably arranged, Dumont appeared. The Van Wagenens were surprised when Isabella announced that she was leaving with him. Although John Dumont intended to take his best laborer back, at first they briefly played a verbal game of wills. Teasingly, Dumont said, "I shall not take you back again; you ran away from me." Ignoring this unconvincing rebuff, Isabella continued to ready herself and her baby for the wagon trip.[13]

Isabella's decision is all the more perplexing, given her relationship with Elizabeth Dumont and her sister, but especially because of John Dumont's behavior. In the midst of struggling to get her son back, the wonder is that Isabella talked to Dumont at all. Yet despite his unbending commitment to oppressing her, the rapprochement between them remained, and they bantered with playful familiarity. Despite her "liberation," Dumont still had the upper hand out of a long pattern of domination and subordination. At the Van Wagenens' she may have attended camp meetings more for the sake of their freedom, openness, and spontaneity than for the sermons. She later compared her wanton desires at that time to the ancient Hebrew people who were delivered from bondage, but looked "back into Egypt," grumbling and reminiscing about sitting "by the flesh pots" and eating "bread to the full" in slavery. Isabella so longed for Pinkster's pagan celebration and the world of the flesh that she chose to jeopardize her newly acquired, God-granted freedom. Both Isabella and the ungrateful Hebrews desecrated God's favor. In both instances, the glory of God was revealed.[14]

Isabella's note dated her conversion as winter 1827, but the *Narrative* fixes it as Pinkster time. In 1827, Paas (Easter) occurred on April 15 and Pinkster Sunday on June 3. March was a frigid month, and even early April was too raw and rainy for outside activity. Pinkster preparations began far ahead of time, and Isabella apparently planned to participate. It was at least April when her "experience" occurred. Just as Dumont's visit was not coincidental, neither was Isabella's rebirth during Pentecost season.[15] But whatever her own and Dumont's intentions were, Providence intervened.

As Isabella approached the rear of the wagon, but before she could get in, "God revealed himself to her, with all the suddenness of a flash of lightning." His presence surrounded her, "and there was no place where God was not." She was now confronted with "her great sin in forgetting her Almighty Friend." Her deceptions and broken promises loomed before her, and for the first time, she cowered in response to an "awful look" from one she had spoken to on an equal footing. She wanted to hide, to escape the dreaded presence, but she felt that even the bowels of hell could not conceal her. She saw God, but God moved away after the first incriminating look. If the look came again, she thought, its force would extinguish her forever, as one "blows out a lamp." The second look did not come, and Isabella felt relieved and reprieved. Stricken to the spot near the back of Dumont's Dearborn, she lost track of time. When she emerged from her spiritual trance, Dumont was gone. The *Narrative* is silent on events between the time God struck her and Dumont's departure.[16]

If this was not Isabella's first visionary encounter, it was the first realization that her omnipotent God could be judgmental and angry; the magnitude of her transgressions loomed large. While everything transpiring in the yard seemed to happen in a flash, her mental reverberations appeared perpetual; the remnants of God's presence and fiery breath remained while the spiritual image took flight. God "burnt me," she later recalled, making her "melt like wax before the flame," and "wilt like a cabbage leaf." Finally, the Force disappeared. Puzzled and transfixed, Isabella could only proclaim, "Oh, God, I did not know you were so big."[17]

Chastened by this awesome manifestation, Isabella was at least comforted when the second look did not come. She relaxed, and Jehovah was again like distant Nzambi. As her anxiety and fear changed to wonder, she returned to the house to finish work she had intended to leave undone. It was not Nzambi's breath she had experienced but that of wrathful Jehovah. Her temptation was unacceptable; God demanded transformation, or she would reap eternal damnation. The Force dogged her movements mockingly throughout the house. Troubled and unable to concentrate on her chores, she thought of bargaining with God as before, but caught herself. "What! . . . shall I lie again to God? I have told him nothing but lies; and shall I speak again and tell another lie to God?"[18]

This confession was Isabella's first step toward justification (conversion), and prepared her to receive the redemptive power of Christ. God's breath, according to the New Testament, punished as well as rewarded, brought judgment as well as purification. Whoever refused the blessing of the Holy Ghost would be judged. Isabella's first scorching by the fiery breath only began her epiphany. Within a few minutes, the "second look" appeared that she had hoped to avoid. As before, it took form as God's consuming, fierce breath. But then a space opened between Isabella and God's accusatory presence. It was filled by a friend "worthy in the sight of heaven," and offering a way out. Because of her cursory knowledge of Christianity and flair for rhetorical imagery, Isabella at first thought the mediator was Deencia, "who had so often befriended her." However, no human confidant had such authority or protective capacity, and the vision of Deencia, covered with "bruises and putrefying sores," was as unclean as Isabella herself. Then Isabella envisioned a second being, whose presence refreshed her as a cool breeze on a hot day, or an umbrella between "her scorching head and a burning sun." As this mysterious vision "brightened into a form distinct, beaming with the beauty of holiness, and radiant with love," Isabella asked aloud, "Who are you?" Not sensing the foreboding she experienced with God, Isabella attempted contact. When she uttered, "I know you," the vision remained quietly in her presence. When she professed to not know who it was, the vision "moved restlessly about like agitated waters."[19]

Though bathed in the glory of visionary light, love, and new awakenings, Isabella could not at first name the being. Her mind struggled to discern who it was and to place it in her belief system: "her whole soul was one deep prayer that this heavenly personage might be revealed to her, and remain with her. At length, after bending both soul and body with the intensity of this desire, till breath and strength seemed failing, and she could maintain her position no longer, an answer came to her, saying distinctly. 'It is Jesus.' 'Yes,' she responded, 'it is *Jesus.*'"[20]

Isabella now believed Christ dwelled within her, as he had within his disciples, and that she received the Holy Ghost. In the Bible, the first sign was a swift rushing noise, so overpowering and unexpected that it attracted everyone's attention: "And when the day of Pentecost was fully come, they were all with one accord in one place. And suddenly there came a sound from heaven as of a rushing mighty wind, and it filled all the house where they were sitting." The second sign was even more stunning: "cloven tongues like as of fire," filled them with the Holy Ghost. They began speaking in different languages, "as the Spirit gave them utterance." Hence, the Spirit endowed the disciples' authority to spread the Gospel. As witnesses for Christ in a new state of grace, followers spoke *differently* from the multitude. For Isabella, the Holy Spirit, like Jesus' presence, symbolized God's power and the agency of purification. The brilliance and the splendor of fire also signified the glory of God. "Then did I come to know de Lord! Saw him Child—Yes I could see, feel a big, big light."[21]

It was not enough that Isabella perceived intimacy with the Creator, or that her traditional spiritual heritage promised an afterlife of transient brilliance similar to the fiery Holy Ghost. She lacked justification: entering communion with God as a pardoned, transformed sinner saved by Christ, embracing a testament of faith, and endowed with grace through the Holy Spirit. Only through this approved transformation (even imperfectly) could she be righteous in God's sight and receive salvation. At some point, as a result of the Methodist meetings, Isabella realized that while she might "talk to God," receive counsel, and achieve favor, the real reward eluded her until she accepted God's power and embraced the intercession of Jesus Christ. Like many Christians of the oppressed classes, Isabella now claimed Jesus' suffering, the soul force of his invisible messenger, and the Christian concept of life beyond human existence. She also accepted the Methodist emphasis on a "God-fearing" mind-set. "Fear of God," Freeborn Garrettson preached, was the first step to salvation. This was a crucial trepidation in securing "the convicting, justifying, and sanctifying grace of God," whereby the soul "solemnly and reverently reflects upon the perfection of the Deity, and the redemption which was purchased by Jesus Christ." Isabella's submission to divine will was her entry to an "internal principle of genuine piety," and a true "union and communion with the divine Spirit."[22] Accepting justification, which meant completely relinquishing her old way of life, took time, understanding, and contemplative mental debate. Eventually, her early training, the themes of Pentecost, and revival preaching all found their mark.

Isabella's justification by faith, forgiveness of past wrongs, and deliverance from her own sins came through Dutch Pietism and Methodism. Both embraced Arminianism and interpreted religious transformation via enrichment of the Holy Spirit. This cleansing, energizing, and divinely inspired experience was the capstone of holiness. While embracing an angry Jehovah, Isabella integrated something of the mystical Nzambi. Her God was supreme, wrathful, overwhelming, yet also loving.[23] Her previous exposure to religious conversations, if not doctrinal pedagogy, had not been devoid of the slaveholders' self-serving rhetoric and social-control baggage. But her heart was won by her own dramatic personal experience of love, fellowship, and the promise of "works."

II

Many mystics and visionaries achieve salvation in isolation and without denominational affiliation. Isabella did not quiver on an "anxious seat" at a revival, or in church with a minister preaching hell and damnation over her. And she was not baptized in a "watery grave." Instead, she merged the simplicity of camp meeting messages, the power of spiritual baptism, and practical dealings with God in critical struggles, to arrive at an interpretation of faith. Moreover, her awakening and acceptance of the Trinity led her beyond justification. Her intense experience and overpowering spiritual thirst inspired in her an unflinching desire to test her new confidence. From that time forward, she grew in faith, listening to all she heard, formulating interpretations on the nature of God, Jesus, and the Holy Spirit. Jesus, she believed, was one from whom "love flowed as from a fountain." Jesus was not God but stood between her and God as mediator and savior. She feared God, because of her "vileness and God's holiness and all-pervading presence, which filled immensity, and threatened her with instant annihilation." She also prayed to God, who, through the love of Jesus Christ, answered her prayers. Her faith in prayer equaled her faith in the love of Jesus. "Let others say what they will of the efficacy of prayer, I believe in it, and I shall pray. Thank God! Yes, I shall always pray."[24]

Isabella's conversion, a soul-grappling, all-encompassing realization that divine power supersedes human will, embraced the tradition of African American female spiritual narratives, in which the traumatic decision to follow Christ often occurred in a dream or trance, sometimes setting miraculous events in motion, and leading to a calling outside of church denominations. Isabella joined other visionary black women, all freeborn. Shaker eldress Rebecca Cox Jackson said she received literacy "by the power of God." Methodist visionaries included Jarena Lee of New Jersey, fourteen years Isabella's senior, and Zilpha Elaw of Pennsylvania, born in 1790.[25]

White Primitive Methodists, including the Wesleys, and Dutch Pietists also recorded miraculous visionary transformations, thereby encouraging ecstatic and hallucinatory practices. Isabella's exemplary experiences were also similar to those of white Dutch women such as Dina Hardenbergh. "It now was Wednesday, the first of February, and it was five years since my soul was set free," Dina wrote in 1747. Like Isabella, Dina also communicated directly with God, and viewed prayer as a two-way conversation: "It seemed to me that the Lord said to me, 'Did you waver? Did you not unconditionally surrender yourself to my guidance and control?'" Both Dina and Isabella emphasized the power of prayer and the significance of Pentecost. On Pinkster, Dina wrote, "the Lord was very close to me . . . he freely imparted the Spirit of prayer. I was particularly impressed with the great outpouring of the Spirit on the day of Pentecost." After Dina's divinely inspired marriage to Johannes Frelinghuysen, en route to America their vessel sprang a leak during a terrible storm and began sinking. "Dina calmly sat in a chair tied to one of the masts and prayed for their safety. As she prayed the water stopped rushing into the hold. . . . The ship was saved." A swordfish was "wedged in the open seam of the hull, effectively stopping the leak." Throughout her long life, as counselor, teacher, and adviser, Dina greatly influenced rural Dutch women of faith in New York and New Jersey.[26] Thus traditions of female spirituality also grounded Isabella's sense of prophecy.

Engaging the Holy Spirit represented Isabella's awakening, not her complete fulfillment, for she was not sanctified. She still had an appetite for passion and pleasure. Progress toward sanctification required that the soul control the body's actions and the body be subordinate to the soul. Isabella's profound spiritual baptism at least prepared her for sanctification, and her struggle against sin was the first step on a journey that for some people took years. Jarena Lee took four years. Zilpha Elaw was nine years past her conversion when "God was pleased . . . to sanctify me as a vessel designed for honour."[27]

Isabella began her path to sanctification and "perfection" as she experienced another major crisis. After over one year of unremitting struggle against "formidable enemies," she had her boy once again, and he was free. But in court, seeing his scared face, she hastened to examine him entirely and privately. Away from the white people, she removed his clothing. "Heavens! what is all *this*?" she cried. Peter's back was ridged with swollen, raised skin, "like her fingers, as she laid them side by side." Isabella cried out in alarm and agitation, "Oh, Lord Jesus, look! See my poor child!" Peter explained: "It is where Fowler whipped, kicked, and beat me." Isabella was beside herself with shock and anger. "Oh my God! Pete, how *did* you bear it?" He answered bravely, telling his mother, "Oh, this is nothing." But his enslavement was a horror story. If Isabella had seen Phillis, another one of Fowler's enslaved victims, Peter said, "I guess you'd scare!" Phillis was a nursing mother, and Fowler so lacerated her breasts that "the milk as well as blood ran down *her* body." Isabella wanted to know, "What did Miss Eliza say, Pete, when you were treated so badly?" While Fowler slept, Eliza surreptitiously comforted Peter. When the bruised and bloodied child crawled under the porch and his back stuck to the boards, Eliza coaxed him out and put salve on his sores. She pitied him, and said she wished "I was with Bell."[28]

Eliza Gidney Fowler's assistance and sympathy toward Peter did not mitigate Isabella's fury, as she looked on her little boy's mutilated back. Rejecting her newfound Christian lessons on forgiveness and compassion, she came as close to invoking the power of conjuration as any South Carolina root doctor. She cursed the Gidney family in the tradition of BaKongo *kindoki* (wrath or force, according to African scholars). She called for assistance from the Other World. If done for positive rather than selfish reasons, *kindoki* was not witchcraft. Consumed with rage, Isabella wanted vengeance for Peter, and for generations of terrible wrongs done to black people. She could not yet look beyond the suffering whites caused. Her son's agony was real; she did not view it through fatalistic, philosophical Christian eyes. This was one of the occasions when she begged God to kill all white people. Moreover, she called for special damnation on the Gidneys. "Oh Lord, 'render unto them double' for all this!"[29]

Surely some personal motherly guilt mixed in with Isabella's outrage against whites, since her leaving the neighborhood had helped make Peter's removal possible. Seeing his deplorable physical condition, she could only imagine what such brutality had done to his heart and mind. Peter was never the same, and his childhood tribulations were forever ingrained in his mother's memory. His ordeal surely contributed to his ungovernable behavior as a teen.

After the 1827 court decision, Isabella's stock rose among whites, including Gidney relatives. She even briefly worked for Fred Waring, Solomon Gidney's uncle, which surprised and disgusted John Dumont. He called Isabella "a fool," and reminded her that in court Fred Waring had called her "the worst of devils."[30] Yet Isabella understood her vulnerability as a poor black woman, and as a veteran of patriarchal slavery, she knew the power of negotiation. She kept options open, thinking she needed them now more than ever. Having triumphed over slaveholders and proven herself, thereby gaining a measure of respect, she had made enough enemies among white folk. After recovering Peter, she maneuvered to mend fences for the future.

Her careful strategy began with accepting the Warings's offer to work during a family illness. She had forgotten her "curse," but believed Providence had placed her in the Waring home. A letter arrived for Fred Waring, the brother of Mary Gidney and Elizabeth Dumont. Waring's young daughter blurted out its contents to Isabella: "Fowler's murdered Cousin Eliza!" Believing the child spoke rhetorically, Isabella sardonically answered, "*that's* nothing—he liked to have killed *my* child; nothing saved him but God." Isabella realized the allegation was serious when Solomon Gidney and his mother rushed into the house. As they proceeded to another room to see the letter, an inward voice pressed Isabella, "Go up stairs and hear!" "Go up stairs and hear!" Placing an ear against the closed door, she heard chilling news; John Fowler had indeed murdered his wife. According to Isabella's version of the letter, Fowler "knocked her down with his fist, jumped on her with his knees, broke her collar-bone, and tore out her wind-pipe!"[31]

Isabella recalled her pronouncement, "Oh God, render unto them double." Either Jehovah had answered her prayers, or Nzambi had brought *kindoki*. The same hands that had maimed Peter had destroyed Eliza, and Peter's successful return to Ulster County probably had fueled the fire that had put an end to his young supporter's life. Mary Gidney, who had laughed at Isabella's distress and dismissed her heartache, was experiencing what thousands of enslaved mothers endured daily—the loss of a child. The sins of the mother were upon the daughter—a kind young woman who had soothed the bleeding back of Isabella's child. Now the innocent Eliza was dead, her murderer in prison, and *her* children orphaned. Shocked and conflicted, Isabella's heart bled for Eliza's children, as well as for the relatives who laughed at her calamity and mocked her. She reflected much on the wondrous events and the special providence of God. But she recoiled at the thought of poor Eliza's fate. Of course, Isabella could not question God, who had "answered her petition." Nevertheless, "the language of my heart was, 'Oh, my God! that's too much—I did not mean quite so much, God!'"[32]

Isabella believed that her curse—her prophetic, telepathic, supernatural power—had caused Eliza Gidney Fowler's death. Evidence verifies that Eliza died in 1828 at the hands of her husband following Peter's return; that Eliza's mother, Mary Waring Gidney, died about a year and a half later; and that Eliza left two young children. Her daughter, Mary Charlotte, later wrote poetry that bespoke a painful childhood.[33]

In these early years of refining her religious development, Isabella frequently merged African and Christian traditions. Pronouncing her prophecy of retribution on the Gidneys, she had assumed the role of African priestess, prophetess, or *nganga*, cursing and blighting the white family responsible for her boy's abuse. Yet she then shrank from the fulfillment of this powerful damnation. Thereafter, Christianity guided her spirituality. Though she still claimed a mystical power beyond the white man's authority, she replaced hatred with love and forgiveness, even toward "white folks." She asked God to show people that she was under a special sign. "And he *did*; or if he did not show them, he did me."[34] Isabella now felt that in God's name, her possibilities were limitless.

Some time in the summer of 1827, while working in Kingston and waiting for Peter, Isabella walked down the street and heard singing. Peering into the window of a private house, she observed a Methodist meeting. The minister, Ira Ferris, lined out a hymn: "There is a holy city, a world of light above." The singing stirred Isabella, as did the Scripture "Behold, I come quickly, and my reward is with me to give to every man according as his work shall be." Blacks did not attend white private gatherings or churches unless seated separately. Isabella's attire was probably meager, and she usually went barefoot. These Methodists, unconcerned about social formality or outward appearances, invited Isabella in. She soon joined Kingston's St. James Methodist Episcopal Church.[35]

Isabella's faith and charisma impressed the small Methodist band, and there her public ministry began. Although a rough, raw, unimproved farmwoman, she possessed a natural spirituality and confidence. She found a religious denomination that accepted her voice, despite her color, sex, condition, and lack of education. She formed positive relationships with white women for the first time, and they encouraged her to seek broader horizons. She began learning Scripture, doctrine, and hymns, fusing exegetical association with practical experience. Flush from her encounter with the Trinity, by 1828 she had a passion for God and was sanctified. Believing that the sign of her true holiness was the horrific tragedy that befell Peter's tormentors, her practical spiritual witness surpassed doctrine and related directly to God's grace. Moreover, she was a gifted communicator. On the itinerant Methodist circuit, Isabella Van Wagenen became a mouthpiece for God.[36]

But I suffer not a woman to teach, nor to usurp authority over the man, but to be in silence. — 1 TIM. 2:12

Isabella, the coloured woman . . . is well known among the Methodists, and . . . was much respected by them. Mr. Latourette assured us the influence of her speaking was miraculous; even the learned and respectable people were running after her. — GILBERT VALE

And now abideth faith, hope, charity . . . but the greatest of these is charity. —1 COR. 13:13

CHAPTER 6

Sanctification and Perfection

BECOMING A RELIGIOUS RADICAL

Isabella migrated to New York City with a "Mr. and Miss Gear" in 1828. She was more fortunate than most freed women relocating to urban centers. She quickly found employment because Miss Gear, a schoolteacher, introduced Isabella to "respectable" Methodist families, and she had excellent letters of recommendation. Isabella left three daughters behind. Getty Dumont recalled that Isabella tried to leave two-year-old Sophia with John Dumont, but he said the child was too young; but later he did take Sophia. The two "colored" females listed in John Dumont's household in 1830—one "under ten" and another "over ten"—were Diana and Sophia; Elizabeth went to a Gidney family member. Isabella took her troublesome, traumatized son, Peter, to New York. She envisioned better opportunities for him and, typical of the times, thought her son rather than her daughters needed education.[1]

Isabella's removal further fragmented her family and ensured her daughters' neglect and lack of education. Although New York law stipulated that enslaved children be educated, few rural whites obeyed this edict. Diana actually went to school once in Ulster County, but had no idea why she was there; she was ignored by the teacher, so she left. Educational deficiency handicapped Isabella's daughters, though not because they worked as domestics. Even some unmarried middle-class black women were domestics. However, nonliteracy coupled with rural backgrounds deprived Diana, Elizabeth, and Sophia of higher aspirations and independence.

Isabella's former partner, Thomas, was broken in spirit and worn out physically. The couple's early visions of a family home had turned to "thin air." Forced off the Dumont place after emancipation, Thomas had worked odd jobs for a while, but died in the Ulster County poorhouse. Had freedom come earlier, or had Thomas been younger, the couple might have accumulated property and realized modest dreams, as other nonliterate blacks of their generation had done.[2] But Isabella Van Wagenen had a gift, a message, and a calling. She would not have been satisfied with obscurity.

Isabella did not abandon her children and did not distance herself from them, as some writers suggest.[3] New York City was no place for her young daughters. White social services did not accept black children, with the exception of the abusive Municipal Almshouse. Black churches had no support system for working parents. Poor children often wandered the streets; the city had its share of twelve- and fourteen-year-old sex workers. Women such as Isabella faced enormous urban pitfalls. Emancipated without compensation, uneducated, unwise about freedom, and impoverished, they were separated from their children by statute. But New York and New Jersey mothers frequently returned to the "old place," while wealthy urban whites lamented the dearth of "good help." They called this black female "floating" population erratic, lazy, and morally loose. In actuality, these women tried to improve their circumstances and maintain ties with their children. For black women, historically, geographical distance from family was often necessary during freedom migrations. This rarely translated into desertion, although distance created vulnerability. By 1849, two unwed daughters had made Sojourner a grandmother. Her inability to provide them with better protection and support was a consequence of slavery.[4]

Isabella witnessed volatile mob scenes in New York City, whose black population rivaled Philadelphia's (about fifteen thousand). "Class geography" also characterized New York—a holdover from Dutch days when the free poor, the enslaved, and the master class might live in close proximity, but with the strictest hierarchy. The arrival of Irish Catholics in the nineteenth century brought new tensions. Blacks and Irish were neighbors, labor competitors, and political foes. During Isabella's first year in New York, the city celebrated the presidential election victory of Andrew Jackson, a Tennessee slaveholder who embodied the Jeffersonian ethos: white farmers and workingmen as the "bone and sinew" of America, universal white male suffrage, states' rights, African colonization for free blacks—and slavery for the rest. New York's Martin Van Buren and his

Albany associates, called the "Regency," orchestrated Jackson's victory and soon ushered in a second American party system (Democrats versus Whigs). The Democrats' New York City stomping ground was Tammany Hall (a fraternal club transformed into a political machine). The party's glue was a white nationalism that embraced racism just as Northern blacks were seeking to position themselves as a free people.[5]

The growing political clout of Irish immigrants eroded most labor opportunities for Federalist-oriented African Americans. Twice as many black women as men lived in New York and possessed unmarketable skills. Racism prevented their working in factories with white women in the emerging clothing industry, or doing the non-specialized sewing at home (outwork). Besides domestics, poor black women were vendors—selling pastries, hot chocolate, hot buttered fruit, chestnuts, vegetables, and cider. Chanting their wares on streets and in markets, these women contributed to the city's roguish reputation.[6]

The black middle class operated small businesses, ministered black churches, taught school, and acquired real estate. New York blacks also established their race's first newspaper, *Freedom's Journal*. The editors spoke for the middle class in opposing rural black migration, fearing that the city's vices would entice country people's "uncultivated minds" away "from the line of duty." Stay with agriculture, *Freedom's Journal* urged. Only suffering awaited blacks in the cities. Nonetheless, Isabella joined thousands who flocked to New York, and sometimes met "force with force" in racial confrontations. Blacks not only paraded in honor of abolition, they organized street fights against slave catchers, and protested harassment of their institutions.[7]

A small number of whites supported black uplift. Reverend John Stanford, who supervised the city's "humane institutions," maintained close ties to the black community, promoted moral improvement and relief, and organized little chapels among the black poor. Instrumental in establishing the First African Presbyterian Church, Stanford also introduced wealthy silk merchant Arthur Tappan to black religious leaders and nudged him toward black causes. Through Tappan's influence, Theodore Wright, later a noted Abolitionist, was admitted to the Presbyterian Seminary, and later founded New York's Second African Presbyterian Church. Stanford's revivalist zeal and focus on downtrodden blacks would soon attract Isabella.[8]

Isabella's Methodist friends immediately introduced her to James La Tourette, a prosperous, middle-aged fur merchant and speculator from a large, wealthy Staten Island (Richmond Hill) family of French Huguenot and Dutch Reformed extraction. La Tourette, who had recently left John Street Methodist Church, was also a popular, unordained preacher whose home was a nerve center for enthusiastic religion. The family eagerly employed Isabella. La Tourette's young wife, Cornelia, had recently lost one baby and had another on the way and a toddler. For servingwomen such as Isabella, good domestic employment in a generous family ensured a certain standard of living. They had their own quarters and received a salary, daily necessities, a refuge during illness, and protection from the dangerous streets. Isabella's letter from St. James Church in Kingston also ensured membership in the John Street congregation. For the next two years, she worked and worshipped among white Methodists and frequented La Tourette's separate meetings.[9]

Like other blacks refusing to tolerate Jim Crow indignities, Isabella would not ride streetcars because she had to sit outside. She was accustomed to walking, and it helped sharpen her recall of place names, streets, and landmarks. The fact that her employers were clustered near each other facilitated her geographical adjustment. Her English improved; she maneuvered well in her part of the city, and she prospered. She saved money and furnished her own living quarters. She still enjoyed dressing well and wore a fancy cape of which she was quite proud. She remained attached to her Dutch pipe.[10]

Isabella formed friendships with other now-forgotten black female "doers of the Word": Mary Simpson Washington, formerly enslaved by George Washington (some said he fathered fair Mary), was a popular shopkeeper, vendor, and pleasant "do gooder" affiliated with St. George's Church. "Elegant" Mary nursed the sick "whether cats or people" during epidemics and shared her "fund of anecdotes respecting her old master," particularly on Washington's Birthday. She and Isabella were "intimate" friends until Mary's death in 1836. Katy Ferguson was another role model for Isabella, and their early lives had parallels. Katy was born into New York slavery about 1775, and her Virginia-born mother grounded her in spirituality before the two were painfully separated. After Methodists helped Katy obtain freedom, she married young and had two children, but she lost her entire family. As a young widow she became a sought-after confectioner who cared for orphans and poor children with her own resources. On Sundays she invited children into her Five Points home for Christian teaching. This began "a great and good work." With help from Reverend John Stanford and reformer Isabella Graham (whose Relief Society only aided children of impoverished genteel whites), Katy established the first Sunday school in the city. Her home was also the site for adult weekly prayer meetings where women such as Isabella could bear witness. Isabella's spiritual horizons broadened through these friendships, her religious affiliations, camp meetings, black celebrations, and membership in a woman's lodge.[11]

White Methodist women employers also helped Isabella's religious development. Belinda Gatfield and Cornelia La Tourette taught in the John Street Church "coloured class"; Isabella heard Bible lessons there and learned about Methodism while simultaneously polishing her English. However, even before she arrived, many African Americans had abandoned John Street church membership. New to the city and cautious, she remained with her white benefactors for a time, to "learn all she could."[12]

Perfectionist James LaTourette probably gave Isabella her first opportunity to speak publicly in New York City. Labeled a Methodist maverick, La Tourette was reportedly the "emperor" of the growing Perfectionist movement, which he called a "faith." Local and out-of-town believers gathered at revivals and in La Tourette's home for emotional meetings. Every early Methodist itinerant and bishop once preached Perfection. The doctrine appears throughout Scripture, beginning with Adam and Eve—created perfect, but falling short of God's demands and expectations. Nineteenth-century exegetical debates over Perfection were rooted in antiquity. Over the centuries Christianity has vacillated between Augustinian predestination (preordained salvation depending on the grace of God) and Pelagianism (free will). While Martin Luther's Augustinian views became the basis of America's Protestant predestination heritage, the pendulum swung the other way in the eighteenth century when John Wesley, founder of Methodism, urged Christians to strive for earthly Perfection ("perfect love" flowing from salvation). Wesley insisted that both the Old and New Testaments proclaimed the possibility of Perfection; it was central to his theology. But John Street pastor Nathan Bangs was priming the Methodist Episcopal Church for respectability and deplored liberal doctrines such as Perfectionism, which accepted female public witness, sermons based on practical dealings with the Holy Spirit, and emotionalism. However, James La Tourette welcomed Isabella Van Wagenen's spiritual gifts.[13]

Since not everyone achieved perfection, Isabella, successfully overcoming spiritual weakness and Satan's many taunts, considered herself blessed with holiness and sanctified. Perfection was essentially a "striving." (Even Christ was tempted.) Hence revitalization through worship, prayer, praise, and service not only won souls and nurtured converts but sustained sanctification. While Perfectionism was too radical for Methodism's new image, others considered Christianity's work only half done without this striving. Isabella was comfortable among religious enthusiasts who believed in miracles, spirit possession, the gift of prophecy, interpretations of visions and dreams, and a simple apostolic lifestyle. Perfectionists also dealt in signs, wonders, and mighty deeds through prayer.[14]

Perfectionism, which guided Isabella's spiritual development and reform interests, was the most significant of the many isms emerging from this era. Perfectionism was the guiding force behind the Great Western Revival, begun under the inspirational preaching of Charles Grandison Finney, and the movement was in full force when Isabella arrived in New York. Finney breathed so much fire and life into "cold, languid" western New York churches that the region was labeled "burned-over." This revivalism spread throughout white America north of Dixie. Calling his strategy "new means" and "measures," this magnetic Presbyterian's preaching style was extemporaneous, lively, and conversational; his sermons fused Scripture with experience, as he bore down on listeners with steely, piercing eyes, sometimes singling out individuals. He led or lined out hymns in a fine singing voice. He also conducted collective and private prayer sessions and discussions. Although he did not rant, he embraced the enthusiasm of common folk, welcomed spiritual paroxysms, and provided a good dose of hellfire.[15]

"New men" spread Finney's new measures throughout the Northeast and Canada, where, reportedly, people "on every side . . . rage like mad men." Some in Finney's Perfectionist "fifth column" were barely literate; others were intellectually accomplished.[16] While most of the established clergy opposed Finney, New York's leading evangelicals, Arthur and Lewis Tappan, hoped that Finney could merge religion with reform in their city, where he held massive revivals. In 1829, the Tappan brothers transformed Chatham Garden, a huge old theater in the middle of the impoverished Five Points district, into a sanctuary. With Finney as pastor, Chatham Street Chapel became the Second Presbyterian Free church, where urban worshippers included clerks, small tradespeople, midlevel merchants, and the laboring classes whom established churches ignored. Finney reportedly initiated "ultraism," defined as an "amorphous . . . combination of activities, personalities, and attitudes creating a condition in society which could foster experimental doctrines." The ultraists, however, took their Perfectionism far beyond Finney's. Disenchanted preachers were leaving him and beginning to communicate with the more radical James La Tourette at the time that Isabella worked in his home and preached at his meetings. Some of these ministers later became the most ardent reformers and Abolitionists. Finney was soon wooed away from New York City, with the Tappans' blessings, to teach theology at the newly established Oberlin Institute in Ohio.[17]

Thus, from the beginning of her New York City years, Isabella connected with ultraism, Perfectionism, and remnants of Finney's movement. Finney's measures, like his brand of Perfectionism, were not new; they came from Primitive Methodism, and were still being practiced by female messengers attempting to reclaim a spiritual status they once enjoyed. Prior to 1830, over one hundred unordained women had traveled throughout the country "thundering out their condemnations of sin." Yet once dissenting sects had become mainstream, they had attempted to silence women and written them out of church histories. Although women were more active and numerous than ever in the churches, they could not preach, except among free will Baptists, Quakers, and Perfectionists. In particular, the black male religious hierarchy discouraged black women preachers. Nonetheless, women preached, especially at camp meetings, and a few left personal accounts.[18]

Isabella Van Wagenen, the Methodist, did not need Finney's example to apply the measures effectively. She was naturally endowed with a powerful presence—an impressive sinewy frame, large, penetrating eyes, and a commanding voice that carried a congregation. Her contralto singing was called sonorous, rich, and deep, but also sweet, melodious, and moving. Merging the sacred and secular in her preaching, Isabella possessed the measures' raw material—personal experiences documenting the miraculous saving power of the Cross, even in the darkest hour, and living testimony that God, for the sake of the faithful, would rain down destruction. She cultivated and wielded well other tools of the new measures trade: mannerisms, movements, gesticulations, shifting of voice from shouts to whispers, and visual and auditory sensations that roused the audience. She began committing biblical passages to memory and debating with ministers. She merged scriptural parables with life, and presented her message in a vernacular style that was especially appealing to rural folk of the hinterland.

Isabella was a mystic before becoming a Methodist, and her "gifts" went beyond new measures. She directly connected spirituality with cosmology and combined Africanity with Christianity. Mysticism prepared her as a messenger. James La Tourette described Isabella as endowed in "spiritual mysteries" and "exemplary—a child of God and eminently gifted and favoured by God." She was, he said, noted for "long and loud preaching and praying remarkable for their influence in converting." The Methodists called her speaking influence "miraculous." At camp meetings, Isabella Van Wagenen "commanded a larger audience than the celebrated [Irish revivalist] Moffit, when both were preaching on the same ground, at the same time." Isabella's heritage, training, trials, and faith in her own ability to bear witness coincidentally meshed with Finney's movement and measures. She had charisma—the "pneuma" of the Holy Spirit, which she and others believed was divine grace bestowed by God.[19]

Isabella probably met Jarena Lee and Zilpha Elaw, who were preaching in the vicinity between 1828 and 1830. Both Isabella and Zilpha shared preaching grounds with Reverend John Moffit, whom Isabella reportedly outshone. The self-proclaimed white prophetess Harriet Livermore was James La Tourette's guest while Isabella lived in his home. The daughter of a United States Senator, Livermore preached to black women in prison, reportedly with great effect; later she published her sermon and presented a copy to each woman. Yet religious publications never mentioned these women.[20]

In fact, Methodists and other denominations condemned female preaching, even as women continued to attract large audiences. In 1828, a Methodist wrote an article lamenting "living in a place where I am doomed to witness *frequent* violation of propriety and female delicacy." The writer urged all denominations to rally in a common cause and to establish an "American Society for the Prevention of Women's Speaking and praying at improper times and places." No person whose wife or daughter prayed or spoke in public would be allowed to join. Presbyterians urged women to use only "proper means" to propagate religious knowledge. Ministers quoted the apostle Paul's dictate that women keep silence in the churches, and "be subordinate. . . . If there is anything they desire to know, let them ask their husbands at home." Furthermore, in no case should women "be public preachers and teachers, in assemblies promiscuously composed of the two sexes." Women should practice evangelical piety at home; outside the home they could do charity, do certain benevolent work, and form "associations for prayer among themselves." Noting that Paul sometimes favored women's public "praying and prophesying," ministers rationalized that in ancient times women were under miraculous dispensation and supernatural inspiration.[21]

Isabella's ultraist associates rejected this perspective and encouraged her preaching. And in conformity with the doctrine of free will inherent in Perfectionism, most ultraists viewed women as the unrecognized promoters of virtue. Through her friendships with Perfectionists, Isabella became a preaching woman and a moral reformer.

II

As a member of the New York City black community, Isabella also obtained an education in identity politics. *Freedom's Journal,* the voice of black protest, progress, unity, and culture, launched a frontal attack on the American Colonization Society (ACS), an upholder of slavery and opponent of black citizenship. The creation of the ACS in late December 1816 had coincided with the anticipated passage of New York's abolition law. Not coincidentally, when the law passed in 1817, New York newspapers extolled colonization as the "solution" to the black "problem," and ACS branches spread rapidly. Members had various agendas, but the basic goal was to rid the nation of free blacks, reduce threats to slavery, and keep the volatile subject out of national politics. Noted slaveholders, national statesmen, Supreme Court justices, and the major religious denominations all supported colonization. So did mainstream newspaper editors, including New York's James Watson Webb and William Leete Stone, and progressive whites, including the Tappans. Even a few black leaders rationalized that an African colony would enhance commerce, spread Christianity, and be a safe haven for victims of the illegal Atlantic trade. Ordinary blacks wanted none of it. At public meetings they expressed open hostility toward anyone supporting the white-sponsored, slaveholder-dominated colonization scheme. Black leaders followed their people.[22]

By 1831, Isabella had united with the African Methodists, who had founded the first black Methodist congregation in New York, called "Zion Church" and later Mother Zion, because from it sprang a new denomination—African Methodist Episcopal Zion (AMEZ). New York black Methodists formed their church independently of Philadelphia's Bethel African Methodist Episcopal Church ("Mother" Bethel); but both denominations represented blacks' long-held desires for autonomy from white spiritual and secular control. Black New Yorkers had met separately for worship since 1780. In the 1790s, they publicly organized an African Society amid growing racism within John Street Church. Whites controlled black classes, refused to license black preachers, and built separate benches in the galleries marked "B.M." (black members). In 1796, when John Street whites opposed the Saint Domingue Revolution, a group of angry blacks followed John Varick and Peter Williams Sr. when they left the church. They rented a meetinghouse in the heavily black Sixth Ward, near the Collect Pond and the Bowery, land once owned by the first group of African Dutch freed people. Black leaders petitioned the Common Council for assistance in purchasing land for a place of worship and for a cemetery, to replace the Old Negro Burial Ground, which had been in existence since before 1640.[23]

When Isabella arrived, black Methodists had a fine new edifice at Church and Leonard streets. They had also broken completely from the white Episcopacy and established a separate denomination with James Varick as the first bishop. It seemed a good church for Isabella. New York's Methodist Conference grew increasingly white, conservative, and isolating for blacks; (Zion was conveniently located near Isabella's new employers on Duane Street; and although both the AME and the AME Zion churches were activism-oriented, the latter was reportedly more radical. At one time, leaders such as David Ruggles, Frederick Douglass, Harriet Tubman, Jermain Loguen, and of course the future Sojourner Truth were all affiliated with the AME Zion denomination.[24]

Zion, was the church of the black working class at this time and a center for important social and political discourse. Isabella heard debates and speeches affecting the general black population, including the organization of the first black national convention. At Zion, Isabella also had a reunion that was both sad and joyful. When her sister Sophia moved to the city, she introduced Isabella to Michael, a brother she knew only through their parents' sorrowful stories. Michael and baby sister Dinah had been taken away one snowy morning, and the little boy's vain struggle to hide was embedded in the family's history. Dinah, whose name had been changed to Nancy, had recently died in the city. Through Michael's description, Isabella realized that she and Dinah had held hands at Zion's altar, never knowing that they were blood relations. Isabella should have sensed it. "Was not I . . . struck with the peculiar feeling of her hand—the bony hardness so just like mine? And yet I could not know she was my sister; and now I see she looked so like my mother!" Out of ten or twelve siblings, three lived to find each other. They wept, laughed, exchanged stories, and cursed the bondage that had shattered their family. Each emancipation, whether gradual or immediate, North or South, created similar pathos. Yet these children of James and Elizabeth were fortunate. Isabella and Peter now had an extended family.[25]

According to Isabella's Perfectionist beliefs, human love was a medium to celebrate divine love: "Pure and undefiled religion before God and the Father is this: to visit the fatherless and widows in their affliction." Her charge was outreach—to rid society of sin before the Second Coming—and her desire was to "be up and doing." Neither Zion Church nor camp meetings satisfied her calling. Service was a conscious manifestation of Christian charity, and good works meant bestowing love beyond the margins of those who returned it or who were easy to love. It required a special, extended form of giving. Yet Isabella was a poor, Dutch-speaking, uneducated domestic from the country; she did not fit in with middle-class black women's race-based benevolence. She began to search for a way to bring about broader, biracial reform, which emphasized sacred, secular, and feminine issues; in doing so, as will be discussed, she was ahead of her time. At least one other black female ultraist joined her—a woman named Katy (not Katy Ferguson), whom Isabella met at Zion. Katy had fled Virginia bondage via the Underground Railroad, leaving children behind; she kept house for a religious zealot named Elijah Pierson. Like Isabella, Katy was a Perfectionist who followed teachings of the Spirit and engaged in reform work.[26]

Isabella's reform work first began when she joined white Methodist women involved in the gritty Five Points Project, which was led by John McDowell, a young Princeton Seminary student and city missionary. The Five Points was situated on the swampy, filled-in, polluted Collect Pond, where brewers, tanners, potters, and tobacco manufacturers had once had shop-homes. Some streets were "foul, muddy lanes," with "refuse-choked pools of slime and silt" washing down from the surrounding hills. When it rained, cellars, kitchens, and backyards filled with unclean water and green, stinking muck. Known for rampant disease, "naked depravity," and "moral leprosy," Five Points owed much of its bruising notoriety to a "social melting pot" ambiance, where the "vilest rabble, black and white," publicly caroused together. The Points reportedly was made up of the city's worse elements: working and unemployed poor, homeless urchins and beggars, elegant brothels and dilapidated sex houses, streetwalkers and dandies, fops and pimps, theaters and dance halls, saloons, gangs, alcoholics, roaming pigs, and wild dogs. Casual, sometimes racially motivated violence commonly erupted into riots. Yet, despite antipathy, "black and white promiscuously mingle and nightly celebrate disgusting orgies." They shared the urban sex trade—whites frequented black-run establishments, and black men sometimes controlled white female sex labor. Writer George Foster, reflecting on the Five Points interracial phenomenon in the 1850s, noted that some white women preferred black men as "desirable companions and lovers."[27]

Isabella preached in this "seat of Satan," enduring the sexually and racially charged "language of the street" and the crude, suggestive "behavior of the street." People stood half-naked in doorways or windows, brazenly taunting, jeering, and beckoning women reformers. The Points, called the most notorious slum in the Western Hemisphere and located in the lap of City Hall, challenged powerful and privileged New Yorkers in their access to the streets. Any man "hazards his good name" one report said, if seen in the vicinity of the Five Points, and a "virtuous female cannot go out at certain hours without being insulted." Nonetheless, by the spring of 1831, Isabella was recruiting female prostitutes who vowed to reform and enter John McDowell's recently established Magdalen Society. McDowell understood women's crucial role in this moral reform movement. "Ladies, ladies," he implored, "your suffering sex demands this at your hands—the Savior demands it."[28]

McDowell had enlisted the support of influential Arthur Tappan to organize the Magdalen Society for the repentant prostitutes Isabella and other female reformers recruited. The two men walked the "deplorable" Five Points; the Fourth Ward's Battery slum on the wharf ("the Hook"); and the black Bancker Street slum. Unlike McDowell but like most male evangelicals, Tappan considered men the spiritual interpreters and guardians of morality, and used biblical exegesis to represent human iniquity in female terms. Women symbolized humankind's vile and blasphemous element, destined to perish in the great apocalyptic fire. Indeed, the Bible's beginning and end used women as tropes for the power of unbridled, unredeemed sexuality. In the Book of Revelation, a sinful world was "the great whore" of Babylon, who drank "the blood of the saints" and "martyrs of Jesus." But McDowell convinced Tappan that by also focusing on perpetrators of prostitution—young male seducers, "men of fashion and profession," and a host of "sailors and Negroes"—and with help from reform women such as Isabella, "harlots" could be saved.[29]

The Magdalen Society emerged from an already established female asylum run by Pearl Street merchant Elijah Pierson, the religious zealot who employed Isabella's friend Katy. Pierson ran the asylum in his Bowery Hill home, but after his wife's death, the enterprise languished. The grieving widower agreed to move and relinquish the Bowery Hill property to Tappan; he formed an all-male board and reconstituted Pierson's asylum as a home for penitent prostitutes. The board, mostly nouveau riche merchants, was 90 percent High Church, with Tappan as president and McDowell the only minister. Several board members, including Elijah Pierson, provided the women with daily religious instruction and supervision on a rotating basis. The board also established a probationary halfway house in the Five Points.[30] Before long, Isabella Van Wagenen would go to Bowery Hill.

She, Katy and a very small group of white women, making up "the most extreme wing of evangelical Protestantism," courageously worked in Five Points. Isabella boldly entered "the most wretched hovels," "dens of iniquity," and underground businesses, where her white sisters "dared not follow." A tall, quick figure in her dark cloak and turban, she slipped into out-of-the-way bailiwicks and dismal medieval haunts well known for "miscegenation sexual intercourse": "Yankee Kitchen," "Cow Bay," and "Squeeze Gut Alley." The fiery-tongued black woman preacher would certainly have censured Hannah Lewis, the popular black madam who employed only white women. Respectable black churchmen who used their "grocers" (liquor stores), oyster houses, gambling joints, and grogshops for illicit purposes came under attack. No establishment or individual was off limits, McDowell told the female brigade, whether businesses, brothels, nightwalkers, pimps, or customers. Reformers admonished, reproved, and counseled. They heard stories of shame, seduction, and abandonment; argued with madams; and gathered up intoxicated women from the pavement.[31]

Thirty years of enslavement and sleeping on pallets in Dutch kitchens shaped Isabella's understanding that neither unfortunate circumstances nor proximity to "evil" was synonymous with moral degradation. The Five Points housed more than pimps, sex workers, and the destitute. The "best-known [white] madam in ante-bellum America" kept her establishment and home right next to Isabella's Zion Church. So did the Garnets, a respectable, Maryland-born, self-emancipated family, whose son Henry became a noted Presbyterian minister and Abolitionist. Alexander, son of the Crummells, who lived next to the Garnets, became a leading black intellectual and Episcopal priest. Isabella was especially eager to "get among her own colored people." Recently emancipated Sixth Ward residents lived in miserable, ill-heated garrets and cellar homes, possessed little furniture, and slept on hay mattresses with heaps of rags as bedcovers. Just as Isabella refused "to bow to the filth of the city," so could her personal example encourage others spiritually, and mitigate their hopelessness. She visited the Mission House, held private prayer meetings, catechized families, visited deathbeds, organized and taught Sabbath schools, and handed out Bibles. This antebellum womanist consciousness was not modern feminist consciousness, but nonetheless struggled against white patriarchy. Historically, black women have expressed their consciousness through activism involving family and community, thereby not challenging black men. Isabella followed, as well as extended, that trajectory. However, some blacks in the Five Points preferred to hear whites. This pained Isabella to tears, but did not deter her efforts within the female spiritual army.[32]

Although most black people rejected Isabella's social and spiritual counseling, she nonetheless continued teaching and preaching. Her preaching style was intense, extemporaneous, and call-and-response. But she believed that God spoke in a "still small voice." Wild, unruly, unhinged physical ecstasy at Five Points meetings seemed to stem from sources other than a work of grace. At James La Tourette's noisy mission assemblies, overwrought worshippers wept, prayed uncontrollably, and expressed penitence with physical gyrations. Once, when the packed-in congregation became "delirious with excitement," they jumped on Isabella's cloak and threw her off balance. Landing on the floor unceremoniously and unexpectedly, she tried to right herself. But the worshippers, thinking she was in a state of possession, rejoiced "over her spirit" with even more frenzy. A weaker person might have suffocated. But the black lady preacher was muscular and strong. She struggled against the enthusiastic worshippers, no doubt losing her turban as well as her cloak. Finally free, and suffering from "both fear and bruises," Isabella ended her participation in boisterous, foot-stomping spiritual demonstrations in the Five Points.[33]

In spring 1831, at the urging of Daniel Smith, a storekeeper and Perfectionist preacher from Kingston, and Abijah Smith, also from Kingston and a class leader at John Street Church, Isabella joined their work at the Magdalen Society. Elijah Pierson's housekeeper, Katy, took Isabella to Bowery Hill, a lush, bucolic, country-like enclave overlooking the Hudson River. This sequestered neighborhood attracted wealthy ultraists interested in alternative lifestyles. Isabella made an immediate impression on board member Pierson. Had she been baptized? He inquired. Yes, replied the African Dutch mystic, "by the Holy Spirit." To Pierson, her answer was indeed appropriate. In the Pentecost tradition, Isabella's calling was superior: God the father "baptized with the Holy Ghost." Moreover, had not God "chosen the poor of this world to be rich in faith?" Isabella became a regular preacher at the Magdalen; Pierson believed that Providence and prayer had brought her there. He needed a spiritually endowed housekeeper to replace Katy.[34]

The Magdalen Society's hidden dynamics, and Elijah Pierson's religious proclivities, which Isabella soon embraced, need some explanation. The former Presbyterian elder's intense quest for "true" holiness dictated insularity. To "keep oneself unspotted from the world" and reinforce spiritual strength, Perfectionist "saints" gathered in "little circles for social worship" or "holy bands." Before his wife Sarah's death, Pierson had created a Bowery Hill worship circle. His followers included Sarah, Katy, and two married couples who were cousins: Ann and Benjamin Folger and Frances and Reuben Folger, who also moved to Bowery Hill. This Perfectionist band practiced personal rectitude, asceticism, and plain living. They abhorred invidious distinction, including disdain toward blacks and the poor, segregated church seating, special pews, and church collections. They worshipped together several times daily, fasted to the point of emaciation, witnessed through visions, spoke directly to God, and prayed extemporaneously. Elijah Pierson, a shrewd businessman and "very rational and intelligent" in monetary matters, became a puzzle to his financial and religious associates. His former pastor, Reverend Gardiner Spring, tried unsuccessfully to wean Pierson away from his "delusions." Before his wife's death, Pierson claimed a call to preach. When he was denied ordination, Pierson's Bowery Hill home became his church. Within months of opening their female asylum, thirty-four-year-old Sarah lay dying of tuberculosis. Pierson believed her illness was God's test to see if he had "faith" enough to continue his mission despite "Christian" mockers.[35]

Pierson expected a miracle. "June 18, 1830, Day of fasting and prayer for Sarah," he wrote in his diary. "It seemed the Lord said, "Sarah thy wife shall recover.'" Two days later, while riding to his office, Pierson had a profound revelation and dispensation: God said: "I have named thee this day Elijah the Tishbite and thou shall go before me in the spirit and power of Elias, to prepare my way before me." Pierson was to "Gather unto me all the members of Israel at the foot of Mount Carmel," assemble his "elders," and form a new "kingdom." Elijah, the great Old Testament prophet, was acknowledged in the New Testament as John the Baptist, the "spirit and power of Elijah." John's ministry of repentance was forerunner to the messianic age. Rather than dying, Elijah ascended to heaven in the flesh. The Book of James invokes Elijah as a wonder-worker. If anyone was sick, "Let him call for the elders of the church and let them pray over him, anointing him with oil in the name of the Lord." Prayers of faith would save the sick, "and the Lord will raise him up." So Pierson gathered followers around his wife's sickbed; they prayed and bathed her in oil. Her death on June 29, 1830, only enhanced Pierson's faith. At her funeral, Pierson and his followers attempted to resurrect Sarah.[36]

At the time of these events, Isabella had not met the Piersons. Yet later, she was accused of being "one of the principal actors and speakers in the religious rites and ceremonies" surrounding Sarah Pierson's deathbed anointing and bizarre funeral. Two hundred friends and family members observed the ritual over Sarah's coffin. Gardiner Spring and Sarah's father, minister John Stanford, were among the stunned clerics who witnessed Pierson reading passages on miracles and healing, praying over Sarah, and pathetically attempting to revive her. The spectacle left Stanford "ill and depressed in mind." Such "faith of miracles" and "miraculous power," Gardiner Spring said, like female preaching, belonged only to ancient times. Spring blamed Pierson's behavior on Charles Finney, Perfectionists, and other enthusiasts who encouraged pursuit of miraculous promise. Years later, Spring wrote: "There are men and women still alive and among us, who remember the circumstances of the death of Mrs. Pierson, around whose lifeless body her husband assembled a company of believers, with the assurance that if they prayed in faith, she would be restored to life. Their feelings were greatly excited and their impressions of their success peculiar and strong. They prayed, and prayed again, and prayed in faith. . . . She slept the sleep of death."[37]

When Isabella met Pierson, he still believed in his wife's resurrection; his delusion was fed by follower Ann Folger, who secretly wrote him that Sarah would return via another woman's spirit—Ann's cousin-in-law, Frances Folger. Ann even had a vision that the pair would conceive a son named James. Inspired by these beliefs, Pierson continued his spiritual and humanitarian efforts. As Isabella was going to work for the Magdalen Society, Pierson was organizing his new home on Fourth Street into a Perfectionist commune, enclave of holiness, and precursor to a "kingdom of God on earth."[38]

Isabella found the Magdalen Society thriving, despite some sectarianism tensions among board members. They resented Elijah Pierson's Perfectionist views, though only the "saints" knew he also claimed transmigration. Things went well on the surface until McDowell's first annual report hit the press. It drew a howl of protest from religious conservatives, Democrats, and the "sporting" community. These protesters were outraged that the report placed the number of sex workers in the city at a staggering ten thousand, presented women as sympathetic victims, contained frank personal vignettes implicating "respectable" male citizens, and revealed the prevalence of interracial sex. "The city has been slandered," the penny press screamed; McDowell had brazenly exposed "virtuous women" to horrifying details of sexuality in the infested slums. The Magdalen evangelicals had defamed the city with inflated statistics. Although McDowell defended and tried to explain his information, the embarrassed High Church board devised an exit from the project, and Tappan soon transferred the Bowery Hill properties back to Elijah Pierson. Even McDowell eventually abandoned both the Magdalen Society and Elijah Pierson.[39]

In the midst of this furor, Katy and Isabella left for the summer to visit their children. Isabella agreed that on returning to New York, she would work for Pierson at his Fourth Street home. In the fall of 1831, she moved into this commodious property. It had ample living quarters, room for a small progressive school, and a chapel, called the "kingdom." Imagining himself as Christ's biblical forerunner and the incarnation of John the Baptist ("Elijah the Tishbite"), Pierson embraced mystical apostolic Christianity. Reportedly, his kingdom attracted "many worshipers" and maintained a "selected community of God's favorites," including Katy, a reformed sex worker from Bowery Hill named Mrs. Bolton, and Sylvester Mills, a wealthy, unbalanced Presbyterian merchant. Although the Folger couples had moved, Ann and Benjamin Folger still considered Pierson their spiritual leader. Isabella not only joined the household, she became Pierson's preaching associate at the Fourth Street chapel and at the Magdalen Society. Pierson and Isabella preached repentance, the mystery of faith, healing miracles, and "teachings of the Spirit." The Magdalen Society remained open until April 1832, when finances forced its closure.[40]

Besides supporting female preaching, Perfectionists also believed that slavery, which hindered God's kingdom on earth, was evil. Both the domineering, "tyrannical" James La Tourette and the sensitive but spiritually forceful Elijah Pierson praised Isabella's preaching. Yet they differed on slavery. While LaTourette favored African colonization, Pierson supported abolition. He had hired Katy when she was a "fugitive," eventually purchased her freedom, and reportedly gave her a stipend to live on.[41]

Thus, for Isabella, the kingdom's appeal was socioreligious. It became her home, church, and community, where she was more than a domestic. Pierson called Isabella a "master spirit." Her intense faith, her amazing experience with the Holy Ghost, her sanctification journey and service made her equal, if not superior to other kingdom members. They washed each other's feet ("If I then, your Lord and Master, have washed your feet; ye also ought to wash one another's feet"), and greeted each other with a kiss ("Greet all the brethren with an holy kiss"). The spirits sat, ate, and worshipped in common, embracing a leveling that disregarded the larger society's racism and sexism.[42] For Isabella, this Christian communalism with an egalitarian base was a satisfying life.

Pierson and Isabella learned from each other. Despite his grief-stricken literal biblical interpretations, Pierson was not insane. Isabella absorbed the Presbyterian elder's vast scriptural knowledge and emulated his practices. For example, Pierson fasted weekly for three days and two nights because it created "great light in the things of God." Isabella, with her intense personality and rationalism, believed she needed even more light than Pierson. She fasted three days and nights without water. Ravenous on the fourth day, unable to walk at first, she weakly got to the pantry and ate an entire loaf of bread, hoping her voracity did not offend God. Admitting she was lighter in body than mind, she nonetheless enjoyed feeling that she "could skim around like a gull." On the other hand, her miraculous personal experiences went far beyond Pierson's. Unimpaired by theology, unfamiliar with theological arguments and debates, accustomed to spiritual introspection, she infused religion with life. The sacred-secular convergence that framed her mysticism, and Pentecostalism, had been tested. She also connected Christianity with African animism, in which miracles, devils, spirit possession, and transmigration of souls were not incongruous but common. One of Isabella and Pierson's many "bearing witness" sessions in 1832 could have certainly produced the slip of paper documenting her baptism in the Spirit.[43]

Ultraists' attraction to African American religious expression was not simply condescension or paternalism. Most blacks were fervently spiritual and rarely placed limits on mystical power. Nor did primitive Methodists and Perfectionists.

However, what most whites studied and practiced was natural within African heritage. The spontaneity of *African* American worship was born of mysticism, oral tradition, and a numinous cosmological ethos that eschewed rationalism in spiritual if not practical matters. Although mystical events had created and propelled early Christianity, mysticism had grown less significant. Whites who wanted to reconnect with altered states of mystical holiness or consciousness emphasized fasting and other methods for communicating with a transcendent influence or divine presence. So mystically inspired people like Isabella and Katy gave Pierson evidence that Scripture remained spiritually legitimate. If Isabella could retaliate successfully against the Gidneys by invoking a death curse, the "Spirit" could also empower Elijah Pierson to transmigrate as "John the Baptist." Moreover, if Pierson had faith enough, Sarah's "spirit" could conceivably enter another woman. Although incongruous to an outsider, such supernatural beliefs bound members of the kingdom together.

William James's analysis of mysticism is useful in distinguishing the Perfectionists in Pierson's kingdom from evangelicals and from other ultraists. According to James, mystical understandings had the following characteristics: sacred meaning that words cannot capture fully; insight above doctrine or discursive intellect leading to revelations and illuminations; recurrent altered states of consciousness, creating a rich, numinous development; and passivity, the most significant characteristic, wherein the higher power or Spirit takes possession.[44] Some religious radicals believed some of these principles; Kingdom followers accepted them all, and were labeled "fanatics." They believed that everything came through direct teaching of the Spirit, or God, who bestowed enlightenment on favorites. Saints "could see farther than other people into the Scriptures and the will of God." Pierson's followers believed that he, a man of old Presbyterian stock, possessed superlative knowledge. Isabella absorbed that scriptural wisdom, while he benefited from her peculiar, intuitive mystical insights. This extrasensory perception often came after fasting, which brought more intense dreams and visions with divine messages, thereby enhancing receptivity and communicative powers. As mystics possessing the characteristics of their different individual callings, Isabella and Pierson nonetheless shared theological principles. More significantly, as Perfectionists, they claimed the teaching, guidance, and at times possession by God, whom they called the "Spirit of Truth."[45]

Isabella's star might have risen higher in the city had she remained among Methodist Perfectionists and reformers and at Zion Church. Instead, she preferred the egalitarian spiritual niche of Pierson's kingdom. In so doing, she chose a religious trajectory too radical even for her former associates. This decision soon led her down a deceptive religious path.

A good name is rather to be chosen than great riches, and loving favour rather than silver and gold. — PROV. 22:1

The original members of this church were about a dozen. . . . Among them was Isabella, a black woman; who . . . was probably, before the end came, among the most wicked of the wicked. — WILLIAM LEETE STONE

CHAPTER 7

"I Will Crush Them with the Truth"

THE COMMUNE OF MATTHIAS

I

Isabella did not like Mrs. Bolton, and resented the reformed sex worker's influence on Elijah Pierson. "Fair, fat, and forty," well-dressed, and "pleasing and genteel in her manners," Bolton secured the position of matron at the Magdalen Society by manipulating Pierson. When the Magdalen closed, Pierson hired Bolton to do needlework in his home. Isabella also questioned Mrs. Bolton's spiritual reformation; she revealed almost proudly that she was a seasoned seducer of men and had "lived in fornication," and she named various gentlemen who had paid her large sums of money for sex. Bolton also confessed to joining the Methodists only to hide her lewdness. At camp meetings, she "had fainted, foamed, been carried into tents, and expressively *carried on*," only to entice men. After recounting sordid, unsolicited details of her iniquities, Bolton then inquired, "now do you think I *can* be forgiven?"[1]

Pierson answered affirmatively, quoting Scripture on "harlots entering the kingdom of heaven before others." But Isabella found Mrs. Bolton's actions immoral and shockingly heretical. She who "had played the hypocrite so well at camp meetings might be playing the hypocrite now," and "she who had seduced so many men with such skill, might be seducing Mr. Pierson." Although Pierson rebuked Isabella for lack of charity, she remained convinced of Mrs. Bolton's disingenuousness. Bolton's example reveals prostitution's complexity. Men often seduced women, led them astray, and abandoned them. Some female sex workers saw their trade as like any other, some as a form of power. Isabella believed Mrs. Bolton still had a harlot's "spirit."[2]

The two women maintained an uneasy truce. In the spirit of love, they worshipped together, washed each other's feet, and embraced. Isabella ran the house, supervised Pierson's two daughters (about eight and ten), and was a master spirit in the kingdom; she sometimes accompanied Pierson on preaching missions around New Jersey. Bolton distributed tracts, solicited audiences for kingdom sermons, and carried Pierson's message to the city. His following grew large as she gained access to homes and walked the streets, calling "Come and hear Elijah, the Prophet."[3]

Bolton's appeals apparently attracted a bearded stranger to Fourth Street. Unfortunately, Isabella's skepticism of Mrs. Bolton did not extend to this stranger when he appeared on May 5, 1832, at Elijah Pierson's door. Tall and slender, he had small, wild-looking gray eyes with a piercing intensity. His dark curly hair, parted down the middle, was mixed with gray, and below shoulder length. Only men in the Bible had such hair, Isabella thought. But even more stunning and so like biblical pictures, was the stranger's long, full beard of equally dark curly hair covering his breast. Isabella thought of "Jesus in the flesh."[4]

Editor Gilbert Vale, who had previously met Robert Matthews and heard him lecture, said he looked the part of Jesus, and also adopted the Nazarene's style of sitting rather than standing while sermonizing. Matthews "dealt in unconnected sentences sometimes much to the purpose, and others very flat," and he "displayed no marks of great genius; or much learning."[5] Nevertheless, Isabella was drawn to him. She invited the stranger into the parlor and they engaged in conversation. She stated her own religious opinion and inquired of his.

He called himself "Matthias," and if such naming was not ingenious, it certainly reveals his cunning and foresight: Matthias was the name of the disciple in the Book of Acts who replaced Judas after Jesus' ascension. Conveniently for Robert Matthews, after Matthias's ordination, he disappears from Scripture. Yet much significance was attached to his existence. First of all, the Holy Ghost, representing God's spirit, appeared only after Matthias's ordination. Second, Matthias had personal companionship with Jesus. Third, all twelve disciples received the Pentecostal breath, thereby having the numinous powers of the Spirit of Truth. Thus Robert Matthews was the lost apostle returned as prophet. Finally, Matthias's ordination reconstituted the group of twelve eyewitnesses to the Resurrection. Matthews used that number to suggest a symbolic restoration of Israel (twelve tribes) and hence a "kingdom of God on earth," something he actually wandered into. Matthews also used the number 12 to represent his own predictions of coming doom.[6]

Isabella queried the imposing stranger further. Why the beard? Devout men in the Bible did not cut their hair, he said. She asked why he called himself a Jew? All the disciples were Jews, he answered, and represented the Spirit of God the Father. "Do you not remember how Jesus prayed?" he reminded her. He prayed, "Our Father"; it was the Father not the Son's kingdom that would come to pass. This supplication was the foundation of Isabella's early faith. She could not argue against the literal representation of the Father as supreme. Matthias heard Isabella's experience, and learned all about Pierson. At the conclusion of their conversation, Isabella "felt as if God had sent him to set up the kingdom." Matthias promised to return on Saturday evening, when "John the Baptist" was home.[7]

Robert Matthews was born in 1788 into a large Scottish Presbyterian family in Washington County, New York. Orphaned at age seven and apprenticed in farming and carpentry, he grew into a young man of good habits, strong faith; he was "strictly temperate, careful in his observance of the Sabbath, and regular in his attendance." His wife, Margaret, said that initially, he was a kind, affectionate, and attentive family man. Yet he had "strange monthly turns" accompanied by leg spasms, violent headaches, and vomiting. The deaths of three children, his own near-fatal illness, and failed business enterprises in New York City affected his character negatively. His monthly turns increased, causing outbursts of anger and confusion over the "least thing." Matthews ceased work at his carpentry trade during these episodes, and became abusive toward his wife and children.[8] Searching Scripture to explain his personal calamities and failures, Matthews devised unconventional, bizarre biblical interpretations.

While the family lived in New York, Matthews attended Zion Church, and claimed it was the only time "he had ever seen the spirit of religion; that the time was near when the blacks and whites would associate." He also proclaimed himself a Jew through his grandmother having transferred her "spirit of prophecy" to him and blessed him on her deathbed. Margaret Matthews believed his Jewish notions came from Tammanyite Mordecai Noah, who actually was a Jew, and who was building a new city, Ararat, in upstate New York. But Matthews's model for a Temple of God and Holy City came from the Book of Revelation, and he would not have agreed with Noah's racist antiblack pronouncements. Matthias's religious enthusiasm and fits of insanity increased after the family returned to Albany and another son died a painful death from smallpox. Matthews greatly admired Edward Kirk, Albany's bold, antiestablishment Perfectionist Presbyterian minister, who was labeled a fanatic for helping the poor, supporting temperance, and for his strident Abolitionism. Kirk aided and befriended

Robert Matthews's destitute family but, like the Albany Methodists, shunned Matthews and denied him membership in the Fourth Presbyterian Church.[9]

Like the carpenter Jesus of Nazareth, the "Spirit" compelled Matthews to relinquish his chisels. He preached on street corners and interrupted church services with doomsday harangues. Long-suffering Margaret drew the line when Matthews attempted to baptize her. She threatened to "jump out of the window." Matthews cursed her for refusing to obey him as her husband and as a "holy man." Margaret kept her family together by accepting handouts, sending her little boys to beg, while she and their teenage daughter Isabella worked at shoe binding at home. Matthews disappeared during warm months and spent cold winters with his family, until Margaret resolutely refused to feed him. He vanished from Albany in the winter of 1829.[10] Isabella and Pierson knew nothing of his previous background.

As Isabella had advised, Matthews returned to meet Pierson. Eager to sit in on their conversation, Isabella finished her work early. If Elijah Pierson had branded Matthews an impostor and sent him away, that would have been enough for Isabella. But Pierson was no match for the striking, biblical-looking, quick-thinking prophet who twisted scriptural meanings deftly and persuasively and boasted the humble occupation of the Nazarene. He also wooed Pierson with the synchrony of their beliefs and experiences: direct influence of the Spirit, metaphysical transmission from one body to another, establishing a kingdom of God on earth, and damnation of "Christians" (people tied to traditional churches who condemned Perfectionism). Pierson's call as Elijah the Tishbite had taken place on June 20, 1830. Miraculously, Matthews claimed to have "completed" his call on that exact day (in reality it was early June), in "Argyle," New York (actually in Albany). The transmigrated prophets were about the same age, and from devout Presbyterian families. But Matthews declared superiority. The kingdom coming was not of the Son, but of the Father, and Matthews said he possessed the spirit of the Father. "He was God upon earth, because the spirit of God dwelled in him." John baptized with water in preparation for "the Father," who baptized with the Holy Ghost. Thus, the Father's presence transcended water baptism. Matthews was "Father Matthias," and their mustard-seed kingdom would spread throughout the earth. "Our creed is truth, and no man can find truth unless he obeys John the Baptist, and comes clean into the church."[11] Hereafter, Pierson's role was to lead converts to Father Matthias—the "Spirit of Truth." After the two spirits reached this understanding, they washed each other's feet, and all sat down to dinner.

Elijah Pierson preached once more, and announced that Father Matthias would deliver all sermons. Matthias immediately declared certain people to be blasphemers, including those who said the Jews had crucified Jesus; those who said the Sabbath was the first day of the week; those who immersed (baptized) converts fully clothed; and those who said sprinkling was baptism. Matthias instituted same-sex communal bathing to combat a sense of "shame" and because he believed that personal modesty bred individual "pride." Some of Matthias's pronouncements greatly affected Isabella's and Pierson's previous work. He disallowed praying and all reform activities and closed Pierson's and Isabella's Sabbath school. For Isabella, Matthias's attitude toward women was especially limiting. All who taught women were of the wicked; no females should lecture to their husbands or any men; everything with the smell of women would be destroyed; women were "the cap sheaf of the abomination of desolation—full of all deviltry." Women's role was simply to be obedient; otherwise, they were spirits of the wicked.[12]

Matthias's views on women were merely extreme versions of High Church doctrines. Isabella Van Wagenen's acceptance of this silencing reflects her Pentecostal understanding. Matthias represented forces that defined her conversion—the Father and the Holy Ghost—and legitimated her baptism of the Spirit. Although Jesus was the interceder for Isabella, the Father was greater than the Son. Since Elijah Pierson, Isabella's reference point, embraced this interpretation, so did she.

Matthias also mesmerized others. Widower Sylvester Mills offered the prophet his lavish Franklin Street home. This worked out well for Matthias and Isabella. At Pierson's, the schoolteacher-border known as Mr. Sherwood persecuted Matthias by pulling his beard, taunting him verbally, and calling him an impostor. Likewise, Mrs. Bolton vexed Isabella. Thus in the early summer of 1832, Matthias and Isabella moved to Mills's home. Katy—back from Virginia—went to Pierson's, while Mills's Irish domestic couple (John and Catherine Galloway) remained with him. The kingdom, now in Lower Manhattan, attracted even more attention.

Having spent so many years in want, Matthias preached material abundance. Since good things in life were for enjoyment, the spirits lived well. Isabella and Catherine Galloway sat a stupendous table. The commune ate plain good food: all sorts of meats (boiled only) except swine, varieties of vegetables, plain sweet cakes (but no rich pies), coffee and tea (but no alcohol). Worshippers were always fed, which increased their numbers. Editor William Leete Stone described Matthias's clothes as gaudy and ostentatious, including a crimson sash with the symbolic twelve tassels and Wellington boots (or sandals). His personal pomp, riding carriage, and long hair, as well as his beard in an age of clean-shaven men, attracted much attention. His outings along Broadway or the Battery drew crowds.[13]

Capitalizing on his benefactors' sheepish attitude about being "merchandisers," (parasitic, stingy, rich men), Matthias incurred huge clothing and food bills. He and Mills also developed a blueprint for a "temple." Mills ordered ornaments inscribed with the Lion of Judea, and a silver chalice to adorn the temple. When Mills's female relatives appeared, Matthias drove them away. Matthias was attracting larger audiences, particularly women. But he tolerated only obedient women—Isabella, Katy, Catherine, and Mrs. Rosetta Dratch, Pierson's elderly Jewish convert. The presence of women, Mills's spending sprees, the interracial character of the kingdom, and Matthias's sermons gave rise to rumors of licentious behavior.[14]

That summer, Asiatic cholera raged in the city, and the Sixth Ward was hardest hit. The cholera had migrated from Canada; in Quebec it had claimed twenty-two hundred people out of a permanent resident population of twenty-eight hundred. Despite physicians' warnings, New York officials, editors, and merchants did not alert the public in a timely fashion. By early July, the word was out, but too late for successful quarantines or emergency measures. In that month alone, the death toll was two thousand; it would have gone higher if more than a thousand New Yorkers had not fled the city. Elijah Pierson and his children escaped to Morrisville, N.J., but the other kingdom members remained. Evangelicals declared that the cholera epidemic was a scourge from God; Matthias preached that "sick devils" caused cholera, only entering those of little faith. Miraculously, no one in the kingdom was stricken, a further sign to followers of Matthias's divine favor. "The angels of destruction are making dreadful havoc, but do not be troubled," Mills wrote Pierson on July 20, 1832. "They are reaping the tares," but all was well in the kingdom. "The harvest is begun, and not a single blade of wheat can fall or be injured." The tares (biblical term for a noxious weed representing wicked people) were those outside the kingdom. The wheat (those within) were saved from cholera. Mills reported that "Katy is well, and at the Lord's house often. Isabella is also well. Matthias is still with us, thank God! . . . Surely this is 'the Kingdom of God.'"[15]

By October, the official death toll was 3,516, not including those undiagnosed and the sick who left the city but died later. Among the victims were John Jacob Astor's daughter (America's richest man had fled to Europe), prominent business leaders, doctors, and clergymen. The greatest trials fell on the poor, and perceived causes for the disease ranged from immorality to tobacco, alcohol, and unhealthy diet. It was 1849 before a British doctor theorized that cholera was contracted orally from water, usually through sewage contamination. New York's drinking water supply came from impure, polluted neighborhood wells. Few could afford the spring water carted from upstate. Undoubtedly, the secret to the kingdom's amazing health during this calamity was Matthias's insisting that they drink only clean spring water and eat fresh, unrefined, nonfried foods. The merchants in the kingdom willingly paid the $20 annual fee for fresh water.[16]

Matthias, who upheld female morality and "purity," seemed above seduction, though women tried. He whipped a Methodist teenager who claimed she spoke to God. He proclaimed Mrs. Bolton a devil and a lewd woman when she employed her wiles; to Isabella's great satisfaction, Pierson banished Bolton from the kingdom. Still, Matthias's unorthodox and unconventional views on marriage and reproduction drew attention. He preached against the commandment "increase and multiply," saying "God had never authorized wicked people to multiply." As the ideas of seventeenth-century Swedish mystic and philosopher Emanuel Swedenborg gained currency in America, some Perfectionists disavowed marriages without a spiritual base and advocated spiritual marriage over civil marriage. James LaTourette's former associate John Humphrey Noyes not only proclaimed a "second coming" but a "doctrine of security" from sin as an extension of Perfectionism. This concept evolved into couples attempting unsuccessfully to illustrate their firmness of spirit by sleeping together without carnal contact. The lines between religious enthusiasm and sexual excitement sometimes blurred. Matthias's support of spiritual wifery and attacks on traditional marriage nearly caused a riot. His sermons, his forcing out of Mills's female relatives, and Mills's wanton generosity all incited Mills's family into action.[17]

In September 1832, the kingdom came under siege. Sylvester Mills's brother Levi, his business associates, a "Christian" mob, and the police stormed the kingdom. After leading away meek Sylvester, the mob turned on Matthias. While Isabella tried to prevent their entrance, John Galloway, Mills's servant, let in the disrupters. They violently pushed Isabella out of the house and locked the doors. Matthias cursed Galloway for his "treachery," but like the Nazarene, he offered no resistance. Isabella reentered through another passage. The "powerful and energetic woman" tried to rescue Matthias. She was again roughly hauled out, but found another entrance and continued to intercede. The frustrated men now resorted to physical abuse. Isabella was "struck violently by Mr. [Levi] Mills." Badly injured by the blow, she nevertheless found another entry and tried unsuccessfully to protect Matthias. Some men held Isabella while others shaved Matthias clean, cut his hair, took his money and his watch, stripped off most of his clothing, and generally humiliated him. While the "Christians" restrained Isabella, they also lectured her. When satisfied that the prophet was sufficiently ridiculed, they and the police took Matthias to the "apartment for the insane" at Bellevue Hospital, as he reportedly screamed he was "God Almighty."[18]

Editor Gilbert Vale condemned the "Christians" and denounced the police for taking bribes to violate the peace. The law, Vale wrote, had behaved in a disgraceful manner, interfering in a private matter, attacking residents of a home, and manhandling a defenseless colored woman and an obvious fanatic. Sylvester Mills was committed to Bloomingdale Lunatic Asylum, and his house was closed. The now homeless Isabella received many offers of "asylum," including one from the apologetic Levi Mills. She desired no charity from "Christians," and spoke out harshly against them. She insisted that their lecturing to her about religion and Matthias and denouncing him as an impostor was pharisaical. She compared their inhumane treatment of Matthias with his humble submission. She paralleled events to the old story of "Crucify him, Crucify him." This persecution riveted Isabella more closely to Matthias than ever, for as Jesus said, "A prophet hath no honor in his own country." "It had the same effect on others," according to Gilbert Vale.[19]

Isabella convinced a hesitant Elijah Pierson to help Matthias. With the assistance of Matthias's brother George, they filed a habeas corpus writ. Matthias was discharged, but rearrested immediately for blasphemy—he claimed to be "God Almighty," Levi Mills asserted. He was freed on bail (no doubt Pierson and Isabella's money), and the charges were eventually dismissed. Isabella also visited the pitiful Sylvester Mills, who remained incarcerated for some time, but seemed steadfast in "faith."[20]

Pierson rented a house for Isabella and Matthias and gave the prophet a monthly allowance. Isabella purchased furniture, and Matthias's brother, George Matthews, also moved in. Matthias sent him with money for Margaret and instructions to join him. Rakish George kept the money but visited Margaret, who had heard that her husband was "in [the] company of a few gentlemen in N.Y." George lied, saying he had not seen his brother but had heard that he "had died at Philadelphia." Isabella and Matthias soon evicted George because of his alcoholism. When he left, he also stole some of Isabella's furniture.

Thus, the kingdom dissolved. Isabella went back to her old employers; Matthias returned to his street harangues. Suggestions made later that the African Dutch mystic and the prophet were lovers seem improbable. Both considered themselves married, and Matthias was not naturally a lascivious man. Isabella viewed him as a spirit guide above carnal behavior. Certainly much preaching, Scripture lectures, and dissemination of wild interpretations occurred in the Clarkson Street house. But in May 1833, moving time in the city, the "Spirit" told Pierson to close the Clarkson house. Matthias rented a room. Isabella stored her remaining belongings with her employers, Lucy and Perez Whiting, and then left for Ulster County to see her children.[21]

While she was away, Pierson introduced Matthias to Ann and Benjamin Folger. That fall, Isabella worked for her former Methodist preaching associate Daniel Smith, and also took in laundry, including Matthias's. One day, Matthias came for his laundry, and told Isabella that the Folgers had invited him to their country home for a while. Soon afterward, Ann Folger and Pierson's youngest daughter came for Matthias's laundry. Matthias was "well pleased" in the country, Ann reported, and Pierson was also moving there. Two weeks later, Matthias himself appeared. Elijah Pierson, who was prone to fits, was ill and needed

Isabella's help. And Matthias was reconstituting the kingdom at the Folgers' estate in Sing Sing (Westchester County). He wanted Isabella to join them and supervise the house along with Mrs. Folger. There were no wages to be earned but no expenses either. According to Scripture, "them that believed were of one heart and of one soul: . . . they had all things in common." Isabella accepted the offer and removed her furniture from storage, and Benjamin Folger shipped it to Westchester. Managing a large household without wages was a major concession for Isabella. How long she planned to stay was unclear. But the religious mystic was following apostolic Christianity. The concept of communal living was spreading, and in utopian communities, members commonly relinquished wages.[22] The Sing Sing community, in Mount Pleasant Village, was called Zion Hill or Mount Zion. It was beautiful, spacious, scenic, and isolated. No prying eyes would interfere with Father Matthias's preaching and teaching, or observe his rages. But Isabella later said it seemed strangely wrong from the beginning. Watching an incredible drama unfold, Isabella claimed that she remained at Zion Hill more out of curiosity than commitment.[23]

II

The Zion Hill kingdom originally included Father Matthias; Isabella; the Folger couple and their three children; Pierson and his daughters; Henry, an English tailor; Lewis, a German coachman; and Catherine Galloway, the Irish domestic. Catherine's husband had died an agonizing death, which kingdom members attributed to Galloway's part in the Father's arrest and humiliation. Much like Isabella's curse and Eliza Gidney's death, Matthias's hex suggested a power beyond human agency, and reinforced his hold on the kingdom. Other members came and went. Some people worked on the farm but were not in the "family." Generally, more than twenty people were on the estate. Elijah Pierson, who had now grown a beard and sported long fingernails, retired from his Pearl Street business. He kept a house in the city on Third Street where Benjamin resided on weekdays and Catherine kept house. While Ann, Isabella, Pierson, and Matthias were often the only three adults at Zion Hill, the entire family gathered there toward the week's end.[24]

Matthias's reputation as "Jumping Jesus" (because of his quick temper, rages, and professions of divinity) preceded him to Mount Pleasant. Yet local people observed that Matthias managed his affairs well, and supervised agricultural activities successfully. Farmers said Matthias was as "sharp at a bargain as any man," skillful at procuring good laborers and in selling his produce. Everyone worked at Zion Hill. Matthias divided the household into "departments" and reportedly introduced improvements. Isabella, accustomed to managing large households, oversaw the domestic work routine. She was efficient, and knew Matthias's taste and temperament. The black woman did the "common" work—starting the heating and cooking fires, preparing the meals, washing, and sometimes gathering coals and wood. The "delicate" white woman assisted in the light work, such as making beds; setting, serving, and clearing the table; tending the children; and sewing.[25]

At Pierson's urging, Benjamin Folger placed Zion Hill in Pierson's name, and Pierson then supposedly (but not truly) deeded the "mansion and farm, lately known as Heartt Place, to Mr. Robert Matthews" for setting up and establishing "the Father's House." This action was more slick than zealous. Pierson reasoned that creditors could not hold the two merchants liable, yet any financial success came from Father's blessing. Using Pierson's money, and believing in Matthias's power, the merchants also enhanced the commune's portfolio. They purchased undeveloped lots in the city, reselling them at sometimes $8,000 profit; they bought the patent to a "globe stove," renamed it the "Ne plus ultra kingdom stove," and sold it for the huge sum of $70 to $75 each. Pierson wanted no money exchanges in his name ("If you would be perfect, go and sell what you own and give it to the poor"). Hence, all accounts bore Folger's signature. Already facing economic embarrassment from unwise investments, Folger expected Pierson's business sense to forestall financial ruin. The merchants gave Matthias large sums of money, and granted him full purchasing power for the farm. They bought him a fine carriage and beautiful gray horses for his Westchester County business and pleasure excursions. The family prospered, and life was peaceful, cooperative, and collective at first. As the Spirit of Truth, Matthias's sacred authority protected, blessed, and cursed. Matthias, Pierson insisted, was a prophet sent from God, possessing the spirit of God, and ordained with supernatural power over sickness, life, death, and damnation. The others followed Pierson's lead.[26]

Matthias organized the details of family life. Everyone ate carefully, worked hard, and rested well. A light breakfast, a substantial midday meal, and a small, meatless repast for supper made up the food regimen. Having fresh, unprocessed foods, regular eating habits, and abstaining from alcohol all enhanced good health, which everyone generally enjoyed. Even Pierson's fits were under control. Matthias demanded cleanliness, frequent bathing, and washing of hands at a time when America had not discovered the relationship between hygiene and health. Matthias apparently had no ban on Isabella's tobacco, since he took snuff. Among his elaborate wardrobe articles was a French snuffbox, a gift from Benjamin Folger.[27]

Isabella Van Wagenen and Ann Folger had traveled in similar Perfectionist circles, so Ann concealed whatever racial prejudice she harbored toward Isabella.

Matthias had insisted that Ann dismiss her white housekeeper to make room for the African Dutch mystic. Along with spiritual influence with Matthias, Isabella expected equal family membership. Yet the estate was purchased with Ann's inheritance, and events soon revealed that she was not satisfied with her position in the kingdom. Perhaps because of Isabella's centrality there, Ann sought to neutralize and outstrip her. In addition, Ann's physical attraction to Matthias and his previous relationship with Isabella, though apparently not sexual, caused uneasiness and tension. Isabella soon noticed that Ann was extremely attentive toward Matthias, and "particularly desirous of pleasing" him. The bourgeois woman's doting flattered Matthias's considerable vanity. Crafty in furthering her designs, Ann asked Isabella about Matthias's doctrinal or spiritual "feelings and opinions on particular subjects," and then represented those ideas to Father as hers. The beguiled Matthias complimented Ann on her wisdom in possessing "the very spirit which he had." If Father disagreed or his countenance darkened, Ann gently retracted or quickly adjusted her meaning to conform to Matthias's.[28]

Each morning at breakfast, as Matthias inspected the family, the once ascetic Ann Folger now appeared highly scented and beautifully dressed. She lavished personal attention on Matthias and took over Isabella's job of preparing his wardrobe. She embellished Father's already gaudy attire with her own hand-embroidered linens, laces, and nightcaps. Isabella insisted that much of Matthias's outlandish regalia described by Stone—colorful trousers, frocks and silk vests—was Ann's doing. She also gave him a "large golden ring." The more knowledge she gained from Isabella about Matthias, the more Ann conversed with him. When the household retired, the two sat in the parlor comparing spiritual revelations, tests of faith, and dreams. These sessions by the firelight were so "tête-à-tête" that Isabella, always valued in such conversations, felt like an outsider. If Matthias and Ann were having an evening "spiritual" dialogue and Isabella entered the parlor, they immediately ceased speaking. Once when Isabella entered the parlor, Ann's hostile eyes "flashed fire," and Matthias made a "careless remark." Surprised and "forcibly struck" by their exclusivity, Isabella quickly retreated.[29]

Isabella and Matthias shared intense mystical experiences; both had overcome persecution and claimed a special relationship with God. Isabella believed that she was more Matthias's "spirit match" than Ann Folger. But her simple faith and loyalty as a religious disciple proved no match for Ann's physical attraction and sexual passion. Nor was Isabella's stature as a reformer, preacher, and master spirit enough to bridge the gaps of color, culture, and socioeconomic difference. Isabella's *place* was in the kitchen, not the parlor, and Ann wanted control over both. Above all, a colored woman should not enjoy, more than Ann, the confidence of the handsome "Spirit of Truth."

Isabella kept her own counsel. Yet as a quick study, privately, she compared Ann Folger's spirit with that of Mrs. Bolton. Foiled in its attempt on Matthias, Bolton's spirit "had left her person and got into the more delicate frame of Mrs. Folger." Just as Matthias saw through Mrs. Bolton, Isabella thought he would eventually denounce Ann. But Matthias was more charlatan than religious zealot, while Ann Folger was not properly a harlot. Raised in the bosom of the Reformed Dutch Church, she possessed enough breeding, vanity, and confidence born of skin, class, and economic privilege to believe her seduction of the prophet was spiritual. Her interest in sexual experimentation under a rubric of Perfectionism predated meeting Matthias. And he had previously denounced marriages with no spiritual affinity. Thus, mutual beliefs formed a base for their union before they ever met. Matthias, quickly appreciating Ann's charm, money, and position, abandoned his own edict that holy men not preach to women outside of their husbands' presence. Thus, the "superstructure," Gilbert Vale and Isabella reasoned, on which Matthias shipwrecked his prophetic character was laid when he encountered the "particularly alluring" Mrs. Folger.[30]

Ann Folger, Vale observed, was "extremely pleasing" in appearance. Her complexion was "light, features good, nose prominent, mouth pretty, amber eyes of great power, and pretty chin." Her figure was "tolerably good." But Ann's voice was her most mesmerizing attribute—extremely soft, insinuating, ostensibly gentle, and innocent. Her demeanor and conversation suggested natural harmlessness, epitomizing the four cardinal female virtues: purity, piety, submissiveness, and domesticity. Indeed, her claim to these virtues infatuated Matthias. However, Isabella insisted that Ann's disarming femininity, including her face, voice, and movements, were deft weapons of seduction. In attempting to convey this to Vale later, Isabella imitated Ann's manner when hovering over Matthias, and tried taking on Ann's air: "*Father*, would you like this? *Father*, will you have that? *Father*, shall we do this?" Isabella only clumsily re-created Ann's "tones, gentle inflections of the head, and bend of the body." Her impersonation of Ann's delicate artifice provoked laughter in both Vale and Isabella. "Oh I can't do it," said Isabella heartily, pretending to be frustrated as she gave up.[31]

Ann's feminine wiles were eventually put on display for the whole family. Matthias insisted that kingdom spirits greet each other with a kiss, and bathe together. Ann and Isabella bathed each other while the female children watched; similarly, the menfolk took communal baths. Although intended to affirm humility and dispel difference, kissing and weekly bathing in a perfect state of nudity, like the late-night spiritual conversations, became part of Ann and Matthias's foreplay. One fall evening, in Benjamin's absence, the family gathered to bathe. Hot water was first prepared for the men and boys. Before Pierson or any males followed Matthias into the bathing room, Ann scurried after him, asking "Father shall I wash you?" and locked the door. They remained in the room for such a surprising length of time that Pierson's youngest daughter quipped, "Father" should certainly be "clean enough."[32]

Within days of this bathing incident, Elijah Pierson and Ann Folger went to New York City to see Benjamin. In the Folgers' bedroom, Catherine Galloway later told Isabella, "there was a terrible to-do nearly all night." Pierson had announced that Ann was Matthias's "spirit match." Judging from the noises and tones, Benjamin was "afflicted with both grief and passion." Benjamin loved his wife and respected Elijah Pierson as a businessman and religious teacher. Two years earlier, Pierson had remarried the Folgers in "Gospel order," to counter their "Christian order" marriage. Yet the outraged husband feared that if he resisted, Matthias would curse him for disobedience. After a full week of persuasion and promises, Benjamin, dejected, agreed to give up Ann.[33]

Isabella was not yet privy to these New York events when Ann returned to Zion Hill. Entering the kitchen with a lighthearted but commanding demeanor, Ann told a surprised Isabella: "Have the house set in order," particularly the master bedroom. She instructed Isabella to wash her new chemises, as well as the nightcap and the shirt Ann had made for Matthias. Isabella, who already had her scheduled duties, was annoyed. She did not take orders from Ann Folger, and "It was not the *time* for washing." Yet Ann proclaimed that she was now "Mother" of the kingdom. She and Father were newly discovered "*match* spirits," and a "union" would occur between them. By Matthias's authority, Isabella would now receive orders from Father and Mother. Isabella sought perfect clarity on what this union and Ann's new status represented in carnal terms. "But are you going to sleep with him?" Isabella pointedly asked. "Yes, certainly," Ann replied.[34]

Elijah Pierson explained to Isabella, "without astonishment," that Ann and Matthias had become *match* spirits through a series of synchronic dreams and visions. Two years before they met, Ann appeared to Matthias as the Mother of the Institution he was about to raise. In addition, since Matthias represented "Adam, the beginner of a new order," God had also made an Eve. Through daily and nightly conversations, "Adam and Eve" had determined they were *matched*. It could have stopped there, since both were married with families. But Ann's vision went deeper. She saw two ascending smoke columns uniting at the top in physical union. "The Lord had shown her that she should take Father to be her husband; and she was to have a holy son." Unsure of how Father would receive this bold, adulterous proposal/vision, and knowing Matthias was the dream interpreter, Ann risked incurring his wrath. Using the identical feigned obeisance and timidity that she had used with Pierson regarding his wife's transmigration, Ann meekly confessed that in revealing her vision, she "had taken up a cross." If she had done wrong, "please forgive me." Matthias, who may have initially entertained a mere flirtation, was taken aback. He needed time to "think of it." He consulted Elijah Pierson, who already believed Ann's prediction that he would soon be united with her cousin. When Pierson approved the match, Matthias advised Ann to follow the dictates of the Spirit. That led to Pierson and Ann's trip to New York City.

Ann wished that "Isabella should suppose her something superior to other women, just as she supposed Matthias superior to other men." If Matthias, as "recipient of the Holy Ghost," was superior in holiness and in "bodily qualities," then so was Ann. Hence, Ann's Christian husband offered her "no satisfaction," while Matthias gave her "great satisfaction." Moreover, despite having borne three children, Ann proclaimed herself a virgin. She and Pierson had convinced Benjamin to attest to her maidenhood and "give" her to Matthias as Ann Disbrow (her maiden name).[35] Within three months, Ann Folger had accomplished her three goals: seducing Matthias, convincing her husband to "offer" her to Father formally, and becoming the spiritual Mother Superior of the kingdom.

What sort of man would "give" his wife to another man? Benjamin Folger of Hudson, New York, was a childhood friend of William Leete Stone. A poor boy whose rich relations set him up in business, Folger became a wealthy, respected hardware merchant and speculator who supported moral reform and embraced his wife's religious beliefs. Gilbert Vale thought Benjamin a handsome but effeminate man whose polite manner and good temperament effectively concealed a defective education, vices, and a weak character, especially his inability to stand up to his subtly tough, well-born wife. He returned to Mount Pleasant and formally gave Ann to Matthias. While temporarily consoling himself with Catherine Galloway, Benjamin expected a more luscious carrot—Matthias's pretty, and presumably chaste, eighteen-year-old daughter, also named Isabella.[36]

In January 1834, Benjamin went to Albany and collected Matthias's three sons and Isabella, his bride-to-be. After sending his own son and Matthias's older boys ahead, Benjamin, Isabella, and her youngest brother stayed at an inn. Benjamin and Isabella had sex in the presence of Matthias's young son, and Benjamin discovered that his "virgin" *match* had married the previous month. At Zion Hill, an outraged Matthias nullified his daughter's marriage to a young man named Charles Laisdell, and remarried her to Benjamin Folger because of the "act on the road." For the next six weeks, passion reigned in the kingdom. Impoverished young Isabella Laisdell basked in her privileged circumstances, and Benjamin Folger behaved like a newlywed. Matthias and Ann, openly devoted to each other, worked at fulfilling the prophecy of conceiving a "holy child." Elijah Pierson waited patiently for his own *match* spirit. Isabella Van Wagenen went about her work, observing events and staying above the fray mainly by circumstance. She might have joined the coupling, she said, but there was no match spirit for her in the kingdom.[37]

In early March of 1834, young Isabella's legal husband arrived, seeking his wife. The white adults were in New York City, and Isabella Van Wagenen sent

Charles Laisdell away. But she sent word to the kingdom family. The already suspicious villagers gave Laisdell liquor and quizzed him; soon thereafter, they spread gossip as he lurked around the estate. The kingdom family returned, and Elijah Pierson gave Charles Laisdell bribe money. Taking the money without ever seeing his wife, Laisdell remained in Mount Pleasant, drinking at the tavern and conversing with villagers about the "mystery within" the house. The kingdom family shuffled young Isabella Laisdell back and forth from city to country, foiling her husband. Public curiosity increased. Large "crowds assembled about the premises, and on a hill overlooking the house." Advised to seek legal recourse, Laisdell had the family summoned before the magistrate. A mob followed their carriage, hooting, hallooing, and taunting Matthias.[38]

In court, Laisdell produced a marriage certificate and claimed his wife, against her protests. Benjamin, having lost his "bride," again consoled himself with Catherine. Back in Albany, Isabella Laisdell told her mother of Matthias's affluent lifestyle and his relationship with Ann Folger. The secret was also out in Mount Pleasant, and the village leaders called on the Folgers. Seeing them approaching, Isabella Van Wagenen quickly alerted the couples, who were still in bed. "Devils," meaning the public, were not privy to the kingdom's sleeping arrangements. The Folgers quickly dressed, politely greeted the visitors as a couple, denied the rumors, and refused to dismiss Matthias from their home.[39]

Throughout the spring of 1834, Isabella Van Wagenen grew more dissatisfied. Benjamin Folger, now facing bankruptcy, was often in New York with Catherine. Matthias, openly enraptured with Ann, paid little attention to orderly domestic supervision. The couple spent most of their time in bed, and Isabella freely entered their bedroom to make a fire before they arose. "See Isabella, this is my pillow," Ann said snuggling into Matthias's massive beard. Since no one could breakfast until Father and Mother appeared, Isabella's schedule was awry. As peace and order declined, her workload increased. When she complained, Matthias insisted that his and Mother's *spirit* helped, so that Isabella should do twice the work in half the time. Isabella was not impressed. The more Ann and Matthias solidified their "union," the more Mother scolded Isabella. Matthias also reprimanded her at Ann's insistence; even gentle Elijah Pierson began reproving Isabella. She was now treated like a "colored" woman. When a new couple, the Thompsons, joined the commune, sleeping arrangements were initially concealed. But soon Ann, now carrying the "holy child," spoke openly to Mrs. Thompson of her relationship with Father, and bragged about seducing him. Catherine Galloway became pregnant but miscarried early. She also spent much time in the parlor, and did little work. Isabella watched angrily as Mother foisted Catherine's duties onto Pierson's daughters, elevating someone Isabella said was "only fit for the kitchen" to the status of a lady. No amount of

Ann's clothing and adornments erased Catherine's natural plainness, or fully appeased Benjamin, who sometimes sulked and challenged Matthias's right to Ann. Pierson intervened, but occasionally Ann pacified Benjamin by secretly sleeping with him. Ann did it for peace, not pleasure, she told Isabella. Benjamin was a child, not a man. It was "like a mother sleeping with her son," because "the Spirit worked with Matthias, but it did not work with Benjamin." Meanwhile, the public storm gathered.[40]

The wonder is that Isabella remained in the kingdom. She scoffed at any spiritual relationship between Ann and Matthias and rejected Ann's claims to virginity and giving birth to a holy child. She received no wages, did most of the work, was belittled like a child and treated like a servant rather than an equal. On several occasions, she threatened to leave, but later said she stayed to see the eventual outcome. There was undoubtedly more. She not only believed Matthias was a holy man; she retained the old patriarchal bond. While she did not believe in Ann Folger as Mother, she believed in a communal vision, and unfortunately, she believed in Matthias.[41] Isabella was also loyal. In that devotion, she was no more gullible than other, better-educated spiritually minded individuals in that era of religious enthusiasm.

Summer approached, and more disputes erupted over the workload. Pierson was listless and distracted. Benjamin Folger, despite his trysts with Catherine, was unhappy. Elizabeth Thompson, eyed as Benjamin's possible match, fled with her husband, who remarked, "there is too much changing of wives here." Rather than confront Matthias, Benjamin poured out his unhappiness to Isabella, his devout Dutch mother-in-law, New York friends, and the Mount Pleasant villagers. Without divulging details, Benjamin complained and sought advice about Matthias's "intrusion" in his family life. Urged to remove his family, one day Benjamin, fortified by liquor, returned to Zion Hill determined to collect his wife and children.[42]

A confused, comical, and frantic scene ensued. Benjamin ordered Ann to prepare herself and the children for travel. "I am not your wife!—Behave yourself!" Ann answered. Matthias tried to intercede, and Folger called him a "damned imposter." The kingdom was alarmed at this blasphemy. Even Pierson could not calm Benjamin, who made a grab, unsuccessfully, for his son's garden knife. He scuffled with Isabella and various family members, who dragged him into the parlor. He rushed to the fireplace, clutched the poker, and shouted at Matthias, "I'll split your brains out!" Someone wrested away the poker. Benjamin ran from place to place seeking a weapon, while family members tried to protect Father. Finally, Benjamin threw Matthias on the sofa, and they wrestled. Although the slight prophet was no good at fisticuffs, he finally extricated himself and ran for the door. Benjamin rushed him again. Isabella stepped in. She seized Benjamin's arms and held him against the door while Father fled. No match physically for the powerful black woman, Benjamin instead tried to assert authority by reminding Isabella of her "place." He shouted "Isabella, Isabella, go down in the kitchen!" She held fast to the squirming, exhausted Benjamin, who was shaking like a leaf and staring wildly. She had long pitied Benjamin Folger, and while immobilizing him, insisted "I have never done you any mischief." But she would not let him hurt Father.[43]

Matthias returned to the parlor with what he called his "miraculously pre-served," beautiful two-edged "sword of Gideon," which was part of his attire. Swinging wildly, he exclaimed repeatedly, "Let that spirit be destroyed!" (Benjamin's violent spirit). This did not cow Benjamin. As Isabella released him, exhausted but still resolute, he ordered Ann, "Fix yourself to go with me," and left to procure a wagon and carriage for his family. Mother and Father sat crying in each other's arms. Isabella prepared lunch. When Benjamin returned, Ann convinced him to eat. The meal mellowed Benjamin, and Ann took him to another room. He "came out like a tamed elephant, with all his passions subdued," and his faith in Matthias renewed. But he had aroused the village, and a crowd surrounded the estate. Fearing for Father's safety, Ann shaved him, and he left Mount Pleasant surreptitiously.[44]

Those events took place on June 3, 1834. With Matthias gone, Benjamin slept with his wife. But now Elijah Pierson assumed the character of Matthias, saying that as Father, he should have Mother. His pretensions were quickly interrupted. Ann pined so for Matthias that the family followed him and moved to Pierson's Third Street home. Benjamin continued to claim his wife occasionally, as well as Catherine, though remaining a "believer." When Benjamin went to work, Ann closeted with Matthias, and Isabella had the demeaning role of sentinel. Ann sometimes avoided Benjamin by sleeping with Isabella. When the two women spoke of Matthias, Ann "actually showed Isabella how Matthias kissed or embraced her." Soon the family, minus Benjamin and Catherine, regrouped back at Mount Pleasant.[45]

Elijah Pierson grew problematic. His seizures increased, and exclusion from the coupling disturbed him. Although a modest, middle-aged merchant, Pierson had an "amative disposition," which increased after his wife's death. He masturbated during "insensible" fits, and instructed Isabella to prevent any "improper behavior" during his seizures. They often erupted at mealtime. Pierson would thrust one hand into his trousers, stretch out the other toward Ann Folger, stare at her wildly, and call out "Ann, Ann, Ann," or "my wife! my wife! my wife." Ann and Catherine were disgusted and called Pierson a "beast," while Matthias gently led him away from the table. Pierson needed a match. Ann finally handled the crisis by reminding Pierson that his match spirit was Frances Folger. Pierson actually approached her; she rebuffed him strenuously.[46]

That 1834 summer in Mount Pleasant provided Isabella with personal safety. It was a year of riots, and blacks were targeted in Lower Manhattan. Urban blacks' opposition to colonization finally won over some progressive whites, particularly twenty-four-year-old editor William Lloyd Garrison. In January 1831, he began to publish a periodical, the *Liberator*, which blacks liberally funded. This partnership spearheaded the nation's first interracial antislavery organization, the New England Anti-Slavery Society (NEASS). That June, the first black convention met in Philadelphia and proposed a national organization devoted to immediate emancipation and black equality. Garrison's 1832 pamphlet "Thoughts on Colonization" was extremely influential. The ACS, wrote Garrison, was not antislavery but anti-Negro, a "creature without heart, without brains, eyeless, unnatural, hypocritical, relentless, unjust." Garrison linked the ACS to the rum trade, which served up "liquid poison" in Africa. From East to West, white antislavery colonizationists, including Arthur and Lewis Tappan, gave up colonization and embraced Garrison's powerful reasoning and "damning clarity."[47]

The Tappans financed circulation of Garrison's pamphlet and a trip he made to England, where he attacked the powerful lobby of the ACS and witnessed the historic passage of Britain's Abolition Bill. He secured a great victory for the cause of immediate abolition by obtaining a letter signed by leading British Abolitionists condemning the ACS. He returned to America in time for the founding of the New York Anti-Slavery Society in October 1833. William Leete Stone, president of New York's Colonization Society, roused the public against "the Notorious Garrison." An angry mob of two thousand gentlemen, drunkards, and Bowery b'hoys prepared to descend on the meeting. The Abolitionists quickly conducted business and adjourned. The enraged mob seized an elderly black man and humiliated him. Two months later, in Philadelphia, a biracial assembly organized the American Anti-Slavery Society (AASS) with Arthur Tappan as president, and immediately put traveling agents in the field.[48] Thus, the new national organization not only challenged slavery and racism, it demolished the ACS's liberal pretensions in America and England.

New York City's summer of unrest and rioting was fed by antislavery mobilization. Sufficiently revved up by articles in the *Commercial Advertiser* and *Courier and Enquirer*, a mob of three thousand attacked black homes, businesses, and institutions. They also singled out interracial couples, white Abolitionists, and white churches friendly to blacks. Mob leaders planned their attacks using messengers and rendezvous points. Different groups converged on the African School, John McDowell's office, and Arthur Tappan's store, where the city watch halted them. One group destroyed Isabella's Zion Church, then made a bonfire of St. Phillips Episcopal Church and parsonage. Although William Leete Stone blamed the violence on attempts to "mulattoize" white posterity and reduce whites "to the condition of mongrels," this was a smokescreen to attack blacks and abolition. Days before the outbreak, Stone published a spoof, "A White Wife Wanted," in which "Bandy Pomp declared: I hab cum to de conclushun dat de gemmen ob culler must exclaim . . . dat dy too be de frind ob equal rites. . . . I hab therefore determine to nnounce to my dopted country, dat I . . . be willing to malgumate and just as lib marry white woman as any. De Ladies will please send in their proposals to de Editor ob de Liberator."[49]

Even the moderate *Journal of Commerce* (once owned by Arthur Tappan) connected Stone to the violence, and ran the headline "Colonization Riot." While Garrison called editor James Watson Webb a virulent, cowardly ruffian, Stone, he said, was the most unscrupulous of all—"a miserable liar and murderous hypocrite." Stone's paper, wrote Garrison, had created the mob. "If any man ever deserved to be sent to the Penitentiary or State Prison for life, Stone is that man." But Stone and Webb, like nearly all New York editors, blamed Abolitionists for the terrorism that devastated the black community. They agreed with Mayor Cornelius Lawrence that Abolitionists were "misguided, misjudging, imprudent men."[50]

The riots caused anxiety in the kingdom, of course, and Benjamin Folger probably limited his trips to the city. It was an anxious time for Isabella, who had family in the Sixth Ward and knew some of those killed and injured and the hundreds left destitute. For two days, rioters had "entire possession of the city." Many black families fled, while others armed themselves and fought.[51]

IV

While the riots raged, the commune tottered. The death of Elijah Pierson eventually sealed its doom. His final illness began on July 28, when he and Matthias picked some blackberries and the family had them for dinner. Pierson devoured two helpings, leaving none for Matthias, who, as Father, was entitled to the "first fruits." Matthias went on a screaming, scolding rampage. The next day, while picking berries, Pierson ate more, and without washing them. He became ill at dinner, with vomiting, diarrhea, and convulsions, his long beard stained with berries. The family fled the dining room in disgust. Only Isabella, scarcely able to restrain herself, attended Elijah Pierson.[52]

His convulsions became almost uncontrollable that week. The family's disavowal of medicine and doctors left only Isabella and young Elizabeth Pierson to care for the ailing man. Father and Mother even scolded Isabella for giving so much attention to Pierson, since she had to take over his outside work and do her regular house chores. Exhausted by nightfall, Isabella nevertheless slept in Pierson's room on a row of chairs. On the last night of Pierson's life, she bathed him in preparation for a visit the next day from his old friend Rosetta Dratch. On August 4, leaving Pierson sleeping peacefully, a tired Isabella obeyed Father's instructions to sleep in her own bed.[53]

Finding Elijah Pierson dead the next morning shocked the family, whose beliefs disavowed illness or death among the faithful. Thus, Matthias explained that Pierson had "lacked faith." Yet though his "devil" spirit had triumphed over his body, his good spirit remained. Mount Pleasant village was astir over the news. Pierson's New Jersey relatives accompanied Benjamin Folger to Sing Sing to claim Pierson's body, and the coroner held an inquest. At the inquest, Ann Folger adamantly affirmed the family's belief in "teachings of the Spirit," including the evil of physicians and medicine. Questions put to Isabella and others involved more about sleeping arrangements than Pierson's death. When the jury surmised that the Folgers did not sleep together, they continued to pry. Isabella's answers became combative, demonstrating the gift for repartee that later made her famous. A juror asked "What had become of Pierson's devil spirit or evil spirit?" Isabella answered tartly that it might have entered one of them.[54]

Pierson's financial affairs were in disarray. His family suspected foul play when they discovered that his property had been signed over to Matthias. Zion Hill, originally Ann and Benjamin's property, was legally Pierson's, and he had actually only leased it to Matthias for $1. Pierson's body, which had been buried immediately in Morristown, New Jersey, was disinterred and examined. The doctors' findings were inconclusive. The Pierson family had legal rights to Zion Hill, and the kingdom family was forced back to New York City. They contemplated a kingdom in the "West." Further dismantling occurred, and Isabella renewed her threats to leave. The Folgers' regular bedding together for the sake of appearances aroused Matthias's suspicions. The couple even traveled together on business, though Ann's pregnancy was in its advanced stages. The sexual quadrangle continued through mid-September. Benjamin slept with Catherine but did not fully give up his wife. Catherine put it best after Matthias caught Ann and Benjamin locked in a room and probably in a sexual tryst: "Did you ever see such a woman?" Catherine exclaimed to Isabella, referring to Ann's sexual appetite. Ann wanted "Matthias all night and Ben (as she said) all day." Ann later explained to Isabella that Folger had "forced her."[55]

Ann's dalliances finally taxed Matthias's limit, and one night he angrily kicked her out of their bedroom. Knowing that Catherine was with Benjamin and fearing Pierson's "spirit," Ann climbed into bed with Isabella. Matthias followed her and ordered Isabella out, because Mother was a harlot: "My Lord and My God, have I had that devil in my bosom!" Matthias insisted that Isabella must not sleep in a bed with Ann. "God will curse you if you do!" Cringing, Ann asked Father where she should go. "Go to the pit from whence you came, you cursed creature," Matthias ranted.[56]

No one wanted breakfast the next morning, so Isabella prepared only coffee, even for the children. After Catherine left Benjamin's room, Ann entered and had her coffee there. When they joined the family in the kitchen, Ann's softness toward Matthias was gone. She called Benjamin "husband," told Isabella to obey him, and spoke to Father with harshness. The spell had broken. Although Matthias now saw through Ann's tender trap, he did not believe that his kingdom rested on her favor. But Benjamin told Matthias to leave the house. Father shed real tears.

Events now transpired quickly. The Folgers schemed to rid themselves of Matthias, deflect suspicion about Ann's infidelity, and conceal Benjamin's financial embarrassment. Folger gave Matthias $500 in silver and gold, supposedly to set up a kingdom in the West. He gave Isabella $25 as payment for her past labor. The two should go "together," advised Benjamin, and seek a new place. The Folgers would join them after the birth of the "holy child." Isabella possessing the money was crucial to Benjamin's scheme, and Catherine warned her that it was a trap. Isabella had her own reasons for refusing to carry the $500 when Benjamin urged her to. She was poor, uneducated, and black; New York City whites were in an ugly antiblack mood. Whether the "amalgamation" (race mixing) issue was paranoia or real, it made framing Isabella and Matthias seem easy.[57]

To facilitate Isabella and Matthias's leaving as a couple, Folger volunteered to take Father's boys back to Albany. Isabella and Matthias foiled him. Matthias went directly to Albany and left the money with Margaret, while Isabella stopped at John Dumont's. The next day, a Saturday, Isabella appeared in Albany, and so did Matthias's sons, whom Benjamin Folger had sent alone in a towboat. The boys revealed that Folger was coming after Matthias with a policeman for "stealing and robbing things." Matthias was unperturbed by this news, but Isabella, immediately sizing up the plot, went back to Ulster County and conferred with John Dumont. When she returned three days later, Matthias was in jail. Convinced by Margaret that her husband was not a thief, armed with Dumont's legal advice, and with Margaret Matthews in tow, Isabella returned to New York City. There the Folgers were busily spinning yarns. Benjamin charged Matthias with theft and told the newspapers that Isabella had tried to poison his family. Evangelical friends, business associates, and even James La Tourette all sympathized with the Folgers. The penny press played up the scandal. The once reputable *Journal of Commerce*, now specializing in stories on sex, crime, and race, reported that Pierson's death had been "very suspicious," and Matthias had threatened the Folgers. They alleged that a "coloured woman" was involved because the white family had become "violently sick" after she served them coffee. Benjamin Folger said he believed that the black woman, under Matthias's influence, had intended "to poison the family." Fortunately, none of the Folgers had died, the *Journal* wrote, but they still had not recovered from the effects of the intended poisoning.[58]

Although not charged, Isabella was under suspicion. Her reputation and vindication were linked to Matthias's fate. Working with Margaret Matthews to find counsel, Isabella rejected so-called Christian attorneys who called Matthias a *"beast"*; the two women settled on Henry M. Western. The first charge that Matthias faced was fraud, which did not overtly involve Isabella. In October 1834, a curious crowd of courtroom listeners heard several days of testimony in which Benjamin Folger admitted that he had "honestly and truly" believed that Matthias had "commenced the Reign of God on Earth." Elijah Pierson's "piety and good sense" had persuaded Benjamin that Robert Matthews was Matthias, the apostle of the New Testament raised again from the dead, who "possessed the spirit of Jesus of Nazareth" and was the second appearance of the Spirit. The kingdom family had believed that "Father" forgave sins, communicated with the Holy Ghost, and brought good and evil. They had lavished money and goods on Matthias under threats of a curse. The bequests from Benjamin to Matthias, Folger said, had been obtained "falsely and fraudulently."[59]

Matthias insisted that he had never said he was "God" but a traveler, a preacher, and a "Jewish teacher-priest of the most high." Although sometimes calling himself the Spirit of Truth, Matthias maintained that he was merely the *"trumpet* for the Spirit of Truth"; he was not the Messiah, only "a servant of God," and a messenger. He admonished all followers to practice "obedience, as did Jesus of Nazareth, and . . . secure eternal life." His role was to prophesy—"that the hour of God's judgment is come." Unable to sustain coherency for long, though, Matthias lapsed into mystical nonsense. He was "the last chosen of the twelve apostles and the first in the resurrection which is at the end of 2,300 years after the building of Jerusalem . . . and 1,260 after the birth of mankind, which terminated in 1830, that being the last . . . of the power of the false prophet . . . and now denouncing a judgment on the Gentiles and that judgment is to be executed in this age." After lengthy tirades, he returned to subjects "much to the point."[60]

He candidly admitted receiving about $10,000, half of it from Ann Folger's own separate estate. Yet he did not "ask" for goods or money; followers did not relinquish *"their* property" but only "property, which they believed belonged to God." It was the merchants, Matthias said—Folger, Pierson, and Mills—who frequently "declared to me, that they believed I was the Father, and that I was qualified to establish God's Kingdom upon Earth, and that Zion Hill (and other property) was transferred to me . . . for that purpose." He accepted money and property only in the name of God, and it belonged to God. Since the merchants had voluntarily transferred their property to him, Matthias asserted that his claim to Zion Hill for God's kingdom on earth was legitimate, and could not be nullified. Matthias did not get the property, but neither did Folger obtain an indictment. His case was so weak that he dropped the charges.[61]

In spite of his embarrassing public defeat on the fraud charges, Benjamin Folger still believed that he had the upper hand. Matthias was remanded to Westchester County jail because an indictment of murder was issued, based on accusations raised by Folger and a medical opinion that "some unknown substance" was found in Pierson's stomach, which had been preserved. Folger personally told Margaret Matthews that he knew Matthias was innocent of murder, but wanted him hanged anyway. Benjamin sought assistance from William Leete Stone, who secretly agreed to edit a book on the kingdom from the Folgers' perspective. Stone was not only assisting a humiliated boyhood chum whose wife had strayed far from the confines of "true womanhood" but also, because of his ties to anti-abolitionist colonization, wanted to discredit African Americans and abolition. Newspaper accounts had already related that Pierson might have been poisoned with blackberries, which, like the coffee, implicated Isabella. Stone prepared to depict Isabella as representing the same forces that had caused the July race riots—black excess, sexuality, and "fanaticism." The coffee and blackberries poisoning stories circulated continuously, while the Folgers secretly narrated their version of Zion Hill events to Stone, who embellished their story in the soon-to-be-published book and in the newspapers. For example, he deceptively placed Isabella, James La Tourette, and Matthias at Bowery Hill worship meetings and Sarah Pierson's anointing and grotesque funeral.[62]

It was a low point for Isabella, who reproved herself for not leaving the kingdom on discovering the hypocrisy. Now, "former friends," including Pierson's Morristown relatives, shunned her and believed the worst.[63] Surely her brother and sister supported her, and other blacks accustomed to white denigration. However, she was an embarrassment to middle-class blacks who probably felt she should have known better. The black community was still enduring great human misery brought by the riots, and defending themselves against amalgamation accusations. This scandal involving a lower-class preaching black woman and a notorious "impostor" played right into the hands of racist detractors and editors such as Stone and Webb.

Issues of racism, crude sexuality, and class privilege dominated the Matthias case. Isabella, an uneducated black domestic, was considered ignorant and expendable. Matthias, a mere artisan, was also inconsequential. In addition, the Folgers despised Matthias because he personified Ann's infidelity and lust and Benjamin's profligate weakness. They coldly looked forward to Matthias's being charged with murder and executed, and Isabella's loss of livelihood and possible imprisonment. Even before Matthias was charged and before the Folgers' book was published, white public opinion believed the worst about the black woman and the white carpenter, including a sexual liaison, conspiracy, and murder. The Matthias case partook of the sensationalism of sex-tinged amusements in racist mid-nineteenth-century America, exemplified by P. T. Barnum's circuses and the black "wench" stereotype in minstrelsy. These amusements titillated whites' greatest fears and desires: they found ridicule of blacks entertaining, as well as—and perhaps because—it was repulsive, alluring, and forbidding. The antiblack riots were an expression of cultivated paranoia about black sexuality and fear of destabilizing the economic and political alliances between New York and slaveholding states. All this encouraged rumors that Isabella was a sex-driven criminal. In the press, she was a minstrel scapegoat—the "wench" character acted out in the theaters of Jacksonian America. Isabella as "wench" symbolized basic, prevalent urban ideologies that cast black women as immoral and foolish. Eric Lott, analyzing the "homoerotic" aspects of blackface minstrelsy and the "transvestitism" of the black female character, misses the simple heterosexual overtones. The only way theatergoing white men of all classes could safely camouflage their sexual desire for black women was through ridicule.[64]

Anticipating having to defend herself in court, Isabella returned briefly to Ulster County, where she obtained more advice from John Dumont. She also secured letters from him, Isaac Van Wagenen, and Kingston Knickerbockers such as A. Bruyn Hasbrouck, a Hardenbergh kinsman, founding president of Kingston's first bank and future president of Rutgers University. "Isabel," Hasbrouck wrote, had lived with his family in 1828. "She merited the entire confidence of my family, by her good conduct and fidelity." Returning to New York, she pressed her case among the Methodists. With James La Tourette she had quite a meeting. Now that she was "labouring under Folger's charge of poisoning," he viewed her differently. He attacked her on religious grounds, preached to her, and lectured her for leaving his Five Points meetings. She maintained that her faith was not the issue, only her character. Would La Tourette pen his knowledge of her behavior *"during the time he knew her"*? He said no; and his stinging, calumnious tongue-lashing reminded her of the narrow-minded, so-called Christians who had persecuted and struck her and abused and mauled Matthias. She concluded that La Tourette was one of the vain, money-grubbing merchants Matthias preached against. He supported the Folgers publicly. Privately, however, he told his wife and others that he believed everything Isabella said. Isabella was "exemplary," he noted, and possessed the "best character for morals, truth, industry, and intelligence."[65]

Isabella was caught between class and ideological divides among her Methodist associates. Fur merchant La Tourette was more loyal to his class and his business ties in the South than to the wronged black lady preacher he had once helped cultivate. But her midlevel employers championed her. Shopkeeper Daniel Smith thought Isabella "worthy of any trust." Painter John Gatfield's wife Belinda, one of the Five Points evangelical women, said her family "never had a servant that we could place such implicit confidence in." Jeweler John Downing wrote that she was "a strictly honest moral woman, and her equal I have not found since she left me." The recommendation from Lucy Whiting and her shoemaker husband Perez suggests their awareness of the stark contrast between Isabella Van Wagenen and Ann Folger. They had never had a domestic in whom they placed "such implicit confidence." In fact, the Whitings said, "we did, and do still, believe her to be a *woman of extraordinary moral purity.*" These employers were progressive New Yorkers who opposed racial violence and signed antislavery petitions. Thus, rather than hurting Isabella, La Tourette's behavior rallied her defenders.[66]

The murder trial, set for November, was postponed because of Ann's confinement and because she and her (female) "holy child" contracted smallpox. Meanwhile, Benjamin kept spinning yarns about Isabella and Matthias. Henry Western encouraged Isabella to sue Benjamin Folger for slander and defamation of character; otherwise her courtroom testimony would be compromised. This so alarmed Folger that he personally retracted statements he had made to friends about her. He and Ann went to La Tourette, confessed their duplicity, begged his "forgiveness," and asked him to intercede. He had burned his bridges with Isabella, however, and still would not support her. The Folgers also contacted Isabella's current employer, Perez Whiting, and asked to settle privately with her. She wisely refused. Even as they attempted to make amends with Isabella, Ann and Benjamin intended to exonerate themselves among "respectable" whites through the pen of William Leete Stone.[67]

Stories and innuendoes about Isabella escalated. The penny press, playing up a conspiracy between "the coloured woman" and the "impostor," described how Isabella, under Matthias's orders, had given the Folgers and Pierson poisonous blackberries that neither she nor Matthias ate. All the other family members became ill, and Pierson died because he had eaten the most blackberries. According to Stone, she had continued to try to poison the Folgers, now with coffee: "We have . . . learned beyond doubt" that "an attempt was made to poison Mr. Folger and his family . . . and had well nigh succeeded." Pierson's body was again disinterred for the trial. Although no definite signs of poison were apparent, four New Jersey physicians testified that they had found a "large quantity of unwholesome and deadly substance" in Pierson's bowels. This was more fodder for the press. But Isabella also had a story, and in a closed inquiry in late November, she gave the Westchester County Grand Jury a sample. The jury called Rosetta Dratch, Benjamin Folger, and Isabella as witnesses. (Catherine was attending Ann Folger's delivery.) Isabella took the stand after Benjamin.

The jurors ridiculed her and insinuated a sexual relationship with Matthias. Had she ever kissed Matthias, they asked knowingly. Yes, Isabella answered, understanding their meaning. "Now don't he kiss sweet?" was the next inquiry. Isabella was ready: "No sweeter than Ben Folger," she sallied, knowing that Folger had suggested the question. Clearly, if the white jurors pushed her, they would hear testimony that condemned not the black domestic but the pillars of their respectable little community. Isabella's retort ended that line of questioning.[68]

Stone divided his editorial energies between denigrating Isabella and attacking Abolitionists. A visit by British Abolitionist George Thompson in October 1834 created more virulent press and riotous behavior. "He must not be suffered to speak," Stone proclaimed. "He must not be heard." But Thompson spoke to huge Northern audiences, and his eloquence moved many prominent people closer to supporting immediate abolition. For Isabella, however, the year ended without a trial and without closure on her involvement with Matthias.[69]

Meanwhile, Ann, having recovered from smallpox, and suspicious of Benjamin and Catherine, let Catherine go at Christmastime without a penny. Isabella shared her food and money with the destitute Irish woman and her children. This generosity loosened Catherine's tongue. The two domestics concurred that Ann had been the master of deception. The Folgers, Catherine informed Isabella, were busy regaining friends and concocting lies about Isabella. "You know how she can smooth it so." Isabella first heard about a slanderous book being prepared from Catherine. "All this blessed winter Mrs. B. Folger has been writing against you and Matthias. . . . She will overcome you, and Matthias will be hung; and all the Christians have been helping her." Isabella was resolute and angry, but not frightened. "I have got the *truth*, and I know it," she told Catherine. "and I will *crush* them with the *truth*."[70]

Isabella convinced Catherine to give a deposition to Western; she corroborated Isabella's story and confessed to repeated intimacies with Benjamin Folger. This armed Western with "white" evidence to buttress the black woman's testimony. As the trial approached, Ann, unaware of Catherine's deposition to Western, wooed her back into the Folger camp. Catherine, who seems to have been as impulsive and erratic as her white mistress, now told Ann of Isabella's vow to "crush" the Folgers. The two white women walked arm in arm into the Westchester courthouse.[71]

The trial began on April 16, 1835. The physicians, under Western's cross-examination, admitted they had no conclusive evidence that the "something white" in Pierson's stomach had been poison. Ann Folger and Catherine Galloway testified at length about Matthias's strange doctrines, his control of Zion Hill, and Pierson's illness after eating blackberries. Isabella, Ann said slyly, had been Matthias's "housekeeper," a term often synonymous with "sex worker." However, Charles Ruggles, the Superior Court judge, knew Isabella from Ulster

County; he had been the district attorney in her son's kidnapping case, and he was John Dumont's nephew. Isabella also possessed Dumont's recommendation and one from A. Bruyn Hasbrouck, Ruggles's former law partner. Local employers further insisted that Isabella's character was inculpable. Clearly, if placed on the witness stand, this articulate paragon of honesty would indeed "crush" the Folgers's testimony. There was plenty of malice, but no real evidence to convict Matthias or to link Isabella to murder. Judge Ruggles, the prosecution, and the defense worked out a backroom deal. Western motioned to dismiss the charges for lack of evidence, and Ruggles so instructed the jury. They immediately acquitted Matthias.[72]

Isabella was "grievously disappointed." Truth had not been served; she had been deprived of the opportunity to present her "simple but fascinating narrative." Winning her slander suit against Folger was only a partial victory. What has been argued for enslaved black women of the South was also true for the North: the characterization of "jezebel" was embedded in Northern white mythology about all black women. At the trial, Ann had fed that libel and used Isabella to conceal her own infidelity. Stone's *Matthias and His Impostures*, published two months later, and his articles in the *Commercial Advertiser* continued the stereotyping. Stone suggested that a romantic link had existed between Isabella and Matthias since 1833. When they had lived together, Stone wrote, "she gave the avails of her labor to him, besides at times borrowing money for him." Although Matthias paid Isabella for washing, this implication that he was her pimp classically rendered her capable of prostitution, theft, murder, and conspiracy. Stone, living up to Abolitionists' characterizations of his dishonesty and racism, said that among all within the kingdom, Isabella was "the most wicked of the wicked."[73]

She was bombarded from many angles: Ann's subtle, genteel testimony against her; penny press accusations of murder; Stone's assertion that blinding love for Matthias had led her into fanatic, devious, and even cruel behavior such as slapping poor Pierson in the midst of a convulsion. Stone in particular kept her in public view for months through the *Commercial Advertiser*, covered the trial prejudicially, referred to her disparagingly, cleverly noted the presence of Matthias's wife to suggest a triangle, published a book, and tracked Matthias even after his release. No one exposed Ann and Benjamin Folger's deceits and moral lapses. Gilbert Vale suggests that by not allowing Isabella to testify, the defense as well as the prosecution attorneys, Judge Ruggles, and the jury had all favored "whiteness" and the Folgers, because "right" and "truth" had come from a Isabella, a black woman. Once again, Isabella's marginality was crystal clear. The Folgers had the courts, the press, the so-called Christians (including the evangelicals), the public, and a juicy, widely read, prejudicial book. But Isabella, refusing to go down without a fight, sought her own voice.

And so, by "application of a gentleman," British editor Gilbert Vale met and interviewed Isabella Van Wagenen. Her sponsor assured Vale that he "could rely upon her statements" and her narrative never varied. After listening to Isabella, Vale agreed. Her recall was impeccable and her version of the scandal irreproachable. She wove an intriguing historical account of the rise and fall of a religious commune. Vale loved a good fight for justice, particularly when marginalized people challenged power; he also loved a good story. He got both after gaining Isabella's confidence through his candor and openness. She, too, fascinated Vale, as he compared Isabella and Ann. The two strong women were studies in contrast—each not what they seemed. Vale thought Ann was extremely attractive physically and possessed visible "softness and delicacy." But at her core she was selfish and hard-hearted. Isabella was "the reverse of Mrs. B. Folger" physically but had a superior character. She also possessed shrewd common sense and a feisty personality and despised artifice. Isabella had a private opinion on everything, Vale observed, "and these opinions of her own we have frequently found very correct." Vale surmised that in the kingdom, Isabella had practiced the four cardinal female virtues, while Ann's inherently "warm constitution," restrained previously by education and religious training, had got the better of her. The "lady" on the witness stand was the femme fatale in the kingdom of Matthias, "an adulteress of no ordinary appetite."[74]

Vale and Isabella may not have been such "unlikely allies" as some have suggested.[75] A Londoner educated for the ministry, after his arrival in New York in 1829 he became a publisher, professor of navigation, labor agitator, critic, and literary writer. He edited and published a journal on political economy, the *Diamond*, a literary and scientific journal, the *Beacon*, and a radical newspaper, *Citizen of the World*. He modeled his democratic values after Thomas Paine rather than Andrew Jackson or Martin Van Buren. Before publishing Isabella, he had published British woman's rights advocate Mary Wollstonecraft. In 1836, Vale published a major political exposé involving women. As a freethinker, Vale had no love for evangelical Christianity, revivalism, or its spiritual offshoots. He also despised Democratic Party conservatives such as William Leete Stone, James Watson Webb, and Mordecai Noah. In 1832, Vale criticized the evangelicals and the police for mauling Isabella and Matthias, and in 1835 challenged Stone's prejudicial account of the Matthias commune. Vale was also an Abolitionist; he and his son, Gilbert Vale Jr., signed antislavery petitions, and his son also printed the monthly *Mirror of Liberty* for the young black Abolitionist David Ruggles.[76]

The Simple Narrative of Isabella, coauthored by Vale and Isabella, was a triumphant counterattack against Stone and the Folgers. Isabella certainly received some money from sales of the widely circulated narrative, and was awarded $125 in her slander suit against Benjamin Folger. Public vindication was a sweeter victory. Sweetest of all was Stone "repenting his late publication." Once again, the

African Dutch mystic had proved herself God's ambassador. Ann and Benjamin Folger slipped back into middle-class obscurity after a period of extreme embarrassment. Isabella continued working for the Whitings. Public outcry demanded that Matthias be convicted of something, so he served time for contempt-of-court outbursts and for whipping his married daughter. On his release, he met with Isabella and spent a few weeks in the city. Although no longer a follower, she still viewed their triumph against the Christians and the Folgers as prophetic favor from God. At last report, Matthias was with the Mormons.[77]

In the end, Isabella recognized Matthias's failings and delusions. He, like the Folgers, had used her, manipulating her desire for a beloved community of like-minded believers. Her "ancient" faith had been shaken, she told Vale. Yet it was the dogma of patriarchal Protestantism, represented by John Dumont, James La Tourette, Elijah Pierson, and Robert Matthews that she shed. She also henceforth rejected scriptural exegesis at face value, relying instead on her own interpretations. She remained critical of denominational Christianity. She was convinced that Elijah Pierson's fanaticism had been mixed with true piety, and Matthias's cunning with sincerity and sound religious principles. Matthias's greatest weakness, she reasoned, was not his beliefs but his maleness and vain, egotistical susceptibility to the charms of a deceitful woman. Isabella likened him to the Old Testament David, who was "after God's own heart" but when tempted by a woman was brought down nonetheless. Isabella believed that Matthias, like herself, had never been false to spiritual truth.[78]

Within five years of her freedom, Isabella Van Wagenen's life had changed dramatically. In Ulster, she had successfully challenged the courts for her son. In New York, she had become a preacher and moral reformer and had become involved in a criminal investigation and almost lost her good name. She had won a slander suit and published a book about her experiences. She had no more allowed herself to be mistreated in "Babylon" than she had in Ulster County. True, the label "morally degenerate" was a weight even after acquittal. Elijah Pierson, a good if misguided man, was dead. Robert Matthews, the spiritually ingenious rogue, had dropped out of history. Even John McDowell, "champion of moral reform," died impoverished—hastened, Garrison said, "to a premature grave by ecclesiastical oppression."[79] But the story of the woman named Isabella was beginning anew.

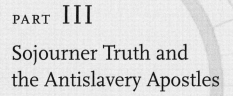

PART III

Sojourner Truth and
the Antislavery Apostles

I told the Lord it would be all right,
if he changed my name.
— AFRICAN AMERICAN SPIRITUAL

Sojourner Truth, Abolitionist, in traveling clothes with carpetbag. Photographs and Prints Division, Schomburg Center for Black Research and Culture, New York Public Library.

Amy Post, radical reformer, Rochester confidant of Sojourner Truth. Courtesy of the Department of Rare Books and Special Collections, University of Rochester Library.

The Broadway Tabernacle in Anniversary Week, when radicals and "fanatics" of all persuasions gathered for their national meetings. Collection of the New-York Historical Society.

The Broadway Tabernacle in Sojourner Truth's time. Collection of the New-York Historical Society.

Sojourner Truth's carpetbag and tobacco pouch. Community Archives of Heritage Battle Creek.

Sojourner Truth's Northampton house, c. 1900. Historic Northampton Museum.

The Five Points, as it appeared when Isabella moved to New York City and engaged in reform work. Collection of the New-York Historical Society.

The Northampton utopian community boardinghouse where Sojourner lived and worked. Historic Northampton Museum.

Freedmen's Hospital, where Sojourner Truth worked for almost two years during Reconstruction. Courtesy of the Moorland-Spingarn Research Center, Howard University Archives.

William Lloyd Garrison, Wendell Phillips, and George Thompson, leaders of abolition in America and England; Sojourner Truth had a close friendship with this triumvirate. Courtesy of the Trustees of the Boston Public Library.

Sojourner Truth in Battle Creek, seated and knitting. Photographs and Prints Division, Schomburg Center for Research and Black Culture, New York Public Library.

Signature of Frederick Douglass. Author's personal collection.

Sojourner wrote this signature around 1876, in response to the request of a Massachusetts admirer. Courtesy of Historical Society of Battle Creek. Community Archives of Heritage Battle Creek.

The Lord appointed . . . seventy also, and sent
them two and two . . . into every city and place.
— LUKE 10:1

We are thy sisters. God has truly said,
That of one blood the nations he has made.
Canst thou unblushing read this great command?
O, Christian woman! In a Christian land.
Suffer the wrongs, which wring our inmost heart,
To draw one throb of pity on thy part!
Our skins may differ, but from thee we claim:
A sister's privilege and a sister's name.
— SARAH FORTEN, "WE ARE THY SISTERS"

CHAPTER 8

The Antislavery Vanguard, 1833–1843

I

    When Isabella returned to her previous lifestyle, the Abolitionist move-
ment was in full throttle. Although she had learned not to place her faith in
religious leaders, and was never guided by institutions, her association with Zion
Church placed her in the center of antislavery activism. She apparently did not
join the Abolitionists while in New York City. Yet the movement into which she
would step as Sojourner Truth was already well established there. The birth pangs
of the early antislavery movement, though preceding the emergence of Sojourner
Truth, are the subject of this chapter; they are important to understand as the
context of her involvement in antislavery, woman's rights, and other reforms.
    New York City was the national headquarters of the antislavery movement in
the 1830s, but Massachusetts was its birthplace. First, black Yankees transformed
and expanded their lodges, benevolent associations, and literary societies into
antislavery groups. This inspired white men and women to take up the cause.
The new movement's most unique and unprecedented aspects were its biracial
makeup and call for immediate emancipation and for Northern blacks' social
equality. New York provided the financial backing for the national movement.[1]

New York also replaced Philadelphia around this time as the national black capital and nucleus of cultural, political, intellectual, and ecclesiastical leadership. The *Colored American* replaced *Freedom's Journal* as the nation's only black weekly; the *Mirror of Liberty* was a black monthly; and the *Emancipator*, the New York organ of the AASS, covered black community events. The clergy-dominated black leadership controlled most community activism; the *Colored American* listed ten black churches in 1840. Reverend Peter Williams Jr.'s elite St. Phillips African Episcopal Church was rebuilt from ashes after the riots with a seating capacity of two thousand. Reverend Theodore Wright's middle-class Shiloh Church (First Colored Presbyterian) seated sixteen hundred. The most thriving Baptist church was the working-class Abyssinian.[2]

Zion Church, "Mother of the rest," adopted an antislavery creed in its founding Book of Discipline; its membership was made up of a black working-class majority, and it had the most militant leadership. Zion's bishop, Christopher Rush, a self-emancipated North Carolinian, was a conspicuous Abolitionist who also presided over the biracial Phoenix Literary Society. When a suspicious fire destroyed Zion in 1839, Rush led a massive restoration campaign; the new three-story structure was reportedly the largest black-owned Protestant house of worship in the world. Under Rush's tutelage, Zion churches expanded into a conference in 1848. Yet Rush was intolerant of women preachers such as Isabella. In fact, he spearheaded the conference's conservative position on female ordination.[3]

For Isabella and other black New Yorkers, the streets held an outside as well as a homegrown danger. The city was a kidnapping hub; kidnapping rings and syndicates were linked to police and local officials, and armed blacks vigilantly fought slave-hunting abductors and their henchmen. Editor David Ruggles, another Zion communicant, believed that "more blacks were seized in New York City than on the West African Coast." Ruggles cofounded the New York Vigilance Committee, headquartered at Zion, which sheltered, fed, clothed, transported, and counseled self-emancipated people on the run. The black lady preacher certainly knew the ubiquitous Ruggles, whom slave hunters pursued "as though he were an outlaw, or a wild beast," vowing to "get rid of him by foul means." Always in trouble with the corrupt legal system and frequently arrested, Ruggles was severely beaten in jail. Singular among black leaders in his support of outspoken women, Ruggles may very well have been the "gentleman" who introduced Isabella to Gilbert Vale.[4] Although Zion's gender conservatism constrained Isabella's discipleship, she was in the lap of black radicalism.

Isabella returned to Zion at a point when black women were broadening their benevolent and community outreach activities into antislavery work. Adopting mottoes such as "Let the oppressed go free," these women pledged to work in a spirit of "charity and union," putting aside class difference for the sake of race progress. They raised money and organized sewing circles and "free produce" (non-slave-produced goods) bazaars. "Like Rachel mourning for her young—by the hand of the white oppressor," as one observer said, these women determined to "heed the enslaved mothers' cry for children torn away." At Zion, Isabella worshipped with activists such as Eliza Day, a spiritual leader who had been barricaded in her home for days with an invalid son during the violent rampage of the rioting mob of 1834. Hester Lane, another of Isabella's associates at Zion, transformed strong religious feelings and principles into social protest. Because the home of this fifty-something widow and entrepreneur was one of the community's "free homes" (underground stations), the 1834 mob had targeted it for destruction. The Colored Sailors' Home was another busy underground depot. "My parents were only samples," Mary Lyons's daughter, Maritcha, recalled, "of the great majority of our people in the free states who worked, suffered and prayed, that no one who had the courage to start [toward freedom] should fail to reach the goal." Her mother kept a vigilant eye out for refugees and eagerly sped them on "in the journey toward the North Star."[5]

Isabella was a moral reform activist prior to her Matthias missteps. Afterward, the urgency of the times pushed her farther. Aiding black women's underground activity at Zion, and keeping a vigilant lookout for "man stealers" were also survival strategies and political statements involving everyone. Supporting self-emancipated people and antislavery and protesting discrimination and furthering race uplift enhanced individual safety while serving the community. With "runaway slaves" active in Northern black leadership and black congregations and making up part of the working poor, the struggle was everywhere, and all black Americans were at risk. Although black men insisted that women work behind the scenes, sometimes women moved beyond their "sphere" or "proper place." When black women in New York attempted to rescue self-emancipated women from a courtroom, black men were outraged, angry, and embarrassed. Such public displays were unacceptable, the *Colored American* said, and brought "everlasting shame and remorse" on the community and the women themselves. "We beg their husbands to keep them at home and find some better occupation for them."[6]

In Boston, however, Garrison was eager for a female voice; African American Maria Stewart was one of the first to write in the *Liberator*'s "Ladies Department" column. "One of the most beautiful and loveliest of women," Maria and her husband were friends and neighbors of radical activist David Walker. His powerful "Appeal, in Four Articles," was called "incendiary propaganda," and a bounty was placed on his life. Masterfully dissecting the hypocrisy of American institutions and the cause of black wretchedness, Walker urged black men to throw off their fetters, act like men, and "kill or be killed."[7] Walker's "Appeal" radicalized Maria Stewart; her husband, a whaling vessel outfitter, probably worked with Walker to distribute the pamphlets to black sailors.

David Walker's "mysterious" death in 1830 and the death of her husband in 1829 engulfed Maria in poverty, grief, and uncertainty—until the "divine influence of the Holy Spirit" spoke to her. Vowing even to die for "the cause of oppressed Africa," she began preaching. In October 1832, Garrison published her treatise "Religion and the Pure Principles of Morality." Like Jeremiah, the "weeping prophet," she lamented the condition of black women and encouraged them to seek fulfillment through wisdom. They should found a high school, own businesses, and "possess the spirit of men, bold and enterprising, fearless and undaunted." Writing only three months after Nat Turner's rebellion, she asserted: "WE CLAIM OUR RIGHTS" as women and men, and "we are not afraid of them that kill the body." God would cut them down like grass, and the wickedness of slavery would suffer retribution. She proclaimed that the God who raised up a Walker and a Garrison was not mocked; Walker "lived though he slept."[8]

The black middle class soon forced Maria out of Boston. Her emotional but unrepentant farewell sounds much like the speeches of the future Sojourner Truth. God had unloosed her tongue, Maria said, drenched her with holy zeal, and made her an instrument. She had but dutifully answered the call on her people's behalf. She asserted that throughout history, women had been seers, negotiators, prophetesses, diviners, mystics, philosophers, and scholars recognized for "the sagacity common to the sex." Why, then, "cannot a religious spirit animate us now?" Admitting that her own race's crushing contempt, jealousy, and prejudice had silenced her, Maria nonetheless predicted that an eminent spiritual woman would "arise among our sable race."[9] Although Maria Stewart envisioned a woman from the black intelligentsia, it was Sojourner Truth who emerged.

Maria moved to New York just as the Matthias scandal was placing black womanhood on the defensive. Keeping a low profile, she taught school, joined St. Phillips Church, and worked quietly in women's organizations, but she also may have secretly authored David Ruggles's anonymous column on woman's rights.[10]

In these heady times in New York City, activist churches, friends in the community, and the practice of literate people reading to the nonliterate all contributed to Isabella's knowledge. Sojourner Truth later said that children made the best readers because they "would re-read the same sentence to her as often as she wished, and without comment."[11] Employers who signed antislavery petitions and subscribed to antislavery newspapers were another source of information. However, the penny press was just emerging, and the public relied more on speakers and visionary spectacle than print culture. Sojourner was fond of saying, "I cannot read, but I can hear." The oversized, ornate Broadway Tabernacle hosted antislavery conventions, temperance meetings, famous speakers, and concerts by the famous (Abolitionist) folk singers the Hutchinsons. At the Tabernacle, Isabella heard dietary reformer Sylvester Graham, whose regimen she later adopted, and the popular Adventist visionary William Miller, whose predictions she rejected.[12]

Attribution to Isabella, on the basis of her nonliteracy, of "lack of . . . culture" and "ignorance," is incorrect and misunderstands the historical context.[13] Since no public education existed, most blacks and many whites were unschooled. Isabella's cultivation of exceptional verbal communication in English suggests an equal lucidity in Dutch—her first language. The manner in which she challenged her adversaries reveals that she was highly articulate, not to mention intelligent. She also had educational opportunities. As noted, a schoolteacher brought her to New York, and she took Bible classes at John Street Church from her female Methodist employers. After state emancipation, the churches, the black community, and the Manumission Society conducted evening schools for "colored adults of both sexes." The price was $1 per quarter, and generally more women than men enrolled. Sojourner tried to write her first name on two occasions, once on the back of a carte-de-visite and once for an admirer. She admitted that her words got all scrambled, and she grew discouraged.[14]

Rather than a "learning disability," other reasons may explain this difficulty.[15] She was a full-time domestic from a rural Dutch background, a single parent, struggling to adjust to the metropolis, and struggling to master *spoken* English. Furthermore, she felt herself under divine dispensation to preach the gospel and spread Christian charity. Black itinerant preacher Julia Pell told writer-activist Lydia Maria Child that trying to read "dragged my mind down"; rather than elevating her spirit, the effort made her thoughts scatter like smoke, and she could not preach. Hence, Pell abandoned literacy.[16] Finally, while English Americans saw education as a foremost aspiration, Dutch Americans did not, especially for females. This lack of education would later constrain the directions of Sojourner Truth's activism; nevertheless, she possessed refined domestic skills, was verbally gifted, and astutely presented herself in court, in print, and as a preacher. She traveled around the Hudson Valley region on steamboats and other public conveyances. Her memory was sharp, her analytical and interpretative abilities highly developed. Conventional literacy would have been of enormous value to her, but it is not the only measure of culture, knowledge, and influence.

II

The upsurge of biracial female antislavery activity certainly drew Isabella's attention. Although black women founded the first female auxiliary under the AASS in Salem, Massachusetts, the most influential societies were biracial and in larger cities. Both the Pennsylvania and Boston Female Anti-Slavery Societies (PFASS) and (BFASS) had a number of black women members, some of whom were founders and held office. These included the Forten-Purvis women of Philadelphia and the Ball sisters of Boston. White members such as Lucretia Mott, the Philadelphia Quaker preacher, and Abby Kelley, a young Massachusetts Quaker schoolteacher, later became reform associates of Sojourner Truth. Child gave the movement literary acclaim, although her activism and her antislavery book dampened her popularity. The dedicated but haughty Weston sisters—Caroline, Deborah, Anne, and Maria Weston Chapman—brought wealth and radical chic to the BFASS. At the same time, the Ladies New York Anti-Slavery Society (LNYASS), organized by evangelical women, had no black members.[17]

Efforts led by Angelina Grimké of the PFASS to form a national female antislavery convention in 1837 laid bare the racism among female Abolitionists. Angelina, the daughter of a South Carolina slaveholder, joined the Abolitionists during the 1835 "reign of terror," when Garrison, poet John Greenleaf Whittier, and others were viciously mobbed. Angelina's eloquent public letter and her treatise "An Appeal to the Christian Women of the Southern States" vaulted her into antislavery prominence just as blacks ostracized Maria Stewart. The AASS invited Angelina and her older sister Sarah to New York to organize a national woman's society and train with Theodore Weld's male "anti-slavery apostles." Angelina and Sarah met with the LNYASS and black women separately. The sisters—both gifted speakers—drew huge audiences.[18]

Theodore Weld was the leader of the Lane Seminary "Rebels," who defied the seminary's faculty and president Lyman Beecher, who supported colonization and objected to student activism in the black community. The protest culminated in the founding of Oberlin College. Weld, called the most mobbed man in the movement, used Christ's outreach method to spread antislavery in the West: living, eating, sleeping, and teaching in black homes, hamlets, and communities; worshipping in black churches; speaking in black lodges; and preaching among whites. Called to New York by the AASS, this "master spirit and chief organizer" trained forty college and seminary men, mainly white, to fight for the cause of abolition. He taught them about the history, philosophy, and profitability of slavery; biblical arguments; and antislavery tactics and strategies. Black Abolitionists led discussions on racism. He commissioned a group, known as the "seventy," who were to travel "two by two" and spread the Word as in the Bible. Weld's methods became the model for the campaigns of Sojourner Truth and her associates in the American West.[19]

Angelina and Sarah encountered pervasive "wicked prejudice" and segregation among most New York evangelical women. The sisters met this racism head-on, speaking in black neighborhoods and urging skeptical black women to participate in the upcoming national convention. Campaigning throughout New York and New Jersey in the winter of 1836, the Grimkés condemned race prejudice before both "promiscuous" audiences and those segregated by race and gender. Angelina published an anonymous "Appeal to the Ladies" in the *Evangelist* and the *Colored American* in which she attacked the LNYASS for its color prejudice. She implored her black Philadelphia sisters to attend the convention despite the racism. Only a black presence would help white women overcome prejudice, and only black intellectual input on black issues could ensure the convention's success.[20]

In 1837, at a little church on Houston Street, New York City women hosted the first biracial Woman's Convention. Yet New York had no black women delegates, while the BFASS and PFASS each had two among their four. Despite being excluded from the LNYASS, numerous local and out-of-town black women registered for the convention as individuals or corresponding members or through organizations. In fact, 1 in 10 women at the convention were African American. Local black women provided the lemonade and lunches, but their interest was politics rather than hospitality. The convention was closed to all except registered participants, but Isabella probably knew quite a few of them because she worshiped with some of the black women, she had worked in moral reform with some of the evangelical women, and her antislavery female employers probably registered for the convention. The tension over racism was strong enough for the Forten-Purvis women to decline offers to board with a white evangelical family who were opposed to all biracial antislavery activism.[21]

Angelina Grimké's compelling pamphlet "An Appeal to the Women of the Nominally Free States" framed the Arrangement Committee's race prejudice resolutions. The racial divide was a pillar of slavery, the committee reported, and white antislavery women, either through silent complicity or open bigotry, were primary culprits. Committee members, including Child and Mott, insisted that interracial mingling would awaken white sensitivity to Northern "anti-Christian" prejudice. If "peculiar sympathy" and solidarity were not extended to black women, the committee cautioned, "We will be termed 'the white slaves of the North.'" Black women in the audience, including Hester Lane, Maria Stewart, and the Forten-Purvises, gave moving accounts of experiences with racism. The title page of Angelina's "Appeal" displayed the poem "We Are Thy Sisters," written by Sarah Forten for the convention.[22]

Angelina Grimké introduced an even bolder direct-action resolution: woman would use "her voice, and her pen, and her purse, and the influence of her example, to overthrow the horrible system of American slavery." The resolution passed after an animated debate, but twelve LNYASS women and a few from Boston went on record as opposed.[23]

This first convention, and two subsequently held in 1838 and 1839, addressed the problem of biracial activism that historically, American women have never solved. Few lasting results came from resolutions on crossracial solidarity. Rather than integrate or support female antislavery agents, the LNYASS women soon dissolved their organization. Angelina married her Abolitionist mentor, Theodore Weld, and Sarah joined them in semiretirement to a New Jersey farm. These early conventions laid the groundwork for Sojourner's later antislavery activism and her calls for biracial cooperation in woman's rights.

Other events nudging Isabella toward antislavery included the tragic death of Elijah P. Lovejoy in Alton, Illinois, in 1837. This editor and Presbyterian minister had fled Missouri after mobs destroyed his press because he had protested the barbaric burning, mutilation, and decapitation of a free black man. In Illinois, Lovejoy was attacked after organizing a state antislavery society. When local authorities refused to protect him, he armed himself. The proslavery mob "smoked out" Lovejoy, shot and killed him, and destroyed his press. While Garrisonians and evangelicals argued over whether Lovejoy's use of "weapons of destruction" made him a "Christian martyr" and politicians emphasized the damage to constitutional freedoms, the *Colored American*'s front-page story read "Spirit of Slavery Triumphant." Like the murdered black man he had defended, Lovejoy had been a "victim of a mob, thirsting for his blood, because he dared to lift up his voice against the oppression of the poor slave." Blacks held memorials, church services, prayer meetings, mass rallies, and fundraising events for Lovejoy's widow and baby. "The gun which aimed at the breast of Lovejoy brought me to my feet," Boston patrician Wendell Phillips declared. In Hudson, Ohio, after Lovejoy's death, thirty-seven-year-old John Brown stood in a prayer meeting and declared: "I pledge myself, with God's help, that I will devote my life to increasing hostility toward slavery."[24]

The historic 1839 AASS meeting changed the course of abolition and opened a path for Sojourner Truth. At the Broadway Tabernacle, five thousand antislavery advocates and some enemies assembled. A split between radical Garrisonians and evangelicals had been brewing for three years. Led by Lewis Tappan, the evangelicals proposed a resolution against Garrisonian "heresies," which was defeated. Garrison struck back and proposed that women be voting members, be delegates to national meetings, and hold office. The evangelical-controlled Executive Committee objected strenuously to "hens crowing." The New York black clerics and black women supported the evangelicals, while secular leaders, including David Ruggles, voted for full female participation. Garrison's resolution carried, despite New York's strong nay vote. Both sides of the debate marshaled their supporters for next year's election of officers.[25]

"More than the usual handful of black men" and a host of women "shouted, hissed, and complained" at the volatile 1840 showdown. "The question of 'woman's rights' is not the only matter of difference," the evangelicals asserted. "Nor is it the chief cause of the difficulty." They could not stand Garrison's radicalism and Perfectionism, and the delicate alliance between the radicals and the evangelicals collapsed under this weight. As did Isabella and John Humphrey Noyes (who later founded Oneida Community), Garrison believed that earthly holiness was attainable—but not through the churches or the parasitic clergy. Garrison also disavowed celebrating a special holy day (Sunday), advocated complete pacifism, and opposed a standing army, military service, and capital punishment. While Noyes had a separatist vision similar to that of Matthias, Garrison's godly "peaceable kingdom" on earth was possible through activist engagement. Above all, Garrison said, people must protest state terrorism (slavery) by not voting or holding office. No law was binding if it conflicted with commands of the Gospel. The evangelicals were furious when Garrison founded the New England Non-Resistance Society in 1838 and used the *Liberator* as a forum. He changed the motto on the *Liberator* masthead to "OUR COUNTRY IS THE WORLD—OUR COUNTRYMEN ARE ALL MANKIND."[26]

When Garrison's forces easily elected Abby Kelley to the powerful Business Committee, the evangelicals walked out. That evening, Lewis Tappan and thirty supporters formed the American and Foreign Anti-Slavery Society (AFASS), known as the "New Org," or New Organization. White women within the Old Org, or Old Organization (the Garrisonians), now assumed the highest national offices, with Maria Chapman taking over the finances. The Old Org lost the New York *Emancipator* and established the *National Anti-Slavery Standard*, with Child as editor. The Old Org also elected women delegates to London's 1840 World Anti-Slavery Convention. However, the evangelicals arrived there first, and successfully lobbied against seating the women. Although black clerics were skeptical about some New Org individuals, they felt bound to evangelicals such as the Tappans by friendship, spiritual association, economic support, and vision. The also supported New Org individuals who favored a political antislavery program.[27] Isabella was not involved in these organizational battles; Sojourner never traveled abroad. But these early struggles opened the way for her involvement in woman's rights, and her reputation would cross the Atlantic.

The split divided both blacks and women. Some black clerics continued to work with the Old Org, because Garrison remained wildly popular with the black masses. The LNYASS disbanded, and antislavery women in the city remained largely unorganized. The Pennsylvania women remained thoroughly Garrisonian. In Boston, Old Org adherents Kelley, Child, and the Weston sisters led a nasty struggle against a well-positioned New Org biracial minority, including BFAA president Mary Parker (white) and African American officeholders such as the Ball sisters. The Ball sisters labeled the Weston sisters arrogant, elitist, and racist. Maria Chapman scornfully dismissed the dissenters as "Spiritual wives" in the harems of "wicked" evangelicals.[28]

Thus, no antislavery organization existed in New York for Isabella, since Garrison's Old Org radicalism suited her concept of a peaceable kingdom and humanitarian reform. Many New York evangelicals abandoned abolition rather than associate even with middle-class blacks as the Tappans urged. But the Tappan brothers remained committed to immediate abolition and working for racial equality. Lewis Tappan's greatest achievements were in promoting educational evangelicalism, and financing the famous *Amistad* case, which, like Elijah Lovejoy's death, awakened blacks such as Isabella to the antislavery cause. Tappan's *Amistad* Committee financed the captured Mende Africans' legal fees, Christian instruction, English lessons, and tours. Ultimately, former president John Quincy Adams successfully argued their case before the Supreme Court. Tappan transformed the *Amistad* Committee into the American Missionary Association, an organization that became far more significant to blacks than his AFASS.[29]

Black communities united around the *Amistad* Africans. Freed without resources, they raised money by touring. Their unblinking boldness and heroism touched black people deeply, instilling respect, pride, and a sense of personal triumph. The deeds of the young leader Cinquez inspired men such as Charles Lenox Remond, Frederick Douglass, and Henry Garnet. Black Abolitionist Robert Purvis commissioned a portrait of the handsome rebel. Ministers preached sermons about the Africans, intellectuals wrote pamphlets, the masses held rallies, and everyone gave donations. Isabella, who frequented Tabernacle events, was probably present at the November 1841 farewell service there. Cinquez vividly narrated the heroic mutiny; his compatriots movingly recounted their two years of troubles and suffering and the tragedy of slavery. They sang emotional Abolitionist hymns. But open weeping erupted when the assembly joined them in lining out the Methodist hymn:

> When I can read my title clear
> To Mansions in the skies,
> I'll bid farewell to every fear,
> And wipe my weeping eyes.[30]

The *Amistad* case was significant for Isabella, just two generations removed from Africa. But the American government made clear its proslavery commitment. As the Africans sailed for Sierra Leone, enslaved Madison Washington led 135 black Virginians to commandeer the *Creole,* a vessel taking them to New Orleans. They killed the slave trader and sailed to British Nassau and freedom. The British salvaged Anglo-American relations only by fully compensating the slaveholders. In *Prigg v. Pennsylvania,* the Supreme Court denied a state's right to extend personal liberty laws, such as trial by jury, to blacks accused of being "escaped property." This resounding defeat set back underground work and put thousands of Northern blacks at risk.[31]

As Isabella prepared to rededicate herself as God's messenger, the voice of the enslaved became a mobilizing force. In May 1843 the main attraction at the annual AASS meeting was a newcomer named Frederick Douglass. As an enslaved Maryland boy, he was jostled between plantation and urban life; a tolerant Baltimore mistress's brief instruction sparked his interest in education and set him on a path of literacy. At twenty-one, he fled bondage and settled in New Bedford, Massachusetts. When he was twenty-five and already a local black leader and licensed AME Zion preacher, Garrison recruited him to join freeborn Charles Lenox Remond as the AASS's only two black agents. Describing himself as initially "green and awkward and embarrassed" in 1841, by 1843 Douglass was polished, articulate, and persuasive. His presence was imposing—tall, bronze, with chiseled African features and a mane of thick, wavy hair. His deeply set eyes and painfully brooding gaze made him seem older than his years. He drew a huge black attendance. And the occasion of white women mixing with "sable-complexioned sons of Africa" prompted the Broadway Tabernacle proprietors to refuse use of the building.[32]

Douglass was a new kind of race leader—southern-born, bondage-bred, and self-taught. A captivating orator, he spoke with deep resonance and impressive diction, and his voice carried well over a large assembly. No address, wrote the *National Anti-Slavery Standard*, received more "loud and protracted applause." Within a month of his New York City appearance, Isabella also spoke publicly of her enslavement. Like Douglass, she could say, "I have myself been a slave."[33]

The arrival of Henry Garnet on the Abolitionist scene also stirred up power-ful forces from within the black community, exemplifying the complexities that would come to divide black activists, including Sojourner Truth and Frederick Douglass. Garnet, the grandson of a Mandingo chieftain, was a brilliant young intellectual, Presbyterian pastor, and founding member of Tappan's New Org. Incensed over the disturbing post-*Amistad* events, Garnet urged that "brethren of the North, East, and West . . . meet together . . . to sympathize with each other and to weep over your unhappy condition." At the National Black Conven-tion in Buffalo in 1843, Garnet moved his audience to tears and clenched fists, invoking black martyrs—Denmark Vesey, Nat Turner, Cinquez, and Madison Washington—noble men who had left cherished counsel: "RATHER DIE FREE-MEN, THAN LIVE TO BE SLAVES." From their graves, Garnet said, dead fathers urged men to forsake patience and rise up: "Let your MOTTO be RESISTANCE! RESISTANCE! RESISTANCE! No oppressed people have ever secured their Liberty without resistance. What kind of resistance you had better make, you must decide by the circumstances that surround you, and according to the sug-gestion of expediency . . . and remember that you are three millions."[34]

This militancy created a showdown at the Buffalo Convention. The split was partly regional. New Englanders and many central New Yorkers—including a young Buffalo resident and self-emancipated Kentuckian named William Wells Brown—backed Douglass, who argued forcefully against encouraging rebellion among his unarmed people. After two votes and three days of intense lobbying, Garnet's resolution was decisively rejected. This convention, while not eclipsing Henry Garnet's leadership, showcased Frederick Douglass and William Wells Brown among blacks throughout the nation.[35] Years later, Sojourner Truth and Frederick Douglass would disagree on the same issue. All these events, and more, before and during the pivotal year 1843 inspired Isabella's call to be a sojourner for truth and justice. Like other activists, black and white, she identified with and embraced the spirit of the intrepid phrase "Let Your Motto Be RESISTANCE!"

His [Peter's] letters are inserted here for preservation, in case they prove the last she ever hears from him in this world.
— *NARRATIVE OF SOJOURNER TRUTH*

As a sojourner, he shall be with thee . . . unto the year of jubilee. . . . For they are my servants, which I brought forth out of the land of Egypt: they shall not be sold as bondmen. — LEV. 25:40, 42

Even the Spirit of Truth . . . dwelleth with you, and shall be in you. — JOHN 14:17

CHAPTER 9

"The Spirit Calls Me There"

A SOJOURNER IS CHOSEN

I

Isabella's son Peter grew into a tall, well-formed, active young man with a cheerful, mild disposition and a generous and winning personality.[1] But racism stifled his prospects, and unemployment among black males was high. Most worked as porters, peddlers, chimney sweeps, and tub men (night workers who gathered and emptied privies or collected manure). A few semiskilled blacks were cartmen's helpers, horse groomers, and coachmen, but artisan trades and factory work were largely closed to them. Immigrants from Ireland, Scotland, or "from beyond the seas" dominated apprenticeships. Only one black youth appeared on the New York City Apprentice Register for the 1830s; he trained as a "servant," and unlike whites, received no pay for most of his three-year contract.[2] While Isabella urged Peter to become a productive, responsible young man, many forces worked against him.

Economic disadvantage, Isabella's preoccupation with her reform and religious engagements, and the alluring excitement of the streets all contributed to Peter becoming a street urchin and petty criminal. He and his friends roamed the city seeking fun and mischief. They burglarized homes and businesses, stole from private citizens, and fenced stolen loot on street corners and at tavern hangouts. Peter and his associates made up an underclass of black youth culture similar to the b'hoys, their white counterparts—young, tough, swaggering blacks in flashy dress and sporting unusual hairstyles. While modesty was the watchword for the black middle and religious classes, the street people preferred a colorful lifestyle.[3]

Lying to white authority was a part of life for rebellious black youth, who artfully concealed their real identities. They were automatic suspects when crimes were committed, and a white property owner's accusation brought charges, and even conviction. Peter's habitual alias, "Peter Williams," appeared frequently in police records. He also used Jim or James Williams, appropriations of his deceased grandfather's and brother's name. Besides using an alias, Peter sometimes further concealed his identity by misquoting his age, and listing Isabella as "Betsy Williams," a diminutive of his grandmother's and sister's name. Peter's trail of petty crime began at the age of eleven. In July 1830, Peter Williams and George Pine allegedly stole a gold watch and chain. Although found guilty, the boys were discharged. Two weeks later, a bench warrant was issued for Peter "and other black boys unknown to the deponent" for stealing two silver spoons worth $2.50. Again, he was released. In September 1830, Peter reportedly stole nine silver spoons from Cornelius Vanderbilt. He was found guilty and sentenced to six months in the New York City Penitentiary (the Tombs) but again was released.[4]

Isabella aided her son repeatedly, but his brushes with the law continued for some time. Then, for nearly four years, police and court records are silent on Peter. Since he was not with Isabella in either commune, he was probably back in Ulster County, and returned to New York after the Matthias kingdom dissolved. In September 1834, Peter Williams was back in court; he and his friends were convicted of two counts of burglary and sentenced to a total of ten years in state prison.[5]

That should have put him away for some time. Isabella was in the throes of the Matthias imbroglio, and no doubt the legal connections she had at that time secured Peter's release. Later that fall, while the newspapers scandalized his mother, Peter and his buddies struck again. The district attorney charged Peter Williams—"alias Jim Williams"—and others with rowing (in a stolen boat) to Blackwell's Island, breaking into a shoe store, and stealing shoes, leather, and cobbling boots. Despite the seriousness of this accusation, Peter was released. In 1836, Peter Williams reportedly stole a watch, but was discharged. The Ulster County folk predicted that Isabella's son seemed destined for prison or worse. His final brush with the law was in January 1839, when he and his friends were accused of stealing timber.[6]

Peter was Isabella's special child, her only surviving son, who had suffered brutality and trauma when sold away. When he contritely "lay open his whole soul to her," pulling at her heartstrings, she accepted his excuses. Through friends, she secured positions for him. She gave him money to enter navigation school, only to discover that he had spent it. She purchased livery for his coachman training, and he promptly sold it. Her patience ended, she resorted to tough love, thinking that he would never reform so long as she bailed him out of difficulties. The forgiving woman of God left her son in prison and ignored his messages for help. Finally, he called on the black leader whose name he had borrowed.[7]

Reverend Peter Williams Jr. was a noted leader in New York's black community. Born in slavery during the Revolution, his parents worshipped with the congregation that became John Street Methodist Church. After the Revolution, Methodist leaders helped the family obtain freedom. Williams Sr. became sexton of John Street Church and a substantial property owner, tobacconist, and undertaker. While he eventually helped found Mother Zion, Williams Jr. united with the Episcopal Church, becoming the second black priest ordained in America. A learned man and activist, the younger Williams's "Oration on the Abolition of the Slave Trade" was so eloquent that whites refused to believe he wrote it. Isabella's son knew of Peter Williams Jr. because his community service included aiding troubled, rootless, jobless young men. Alexander Crummell, a protégé of Williams Jr., mistakenly called him timid, crushed by the "dark and gloomy days of New York slavery," and awed by Episcopal power. Actually, when Episcopal bishop Benjamin Onderdonk tried to block young Crummell's seminary admittance, Williams Jr. was his champion. In Sojourner Truth's *Narrative*, Peter Williams Jr. is called a "barber," which meant undertaker and medical practitioner, roles that further reveal Williams's importance to black New Yorkers, who called him "Brother Beloved."[8]

The fifty-six-year old cleric assisted young men by helping them go to sea. New York was prime recruiting ground for shipping agents, who haunted boardinghouses, orphanages, churches, and prisons. Directors or city institutions and ministers such as Williams kept a sharp eye out for sturdy young men. Although the economic depression from 1837 through the early 1840s forced agents to turn away applicants, the black lady preacher's son had a strapping physique, constitutional hardiness, size, and muscle. Williams visited him in prison and offered to redeem him if he promised to go to sea. Although life on a whaler paled in comparison to the dangers and delights of the streets, several months in the Tombs with no visits from his mother had changed Peter's mind.[9]

For bondmen and free black men, the waterways represented mobility and strength of character. Black oarsmen and pilots navigated rivers and inlets throughout America. On whalers, blacks and whites received equal pay for equal work. The special training provided was also popular among blacks, allowing them to move beyond the "greenhand" or ordinary seaman level. Gilbert Vale had a science and navigation school, and a black academy offered courses. Some blacks owned vessels; others were officers. The black middle class believed that the harshness, danger, and isolation of seafaring toughened young men and advanced their worldly education. Men from solid backgrounds often returned as mature, seasoned, cosmopolitan individuals. Seafarers such as Paul Cuffe, James Forten, William P. Powell, and Henry Garnet (who lost a leg at sea), all seafarers turned activists, wore the mantle of leadership well. From 1803 to 1860, an estimated three thousand black men sailed on whalers from New Bedford alone.[10]

Although it was Peter Van Wagenen's benefactor who had assumed responsibility for him, he paid a somber parting visit to his mother. He had disappointed her so many times that she was guarded and distrustful of any good intentions. It was not a proper goodbye, because she did not believe Peter was going to sea, and she was still angry. He had lied so much before, how could she believe him now? Even Peter Williams Jr.'s personal assurances did not convince her. The young whaling recruits roomed at the Colored Seamen's boardinghouse, which by 1839 was run by black Abolitionist William P. Powell. A week after Peter's visit to his mother, Rev. Williams called on her and assured her that Peter was gone. Nonetheless, for some time, she expected to see him emerging from some by-place in the city.[11]

"Peter Williams" signed on to the ship *Zone,* which sailed from Edgartown, Massachusetts, on May 19, 1839, under Captain Edwin Hiller. Over a year passed before a letter reached Isabella. Letters to his "Dear and Beloved Mother" give voice to Peter for the first and only time. He had seen more of the world than he ever expected to see—the Azores, the Caribbean, Tahiti—and was writing her from the Off-Shore Grounds near Peru. He got into trouble on board, for "shoving my head in the fire for other folks." He inquired nostalgically about his sisters and cousins. Above all, he wanted his mother's confidence. Before leaving, he had not been able to convince her to trust his resolve. Now, his greatest desire was to return home with enough money to make his parents proud. Fretting over his past behavior and the pain he had caused her, he asked Isabella's forgiveness "for all that I have done." He ended with "Mother, I hope you do not forget me, your dear and only son." He signed his letters "Peter Van Wagener."[12]

Although the black community viewed sea life as a manly pursuit, it was also labor-intensive, oppressive, and hierarchical. The power mechanisms on a whaling vessel, as seamen's protection agencies warned, were as brutal as on an Alabama plantation. In both instances, the master's authority was absolute. A whaling captain, like a slaveholder, defined punishable offenses as "indiscipline, disrespect, insolence, or refusal to perform an assigned task." Captain Hiller was hard on his crew. Within a year, five Americans died on board the *Zone.* Peter did not—perhaps could not—tell Isabella that a mutiny had occurred on the *Zone* sometime between its departure from the Caribbean and before its arrival in Tahiti on March 22, 1840. But he wrote of a dead shipmate whom she knew. Peter Jackson had "died on board the ship Done [*sic*]," in the West Indies, he wrote. She informed Jackson's family. His death was undoubtedly related to the mutiny. The ship's log is lost, but the consul records note a fee paid for "examination of Crew of ship Zone for revolt" and a certificate of punishment issued. The names of those examined and the type of punishment administered are missing. However, Peter being punished "severely" for helping others suggests that while he was not an instigator of the mutiny, he sided with the rebels. The *Zone* mutiny was not an isolated incident. Brutality toward the crew, the lack of whale activity, and fear of an unprofitable voyage gave rise to short tempers and unrest. The treatment of seamen inspired William P. Powell to establish the American Seamen's Protective Union Association. Despite his hard luck, Peter remained upbeat. He looked forward to doing better and returning home within twenty-two months.[13]

Peter's final letter, dated September 19, 1841, was the most touching. He said he had written five letters and received none at all. Had she forgotten him? Was she still angry? Her prodigal son assured his mother that he only wanted to make good and return to her. She long remembered his warning: "If I don't do well, you need not expect me home these five years." Peter closed the letter with a poem, revealing that he was a gifted, thoughtful young man. "When this you see," he wrote, "remember me, and place me in your mind." The poem speaks to the oppressiveness of whaling that gave rise to a collective race consciousness in seamen's boardinghouses, which long voyages nurtured.[14]

> Get me to my home, that's in the far-distant west,
> To the scenes of my childhood, that I like the best,
> There the tall cedars grow, and the bright waters flow,
> Where my parents will greet me, white man, let me go!
> Let me go to the spot where the cataract plays,
> Where oft I have sported in my boyish days;
> And there is my poor mother, whose heart ever flows,
> At the sight of her poor child, to her let me go, let me go!
> Your only son,
> Peter Van Wagener

While Peter sailed the seas, Isabella worked hard, saved, and went to meetings, but remained disenchanted. She certainly never recovered her former stature in the city. And in New York, the Democrats' rise to power, splits in reform groups, and deaths overshadowed the hopes of Abolitionist activism. Even David Ruggles left New York destitute, nearly blind, broken in health, and falsely accused of mishandling antislavery money. As the depression dragged on, Isabella felt even she was becoming competitive and greedy, placing gain above God. Her industry "doubtless kept some poor wretch from paying work."[15] No doubt her only uplifting anticipation was her son's homecoming.

On May 19, 1843, the *Zone* returned to New Bedford without Peter. His nostalgic letters indicate that he would not have jumped ship. Most likely, he had died during the smallpox epidemic that raged in the South Pacific from the summer through the fall of 1841. Ships' logs contain distress signals from Tahiti, where Americans and islanders died rapidly. On September 2, the first mate of the *Moss* wrote of the pox, "I hope it all Over." However, it was not. In Peter's September 19 letter to Isabella, he wrote from Tahiti that his health was good. Disease ravaged men all around him. More humane captains began vaccinating their crews—a dangerous procedure accompanied by illness, but an alternative to the deadly disease. Captain Hiller probably did not vaccinate his crew. Moreover, the disease continued, and ships could not leave Tahiti. Although records indicate that the *Zone* left port in October, the contagious quality of smallpox and the insular nature of a ship were not conducive to survival in such conditions.[16] Peter's demise, like that of his friend, went unrecorded.

In February 1842, the registry book of Pitcairn Island lists the arrival of the "Ship Zone of Nantucket, 33 months out" with 1,650 barrels of sperm oil. The *Zone* took on only 25 percent more in the remaining fifteen months of its journey. Still, 2,061 barrels of sperm oil was a respectable total. Peter's share after expenses would have been just over $100 for the entire voyage. Something on board the *Zone* was awry, as the mutiny reveals.[17]

Peter's disappearance, whether caused by smallpox, punishment, or an accident, was the great mystery and tragedy of his mother's life. The little boy whose kidnapping had caused her so much anguish, the teenager whose misbehavior had nearly broken her heart, was gone. Yet Peter was Isabella's miracle child—living proof of her divine favor, covenant with God, and defiance of slavery. God, she believed, had scripted her child's return to New York. Regaining Peter had been her first victorious test of faith after her conversion; her curse on the Gidneys, the supreme authentication of her sanctification, had come through Peter's bruised and broken flesh. In 1843, she could not believe it had been for naught, and hoped that God would spare him once again. But her distressed inquiries were hampered. Young black men commonly died at sea, she could not read or write, and her main contact, Peter Williams Jr., had died in 1840. Although she had lost Peter twice in earthly life, as Sojourner dictated her *Narrative* in 1849, she still hoped for his return. She also now embraced a new faith—Spiritualism, a belief not only in life after death but human contact with departed loved ones. As he had once implored her to believe in him, she now insisted that whether in heaven or on earth, he was reformed. "He is good now, I have no doubt," she insisted. "I feel sure that he has persevered, and kept the resolve he made before he left home—he seemed so different before he went, so determined to do better."[18]

II

On May 11, 1843, a notice appeared in the *National Anti-Slavery Standard*:

A COLORED LADY PREACHER

Last Sabbath afternoon, we had the pleasure of listening to a very touching discourse from a colored woman, in the Sixth-street Methodist (colored) church. She was once a slave, and is a fine specimen of natural oratory. In propriety, energy, and grace of action, she beats any teacher of elocution we ever heard.[19]

This had to be Isabella Van Wagenen, the only known unlicensed black woman preacher living in New York and born in slavery. The Sixth Street Methodist Church was within the Methodist Episcopal denomination, and its black pastor, Luther Mead, allowed women to speak. Isabella delivered this antislavery sermon just before Peter's scheduled return. But Peter did not return, and she faced another test of faith. Should she remain in the city, or follow the voice of God?

Personal crossroads and crises seem to have led Isabella to spiritual regeneration. After her deliverance from the Matthias debacle, she reconnected with the "ancient faith" that had always been her mainstay. She returned to church meetings, but continued to be guided directly by God and prayer. But she was mentally tormented and troubled by her own lack of a place in the city, even more so in light of the mystery of Peter's whereabouts. One night, after leading an apparently wrenching prayer meeting, she felt especially spent and spiritually malnourished. Self-doubt, depression, and indecision dogged her through a sleepless night. "Lord what wilt thou have me to do?" she asked. Finally, an epiphany came. She must do more than clean houses and boil beef. She must leave the city, the Voice said. "Lord whither shall I go?" The Voice spoke as plain as her own: "Go East."

For Isabella, this life-altering decision was as cathartic and fateful as her flight from the House of Bondage. She was God's "chosen vessel." Next morning, she put together a few belongings and announced her imminent departure to Lucy Whiting:

"The Lord is going to give me a new home, Mrs. Whiting, and I am going away."

"Where are you going?" asked her employer.

"Going East," answered Isabella.

"What does that mean?"

"The Lord has directed me to go East, and leave this city at once," Isabella answered. Mrs. Whiting was shocked.

"Bell, you are crazy."

"No I ain't," assured Isabella.

"The Spirit calls me there, and I must go."

Lucy Whiting explained Isabella's amazing decision to her husband, Perez, who did not think Isabella was crazy. "But," his wife insisted, "I tell you she is; she says she's going to have a new name too; don't that look crazy." Perez Whiting replied, "Oh no," but asked Isabella to at least have breakfast, which she refused. Since witnesses for Jesus also took vows of poverty, the Sojourner would travel light and trust God for her needs. She left money with the Whitings, which she had intended to deposit in the bank. "I just put a change of clothes in a pillow-case and started. All the money I had with me was twenty-five cents given to me by a good man at prayer meeting."[20]

At age forty-six, Isabella Van Wagenen, nearing the end of the average African American life span, entered a third stage of life. Enslaved for one generation, freed during a second, she now contemplated a future mission. Blessed with spiritual gifts and believing she was summoned to apostleship, she determined to work out her salvation through usefulness. Her oration at the Sixth Street Church had been a public testament, but she left the "Second Sodom" quietly, secretly, and unannounced on June 1, 1843, Pentecost Sunday morning.

As a "Sojourner" for the "Spirit of Truth," she drew on her New York City experience, even Matthias, whom she still believed was a messenger of God. But just as she had censured his weakness for Ann Folger, she broke with him by reclaiming her status as a holy woman. She was among a small number of black female itinerants claiming scriptural justification for their missions—reminding male ministers that a woman (Mary Magdalene) first preached of the risen Savior, and that apostleship did not require literacy. Unlettered women compared themselves to Christ's disciples, who "though they were fishermen, and ignorant of letters too," were inspired to preach. Responding to Paul's edict against preaching women, female itinerants reminded men that "Paul called Priscilla, as well as Aquila his 'helper.'" Finally, Pentecost justified Sojourner Truth and women preachers, because "women as well as men were . . . filled with the Holy Ghost." Women were among those "who continued in prayer and supplication, waiting for the fulfillment of the promise." Moreover, black preaching women said, if women had lost the gift of prophecy, so had men. Yet they insisted that the Bible resolved this strife by stating "There is neither male nor female in Jesus Christ."[21]

A new name almost always accompanied being "chosen." Elijah Pierson taking the name "John the Baptist" and Robert Matthews the name "Father Matthias" bordered on psychiatric and spiritual delusion. In saner moments, however, Matthews called himself a traveler. Harriet Livermore was a "pilgrim." In the New Testament, Saul of Tarsus had become "Paul." Isabella Van Wagenen becoming Sojourner Truth was an inspired naming. A sojourner was biblically significant, reflecting the manifestation of her mission. "Truth" was divinely motivated; it connected Sojourner's apostleship to the Holy Spirit.

III

As the disciple of Christ left the city, she thought of a biblical story. Lot, Abraham's nephew, obeyed God's instructions to depart wicked Sodom and Gomorrah without looking back on the evil cities' destruction. Lot's wife disobeyed, and was transformed into a pillar of salt. Once before, Bell had also desired to return to a wanton life on Dumont's farm, and "looked back into Egypt." But the power of God had struck her. This time Sojourner Truth dared not turn around.[22]

In Brooklyn, Long Island's largest town, much of the black population was crowded around the squalid ferry district. Kings County was still largely Dutch and still had the highest number of slaveholders and enslaved people in the North. Kings County was also New York City's breadbasket, supplying the metropolis with agricultural grains and vegetables. The servitude clause in New York's Emancipation Act kept young blacks on Kings County farms well into the mid-nineteenth century. Freed adults worked on Dutch farms as day laborers, tenants, and domestics. In Brooklyn, blacks had more opportunities in semiskilled and skilled occupations than in Manhattan. Politically, the Kings County Dutch sustained an intractable conservatism and joined immigrants in supporting the Democratic Party.[23]

The Sojourner quickly headed for the country, probably taking the well-traveled post road through Brooklyn, Bushwick, Flatbush, and other rural towns. This route was safer and more populous, and she could find work. Besides farms, hamlets, and villages, the landscape was studded with camp meeting sites and occasionally a utopian community. The countryside also hosted various spiritual travelers, wayfarers, vendors, and vagabonds. In this rural county, Sojourner's Dutchness and skills were advantageous, and she found employment immediately. One family offered her a great deal of money to stay, but she remained only a few days, and on leaving, accepted only enough money to "pay tribute to

Caesar." She remained in this predominantly Dutch western area of Long Island, no more than ten or fifteen miles from Manhattan, for about one month.[24]

Fifteen years in the city had not obliterated Sojourner's familiarity with the outdoors or country life. The sun was her compass and her timepiece. The many hours of daylight during that seasonable eastern summer gave her time to find a night's resting place. It was not always easy. In one evening, miserly folk refused her a night's lodging twenty times. She generally found blacks more welcoming than whites, and the poor of both races more hospitable than the well-off. Conscious of racism, she never told strangers that she was alone. After one weary day of walking, she went to a tavern that also served as a courthouse and jail. The tavern keeper refused to rent her a room, but offered to lock her up. Preferring freedom under the cope of heaven to sleeping in jail, she walked on. It evidently began raining, for she soon joined a couple sheltering under a shed. The wife offered Sojourner lodging if she first accompanied them to a "ball." The revelers, Sojourner said, were dregs of society, and the ballroom a dirty hovel filled with abundant whiskey and powerful fumes. Her prospective hostess passed out from too much alcohol. It was useless, even dangerous, to lecture these inebriated carousers, so Sojourner sat in a corner and observed the spectacle. Finally, the husband aroused his wife, and all three departed. Their abode was a "miserable cabin" with one pallet, which they generously offered to their guest. Declining to take their only bed, she sat waiting for the "eye of day."[25]

Although reform was not popular in western Long Island, Sojourner Truth found enough listeners to hold protracted meetings. Temperance became a popular cause among black leaders, who condemned alcoholism as a source of moral lapses, criminality, and a major killer of the race. In Brooklyn, Presbyterian minister James N. Gloucester and his wife Elizabeth were both militant Abolitionists and temperance advocates who welcomed radical reformers into their church. Sojourner was a guest of the Gloucesters after the Civil War, and she may have met them in 1843; both frequented summer temperance meetings. She soon continued east, preaching "religion and abolition all the way."[26]

Approximately eight thousand African Americans lived on Long Island, but the paucity of black churches reportedly hindered their intellectual, moral, or spiritual improvement. In 1843, Nassau County had only four and Suffolk County five black Methodist churches. Their aggregate membership even in 1845 was 941; numerous secessions and rivalries created tiny separate congregations, sometimes under one "bishop." Sojourner found that this was a region of rural Quaker towns dotted with black property owners and separate black communities. They usually held church service monthly and were often without pastors for extended periods, but they would not allow female preaching. Sojourner held outdoor meetings near towns on the turnpike or post road, and "had a good time" among these country folk.[27] She was not simply "wandering."[28] She was spreading a message.

She felt less welcome in some densely settled areas, including the village of Huntington, which had a white Methodist and an AME church. But in Cold Springs, a quaint, thriving little Quaker village on Long Island Sound, she found numerous kindred spirits. There her cooking as well as her preaching won favor. She helped organize a mass temperance meeting, and the assembly raved over her "dishes *a la New York*."[29]

Like Sojourner, the early Hicksite Quakers emphasized the spirit over the letter of Christianity and interpreted Scripture as mystical revelations and moral directives rather than erudite rationalisms. Like Sojourner, they believed that salvation freed humanity from the sacraments; they stressed Christ's moral example and the fullness of his spirit through the greatness of each human heart. For Sojourner as for the Hicksites, the Spirit was an "Inner Voice" and guiding light. These Quakers also had a tradition of "traveling Friends," including Elias Hicks, who spread the message of reform. Finally, Hicksite emphasis on equality of the sexes, a female ministry, and temperance and their historical role in abolition placed them squarely within the religious radicalism of Sojourner Truth.[30]

By the time of Sojourner's trek, the Hicksites had split between those opposing "worldly" reform outside the meeting and those viewing reform as a logical extension of their faith. Many radical eastern Hicksites migrated west and called themselves Congregational Friends, Friends of Human Progress, or Progressive Friends. They advocated social activism, particularly abolition, peace, temperance, and woman's rights. They invited non-Quakers into their midst, and their meetings became increasingly ecumenical. When Sojourner Truth said she would find friends in the East, this might have been based solely on faith, or perhaps on connections with a larger reform movement, which included Quakers. Her friend Eliza Seaman Leggett was a Long Islander whose Abolitionist father, a noted Manhattan physician, worked the Underground Railroad. In 1843, the Leggetts lived in Roslyn (called Hempstead Harbor), directly in Sojourner's path. Like many excommunicated Long Island Quakers, the Leggetts moved west and joined the Progressive Friends. Such people became Sojourner Truth's closest associates. "I have always loved the Quakers," she said.[31]

IV

Sojourner crossed Long Island Sound into Connecticut, a state tied to the South economically, and unfriendly to both antislavery and to blacks. Nonetheless, the state's New Org antislavery society represented eighty-seven towns, and its New England Methodist Anti-Slavery Convention, which challenged the proslavery Episcopacy, was made up of seventeen hundred preachers, class leaders, and stewards. Communities such as Brooklyn, Middletown, New Haven, and Hartford were important Underground Railroad stations. Sojourner soon had impressive audiences.[32]

She traveled to various communities around New Haven, holding "communion of spirit" with all listeners. Preaching the Perfectionist views of her old teachers, she replaced Matthias's misogyny and literal orthodoxy with her own biblical reasoning, experiences, and personal testimony. Moving on to the Hartford area, she encountered little prejudice against her views, or against woman preachers. The Adventists (called Millerites) had three "great tent" meetings in Connecticut that fall, and she attended two held late in September. Her reputation began to precede her, and soon she traveled by invitation and with recommendations. A "zealous sister" of Bristol requested her presence at a meeting there. Afterward, Henry L. Bradley, a "spiritually minded brother," directed her to the care of "Sister Dean," who then entrusted her to two others in another community. Brother Bradley's letter gives some sense of Sojourner's speaking impact and range of topics: "Sister—I send you this living messenger, . . . Ethiopia is stretching forth her hands unto God. You can see by this sister, that God does by his Spirit alone teach his own children things to come. Please receive her, and she will tell you some new things. Let her tell her story without interrupting her, and give close attention, and you will see she has got the lever of truth, that God helps her to pry where but few can. She cannot read or write, but the law is in her heart. . . . Send her to brother—, brother—, and where she can do the most good."[33]

Sojourner's new friends of the "'second advent' excitement" followed William Miller, a Baptist minister who in 1831 prophesied Jesus' physical reappearance. Christ would soon come—to damn all sinners, glorify the saints, and then begin his thousand years of rule on earth. Miller's message spread to isolated, economically depressed rural communities, where frenzied tent revivals occurred. "Father Miller" published his lectures, which included bizarre formulas and biblical charts predicting the exact time of Christ's apocalyptic appearance. Miller's primary promoter, a prominent young Boston Abolitionist minister, popularized Miller in major cities, introduced his lieutenants to influential reformers, and launched two popular publications: *Sign of the Times* and the *Midnight Cry*. The clergy and the secular and religious presses supported Miller. In 1840, two hundred renowned ministers met to strategize about speedily warning the people of the last days. By 1841, Millerism was a cottage industry. On January 1, 1843, Miller predicted that Christ would return between March 21, 1843, and March 21, 1844. Then the saints would ascend to heaven while hell's catastrophic fires consumed the earth and the wicked.[34]

Anxiety, fear, confusion, and schism escalated as the date neared. Miller's general conference had built a "great tent" 120 feet in diameter, with a fifty-five-foot pole and six doors. Its four-thousand-seat capacity, with room for another two thousand in the aisles, was not enough—over twelve thousand worshippers gathered. As "the last year that Satan will reign in our earth closed in," doctors, teachers, artisans, students, housewives, and laborers gave away their belongings, left their homes, and even deserted their families. Tent sites also attracted curiosity seekers, rogues, and "young blades" determined to go home with a fair young "angel" on "her last *night*."[35]

Sojourner Truth was not a Millerite.[36] Having heard William Miller in New York City, she dismissed his predictions. She believed that the kingdom of God came after achievements of human instrumentality, so that the Second Advent followed the millennium. In preparation for receiving Christ in a *post*millennialist era, Perfectionists strove to replace sin and inequality with goodness and social justice.[37] Both interpretations had scriptural support. Yet Millerites' premillennialism and their belief that Christ would come before reformers had paved his way dominated the times, and Advent camp meetings attracted thousands.

Miller's prediction, Sojourner said, was "shaking the very foundations of the universe" as the proposed October 22 Advent date approached. At a meeting she attended in Windsor Locks in Hartford County, people were restraining a woman who believed that as Peter had walked on the sea by faith, she could walk across the Connecticut River. Amid this disorder and excitement, Sojourner gained the worshippers' attention. Characteristically, she listened patiently to discern and interpret for herself whether there was "any good ground for expecting an event, which was, in the minds of so many." Going among various groups, mellowing them with her singing and talking with them, she concluded that they were laboring under a delusion. When they asked if she believed that soon "the Lord is coming," she did not refute the doctrine directly. "I believe," she answered, "the Lord is as near as he can be"—wisely supporting Christ's spiritual rather than literal presence. The distraught people eagerly seized on a reason to be less agitated and terror-stricken. Sojourner's witness so inspired the Windsor Locks Adventists that they sent her on to Hartford associates. There, she urged the frightened worshippers to calm themselves, to watch, and to pray, for Christ would not appear in such confusion. "The Lord came still and quiet," yet they were so raucous that Jesus could come, move all through the crowd, and leave again and they would never know it.[38]

When the predicted date passed, William Miller moved the end of time ahead to March 22, 1844. This further increased public trepidation and also heightened Sojourner Truth's skepticism. In Hampden County, near Springfield, Massachusetts, she spoke to another large, terrified assembly. Addressing the ministers responsible for the anxiety, she fused secular wit and common sense with an irrefutable biblical parable to illustrate that people of God need fear nothing. First, she described a graphic, uninviting scene of saints returning "to walk in triumph" on the new earth but stumbling over the burnt ashes of sinners. "This is to be your New Jerusalem!!" she said sarcastically, "coming back to such a muss as that will be, a world covered with the ashes of the wicked." Then, turning to a spiritual rationale, she reminded the ministers of "Shadrach, Meshach and Abednego," the three Hebrew men refused to worship a golden image and survived being bound and thrown into a fiery furnace. Nothing belonging to God can burn, she proclaimed, any more than God himself. Sojourner Truth could stand a burning earth, because "Jesus will walk with me through the fire, and keep me from harm." She also struck a chord in recounting that instead of three bound men walking through the flames, the Babylonian king Nebuchadnezzar saw "four men loose, walking in the midst of the fire." They had "no hurt," she said, and "the form of the fourth is like the Son of God." A true servant was not afraid of fire or the end of time. "Do you mean to tell me that God's children can't stand fire?" she asked rhetorically. "It is absurd to think so!"[39]

It was quite a sermon, and the ministers "were taken quite aback." An unschooled black woman had employed her own scriptural hermeneutics to examine and reject their doctrines. Their encounter with Sojourner harked back to James LaTourette's observation that learned and respectable people followed the African Dutch mystic. Likewise, the Millerites "drank in all she said." Wherever she went during that camp meeting season, she found audiences eager to hear new and strange things. When she arose to speak, her commanding figure and dignified manner reportedly hushed every trifler into silence. She was a great favorite because of her amazing gift in prayer, her extraordinary singing talent, "and the aptness and point of her remarks," which she expressed with great originality.[40]

As winter approached, Sojourner sought "an abiding place" that would complement her lifestyle, philosophy, and spirituality. She knew of Bronson Alcott's Fruitlands near Boston. Like Sojourner, Alcott had also set out on June 1, 1843, with his long-suffering wife, Abigail, his children, and a few followers, to set up a commune. This brilliant but "wild" philosopher-transcendentalist was a Garrisonian Abolitionist and Perfectionist. Fortunately, Sojourner's friends discouraged her from going to Fruitlands, which did not last the winter. Later Sojourner and the Alcotts would work together in reform.[41]

Sojourner also considered the commune in Enfield, Connecticut, organized by the Shakers, who believed in God's dual nature—male and female. They believed the first coming had been through Jesus, and the Second Coming through their founder, Mother Ann Lee. When her spirit or that of another departed person took possession of Believers, they shook, quaked, danced, and spoke in tongues. Shakers condemned alcohol, war, tobacco, and corporal punishment. They practiced celibacy and fictive family arrangements, and they welcomed industrious seekers after holiness. Their prosperous community had abundant crops (including tobacco to sell); rich and beautiful grounds; exemplary artisans; sober, neat, assiduous Believers.[42]

But the Shakers' ecstatic religion, abhorrence of politics, and withdrawal from society were incongruous with Sojourner Truth's beliefs. Moreover, the Shaker incarnation of Mother Ann as Jesus seemed dangerously close to Father Matthias. Finally, the Shakers amassed more wealth and lived better than many people in the "outer world." Even the black Shaker eldress Rebecca Cox Jackson wondered how the only "people of God" could save society by focusing on their own temporal concerns. Sojourner Truth wanted to engage actively in universal human progress, improving the human condition, and reforming the world. Shaker Perfectionism veered to the religious right, and Sojourner to the left. She did not go to Enfield.[43]

She spent most of the winter around traditionally rural Hampden County. Blacks here worked as day laborers for former white slave owners; a few had substantial farms; and others were self-emancipated Southerners. By 1843, African Americans had gravitated toward towns—Springfield, Holyoke, and Westfield—living in enclaves called Jamaica and Hayti. In 1844, the railroad connected Springfield to the South, creating white prosperity and population expansion. Blacks also established more barbershops, eating saloons, laundries, and whitewashing businesses. However, Springfield did not have a single black church, and certainly Sojourner Truth deserves some credit for the new AME Zion place of worship established in 1844. It became a forum for black leadership and a center of Underground Railroad activity; Abolitionist and Springfield resident John Brown frequently attended. Judging from Sojourner Truth's impact since leaving Manhattan, her decision to follow the dictates of the Spirit seemed divinely inspired. A "colored woman," Rachel Stearns wrote, was "taking Springfielders by storm."[44]

What say you to a little social community among ourselves?
— WILLIAM LLOYD GARRISON TO GEORGE W. BENSON

When existing institutions are found inadequate to promote
the further progress of society, it becomes the duty of those
who perceive the necessity of reform to associate together
upon principles, in their opinion, the best calculated to fulfill
the designs of God in placing man in this life.
— NORTHAMPTON PRELIMINARY CIRCULAR (1842)

There is a holy city,
A world of light above,
Above the starry regions
Built by the God of love.
—SOJOURNER TRUTH'S FAVORITE HYMN

CHAPTER 10

A Holy City

SOJOURNER TRUTH AND THE NORTHAMPTON COMMUNITY

I

An amazing "colored woman" was inspiring an unusual flurry of liberalism in Springfield, Rachel Stearns wrote Maria Weston Chapman in February 1844. The black preaching woman could not read or write, Stearns added, but "the spirit has taught her." She was especially effective in preaching tolerance in local churches. In that conservative town, black people attending the white Wesleyan church were being treated courteously; Episcopalians had even admitted a "respectable colored man" to devotion and listened attentively to him; and a nonresistant Garrisonian calling himself a "2nd advent lecturer" had gained a sizable following. The preaching woman was Sojourner Truth, and Springfielders asked her to remain. But she still sought a communal living arrangement, and her friends knew just the place. She would "go to the Northampton Asso[ciation] next week," Stearns wrote.[1]

Situated in Hampshire County, Northampton, Massachusetts, was home to men of mark in church and state. This seat of (Federalist-Whig) "intelligent conservatism" was the birthplace of Great Awakening preacher-thinker Jonathan Edwards and of the influential Tappans. Northampton also mirrored Springfield in prejudice, and was a favorite vacation spot for slaveholders. Abolitionists David and Maria Child had settled near Northampton to cultivate free-produce beet sugar as a replacement for slave-produced cane sugar. "I have never been so discouraged about abolition," Maria wrote in 1838, "as since we came to this iron-bound Valley of the Connecticut." Native-born whites and Irish immigrants created an aura of intolerance and anxiety. "Oh the narrowness, the bigotry of man!" Child proclaimed. She predicted that hostility toward blacks would last many generations.[2]

Nonetheless, the scenic spot enveloped by lush countryside and rising hills drew praise even from William Lloyd Garrison. During his summer visits, he marveled at the sublime beauty and perfumed summer air in Northampton, "the most charming place" in the Commonwealth State. Unfortunately, Sojourner Truth's first impression was not of such beauty. With railroads unfinished and waterways frozen, she endured a frigid, uncomfortable, midwinter trip of twenty miles by horse and buggy. She also arrived quite ill. Her Springfield friends entrusted her to their relatives living in the commune outside Northampton. Unable to imagine remaining in this stark setting, she agreed to "tarry with them one night."[3]

Sojourner had come to the most exceptional and progressive commune established during America's "communitarian moment." Founded in 1842 on principles of activism, spirituality, equality, and liberty of conscience, the Northampton Association of Education and Industry, called "the Community," had some of the most radical reformers among its founders. They included George Benson, Garrison's brother-in-law; Samuel Hill; Hall Judd; and Theodore Scarborough, Olive Gilbert's uncle. The Community was located three miles from town on Broughton's Meadow, a sandy, flat plain with a few trees, good meadows, and a river running through it. The investors had made a bargain down payment of $20,000 on 420 acres and the buildings of a large silkworm farm and manufacturing company. When Sojourner arrived, about 130 people lived in the Community; that soon increased to 200. Most residents lived in a large, new, four-story brick structure near the Mill River. This building also housed the Community kitchen and dining room, a reading room, the Community store, a basement laundry, and the main operations of the silk factory. Other buildings contained departments of lumber, agriculture, cutlery, domestics, mechanics, accounting and education. The rustic, plain, factory-farm living quarters offered little privacy and few personal comforts. Nonetheless, the Community had an extensive waiting list of reformers anxious to live among like-minded folk. The Community apparently accepted Sojourner Truth over other applicants. And regardless of her initial misgivings, she warmed to the Community. She sent word to Springfield friends that "she had found the quiet resting place she so long desired."[4] Northampton would change Sojourner's life.

Embedded in the Northampton emphasis on spirituality and "millennial foreshadowing" was a commitment to revolutionize civilization. The Northampton air was full of "isms," Frederick Douglass recalled: "Grahamism, mesmerism, Fourierism, transcendentalism, Communism, and Abolitionism." The Community's dedication to emancipation alone, Douglass said, was enough to secure respect from black activists. Sojourner was certainly delighted to see David Ruggles there; the Childs had brought him to the Community soon after it opened. Despite his illness and failing eyesight, he remained a leader among Garrisonians.[5]

Most Community members had humble farming and artisan backgrounds, although a few large investors were former merchants. A few clerks, teachers, ministers, and intellectuals, two physicians, one lawyer, and a professional portrait painter named Elisha Hammond were also members. Economically speaking, the Community was partly a "Stock Company" investing in silk manufacturing and partly an "Industrial Community" composed of workers in various departments. Stock investors shared income according to outputs of capital, labor, and skill. Most Industrial members owned no capital investment but had an equal voice and vote. However, investors could remove their shares and withdraw from the Community at any time. Services such as simple meals, washing, education, nursing, and baths were free within reason. The Community store provided goods priced reasonably.[6]

At the Community, Sojourner Truth was noted for hard work, helpfulness, and activism, and she became an authority figure. Both she and David Ruggles were vigilant in confronting slackers, especially black ones. Sojourner "turned Johnson the old colored man out of doors" for not pulling his weight. She demanded an accounting from a lazy young self-emancipated man and eventually insisted that he also leave. She asked no more of others than she did of herself. Yet her physical energy was extraordinary. Young Giles Stebbins observed that she did more housework of the heaviest kind than two ordinary women. She was also known for kindness. She nursed the sick and may have been the seamstress for single black men. Community store debits indicate that the men actually purchased more fabric than most women, and had more flamboyant taste. Sojourner's self-emancipated friend Basil Dorsey was fond of silk, "cassimere," and "kersey plaid." A frugal seamstress, she made major fabric purchases of sturdy materials good for traveling such as calico, gingham, cambric, and shirting; her frivolous purchases were ribbon and tobacco. Northampton founders George Benson and Samuel Hill used their homes as Underground Railroad centers, where self-emancipated people received shelter, food, fresh garments, and spiritual comfort. Sojourner Truth was their frequent overnight guest, and was certainly involved in the underground work that Abolitionists simply called "the business."[7]

The Community prided itself on gender equality. Women selected their own work department (everyone chopped mulberry leaves and fed silkworms in summer). They preferred conventional domestic roles, and men often assisted. Dolly Stetson, wife of the traveling silk agent James Stetson, did most of the cooking for the Community boardinghouse, yet labor cooperation greatly lightened her work. "Aunt Mary" Benson (her sister-in-law) watched over Dolly's infant, made her beds, and kept her rooms in order. Stephen (a self-emancipated resident) made the fire, put on the kettles, cut the bread, stirred the pudding, and helped with other kitchen chores. The "Hayden girls" set the tables and washed the dishes. After breakfast, David Ruggles and "Mrs. Bradbury" brought in wood, shelled peas, stringed beans, and prepared potatoes. Dolly sometimes made "bread, gingerbread, pies, etc." and cooked dinner while Mrs. Bradbury made tea. Sojourner Truth soon became director of the laundry department. Silk dyer James Atkins wrung out the clothes for Sojourner when his own work was "dull." She and Atkins, a former stereotyper in the Harvard University printing office, were the only two smokers in the Community. When she traveled, other members filled in for her. "You ask if Sojourner has returned," Dolly wrote her concerned husband. "She has been absent two weeks in which Stephen, Mrs. Small and myself did the washing." The work proved burdensome, and when Sojourner returned, she received a male assistant.[8]

She bonded with women from rural Connecticut farm backgrounds similar to her own in the Hudson Valley. At meetings, women held forth on "the anti-slavery enterprise, non-resistance, woman's rights, religious liberty, &c &c." At one gathering, women argued for their rights and entitlements by using the theme of Christian equality from the Book of Galatians. However, some of the middle-class women had only joined the Community because of their husbands' commitment. These women disliked the workload, rural conditions, stoic outlook, and absence of domestic servants. Not every woman wanted freedom of thought. At an important decision-making meeting, one woman insisted that her "opinion" (her husband) had gone "to the West." Yet for most women, Northampton represented a superior, freer lifestyle. Women gained strength from each other, from male encouragement, and from the high-profile role of women in radical reform. Three women sat on the executive board of the AASS. Abby Kelley remained the lone female antislavery agent, enduring with her young traveling companion, Jane Elizabeth Hitchcock, mobbings and persecutions that reinforced Community women's insistence on speaking out. Northampton became the launching pad for Sojourner's articulation of gender issues.[9]

Northampton Community members were "Come-outers." This movement had begun among Methodists who opposed slavery and soon came to include anyone who left their church or was excommunicated. Rooted in Perfectionism, Come-outerism exemplified the scriptural edict in the Book of Revelation warning the faithful to leave Babylon: "Come out of her, my people, that ye be not partakers of her sins, and that ye receive not her plagues." Sojourner easily embraced the Community's "infidel" philosophy that Sunday was a time for private meditation, open discussion, and group criticism rather than engaging in traditional religious doctrine. After the children's Sunday morning instruction, adults held an afternoon "free meeting" in the dining hall or in fair weather, under a "beautiful spreading pine, standing on the high ground." Come-outers were sometimes harshly critical toward each other; these Sunday meetings, Giles Stebbins said, were always provocative and thoughtful but never mean-spirited.[10]

At Community forums, Sojourner held audiences "spellbound" with stories of her bondage, her persecutions by so-called Christians, her dealings with the Holy Spirit and with false prophets, and her interpretations of Scripture. Any topic was welcome, but the Spiritualism of Andrew Jackson Davis, the "Poughkeepsie Seer," was wildly popular. As a twelve-year-old impoverished Dutchess County shoemaker's apprentice, Davis had claimed spirit communication. In 1844, when he was nineteen, two handlers skillfully promoted him as a traveling clairvoyant and healer; in 1848, he published his two-volume *Principles of Nature, Her Divine Revelations*. This first work of American Spiritualism, though considered a "verbose and redundant derivative conglomeration" of Fourierism, Swedenborgianism, natural rights philosophy, and economic radicalism, remained the most famous. Sojourner Truth rejected Davis's denial of miraculous conception, original sin, and the Trinity. Yet she agreed that Isaiah was the best and most radical prophet; death was spiritual freedom in heavenly spheres; and deceased spirits communed with in-the-body spirits. Sojourner and Davis both considered themselves spirit mediums and thought utopian living the best means of social happiness and spiritual elevation. Both were antiauthoritarian and antidogma. His abolitionism and commitment to social and economic equality further enhanced his appeal at Northampton. Sojourner Truth used his beliefs to fuse the communitarian movement with an Abolitionist-Spiritualist component.[11]

To the outside world, the Community's insular utopian ambiance might appear similar to Sojourner's kingdom experiment. Resident physician and Abolitionist lecturer Erasmus Hudson called the Community a "moral reform depot or headquarters for antislavery, non-resistance, holiness, etc." from which advocates spread east, west, north and south. Sojourner Truth's moral reform impulse found fruitful ground there, where "bearded wonders" and "bards for the Holy Ghost" embraced Garrisonian abolition. Among them was colorful, contentious C. C. Burleigh, who had put aside his plow and legal studies to join the Abolitionists of Windham County, Connecticut, after a local white teacher and her black students had been persecuted. Sporting a beard and backpack, he had blond hair that flowed in ringlets past his shoulders. He usually returned to Northampton with thrilling stories of antislavery successes, but also bruised from clubbing and rocks, and smelling of rotten eggs. Sojourner later traveled with him in the West. Samuel Hill, a Quaker turned Baptist, had been driven from the same Windham County by a church mob for inviting Wendell Phillips to speak. A well-read schoolteacher and proponent of communism, Hill almost single-handedly kept the Community together. Sojourner called Hill "one of the best antislavery men in that abolition community."[12]

Sojourner's connection to James and Laura Boyle went back to New York City, where they had briefly moved in the same Perfectionist circles. In 1838, after breaking with Charles Finney and the clerical Abolitionist evangelicals, Boyle had published sophisticated works on slavery, political theory, religion, politics, and class-labor-capital relationships. Garrison considered Boyle's voice and pen invaluable. Northampton became his springboard for antislavery jaunts around the Northeast and the Ohio Valley. A true eccentric, he had a full beard and dressed in an outrageous "continental costume, including knickerbockers and cocked hat." His philosophical flights, encyclopedic knowledge, and loud, fast-talking style offended some residents who also thought him "coarse and vulgar." But Sojourner liked to match wits with him and compare his unorthodox views with her own eclecticism, personal experience, and practical reason. He remained a devoted associate of hers throughout her life.[13]

Northampton visitors who became part of Sojourner's activist years included the "notorious" Abby Kelley, with whom she later joined forces on the antislavery trail. She met freeborn black Abolitionist Charles Lenox Remond, a passionate, accomplished speaker. When he later traveled to the British Isles for the AASS she covered much of his New England circuit. Within a few months of her arrival in 1844, she also met Frederick Douglass, by then probably the most popular antislavery agent.[14]

Sojourner Truth met two other future traveling companions: Parker Pillsbury and Stephen Foster, whose biting anticlerical "speak-outs" inspired friends to nickname them the "New Hampshire Fanatics" and the "steeple-house troublers." As an Andover Seminary student, Pillsbury had heard Garrison and British Abolitionist George Thompson. Later, he left his parish ministry for the Abolitionist circuit, and became famous for his irreverent, uncouth, "splendid vehemence" against the churches. Foster, who later married Abby Kelley, had joined the Abolitionists after graduating from Dartmouth College and Union Theological Seminary. His confrontational tactics included interrupting prayers, challenging sermons, and publicly denouncing churches as "brothels" complicit in the sexual exploitation of enslaved women. When ushers attempted to lead him from sanctuaries, he went limp, forcing them to drag him. Repeatedly jailed and thrown out of windows, he also once received such a vigorous "evangelical kick" that he could not walk for weeks.[15] Sojourner would learn to match Pillsbury and Foster's antislavery Come-outer confrontations.

Spirituality was a guiding force at Northampton, and Sojourner Truth was considered a gifted preacher, seer, and mystic. The "Lord reveals everything to her," one of the Stetson teenagers wrote. On one April Sunday in 1844, singing, laughter, preaching, and praying filled the Community Hall all day. That morning, the Hutchinsons performed before a full house, and Douglass preached; Sojourner Truth, James Boyle, and Asa Hutchinson sang and preached in the afternoon. The Hutchinsons' fourteen-year-old lead singer, Abby, and Sojourner formed a special and enduring bond of friendship. Sojourner also preached when the young child of the newcomers Elisha and Eliza Hammond passed "to the spirit land" after much suffering. At the "solemn" funeral, Sojourner Truth "spoke with much feeling and sang something on the death of an infant," an experience familiar to her own heart. When Hall and Frances Judd's baby died, Sylvester Judd, refusing to enter the commune of "infidels," attended his grandson's funeral in a tavern keeper's home. "Many of the community, and others in the neighborhood attended," he wrote. At the brief, grim service, Samuel Hill read from the book of Hebrews, and a hymn was sung. Then "a colored woman" made remarks that deeply impressed Judd. She also sang "2 or 3 verses" of a moving song, before the child's father closed the service with a short prayer, and they carried the little coffin to the grave.[16]

Though there is no evidence of scandals or sexual misconduct there, gossip and accusations of free love, promiscuity, multiple marriage, and spiritual wifery dogged the Community. Townspeople whispered about the boys' and men's communal bathing in the Mill River, and the solemnization of marriages without a clergyman or justice of the peace. Community founder George Benson, although not a minister, married one young couple under a tree. A mature couple were wed at the boardinghouse breakfast table, and afterward Dolly Stetson served brown bread and water. Most Community residents supported traditional family arrangements, and Sojourner Truth, having seen the dangers of spiritual marriage, emphatically supported "enlightened self-restraint." Yet opinions differed on "free love" and the "marriage question." One young couple argued against relations held together by "legal punishment" and wanted a "true marriage" of personal and sacred bonding. Even members who agreed with this principle still refused to jeopardize conventional marriage. When the unheeding "free love" couple consummated their union without any semblance of marriage vows, but simply by spending the night under the Community oak tree, Sojourner led the majority in appointing David Ruggles to banish them.[17]

In July 1844, Sojourner's daughters Elizabeth and Sophia arrived. The reunion of mother and daughters was "prodigal" and "very affecting," Dolly Stetson wrote. Sojourner and Sophia had become estranged because she had defied her mother and moved in with a widower. The man had promised marriage but instead had "shamefully" abused Sophia even while she cared for his children.

Sojourner's friends had wrested Sophia from the man's grasp and sent both daughters to Northampton. Sophia and Elizabeth were "energetic like their mother," Dolly observed, and "two fine looking negresses as you ever saw." Like young Isabella, Elizabeth and Sophia loved to dance. One day soon after their arrival, all the young people gathered for recreation during the day at "Paradise," the Community's recreation grounds. After they returned to the boardinghouse hall at dark, Sophia and Elizabeth introduced them to the waltz. Their young audience was delighted. The elders called this "touch dancing" wrote Dolly, and it "was quite a wonder to the people here."[18]

This incident soon ignited internal dissension over the effect of "amusements" on male-female social behavior. Members and guests debated the propriety of recreations and dancing. Those Dolly called rigid "puritans" included Sojourner, Samuel Hill, James Boyle, George Benson, and the Judds. The "liberals" included Dolly and other parents; teachers Charles May, Sophia Foord (formerly of Fruitlands), and David Mack; and William Bassett, director of the silk department. "Last week we had a regular blow up from Sojourn and Boyle about the young people," Dolly Stetson wrote her husband. The "puritan" element condemned touching, dancing, cards, and any games. James Boyle described the young people's recreation with "vile" language and "cursing"; this led to such intense criticism from parents that the Boyles soon left the Community. Sojourner also thought amusements encouraged wild, loose behavior; she even castigated Charles May for using playing cards as a mathematical teaching tool. Challenging Sojourner, Sophia Foord called eating meat worse than card playing.[19]

Dolly Stetson considered this controversy a test of wills and leadership and a great philosophical divide that defined the Community's social structure. At a private meeting in Samuel Hill's home, the elders accused the "liberals" of introducing bad influences. Hill greatly upset Stetson by encouraging some teachers to leave the Community. This would be "the death blow to our association," she wrote. The amusements issue again arose at the picnic celebrating the new Community kitchen and dining room. Sojourner Truth, George Benson, David Mack, and Samuel Hill spoke, and left. The young people brought Mrs. Hammond's piano into the hall, and "a few brave souls" including Dolly Stetson, began dancing. Samuel Hill reappeared. It was nine o'clock, he announced, and all "reasonable beings" should be in bed. Everyone left grumbling. The liberals again tried unsuccessfully to introduce dancing at the Community's festive third anniversary picnic, which included an address by Frederick Douglass. Disheartened, Dolly Stetson complained that there were far worse things than a game of whist. "I had much rather my daughters should be dancing or playing cards (as wicked as that sounds), in a mixed company of boys and girls than in the language of Sojourner to be lolling on each other or squeezing each others hands or sitting in each others laps." Dolly reasoned that boys and girls in coeducational surroundings should have time for innocent amusements, or they "will be apt to spend it much worse." Although the young people often ignored "puritan" disapproval, and Sojourner softened her position, liberal teachers left.[20]

Sojourner Truth's caution and rigidity over amusements and her concern about moral laxity harked back to her Matthias experience, her own youth, and also disappointment in her daughters. Eighteen-year-old Sophia arrived at Northampton pregnant by her abusive former partner. "Sophia . . . is clearly encienta[sic]," Dolly Stetson wrote, which explained why Sophia began doing her kitchen work "so poorly." Dolly, whose eldest daughter was close to Sophia in age, remained nonjudgmental. But Sophia's out-of-wedlock pregnancy embarrassed Sojourner. She had spent very little time with her daughters as children, and establishing intimacy with them as adults was difficult. Even as Sophia's delivery time approached, Sojourner traveled to meetings. But she was also a doting grandmother; no doubt she chose the baby's name, Wesley, after John Wesley, the founder of Methodism.[21]

Family connection was an important component of the Community's structure, and several extended kinship clusters existed. Following that pattern, Sojourner invited not only her daughters to Northampton but also, it appears, two other kinswomen. "Sophia Gidney," listed in Community account books, could be Sojourner's sister, whom she found as a young woman, and "Jane Gidney" could be Sophia Gidney's daughter. They disappear from record after the Community folded. By the mid-1850s, Sojourner and her sister had again lost touch. However, she and her daughters grew closer. Diana moved to Northampton after 1850 just as Sophia relocated to western New York, and Elizabeth moved to the Boston area. One of Sojourner's daughters always lived with her.[22]

Education at the Community was "so different from the stereotyped training of other young folks." Boarding and resident students had a general academic regimen, work-study, and domestic arts instruction with no gender distinctions. Nature was their laboratory for botany, biology, and geography; David Ruggles was their health and physical education teacher. Extracurricular activities included Sunday forums, visiting speakers, political discussions, dietary ethics, and antislavery rallies. Sojourner Truth and David Ruggles always had an audience among young people and contributed to their unorthodox education with a wealth of stories. In turn, young people read to Truth and Ruggles. Some of these children later became prominent editors, ministers, and educators who remembered Sojourner fondly. In 1857, Garrison's son George Thompson Garrison visited Sojourner in Michigan. In 1870, William Lloyd Garrison Jr. wrote from Boston, "I found Sojourner Truth at Rockledge. . . . She is a remarkable woman, very bright and smart. . . . I remember her very well in Northampton days." Giles Stebbins entered Northampton as a conceited boarding student and prospective Unitarian clergyman. He engaged Dolly Stetson in biblical proslavery discussions, "unlearned, as I supposed, in clerical lore." Her provocative expostulations on "Scripture in the light of liberty" helped transform him into a radical Abolitionist within a year. Northampton, he proclaimed, was a "'city set on a hill,' to give light all around." Sojourner Truth also had a profound impact on him, and the years deepened the friendship of these two radical reformers and lifelong Spiritualists; both eventually settled in Michigan many years later.[23]

II

Residents remembered that Sojourner Truth wore many hats at Northampton and that her conversation and speeches were laced with humor, anecdotes, and spirituality. "Three thirds of the people are wrong," she once said, preaching to the Community. "That takes them all Sojourner," someone shouted. Undaunted by her own faux pas, she quipped, "I am sorry. I had hoped there were a few left." Samuel Hill's son Arthur recalled her excitable and wonderful imagination. Normally skeptical, she wondered if a shooting star was a sign of the Second Coming, and she roused the elder Hill out of bed in the middle of the night. "Samuel Hill, Samuel Hill," she shouted, "Come out here," and "never mind your breeches!" If it was the end, he had no need of clothing. Another Sojourner story became part of Community lore when self-emancipated George Washington Sullivan fell from the factory belfry. Dolly Stetson wrote that he landed on his feet, and after many applications of cold water, seemed fine. Mary Stetson added to her mother's letter: "Sojourner says that if it was the Devil that made him fall it was the Lord that prepared a place for him to fall upon for he came right between a large rock and the platform and on the softest place." Years later, a revised version related that a child had fallen off a dam and landed uninjured in a pool of water only several feet long. In that account, Sojourner asserted, "If the Devil made him fall the Lord had a fixed place for him to light in." Sojourner loved the Community. "What good times we had," she recalled. "If any were infidels, I wish all the world were full of such infidels. Religion without humanity is a poor human stuff."[24]

Northampton was an ideal central location for Sojourner's travels. In April 1844, just two months after her arrival, "Mrs. Sojourn" borrowed a horse for 25 cents from the Community store and purchased traveling shoes for 50 cents. She held meetings throughout the region and, the consummate Come-outer radical, often asked to speak in a church. The answer was usually no, and she preached from a stump, a wagon, or a hastily constructed platform. Community folk kept track of her whereabouts, and if she went too long unaccounted for, Samuel Hill sent someone to search for her. She welcomed the sight of Hill's teamster and pair of white horses. Itinerant preaching was not always safe. Denominational rivalry created arguments; gamblers and "peddling tents" stood right next to prayer tents. "Numerous men, and boys, and sometimes women, white, black, and speckled," cavorted at night, eating, drinking, smoking, swearing, singing, jesting, and blackguarding. Worst of all, drunken, hostile "rowdies," also nick-named "Cainites" or "Cain Family," plagued worshippers, disrupted meetings, and threatened speakers. Rowdies carried clubs and brickbats and threatened bodily harm, especially toward black camp meeting participants.[25]

In 1844, Sojourner had a frightening experience outside Northampton. Scores of Cainites appeared, and she joined other preachers scurrying into a tent. She even hid behind a trunk, fearing that as the "only colored person," the Cainites' "wicked mischief" would befall her in double measure. As they shook the tent from its foundations, Sojourner's faith returned. "Shall I run away and hide from the Devil?" she asked herself. "Me a servant of the living-God?" Reemerging and facing them, she urged others to appear, but everyone refused. Recalling the Scripture "one shall chase a thousand, and two put ten thousand to flight," she walked out alone amid the noise and confusion and past the preachers' stand, where the woman scheduled to speak stood trembling. Sojourner found a piece of high ground, and "with all the strength of her most powerful voice," she sang: "It was early in the morning . . . Just at the break of day—When he rose—when he rose—when he rose, and went to heaven on a cloud." Relating the incident to Olive Gilbert later, Sojourner sang the hymn for Gilbert. Her deep contralto voice, her brogue, her style, and her animation, Gilbert wrote in 1849, were unforgettable; anyone hearing her sing that song would remember it as long as they remembered Sojourner Truth. Whether the music made the moment or vice versa, on a moonlit night in an open-air clearing, the tall, angular black woman stood above the fray, intent on singing until the power of God overcame the Cainites' devilish intentions. (Sojourner's retelling, Gilbert said, was "truly thrilling.")[26]

Crowding around her, the rowdies said they meant no harm, but only wanted to hear her. "Sing to us, old woman," said some. "Talk to us, old woman," said others. "Pray, old woman," they called out. "Tell us your experience." She asked them to stand back, and the leaders forced the enlarging crowd of mostly young white men to give her space. As they listened attentively, their preoccupation with her allowed other parts of the camp meeting to continue. The leaders pressed her for more, garnering a wagon so that those in back could hear. They dared anyone to touch her, but she felt more captured than protected. From the wagon, she spoke and sang for another hour. She recalled part of her sermon for Gilbert: "'Well, there are two congregations on this ground. It is written that there shall be a separation, and the sheep shall be separated from the goats. The other preachers have the sheep. I have the goats. And I have a few sheep among my goats, but they are *very* ragged.' The sermon 'produced great laughter.'" Finally growing weary, she agreed to sing one more song, and the rowdies agreed to disperse afterward. When she finished, they kept their word, going across the campgrounds like "a swarm of bees," inciting fear but harming no one.[27] Fiercer antislavery mobs awaited Sojourner Truth; God had chosen her to preach to the unconverted.

The Community's biracial egalitarianism was exceptional. Not only was bigotry alive and well in the North but also all the utopian communes (except Hopedale) either ignored blacks or viewed them paternalistically. Fourierist communities considered chattel slavery a mere by-product of capitalism, no worse than "wage slavery." However, the actual ideological fault line was deeper than economics. Fourierists called Abolitionists "nigger-loving and white-man hating fanatics," who practiced "selective compassion." Fourierist opposition to slavery during the Mexican War was under a banner of free land, free labor, and free soil for free white men. But at the Community, Frederick Douglass recalled, "neither my color nor my condition was counted against me." Asa Hutchinson's account of a reunion with Douglass bears this out. One spring afternoon in 1844, at around three o'clock, the visiting Hutchinsons heard "a rap" on their door, and in walked Douglass, whom many whites insisted on calling Fred. "Then came shaking hands, pulling and hauling, loud talking, laughing, embracing, etc." They had not seen "Fred" for nearly a year. He looked great, Asa Hutchinson wrote, and was "full of anecdotes." Douglass and the Hutchinsons ate supper together, played "bat-ball" with the young men, sang, and talked with the ladies. At bedtime, Judson Hutchinson "went to the next house and slept with Douglass."[28]

The Community's liberal views on race, like their politics, vexed most whites. Although young Abby Hutchinson stayed in a hotel, the Community still drew criticism. A local newspaper complained that Abby was "gallanted to her hotel by one of its [Community] members, and he a huge black man!" On another occasion, the Community welcomed a *Journal of Commerce* reporter, who later wrote a contemptible article. Any man, he wrote, who took his lovely, educated, refined family of young ladies away from pleasant society "to live in the wood," and associate with "vulgar unionists *of all colors*" was obviously wild, insane, and brutal. He criticized the boardinghouse food as "primitive," the eating tables as rough boards with no tablecloths, and the company as coarse. The racial familiarity and promiscuous seating especially shocked him. Opposite one of the "lovely accomplished daughters of Mr.—sat a *large male negro!*"[29]

The reporter was referring to David Ruggles, who fumed over the "false and scurrilous" article. He dictated a letter to David Child for the *Journal of Commerce*, in which he reminded the press of his previous position as a New York City editor. The "male negro to whom the writer refers," Ruggles wrote, had once habitually dined with the *Journal* editor, "editors of other journals, and with some of the principal merchants of New York" at (black) Thomas Van Rensselaer's popular restaurant. Such eminent men, Ruggles added, "would have sickened had they to dine with such an apology for a man, as the author of that communication." Ruggles, the Garrisonian radical who had ushered so many to freedom, was also "much esteemed" by New Org moderates. In Northampton, he struggled with illness but continued his underground work and created an antislavery base in the commune, the town, and the nearby vicinity. He was certainly instrumental in enhancing Sojourner's position among local Abolitionists.[30]

III

Sojourner had an opportunity to join the black women of Northampton town in organizing sewing circles, fairs, and bazaars to raise money. Local black women in Massachusetts, lecturer William Wells Brown observed, furthered a sense of unity and aided enslaved "females driven daily to the sugar, the cotton, the rice and tobacco plantations." But Sojourner Truth sought more direct action.

Embracing the Community's values, she naturally launched her antislavery activism as a Garrisonian. Although situated in western Massachusetts, the Community was the radical epicenter for Connecticut, where Garrisonians had no state headquarters and no mouthpiece after the 1840 split. New Haven blacks helped Lewis Tappan isolate radicals within county societies and prevent Garrisonians from speaking, voting, or holding office at annual state meetings. Abby Kelley, an Old Org executive officer, was not allowed to speak at New Org meetings. The rivals collaborated occasionally, but in general their grudges upset antislavery programs and funding and sometimes compromised underground effectiveness. Yet Sojourner Truth spoke at New Org antislavery meetings and had close relationships with moderates in Northampton town. Always antisectarian, and displeased when reformers fighting for the same cause conflicted, she stayed above the feuding.[31]

Despite the smallness of Northampton's black Abolitionist presence—Community members, about 150 town residents, and a fluctuating underground population—strategically it was an important testing ground for radicalism. Northampton town was a county seat, a tourist spot for Southerners, an agricultural center, and a fledgling manufacturing enclave. Underground supervisors shuttled charges from Northampton to Farmington, the region's "Grand Central Station." Passengers continued to New York or up the Connecticut River Valley via Vermont to Canada. Connecticut-born Ruggles coordinated both routes, and Community residents protected passengers traveling the "Road." Northampton Abolitionists helped blacks flee from their vacationing owners; in December

1843, David Ruggles, Samuel Hill, and George Benson refused to relinquish a man whom authorities traced to the Community. Self-emancipated Stephen C. Rush was night watchman and defended the Community from slave catchers. Self-emancipated resident William Wilson fled the South and then returned for his grown son; then both returned for Wilson's daughter. Freeborn Community blacks working the underground included Josiah Hayward and his family. An Abolitionist cabinetmaker from Salem, Massachusetts, Hayward invested in the Community early on. After it dissolved, the family remained for their daughter's education.[32]

The summer before Sojourner's arrival, Garrison, after conferring with Community radicals, had prepared to announce his new strategy in Northampton's Town Hall, on July 4, 1843. When locked out of the hall, the Garrisonians had mounted a nearby stump. Townspeople and vacationing slaveholders had hissed and heckled as the radicals had proclaimed their themes: "Churches as Bulwarks of Slavery" and "No Union with Slaveholders." On August 1, David Ruggles had presided over an all-day celebration of West Indian emancipation in Northampton town. Old Org and New Org followers especially, from nearby hamlets and the Community, appeared en masse. Black and white children marched together. Garrison and Boyle headed the list of white speakers. Black orators included Stephen Rush, "from the land of chains, whips and bowie knives," Josiah Hayward, and David Ruggles, both "widely and worthily known." No black women spoke at Northampton antislavery meetings until Sojourner's arrival the following winter.[33]

Frederick Douglass's 1844 visit to Northampton began a long activist interaction between him and Sojourner Truth. The Community turned out in full force when the Hutchinson singers combined a Town Hall concert with a lecture from Douglass to draw a larger crowd. Reportedly, the audience was overflowing, as the singing silenced loud catcalls and generated a "pure moral atmosphere of anti-slavery." It was shattered when one hostile white threw a large rock at Douglass, which barely missed him. He was calm, but the incident created a stir in the Community. The Stetsons kept the rock as a souvenir of Abolitionist persecution.[34] Besides admiring young Douglass's courage and activism, Truth saw her own life in his passionate example.

Garrison also probably met Sojourner Truth in 1844, when he stopped in Northampton en route to the AASS's annual May convention customarily held at the Broadway Tabernacle in New York City. It was a momentous presidential election year, and Garrison was to propose to the convention the resolutions hammered out in 1843. He expected a struggle from proponents of the newly formed Liberty Party. In addition, some radical Abolitionists supported the Henry Clay–Theodore Frelinghuysen (Whig) ticket, thinking the two slippery slaveholders' waffling on the annexation of Texas (a slave state) struck at Democrats, who solidly supported it. Sojourner certainly recognized vice presidential Whig candidate, Frelinghuysen—New Jersey senator, churchman colonizationist, and Hardenbergh kinsman. Having personally experienced this Pietist Dutch family's proslavery activities, she knew the connection between enslavement and clerical hypocrisy.[35]

Even the Hutchinsons' "magnificent" singing did not ease the tension in the Tabernacle. Liberty Party supporters included New Yorkers led by black physician James McCune Smith. Outgoing *Standard* editors David and Maria Child also supported the Whigs. Nonetheless, Garrison, flanked at the podium by Douglass, Remond, and William Wells Brown, eventually won a victory of 250 to 24 votes for his resolutions. They repudiated the Constitution and urged Americans to "come out" of all organizations, especially churches, refusing to stand against slavery. Later that month, at the New England Anti-Slavery Society convention, the Garrisonians unfurled the banner of the era. Its background was red, symbolizing the bloody character of bondage. On it, an American eagle trampled on a half-naked, shackled slave, the Constitution, and the Right of Petition. In its beak the eagle clutched two mottoes: "All men are created free and equal" and "We many are one." One of the eagle's broad wings cradled the Capitol, a slave gang, and an auction block. The American church and black-robed priests huddled under the other wing. The "Eye of the Serpent" frowned down on the entire scene. The banner's reverse side read "Immediate and Unconditional Emancipation—American Anti-Slavery Society—formed December 6, 1833—This Banner presented May 31, 1844—NO UNION WITH SLAVEHOLDERS!"

Sojourner Truth, accustomed to being labeled a fanatic, joined the movement at a "trying" time—for Abolitionists, the most divisive since 1839. They had "passed the 'Rubicon,'" Garrison wrote, and alienated "many from our ranks."[36]

That year, the Northampton Abolitionists engineered a widespread protest against the incarceration of three underground conductors. Charles Torrey, a Boston New Org minister, faced six years in the Baltimore penitentiary. Jonathan Fountain, Torrey's free black accomplice, had escaped without his enslaved wife and child. The Massachusetts carpenter and ship captain Jonathan Walker, the most celebrated conductor, had been caught taking seven escaped men to the Bahamas. Tried, convicted, fined, and sentenced to a year in irons, Walker was also branded on one palm with the letters "S.S." (slave stealer). He was remanded to the pillory, where slaveholders physically abused him, spat on him, and "threw garbage and other foul objects at him." Northampton blacks held meetings in town and raised money for the jailed Abolitionists. "We are here," Stephen Rush wrote Garrison, "to honor liberty and to denounce slavery . . . to proclaim the dictates of eternal justice and to rebuke the wrongs done by man to man." Sojourner joined the campaign protesting the conductors' incarceration.[37]

Her lack of education restricted her organizing and facilitating capacities;

she could not take minutes, write or read letters, or make banners, posters, or leaflets. Yet these activities had long kept women invisible. Sojourner was a mobilizer, and preferred the platform. And so she became the only woman who spoke at a mass countywide convention the community blacks called to raise money. David Ruggles chaired the convention; Stephen Rush and a young black woman were secretaries. The New Org pastor of Boston's Free Baptist Church (later Tremont Temple) spoke first and was followed, the reporter said, "by our Community friend Sojourn," David Ruggles, Josiah Hayward, and several others. Although Sojourner's words and the audience's reaction were not recorded, *Liberator* articles reveal that she was already a well-known speaker and that New Org activists willingly spoke on the platform with a woman. This speech—her recorded entrance into the Abolitionist movement in 1844—was the first public speech by an antislavery black woman in ten years.[38]

Sojourner's race consciousness grew at Northampton, as her people, united through oppression, heritage, and slavery, negotiated "two-ness" in a black and white world. Community and village blacks gathered for social occasions and ignored white efforts to burlesque their activities. Ever careful about conflicting with white celebrations, blacks held "high festival" on July 3 instead of July 4; August 1 commemorated black freedom where it existed and heralded the hope of liberty for those enslaved. Mindful of moral rectitude and white opprobrium, blacks only held "cold water" (no alcohol) events, but with abundant music from a colored band, a huge dinner, and speeches on ancient black history, antislavery, and race improvement. Abijah Thayer, *Hampshire Herald* editor and Underground Railroad agent, promoted their events and publicly praised black conduct. Most white onlookers insulted and mimicked sable citizens.[39]

Even after Sojourner relocated West, she returned to Northampton and visited with people who remained part of her widespread biracial collective of friends. After underground conductor Jonathan Walker was released and briefly settled in Northampton, she and he established a long association. They shared the distinction of eighteenth-century birth, and they were both anticlerics, Come-outers, pacifists, communitarians, and health reformers who smoked. Walker was among a few whites that Sojourner said had truly felt the sting of bondage. He excited passions on the platform by simply raising his hand, revealing "the coat of arms of the United States!" But "S.S." Abolitionists said, really meant "Slave Savior." Walker's disfigured hand was the subject of daguerreotypes, and Abolitionist poet John Greenleaf Whittier immortalized it in verse. Like Sojourner, Walker was not a paid agent; he worked the underground while his family of nine children endured financial hardship. Like her, he worked among the freed people and settled in Michigan, where a statue honors him. In old age, he wrote to her and inquired how she had won her battle against tobacco. The secret, she answered, was "the Spirit that speaks to me."[40]

Sojourner Truth's first known return to her home state occurred in 1845, two years after her hegira. During "Anniversary Week," a convergence of Fourierite, religious, anti–capital punishment, temperance, education, antislavery, and prison reform organizations met in the Tabernacle in New York. These plainly dressed women and unfashionably bearded men carried brown bread under their arms, and Ralph Waldo Emerson waggishly called them "fleas of conventions." The *New York Herald* called them all "abolition fanatics"; nothing would satisfy them "except dissolution of the Union," and they were "more noisy, virulent, vindictive and unreasonable than ever." Sojourner Truth joined the largest contingent: New Englanders led by those the *Herald* termed usual suspects: Garrison, Wendell Phillips, Abby Kelley, the two "New Hampshire Fanatics," and Douglass. Several others who descended on "Babylon the Great" were to become Sojourner's friends and associates as well: Samuel J. May and the militant self-emancipated Jermain Loguen, from Syracuse; Marius Robinson (one of the Lane rebels) from Ohio; free black Robert Purvis and Quakers Joseph and Ruth Dugdale, in the Pennsylvania contingent; and the most renowned underground leaders—Thomas Garrett, from Wilmington, Delaware, and Levi Coffin, from Cincinnati. There were a number of black men on the platform; Sojourner was the only black woman.[41]

Even unfriendly presses praised white Abolitionists from New England's first families while ignoring blacks. The *Herald* called Wendell Phillips "graceful, enthusiastic, mellifluous"; Edmund Quincy was "subtle and logical"; Maria Weston Chapman was "the female Napoleon of young America"; and Abby Kelley was "lovely, intellectual, enchanting, fascinating." Antislavery presses focused heavily on Douglass's thrilling new *Autobiography* and his courageous but dangerous naming from the platform of his Maryland *owner*.[42]

Since 1840, white Abolitionist women had conspicuously assumed leadership positions while black men warned black women against assuming a "Frances Wright" persona (she was a British free love, abolition advocate and communitarian public speaker). Despite their silence, black women were sexually objectified even in the name of antislavery. At the 1845 meeting, Stephen Foster, using black women to denounce the churches and clergy, launched into a zealous tirade about sexual license, and asserted that he could buy any enslaved woman and "do with her as I please." Black women in the audience left, "blushing deeply," and some white women followed. A "general row" ensued, as angry black men accused Foster of bad taste and indiscretion. When Foster reiterated that all churches were the "mother of harlots and the cages of unclean birds" and that no ministers who remained within the churches were truly antislavery, even tolerant people wanted him thrown out. The *Standard* called this a "warm and exciting" debate, while the *Herald*'s detailed account termed it a "Furious onslaught."[43] Neither press mentioned that an affront to black women had created the polemic. Yet clearly black women activists saw themselves and enslaved women as reduced to the status of simple objects.

Moreover, the Abolitionist press raved about Jane Elizabeth Hitchcock's maiden speech, while ignoring Sojourner Truth. Even "slightly colored" newcomer Jeremiah Sanderson praised Hitchcock's "most eloquent and logical speech." His account to Amy Post of Rochester, New York, about "women's progress" ignored the black woman on the platform and Foster's embarrassing outburst. Nor did an African American newspaper exist to document the first black woman speaker before the AASS. Finally however, two weeks later, the *Standard* noted that the convention "was addressed by a colored woman who had been a slave, but more recently a resident of Northampton, Massachusetts. She has no name. Her remarks were characterized by good sense and strong feeling."[44]

Unfortunately for Sojourner Truth, Maria Weston Chapman had replaced Maria Child as the *Standard*'s editor. Otherwise, Sojourner might have received better coverage in her native state. At least a later issue corrected the flippant comment about her name. One of the most "impressive" among the interesting new speakers showcased at the convention, the *Standard* observed, was that "of a colored woman of strong mind, and remarkable gift of language, to whom Slavery had given no name, but who is known among her friends as 'Sojourner.'" Moreover, later that summer, Quaker Abolitionist Benjamin Jones visited Northampton and wrote about Sojourner. "Do you remember her?" he reminded his readers. She spoke twice in New York City, and though "wholly untaught of schools," she "poured forth a torrent of natural eloquence which swept everything before it."[45]

While in New York, Sojourner certainly visited old friends and sought news about Peter. There was no reason to go to Ulster County; apparently Diana was not there. An early reminiscence states that in Battle Creek, Michigan, "Sojourner Truth's daughter" cooked at barn raisings for new Quaker settlers from Ulster County. This coincides with the 1844 birth date of Diana Dumont's son James Caldwell. Diana may have accompanied settlers to Michigan, had James, and returned to the Dumonts, where she again was in 1850 before moving to Northampton. In the 1850s, little "Jimmy" Caldwell attended school in Northampton periodically with Samuel Hill's son Arthur. The 1860 Census for Bedford, Michigan (Battle Creek Post Office), lists James Caldwell as a sixteen-year-old blacksmith's apprentice. When he enlisted during the Civil War, he gave his age as nineteen and his birthplace as Battle Creek, Michigan.[46]

After Frederick Douglass revealed his identity, the Community became his safe haven for part of the summer, before he sailed for Liverpool. By then the "eloquent fugitive" and the African Dutch mystic were friends. Truth and

Douglass had similarities besides race, activism, and previous bondage. Both were gifted extemporaneous orators—partly natural, partly contrived, partly patterned, and always appealing to the higher sentiments. They evoked laughter but also empathy. Douglass's "strangely corrugated brow" and "maddened eyes" held deep sadness, one observer noted. But his friends knew a warmer side. Elisha Hammond painted Douglass's portrait that summer. He "tried to look becomingly grave," Benjamin Jones noted, but the shadow of his smile rested "like sunlight upon his countenance," which "almost speaks." Both Truth and Douglass were great humorists. Indeed, many enslaved people used laughter and satire as healing agents, but for these two slave-born lecturers, humor was strategic. After disarming an audience with laughter, Douglass then stripped off his shirt, exposing whip marks representing slavery's rapacious brutality, and a back muscular from manly labor. Truth employed humor as a revival preacher, and on the Abolitionist circuit, she incited great laughter, then tears when she revealed her scarred back and held up "the cruel stump of a finger that seems ever to tell the story of her slave life." If Frederick Douglass was "cut out for a hero," so was Sojourner Truth.[47]

Benjamin Jones wrote his impressions of the "wild" and "rough" Community for the *Pennsylvania Freeman*, spending much of his time with "the SOJOURNER." Sojourner's commitment to communal living and abolition was stirring, Jones wrote. "Strong in the faith, and with a grateful and hopeful heart, she joys to remain an humble laborer in the anti-slavery cause and a SOJOURNER here." Having found a long-hoped-for abiding place among the "choicest spirits of the age," Sojourner expected that Northampton would always be home.[48]

Wash and be healed.
— COLD WATER ARMY SLOGAN

I did not think you were laying the foundation of such an almost world-wide reputation when I wrote that little book for you, but I rejoice and am proud that you can make your power felt with so little book-education.
— OLIVE GILBERT TO SOJOURNER TRUTH

CHAPTER 11

The Cold Water Army, Olive Gilbert, and Sojourner's *Narrative*

I

Hydropathy was among the most important new "isms" at Northampton, and Sojourner Truth claimed it saved her health. David Ruggles, among the first American practitioners of the European cold water cure, collaborated with Dr. Robert Wesselhoeft, a German immigrant, physician, and political freethinker who opened an establishment in Vermont. After first treating himself, Ruggles introduced his method to six Northampton friends, including Sojourner Truth. Claiming to determine the nature and state of a disease by touch, Ruggles used the skin's condition as a gauge of its electricity, or "vitality of power." In order to treat a patient successfully, he had to sense the patient's body heat—an incessant, regular, energetic emission from the pores. According to former Community member David Mack, who edited the *Water Cure Journal*, Sojourner was seriously ill when she entered Ruggles's infirmary in 1845. Initially, she was an uncooperative, grumbling, and complaining patient who resented the prolonged treatment, immobility, confinement, and regimentation. Even several weeks into her treatment, she called the water cure "a humbug." Ruggles treated her for stomach and bowel problems ("scrophulous humors and dyspepsia"); swollen, abscessed, and inflamed legs; and joint and muscle ailments.[1]

She admitted that she had been practically an invalid when she began treatments, but she hated the chilling wet sheets and the numerous daily baths. "I shall die if I continue in it," she said of the water cure regimen, "and I may as well die out of the water as in it." But Ruggles convinced his ailing friend to stay the course. Her first sign of progress was relief from dyspepsia. She eliminated "much bile and acrid matter from the stomach," Mack wrote, whereupon her strength increased. But then she began failing rapidly, and complained of suffering more from the chilling baths than the painful leg ulcers. Ruggles theorized that pain and discomfort were precursors to a "grand crisis," leading to cure. This finally began six weeks into her treatment, when there appeared "a humor exuding from her legs below the knees, coursing from her feet, and the very ends of her toes." These continual secretions greatly relieved her. After ten weeks, she was "cured" and cheerfully went back to supervising the laundry. Her legs were restored to hearty usefulness, and rigorous diet control eliminated her stomach problems. She thankfully reported that "she has never enjoyed better health in her life."[2]

Her treatment was certainly not pleasant. Ruggles first wrapped her in cold, wet sheets or a sack (the "wet-sheet" or "sack" regimen), then covered her with blankets for one hour. The cold, uncomfortable wet sheet eventually became a warm, soothing poultice. Then, when she was sweating profusely, he unpacked her, and bathed her in cold or tepid water, while she simultaneously drank copious amounts of water. He administered this "rapid change of matter in the system" routine five times daily for many weeks, thereby creating the crisis—extreme perspiration and secretions of poisons. Sojourner Truth became a believer, along with health enthusiasts who called the water cure the ultimate life sustainer and purest form of natural healing.[3]

After his success with Sojourner Truth and several distinguished town residents, Ruggles's hydropath institution was one of the most popular in the country. Patients who came on crutches left walking. One female patient, cured after three months with Ruggles, wrote that he also cured nine of her lady friends, including a slaveholder's wife whose "incurable" illness had "baffled skilled physicians for fourteen years." Abolitionists helped Ruggles expand his operations, and his small staff apparently included Sojourner's daughter Elizabeth. By 1846, the Northampton Water Cure had over forty patients. Women and men from the highest professions, ordinary mechanics, reformers, and foreigners went to Ruggles's "Siloam, to 'wash and be healed.'"[4]

Dr. Wesselhoeft's glitzy establishment up the river in Brattleboro, Vermont, attracted politicians, the rich, genteel reformers, and literati: Harriet Beecher Stowe, Catharine Beecher, Henry Wadsworth Longfellow, and occasionally Olive Gilbert. Yet Ruggles also treated a notable crowd. Besides Sojourner Truth, John Brown's wife, Mary, Abby Kelley (recently married to Stephen Foster), Lucy Stone, Douglass, and Garrison took the cure in Northampton. Mary Brown traveled alone from their new residence in North Elba, New York, to see Ruggles and remained for four months while her husband was in England on business. John Jr. wrote the displeased patriarch that Ruggles treated Mary for neuralgia and "scrofulous humour" of the glands. "I'm glad you told him," Mary wrote her stepson, about Brown Sr. "He has never believed there was any disease about me." But, she added, "I think if he was here now he would change his mind." When John Brown Sr. returned, he stopped in Northampton to fetch Mary. He visited with the Abolitionists and apparently approved of Ruggles's establishment; Brown left while Mary continued taking the cure and enjoying the companionship of other patients such as Sojourner Truth and Lucy Stone. For progressive women, the "water-cure craze" not only restored health but also created friendships and encouraged independence and political awareness. An average stay was about fourteen weeks, but some people remained for over a year. During long walks and lingering talks in their rooms, women at the water cure built bonds of sisterhood. When Mary Brown finally left, she had lost much weight, and said she both looked and felt better.[5]

As a water cure enthusiast, Sojourner Truth embraced Ruggles's larger health counseling, based on the teachings and writings of Sylvester Graham, a Northampton resident. Graham opposed alcohol; rich, salty, highly spiced, or high-temperature foods; sugars; red meat; and tobacco. Stimulants, including too much sex, Graham said, ruined the body, mind, and soul. Exercise and spartan living were keys to physical strength and long life. Most people in the Community boardinghouse followed a "Grahamite" diet. Reportedly, any patient "Doctor" Ruggles treated for gout was "infallibly cured" if the patient obeyed his advice about diet, exercise, and mental rest. In that age of "the great American stomachache," most people ate and drank gluttonously. One meal commonly had several kinds of meat—smoked, salted, fried, boiled, and roasted—with vegetables, starches, gravies, pies, and cakes, all cooked in abundant lard. Diners preferred fermented beverages or bitter coffee to water. Sojourner Truth had practiced fasting and healthful eating in the kingdom. But she continued smoking, while water cure patients such as Garrison secretly and prolifically cheated on food. All enjoyed the physical exercise. Following each treatment and round of water drinking, patients walked for miles in the open air. "We are either in the woods or in the water," Garrison related. Hydropathists also insisted on periods of quiet conversation and reflection, which women obeyed more than men. Ruggles "caught me writing in my chamber," Garrison confessed, and "scolded me emphatically." Sojourner Truth took advantage of the water cure as a respite from the road, a means of furthering female camaraderie, and a time of spiritual peace.[6]

Thus, Perfectionists—from Matthias to Garrison and Sojourner Truth to Abby Kelley—proclaimed "all hail to pure cold water." It became the centerpiece of Abolitionists' health reform, and they tried to begin each day with a cold water body wash. The term "cold water army," once referring to those who pledged to drink water instead of alcohol, also represented temperate, diet-conscious, reform-minded progressives. The Abolitionist cold water army seemingly lived longer, had stronger constitutions, withstood diseases more readily, and withstood the demands of public life as they crisscrossed the North during lecturing seasons. Early antislavery travelers attributed poor health to bad food, poor hygiene, and inadequate exercise. They now carried their own "victuals." This usually consisted of coarse brown "Graham bread," which was sometimes ground up, softened in milk overnight, and eaten hot or cold. It developed into a dry breakfast cereal called "granula." Although Sylvester Graham died in 1851, his health reform ideas became "a declaration of physical independence from the capitalist marketplace." But also, through holistic treatment—body, mind, and spirit—health reform's sociopolitical implications linked it to progressive thought and millennialism. Striving for individual and societal perfection in the wake of Christ's Second Coming meant becoming a purified physical as well as spiritual temple.[7]

Sojourner Truth's Millerite connections were also part of this Gospel of health. Ellen and James White led the largest group of squabbling premillennialist holdovers from the "Great Disappointment"—Sabbath-keeping Adventists who fused progressive political rhetoric with a spiritual lamentation of national decline, worked the Underground Railroad, and condemned proslavery legislation. In 1854, a vision directed "prophetess" Ellen White to Battle Creek, Michigan. There, in 1863, she and thirty-five hundred followers organized the Seventh-Day Adventists around Christ's imminent appearance without a date, health and food reform, and sexual restraint. After the Civil War, their water cure establishment (Battle Creek Sanitarium) became world famous, thanks to White's brilliant young protégé Dr. John Harvey Kellogg. Together they built the first Seventh-Day Adventist empire. Kellogg later became Sojourner's physician, and transformed granula into an instant cold breakfast cereal called cornflakes.[8]

Sojourner Truth and the Adventists moved West independently but almost simultaneously. While she did not join the Millerite-Adventists, she renewed friendships with them because of their social justice beliefs. Antebellum Adventists were not conservative, antiinstitutional, apolitical, or fundamentalists.[9] Although obsessed with Apocalypse, believers also supported abolition. Similarly, crème de la crème Abolitionists such as the Grimké-Welds embraced the doomsday message. Despite Sojourner's association with Adventists, her religious radicalism had a much stronger foundation.[10] She prepared for Christ's Second Coming by challenging social evils. At water cure establishments, she not only took the treatment but also spread the word and made some of her most lasting friendships.

Sojourner also embraced phrenology, an ism popularized by Lorenzo N. and Orson S. Fowler. Phrenologists believed that a certain mental capacity governed each section of the brain, and the skull's shape determined each faculty's mental constitution. Phrenologists attacked pseudoscientific racists' claims that blacks had smaller brains than whites, and disavowed assertions that a female's brain simply could not hold as much knowledge as a male's. Sojourner Truth skillfully addressed the latter theme in her famous 1851 speech in Akron, Ohio: "As for intellect, . . . if woman have a pint, and man a quart—why can't she have her little pint full? . . . We can't take more than our pint'll hold." Women reformers often had their "head read." According to an analysis of Truth's "phrenological character" by phrenologist Nelson Sizer, she had unmatched moral firmness and believed "truth was a jewel." Her cautious self-reliance enabled her to think and plan for herself, thereby augmenting her sense of judgment. "Hence whatever you have to do, you take hold with confidence," Sizer wrote. Her character was deemed very strong in parental affection, friendship, and love. Her memory of faces, places, and facts was extraordinary, as was her capacity for getting on in the world. Though she could not read or write, she had "naturally a good talent for figures—can reckon money, and do it very straight and correctly."[11]

Sojourner did not relinquish tobacco. Smoking was unhealthy, friends scolded, and tobacco, like cotton, was cultivated with slave labor. But she loved her clay Dutch pipe. Nostalgia, habit, and addiction all bound her to a practice developed in childhood and associated with a world left far behind. The upright Sojourner Truth was "a slave to the filthy weed." It bothered her; she prayed over her addiction and waited until the Spirit instilled the "necessity to give it up." Meanwhile, her habit was good for a chortle or two. Black people, no matter how respectable or wealthy, sat in public conveyances with poor whites, smokers, and drunks. Sojourner said she preferred to inhale her own tobacco, and smoked "out of self defense." In Milton, Wisconsin, an Abolitionist friend asked her if she knew the Scripture that declared nothing unclean shall inherit the kingdom of heaven. "I have heard tell of that," she replied, no doubt puffing away. Well, he continued, "Sojourner, you smoke, and cannot enter the kingdom of heaven because there is nothing so unclean as the breath of a smoker. What do you say to that?" She had a witty retort: "I speck to leave my breff behind when I go to heaven."[12]

II

Sojourner Truth's beloved Community was debt-ridden and financially shaky even when she arrived. Some stockholders had already physically withdrawn, and some considered leaving. Other investors believed that the enterprise would eventually pay for itself, while the Industrial Community thought the experiment was at a sociopolitical peak. During the fall of 1844, members argued late into the night over dissolution and talked of little else during the workday. Sojourner Truth and Frances Judd lobbied tirelessly for the Community. Child care responsibilities prevented Dolly Stetson from attending meetings, but her letters voiced the opinions of most women. No place in the world was completely perfect, Dolly wrote her skeptical husband, but community life was better than what they previously had. "If you could be at home with us we might be happyer here than we could be to return to Brooklyn (Connecticut)." The majority won at these meetings. The Association continued, but members left anyway because of conflict over social conduct.[13]

In spring 1845, the boardinghouse was renovated, and new members replaced departed ones. Amid this spurt of optimism, a surprised Dolly Stetson overheard investors say that her family was leaving. After "pumping David Ruggles," Dolly gained more inside information: the Association's financial condition was dire, and Dolly's husband had decided to leave without consulting her. Too distressed even to go into town for Frederick Douglass's lecture, Dolly sat alone at the boardinghouse and wrote James. How could returning to the rural isolation of Brooklyn do "much good to our race"? In that environment, their moral convictions were "rendered powerless" because "we have not the wealth and station to render us worthy of notice." And where else outside of the Community could their children have access to such erudite teachers, or their girls be influenced by such "accomplished women"? James was acting rashly, she wrote. While Sojourner attended the annual antislavery meeting in New York, Community debates grew heated, especially when cofounder George Benson unsuccessfully proposed manufacturing cotton. As Dolly surmised, despite the supposed democracy, investors would "do what they please."[14]

Nonetheless, Sojourner Truth truly believed that the Community would continue. Throughout 1845, stalwart investors remained, and life appeared normal. However, by spring 1846, serious unraveling commenced, and Dolly prepared to leave. "I know not when my spirits have been so depressed," she wrote that March. Others followed, but diehard investors—the Judds, Hammonds, Stebbinses, and Hills—held on. So did Sojourner and her family. Finally, the Community ceased to exist on November 1, 1846; the executive council announced that "no allowances for the subsistence of members would be made" after that date. The Bensons welcomed Sojourner and her daughter Sophia into their home. Elizabeth apparently resided in David Ruggles's water cure establishment. Sophia and Jane Gidney disappeared from history.[15]

Sojourner Truth and other women were bitterly disappointed in the demise of the Community, where they had thrived on the independence, mutual assistance, and mental growth that utopian life had offered. Some, including Sojourner, Eliza Hammond, and Frances Judd, remained in Northampton and continued their activism. But Dolly Stetson, mother of eight, resumed farm life in rural Brooklyn, Connecticut, and for a time went into a deep depression.[16] Sojourner's beloved Community did not endure, but like other former members, she praised its lessons of friendship, equality, spirituality, political growth, and womanist consciousness, all central to spreading social reform.

Her residency with the Benson family was soon in jeopardy. In 1848, George Benson presided over the Anti-Sabbath Convention (protesting obligatory Sunday observance). Vitriolic Henry C. Wright, "the gadfly's gadfly," coined the convention slogan, which even offended some Garrisonians: "Man Above Theology! Conviction Above Authority! Nature Above Art! Self-evident Truth Above Bibles!" At the time, Benson supervised a cotton mill opened by New Org merchants leasing Association property. Although he was manufacturing with slave-grown produce, he hired local black workers and former Community members and operated "Bensonville" as a co-operative. The outraged merchants fired Benson. As he considered relocating his family, Sojourner faced another displacement.[17]

Sojourner Truth had once envisioned "a little home of her own"; her friends made that dream a reality. The idea of her publishing her life story germinated after the Anti-Sabbath Convention. At that time, Garrison, with the contacts to spearhead such a publication, made his longest stay in Northampton. Meanwhile, Samuel Hill was dividing his portion of the Community property into parcels, selling them to former members and using the proceeds to pay off Association debts. He sold land to Sojourner near his own home, built her a house, and trusted her with a mortgage for the full amount in her own name. Windham County Community members had already introduced her to a frequent visitor named Olive Gilbert; she agreed to write the African Dutch mystic's story.[18]

Almost nothing has been written about Olive Gilbert, the woman responsible for committing Sojourner's story to paper. The *Narrative* has sometimes been dismissed as Gilbert's manipulation of Sojourner's lived experience, or as a secondary rather than a primary account of her life.[19] White testimony on behalf of a black subject can be problematic. However, Sojourner Truth's story is as much within the "slave narrative" genre as other works dictated to whites that are considered reliable. A brief exploration of Olive Gilbert's background, her Abolitionist connections, and her reform commitment show that her representation of "Truth" cannot be summarily dismissed.

Olive Gilbert was born in Brooklyn, Connecticut, in 1801. Her father died young, leaving behind his wife, three children (one soon died), and a successful farm. The farm and much of the land belonged to Olive's mother, Mary (Molly) Cleveland. One family member founded Cleveland, Ohio; another later became president. Molly soon married a local farmer named Samuel Scarborough, and they had three sons who reached adulthood: George, Perrin, and Edwin. Olive grew up in a household of boys that included her older brother Joseph Jr.[20]

The Scarboroughs were dissenters in Brooklyn's conservative Congregational Church, and when Unitarianism swept through New England, Olive's mother and stepfather adopted these minority doctrines. In 1823, the Brooklyn church offered a permanent appointment to interim pastor Samuel J. May. Olive Gilbert had a conversion experience the next year and became a member.[21]

Gilbert's association with Samuel May connected her to Sojourner Truth. May, a Harvard-trained Boston Brahmin, was the first ordained Unitarian minister in Connecticut. He rejected a large pulpit in Richmond, Virginia, for Connecticut's rural Windham County, where judges and selectmen, including Gilbert's stepfather, worked alongside common day laborers. May was controversial; he organized the Windham County Peace Society, advocated public education, and established a village lyceum and a Total Abstinence program. The latter condemned practices of "treating" schoolchildren to alcohol and on-the-job drinking among young factory workers. Unpopular even within his congregation, he nonetheless maintained a substantial base of older progressives and eager young converts. Gradually, the large, lovely, white-steepled church prospered under him, as he spread his beliefs throughout southeastern Connecticut. While the powerful Lyman Beecher, among others, declared war on Unitarian "heresy," May, its most eloquent proponent, was nurturing Olive Gilbert.[22]

Like Sojourner Truth the Methodist, Olive Gilbert the Unitarian embraced Perfectionist thought, and both ultimately found their churches disappointing. May's mentor, William Ellery Channing, provided the theological structure of American Unitarianism. It opposed doctrines of election and innate human depravity, dismissed sacramental observances, and embraced "doing justly, loving mercy, and walking humbly." Unitarian perfection followed the teachings of Jesus, New Testament primitive Christianity, and a sense of moral responsibility, even in opposition to governmental authority. However, Channing denounced the radical Abolitionists as counterproductive and reckless. Garrisonians had once courted Channing; they soon dubbed the Unitarian church a "Whig" haven for Northern textile mill owners ("lords of the loom"), Southern cotton planters ("lords of the lash"), and colonizationists sidestepping antislavery. May broke with Channing and became a founding member of both the NEASS and AASS.[23] He led Olive Gilbert to Unitarianism, but she and Brooklyn members of the future Northampton Community deserted the denomination.

The Benson family, in whose home Sojourner later dictated her *Narrative*, was also important to Gilbert's activist credentials. George Benson Sr., of Rhode Island, had been a founder of the NEASS and AASS. In 1823, he retired to a large Brooklyn farm, and George Jr. took over the family's wool business.

Olive Gilbert became intimate friends with Benson Sr.'s daughters; Helen, the youngest, married Garrison. Frances, Mary, Sarah, and Anne all suffered from "protracted bodily infirmities," but were committed activists. At the National Anti-Slavery Women's Convention in New York, the Benson women supported total equality for black women. When Sojourner Truth met the Bensons in 1844, three sisters had died, and Sarah was terminally ill.[24]

Gilbert, May, the Bensons, and others planted radical abolition seeds in Windham County through a local struggle over black education. The fruits of their efforts spread far beyond that conservative corner of Connecticut. In 1831, Prudence Crandall opened a secondary school for white girls in Canterbury, a prosperous bucolic hamlet adjacent to Brooklyn. When she allowed Sarah Harris, a fair-skinned "coloured" young woman, to attend classes, townsmen accused Prudence of promoting "leveling" and "intermarriage between the whites and blacks." She refused to dismiss the student and even told the stunned townsmen that Moses had had a black wife. When whites withdrew their daughters in April 1833, Crandall advertised her facility throughout the North as a secondary school for women of color.[25]

The "nigger" school in beautifully manicured Canterbury outraged its whites. Their leader, Andrew Judson, called Crandall a fanatical tool of outside agitators, seeking to "mongrelize" the town. Residents taunted the students, threw animal feces in Crandall's well, broke windows, blew horns, and shot off firearms outside her residence; Churches closed their doors and shops refused entry to her and her students. Abolitionists rallied around her. Garrison scorched the "Canterbury Junto" with his pen and labeled Connecticut the Georgia of New England. May attacked prejudice from his pulpit and wrote pamphlets on black education and on ancient African civilizations. The antislavery movement had not yet split; Arthur Tappan paid Crandall's legal fees, and Benson Sr. financed a local Brooklyn newspaper. Persecutions notwithstanding, one student wrote that "the happiness I enjoy here pays me for all." Nonetheless, Connecticut's General Assembly legislated that blacks could not enter the state for education. Crandall's arrest under this "Black Law" horrified even non-Abolitionists and placed Windham County under an unwelcome national microscope. On appeal, the state Supreme Court convicted Crandall within thirty minutes, maintaining that black people "are not citizens within the obvious meaning of the Constitution." In 1857, Chief Justice Roger Taney used this decision to argue against black citizenship in the Dred Scott case.[26]

The virulent hostility that arose during this eighteen-month conflict radicalized Gilbert and May's inner circle. Many joined the May-Benson underground, and Brooklyn became "a busy station, for most of the East Connecticut lines converged there." David Ruggles had begun his underground work in his native southeastern Connecticut, and it now spread, as Crandall's local nucleus connected with out-of-town Abolitionists and students' parents. They all gathered in the Benson home, which Crandall named "Friendship Vale," the "asylum of the oppressed." Even after Crandall lost her case, Brooklyn remained a reform hub. Abby Kelley frequently traveled the eastern Connecticut circuit, "making George W. Benson's [Jr.] my headquarters." The Crandall struggle also spawned a network of marriages, most notably that of Helen Benson to Garrison and May's sister Abigail to Bronson Alcott. It was no accident that when George Benson Jr. eventually sold Friendship Vale to invest in a utopian ideal, many Brooklyn residents followed him to Northampton, where they met Sojourner Truth.[27]

Gilbert led in organizing the Female Anti-Slavery Society of Brooklyn and Vicinity, which grew out of the Crandall network. Women in the Brooklyn area sheltered Crandall's students, escorted them to May's church and to trial, purchased their supplies, taught them, and visited their head teacher in jail. Like the students, these women endured criticism and ridicule. When the struggle ended unsuccessfully, they transferred their political energy to an antislavery society that preceded the men's by three years. During its existence, the female society had more than sixty members and kept pace with sister organizations in Salem, Boston, and Philadelphia. Acknowledging a special responsibility to enslaved women, the Brooklyn female Abolitionists declared open opposition to any institution whose principles were contrary to the humanity, honor, and religion of "more than a million of our own sex" who were "groaning under the yoke of . . . degrading bondage."[28]

Gilbert was the engine of the Brooklyn organization. She kept minutes, communicated with other northeastern female societies, arranged meetings, solicited speakers, and ordered antislavery literature. The society organized petition drives and bazaars and raised money for the *Liberator*. They held special meetings to sew, knit, and darn for impoverished free black families and for the Underground Railroad. Gilbert and the Brooklyn women supported the Grimkés, discussed their pamphlets, and sent representatives to the annual meetings of the AASS. In those early days, only men spoke at women's meetings. Men counseled women about withstanding opprobrium and condemnation as ultraists, fanatics, and amalgamationists, and emphasized women's significance as instruments of moral reform. The rural Brooklyn women accepted this challenge as Crandall's final trial unfolded amid waves of publicity and unremitting persecutions. Garrison wrote his bride-to-be that the women's meetings "gave me real pleasure. . . . There is no zeal, no liberality, no devotion, like Woman's!" The female society's last record was written in August 1840; Gilbert, its secretary, wrote that most active and reliable members had moved, were ill, or had simply stopped coming. Since much time had lapsed since the last meeting, they could no longer be considered an organization. The women decided to "go on as a band of volunteers."[29]

Gilbert's polite final words gloss over the ideological controversy and religious factionalism that destroyed the Brooklyn Society. Most Brooklyn women backed Garrison in 1839–40, but Connecticut's state organization was solidly New Org. Moreover, May, disgusted with the racism and the church elders' resentment of his activism, soon resigned. Ultimately, he became pastor of Church of the Messiah in Syracuse, New York, where he remained throughout his public life. He met Sojourner Truth at Northampton, and their friendship deepened over the years. His departure from the Brooklyn church prompted the exodus of Garrisonians such as Gilbert and her Scarborough brothers. Gilbert traveled wherever she had close friends or family, using the Cleveland—Scarborough farm as a home base. Fortuitously for Sojourner Truth, Gilbert had reasons of kinship, friendship, and politics to be in Northampton. Windham County residents nurtured on Garrisonian radicalism represented the core of the Northampton Community.[30]

III

The "friend" in the Community who introduced Gilbert to Sojourner Truth was either Sarah Benson or Dolly Stetson. When she met Sojourner, Olive was advised that she was in the presence of a remarkable woman. Yet Gilbert had no idea "that we should ever pen these 'simple annals' of this child of nature."[31] Nonetheless, this private, quiet, and diffident Connecticut Yankee was an appropriate choice. Gilbert was a soldier in that "silent army" of antislavery women who also made up the cold water army.

Although certainly in better circumstances than Sojourner Truth, Gilbert also lived on her own resources and was independent. Olive and Joseph Gilbert inherited separate lands from their father and had "equal standing" with the Scarborough siblings for their mother's inheritance. Joseph Gilbert, who was not involved in antislavery or in the Brooklyn church during May's tenure, worked for his stepfather under legal compulsion until 1832. He then sold most of his inheritance to Samuel Scarborough and left Brooklyn. In 1827, Olive received an undisclosed "personal estate," a "family settlement," and $500 in exchange for relinquishing her rights to any Cleveland-Scarborough property. In 1835, Gilbert sold her father's remaining lands for $800.[32] This modest inheritance sustained her; she remained single, lived frugally, and accepted hospitality. An avid reader, thinker, and correspondent, she avoided Prudence Crandall's mistake of marrying a spouse who curtailed her mobility and her intellectual pursuits and controlled her property. Marriage also interfered with personal achievement, while childbirth imperiled female health and life. Only in utopian communities or at water cure establishments did family women openly assert their collective gender sensibilities and self-expression and proudly claim their intellect. Both Gilbert and Truth valued freedom more than marriage.[33]

In Sojourner's *Narrative*, Gilbert maintains that she has more knowledge of bondage than most Northern Abolitionists and has witnessed slavery in "D_____ County." This mysterious notation refers to Daviess County in western Kentucky, where her brother George Scarborough lived. George had also rejected farm life as an adult, and studied science at Rensselaer Institute in Troy, New York, and theology at Harvard Divinity School and then traveled South for his health. In Owensboro, Kentucky, he became headmaster of an elite school owned by a wealthy slaveholder, created a thriving coeducational institution, and married his employer's daughter. Daviess County was situated on the Ohio River, and over a third of its population was enslaved. [34]

Slavery was harsh in Owensboro. Blacks could not buy, sell, or own so much as a chicken or a dog. Fear of the Underground Railroad was rampant, black mobility was heavily restricted, and slave patrols were constantly active. George Scarborough was a tall, quiet, well-liked scientist who was also a Unitarian and, according to Owensboro residents, an Abolitionist who "held his peace." But his sister did not; Olive expressed open disapproval of slavery while visiting Kentucky, and Northern friends feared for her safety. One Yankee woman, Delia Webster, was already languishing in a Kentucky prison for underground activities. "Olive was going to Kentucky to see George S," Dolly Stetson wrote. "I hope she will keep clear of the penitentiary." The unexpected death of Scarborough's father-in-law made him a slave owner. He hired out the slaves, specifically ordering proper treatment, accommodations, and clothing. After his wife died, leaving him childless, he left Kentucky. Whether he freed or sold his inheritance is unknown.[35]

Olive spent the longest periods on her visitation rounds with her "cherished friend and sisterly companion" Sarah Benson, when Sarah was ill with breast cancer. A compassionate nurse and spiritual supporter, Olive also accompanied Sarah to water cures, hoping to restore her health. When Sarah became bedridden, the Benson home became a female center. Sojourner Truth also helped nurse Sarah, and even Helen Benson Garrison journeyed from Boston. Under different circumstances, Sarah Benson, who knew Sojourner Truth more intimately, would have written her story. It is interesting to speculate that while Gilbert was ultimately responsible for the chronicle, Sarah may have been partially involved in editing Sojourner's *Narrative*, in whatever capacity her health allowed.[36]

The two unmarried white women adhered to conventions of female morality, and certainly cautioned Sojourner about revealing her sexual history, thereby leaving that part of her life open to historical speculation. But Sojourner Truth participated in this decision, since divulging moral improprieties would expose herself, those she loved, and those she had forgiven. While sexual exploitation was merely implied, the bitter brutality of Dutch slavery was explicit. "I can't read, but I can hear," Sojourner was fond of saying. And her consistent verification of the *Narrative* confirms that she exerted more control than modern writers have acknowledged. She hid darker secrets even from white women friends because, she said, no one would believe her. Her systematic, extended oral recounting of her former life for posterity was a kind of renewed mourning, an odyssey both dramatic and emotional. Although bondage was the real culprit, detailed remembering also required that she revisit her own mistakes and guilt. Isabella had been "a slave in N.Y. state, called a nigger wench, and treated as less than human." Surrounded by those who "regard her as a woman and an equal sister," when Sojourner Truth compared her position at Northampton with her "wench" status in Ulster County, it made "tears spring from her eyes."[37]

In the *Narrative,* Sojourner claimed a voice for her family and the African Dutch people. Hers was the only black perspective ever recorded on slavery among the insular, tight-lipped Dutch New Yorkers. The setting in which she told her story—in the Benson home and at Ruggles's water cure—also reinforced black-white female bonding. Sojourner Truth the narrator, Olive Gilbert the stenographer, Sarah Benson the invalid-adviser, and a host of female listeners shared a radical vision that transcended the racial divide that the larger society tried to impose.

Abolitionist publisher James M. Yerrinton printed Sojourner's *Narrative* on credit. Garrison's brief preface to the work said little about the author, thus giving weight to a misconception that developed later that Sojourner's *Narrative* was more Abolitionist propaganda than lived experience. George Benson and Samuel Hill added notes to vouch for this impoverished uneducated black woman with the lofty name of Sojourner Truth. Her influential friend Abijah W. Thayer, editor of the *Hampshire Herald* and a New Org Liberty Party man, also publicly endorsed the *Narrative.*

After the 1849 annual meeting of the AASS, Sojourner visited Ulster County, where her daughter Diana and grandson James lived with John Dumont. Now a widower, Dumont professed regret for having owned slaves. Sojourner was forgiving. Although her *Narrative* contained no personal disclosures about their relationship, it nevertheless caused Dumont some angst and embarrassment. He and his children moved to central New York. From 1851 on, when visiting friends in Cayuga County, Sojourner Truth passed by the Dumont homestead. She certainly looked in on her former owner, and he probably followed her antebellum exploits. He was still alive in 1863 when Harriet Beecher Stowe published her article "Sojourner Truth, the Libyan Sibyl" in the *Atlantic* and made Sojourner Truth a household name in the North. Above all, John Dumont, lawyer, Whig, and later a Republican, was undoubtedly most impressed when Truth had a private audience with President Abraham Lincoln. Dumont had enslaved Sojourner, and exploited her both physically and sexually. But even as a free woman, she called on Dumont in times of trouble, and he helped her. Perhaps the complexity of their emotional attachment remained until his death in 1869 at age ninety-four.[38]

Illness and death plagued the Abolitionist community. The Garrisons lost children in 1848 and 1849; in December 1849, Sojourner's old friend David Ruggles died. To the very end, he dictated articles and made expansion plans, and his infirmary full of patients included Lucy Stone and Sojourner Truth, Mary Brown having recently left. While many former patients experienced "blessings of health at his hands," he had not been able to cure himself. He ignored physicians' advice to slow down, and they insisted that "over-exertion, mental and physical," prevented the restoration of his health. His ailments included inflammation of the optic nerve, inflammation of the bowel, and a recurring liver ailment. His death was an "irreparable" loss to hydropathy, the antislavery movement, and humanity, the *Water-Cure Journal* wrote. "We look in vain for another to fill his place."[39]

The antislavery movement had lost the most, Douglass wrote, for Ruggles was still "in the midst of his years and usefulness." His memory lived among thousands who "escaped the yoke of slavery by his aid." Douglass was among that number; Ruggles had been a young editor and race leader when he had rescued the bewildered Marylander from the New York City streets teeming with slave catchers. Later, when Douglass himself struggled with the *North Star*, he often stopped in Northampton, took the cure, and communed with his noble friend. "I owe my life" to his "skill and attention," Douglass wrote. Ruggles had "literally worn himself out in humanity's service."[40]

Ruggles's death must have been especially difficult for Sojourner Truth. They had arrived in New York City around the same time, where the young urban freedom fighter had been "known, honored, and feared by the whole kidnapping police" and as familiar to the New York press as "the most notorious politician in the country." At Northampton, Ruggles and Truth were compatriots. Sojourner knew and loved Ruggles as a younger brother, and she experienced his sympathy, example, and gentleness. He had patiently nursed her back to usefulness and reintroduced her to healthful living. An early supporter of woman's rights, he had inspired and encouraged her Abolitionist education and her race consciousness. He "identified with the colored population by complexion and destiny" Garrison wrote. With the spirit of a hero and the courage of a martyr, Ruggles had conquered obstacles, performed exploits, and suffered for his people. Even his ailments seemed directly related to his New York activism. In fights with thugs, kidnappers, proslavery muggers and jailers, Ruggles had been kicked, had bones broken, and endured hard blows to his body from bricks and bats. He had been thrown into dank, cellar-like jails with no light or sanitation. Such treatment easily led to a severely damaged constitution, ruptured internal organs, and failing eyesight. The Abolitionist community mourned David Ruggles, from east to west, as the most effective and daring underground conductor of the era. Sojourner Truth and her daughter Elizabeth no doubt helped his grieving mother and sister nurse him during his final days. His family carried him back to Norwich, Connecticut, his birthplace, for burial. Ruggles and Truth's leadership in the Community revealed that they shared a broad love of humanity that was beyond race.[41]

Sarah Benson's quiet suffering soon ended, though she lived to see Sojourner's *Narrative* published. Shocked beyond measure on seeing Sarah's "cancerous affection [*sic*]," Garrison was amazed that she had lived with such rotting flesh, completely decayed with disease. Because of her courage and the women rallying around Sarah so faithfully, the menfolk had "had not the slightest idea as to the ravages it had made until after her death." Encircled by her women friends, Sarah remained "eminently conscientious, kind, amiable, sympathetic, disinterested, benevolent" to the end. Her impact on the *Narrative* and Sojourner Truth seems clear: a "sense of propriety . . . discriminating without being prudish"—a simple, solemn piety rather than a wordy, loud-tongued, or ostentatious religiosity. Sarah and Olive were "as one in sympathy, affection, suffering, and goodness." Just as Sojourner and Olive shared Sarah Benson's friendship and bereavement over her death, the three shared in reconstructing the African Dutch mystic's life.[42]

Gilbert and Truth's paths diverged after 1850, each making their own unique mark in the world. Gilbert's was the "quiet mark" of a thinker and teacher. Truth's was the public mark of a mobilizer. However, the Northampton experience and the *Narrative* created an intimacy between them that the years did not alter. Gilbert followed Truth through the newspapers. The Sojourner heard of Olive from the Garrisons, Bensons, Mays, and other mutual associates. Years later, when they were old women, Olive wrote Sojourner, "believe me to be your true friend and well-wisher, now and forevermore."[43]

Sojourner Truth made her maiden speech before the AASS sixteen months after Rachel Stearns wrote Maria Weston Chapman about the astonishing colored lady preacher in Springfield. She spent six years traveling local junkets through rural hamlets, small towns, and communities around Springfield, Worcester, Providence, and Boston. The *Standard, Liberator*, and *Freeman* took note as she preached, prayed, sang, traded barbs, matched wits, and told her story with such aplomb that Yankee audiences forgot their aversion to Dutchness. She always had detractors, some from her own race. But she was never isolated from black people, however much she fascinated whites. Perhaps because she dictated her story, Douglass never advertised or acknowledged Sojourner's *Narrative*. But he recognized and certainly appreciated her impact, popularity, and witness.[44]

Thus, her decision to follow her calling of the Spirit by going East had been prophetic. Her elation about the *Narrative* had to be mingled with sadness over personal loss and because she could not read her own story. Yet the *Narrative* was Sojourner's truth, despite some transcribing mistakes and intended omissions. The work proved her bondage, her age (fifty-three), which new friends soon insisted on increasing, and her freedom. It recounted her passion for God, her justification, her sanctification, and her calling. "Read my little book," she told the public. "It's all there."[45]

O brothers, awake! for the time has come
To brighten the blood-hound's fame;
They've opened a nobler field for us,
To follow our human game.
— C. SHIRAS, ESQ., "THE BLOOD-HOUND'S SONG"

The hounds are braying at my back;
Oh, Christians, will you send me back?
— AUTHOR UNKNOWN

CHAPTER 12

The Bloodhound Bill
and Intensified Activism

I

Prepublicity advertisements for Sojourner's *Narrative* began in April 1850, with the following statement in the *Liberator*: "*JUST PUBLISHED. And for sale at the Anti-Slavery office at 21 Cornhill, NARRATIVE OF SOJOURNER TRUTH, a Northern Slave emancipated from bodily servitude by the state of New York in 1828. With a Portrait.*" In the week before the May convention in 1850, Garrison added a postscript to the announcement: "This is a most interesting Narrative of a most remarkable and highly meritorious woman, the sale of which is to be for her exclusive benefit. We commend it to all the friends of the colored population—Ed.Lib." Abolitionists from across the nation anticipated the largest annual gathering ever.[1] And Sojourner Truth looked forward to the public announcement of her *Narrative* in her home state. But it was not to be.

The times were "fearful, stirring, and terrible," as national furor erupted when California's application for statehood included a ban on slavery. In response, Southerners mounted a confrontation, fueled by the invective of dying fire-eater John C. Calhoun and intensification of Abolitionist "No Union with slaveholders" agitation. Moreover, a new, increasingly powerful Free Soil party, dissatisfied with slavery's expansion, challenged the Whigs. To calm the sectional fury and neutralize abolition, congressional leaders Henry Clay of Kentucky and Daniel Webster of Massachusetts orchestrated a compromise. Congress would admit California without slavery, but enact an ironclad fugitive slave law, permitting the immediate arrest without a warrant and return of any *alleged* fugitive. Such persons could not testify or appeal, but hearsay testimony against them was admissible. The legislation also provided for a payment of $10 to federal commissioners who granted certificates to slaveholders permitting them to take back alleged fugitives, while commissioners who denied such certificates to slaveholders would receive only $5. Commissioners could deputize any citizen and use any measures to prevent interference.[2]

In 1850, radical Abolitionists seemed stronger than ever—more pristine, above self, party, race, and government. Ten years earlier, in 1840, Lewis Tappan and the clerical Abolitionists had predicted that the "no-marriage perfectionist" Garrison, who embraced "every infidel fanaticism which floats," was losing influence. Instead, Garrison's base had grown in the British Isles and America, especially among women. And in 1850, he promoted Sojourner Truth as he once showcased Frederick Douglass and William Wells Brown.[3]

Sojourner Truth and Garrison were kindred spirits. As seekers of a kingdom of God on earth through moral reform, both initially embraced but then rejected the church. Faith and the spoken word was her strength, while he, indentured to a printer in childhood, used the press to transform words into spiritual and moral weapons. Her circle of urban associates exposed her to reform and Perfectionism, while his young male cohorts included intellectuals such as Alcott and the humanitarian Quaker poet Whittier. Garrison's impoverished family background, including ancestors who immigrated to America as bond servants, was closer to hers than to those of his elite Boston associates. His mother had been a servant, and his alcoholic father, a mariner, had deserted the family. Like Sojourner's Mau-mau Bet, Garrison's devout mother had taught "Lloyd" to value faith, honesty, steadfast duty, and firmness as a Christian soldier. Garrison and Truth—two hymn-singing, Bible-quoting Perfectionists of humble birth—were friends for life.[4]

Besides his appreciation of Sojourner Truth as a reformer, their friendship also reflected Garrison's closeness to blacks. He was hated as much for his association with African Americans as for his caustic pen. African Americans provided seed money to start the *Liberator* after he left Quaker Benjamin Lundy's colonization-oriented *Genius of Universal Emancipation*. Blacks sustained the *Liberator* in its struggling years, and the NEASS was founded in a black church. Although Garrison's singleness of purpose led even some friends to call him an egomaniac, he was not a "romantic racialist" who idealized blacks or a "night-time Abolitionist" who avoided blacks publicly. He traveled, boarded, and ate with blacks so much that whites derisively called him a mulatto.[5]

Sojourner Truth and Garrison gloried in pitting "the strife of Christ against the empire of Satan." Their faith was tested in New York, where newspapers busily denounced the annual 1850 "congresses of fanatics" as a host of "Disunionists, Socialists, Fourierists, Communists and other Abolitionists" descending on the city like locusts of Egypt. Weeks before the meetings, James Gordon Bennett's *Herald* printed "Mob Instructions"—a direct appeal to violence that created the largest, angriest opposition ever. The *Herald* urged whites to support the Union and the Constitution by rebuking and silencing Abolitionist fanaticism. Merchants, they advised, whose fortunes were interwoven with the South should leave their counting rooms and stores; mechanics, laborers, and any citizen who valued the city's honor and the "safety of his race" should cease work and show loyalty to "country, to humanity, and the safety of his fellowman in another section." Most local black Abolitionists stayed away. On the platform, Sojourner Truth joined Abby Kelley Foster, newcomer Ernestine Rose, and Mary Grew, who opened the meeting with a prayer.[6]

The police watched as Tammany Hall captain Isaiah Rynders led workingmen, b'hoys, and street thugs into the Tabernacle. Interrupting Garrison's opening speech, Rynders loudly demanded to know if Abolitionists approved of any religious denominations. None were friends of the enslaved, Garrison answered. "Are you aware that the slaves in the South have their prayer-meetings in honor of Christ?" Rynders shouted. "Not a slaveholding or a slave breeding Jesus," Garrison countered. Ignoring the mob's gasps, Garrison added that Jesus was obsolete in America. "Who objects to his course in Judea? The old Pharisees are extinct, and may safely be denounced. Jesus is the most respectable person in the United States." Warming to his own invective, Garrison insisted that Jesus sat in the chair of the United States president, since Zachary Taylor believed in Jesus. "He believes in war, and the Jesus that gave the Mexicans hell." Loud applause from Abolitionists was mixed with deafening cries of "shame, shame" from the horrified mob. Rynders jumped onto the platform, shook a clenched fist at Garrison, and shouted, "I will not allow you to assail the President of the United States. You shan't do it." Children screamed and frightened women attempted to leave. In answer to the Abolitionist men's plea to "Have some respect for the ladies," Rynders blared that "White women who cohabit with and mix with the wooly-headed negro" did not warrant respect.[7]

As the subject turned to race, it was clear that no one, especially Sojourner Truth, would be able to speak. Douglass bantered with a mob representative who proclaimed that "blacks were not men, but belonged to the monkey tribe." Horace Greeley's *Tribune*, reporting the Abolitionists' side, noted that Douglass's humor, reason, and "relentless eloquence" literally "skinned" his opponent. "You're not a black man," Rynders shouted angrily. "You are only half a nigger," referring to Douglass's mixed-race ancestry. Douglass smiled wryly and replied, "I am indeed, only half a negro, and half a white man. I am half-brother to you." The Abolitionists convulsed with laughter at Douglass's bon mot, while the seething mob roared to Rynders, "Knock him down." Then Samuel Ringgold Ward, tall, majestic, articulate, and "black as the ace of spades," rose to challenge the rioters' claims of black inferiority. Although Ward "fairly extinguished the Rynders party," few could hear him. Feisty Ernestine Rose tried to speak but was shouted down by catcalls and insults. That evening, the mob returned, drowning out speakers by playing bagpipes, beating kettles, using other disruptive objects, while they screamed for "nigger" Douglass to return to the podium.[8] Apparently, Sojourner did not attempt to speak.

The second day was worse, and if women were originally on the platform, they quickly vacated. With an audience of about half Abolitionists and half mob, drunken, swaggering men stormed the platform. Race-baiting again took the forefront: "Whar's Pete Williams" (noted black dancer), "Garrison's nigger minstrels," and "Get off dat black gal's heels," rang through the hall. As two black women were escorted out, Rynders's men shouted, "Get along, yeller gals!" By the time Wendell Phillips arose to speak, all the women had left the building. Phillips was determined, but the mob drowned him out with "three cheers" for Mississippi, Alabama, South Carolina, Henry Clay, Daniel Webster, and the Constitution. The Constitution, Phillips shouted above the hecklers, "should be trampled under foot." Mayhem ensued. The mob within was completely out of control; the mob without clamored for entry, even climbing through windows. The scene became a brawl, and Abolitionists fought back amid cries from the mob of "tear down the building—Set fire to it." Finally, the police chief and his detachment escorted the Abolitionists out. They finished their business at William Powell's Colored Sailor's Home, and adjourned one day early.[9]

If Sojourner Truth had attempted to speak in New York, she might not have been mobbed, but certainly would have been grossly insulted. The venomous anti-Abolitionist scenes embarrassed the entire North, and even moderate newspapers decried the affront to free speech. Complicit local presses denied that Rynders represented them, while the Tribune insisted that officials had ordered the "grossly derelict" police chief not to interfere, even when women suffered "beastly insult," white men were beaten, and Frederick Douglass was threatened with assassination. It was a learning experience for the Sojourner, who would later face hostile mobs, and who adopted some of the rhetorical themes that both Garrison and Douglass expressed.[10]

Following the failed New York meeting, an unprecedented number of Abolitionists converged in Boston; other free blacks and self-emancipated people joined Sojourner Truth on the platform for the New England Anti-Slavery Convention. Henry "Box" Brown had shipped himself north in a freight crate. Ellen and William Craft had fled Georgia in 1848, with nearly white Ellen disguised as her husband's young master. Garrison began the afternoon session with Sojourner Truth by his side. The *Narrative* was announced in her adopted state, not her native state. Her six-foot frame seemed even taller next to Garrison, who was "quite a short, and small sized man." Although most of those present already knew her, he wanted the national antislavery audience to take special note of the *Narrative*.

He "asked leave to introduce to the Convention a woman, who had formerly been a slave, but was now residing in Northampton in this State. Her former name was Isabel but she had taken the name of Sojourner Truth. She spoke for about half an hour with great earnestness, evincing an extraordinary natural shrewdness and wit—The Convention was deeply interested by her remarks. She has recently published a little work, giving the narrative of her life."[11]

The AASS's endorsement and publication of Sojourner's *Narrative* under its auspices identified her with the Garrisonians as they embraced a bold repudiation of American laws and institutions. Since slavery was war, the New England resolutions said, Abolitionists urged blacks to use every weapon they could snatch, and their friends would challenge the rule of law on their behalf. That included trampling on the Constitution and any legislation, judicial decisions, or precepts demanding "the rendition of fugitive slaves." If Congress ignored justice and equal rights by passing such laws, and required citizens to aid slaveholders or U.S. Marshals in apprehending those in search of liberty, then the Abolitionists would consider such laws "null and void." Already regarded as godless, the Abolitionists also addressed biblical edict. If the Bible sanctioned slavery as Southerners maintained, and thereby opposed the self-evident truth that all people were created equal, then "the Bible," Abolitionists asserted, "is self-evident falsehood." But Sojourner Truth and most Abolitionists believed that the Bible's terrible warnings and fearful judgments denounced injustice and oppression. Despite some "rowdyism" at the convention where Sojourner spoke, black Abolitionist William C. Nell called it a glorious meeting, and a "brilliant triumph for the friends of humanity."[12]

II

That summer and fall, Sojourner Truth traveled throughout New England. She was at the massive July Fourth picnic celebration in a beautiful pine grove in Abington, Massachusetts. In an ambiance of recreation, singing, and poetry reading, Abolitionists deprecated the contradiction of a republic founded on equality but holding people in chattel slavery. Garrison preached from his favorite texts—Isaiah, who enjoined "Let the oppressed go free; break every yoke," and Jeremiah: "Ye have not harkened unto me in proclaiming liberty, every one to his brother, and every man to his neighbor." Like the Hebrews whom Jeremiah threatened with divine judgment, the American republic was also doomed. After lunch, Garrison introduced the "well known" and "remarkable colored woman" who spoke from personal experience "in her own peculiar and impressive style and dialect." Using her life as exemplar, Sojourner chronicled slavery's wickedness, emphasizing the buying and selling of children, and separation of families. Afterward, she had a brisk sale of her books. Her next large recorded presence was the annual First of August West Indian Emancipation celebration in Worcester. There she joined local residents, including the Fosters and Unitarian minister Thomas Wentworth Higginson.[13]

Despite Northern protests, the Compromise Bill passed in Congress. This rocked black America, although no one was surprised when President Millard Fillmore signed it on September 18. Because of the fugitive slave provisions, Douglass aptly dubbed it the Bloodhound Bill. "The night is a dark and stormy one," he wrote; blacks were fearful, dismayed, and utterly disillusioned, and many fled to Canada. Everyone was a potential victim of either kidnapping or re-enslavement, including black America's "pride and hope." Sojourner knew most of these prominent men. Her former Zion pastor, Bishop Christopher Rush, had lived free for thirty-six years. Henry Bibb, a Detroit itinerant preacher and major underground leader, dodged his owner and fled immediately to Canada; Congregational preacher and publisher Samuel Ringgold Ward of Cortland, New York, also went into exile; Jermain Loguen, the intrepid underground superintendent and Zion minister in Ithaca and Syracuse, New York, was "hunted down" and fled to Canada, but he returned and continued the struggle. Self-emancipated blacks visiting Europe, including Henry Garnet, J. W. C. Pennington, and William Wells Brown, were advised to remain abroad. Freeborn intellectual Alexander Crummell was so distraught over the Bloodhound Bill that he demurred about ever returning to America. Henry "Box" Brown fled to England; the Crafts went into hiding separately.[14]

In an exodus of ordinary folk, the black population of some towns was cut in half as domestics, waiters, laborers, and artisans fled under great hardship. Two weeks after the bill's signing, nearly all the waiters (about three hundred) in Pittsburgh hotels had fled to Canada. In Boston, Leonard Grimes's Twelfth-Street Baptist, or "Fugitive Slave," Church lost 60 of its 141 members. Disposing of property at a loss, desperate blacks went "almost penniless and nearly naked" to a climate with winters more severe than they thought possible. Carrying pistols and bowie knives, they pledged to resist reenslavement "even to death."

The devil would "do well to rent out hell and move to the United States," said an armed Cincinnati pastor leaving for Chatham, Ontario. Between September and December, over three thousand black people arrived at St. Catherine's alone. In the ten years after 1850, over twenty thousand people reportedly fled to Canada. The influential young Ohio lawyer John Mercer Langston advocated not Canadian but African emigration for his people.[15]

As every day brought reports of people being snatched, arrested, and placed in irons, black Americans embraced Henry Garnet's 1843 appeal: "Let Your Motto be Resistance." Everyone, whether legally freed or freeborn, was advised to carry a weapon. Pittsburgh's Martin Delaney vowed to transform into "a lifeless corpse" any slaveholder who crossed his threshold. Normally mild-tempered Robert Purvis, president of the Pennsylvania Anti-Slavery Society, forced to destroy his meticulous underground records, "thrilled the whole assembly," Parker Pillsbury reported, "as I never saw it done before." Purvis's eyes flashed as he pledged to shed the blood of "any palefaced specter" attempting to execute the law in his home "though the lives of myself and my family should be sacrificed." Although this Quaker-dominated antislavery society repudiated his militancy, at a mass black protest, wealthy Robert Purvis and others of his class joined freeborn and self-emancipated workingmen in vowing "death" to all invaders of their community. In New York City, blacks of both sexes, all ages, all classes, and all strains of antislavery held an October meeting far beyond Zion's fifteen-hundred-person capacity. Affirming that resistance to tyrants was obedience to God, New Yorkers collected $800 for a man already arrested under the new law. At the Western Anti-Slavery Society meeting in Salem, Ohio, Garrisonian Henry C. Wright called for death to kidnappers. Although many in Ohio worshiped an "almighty slave driver," others, Wright said, urged fleeing bond people to "'Stop here—we will protect you—and you shall be taken back to bonds only over our dead bodies.'"[16]

The Fugitive Slave Law also spurred the emergence of new black women activists. A twenty-seven-year-old schoolteacher named Mary Ann Shadd (Cary) and petite, thirty-year-old, self-emancipated Harriet Tubman emerged almost simultaneously in 1851. Shadd's activist family worked the underground in Delaware and Pennsylvania. As strident and "peculiarly eccentric" as Sojourner Truth, Shadd relocated to Canada and became a speaker, writer, Come-outer, and editor. Uneducated Tubman escaped from Maryland just in time to light up the underground, returning South for her family and others, using Philadelphia and Wilmington as bases. With a price on her head, Tubman made harrowing trips to the South and shepherded her charges all the way to Canada. Frances Ellen Watkins, a modest young freeborn poet who had moved to New England from Maryland, began writing resistance verse and frequenting Abolitionist gatherings.[17]

Truth and Tubman, both slave-born and uneducated, were easily the most visible black women agitators. Both relied on faith, intuition, geographical knowledge, and pragmatism. Like Sojourner, Harriet insisted that "she talked with God, and he talked with her, every day of her life." Her Quaker coadjutor, Thomas Garrett, declared that he never met with anyone who "had more confidence in the voice of God, as spoken to her soul." As chosen instruments of Providence, and under special protection, Truth and Tubman went wherever God sent them. Harriet preferred direct action, but occasionally made impressive speeches. Sojourner was a mobilizer via the public stage, but said she also worked the underground. Some writers dispute this, since William Still did not mention Sojourner in his monumental volume. However, Still omitted many important underground workers, reportedly for personal reasons. Given Sojourner Truth's own statements, and close association with major national underground leaders, local agents, and station keepers ("break men"), there is no reason to doubt her veracity about being a conductor.[18]

Sojourner's close friendship with Lewis Hayden, a self-emancipated Kentuckian, also ties her to the underground. The "Great Compromiser," Henry Clay, owned Hayden's first wife and child and sold them "down the river." Hayden remarried and escaped to Canada in 1844 with his family, through the ingenuity of two white Abolitionists. Calvin Fairbank, a New York Methodist minister and Oberlin graduate, and Delia Webster, a Vermont schoolteacher, were both caught and imprisoned. Webster was eventually pardoned, but Fairbank was sentenced to fifteen years in prison. Hayden soon returned to America and settled in Boston. As a celebrated, gritty leader, he was Garrison's "staunchest ally" and black Boston's "tavern of strength." His residence on Beacon Hill (then called "Nigger Hill") had a secret entrance leading to a tunnel. In 1853, when Harriet Beecher Stowe sought witnesses for her "Key to Uncle Tom's Cabin," Abolitionists took her to Hayden's home. "Thirteen newly-escaped slaves of all colors and sizes were brought into the room for her to see."[19]

Truth and Hayden shared Abolitionist sentiments and the platform, but he was not a pacifist or strictly a Garrisonian. Swearing to blow up his family rather than surrender to slavery, he kept two kegs of gunpowder ready. Yet his home, called the temple of refuge and citadel of liberty, was a gathering center for humble and middle-class black and white Abolitionists. The arrival of British Abolitionist George Thompson coincided with the appearance of Georgia slave catchers hunting the Crafts. At Belknap Church, Lewis Hayden, William C. Nell, and Charles Remond angrily threatened the "human bloodhounds." Late that night, Garrison and Thompson went to Hayden's home, where Ellen Craft was hidden. Thompson observed that the double locked doors were also barred, and windows barricaded. Hayden, his young son, and others sat around a table covered with loaded weapons. Nearby stood "a band of brave colored men armed to the teeth and ready for the impending death struggle with the United States Marshall and his armed posse."[20]

Late in 1850, Hayden secured Calvin Fairbank's release by raising $650, and he headed east in time to witness two unforgettable events. In Cazenovia, New York, Fairbank, a New Yorker, observed the "most exciting, instructive convention of my life." Abolitionists Gerrit Smith, Douglass, May, Loguen, and others dubbed their gathering a "Fugitive Slave Convention" and challenged the new law by sitting on the platform with self-emancipated people. Later, in Boston, Fairbank was Hayden's houseguest and observed the "most memorable of all the great lights of the time." On November 6, the Vigilance Committee prepared for a confrontation with slave catchers seeking the Crafts. Sojourner, staying with the Garrisons, was most likely among the crowd of noisy, passionate, and angry black women and men in Hayden's home that evening. Executive Committee member Hayden, a "born leader of men," issued an eloquent call to arms as his black base answered in call-and-response style. While he was lost in the urgency of his appeal, his eyes flicked past the sea of familiar black faces and rested on a far corner of the room, where he noticed for the first time Wendell Phillips, Garrison, Ralph Waldo Emerson, Senators Charles Sumner and Henry Wilson, and Unitarian minister Theodore Parker. Startled, perhaps doubting his own oratory ability compared to "those noble men, embodying the lore and wisdom of the Bay State," Hayden "sank into his seat abashed and silent," according to Fairbank. But his message resonated with his people, and with Wendell Phillips. Other white leaders proposed a different course, to which the assembly finally consented, and then raised a large sum of money for the Crafts. The next morning, Fairbank recorded, Theodore Parker remarried the couple as free people in Hayden's home. Parker handed William Craft a Bible. "Make it the man of your counsel," he advised. He then gave Craft a "poniard of fearful length and proportions, and holding it by the shining blade, extending to him the hilt, said: 'Take this and defend your wife.'" The Crafts left for England via Canada. Fairbank met Sojourner Truth in Boston and was exceedingly impressed with her "practical wisdom." He briefly became her Northampton neighbor, but returned to his underground work, and eventually was again imprisoned.[21]

After the Crafts' departure, representatives from all over the nation gathered in Rhode Island for the first annual antislavery convention since the Bloodhound Bill had become law. The secretary called this highly charged state convention the most interesting and effective anniversary they had ever held. Sojourner, the first speaker, said that because she had been a bond slave once, the Bloodhound Bill meant that she was "not now entirely free." Prospects for black emancipation seemed to be at rock bottom, forcing crisis and confrontation. But at least evil was shorn of its cover, and she predicted eventual victory. She "thanked God that the law was made—that the worst had come to worst; now the best must come to best." She argued that blacks should stay in America. Former Oberlin president Asa Mahan agreed that the Bloodhound Bill had accomplished "great good" in Ohio by creating great agitation. The Executive Committee also urged blacks to remain and struggle peacefully, and whites resolved to disobey unjust laws that interfered with duty to heaven and humanity. Henry Bibb, returned secretly from exile, reported on a desperate situation at Sandwich (now Windsor), Ontario, on the Canadian side of the Detroit River, where between fifteen and seventeen people were arriving daily. Douglass and Charles Remond applauded white willingness to put their own lives and property at risk. But ultimately, black people paid the price, and black leaders needed more flexibility than whites in responding to the Bloodhound Bill. Some causes were worth dying for, Douglass said, and "freedom" was one. The patriots of the American Revolution had proclaimed, "Tyrants and despots have no right to live," he said. "Slaveholders, being such, have no right to live." Remond agreed. It was the black man's only resort. Sojourner and other participants debated, without resolution, on peaceful versus forcible resistance.[22]

What with the sea of slave catchers, New England's heightened alert, and black promises to meet all recapture attempts with bloodshed, Sojourner kept a busy pace. In early December, Plymouth's Old Colony Anti-Slavery Society celebrated the two-hundred-thirtieth anniversary of the Pilgrims' landing. Truth, Thompson, Douglass, Garrison, Phillips, the Fosters, and C. C. Burleigh spoke to overwhelming numbers crammed in a spacious church; people eagerly sat through six long meetings over two days. The speakers' eloquence was unequaled, a Boston reporter observed, noting the "capital hits" of Sojourner Truth, "a colored woman, formerly a slave, and now a resident of Northampton Community." Antoinette Brown, a recent graduate of Oberlin's theology school, wrote to Lucy Stone that Sojourner would be speaking in Fry Village, outside Andover, that December. Although Antoinette went to Emerson's Lyceum lecture instead, Sojourner told the young minister that her lecture had been well attended and she had sold many books. It was a "blessed meeting, a blessed meeting," she insisted. Her other end-of-the year engagements included appearances in Dover, New Hampshire; Fall River, Massachusetts; Woonsocket and Valley Falls, Rhode Island. In true Garrisonian fashion, she condemned the churches' role in slavery, but then requested access to "God's house." She was rarely successful, even though by 1845, Southern denominations had seceded from national bodies. Northern churches' disdain for antislavery led fifteen thousand Methodists to establish an antislavery Wesleyan Connection. Yet Sojourner maintained friendships with Abolitionists still within the regular denomination, and always considered herself a Methodist.[23]

During this period of escalated black protest, a national woman's convention was organized. For Sojourner Truth, combining race and gender was consistent with her lived experience, and her speeches often reflected this duality. At the July Fourth commemoration in Abington, she linked white and black women's maternal sentiments. "Do not white women . . . love their infants?" she asked. "Are not we colored women human?" Black women had the same feelings as whites, she asserted. "We suffer as much when our little ones are torn from us, as you white mothers do." Like Sojourner Truth, Abby Kelley Foster consistently emphasized the plight of enslaved women, and believed that confirming universal female sensibilities was a major step in promoting antislavery. Newly appointed agent Lucy Stone lectured so much on women's issues that general agent Samuel May objected. "I was a woman before I was an Abolitionist," Stone protested. "I must speak for the women." She finally agreed to address woman's rights on weekdays and antislavery on weekends.[24]

Although a number of previous regional women's meetings had occurred, including the one at Seneca Falls, New York, in 1848, the call for a national convention arose in 1850, immediately after the NEASS convention. Nonliterate Sojourner Truth could not sign the endorsement, but other black women were among the one hundred plus signers. The National Woman's Convention was set for October 26–27 in Worcester. New Englanders, then, actually laid the groundwork for a radical woman's movement, although Worcester participants such as Lucretia Mott had also been at Seneca Falls. Yet this national call was the first time black women participated in a woman's convention. Some women showed their independence by appearing in the bloomer dress, a knee-length skirt with ankle-length pantaloons. Reportedly, Elizabeth Smith Miller first wore the "shocking" outfit in 1848. By 1850, daring woman were appearing in bloomer dress at conventions and private parties. For white, but not black, women, dress reform became a political statement and shock tactic. And while "several dark colored sisters" sat on the Worcester platform, Sojourner Truth was the only one of them who addressed the convention.[25]

She and other speakers were already seated when Douglass arrived and was immediately ushered to the platform amid loud applause. Truth and Douglass had spent much time together that fall, condemning the Bloodhound Bill from the same platform. Before taking his seat, Douglass hurried over to her and grasped her hands—as if to recognize that their common bond, race and slavery, was far more urgent than woman's rights, but that the Worcester Convention highlighted connections between both reforms.[26] White male Abolitionists did not let the audience forget the Bloodhound Bill, while Douglass and Truth made sure that convention resolutions recognized black women.

The sessions were so crowded that every seat, the aisles, and all spaces around the platform were taken. Presiding officer Paulina Wright Davis, a recognized female physiologist, spoke on the wrongs and rights of women. Next, refined radical socialist Ernestine (Potowski) Rose, according to the *Herald* an attractive, dark-haired Polish Jew with a thick accent, issued a call for women's political, legal, and social equality. This irritated some male clerics who opposed woman's suffrage. But Lucretia Mott agreed, and wanted a resolution affirming woman's freedom and independence in all areas, as a "yielded" not a bestowed right. Rather than men *"giving"* and *"permitting"* rights, women were *"demanding* them in the name of our common humanity."[27]

The *Herald* sneered at all the conveners as socialists and infidels, and was noticeably harsher toward older women. Fifty-seven-year-old Lucretia Mott, the most influential woman present, was all "bone, gristle, and resolution." This "great Ajax of the sisterhood," the *Herald* wrote, had a countenance of "hard iron" and a will as indomitable as Caesar. Mott had criticized Davis's opening address as a tepid "milk and water policy of action." Mott advocated the Garrisonian example—speaking truth plainly, regardless of the consequences. Certainly the two women's politics also influenced the *Herald*'s disparate portrayals of them. The reporter said thirty-seven-year-old Paulina Davis was tall and handsome, with blue eyes, a fair complexion, and ringlets. She wore a "very amiable expression." Mott, a veteran activist and social critic, insightfully analyzed how the *Herald*'s reports mirrored society's treatment of older women. Once youth and outward semblance faded, a woman had nothing in her favor. "An old woman is simply an object of ridicule, and anything that is ridiculous or foolish is said to be only fit for an old woman." Society, "in no respect," recognized the rights of women, Mott said. Hence, women should set their own standards.[28]

When the debates again shifted to equal rights, Ernestine Rose blamed women for complicity in their oppression, because they "play the puppet in the parlor, or the drudge in the kitchen." Mott's hard-hitting response connected female oppression to black slavery:

> Mrs. Rose has made a better apology for man than he could make for himself. (Laughter) Woman is crushed, but nobody is to blame; it is circumstances that have crushed her. So of the poor slave. He is crushed, but nobody has crushed him. It just happened so. (Laughter) It is an abstract evil, that's all. When we begin to denounce the slaveholder as a man-stealer, all scripture had to be searched before people would believe it. . . . Men are cunning and crafty. . . . It was the agitation of the slavery question that had shaken the capitol to its foundations, and that was the cause of the good fruit it will bring forth, in the liberation of the Southern slave. (Applause)[29]

These floor debates helped the Businesses Committee craft resolutions, and Sojourner Truth's inability to serve in such capacities exemplifies how nonliteracy impeded her role as a policy maker. Yet her deficiency also rendered her verbal persuasion and experiential wisdom all the more significant, because she influenced resolutions from the platform. As the slavery of sex dominated convention rhetoric, Abby Kelley Foster compared an enslaved man with a woman bound to "her husband, her lord and master." Douglass reminded the debaters that women and the enslaved both wanted the tyrant to take his foot off of their necks, let them get up, and elevate themselves. Amid much naming of woman's wrongs, rights, duties, and comparisons with slavery, no one mentioned black women in the record until Sojourner spoke. On the first day, from her seat, she urged that black women, the real slaves, not be forgotten.[30]

On the second day, the three women preachers—Sojourner Truth, Lucretia Mott, and Antoinette Brown—engaged the issues of scriptural authority and the Bible's divinity. Sojourner believed that "the Spirit of Truth spoke" through the Bible, but "the recorders of those truths had intermingled with them ideas and suppositions of their own." Similarly, Brown challenged Paul's edicts against women, and she condemned biblical interpretations that victimized women as evil. She quoted passages of Scripture to prove that women had been teachers and speakers in biblical times. Mott elaborated that Paul's injunctions against women applied only to situations in certain churches of his historical time. She further suggested that perhaps Paul and other apostles had "imbibed some of the spirit and ignorance of their age" on the subject of women, and she questioned whether he was a competent authority, since he never married.[31] In essence, the women challenged the Bible's divinity, since certain portions were heavily chauvinist.

Sojourner Truth, Stephen Foster, and Wendell Phillips led discussions on enslaved women. Foster objected to Mott's urging women to avoid weapons in obtaining their rights. The million and a half enslaved women, living "in a condition which makes us shudder to think of," had a right to use the sword, he said. And no one should tie their hands in that freedom struggle. It was also Foster who called for a motion to put Douglass on the Business Committee (which drafted resolutions), after it was formed without any black representation. Wendell Phillips called for the Business Committee to draft a resolution on slave women. As Sojourner Truth spoke for all black women, the *Herald* ridiculed her as it had "Generalissimo" Mott. But the paper also gave insights into Sojourner's remarks:

> Mrs. Sojourner Truth (a lady of color, doubtless of New England origin from the Puritanical title she has the honor to bear) next came forward. And why not? In a convention where sex and color are mingled together in the common rights of humanity, Dinah, and Burleigh and Lucretia, and Frederick Douglas, are all

spiritually of one color and one sex, and all on a perfect footing of reciprocity. Most assuredly Dinah was well posted up on the rights of woman, and with something of the ardor and the odor of her native Africa, she contended for her right to vote to hold office, to practice medicine and the law, and wear the breeches with the best white man that walks upon the earth.[32]

The *Tribune* provided a more respectful sense of Sojourner's remarks. Horace Greeley, a "Conscious Whig" and reformer, scrutinized everything printed in his newspaper.[33] He certainly knew that Sojourner Truth had been Isabella Van Wagenen. During the Matthias scandal, Greeley had been a struggling young printer working for William Leete Stone's *Commercial Advertiser*. He began the *Tribune* in 1841; by 1850, it was the most important newspaper in the North, and Greeley was a major political power broker who corresponded with Garrison and James Yerrinton, Sojourner's publisher. Sojourner's native New York and Dutch cultural background were unusual and made good newspaper copy. While the *Tribune* reporter did not suppress his racism, he nonetheless documents her expanding reputation and reveals her repertoire of commentary on woman's rights: "Sojourner Truth, a colored woman, once a slave, spoke, and gratified the audience highly. She showed that beneath her dark skin, and uncomely exterior, there was a true, womanly heart. She uttered some truths that told well. She said woman set the world wrong by eating the forbidden fruit, and now she was going to set it right. She said Goodness never had any beginning, it was from everlasting, and could never die. But Evil had a beginning, and must have an end. She expressed great reverence for God, and faith that He will bring about His own purposes and plans."[34]

Sojourner's remarks in Worcester resembled the famous speech she delivered the following spring in Akron, Ohio. She spoke of her rights as a woman who worked like a man, of woman's capacity both to upset the world and correct it, and her trust in God's plan. She offered original interpretations of woman's status from Scripture, to "great applause." She so stirred the two other women preachers that in the final session they embraced her remarks. Brown, still chafing from the refusal of Oberlin president Charles Finney to ordain her, quoted biblical passages upholding a woman's right to teach and preach. Mott, speaking on female spiritual authority in the Pentecostal tradition, reminded the audience that women preached the gospel during Christianity's early days. She quoted a passage familiar to Pinkster observer Sojourner Truth: "'I will pour out my spirit upon all flesh, and your sons and daughters shall prophesy.'" A prophet or a prophetess was also a teacher, she insisted. She cited several more passages that supported woman's equality and the ministry of Antoinette Brown, Sojourner Truth and herself.[35]

Mott's parting admonition to the audience was to heed "the simple and truthful words of Sojourner Truth," rich with optimism and faith in the ultimate victory of right. Offering a "most affectionate valedictory" to a full assembly and many outside, she paraphrased Sojourner. Mountains of difficulties stood in woman's path. But in the end they would triumph because the true tenor, spirit, and teachings of Christianity all favored woman's rights. Mott also chose a favorite Sojourner Truth expression for the benediction: "'And now Lord, let thy servants depart in peace; for our eyes have seen thy salvation.'" Black women such as Sojourner had borne much, but retained a spirited faith. "Are ye able to bear all of this?" Mott asked her female associates.[36] Only the test of time would tell.

With Sojourner Truth exerting pressure from the platform and Douglass on the Business Committee, the final resolutions included enslaved women. The convention resolved that among women, those in bondage were "the most grossly wronged of all." Wendell Phillips wrote the "color" resolution that was unanimously adopted: "Resolved, That the cause we are met to advocate, the claims for Woman of all her natural and civil rights, binds us to remember the million and a half wronged and foully outraged, of all Women; and in every effort for an improvement of our civilization, we will bear, in our heart of hearts, the memory of trampled womanhood of the plantation, and omit no effort to raise it to a share in the rights we claim for ourselves."[37] The convention had been a "great success," William C. Nell and Douglass wrote to Amy Post. Indeed, events had transpired so rapidly, they were "beyond description." Neither man commented on Sojourner Truth's role in the convention's success in terms of including black women, yet both were well aware of it. Neither Sojourner Truth nor Douglass attended the 1851 national woman's meeting, which a disappointed Abby Kelley Foster likened more to a fashion parade than a radical woman's movement.[38] The movement would grow increasingly conservative.

Assaults on Abolitionists, passage of the Bloodhound Bill, commitment to the underground, and the creation of a national woman's organization all revitalized the struggle to reform America. Although the Garrisonians seemed united, ideological undercurrents soon troubled the waters. But Sojourner Truth's reputation and public image was growing. The preacher, reformer, teacher, and traveling Abolitionist was now an author, who could speak from her own authenticated source. Carrying a carpetbag of books, possessing unqualified faith and commitment to social justice, and gifted with amazing oratory, the African Dutch mystic eagerly embraced a quickened pace of life.

I heard the voice of the Lord saying, whom shall I send, and who will go for us? Then said I, Here *am* I; send me. . . . Go and tell this people, Hear ye indeed, but understand not; and see ye indeed, but perceive not.
— ISAIAH 6:8–9

She possesses a mind of rare power, and often, in the course of her short speeches, will throw out gems of thought. But the truly Christian spirit which pervades all she says, endears her to all who know her.
— GEORGE PUTNAM (ROCHESTER, NEW YORK, 1851)

CHAPTER 13

The New York Campaign

I

In February 1851, Sojourner Truth prepared to join the campaign through central and western New York. "I am going with George Thompson on a lecturing tour," Garrison had told her. "Come with us and you will have a good chance to dispose of your book." The AASS would cover her expenses. Although now a traveling Abolitionist, she lived on her own resources. Samuel Hill was patient about her mortgage, but she was anxious about her printing expenses. "I had been publishing my *Narrative*," she recalled, "and owed for the whole edition, a great debt to me! Every cent I could obtain went to pay for it." She was to join the traveling group in Springfield. However, Garrison became gravely ill, and a surprised Sojourner found George Thompson alone at Springfield's Hampden Hotel. A man of working-class origins, Thompson also lived off his own resources. Nevertheless, he said, "'I'll bear your expenses Sojourner. Come with us.'"[1]

Conservative Springfield had a New Org antislavery society, a Garrisonian presence, and a cluster of black activists tied closely to the wool merchant John Brown. He had resided there until 1849, and in his home, a gathering place for black leaders far and wide, had shared his ideas about setting up a provisional black state in the Allegheny Mountains. He certainly had encountered Sojourner's familiar face among Springfield activists, even before he stopped at Ruggles's water cure. Brown had attended the Zion Church she helped organize, and frequented Garrisonian conventions where she spoke. Springfield was a major underground point in the Connecticut River valley network, and Brown's warehouse sheltered many freedom seekers. He closed his wool business in early 1851, though, and joined a group of black men and women who set up an armed protective organization called the League of Gileadites. Brown was still in Springfield when Sojourner arrived.[2] One of the Springfield leaders was Sojourner's friend John Mars, the popular Zion preacher.

The Springfield town fathers considered George Thompson a catalyst for violence. During Thompson's 1835 tour, he had had so many threats on his life that he had gone into hiding, shortened his planned one-year stay, and left America secretly. Yet that tour had been a major success, leading to the formation of hundreds of antislavery societies. He was now a member of Parliament and an international social justice advocate; his activism included condemning imperial oppression of all colored people, the Irish, and working-class Britons. Though this second tour had been arranged long before the Bloodhound Bill was passed, Thompson's presence placed a timely emphasis on the urgency of abolition.[3]

Sojourner Truth had lectured with Thompson that fall, and considered him a true friend of the oppressed. She was on the platform at his giant Faneuil Hall welcome reception when, just as Garrison assured the audience that "the Boston of 1850 was not the Boston of 1835," a disruptive mob took over. She had then joined Thompson, Douglass, and others on the platform at black Belknap Street Church, where they were undisturbed. She and Thompson had both spoken at Tremont Temple and in New England farming communities. He was reportedly a sensational orator who possessed "brilliancy, versatility, and captivating power." Gracious and popular with women, he treated Sojourner Truth with courtesy and cordiality, "as if I had been the highest lady in the land." She recalled that he insisted that she sit next to him at meals, accompanied her to the rail cars, carried her bag, "and never seemed to know that I was poor and a black woman."[4]

Prior to Springfield, in Worcester, Thompson had received royal treatment from the mayor and aldermen and lectured at City Hall. But in Springfield, his last New England stop, anti-Abolitionists mounted a protest. "Are you going to allow an English Serf to come among you and create a civil war?" the *Springfield Daily Republican* advertised. "Fellow citizens, be at your posts at Hampden Hall at 6 o'clock on Monday, Tuesday and Thursday Evenings." Effigies soon appeared, and citizens pasted death warrants on tree trunks. After pumping up the community against Thompson, the *Springfield Daily Republican* beat a hasty retreat, proclaiming that empty seats and bare walls were more effective "than a thousand yelling, screeching, hissing, hooting enemies." The owner of Hampden Hall locked out the Abolitionists, while a local delegation named the "Terrifying Committee" visited Thompson and urged him to leave. The evening of Sojourner's arrival, over two hundred men fortified with alcohol circled the Abolitionists' hotel and made a scene with firecrackers, tar barrels, bonfires, drums, fifes, bells, and shouts. They built one fire near the hotel; then, around a bigger "patriotic fire" in the center of the square, they performed a "war dance" into the night.[5]

Sojourner had confronted Springfield rowdies at least once before; in 1848 she, Lucy Stone, the Fosters, and others had faced down a disruptive, angry crowd. The Abolitionists' treatment, the *Springfield Daily Republican* had noted, was so slanderous, disgraceful, and disreputable that it was beyond description. The interracial quality of Abolitionist meetings, the novelty of a black woman on the platform, and the drunken excitement all spelled personal danger. And in 1851, the *Springfield Daily Republican* predicted a serious disturbance if Thompson and his friends spoke. The rowdies, the paper claimed, were the mere instruments of the influential, respectable citizens who fanned the excitement, planned the disruptions, and inflamed passions. When Wendell Phillips, Edmund Quincy, and others arrived the next morning, Thompson and his group were preparing to leave the town. But the Bostonians and local black activists strongly opposed abandoning the meetings. Leaders from the League of Gileadites secured a small meeting place near their Zion Church. The forenoon meeting was not advertised, the sheriff attended to preserve order, and the Gileadites were also armed. The small audience consisted of two hundred faithful blacks and a few white "women and children."[6] Apparently Sojourner did not speak in this charged atmosphere.

The afternoon meeting in Zion Church attracted a larger, "more respectable" (i.e., more white) audience, including a sizable number of women. Again, only the male Abolitionists spoke, and they vehemently attacked the press, the clergy, and the Whigs as instigators of violence. They heralded events in Boston, where Abolitionists had successfully removed from police custody a self-emancipated waiter named Frederick ("Shadrach") Wilkins. Although Lewis Hayden and others were on trial, Quincy boasted, "no fugitive slave had been sent back from New England." Springfield anti-Abolitionists discovered the meeting, and an evening session in the black community was deemed too risky. The "convention" therefore adjourned.[7]

As news of the two meetings spread, indignation against Thompson and his associates escalated. That evening, an even larger drunken horde gathered around the Abolitionists' hotel, hung an effigy of Thompson, and howled beneath the guests' windows. Rotten eggs, rocks, and "other missiles" sailed through glass windows and curtains. The Abolitionists were trapped inside, but the sympathetic hotel proprietors "protected the party from insult within the house." Although local newspapers blamed the "shameful outrage" on the Irish, *Liberator* correspondent George Putnam disagreed. Standing anonymously within the crowd, he saw no more than twenty Irishmen. "The work was done by Yankee voters, led by the editors and their Hunker friends," he insisted. Finally, the rioters disbanded. At midnight, Springfield blacks appeared outside the hotel, and a group of them serenaded the Abolitionists with instruments and vocal music.[8]

Sojourner Truth, Anne Phillips, and another Boston female Abolitionist present during these incursions were not mentioned by name. Even Putnam's *Liberator* accounts emphasized only that Abolitionists were subjected to shameful treatment. Writing to Anne Weston, Thompson cavalierly treated the entire event as an impromptu farce. The "effigy, tar barrels, band, broken windows; &c &c [added to] our merriment," he said, and mimicked the tormentors. He was more serious in writing to Kelley Foster however. One wonders if the Abolitionist press's silence about Sojourner's presence was symbolic of her invisibility or was a form of protection, since no women were mentioned. In any case, early the next morning, the out-of-towners left Springfield. The Bostonians returned east; Thompson sent Putnam to buy three tickets to Albany for himself, Thompson, and Sojourner.[9]

II

When their train reached Troy, New York, a grim-looking Quaker boarded and, expecting the *Liberator* editor, walked through the cars loudly calling for "William Lloyd Garrison." Thirty miles and eight hours later, the travelers arrived by wagon at Schagticoke-on-the Hudson in Rensselaer County. "Oh that ride!" Thompson wrote. "Heaven preserve me from another such." But they had a restful night at a nice hotel, and two white men traveling with a black woman posed no problem to the management. However, the next morning, citizens lined the hotel piazza and stared at the threesome with curiosity and consternation. Traveling twelve miles by wagon to Union Village, Thompson was struck by the Hudson Valley's beauty, even in snowy midwinter. They met the Fosters for a two-day convention. News about Springfield had preceded them. Thompson's treatment had evoked international attention and national embarrassment. European presses had labeled the American republic barbarous and savage; from Sunday pulpits, American ministers lamented that some mob perpetrators were clergy. In Brooklyn, New York, Henry Ward Beecher, pastor of Plymouth Congregational Church, preached a scathing sermon against the Springfield mob, slavery, and the Fugitive Slave Law. No one mentioned the black woman traveling with the member of Parliament.[10]

Even after 1850, the descendants of the "Holland-Dutch" in Sojourner's native region were proslavery, and considered "slow and conservative." Privately assertive Dutch women were especially scandalized and shocked by Abby Kelley Foster, who not only led public discussions but was "able and fearless" in critiquing men. Women greeted her with "icy coldness," while men broke up her meetings and shelled her with "unmerchantable" eggs. Going into the Hudson Valley, she said, was like "going into the arctic circle to sow wheat."[11]

But she and Stephen had long-standing friendships within Quaker communities in the Hudson and Mohawk valleys. At Union Village, antislavery converts greeted them heartily, proudly showing their newest family additions. Speeches by the satirical British minister, the Fosters, and the "quaint" Sojourner Truth assuaged local disappointment over Garrison's absence. In a spirit of harmony, astutely political antislavery citizens listened and debated various issues such as disunion and anticlericism. Afterward, people served delicious foods, and Thompson regaled the assembly with his chilling but humorous account of the Springfield mobs. Then Abby introduced "the aged Sojourner Truth," who spoke "in her peculiar manner" about her own bondage experiences in that very region. The audience "received her with great interest," Putnam noted. Afterward, they "pressed around her to purchase her books" and hear her antislavery melodies. She was "proof of the natural equality (to say the least) of the Negro and white," Putnam said. Indeed, he "devoutly . . . wished, that all whites *were* her equal."[12]

Sojourner met a nineteen-year-old Quaker named Aaron Powell who was attending his first antislavery convention, against the wishes of his father, a "proslavery" Democrat. The year before, Aaron's father had debated Stephen Foster; believing that Foster had won the argument, Aaron had begun subscribing to antislavery newspapers. Sojourner changed the young college student's life when she "laid hands" on him at the convention. While he was in earnest conversation with a group of friends during intermission, "Sojourner Truth, who had been standing alone by the pulpit, came slowly down the aisle." Midway in the church, she reached out her "long, bony arm, placed her big black hand on my head, saying as she did so, with prophetic tone, in her peculiar dialect, 'I'se been a lookin' into your face, and I sees you, in the futur,' pleadin' our cause!'" He soon became an antislavery agent and devoted his entire life to activism. Crediting his calling to this "Mother in Israel," he also became one of her closest younger friends. Throughout the years, he wrote, "I was frequently reminded of Sojourner's prophecy."[13]

The traveling Abolitionists, a motley, unconventional, slightly bohemian quintet, contrasted strikingly with local rural folk. The two women had confident regal bearing and strong faces. Sojourner Truth, taller than the average man, was angular and muscular. Underneath a bonnet, she wore a colored scarf tied in back, dark traveling clothes, and heavy shoes. She was now about fifty-three; her smooth, dark, blemish-free skin showed that she was more ageless than "aged," as the press described her. Forty-year-old Abby Kelley Foster was tall for a woman, slender, and attractive, with black hair pulled into a simple bun away from her sunburned face. She was considered immodest because she never covered her head or buttoned down the top of her Quaker collar as was customary. Foster and Putnam were plainly dressed and bespectacled; Foster sported unfashionable whiskers. In contrast, Thompson, who thought himself quite handsome, wore natty, somewhat foppish outfits. "Behold us in our triumphant car," he wrote, "boxes, bags, buffaloes,[sic] broad-brim and narrow-brims." They battled poor weather, and primitive road conditions, and exhaustion, but remained on schedule. In the "pleasant and scenic" Mohawk River valley, they covered an amazing 120 miles in one day, including eight hours in a closely packed stagecoach. Sojourner's health was normally precarious in the winter months, but she kept pace with her younger companions.[14]

Moving into central New York, they encountered "local prejudice," horrible weather, and mixed successes. Although the manufacturing town of Little Falls was considered proslavery, the Abolitionists secured a building with a capacity of five hundred, which "instantly filled with a fine audience though an admission fee was required." Sojourner and Abby took the platform in the forenoon while Thompson rested. Sojourner's book sold well that afternoon, and she spoke again in the evening. Next morning, it took five hours to go 16 miles by carriage to West Winfield. Traveling in a dangerous, hard-driving rain, the drenched companions remained cheerful—diverting their minds with anecdotes and enjoying the picturesque countryside—"the finest scenery I have yet looked upon in the United States," Thompson wrote. A supportive assembly crowded into the West Winfield Baptist Church. In East Winfield the next day, a larger but less harmonious audience greeted the lecturers. The program began as scripted—emotional singing of the famous "Bloodhound's Bray," passing resolutions against the Fugitive Slave Law, and supporting the underground. But the "true hearted" East Winfield Abolitionists, greatly influenced by Liberty Party and Free Soil man Gerrit Smith, advocated "voting down" slavery through the electoral process, something Garrisonians rejected because politicians were considered corrupt. While they supported antislavery presses and admired Garrison, the divisions and tensions among them would later erupt at the annual meeting.[15]

After three more conventions in Herkimer County, the Abolitionists continued into the heart of the Burned-over District. Once the center of the Iroquois Confederation's vast homeland, the "Finger Lakes" region, so named because the lakes resembled the fingers of a hand, still bore Native American names—Canandaigua, Cayuga, Keuka, Owasco, Seneca, and Skaneateles. Syracuse, the largest manufacturing town, was also the home of the two most valiant central New York Abolitionists, Samuel May and Jermain Loguen. The region was overwhelmingly proslavery Democrat and colonizationist. Nonetheless, blacks, Quakers, political Abolitionists, and other reformers made the mysterious "underground" a watchword. Their "trackless road" of secret tunnels, cellars, covered wagons, and waterways was one of the most shrewdly organized and well-chartered cloak-and-dagger thoroughfares of the North. After clearing the Susquehanna Valley, passengers found several routes to freedom. Some journeyed 25 miles to Ithaca, "the chief Underground Railroad in the county." Here the main stationmasters were members of Zion (St. James) Church, once Loguen's pastorate. The local blacks, led by George Johnson, often worked with sympathetic whites hiding people until the steamboat *Simeon DeWitt* could take them up Cayuga Lake (northwest) as far as Geneva, New York. Others in flight from Ithaca traveled due north to Auburn on Lake Owasco, en route to Syracuse, central New York's main hub. There, Loguen and May either spirited them north to Canada via Oswego, on Lake Ontario, or west to Rochester. A more directly northwestern passage was through Watkins Glen on Lake Seneca, then straight to Buffalo and Canada. Less-traveled clandestine safe havens included tiny hamlets, such as Sherwood, that had engaged in the underground business for decades.[16]

Sojourner Truth's new central New York associates included these black and white underground supporters. She met rural blacks in small farming settlements called "New Africa" and "New Liberia" whose local support for abolition went largely unnoticed but whose zeal attracted Douglass to the region. At agricultural fairs, black women sold produce and homemade artifacts to support the black press and the underground. Blacks bore the brunt of the danger and the expense in underground work. Since men were often away, women carried out the daily labors related to "the business." The women in Loguen's family once fought off slave catchers by themselves. Harriet Tubman, who settled in Auburn, sometimes operated out of Ithaca's Zion Church, and like Harriet, some fleeing Southern blacks also settled in central New York towns. Besides meeting local folk, Sojourner knew the black leaders, Douglass, Samuel Ringgold Ward, Loguen, and others who made solitary dangerous jaunts through the proslavery Adirondacks and Catskills.[17]

Gerrit Smith, New York's richest Abolitionist, sent a three-seated wagon for the five travelers; after seven hours of bad roads, they reached his mansion in Peterboro. Smith had prepared a "most hospitable" reception for the exhausted group. He was a wealthy Livingston on his mother's side; his Dutch father had amassed a fortune in partnership with John Jacob Astor; and his Southern wife, also an unlikely Abolitionist, was Ann Fitzhugh, kinswoman to Robert E. Lee and to proslavery apologist George Fitzhugh. A mobbing in Utica, New York, that involved Ruggles and others in 1835 transformed Gerrit Smith. Henry Garnet called this philanthropist "the unflinching friend of my people." Smith knew of Sojourner through his daughter, Ann Smith Miller, a noted woman's activist who popularized the "bloomer costume"; she had met Sojourner at the

Worcester Woman's Convention. Reform interests sealed Sojourner and the Smiths' friendship: abolition, woman's rights, temperance, water cure, perfection, and the much-discussed Spiritualist movement. Smith and Truth were also the same age. Although she chose moral suasion while Smith used politics and later armed resistance, the difference in their approaches did not mitigate their antislavery alliance and lifelong friendship.[18]

Although harsh weather made road conditions extremely hazardous, "wagons and sleighs from the country" poured into the village near Smith's home, and twelve hundred people filled the spacious Presbyterian Church. Thompson was the major attraction, while Douglass, the Fosters, and Truth added their powerful and persuasive voices. In Syracuse, May and Loguen assembled the largest audience thus far, consisting mostly of blacks. Thompson introduced Sojourner, urged the audience to listen to her story and buy her *Narrative*. She spoke on how slavery destroyed the lives of both whites and blacks.[19]

Continuing through the region called the "psychic highway," because it was home to Spiritualism and religious revivals, in Auburn, the travelers enjoyed the hospitality of prominent lawyer David Wright and his wife, Martha Coffin Wright (Lucretia Mott's sister), whose home was an underground center. The Auburn audiences even surpassed Syracuse. Indeed, the Abolitionists wrote, all the central New York meetings were "beyond the most sanguine expectations." The crowds were rousing and the receptions "glorious," and the campaign was declared a "brilliant success." Even Syracuse's conservative *Daily Standard* admitted that the Abolitionists received overwhelming "marks of approval" from zealous, overflowing audiences. But the paper said the speeches were too spirited, too provoking, too inflammatory, and marked with "intemperance of language or extreme ultraism of sentiment."[20]

Sojourner Truth was just a few miles from John Dumont's residence in Scipio, and her presence in this largely Quaker neighborhood could not have escaped his knowledge. The Dumonts knew about her *Narrative*, but they would have been surprised to learn that their former bondwoman was traveling with a British MP and sharing the platform with one of the wealthiest men in the state. Yet she had nursed the younger Dumont children, befriended the older ones, and once had high regard for her former owner, now in reduced circumstances. She sometimes expressed concern for slaveholders, who bore on their souls the weight of a great sin. Her home, she said, was open to the man who enslaved and wronged her. She would feed him and care for him if he were hungry and poor. "Oh Friends," she said in Syracuse and in Rochester, "pity the poor slaveholder, and pray for him . . . in all his guilt and all his impenitence." Where, she pondered, "will the slaveholder be when eternity begin?"[21]

While Sojourner Truth preached moral forbearance, Douglass grew more political and militant. "I have about decided to let slaveholders and their Northern abettors have the laboring oar in putting a proslavery interpretation upon the Constitution," he wrote to a greatly pleased Gerrit Smith. Disunionists were correct about the "intentions of the framers," Douglass insisted. However, "legal rules of interpretation override all speculations as to the opinions of the Constitution makers." He said nothing publicly during the western campaign, but seemed "depressed," and spoke privately of his new position to Stephen Foster and Samuel May.[22] Sojourner, like her associates, certainly noticed that Douglass was morose, and he may have explained the source of his pressure. Although she abhorred violence, her moral suasion philosophy did not preclude political antislavery engagement. Hence she never censured Douglass on such grounds.

III

Rochester, New York, called the Boston of the West, was famous as a "hot-bed of isms." Founded by Maryland-born Nathaniel Rochester and his twelve enslaved people, "Rochesterville" began as a small frontier village, and evolved into a large, thriving town, thanks to the Erie Canal, agriculture, and geography. As a market and manufacturing entrepôt, Rochester was the nation's flour-milling hub and gateway to the Midwest and the Mississippi. In the 1820s, Rochester was also the nerve center of Charles Finney's evangelical movement. As it grew in economic and social significance, Rochester also grew in radicalism, thanks mainly to blacks and Quakers. Rochester was New York's major Underground Railroad terminus and former headquarters of the Western Anti-Slavery Society. By 1847, the city was also home to the most prominent national black leader and the only black newspaper, and a place where all Abolitionists felt welcome.[23]

In Rochester lived Amy and Isaac Post, Old Westbury Hicksites whose hospitality was renowned and whose egalitarian principles were unassailable. For three months, Sojourner Truth was the guest of these reformers whose kinship and friendship networks embraced all Abolitionist persuasions, religious sects, Come-outers, dissenters, agnostics, and foreigners. Amy's matronly, gentle, and self-deprecating veneer camouflaged a keen intellect, sharp political sense, and masterful organization skills. A leader at the Woman's Conventions in Rochester and Seneca Falls in 1848, she was an excommunicated Quaker preacher, and also helped establish the breakaway Genesee Yearly Meeting of Congregational Friends. She and her husband prioritized abolition, helping Abby Kelley Foster fashion the Western Anti-Slavery Society into a powerful voice that encompassed the northwestern states and Canada West. The couple's spacious home was the Rochester underground's central station. Fifty people once reportedly waited there for transportation to Canada. Isaac Post, a farmer turned druggist, supplied the often ill self-emancipated people with healing medicines, remedies, and poultices. The radical couple also represented "true love and perfect union." Amy Post wrote, "I wish that every woman was as happily yoked as I am."[24]

Sojourner Truth joined many black Abolitionists who spoke reverently of "36 Sophia Street," the Posts' home. Young Frederick Douglass's first trip west in 1842 had begun an enduring friendship with the Posts. They nudged Douglass toward Rochester while he was in England, encouraging his idea of an independent newspaper. Eastern Garrisonians said another New York antislavery newspaper would "injure if not destroy the *Standard*." Amy Post tirelessly supported the *North Star* and was fiercely loyal to Douglass and to his family. William C. Nell, of Boston, a handsome hypochondriac bachelor, with whom Amy shared a birthday, lived with the Posts in 1847 and helped edit the *North Star*. Later, Nell's effusive, gossipy letters from Boston about his love life, health woes, and reform expressed an intimacy between blacks and whites rarely found in letters. Amy Post befriended the self-emancipated Harriet Jacobs and convinced her to publish her personal story of a sexual "indiscretion" that had produced two children with a white man. Although Harriet left Rochester just before Sojourner's arrival, they had numerous opportunities to meet. In 1850, both were in New York and later were in Boston when Garrison announced Sojourner's *Narrative*. Jacobs may also have been one of the "several dark sisters" who sat with Sojourner on the platform at the Woman's Rights Convention.[25]

The Abolitionists loved gaiety and socialization, however dour and grim they may appear in early photographs and daguerreotypes. In Rochester, over fifty friends spent a "a very pleasant" evening at the Douglass home. Guests told stories, mimicked detractors, and sang Abolitionist ballads, plantation melodies, and their favorite friendship anthem, "Auld Lang Syne." Truth and Douglass were both known for song, repartee, and humor. While he publicly suppressed his high spirits, her less-restrained off-color retorts sometimes caused unmarried women to blush. Although jovial warmth of feeling pervaded the party, Thompson privately fed Boston's gossip mill. The "enjoyable evening," he wrote to Anne Weston, was "irradiated by the mild splendor of a certain Julia—(not Byron's)," who accompanied Douglass's violin at the piano. Julia Griffiths—white, articulate, and a gifted editor, had come from Britain to be Douglass's editorial associate; she also became his occasional traveling companion. Anna Murray Douglass, as wife, mother, and helpmate, took the silent high ground, but Julia's extended stay in Douglass's home and her evangelicalism raised radical eyebrows. Besides Thompson's snide remark, white women's comments describing Anna as "uneducated and ignorant," "completely black," and "stout and plain" suggest jealousy and racism.[26] As Anna was once active in New England's antislavery community, it is very likely that she and Sojourner had met previously. Sojourner's Rochester stay and Anna's hosting of the weekly antislavery sewing circle was a chance to become reacquainted. The two dark-skinned women, whom whites considered "not handsome," could find much to talk about.

Sojourner used the Posts' home as a lecturing base and traveled to surrounding towns. Her meetings attracted large groups of black and white rural listeners, drawn to her captivating story of bondage and witty homilies and charmed by her Dutch accent. She also spoke in Rochester's Corinthian Hall, the largest meeting place in the city, and at Zion Church, the black community's activist headquarters. The church basement often served as a barracks, where under cover of darkness, local "station masters" brought blacks to await passage to Canada. Self-emancipated men were prominent in Zion's leadership, and black women kept the Monroe County underground active. Sojourner had an appealing simplicity and was "of the people" but embraced all of humanity. In a Rochester church, she once refused to stand in the pulpit. "I prefer," she told the audience, "to be no higher'n what you are."[27]

Sojourner's lack of education seems more of a problem for modern historians than it was for her contemporaries. Like her, most native black New Yorkers were either slave-born or one generation removed from bondage, and unschooled. Few ordinary women—wives, workers, and mothers—had time for the three Rs. Working parents focused on educating their children, which itself took great effort. For women especially, adult education was a double hardship, requiring concentration and time-consuming study. Both Sojourner Truth and Anna Douglass attempted literacy unsuccessfully. For Anna, organizing an efficient household, raising five children, antislavery work, and hosting visitors made literacy a low priority even "for Frederick's sake." Literacy was not a prerequisite for activism, and Sojourner Truth became the most committed race woman on the scene. Audiences cared more about her message and spiritual power than her inability to read.[28]

Sojourner Truth's reform impulse created for her a deeper bond with the Posts than other black Abolitionists, except for perhaps William C. Nell. Like the Posts and Nell, she was a "whole hog reformer" whose causes included nonresistance, temperance, anti-Sabbatarianism, anti–capital punishment, woman's rights, health reform, water cure, and a deeply intense Spiritualism—all linked to social justice. She believed that certain people, such as herself, communed with departed ones who lived a structured heavenly life. The phenomenon of manifested "rappings" (communicative noises made by departed spirits) permeated reform circles, and Spiritualism became a moral and political reform.[29]

Although she had embraced Spiritualism at Northampton, her faith flowered through friendship with the Posts and the Fox sisters. Kate and Margaret Fox of Hydesville, New York, woke up screaming one night in 1848 after hearing raps (or taps) throughout the room. Fear soon turned to intrigue as the teenagers reportedly conversed with the sounds and received responses through a sequence of numerical "raps." Word spread, and the little farmhouse became a local sensation. Burned-over District folk were not incredulous, since their region had spawned many unorthodox beliefs, sects, and Protestant offshoots. The parents sent Margaret to her brother in Auburn and Kate to her young widowed sister, Ann Leah Fish, in Rochester. Supposedly, the poltergeist followed Kate the clairvoyant, and multiplied its voices. Kate converted many Rochester residents, including the Posts. Isaac became a devoted believer, medium, and spirit writer. Sojourner always believed the "Spirit of God" spoke to her; she and the Fox sisters became fast friends. The three sisters had a successful New York tour and received glowing write-ups from Greeley, who became a Spiritualist along with his wife.[30]

Sojourner Truth and Thompson joined in séances at the Post's home, and witnesses insisted that the "spirits" converted him into "a life-long Spiritualist." Privately, however, he ridiculed principle members of the Western Anti-Slavery Society and the "rapping spirits." At one séance, he wrote to Anne Weston, the spirits directed everyone "to turn into *one bed* together." They placed several beds "side by side," and the "'believers' tumbled in side by side!!!!" Rochester Abolitionists also consulted the spirits about Julia Griffiths, and the "great uneasiness" over her relationship with "a certain distinguished orator and editor of this city." The spirits answered "that the lady was in her right place. Since then, the lady . . . has been the oracle of true believers." Rochester Abolitionists, Thompson joked, were too "full of the spirit world." Sojourner, like her Rochester friends, was a "matter-of-fact," straightforward believer. According to Ohio Abolitionist Esther Lukins, she placed her ear to the floor during one séance, and implored the spirit to "hop up here on the table, and see if you can make a louder noise." While Lukins found Sojourner "amusing beyond description," other "believers" took the event seriously.[31]

In western New York, Sojourner renewed some old acquaintances as well as forming new friendships. Giles Stebbins, the former Northampton schoolboy, was now a Garrisonian agent and married to Catherine Fish, a Rochester activist and signer of the Seneca Falls Declaration of Sentiments. Perfectionist Margaret Prior in Waterloo, formerly a Magdalene Asylum supporter and Elijah Pierson's Bowery Hill neighbor, was now an Abolitionist and Seneca Falls endorser. Sojourner's new associates included Isaac Post's cousin Esther Titus of Lockport, a watercolor artist and Spiritualist. Esther's sister-in-law Frances Titus of Michigan would become Sojourner's devoted friend, traveling companion, and biographer. Sojourner Truth and Lucy Colman, a skeptical transplanted New England activist, would work together in the West and in Washington, D.C., where Colman would accompany Truth on her visit with Abraham Lincoln. Sojourner met Susan B. Anthony, a thirty-one-year-old unemployed schoolteacher and Rochester newcomer, whose parents' farm was an underground station. Initially, Susan's reform interest was temperance; in 1852, she advocated woman's rights, and in 1856 became an agent for the AASS. Truth and Anthony's divergent positions on black male suffrage would test their friendship.[32]

The 1851 annual meeting of the AASS was held in Syracuse, and westerners in attendance were especially impressed with Sojourner. "I have spoken of Sojourner Truth in a former letter," reported Ohio *Bugle* correspondent Esther Lukins, who had written about Sojourner's Spiritualism. "But before I had any true appreciation of her *great strong* character." Her heart, Lukins wrote, is "as soft and loving as a child's, her soul as strong and fixed as the everlasting rocks, and her moral sense has something like inspiration or divination." On the surface, Sojourner seemed "simple and artless," but one dared not "play a bo-peep game with truth." Her eyes "will see your heart and apprehend your motives, almost like God's." What some might consider Sojourner's deficiency, being an unschooled former slave, was actually, Lukins argued, "the shield to guard her rare intuitions, her great pure heart and strong individuality from any worldly tint." Sojourner Truth's energy and overwhelming power, Lukins noted, was all the more remarkable for "a woman 65 [*sic*] years of age."[33] Lukins adopted Putnam and Kelley Foster's erroneous exaggeration of Sojourner as "aged," which followed her throughout public life. Yet Sojourner was younger than coadjutors Lucretia Mott, Isaac Post, and "Branded Hand" Jonathan Walker, and was the same age as Gerrit Smith, all of eighteenth-century birth. Sojourner was only ten or twelve years older than most of her friends and collaborators, as anyone reading her *Narrative* could determine. Yet whites distorted Sojourner's age, and it became part of their lore in endowing her with a superhuman image of exceptionalism.

Abolitionists of all persuasions, including delegates from the Far West, attended the largest national meeting ever and the first since the passage of the Bloodhound Bill. Denied their usual space in the Tabernacle or any other public hall in New York City and Brooklyn, the Executive Committee had relented to pressure from the western wing and agreed to meeting in Syracuse. It was one of those "especially pleasant seasons of enjoyment and refreshment," Giles Stebbins recalled, when moral suasionists and political Abolitionists affirmed their mutual goals. Disagreements over principles and perspectives receded amid declarations of lofty aims, future struggles, and "Auld Lang Syne" recollections. Sojourner Truth was among the ubiquitous "gifted" and "noble" speakers. Thompson added luster to the stellar cast of eastern and western "convention fleas." After one of Thompson's spellbinding "thunderbolts," May invited about twenty people to his home for evening tea. Stebbins called the scene memorable. Though it was late spring, snow had blanketed the region, but the one-mile walk to the northeast section of Syracuse was pleasant. May's residence, overlooking "town and country, mansions and cottages, shops and green fields," rendered a stunning panorama. Among the luminary cast of characters were Garrison,

Thompson, Edmond Quincy, Charles Remond, J. Miller McKim, Stebbins, the "quaint and striking" Sojourner Truth, Gerrit Smith, and Douglass. The Mays and Abby May Alcott graciously served delicious afternoon refreshments. These ultras, Stebbins remembered, were "the best society," with a much higher attainment than anyone in the fashionable world could reach. At the tea table, "what flow of fine humor softening the deep earnestness of speech, what grace and ease, naturalness and fraternity!"[34]

However, the day after this "brilliant tea party," a series of "long, loud arguments" dominated the convention, as Gerrit Smith challenged Garrisonians on the Constitution, antislavery political activism, and the likelihood of bloodshed over emancipation. Then, just before adjournment, Douglass dropped his bombshell. Responding to Edmund Quincy's resolution to fund only antislavery presses supporting disunion, Douglass announced that his paper would no longer support this Garrisonian centerpiece. A collective "sensation" rippled through the assembly, and Garrison shouted, "There must be roguery somewhere." Yet this was not the first time Douglass had opposed a proslavery interpretation of the Constitution. Garrison undoubtedly referred to Douglass's not-so-confidential arrangement to merge the *North Star* and Smith's *Liberty Party Paper* into *Frederick Douglass' Paper*, as an organ of political abolition. As a race leader, Douglass demanded the independence to act without Garrison's scrutiny. Black people's "relations to the Anti-Slavery movement must be and are changed," he asserted later. The battle "is emphatically our battle; . . . and with God's help we must fight it our selves."[35]

Sojourner Truth sat in the front row during the exchanges and interjected her opinions in support of Douglass. Her antislavery message to the people was not overtly political, but she believed that such a strategy could coexist with the moral and spiritual imperatives of her own mobilization methods. Many others agreed, especially since Garrison's intimate friend Samuel May was embracing the Liberty Party and Gerrit Smith was running for office on the ticket. "Why should we censure him [Douglass] more than Gerrit Smith?" a white Rochester Garrisonian wrote the Posts. Unfortunately, Garrison's attitude toward Douglass suggests a dangerous paternalism, which some African Americans called an affront to black manhood. Sojourner Truth and other blacks continuously dealt with paternalism but did not view it as necessarily racism. And it was not Douglass's political abolition that created the eventual Douglass-Garrison rift. For some time afterward, Douglass publicly regarded Garrison with "gratitude and veneration." In Syracuse, he forgave his mentor's "hastily expressed imputation." The heated debate was an enlightening experience for Sojourner Truth, as a prelude to future antislavery and woman's suffrage complexities.[36]

"Well, we have had it, good and strong, hot and heavy, from all sides and parties," Ohio Abolitionist Joseph Treat informed *Bugle* readers. As a westerner,

Treat knew that Douglass had been "verging toward this ground for at least two years." But Treat added, "we shall love him none the less." Indeed, "Fred," previously being offered but refusing to take over the *Anti-Slavery Bugle,* remained a deep disappointment to Ohioans. Music brought the Abolitionists back to their main goal before adjournment. The newly freed Edmondson sisters sang the "most affecting" verses "The hounds are baying on my track; / O Christian, will you send me back?" Then all joined in singing the Spiritualist song "From all Who Dwell below the Skies." "Such a meeting together of Anti-Slavery Spirits!" the *Bugle* reported. Despite some heavy-heartedness over Douglass's disunion defection, everyone declared the convention an antislavery jubilee of "perfect understanding and the most delightful harmony."[37]

However overly sanguine that assessment, Abolitionists put differences aside in preparation for the lecture season. "We are in the midst of a Revolution," Parker Pillsbury proclaimed, "which as much transcends in greatness the revolution of 1776 as eternity is greater than time." The most important field was Ohio, a border state "of incalculable importance" because of its intercourse with and influence on the Mississippi Valley slave states. "Bloodhounds in the shape of human beings" plagued Ohio's Underground Railroad thoroughfare more than any other state. Ohio Abolitionists felt the dearth of a western presence in Syracuse. Ohioans *need to be here,* Esther Lukins declared, linking Spiritualism to abolition: "For many think we are *dead and gone to heaven,* and so, since our friends cannot be with us in Heaven, our spirits wish to 'rap' to them." Sojourner Truth "talks of visiting Ohio," Lukins noted from Rochester, and western Abolitionists anxiously hoped she would join the lecture circuit. "If she should," Lukins added, "my heart cries out, O people of Ohio, appreciate her, and take her into your hearts." The Sojourner had been on the road for a full year. It probably took some soul-searching talks with God, but finally, from Cazenovia, Joseph Treat informed *Bugle* readers, "Sojourner Truth will spend the summer in Ohio."[38]

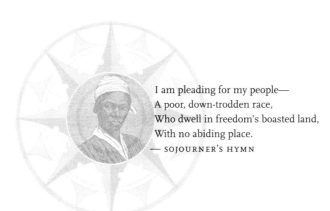

I am pleading for my people—
A poor, down-trodden race,
Who dwell in freedom's boasted land,
With no abiding place.
— SOJOURNER'S HYMN

CHAPTER 14

"God, You Drive"

THE SOJOURNER IN OHIO

I

"I got to Buffalo on the evening of the same day I left you," Sojourner Truth informed Amy Post by letter in early June. She had "a beautiful passage up the lake" (Lake Erie) that night, and arrived in Cleveland the next morning. Cleveland, like Rochester, began as an insignificant little village. In 1796, a black New York pilot and Iroquois interpreter ("Black Joe of Buffalo") guided Moses Cleveland (Olive Gilbert's great-uncle) to the site that bears his name. By 1850, thanks to the Erie and Ohio canals, Cleveland was the most important city in northern Ohio, called the Western Reserve.[1]

From early statehood, Ohio denied civil and educational rights to blacks, forbade settlement without freedom papers, and required a $500 bond and a white patron. Harboring a self-emancipated person carried a $500 fine. In 1850, northern Ohio's reported black population was small and scattered: 224 in Cleveland and 350 in all of Cuyahoga County; 264 in Lorain County, home of Oberlin College; 202 in Erie; and 212 in Summit County. Other Reserve counties reported fewer than one hundred African Americans. These figures exclude hosts of self-emancipated people, the "illegal aliens" of the time, mostly living in agricultural communities. Southern Ohio's much larger black population faced intense white hostility. Bloody attacks on Cincinnati blacks in 1829 and 1836 spurred a mass exodus to Canada. But oppression inspired activism. In 1834, Chillicothe blacks founded the Colored Anti-Slavery Society, and Cincinnati whites edited a colonizationist-antislavery newspaper. Moreover, in 1841, Cincinnati blacks counterattacked with a vengeance when whites invaded their community.[2]

In Cleveland, Sojourner "stopped among the colored friends and was treated with great kindness." One young black activist, William Howard Day, was a longtime acquaintance from New York. Day's activist mother Eliza had helped found Zion Church and had been targeted by the 1834 mob. Like Sojourner Truth, William Day settled in Northampton in 1844; he studied under the guardianship of her friend the Abolitionist editor John P. Williston before going to Oberlin. Day now worked for *True Democrat*, a Free Soil newspaper in Cleveland. Sojourner must have also met Day's fiancée, Lucie Stanton, reportedly the first black female college graduate. Stanton's wealthy stepfather financed the Underground Railroad, posting bail and paying legal fees for conductors and apprehended blacks. Fifty-six-year-old John Malvin was another black leader Sojourner probably met. A self-educated, self-emancipated Virginia carpenter, he was black Cleveland's "leading spirit" and most significant underground station keeper.[3]

In Cleveland, Sojourner did not witness the nurturing spirituality among African Americans that bridged socioeconomic barriers. Instead, most of Cleveland's small black middle class integrated into white churches. The lone black church, St. John's A.M.E., had been established in 1830 and purchased its own building in 1848. Since three of St. John's five trustees could not write, the little church was said to lack an "elevated" membership; it serviced the uneducated, poor, and self-emancipated blacks living in and around the river-front shanties and in settlements outside the city. Black churches were conservative about female preachers, in any case. Nonetheless, Sojourner Truth spoke at an antislavery meeting held during her four-day stay; before leaving, she sold $3 worth of books among her people.[4]

She moved on to Akron and the Woman's Convention. After arriving at the hotel where the participants were staying, she paced up and down the lobby, no doubt seeking friendly or familiar faces. Two Ohio women, Frances Dana Gage and Hannah Tracy Cutler saw the "tall colored woman" carrying a basket on her arm, "in which she carried some little books." As Lucius Hine, a convention vice president, joined the two white women entering the parlor, he joked about Sojourner Truth: "This I suppose is one of the delegates to your convention." Both women "disclaimed any knowledge of this particular delegate." Cutler, the convention's secretary, was a widowed schoolteacher; Gage, the presiding officer, was a homemaker who also wrote poetry, short stories, and a column called "Aunt

Fanny" for Jane Swisshelm's family newspaper, the *Pittsburgh Saturday Visitor*. Having no idea who she was, Cutler later recalled that the embarrassed women tried to avoid Sojourner and move quickly into the parlor. But she followed and accosted them. Lucius Hine, equally ignorant of who she was, found a chair and "sat grinning behind his newspaper" as she engaged Cutler and Gage in conversation. "She told us that she was Sojourner Truth," Cutler recalled, and was in Akron for the convention and in Ohio to lecture on antislavery. She sold books about her life to help with expenses. Gage and Cutler, unaccustomed to black women as convention participants, felt awkward but conversed with her, and each purchased a copy of her *Narrative*. Neither woman took Sojourner Truth seriously. "I fear," Cutler admitted, "we did not feel ready to give her as royal a welcome as her merits deserved."[5]

Gage and Cutler claimed to be woman's rights novices who had never heard of Sojourner Truth. This means that these easterners living in southern Ohio had not read accounts of the national woman's meeting in Worcester. That is puzzling, since Gage and Cutler had joined other Ohio women who had protested their lack of civil rights and implemented a petition campaign for suffrage. Moreover, both women were antislavery Free Soilers, and Garrisonians continuously placed the plight of enslaved women before western audiences. "Who . . . will plead the cause of the slave woman?" Abby Kelley Foster had asked at Oberlin in 1850. Sallie Holley of Rochester, New York, had timidly raised her hand, and on graduation in 1851 immediately joined Sojourner and others as a $10-a-week lecturer. While it is hard to believe the women had not heard of Sojourner Truth, her presence in Akron and her impact surprised them and many others.[6]

Cutler and Gage were both influenced by Jane Swisshelm, novelist and Free Soil editor of the *Pittsburgh Saturday Visitor*. Argumentative and hypercritical, she favored expanding women's legal position regarding property and marriage but opposed woman's suffrage or any issues she perceived as radical. In the *Pittsburgh Saturday Visitor,* she denounced Douglass and Pillsbury for linking woman's rights and slavery at Ohio's first woman's convention in May 1850. Then she rebuked the Worcester Convention's resolution on enslaved women. Woman's meetings were "not called to discuss the rights of color," she scolded; race was "irrelevant" to woman's issues, and introducing that question was "unwise." Instead of allowing "the rights of colored people [to] work out its own salvation in its own strength," the white man, she complained, placed "his boot-black" ahead of his wife and mother; favored emancipating every Southern slave and giving rights to every free negro but gave no thought to white women. In a rancorous war of pens, Pillsbury shot back: why was it "an unpardonable sin" to insist, at a woman's convention, "that we mean women of sable as well as shallow complexion? Of the carved in ebony as well as the chiseled in ivory?"

If that was the meaning, he argued, "it was absolutely demanded that we say it." Outgoing *Bugle* editor Oliver Johnson wondered out loud if Swisshelm was "so dull" as not to see the difference between declaring "the Woman's Right movement is . . . without color distinction, and turning the Convention into an 'abolition meeting.'" Had she so little sympathy toward black women that a resolution asserting "Equality before the law, without distinction of sex or color" incited her "shallow sophism"?[7]

Swisshelm was not cowed. Black women were simply women and should not be especially named. "Of what sex are black women?" she asked sarcastically. "Are they female women or feminine ladies?" Nor did she comprehend that while white women could place womanhood first, for black women such as Sojourner Truth, womanhood was defined by race, just as manhood was so named in American society.[8] Swisshelm refused to see race and prejudice as a black-white great divide. Hence, since the "color question" had no right to a hearing at a woman's convention, Sojourner Truth was the last person Swisshelm expected or wanted to see in Akron. Nonetheless, Sojourner's appearance and the words attributed to her made this relatively insignificant regional woman's convention a memorable historical event.

For many years, Sojourner Truth's 1851 speech, called "Ar'n't I Woman?" was known only through Frances Gage's article written in 1863 for the *Anti-Slavery Standard*. It was reprinted in Truth's 1875 *Narrative and Book of Life* and again in *History of Woman Suffrage*, by Elizabeth Cady Stanton, Susan B. Anthony, and Matilda Joslyn Gage (1881).[9] Sojourner Truth biographer Carleton Mabee offers the most in-depth critique of Frances Gage's famous rendition, which was apparently inspired by Harriet Beecher Stowe's 1863 *Atlantic Monthly* article "Sojourner Truth, the Libyan Sibyl," based on Stowe's meeting with Sojourner Truth. After examining twenty-seven notices of the Akron meeting, most of which ignored or said little about Truth, Mabee concludes that she could not have caused much of a stir. He disputes Frances Gage's recollection that "timorous and trembling" women urged her not to recognize Sojourner Truth, thereby linking woman's rights with "abolition" and "niggers." Mabee furthermore believes that Gage fabricated white female and male hostility toward Sojourner, as well as white male objections to woman's rights. Essentially, he claims, Frances Gage wrongly transformed Ohio's tranquil, liberal geographic setting into a rowdy, racist terrain. The Western Reserve and the town of Akron, Mabee says, were part of a "belt of Yankee settlements" stretching from Boston west through central New York into northern Ohio. This "Yankee Dom" actually "spawned the movements for both blacks' and women's rights." Thus, white women would not have objected to Sojourner Truth because of her race. Finally, since the Universalist Church hosted the woman's convention, Mabee believes that Gage also invented her assertion of clerical intolerance.[10]

Gage made other "key" errors, according to Mabee. She reported Sojourner saying "I have borne thirteen chilern and seen 'em mos' all sold off into slavery." Her assertion that Sojourner challenged male authority was unbelievable: "Dat man ober dar say dat women needs to be helped into carriages, and lifted ober ditches, and to have de best place ebery whar. Nobody eber help me into carriages, or ober mud puddles, or gives me any best place." These statements were part of Gage's grand design to introduce the ringing rhetorical phrase "Ar'n't I a woman?" This linchpin of modern feminist rhetoric was a figment of Gage's imagination, Mabee writes, borrowed from the slogan "Am I Not a Woman and a Sister?" Nor was Truth's impact so "magical" that it incited "roars of applause," turned "the whole tide" of the convention, subdued "the mobbish spirit of the day," or had tears "streaming" down women's faces. Sojourner herself never "hinted" at such an impact, Mabee writes, nor did contemporary descriptions. Thus, Gage's statement that Truth was a "star" at the convention is a myth that blacks and modern feminists use to elevate Truth into a "heroic figure." This raises questions, Mabee says, "not only about Truth and her place in history, but also about early black-white relations at large." Mabee argues that by unjustly claiming white women's hostility toward black women's participation in the woman's movement, Frances Gage's account represents a twisting of the facts comparable to the tale of George Washington and the cherry tree. Rather than offering a "serious understanding of Sojourner Truth and her times," Mabee believes, the "Ar'n't I a Woman" speech is "folklore."[11]

Contemporary accounts contradict Mabee's assessment in a number of ways. His view of northern Ohio during Sojourner's first lecture tour conflicts with that of Sallie Holley, the Oberlin student; she remembered race prejudice at every turn. She received permission to teach black children in nearby Sandusky, but could not "accept any invitation to stay in a coloured man's house." When she nominated her African American friend Lucie Stanton for president of the campus Ladies Literary Society, she created "a great outcry." When she joined Sojourner Truth, Parker Pillsbury, and others as a lecturer, the faculty and administration feared the "anti-slavery gospel" and did not welcome the Abolitionists. Even Garrison's Oberlin visit attracted only "a beggarly handful" instead of the throngs of students who usually filled the immense hall.[12] If the most progressive college in the country was uneasy about antislavery, the presence at the Akron Convention of Sojourner Truth caused equal consternation among some participants.

Most Ohio churches were also intolerant. Even years before the Akron Convention, reformers lamented that the "crucible of Old School Orthodoxy" plagued them on the Western Reserve. Hannah Cutler recalled that Akron's Universalist Church was "the only church in that prosperous town that would have opened its doors to such an unpopular set of people." According to Cutler, it was a "very incongruous audience," and contention arose immediately between radical and moderate women and among men in the audience. One clergyman told the women to go home to their husbands and children, for Christ and apostles were men. "Our opponents," Cutler recalled, "claimed the right to free speech, and hurled the apostle Paul at our heads with great violence." Even Swisshelm repudiated the notion that "the sexes are perfectly equal." She and Michigan's Emma Coe engaged in heated disagreements over the resolutions on equality of the sexes. Sojourner Truth sat on the steps leading to the pulpit, "fanning herself with her slat sunbonnet" and watching everything that "fell from the lips of the speakers." Just before adjournment, Swisshelm's resolutions were laid on the table, setting the stage for an exciting second day. Coe used scathing rhetoric to vent the women's anger over Ohio's 1850 state constitutional convention, which had denied black or woman's suffrage. She made a brilliant comparison between women's condition and "the slave," over Swisshelm's and some men's objections. Sojourner was silent the first day, but on the second, she joined the fray from her seat near the platform. "You men claim all for your selves," she shouted at a clergyman, "you feel very important 'cause your Lord Jesus Christ was a man. But where did de Lord of Glory come from?" Coe continued from the podium: "Pile Bibles as high as the sky, and tell me the Bible teaches such doctrines, and I will not accept it." The audience, Cutler recalled, "was greatly disquieted."[13]

Once scholars began seriously researching Sojourner Truth, they discovered a forgotten eyewitness report of the Akron Convention recorded in the *Bugle*, probably by its new editor, Marius Robinson. But other accounts—those in the *Ashtabula Sentinel* and the *New York Tribune* and one by Hannah Cutler—all reported that Sojourner Truth spoke out at intervals, employing "good hard sense," from her perch on the stairs. Truth and Coe disagreed with Swisshelm over the relations of the sexes and equality of the sexes. Coe was sarcastic, caustic, and bitter. Unlike woman's, man's "sphere" was boundless, she complained, especially if "there is a copper to be turned." Man controlled woman's sphere "down to the minutest details of a ladies' toilet," including "hair-pins, combs, brushes, breast-pins, finger-rings, doll-babies." Man was guilty of a twofold injustice toward woman, Coe proclaimed: first, "crippling the energies of her mind" by depriving her of education, and then "sneering" at her lack of learning. This, Coe added, was grinding with the heel, and then spurning with the hand. Women's presumed inferiority was the best argument for a superior education.[14]

After the raging debates in the morning session, Sojourner Truth asked to speak that afternoon, certainly over Jane Swisshelm's protests. Swisshelm vehemently objected when the convention adopted resolutions stating men and women were "perfectly equal" in "legal, political, pecuniary, ecclesiastical and social rights" as well as mind and body. She used her newspaper to publicly criticize Gage. Having "Aunt Fanny" as presiding officer was a "mistake,"

Swisshelm wrote, because Gage misrepresented the convention's objectives. Although Swisshelm's message was coded, her meaning was clear: Gage's biggest mistake was allowing the black woman to speak. Yet both the *Tribune* and the *Bugle* maintained that Sojourner was genuinely impressive. Moreover, most of the themes Gage attributed to Sojourner are reflected in those accounts. Gage remembered Sojourner as saying: "'If my cup won't hold but a pint, and yourn holds a quart, wouldn't ye be mean not to let me have my little half-measure full?'" Similarly, the *Bugle* reported: "'As for intellect . . . if woman have a pint, and man a quart—why can't she have her little pint full?'" The *Tribune* attributed "some of the shrewdest remarks" to Sojourner: "if she had a pint of intellect and man a quart, what reason was there why she should not have her pint *full*." In all three narratives, she also mocked the concept of a separate woman's sphere and emphasized her life as a worker.[15]

Sojourner did indeed challenge clerics, according to Sallie Holley. She and two "ultra" friends rented the best horse and buggy they could find at Oberlin for 50 cents a day and spent three days in Akron. Holley recalled that Sojourner Truth confronted ministers who claimed Christ's manhood was evidence of male superiority. The young women "were vastly entertained" by "Sojourner's discomfiture and rout of a young preacher who had the temerity to come up against her." According to Gage, Sojourner said, "'Whar did your Christ come from? From God and a woman! Man had nothin' to do wid Him.'" The *Bugle* reported her as saying, "'And how came Jesus into the world? Through God who created him and a woman who bore him. Man, where is your part?'" Apart from Gage's presentation in dialect, her account and the *Bugle*'s contain the same message. Holley also recalled that rowdy audience behavior, angry ministers, and the split among women stirred up an out-of-control atmosphere. Biblical edicts against women were common in American religious culture, and ministers opposing abolition certainly opposed woman's rights. The clerical support for "the right of property in human flesh" and castigation of women "might make an angel weep," one Ashtabula County antislavery woman wrote.[16]

According to contemporary accounts, the tabled resolutions (of Swisshelm) led to another "public meeting." Some women, the *Ashtabula Sentinel* noted, refused "to go on a wild crusade after imaginary good in the shape of political franchise and privileges." Hence, the convention adjourned after the Akron meeting and immediately "held a sort of union at New Marlborough," a little Quaker village nearby. Here Jane Swisshelm tried to overturn the equality resolutions in favor of more limited goals. At the New Marlborough meeting, Cutler wrote, "I recall Mrs. Swisshelm as insisting that woman should claim her right to be helped over bad roads and to be fed whether she worked or not." Cutler also recalled, "But Sojourner Truth replied that she never found any man ready to carry her over mud puddles."[17] Although Cutler did not say so, Truth could easily have added "And ar'n't I a woman?" In any case, Emma Coe, Sojourner Truth, Ohio's Emily Robinson and Josephine Griffing, and others successfully challenged Jane Swisshelm, and the Akron resolutions remained.

Thus, Frances Gage's recollections of Sojourner Truth came from two separate woman's rights meetings, and Gage captured the essence of Sojourner's remarks: she challenged the patriarchy through a focus on female intelligence, education, work, and religion. But Gage did ad lib: no account mentions Sojourner speaking of motherhood and having thirteen children sold into slavery. This material seems to reflect an effort on Gage's part to build on Stowe's cloying sentimental literary fabrication. Sojourner later insisted that she had told Stowe a story, probably about Mau-mau Bet's experience, and "she put it on me." Gage's exaggeration and invention at Truth's expense also conformed to Stowe's equally extremist misrepresentation. And both writers assigned the pejorative term "nigger" to Truth's vocabulary ("Twix the women of de Norf and de niggers of the South"), which some whites also later adopted when giving voice to her. Both women endowed Sojourner with a thick Southern dialect, complete with the term "honey" ("das it honey"), which again, whites later adopted and even added a plural ("honies"). Sojourner never called her people "niggers." Gage and Stowe's expropriation of Sojourner's voice was anything but sisterly; it speaks volumes about their "class and skin privilege" and sense of literary "ownership."[18] Yet despite its form, the content of Gage's narration is not as questionable. Gage assuming control of Sojourner Truth's discourse and minstrelizing her language seems more significant than whether or not she said, "Ar'n't I a woman?"

The declaration that "no available evidence" reveals that "white women advocating women's rights were hostile to black women's participation in the women's movement" ignores historical evidence.[19] Jane Swisshelm had already protested including black women. Moreover, she refused to acknowledge Sojourner Truth in her convention coverage, except to say that "a large black woman" was there "selling books." Few black women attended women's conventions, and none except itinerants spoke publicly. Indeed, even radical white women "shrank from the publicity of the platform," and their white sisters "crossed the street" to avoid greeting them. Sojourner's participation was indeed newsworthy. Yet Swisshelm refused to recognize black women's claim on the woman's movement. Although Sojourner Truth had champions in the audience, she was not part of the program and was not mentioned in the official 1851 proceedings. Gage, silent for twelve years, was prompted to write her article by a desire for public attention. Yet Sojourner's remarks at Akron and New Marlborough were both universal and specific, illustrating that black women did not necessarily attend white women's conventions because they identified with white women's agendas.[20]

History will never know Sojourner Truth's exact refrain, and perhaps Gage did take the phrase from the antislavery motto. However, the *Bugle* reported that Sojourner began with "I am a woman's [sic] rights." The *Tribune* reporter noted, "She said she was a woman." In one of Lydia Maria Child's scrapbooks of newspaper articles is a small section entitled "Too Good to Be Lost—Sojourner Truth." One article is an 1851 newspaper clipping about the Akron speech. Besides affirming the similarity of both Gage and the *Bugle*'s accounts, including audience reaction, the article begins like the *Tribune*: "She said she was a woman . . ." Certainly then, Sojourner's remarks reflected her thoughts on race and gender. Moreover, in keeping with her defiant character, rather than asking, "*A'rn't* I a woman?" Sojourner boldly asserted, "I *am* a woman."[21]

II

Sojourner Truth's Akron appearance seemed perfectly scripted, because it was so apposite an introduction to the state's most progressive women. Leading Ohio antislavery women attending the convention included Jane Hitchcock, Josephine Griffing, and Esther Lukins from Columbiana County, home of the Western Anti-Slavery Society. Betsy Cowles, of Ashtabula County, well known as an educator, had organized the Ashtabula Female Anti-Slavery Society in 1835 and presided over Ohio's 1850 woman's suffrage convention, and probably knew Sojourner from anniversary meetings. Largely owing to Betsy's organizational skills, the Ashtabula Female Anti-Slavery Society was the largest in Ohio. Mary Ann Skinner led a contingent from Portage County, which had the next largest female abolition society in the state. Sojourner's words and wisdom impressed women from other western states, including Michigan's Emma Coe. Sojourner also saw esteemed old friends—the Hutchinsons, and former Community associates Dr. Erasmus Hudson and the Boyles. Hence, despite some moderate Free Soil women's protests, an audience of old and new supporters welcomed Sojourner Truth's remarks, as Amy Post had predicted. Indeed, Sojourner found so many "kind friends" and received so many invitations that she informed Amy, "I hardly knew which to accept first."[22]

Sojourner strategically accepted the invitation of Mary Ann and John Skinner of Ravenna, Portage County, where a huge Free Soil meeting was convening, with special trains bringing folk from Cleveland, Hudson, Akron, and even Columbus. Many Akron participants joined the over three thousand people who listened to speeches by Ohio Abolitionist congressman Joshua Giddings, who had recently lost his bid for the Senate, Governor Samuel Lewis, and Senator Salmon P. Chase. William Day joined "Freedom's Minstrels" (the Hutchinsons), in singing antislavery songs; Frances Gage read antislavery poetry; Sojourner Truth worked the crowd telling her story and selling her *Narrative*.[23]

Sojourner would form close friendships with Garrisonian Abolitionists who worked in the trenches, such as Emily and Marius Robinson. As a young New Yorker, Marius had been inspired by Charles Finney's message of faith and humanitarian usefulness. Robinson moved West and taught the Cherokees, graduated from the University of Tennessee, enrolled at Lane Seminary, and withdrew with the other protesting students. In Cincinnati, he worked on the antislavery *Philanthropist*, developed black "freedom bureaus," and taught in freedom schools, where he met Emily. After his training with Theodore Weld in New York, Robinson's Ohio assignment was the most hazardous field of all. Traveling on horseback and on foot, he endured mobbing, stoning, and clubbing. On the Western Reserve, Trumbull County whites nearly killed him when Quakers invited him to speak. A mob dragged him over a rack of scythes, then covered the bleeding man with hot tar and feathers, burning his flesh and tearing a piece of his arm "an inch square." Sympathizers, including a female, were also beaten for attempting to protect him. The mob carried "the little brown devil" to another town and dumped him in a field, where a "good Samaritan" passerby saved his life. Although his severe injuries kept him from lecturing for ten years, he worked the underground with Cincinnati's Levi Coffin; the Robinsons' farm in Putnam, Ohio, became an Abolitionist headquarters and underground center. "The spirit of slavery is not confined to the South," Robinson said, and "the spirit is identical in character wherever found." If it is not crushed, "we shall all become its victims."[24]

The 1840 split fragmented but did not destroy Ohio antislavery. The heart of radical abolition was Ashtabula County, where Jefferson law partners Joshua Giddings and the more moderate Salmon P. Chase became Lane rebels converts who took their Abolitionist views to Congress. In Austinburg, Betsy Cowles, a committed young teacher and daughter of a Congregational minister, kept the female society going with help from her siblings, Giddings's wife, other local women, and some men. At first, women worked mainly in black education, the underground, petition campaigns, and writing antislavery literature. Theirs was a struggle against not only proslavery elements but also the churches, indifference, and colonizationists calling themselves Abolitionists. When young Abby Kelley made the Western Reserve her special mission, she was deeply hated by women as well as men. Even people espousing antislavery labeled her "vulgar and coarse." Hicksites once tore her clothing nearly off by violently dragging her out of the meeting and thrusting her from the churchyard. But her magnetic speaking power, Cowles's unflinching approval, and Ashtabula friends in high places challenged the opposition. Kelley, Cowles, and Elizabeth Jones established a Garrisonian newspaper, the *Anti-Slavery Bugle*, on the Reserve and convinced the Executive Committee to send its best speakers—Pillsbury, Stephen Foster, C. C. Burleigh, Henry C. Wright, Stebbins, and the mercurial Douglass—into "priest-ridden" Ohio. It remained a tough field. In 1846, newlyweds Abby Kelley and Stephen Foster spent the night in jail for "Sabbath breaking"—selling antislavery literature on Sunday. Western Reserve residents once struck Giles Stebbins with a rotten egg so forcefully in his left eye that it bled profusely and left him blind for some time. Ohio also had several homegrown Garrisonian firebrands: vitriolic J. W. Walker, a British Methodist minister who left his Cleveland church; refined but forceful Josephine Griffing and her husband, Charles—a minister, mechanic, and close John Brown associate.[25] These stalwarts had paved the way for the first black woman Abolitionist speaker. But the Western Reserve was far from antislavery, and Sojourner Truth's mission, preaching to the unconverted, required going into unfriendly territory.

Following the Free Soil convention, Sojourner headed for the annual meeting of the Western Anti-Slavery Society in Salem, the "western citadel of the antislavery forces" and home to the Ohio *Bugle*. Benjamin and Elizabeth Jones had forsaken Pennsylvania to live in this Quaker village of two hundred souls, almost all Garrisonians. But the diverse Western Anti-Slavery Society, organized in 1845 during Texas annexation and the Mexican War, embraced western New York, Pennsylvania, Ohio, and regions west of the Alleghenies. It was ideologically united on immediate emancipation but not the "no union with slaveholders" platform of the Garrisonians and their position that the Constitution was proslavery. When Pennsylvania congressman David Wilmot added Free Soil to the mix (no slavery in the territories taken from Mexico), some political Abolitionists in the Western Anti-Slavery Society supported what Garrison derisively called "a white man's antislavery." Instead of freeing all of the enslaved where they were, Free Soil proposed freeing them where they did not live and keeping them out of western lands. Nevertheless, by 1848, when slaveholding Whig Zachary Taylor won the presidency, Liberty Party men joined with dissatisfied Northern Whigs and Democrats in creating a Free Soil Party. Thus, the new party had a significant racist element, including presidential candidate Martin Van Buren, and a progressive presence, including Congressman Joshua Giddings.[26] By 1851, the Western Anti-Slavery Society was struggling to remain purely Garrisonian as the Free Soil forces gained power within its ranks.

"One of the largest audiences we have ever seen in Ohio," the *Bugle* wrote, gathered for the Society's revival-style tent meeting. Here Sojourner reconnoitered with her traveling companions. Picnic lunches, recreation for children, singing, peddlers, hawkers, even beer and cider all seemed to add lightness to the event. "The people in this region are reformers," wrote the Free Soil *True Democrat*. They not only were intelligent, independent-minded, and well-read but were not tied down by "fashion, party or sect." At least two hundred women wore "Bloomer dresses." The festive atmosphere turned serious once speakers began recounting scenes of auction blocks, painful separations, and bleeding backs. The Garrisonians had invited Joshua Giddings, Free Soil Abolitionist, to speak despite their differences over the Constitution and disunion. He vigorously condemned the Northern Whigs and Democrats for their role in passing the Fugitive Slave Law. "Thousands of responding countenances" heard Sojourner Truth for the first time, the *Bugle* wrote, and listened to "every word of the great truths she uttered." They had heard Douglass speak of Southern bondage, but none of them knew about the cruelties of slavery in the rural North. In the Business Committee, Parker Pillsbury met stiff opposition from Free Soilers attempting to build on Douglass's unsuccessful effort from the previous year, to push a pro-Union plank. Now Douglass was home nursing infected vocal cords, and Sojourner offered an "eloquent discussion" in support of "no union with slaveholders" resolutions. On the second day, she and Josephine Griffing spoke on the importance of underground work and their individual duties to "fugitive slaves." After three days of speeches and debate, the Garrisonian resolutions passed. Abolitionists would continue the moral warfare against slavery until "the last slave shall sing his song of deliverance amid the broken and shivered ruins of this nation's government, and religion." They vowed to labor until a "repentant people" learned to do justice, love mercy, and obey the laws of nature and the dictates of humanity. The symbolic emblem "No Union with Slaveholders" continued to grace the *Bugle* masthead.[27]

After only three months in Ohio, Sojourner had almost sold out her *Narrative*. Although Garrison in Boston and J. W. Walker in Ohio acted as her agents, she kept an accurate mental record of money owed and books sold. Her business sense and determination to eliminate her debts impressed her Ohio friends. From Ravenna, had she contacted Garrison asking for six hundred more books and her publishers' full bill, and wrote, "let me know how many books J. W. Walker received of Mr. Yerrinton." Garrison had not replied promptly; this was apparently her second letter. He always admitted to other correspondents that he had an "inveterate, yes, I will say criminal habit of procrastination." Where was the information she had requested? she asked, and admonished him to "please be particular about Mr. Yerrinton's account . . . I have got to pay him." Anxious about indebtedness, she owed for her *Narrative* and her home, and sent payments on both. As she reimbursed Garrison for shipping expenses, she also complained that his last shipment had been half full of paper and shavings—an unnecessary expense that had cost her $7. "Don't send so much next time," she advised. "Pack them tight" instead, she instructed, with as many books in the box as possible—and "send them by the most speedy, safe conveyance." Sojourner was anxious to have the books before the tour began. If Garrison did not hurry, "I may get out of books before they arrive."[28] Her books arrived on schedule.

Sojourner Truth and her companions called themselves "apostles," sent forth on a unique mission with a special purpose about a new principle. Sojourner Truth, C. C. Burleigh, Parker Pillsbury, J. W. Walker, Sallie Holley, and the Griffings left the comfortable Western Reserve Quaker communities to go into the backwoods among poorly educated hardscrabble folk who were somewhat backward. These rough, unpretentious, rural Buckeyes loved tobacco, corn whiskey, conversation, and crude jokes. Although most were staunch Unionists, some also had a keen ear for truth, and often valued both individual will and the right to keep the proceeds of one's labor. They sometimes made good antislavery advocates when shaken from their social prejudices. As a young lecturer, Abby Kelley understood this and even endured the men's "disgusting" whiskey, chewing, smoking, and crude humor. Sojourner Truth spoke against alcohol, but she still enjoyed a good joke, sometimes told coarse ones herself, and remained a smoker.[29]

The Garrisonians generally traveled in twos, for safety as well as apostolic tradition, and then gathered for conventions. Newcomer Sallie Holley was paired with seasoned Josephine Griffing; Parker Pillsbury often worked with J. W. Walker; Charles Griffing worked with C. C. Burleigh. However, Burleigh sometimes traveled alone, braving the dangerous southern counties on foot. Rural children reportedly fled from this bearded, colorful apostle carrying a backpack full of antislavery literature with his "long curls flying in the wind." Sojourner, new to Ohio, held meetings in communities where she had made friends—Columbiana and Ashtabula counties—and joined her companions later. She most often worked with Pillsbury and Walker.[30]

The early 1850s were "days of outlawry for anti-slavery," Sallie Holley recalled, and hardly a church, hall, or schoolhouse was open to Abolitionists. They considered mixed greetings a sign of progress. Resistance from traditional ministers forced Abolitionists to meet outside, in people's homes or shops. Sometimes opposition backfired on ministers. In the village of Augusta, after supporters prearranged the use of the meetinghouse, church leaders locked the building. The people moved to their schoolhouse, but found the doors and windows locked there too. As evening approached, "a large number of men" forced open a schoolhouse window and unlocked the door. By then, the crowd was so large that the meeting had to be moved outside. This heightened the inspirational effect on that beautiful evening. "Under the softening influence of the full moon," J. W. Walker reported, "we worshipped the Great Father, by laboring to restore the rights . . . of . . . his plundered and tormented children." The meeting far exceeded their expectations, and the audience listened in rapt attention. Pillsbury spoke "with uncommon energy and power, showing how

fertile has been the influence of the clergy against the efforts of the slave."
Walker followed, comparing the state of American institutions with the true
character of Christianity. By the time he finished, the Sojourner was "mightily
moved." She spoke, Walker observed, "as I have never heard her in Ohio." The
audience was "completely captivated." They not only bought many of her books
but "unanimously invited her to return and hold a meeting."[31]

The antislavery apostles faced hostility even when they gained a hearing.
Devoted young antislavery women in Leesburgh, Carrollton County, organized
a convention and fair to honor the Garrisonians and raise money for the *Bugle*.
A large audience assembled, provided supper, and engaged the Abolitionists
in a lively discussion on the Union. Led by the local Methodist "priest," most
of the audience resisted the rhetoric of disunion and the attacks on traditional
denominations. The apostles won no new converts, but were more effective in
nearby New Market, where the "Seceeders' Church" (dissenting Presbyterians)
welcomed them. Speeches by Truth, Holley, and Griffing had the most impressive effects; a crowded and silent audience gave "almost breathless interest" to
all they said. The Abolitionists also gained a hearing at Akron's "Stone Church,"
and while their rhetoric was unevenly received, the local newspaper noted that
Sojourner Truth spoke "many true words" in "strong rude eloquence."[32]

The best Abolitionist speakers were not necessarily the most polished. While
nearly all were fine orators, Abby Kelley Foster believed that compared to easterners, westerners (except J. W. Walker) were second rate.[33] For one thing, the sheer
number of speeches, debates, and verbal exchanges that eastern lecturers engaged
in enhanced verbal acuity. In addition, their backgrounds were mostly ministerial,
educational, editorial, and legal—all learned professions. Some of the best orators
often wrote out their speeches, while others, equally talented, left few printed
words and mainly spoke extemporaneously. Giles Stebbins called antislavery
lecturing the "best education in America." No university, he said, "could have
given such scope for mental and moral culture." Antislavery lecturers nurtured
each other intellectually on the road and at home. They imbibed the pulse of the
people, which was sometimes light and warm, sometimes prejudiced and contemptible, but always, the apostles insisted, capable of moral transformation. For
Sojourner, singing was important as well. She created songs and sang Methodist
hymns, Abolitionist, and underground songs, such as the crowd-pleasing "The
hounds are braying on my track. / Oh Christians, will you send me back?"[34]

She thrived in this environment. The Bible was the "great book" she relied
on, and as her verbal finesse and knowledge of political issues increased, her
speeches became longer and less one-dimensional. She not only spoke from her
little book about slavery in rural New York; she repackaged other speakers' topics
and metaphorically wove them in with her unique experiences, with her original versatility and performance style. She learned much from Parker Pillsbury,

whom Calvin Fairbank called the most "severe, bitter, sarcastic debater I ever knew." Pillsbury's words cut "rough and deep," like an old kitchen knife. William Lloyd Garrison Jr. likened Pillsbury to Martin Luther, who went among boatmen and sailors to learn new words and ways of attacking the pope and Catholicism. "I have been used to hearing all kinds of antislavery speaking," Garrison Jr. wrote his father from the West, "yet I never before heard such tremendous invective, such a grouping together of hard words." Sojourner was gentler, but she often picked up on Pillsbury's themes. At one convention, Pillsbury held forth bitterly, dissecting the high price the nation paid for "American Union." Afterward, Sojourner's long speech transformed the Union theme from political theory to human bondage. "Sojourner said she knew something of the Union—she had felt it; the scars of it were on her back, and she would carry them to her grave. The Union was not sweet to her, it was very bitter . . . if others would taste it in the same way, they would think it was bitter."[35]

Sojourner continued discussing the Union the next day. As a revival preacher, she understood the power of drama in persuading a congregation. As an uneducated black woman speaking to diverse audiences, she knew the importance of humility. And as a former farmworker, she identified with rural people. Beginning with an emotional account of her treatment and her feelings while enslaved, she spoke of slavery's immorality. Then, employing a metaphor from farm life, she introduced political points about the difference between a Free Soiler and a Garrisonian. She said that she could not explain "very clearly" the difference between Free Soilers and Garrisonians, but "she could feel it." She recalled how in slavery days, "they used to hackle flax." Some "worked by-the-day, by-the-day (while saying it swinging her arms slowly) as though affected with rheumatic pains." Others "worked by the job, by the job, job, job, (making her arm go as quickly as she well could)." Similarly, Sojourner said, Free Soilers "worked mighty slow-by-the-day," while "the Garrisonians worked by the job, job, job." Despite her claims of modesty, she understood politics quite well and expressed them in practical and homespun yet succinct comparisons. Garrisonians worked quickly and efficiently for immediate emancipation. The Free Soilers' antislavery plan called only for halting slavery's extension. This gradualism could take America into the twentieth century as a slave nation. Sojourner Truth's ability to "read the people" and apply political rhetoric to daily life with a down-to-earth quality delighted rural audiences.[36]

In Ohio, she also became a convention "opener"—the first speaker in a morning or evening session. She began with a song, asked for a prayer or prayed herself, and then began her remarks, often mixing singing in with her lecture. She might also "lend a helping hand" as others spoke on the platform. The *Bugle* called her out-of-turn interruptions "stunning one-liners" that were very much to the point, and sometimes became full speeches later. Her mental reflexes were quick, and her verbal deliveries articulate, original, and honest, sometimes setting off roars of laughter. She could engage an audience in such a way as to turn a lecture into a conversation or an extemporaneous persuasive dialogue. Audiences enjoyed her adaptation of the call-and-response tradition and her camp meeting style. As one local aptly reported, her presentation of "truths . . . in quaint and homely form" [would] be longer remembered than if they had been clothed in the most eloquent language of a Pillsbury or a Burleigh."[37]

Nearly everything about the Abolitionist lecture tours was unpredictable—attendance, reception, accommodation, and travel conditions. Conventions might host over three thousand people or fewer than one hundred. Ohio's crippling 1851 drought, which forced many cold water reformers to forgo their daily washings, was a small inconvenience compared to others. Yet the apostles blended with the rustic environment, which might require everyone sleeping in the same room on uncomfortable pallets. As for travel, rather than in "winged palaces over New England railroads at the rate of half a mile a minute," lecturers on the Reserve mostly rode in horse-drawn vehicles and ferries. In those days, any rails that had been laid were "made of wood, a foot in diameter, laid crosswise and sometimes with traps rotted out between them," just enough to "catch a poor nag's fore leg and break it." Rail travel was even uncomfortable for Sojourner Truth, riding in the smoking car. Tobacco-chewing men aiming for a spittoon often found the hem of a woman's dress instead. She preferred a horse and buggy.[38]

According to Pillsbury, Sojourner Truth won the day for abolition in one of the most effective conventions of the season. It was the one time in 1851 when they went to southern Ohio. Church trustees gave the lecturers permission to hold a two-day convention beginning with a Sunday sermon, but the pastor promised to preach antislavery himself. Instead, he sloughed through a sermon on the soul's immortality, which Pillsbury called a piece of stupid, seedy, threadbare "theological twaddle." Afterward, the dissatisfied congregation insisted that the Abolitionists hold their meeting. The apostles rarely made racial distinctions in their reports; however, this church was probably black. Pillsbury, Walker, and Truth were in Ross County, a part of southern Ohio, where African Americans had large separate churches, traveling preachers, camp revivals, and impressive all-black farming settlements. At this meeting, Sojourner Truth delivered the sermon. Taking her text from the Presbyterian pastor, she spoke to an "immense audience" and amazed Pillsbury with her thorough review of the minister's message and attack on his "borrowed, but badly read logic." Pillsbury recalled that she reduced the sermon to nothing, "with a power of discrimination I never in my life saw exceeded if equaled. In the terrible crucible of her criticism, she melted it down and down until it was shown to be nothing to the purpose at all. Though unable to read one word, she exhibited a power of . . . keen analysis, such as most professional critics must covet in vain." She generated a "deeply interesting discussion" that continued until a very late hour, and also dominated the next day's meetings.[39]

The antislavery apostles finished up the lecturing season in Ashtabula County, situated on Lake Erie and the Pennsylvania border. Jefferson, the county seat and home of Free Soil congressman Joshua Giddings, had been Abolitionist since the 1830s. The Jefferson Anti-Slavery Society was organized in 1832 and soon became county-wide. Garrisonians scoffed at most politicians, but they revered Joshua Giddings, religious radical, reformer, and staunch Abolitionist. With the exception of John Quincy Adams, Giddings was the most outspoken member against slavery in Congress. His support for the rebels on board the *Creole* in 1842 (thereby violating the "gag rule" against discussing slavery) had forced a censure vote that led to his resignation, but his constituents had overwhelmingly returned him to Congress. But his unpopularity outside Ashtabula was revealed in 1850, when he lost a Senate seat to Benjamin Wade. Giddings continued to declare his public defiance for the Fugitive Slave law; his hometown was a main Underground Railroad terminus, and he was an underground leader. He kept a hidden back room, and his sons drove fleeing bondpeople to the harbor under cover of darkness. In Congress, Giddings asserted that he had "as many as nine fugitives dining at one time at my house." Obeying the "Divine mandate" to feed the hungry and clothe the naked, "I fed them, I clothed them, I gave them money for their journey and sent them on their way rejoicing." Another Abolitionist, the wealthy William Hubbard, was responsible for Ashtabula County being nicknamed "Mother Hubbard's Cupboard." The cellar of Hubbard's Lake Street brick mansion held large numbers of fleeing bondpeople, as did his lakefront lumberyard. He also built a barn with a tunnel going straight to the water's edge, where rowboats carried people to waiting vessels. Some self-emancipated blacks felt safe enough to remain in Ashtabula County, worked in trades, and purchased land. "The voice of the people is, Constitution or no Constitution, law or no law, no fugitive slave can be taken from the soil of Ashtabula County back to slavery," the *Ashtabula Sentinel* wrote after the Fugitive Slave Law was passed. "If anyone doubts this real sentiment, they can easily test it."[40]

The backbone of radical abolition in Ashtabula County was the Female Anti-Slavery Society, which also had some male members. Giddings's wife, Laura, was a founding member, and his young daughter Maria was a stalwart Garrisonian and great admirer of Abby Kelley Foster. Corresponding secretary Betsy Cowles ran the Society like a well-oiled machine, even when she was an Oberlin student and then a teacher. The members organized conventions, planned the easterners' lecturing tours, hosted them, raised money for the Western Anti-Slavery Society, spoke publicly themselves, and traveled to antislavery meetings in the

East. Betsy and her sister Cornelia were also fine singers and gave concerts for the cause. The Society welcomed the Abolitionists, and for the remainder of the fall the Cowleses' home and the warm hospitality of Ashtabula was their base.

Nonetheless, Ashtabula County had its share of anti-Abolitionists, led by the clergy. In some villages, Congregational ministers locked the visiting Abolitionists out of churches even when members wanted to hear them. Free Will Baptist ministers were more accommodating but totally opposed the Abolitionists' messages. When the Abolitionists organized a county convention and ministers instructed parishioners to boycott it, an overflowing number of Free Soilers, Whigs, and the undecided would brave "mud, rain, and dark evenings" to hear the Garrisonians. Debates were intense, and ultimately participants rejected Garrisonian resolutions against voting, against the Fugitive Slave Law, or favoring disunion. But residents urged the Abolitionists to return "at the earliest possible opportunity."[41]

Sojourner Truth's Methodism was truly challenged in Ohio, as she witnessed firsthand the denomination's complicity in her people's enslavement. In Ohio, Methodism possessed "unusual power," and Northern Methodism remained chained to upholding slavery. Morally speaking, Pillsbury noted, church leaders were in way over their heads when challenging the Garrisonians, hence wanted to silence them. Events in the newly settled village of Dorset exemplify the duel for the hearts, minds, and spirits of the people. Unable to use a church, local residents requested and received permission to have an antislavery convention in the schoolhouse. Yet they found the doors bolted and barred and the windows spiked down with huge nails. After removing these hindrances, the community held a morning antislavery session. However, during the afternoon adjournment, "religion and politics of the town" united to foil antislavery: "By the aid of an outhouse vault nearby, they contrived to cushion over all the seats in the room, with an upholstery peculiarly their own—the odor of which was no doubt sweet incense in the nostrils of the deity they adore; and an offering worthy of both the God and worshippers."

Deacons in the Methodist church had dug feces from the outhouse and smeared them throughout the schoolhouse. "But that was nothing to us," Pillsbury wrote. "If their deity demands such sacraments, and if they are willing to crawl down into a vault to procure the means of celebrating such sacraments, why should we concern ourselves in the matter." Within fifteen minutes, "thanks to anti-slavery zeal and determination," the house was ready for an audience.[42]

The deacons' outrageous behavior inspired the meeting with irresistible power, Pillsbury wrote, and like a good field marshal, he quickly assessed the Abolitionists' advantage. Few speakers, he surmised, could channel a charged-up audience like the preaching woman. Sojourner led off the meeting with vituperation that "scathed like the very lightenings." Josephine Griffing followed her; Pillsbury offered only a tribute, leaving J. W. Walker to "bring up the rear." The Abolitionists considered it the most successful meeting they had in the county, greatly strengthening and confirming old friends while adding new ones. The assembly adopted all the radical resolutions, took numerous news-paper subscriptions, and importuned the apostles to return as soon as possible. The Garrisonians were jubilant. "Methodism made manifest on the seats of the school-house," aided by "political spirits," had helped create an Abolitionist base in a new town.[43]

Most of the apostles said their goodbyes in early November, except Pillsbury and Truth. "I am now . . . alone on the battlefield," Pillsbury wrote from Summit County, "with the exception of Sojourner Truth—though her name is a host." The Methodist gospel preacher and the Congregationalist minister lectured to-gether in Ohio's "wilderness of Wesleyanism." They provoked the "Christians" who were in close communion with slaveholders, waxed long on "doxologies of our Glorious Union," swore allegiance to a slaveholding Constitution, or voted for Whigs. Sojourner's cajoling pathos, dramatic experience, spiritual depth, and biblical understanding complemented Pillsbury's intellectual flair, politi-cal pronouncements, flamboyant clerical insults, and long-winded, theoretical verbosity. Taking their messages into Pennsylvania, the two seemed like a "whole team," one listener said. Interested people were never better satisfied with such "anti-slavery truth," a local Abolitionist wrote, although some of it was strewn on stony ground and shallow soil. The two said hard things about the church and the government, but did not denounce God, the Bible, and humanity, as the clergy had predicted they would. Between Sojourner's "excellent" antislavery gospel and Pillsbury's caustic reasoning, no one would have given "a copper" for the union, "much less shed a tear." Thanks to Pillsbury and Truth, the town of Breeksville, Pennsylvania, had its first antislavery meeting, which opened the way for other lecturers. As for clerical opposition, the reporter noted, "closing the meeting-house doors, never prevents the spread of Truth."[44]

The two parted in late November. Pillsbury's trip back to New Hampshire, he wrote to Robinson, was "a pretty severe winding up of a somewhat severe Anti-Slavery Campaign." Nevertheless, he added, the times were unforgettable. "I shall carry with me the remembrance of them as long as memory performs its office." The memory continued to inspire him. Writing from the frigid Mohawk valley, he reminisced to Robinson: physically, he said, he was "half-way back to Ohio again," and "in spirit, I am all the way." Casting his eyes toward Ohio many times a day, he recalled a Sojourner story somewhat imperfectly. Her mother, thinking of her son sold to Alabama, had looked on the moon to find "a slave's comfort" in knowing the family all looked up at the same galaxy. Reflecting on friends in Ohio, Pillsbury wrote: "I also look at the moon, and think she shines on them as well as on me; and that possibly, some of my loved ones there, are looking at the same object, with emotions similar to my own." Sojourner Truth remained in Ohio, "holding meetings and spreading the glorious gospel." When it came to influencing an audience, her power was beyond "the little medium of letters called an education," noted her Ashtabula friend Esther Lukins. She called Sojourner "a natural." Pillsbury agreed "most emphatically"; she was "a piece of workmanship of which nature need not be ashamed." Sojourner described herself as "fresh from the hand of the great Maker!" Nobody, she asserted, "has been modeling me after any of their patterns."[45]

Like most Abolitionists, Sojourner held meetings in the off season, and after a brief respite, was "eager to be abroad," while her strength held out. Pillsbury was "freezing" in upstate New York; Sallie Holley toured New England; J. W. Walker and Henry C. Wright went "among the Wolverines" in Michigan; C. C. Burleigh struggled in the slave states, encountering not only "old fashioned opposition" of mobs and tar-and-feather threats but "jack-knives into the skirts of overcoats." The worst winter in history gripped Ohio, and the mercury seemed fixed at 10 degrees below zero. Snowfalls averaged five to six feet, rivers froze, and freight sat on wharves. Northern Ohio was hardest hit, but "Porkopolis" (Cincinnati) also closed. With sleighs, snow runners, and jumper sleds the only means of transportation, Sojourner could not travel. Moreover, the swift pace of her life over the last two years had led to exhaustion and health issues. Anxious eastern friends and her family had not heard from her for some time. Finally, word came that she had been ill but was healed and recuperating in Ashtabula and Columbiana counties. In March she was well enough to address "a large audience in the New Lisbon Methodist Episcopal Church." Speaking for over an hour, she made "earnest appeals to the people, for justice to the slave, and to her race." She closed her message by singing nine stanzas of her original song, to the tune of Auld Lang Syne: "I am pleading for my people—/ A poor, down-trodden race, / Who dwell in freedom's boasted land, / With no abiding place . . ."[46]

IV

In the spring of 1852, Sojourner Truth was on the road again, heading to southern Ohio with a new supply of books. Traveling alone, she interacted with free black communities as talk of emigration reverberated throughout the state. In Cincinnati, blacks held a five-day state convention presided over by recent Oberlin graduate John Mercer Langston, a precocious twenty-two-year-old whom Sojourner had met the previous year. The Bloodhound Bill, the incredible rise in kidnappings, and the recent defeat of the black franchise created an angry mood. Langston, "animated and eloquent," articulated the "agricultural interest of our people" and advocated a federal grant for black settlements in the territories. He presented a majority report calling for a national black convention on emigration and appointing an agent to determine the "most suitable point for the settlement of our people, and the establishment of an independent nationality." White radicals dismissed this nationalism as "colorphobia," and eastern black activists refused to call a convention solely to discuss western emigration. The issue did not die; Sojourner Truth's post–Civil War activities toward a black homeland were no doubt rooted in these Ohio debates.[47] For the moment, however, black America had more immediate struggles and a more pressing campaign.

The most important spring convention Sojourner attended was the one organized by the Cincinnati Ladies Anti-Slavery Sewing Society in April. Two hundred male and female delegates gathered for the largest convention ever held west of the Alleghenies. Free Soil Abolitionists contributed generously to the society, and the women organizers urged that all "petty jealousies" as well as "party zeal and sectarian prejudice" be left behind. The star-studded affair attracted "Abolitionists of all stripes"—with an especially impressive showing of black leaders. Although black women reportedly were delegates, none were recorded. Douglass was the man of the hour, and his spellbinding keynote address reflected his new militancy. "The way to make the Fugitive Slave Law a dead letter was to make a few slave hunters dead men," he thundered, amid bursts of applause. He carried the convention for Free Soil, but the moral suasionists (who advocated change through moral persuasion, not political action) still claimed him; Garrisonian delegates who regretted his "advocacy of war" applauded his performance.[48] Like other Garrisonians, Sojourner Truth continued to admire Douglass, but as a nonresistant, she did not support his call for violence.

Soon afterward, the legendary confrontation between Sojourner Truth and Frederick Douglass in which it was recorded that she asked "Is God gone?" occurred at Salem, Ohio. The context was a struggle between opposing factions for moral, political, and spiritual primacy in the antislavery movement.

Both Truth and Douglass were experiencing different kinds of ascendancy. After Douglass's stunning Cincinnati triumph, his quarrel with black Abolitionists developed into a full-scale blowout at the annual meeting of the AASS in Rochester.[49] However, even that did not create an irrevocable break, and Douglass moved on to greater recognition at the national Free Soil convention in August. When Lewis Tappan nominated Douglass for secretary, he was elected by acclamation "amid loud applause." White delegates shouted repeatedly for Douglass and so drowned out other speakers that he finally delivered a powerful impromptu speech about using the Constitution for antislavery. His speech was hailed abroad as a sign of American progress—a former slave overwhelmingly cheered in a massive political meeting of whites. But another former slave was also making her mark. Although she did not display the same new hubris as

Douglass, after fifteen months in Ohio, friends and companions proudly noticed that her star was rising. "Sojourner improves, both in her speaking and in her knowledge of the true means of the overthrow of Slavery."[50] Her speeches reflected her understanding of issues in this presidential election year, including the rise of Free Soil, the fragmentation of old political alliances, and the challenges that moral suasion abolition faced in the West. While Garrisonians were committed to moral suasion and attacking the churches' position on slavery, many were also unwilling to abandon completely a political solution. After a winter among Ohio associates, Sojourner wondered if Free Soil might not be shaken from its gradualism. Yet while she understood the possible expediency of a political solution to abolition, her faith would never allow her to condone violence.

The anticipated power play at the Salem meeting of the Western Anti-Slavery Society between moral suasion and political antislavery made it all the more thrilling. If the Free Soil Party could push through their pro-Constitution and voting resolutions, the national candidates would have a strong western antislavery infrastructure. The presence of so many Free Soilers and their presidential candidates (John Hale of New Hampshire and George W. Julian of Indiana) did not sway the Garrisonians. Unlike radical Abolitionist Julian, few Free Soilers supported immediate emancipation. Yet Douglass seemed confident in his ability to redirect the racist tide, within his new affiliation.

When the August 21 convention began in Salem village's spacious Hicksite meetinghouse, the biracial audience was too large to accommodate everyone, "either sitting, or standing." Many outside could not even get close enough to gaze through the windows. Sojourner Truth and her companions of the previous campaign joined Douglass and other Free Soilers on the platform. Oliver Johnson reported for the *Pennsylvania Freeman*, Benjamin Jones for the *Bugle*, and numerous Free Soil presses were represented. The weather was pleasant, and warmth of feeling was pervasive as everyone sang, loudly and passionately, the movement's signature hymn, "I Am an Abolitionist," written by Garrison and sung to the melody of "Auld Lang Syne."[51]

Behind the show of unity, each side jockeyed for control. Parker Pillsbury advantageously presided over the Business Committee, which created resolutions. But speeches and floor debates persuaded delegates which resolutions to support. The meeting essentially became a duel between two master debaters—Douglass and Pillsbury. Douglass argued for resolutions to meet violence with violence against slaveholders, and he forcefully insisted that Garrisonians could "innocently support the Government and hold office under it." Pillsbury's objections were equally strenuous. Politicians simply could not be trusted, he said, and cited specific examples to show the "seductive influences" of politics. Walker, Wright, and Burleigh acted as Pillsbury's wingmen. Sojourner Truth contributed to the warm debates with stinging parleys from her seat and "very good remarks" from the podium. Intense logic prevailed on both sides, as speakers grew mordacious in articulating their positions. The audience loved it, and each adjournment whetted their appetites for more.[52]

Sunday was high drama, and it seemed as though everyone in the countryside headed for Salem. "From the East, West, North and South came long lines of vehicles." At 10 A.M., the "immense throng" flocked together under a broad canopy of towering oaks, which screened people from the sun. First, Marius Robinson gave a long and tedious but encouraging annual report; then, at mealtime intermission, Sojourner sold her books, sang, and engaged in informal conversation. As the much-anticipated open-air debates began, rain threatened on the western horizon. No building in the village could accommodate half the audience, so the people remained in the woods. The rain "came down in torrents," but speakers held forth nonetheless. The great body of the audience shielded themselves as best they could with umbrellas, remained, and listened. They sang songs during the hardest part of the rain. Finally the rain eased, and the committee introduced resolutions on political action; more debates commenced. As darkness enveloped the grove, the final and most memorable session forced everyone inside.[53]

In the meetinghouse, crowded to its utmost capacity, the "candle light evening session" was tense, and waxed as warm as the August night. Douglass, "at the particular request of his Free Soil friends," made one final impassioned speech in favor of the Constitution and voting away slavery. Using all of his considerable eloquence, Oliver Johnson wrote, Douglass spoke great truths "in a most impressive manner." The master wordsmith moved the assembly to tears. But, Johnson added, he did not sway the old-school Abolitionists. "Turning and twisting" the Constitution, Douglass and his Free Soil friends tried to justify the document, but he weakly admitted that it was "proslavery in several important features." Perhaps out of frustration, Douglass again turned to the subject of violence. Under certain circumstances, he insisted, violence outstripped "moral suasion." Using Russian serfs as an example, he insisted that their circumstances could not change without "shedding of the blood of tyrants." Then, as he substituted slaves and slaveholders for the serfs and the nobility, "in the glow of the candlelight," his biting eloquence seemed to carry away the assembly. His argument reached its climax, Johnson wrote, and the audience was "wrought to a high pitch of excitement by his rhetoric." Sensing he had the audience in his hand, he attacked the bulwark of Garrisonian ideology: "'What is the use of Moral Suasion to a people trampled in the dust?'" Immediately was heard "the voice of Sojourner Truth, who asked with startling effect, 'Is God gone?'" Douglass stood silent for a moment, seemingly "fully conscious of the force of the question." When he did finally reply, he could only affirm: "God was present in the minds of the oppressed to stimulate them to violence!"[54]

It was another of Sojourner's stunning sallies, the kind that left opponents speechless just long enough to impact an audience. The Quaker editor was deeply affected. "Sojourner's arrow," he believed, "was sped by more than human power" and "pierced with deadly effect" the belief that "the Sword is mightier than the Truth." Her riveting challenge helped kill any hope of successfully turning the tide toward political action.[55]

Douglass, whom Wendell Phillips had dubbed the "lion" some years earlier, was living up to that appellation in a manner Phillips least expected. But Sojourner Truth, the pacifist lamb of God, gave her friend something to think about. Oliver Johnson incorrectly labeled Douglass an "atheist" and a "sophist." Both Douglass and Truth were preachers in the AME Zion tradition. Douglass's "spiritual father" had been a devout black Methodist who first fanned into a flame his desire as a boy for knowledge, telling him that the "Lord had a great work for me to do." When thirteen-year-old Frederick protested, "I am a slave, and a slave for life," Father Lawson countered, "the Lord can make you free, my dear. All things are possible with him, only have faith in God." Douglass recalled that while he had had the "letter," Father Lawson had given him the "spirit"; he had accepted the old man's special blessing and "holy promises." Like Sojourner Truth, Douglass believed in prayer and faith. "Pray for me," he urged the black Boston community in 1853, "I believe in prayer." When pitted against Truth's spiritual challenge, Douglass's brilliance at secular rationale failed him that August night. Truth called on Douglass to trust his New Testament faith. He could only answer Truth with Old Testament militancy, that God would guide the oppressed in their violence against the oppressor. For a sublime moment, the lion and the lamb were poised at strategic odds. Both former slaves believed in God, quoted the Bible, and saw the hope of freedom in its messages. Ironically, both their interpretations came to pass. Violence eventually freed the oppressed; and the cause's morality led the nation to embrace emancipation as a crusade.[56]

The Western Anti-Slavery Society meeting ended harmoniously. Many moral suasionists vowed to accept political activism, and Douglass emphasized the organization's continued significance to every western Abolitionist. Resolutions reaffirmed Garrisonian principles even more strongly: rejection of "governmental union or confederation with slaveholders"; repudiation of the federal government; and renouncing "any constitutional obligations" to a government that acknowledged a slaveholder's right to "life, liberty, and pursuit of happiness." Certain resolutions struck directly at Free Soilers. The Western Anti-Slavery Society resolved that no political platform had "any virtue or merit which would tempt us from our present impregnable position as a strictly moral and religious anti-slavery movement."[57] For the next ten years, the antislavery apostles conducted their western campaigns on these principles, making them a hated group in the largely proslavery Midwest. As *Frederick Douglass' Paper* came out boldly for the Free Soil presidential candidates, the editor took a position squarely against exclusive use of moral suasion principles. But he continued to work with western Garrisonians.

Only Oliver Johnson's *Pennsylvania Freeman* reported Sojourner Truth's question "Is God gone?" Even Douglass failed to mention the encounter in his newspaper, although he recalled it later. Nonetheless, the confrontation was long remembered; and like many sayings that become legendary, "Is God gone?" took on a life independent of the person, the time, and the place. Garrison and Phillips read it in the *Freeman*. Phillips, who became Harriet Beecher Stowe's publisher, told her the story. Years later, publishing it in the *Independent,* Stowe took characteristic literary license. Between the two retellings, Sojourner's question became "Is God dead?" and the location became Boston's Faneuil Hall. Another revision occurred in 1890, when the confrontation was switched to Cooper Union in New York City.[58]

Rephrasing and relocation did not change the meaning or spirit of Sojourner's message. In asking "Is God gone?" she may have recalled Paul's letter on faith to the Hebrews. Paul affirms the power and promises of God and the omnipotence of Jesus, the "Great High Priest," over manmade priests. Faith is the key to apostolic acts: "the just shall live by faith; but if any man draw back, my soul shall have no pleasure in him"; or "faith is the substance of things hoped for, the evidence of things not seen." Sojourner Truth reminded Frederick Douglass that faith had worked miraculously even in their own personal lives. Moreover, their Abolitionist mission was also in the Scripture: "Remember them that are in bonds, as bound with them, and them which suffer adversity, as being yourselves also in the body." The Salem encounter exemplifies Truth's prophetic imagination and her appeal among antislavery apostles in nineteenth-century America.[59]

Her words became her own epitaph, and her question had a deep meaning for people of faith. Jesus was not a historical figure but a powerful modern arm of peaceful persuasion. Abolitionists were messengers of that power. Among the many synonyms for "gone" are "absent," "departed" "dead," "lost," and "hopeless."[60] Rather than God being gone, Sojourner Truth believed, God sojourned with her and her people. If, as Scripture maintained, God was hope and life, the opposite was despair and death. If God was gone, where was the hope for humanity? It was no wonder that for a moment the lion lost his roar.

In the spirit of the times, talk of bloodshed was dividing Abolitionists everywhere. In Christiana, Pennsylvania, in September 1851, self-emancipated William Parker hid four people fleeing from Edward Gorsuch, a Maryland slaveholder. In a predawn shootout between an armed biracial group called the Gideon Band for Self-defense and Gorsuch, his relatives, and a U.S. marshal, Gorsuch was killed and his son wounded. Parker escaped to Canada, but many blacks and several whites were arrested. Some Garrisonians participated in the armed rescues of self-emancipated people from their pursuers, while others, such as the Motts, assisted the accused but abhorred the use of violence. Christiana also troubled Sojourner Truth, who hated the Fugitive Slave Law and participated in underground activity but was a pacifist. Just as Douglass and Truth clashed over resistance, so did friends such as C. C. Burleigh and the Motts.[61]

In Ohio, the question of violence arose again for Sojourner Truth. A few weeks after Salem, she was in Cleveland at the Ohio Colored Convention. Vice president John Mercer Langston opened the proceedings by paying a special tribute to her. She addressed the audience, though her remarks were not recorded in the official proceedings. Christiana was on everyone's lips, and the convention hailed black physical resistance. That evening, a resolution supporting the use of violence to fight the Bloodhound Bill initiated intense debate. In her evening speech, Sojourner Truth tearfully called for "peace and forbearance." However, the black male majority contended that since the government had forsaken them and joined hands "with the robber" to enforce slavery, black people would "meet him with his own like weapons." The convention proclaimed a policy of covert civil disobedience including violence and then adjourned for a "general jubilee."[62] Sojourner's pacifism was not a popular approach among her wounded people.

She continued to make her mark in Ohio. Although she sometimes joined her traveling associates that fall, she had trekked on her own for months, and was familiar with the Western Reserve's towns, villages, and geography. According to one account, Marius Robinson provided her with a horse and buggy for traveling the rugged northern Ohio terrain. Another source states that it was black Ohioans who furnished her with the horse and buggy, in which she carried personal belongings, her own "vittles," and copies of her book. She held meetings wherever she found enough interested people, preferring a church but willingly using her buggy as a platform. If she had no lodgings, she could drive into the barn or field of a hospitable farmer, and do her daily cold water bathing in a local creek. The buggy's bottom was bed enough for the woman who had grown up sleeping on the kitchen floor of a Dutch farmhouse. When alone, she was not lonely. She loved composing songs, reciting Scripture, singing hymns, talking to the spirits, and talking to God. Perfectly at home in the natural environment, she arrived safely at her destination without benefit of literacy. She "sojourned" over the Western Reserve not aimlessly but sometimes leaving her itinerary to fate. Reportedly, when she came to a fork in an unfamiliar road, she dropped the reins, allowed the horse and buggy to drift, and said, "God, You drive."[63]

In Pennsylvania, Sojourner's Ohio friends said sad goodbyes. She was now a popular and well-known figure among them, and one whose agitation was widely published. Friends and acquaintances were already adopting her metaphors and phrases. Even "sojourning" became part of the Abolitionist lexicon. All willingly "attest to the good she has done in Ohio," Esther Lukins wrote, "not only in procuring an independence for herself, but in materially and sensibly aiding the Anti-Slavery cause." Sojourner Truth was a special favorite in Ashtabula County, especially with Betsy Cowles, who had presided over Ohio's first woman suffrage convention, only to see both blacks and women lose their franchise bid. Betsy wrote a treatise on how slavery exploited black women and entrapped slaveholding women who supported the white male patriarchy. In Akron, Sojourner not only merged human bondage and the slavery of sex, she brought Northern biracial sisterhood to the table and expressed the potential of unrealized power: "man is in a tight place, the poor slave is on him and woman is coming on him." In recognition of her impact as a champion of both women and the enslaved, the Ashtabula County Female Anti-Slavery Society presented her with a huge silk banner. It bore their name and the AASS's old motto "Am I Not a Woman and a Sister?"[64]

Among Sojourner's many goodbyes, none was sadder than the one with Josephine Griffing and J. W. Walker. Josephine and Sojourner had begun a deep companionship that lasted throughout their lives. J. W. Walker wrote a song for his fellow Methodist preacher and Spiritualist friend to commemorate the poignant memories of their shared field of labor. "A Hymn, . . . at Parting with Sojourner Truth and Others" was prophetic, because Walker would die an untimely death in 1854 in the service of antislavery:

> My dearest friends in bonds of love,
> Whose hearts the sweetest union prove,
> Your friendship's like a drawing band,
> Yet we must take the parting hand. . . .
> I hope you'll remember me,
> If here my face no more you see,
> An interest in your prayers I crave,
> That we may meet beyond the grave. . . . [65]

Sojourner Truth's legacy really began in Ohio, with her speech in Akron, her confrontation with Douglass, and her mighty witness against slavery.

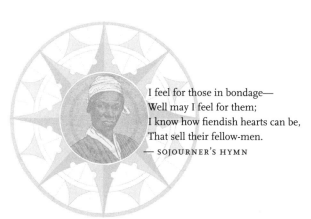

I feel for those in bondage—
Well may I feel for them;
I know how fiendish hearts can be,
That sell their fellow-men.
— SOJOURNER'S HYMN

CHAPTER 15

"I Go in for Agitatin'"

I

Sojourner Truth participated in abolition during momentous times, when the movement made great strides. Many histories insist that abolition's "greatest contribution" and "most difficult tasks" occurred in the 1830s and early 1840s, but in fact the apex of the antislavery struggle lay ahead. In the 1850s, the abolition movement extended its geographical reach, and infused other social movements, showcased women, and those with different ideologies merged strategies. Even so, it was a sinuous and rocky road to national antislavery awareness, leaving in its wake myriad symptoms: broken political agreements; imprisoned, worn out, or deceased activists; desperate "fugitive slaves"; and angry citizens. If the leadership and philosophy of the movement crystallized by the early 1840s, as many historians believe, then Abolitionists fully capitalized on that organizational maturity during the decade before Fort Sumter. Sojourner Truth was one of the movement's most visible crusaders.[1]

Returning from Ohio early in 1853, she stopped in Philadelphia. *Freeman* editor Oliver Johnson wrote that blacks and whites filled Clarkson Hall to capacity to hear this "strong minded woman" whose unusual dialect seemed "rather to augment than diminish her power" and eloquence. Besides championing emancipation "with courage that knoweth no fear and sublime faith in God," she had an amazing facility to delight the audience with laughter, then "move them to tears." Because of numerous invitations, she remained in the city for over a month. Another black woman visiting Philadelphia drew a different reception. When the famous singer Elizabeth Greenfield—called the "Black Swan" by many—sang in the city's whites-only concert halls, black Abolitionists publicly condemned her and labeled her the "Black Raven." Meanwhile, Sojourner Truth, "endowed with great energy of will," spoke to overflowing racially mixed audiences on behalf of her oppressed race.[2]

Philadelphia's black elite, however, apparently gave her a mixed reception. The newly formed AME Church newspaper, *Christian Recorder*, did not cover her lectures. The oldest, largest, and wealthiest black churches—Bethel AME, St. Thomas Episcopal, and Central Presbyterian—remained closed to Sojourner and even to literate black women preachers. This is especially ironic because AME bishop Daniel Payne heartily approved of white women speaking at Bethel. During Sojourner's Philadelphia stay, her friend Ruth Dugdale, a minister of the Society of Friends, addressed an "immense" audience at Bethel. Payne also allowed Oliver Johnson's wife, Mary, to lecture frequently on religion, health, anatomy, and physiology. Moreover, the Abolitionist bishop embraced Garrison, the most notorious Come-outer "heretic," and held a reception in his honor. But Payne, raised in the South as a Lutheran, adamantly opposed a nonlearned clergy, female ordination, and ecstatic manifestations of faith, all of which women preachers embraced.[3]

Sojourner's exclusion was really a snub from the clerical elite rather than an expression of universal class snobbery. She met twenty-seven-year-old Mary Ann Shadd, raised in a privileged activist Philadelphia household and now an expatriate in Canada West. She was in Philadelphia shepherding underground passengers and promoting emigration. She and Sojourner both had confrontational personalities and disparaged the concept of ladylike delicacy that precluded public speaking. The Sojourner also interacted with black and white members of Pennsylvania's antislavery societies, including members of the Forten-Purvis families, and spoke at the PFASS's annual meeting. The hall was full that night, despite unfavorable weather. Sojourner, who followed Lucretia Mott and Mary Grew on the program, launched her riveting witness against the house of bondage by recounting the wrongs that fed her bitter and vengeful hatred "toward her oppressors." She then movingly chronicled her transformation, when a "divine Spirit" had entered her heart. Discovering the strength to love, and the realization that even slaveholders might experience redemption for humanity's sake, she said she desired black liberation "for the master's good as well as the slaves." She urged everyone present to "engage in the good work of emancipation." The assembly listened with great interest and gratification "to a late hour."[4] Although Sojourner Truth was an untrained, unschooled preacher and Come-outer, her audience included those of every class and both races.

Stopping in Boston before going home to Northampton, she had a chance to see Garrison, her editor James Yerrinton, her daughter Elizabeth, and the newest family member, her infant grandson Samuel ("Sammy") Banks. Sojourner also observed that widespread efforts to enforce the Bloodhound Bill had created a new militancy among New England moral suasionists. At the Massachusetts Anti-Slavery Society annual meeting, Charles Remond's angry invective fired up the audience; he rejoiced over Loguen and May, along with Gerrit Smith, leading a daring rescue of self-emancipated Jerry Henry in Syracuse; the death of slaveholder Gorsuch at Christiana; and "the deaths of Calhoun, Clay, and Webster, that trio of defenders of slavery." Gerrit Smith was elected to Congress, where he, Joshua Giddings, and Massachusetts's two senators—Charles Sumner and Henry Wilson—organized a small radical political Abolitionist cadre. Even Whigs and Democrats, formerly lukewarm on antislavery, denounced the government as conspiring with the "slave power." Sojourner finally arrived in Northampton, after over two years' absence. Diana was there with her son Jimmy, but Sophia and her son Wesley had moved to upstate New York. The family reunion was brief, for it was the height of the lecture season. Sojourner soon headed for New York City.[5]

Her activist homecoming was here, in the "Sodom of the East," which had been her starting point. She reconnected with friends, including the Boyles and Bensons, and old employers, including the Whitings. In March, on the platform in the Broadway Tabernacle, at the Woman's Temperance Meeting, Sojourner joined Horace Greeley, Susan B. Anthony, Antoinette Brown (soon to be ordained), Amelia Bloomer (originator of the outfit named after her), phrenologist Lydia Fowler, and others to support the Maine liquor prohibition law. Greeley's *Tribune* also advertised Sojourner's individual meetings. On Sunday, it reported, she would deliver an address on "religion and morals" at a hall on Broadway: "Her style differs from the current literature, as she was never taught to read. . . . But her thoughts are unsurpassed."[6] She now had access to the most influential newspaper in the state and perhaps the North.

After about a month in the New York vicinity, she returned to Boston, where the Garrisons gave her the distressing news that Diana was gravely ill with pleurisy and lung fever. Sojourner went immediately to her daughter's bedside. She nursed Diana for two weeks, but her illness lingered. Unwilling to leave Diana unattended, but needing to be on the road, Sojourner contacted her daughter Elizabeth through their family friend Mary Gale. Elizabeth must come immediately to Northampton, Sojourner insisted, so "I can go to New

York, and other places and do the business that is necessary I should do." Sojourner's letter said nothing about the nature of her business. It may have been lecturing, or making arrangements to secure the rights to her *Narrative,* or financing a new printing. It may also have been underground "business," because instead of New York, she went to Pennsylvania, where she met with Underground Railroad supervisor William Still. He announced that Sojourner Truth was "spending some time" in the Philadelphia area, using his antislavery office as a headquarters and working with him and Lucretia Mott while also conducting individual meetings.[7] Since Still, Mott, and Robert Purvis were the most active underground supervisors in eastern Pennsylvania, most likely Sojourner was transporting underground passengers.

Conforming to her belief that spirituality was a moral prescriptive for promoting the public good, she embraced two other progressive movements. In June 1853, an imposing number of "aged Friends" in Quaker garb and a "fine a company of youths assembled in rural Pennsylvania to found the Longwood Yearly Meeting of Progressive Friends." These mostly excommunicated Hicksites also invited thousands of non-Quakers, Come-outers, agnostics, and others from as far west as Iowa, as far east as Maine, and as far south as Kentucky. Sojourner Truth joined a broad spectrum of "intelligent" Abolitionists, including Douglass, Thomas Garrett, Levi Coffin, Garrison, Thomas Wentworth Higginson, Samuel May, Theodore Parker, Ernestine Rose, and former slaveholders such as Cassius Clay. The Longwood Friends Meeting became a famous nonsectarian four-day annual event at which radicals recommitted themselves to eradicating all forms of social injustice while affirming that human bondage was the most pressing national issue. Sojourner's relationship with these unorthodox Progressive Friends was as close as she came to a religious affiliation.[8]

Her connection to the free thought "Bible conventions" that began to meet around this time, first in Ohio and then in Connecticut, seemed positively "heretical." Renowned Spiritualist Andrew Jackson Davis organized the 1853 Hartford convention, which Truth, Garrison, James Boyle, the Fosters, Parker Pillsbury, Ernestine Rose, and many others attended. (Wendell Phillips and some other Abolitionists refused to participate.) Sojourner always expressed interest in open scriptural inquiry, and the radicals maintained that parts of the Bible were contradictory, were "wrapped in darkness," and bore "no sign of a divine or supernatural authority." No people, Davis proclaimed, had "perpetuated more numerous and more appalling outrages on humanity than those called Christians." Garrison added that to insist that everything in the Bible was God's word and the only rule of faith and practice was "absurd" and "highly pernicious." Such thinking not only injured the intellect and the soul but also was "a stumbling block in the way of human redemption." Women argued that men used the Bible to support patriarchal authority and silence female voices. Everyone agreed that slaveholders justified bondage through the Bible while simultaneously denying literacy to enslaved people. The Bible, participants said, should be "freely examined" because it was as open to interpretation and human error as any other book. But conveners upheld the Old Testament's visionary prophecy and the New Testament's apostolic charge. The "Word" becoming "flesh" was a metaphor for creating a world based on "love" and all this condition implied: equality, liberty, wisdom, community, and peace. Sadly, reformers asserted, in the hands of the "American Church" and the "Priesthood," the Bible had become a weapon against "the rising spirit of religious liberty." But these "ultraists" rejected notions of a *lack of faith*. Hence they denounced and "ignominiously expelled" Ernestine Rose because of her atheist tirades. Nonetheless, the denominations were outraged, and Methodists noted Sojourner Truth's presence at these conventions.[9]

In September 1853, Garrisonians converged in New York City for several conventions, including what they called the Whole World Temperance Meeting—because the earlier National Temperance Convention had expelled female and black delegates who were sent as representatives. Abolitionists crowded into Metropolitan Hall, the city's largest, most magnificent, and most fashionable public edifice. Mindful of public furor over the recent Bible convention, Garrison began with Bible in hand. No book was held in greater veneration, he declared, yet so little understood and so much perverted. However, if rightly interpreted, "I know of no book which is so valuable." He read the fifth and seventh chapters of Jeremiah—the weeping prophet lamenting the tragic fate awaiting his sinful, desolate, unrepentant people. After a female Quaker preacher's simple "blessing" on the audience, C. C. Burleigh and Garrison spoke. "MRS. SOJOURNER TRUTH" closed the session.[10]

She was particularly inspiring that afternoon. Even while conforming to strategic antislavery rhetoric, she was original. Complimenting Garrison and Burleigh's eloquent advocacy for "the rights of my poor, down-trodden race," she nonetheless maintained that no one could plead so vigorously as the sufferers. Time had healed some pain, and "Christ Jesus" had enlightened her mind with a spiritual awareness that transformed anger and hate into forgiveness. The more light she received, the less bitterness she felt, and she wanted harmony between the races. She spoke of enslavement among the "Low Dutch" and how she was not only raised ignorant of letters, ill-clad, and ill-fed, she was called "a brute." White people said "We were a species of monkeys or baboons." Having no knowledge, she had believed it. But now she knew something of her race's history. In Ohio, at a black convention, she had shared the platform with self-emancipated minister J. W. C. Pennington, recently returned from studies in Europe; he had delighted his black audience with information about their ancient African past. She also spoke of the importance of family, and separation as the cruelest aspect of bondage. "I can't read," she told her audience, "but I can feel"; and she invited listeners to take a vicarious journey with her into the emotions of the enslaved:

> "I think I can see my mother now as she stood many a night . . . in the old apple orchard, under the open heaven, when the moon and stars were brightly shining. My poor mother would weep and say in Dutch, 'Oh! Mein Got, Mein Got,' which means in English, my God. "My poor children will be sold into Slavery." I did not know what that meant then, but I have learned since. My mother cried bitterly, and I took the corner of her old apron and wiped her eyes, and asked what she cried for. She said, 'my poor child we are going to be sold, and we shant see one another again; when you are far away; remember that I shall see the same moon and stars that you look at, and when we die we shall both go to heaven among them.'"

Audiences wept over the vision of Mau-mau Bet's dream about fellowship in a future world, and telling her child to ask God to "make bad people good." The people didn't get any better," Sojourner said, so she prayed that God would "kill them for they seemed to die quicker than they got good." Returning to her beginning point, she said that when she finally understood the true meaning of faith, she embraced her mother's spirituality and stopped praying for the death of all whites. Despite this "flow of love" that allowed forgiveness, she concluded with her main theme: what slavery had done to her and her loved ones. "I am the last of my family," she said. "I have got a sister somewhere, if she is alive; but I don't know, it is so long since I saw her." Sojourner said she was around "sixty years old," and her oldest daughter was "forty." Sojourner was only a few years off, but mistakenly believed she had spent "forty" instead of thirty years in bondage. A witty plug for her book ended her painful, personal saga: "I've got a narrative of one part of my life and I take that part to support the other. [Laughter]." When the laughter subsided, Sojourner urged Abolitionists to do everything in their power to ameliorate the condition of her race. She took her seat amid "Cheers."[11]

She was the last speaker to complete an address without interruption. The evening meeting dissolved in a row, as local rowdies and a large number of Southerners stormed into the hall without paying the admission charge of 12 1/2 cents. They poked fun at Lucretia Mott's "colored silk robe, with the Quaker cap," and hissed until she "finally broke off in the middle of her speech" and quietly sat down. Lucy Stone then rose, also wearing a black robe but with "regular Bloomer trousers." Although she initially challenged the rowdies and roared back, their "thunderous shouts," hisses, and deafening torrents of expletives also forced her from the platform. The Abolitionists had to adjourn, the *Herald* wrote approvingly. But the *Tribune* decried the scandalous treatment of "talented and celebrated" individuals committed to "giving freedom to human beings." With undampened spirits, the "whole-hog reformers" held a "Great Temperance Banquet," graced with uplifting singing, good company, and fine speeches. While the *Tribune* called the meal a major disappointment, Sojourner and her associates relished vegetable soups, wheat meal cakes, molded farina, baked sweet potatoes, stewed creamed squashes, custards, fruit, and pure cold water.[12]

In spite of her success at Metropolitan Hall, speaking to New York City black audiences was her crowning achievement. "SOJOURNER TRUTH, a distinguished colored woman," the *Tribune* announced, would speak at the Colored Congregational Church. Unfortunately the *Tribune* gave the wrong address, and due to that "misdescription of the locality," attendance was not as numerous as expected. But the audience "(principally colored with a sprinkling of white folks) made a decent display in the body of the church, and listened with attention to the address and proceedings." The meeting opened with a "well sung" hymn accompanied by the organ. Pastor Levin Tilmon, a local activist, offered "a very excellent and appropriate prayer" and then introduced the speaker.[13]

Having addressed twelve hundred people the day before, Sojourner expressed disappointment in the audience's "thinness." Yet, she said, God promised that "Where two or three were gathered together in His name, He would be in the midst," hence God would extend a blessing to the meeting. She was in rare form, speaking as though the sanctuary was full. The spirit of God had come upon her, she said, and she had preached at a great many meetings, often before large white audiences. Now, she thanked God for the chance to stand before her own people in her home state. Although she had prayed for slave owners—which was hard enough, she said—her greatest difficulty was standing before her own people, with whom she shared the dilemmas of oppression and the quagmire of racism. What could she say to fellow sufferers on the subject of slavery? Many, like her, were "robbed of education . . . rights . . . children . . . father, mother, sister, and brother." They were "strangers in the land, who had had little of God's footstool under their control."

Since this audience knew of slavery's wrongs, she bore personal witness in solidarity. She "was tied up and whipped till the blood trickled down her back"; her young husband was whipped, and his blood had "flowed till it could be traced for a mile on the snow"; and her beloved father had been allowed to freeze to death." Yes, she had begged God "to kill all the white people and not leave one for seed." Although eventually, faith bound her to mercy "in a Christian spirit and in one of forgiveness," blacks really had no choice. God would punish whites, and she "had high hopes" for that time of retribution. For what could whites say on the Day of Judgment? Moreover, in spite of slavery and racism, she said, drawing loud applause, "she lived and God lived in her." She also spoke of her time in New York after her emancipation. Although she had been "ignorant and could not speak English very well," she would "not bow to the filth of the City." She went around with the lady who had brought her there, and determined to learn all she could. Having grown up not even knowing that Jesus Christ was the Son of God, she discovered a wondrous spirituality. She wanted to get among her own colored people, "do good" through love, and teach them. But "they repulsed her and shoved her off. . . . She went away weeping." Sojourner understood that blacks' rebuff of their own kind was part of white brainwashing, for she, too, had once imbibed hatred of things black. She used to ask "Why was I black?" If born white, "I could have plenty of food and clothes." Now, she said, she "gloried her color" and "was well satisfied" with the "color that God had been pleased to give her."

She often wondered, she added, what blacks had done "that they should be hated." The answer was skin color, even though her people "had not made themselves black." Yet whites not only victimized her race, they tried to evade culpability by saying blacks were lazy and careless about their own rights and liberties. Thus, she said, the oppressor bound blacks "hand and foot, and ask them why they did not run." She insisted that even black moral lapses and lethargy were products of prejudice and lack of opportunity. These facts, she said, spoke for themselves. "The blood and sweat and tears drawn from the black people were sufficient to cover the earth all over the United States," and it was difficult to forgive whites. Yet she urged her people to go forward in a spirit of hope and race progress. Her own humble history and presence exemplified the power of faith, strength, and human will. She was purchasing a home, had published her life's story, and had spoken to multitudes throughout the North. And she had begun with nothing—a slave, born in a rural Dutch village, an unschooled non–English speaker. When emancipated, she had had no money, but possessed character, thrift, and a sustaining faith.

She ended with a fervent call for action. Blacks had a responsibility to join white reformers and speak out publicly for their rights. She "exhorted the people to stir and not let the white people have it all to themselves." She denounced smug do-nothing blacks who were seemingly satisfied with their lot and caring nothing for others. There was more than one kind of bondage, and black complacency also restrained her people. She urged black women to take a stand and demand their rights. "As a colored woman," she wanted *all* the rights to which she was entitled. Her address "occupied a considerable time," the *Tribune* wrote, and excited "considerable interest and popularity." Although she did not do a lucrative business among this working-class group, Sojourner passed around her *Narrative* and sold several copies.[14]

She held other meetings in the New York vicinity. Variety, imagination, fullness of experience, sincerity, tragedy, and humor dominated her speeches. Her creativity arose from her skill in narrative and explication and from her understanding of English as a second language. She used old material in new ways, framing her reservoir of stories, metaphors, biblical imagery, and anecdotes into practical themes and political jibes. Though she could not write, reporters captured her words with the new method of phonography while they ignored other Abolitionists' speeches. Sojourner Truth was more than an Abolitionist; she was a personality.

Two days after her uplifting address in the black church, she faced a challenging situation at the meeting of the Woman's Rights Convention, managing it with the genius that was hers alone. For this convention, Angelina Grimké Weld had emerged briefly from her domestic perch, and Frances Gage had traveled from her new St. Louis home. Three years of experience and their recent expulsion from the National Temperance Convention had stiffened the women's resolve. Even the *Herald* admitted that these seasoned reformers were "not wanting in coolness and self-possession." Most women still avoided the platform, but they dominated the audience, and so many had bobbed their hair and donned bloomers that the *Herald* ridiculed the convention as "The Bloomer Comedy." Even as excited rowdies tried to dislodge the convention and create a melee, President Lucretia Mott noted that the women's "calm" was a "beautiful sight." Sojourner was the lone black woman on the platform. "We observed an old colored woman, named Sojourner Truth" the *Herald* wrote, "who, we presume, also demands the rights to vote, for these ladies claim that right for all, without distinction of sex or color." Other "colored ladies of the city" the *Herald* noted, refused "to assist their white sisters in their movement." Sojourner did not wear bloomers, but the *Herald* labeled her talk the "Piquant Speech of a Black Bloomer."[15]

She came forward, amid "hisses, cheers, and the most uproarious laughter," and began with a chaffing African American "toast" meant to insult the rowdies. "It is good for me to come forth to draw out the spirit of the people here for there are some I see with the spirit of the geese and the snake." Throwing insults back, the rowdies attempted to put the speaker in her "place"—that of serving whites. They "called for half a dozen [oysters] in the shell," the *Daily Times* wrote. "I am also a citizen of the State of New York, for I was born in it; therefore I feel at home here," she answered defiantly. "I was a slave in the State of New York. I came forth to speak in behalf of woman's rights, for I know a little mite about their rights, and that little mite I want to throw in while the scales are moving." The rowdies shouted, "Hurry up the stew." She challenged, "I know that it feels a kind of hissing and tickling like to see a colored person thrown down so low that they never expect to come up again; but they are come." The reformers laughed and applauded. Sojourner Truth would have her say.[16]

She framed a satirical metaphor, comparing modern female oppression with biblical times. The Persian King Ahasuerus chose a beautiful young captive Jew named Esther (the *Herald* thought she said "Hester") as his queen. "I was a thinking when I saw women contending for their rights," she said, "I was a thinking what a difference there is now and what there was in olden times, when it seemed that the great kings of the earth would kill a woman if she spoke to them." And yet, Sojourner related, Queen Esther risked her life and complained before the king about oppression and wrong. Esther's courage greatly impressed King Ahasuerus, Sojourner reminded the assembly, and "he raised his scepter up and he says 'half of my kingdom will I grant unto thee.'" Esther's valor saved her people from slaughter and her guardian Mordecai from execution by the evil machinations of Persian Prince Haman (the *Tribune* thought she said "Herrod"). "Should the king of the United States be greater or more crueller or more harder?" Sojourner asked. Women "want their rights as Queen Hester [*sic*] wanted her rights, but the King was so liberal that he said he would give half of his kingdom to her." Woman came to "demand her rights—not the half of a kingdom," Sojourner insisted, yet "you hear how the sons hiss their mothers like snakes because they come to ask for their rights." She reminded the men of the fate meted out to Prince Haman because he plotted wrongfully against Esther's guardian. "Although the great King hung Haman," said the pacifist Sojourner, "I want no man to be killed." The rowdies hissed as she concluded: "I am watching these hisses, and I intend to watch them. . . . When an aged woman comes forth, God says honor your father and mother that thy days may be long in the land of thy youth. You ought to honor your father and mother instead of hissing like snakes and geese. I thank you for hearing me; I want to bring these things before you to show you I am sitting among you and that every now and then I will come and tell you what time of night it is."[17]

Sojourner "sat down amidst great applause" from the reformers, the *Herald* wrote, but she had created "a great deal of fun" for the rowdies. The *Tribune* regretted the disrespectful treatment accorded her, but other papers insisted she had no right to expect anything else. It was not an insult to publicly ridicule a black woman who belonged in the kitchen. But, the *Times* added, the real culprits were the "desexed she-males" whose "shameless self-exposure" aroused the "rabble and disgusted the sensible." Although conservative newspapers proclaimed that inviting Sojourner Truth had turned the event into "a regular breakdown," women at the convention hailed her speech as a great success. The black woman's commanding personality and dynamic, colorful originality attracted even the racist press. Fully aware of the media's power, Sojourner seemed to relish being a subject of their interest. Later in life, she would resent how white print culture misrepresented and distorted her image.[18]

After the Woman's Convention, she spoke in New Jersey and on Long Island. At the Williamsburgh Congregational Church, she expressed her people's growing impatience and the retribution awaiting confirmed white racists at the "bar of judgment." She also "narrated the history of her mother-in-law, who was sold from her native land in Africa, and brought to this country and sold in bondage."[19] Black intellectuals such as J. W. C. Pennington and William Wells Brown had helped arouse in black Americans such as Sojourner Truth a new sense of identity and connectedness to African civilization. She publicly asserted pride in her cultural antecedents and history by relating her mother-in-law and grandparents' West African roots during her remarks.

Some time in 1853, the *Narrative* sold out of its first printing. Sojourner's friend James Boyle, now a New York City preacher, patent medicine distributor, and physician, purchased the plates of the *Narrative* and financed a second printing identical to the Boston 1850 edition. Now she had a new stock of books for the lecture circuit.[20]

She continued to deliver some of her most important addresses at this time. Her November appearance at Abyssinian Baptist Church reflected her growing influence and leadership recognition among African Americans. "We hope she may have a full house," wrote the *Standard*, now edited by her friend Oliver Johnson. "Though illiterate, she is a woman of good natural abilities, and . . . capable of exciting the deepest sympathy of those who hear her." A "respectable audience of colored people" filled the sanctuary for her discourse with her people. Her "inscribed banner of white satin" hung from the pulpit cushion, signifying the prominence of slavery and woman's rights in her message. At the top, it read: "ASHTABULA COUNTY. / Am I not a Woman and a Sister?" Underneath this statement was a kneeling figure of a woman with uplifted hands, and below it the lines "How long, O, Lord! How long, / A Million-and-a-half of American Women in chains. / Shall we heed their wrongs? / Will not righteous God be avenged upon / Such a Nation as this?" An elderly colored man opened the meeting with a prayer, and Sojourner sang her hymn "I am pleading for my people, / a poor, down-trodden race."

Then she delivered her most secular and controversial lecture to a black audience on record. There was a time, she began, when her people did all the common work. But gradually, whites pushed blacks out of nearly every unskilled occupation. Now, "white folks" cleaned boots and waited on tables. Whites "lie about lazy, and beg cold victuals"; but, she admitted amid laughter, "colored people did that sometimes too." Humor was one of her most deft tactics for winning over an audience. Speaking with anti-immigrant bias, she said that since Irish laborers had replaced blacks, the city streets were less clean. Thick layers of dirt covered New York, producing flies that invaded the shops and even got into people's eyes. She observed that dirt, mud, and filth had hardened on the streets and whites had to use "picks and crow bars and pull up the stones to remove the dirt, and then go again." The audience again erupted into laughter.

Unemployment was not funny, however, and she grew serious. Like other leaders, she was concerned about her people's economic plight. "Not long ago nobody but colored people were coachmen and barbers." But "now they have white Pompeys, with the livery coats on and poor black Pompey goes to the wall." Yet she was encouraging. "My colored brothers and sisters, there's a remedy" for unemployment and racism. While Douglass had proposed a black manual labor school, Sojourner followed the black westerners' solution of emigration—not colonization, for they would not be driven out of America. "Where I was lately lecturing out in Pennsylvania," she began, "farmers wanted good men and women willing to work their farms on shares." If blacks went out there, she said, "depend upon it, in the course of time you will get to be independent." They could save money, buy land, and become self-sufficient. She who had witnessed and experienced a lifetime of personal and historical transformations had no patience with blacks who abhorred leaving their home environments. She reminded them of her own personal example. "How long ago was it that a colored woman could address a white audience of a thousand people, and be listened to with respectful attention." She also urged blacks to be law-abiding. Newspapers were replete with crimes *against* blacks but few *by* them. "Continue to put the white people to the blush," she counseled. Blacks should never stoop to the level of whites.

She also used the meeting to promote religious reform, critique clerical hierarchy, and advocate for women. She urged ministers to stop focusing on events thousands of years old, and make the Word flesh by helping humanity. It was so much easier to go to Egypt, "among the bones of dead Pharaohs and mummies," than to deal with the stern realities of the "living present." She criticized the superfluous ostentation of church edifices, "big, lumbering things" taking up costly space and doing no good. Churches filled a third of their capacity once a week while hosts of destitute citizens resided in "low dens and sky lighted garrets." Why not lodge people in these immense, empty structures that were "a dead loss" most of the time? She mercilessly satirized black male clerical opposition to women speaking in public. "Big Greek-crammed, mouthing men," for many a long century, "had been befogging the world, and getting its affairs into the most terrible snarl and confusion." Yet when women spoke, ministers "cried 'shame on women!'" She urged black sisters to seize their special mission, move forward, and not leave it all to white women. In a mocking role reversal, she asserted that women, not men, were "peculiarly adapted to fill the talking professions." Men, she ribbed, should "no longer unsex themselves by leaving the plow and the plane, for the pulpit and the platform." Women, she said, could "set matters in general aright, and then keep them so." They must "set to work and drag the world right side up, disentangling it from the snarl which men have willfully got it into." Women had only to be resourceful, united, and resolutely put "their shoulders to the wheel."[21]

There was certainly no laughter now. Shock was another of her strategies. Few speakers used satire more skillfully. Not since Maria Stewart had a black woman so publicly and scathingly seared black men. And like Maria, Sojourner's biting parody and lambasting of male leaders as narrow, greedy, sexist, and un-Christian undoubtedly stunned her listeners. Just as she wanted whites to "feel" what the enslaved felt, she wanted to jolt her race into a sense of urgency. Although she knew that some might dismiss her as crazy and ignorant, she gave blacks, especially women, much to think about. She may have inspired twenty-three-year-old Elizabeth Jennings. A member of Levin Tilmon's church, where Sojourner spoke, in 1854 Jennings sued the New York public transit system in 1854 for injuries she sustained when she was thrown off a "white only" trolley car. Sojourner's example inspired Canada West activist Mary Ann Shadd in battles over gender issues with Lewis Tappan's American Missionary Association. Sojourner also influenced black women in unknown ways. One definite indication of a positive response to her at Abyssinian was that after her address, she "did a considerable business in the way of selling the first part of her life . . . to support the remainder."[22]

In December 1853, she reunited with western friends at the historic twentieth anniversary celebration of the AASS held in Philadelphia. The Douglass-Garrisonians rift had crested during the last six months, and key Abolitionists avoided the convention. However, general black attendance was the highest ever, and Sojourner's public witness undoubtedly loosened the tongues of other black women. Several left their seats in the audience and briefly took the platform. The audience was "deeply moved" when a Mrs. Williams of Delaware offered emotional praise to the AASS. Wilmington Methodists called Abolitionists "infidels" and "enemies of the colored people," Mrs. Williams said, but now she could personally refute that. She had heard here more truth, been more "enlightened as to the character of God," and had her "heart more stirred with love of God" than from any Methodist preaching. Sojourner Truth joined other blacks who spoke emphatically and convincingly against colonization, which some whites still advocated. "Colored men and women" denounced and debated colonization, Giles Stebbins noted, with "an earnest indignation, a touching pathos, and a spirit of firm and intelligent resolve." Sojourner Truth sang a "plaintive song" about the wrongs of slavery. The convention promised to publish the debates over colonization resolutions, but never did. Instead, with the exception of Lucretia Mott, male New Englanders dominated the entire published accounts.[23] This was the sort of slight that angered black Abolitionist leaders.

Two preaching women—Sojourner Truth and Jarena Lee—sat together on the platform at that meeting. Significant parallels of their lives further underscore the struggles that female preacher-activists endured. Both Lee and Truth were converted and "sanctified" under Methodism, preached without ordination, were camp meeting favorites, and published accounts of their lives (Lee in 1836 and 1844). Lee joined the AASS in 1840, and although after 1849 her whereabouts were reportedly unknown, she was active in Philadelphia. She was certainly one of the insurgent black women who in 1850 unsuccessfully demanded Methodist ordination. Like Sojourner, she remained unrecognized by the AME Church, and Bishop Daniel Payne refused to reprint her memoirs.[24] Years earlier, Lee had been an example for Isabella the preaching woman. In 1853, at seventy, Lee joined Sojourner Truth on the platform and opposed colonization.

II

The AASS began its pivotal twenty-first year during an economic boom. California gold was enriching the national purse; Southern cotton exports reached one billion pounds; 20,000 miles of rail stretched across America; commercial agriculture and urban manufacturing was flourishing; and European immigrants were entering the country in massive numbers.[25]

Progress, prosperity, and population explosion created demands for territorial expansion, which opened old political wounds. In 1854, Illinois Senator Stephen Douglas, chair of the powerful Committee on Territories, challenged the 1820 compromise that had admitted Missouri as a slave state and banned slavery in regions extending north from the latitude of 36° 30′ to the Canadian border and west to the Rocky Mountains. Douglas proposed dividing Kansas and Nebraska into separate territories and called for "popular sovereignty"—allowing inhabitants to vote on slavery. Ecologically, eastern Kansas resembled neighboring Missouri, which had over a hundred thousand enslaved people. Slaveholders immediately began building a proslavery majority in Kansas.[26]

Attempts to eviscerate the Missouri Compromise caused a storm in the North and West, even among some Democrats and Cotton Whigs. Many believed that Douglas had violated the national compact and undermined the Founding Fathers' intent to restrict slavery. Politicians who had supported the Bloodhound Bill as "the price of union" now envisioned a sinister plan to embed slavery in the national future. The old Liberty Party idea of a Slave Power reemerged; everyone followed the bill closely. Churches shook off their lethargy and began expressing antislavery sentiments. In New England, 3,050 clergy sent an interdenominational protest petition to Washington, which New York ministers soon emulated. Even the proslavery *Herald* called Douglas's bill "insane" and predicted a presidential veto, if it passed. Nonetheless, Congress passed the Kansas-Nebraska Bill, and Franklin Pierce signed it in May 1854. Radical Abolitionists fervently reiterated "no union with slaveholders" and called for antislavery revitalization, recommitment, sacrifices, and contributions from "Maine to Wisconsin."[27]

Simultaneously, Sojourner Truth joined thousands of reformers in Boston for the meetings of the New England Anti-Slavery Convention and the Woman's

Convention. Before those meetings happened, however, the entire nation's attention turned to Boston, the "Citadel of Liberty." A self-emancipated man, Anthony Burns, was arrested. Authorities had vowed never to have repetitions of the armed rescues of Jerry Henry in Syracuse and Frederick ("Shadrach") Wilkins in Boston or of the shootout in Christiana. For their part, Boston's Abolitionists still chafed over an unsuccessful attempt they made in 1851 to liberate a self-emancipated man named Thomas Sims. They pledged a revolutionary "Tea Party" to rescue Burns. On the evening of May 26, while over five thousand mostly white Abolitionists convened an angry evening Vigilance Committee meeting, Lewis Hayden took a group of black men to the courthouse. After the meeting, where Wendell Phillips, Theodore Parker, and others had urged calm, Unitarian minister Thomas Wentworth Higginson and shoemaker Martin Stowell, both of Worcester, and a group of whites joined the blacks. Hayden, Higginson, and Stowell led men armed with revolvers, axes, clubs, and cleavers in an attack on the courthouse. After struggling to push a long wooden beam through the heavy door panels, the Abolitionists engaged in a pitched battle with deputies. As the Abolitionists were beaten back and Higginson's face was bloodied badly, Hayden fired pistols to cover Higginson's retreat. In the melee of shots, knives, fists, curses, shouts, and withdrawing protesters, a mortally wounded deputized Irish truck man shouted, "I am stabbed!" The Abolitionists fled; within days, nine were arrested, including Hayden, Higginson, and Stowell, and charged with "High Treason." Phillips, Parker, and others were also indicted.[28]

A week of legal maneuverings and nightly Faneuil Hall protests ensued. Sullen, enraged black Bostonians filled the streets and milled around the courthouse, "watching from dawn till eve, and some of them the long night through." Ignoring the "jeers and insults of pro-slavery Irishmen and pro-slavery Americans," blacks stood daily vigil at great economic sacrifice. Even pacifists expressed militancy. "The arrest of every fugitive may be contested *even unto blood,*" Angelina Grimké Weld insisted. Stephen Foster urged every man to fight slavery, and if his weapons be physical, "let him use them." Predictably, Burns lost his case, and President Pierce called out the Cavalry and Marines. Sojourner Truth was certainly among the throngs of black women who wept as two thousand heavily armed whites escorted the lone black man to a federal cutter in Boston Harbor on June 2. "Shame!" black onlookers shouted. The scene "made my blood boil," young Charlotte Forten wrote, standing with her father and Uncle Robert and Aunt Harriet Purvis. Church bells tolled, some stores closed, and black men stood with clenched fists. However, some whites cheered, and on observing Wendell Phillips and Theodore Parker yelled, "there go murderers" of an Irish workingman.[29]

The Massachusetts Anti-Slavery Society held a July Fourth "Grand Mass Meeting of Friends of Freedom" in honor of "BURNS and SIMS!" They urged all towns and villages of the Commonwealth to challenge "the success of the Nebraska Bill and the fresh insult" occasioned by the "kidnapping of Anthony Burns in the City of Adams and Hancock." Boston's Vigilance Committee urged citizens to ring church bells, hold protests, preach sermons, and evince other expressions of national disgrace and humiliation. The meeting would be a momentous counterdemonstration to support Abolitionists such as Hayden, Higginson, Stowell, Phillips, Parker, and all others free on bail but under indictment for "High Treason."[30]

Boston, Milford, Northampton, Springfield, and Worcester provided special trains to the picnic-rally in Framingham. Carriages, buckboards, and horses also filled the tree-lined grove. It was a community affair; Sojourner may have brought her family. Swings, boat rides, and a refreshment stand gave the occasion a celebratory air. Yet it was called a day of "humiliation and sorrow." A quiet pond graced the background of the speakers' platform, which chief organizer William C. Nell had draped in a black American flag and two banners. One, labeled "Virginia," displayed triumphant insignias and ribbons. The other said "Redeem Massachusetts." Garrison's portrait rested between the state banners, to "break the chain" binding them. Two white flags labeled "Kansas" and "Nebraska" were on the platform. Sojourner Truth was among the cavalcade of speakers, including Henry David Thoreau, who was greatly disappointed because his time, like everyone's, was strictly limited.[31]

A melancholy Garrison spoke first, lamenting that slavery had rendered meaningless the noble promise of the Declaration of Independence. Decrying the harsh treatment of the accused men while incarcerated, he asked: what was an Abolitionist after all "but a sincere believer in the Declaration of 76?" Yet Abolitionists suffered every kind of personal defamation and ostracism. Though he remained committed to turning the world upside down, he wondered if the nation would ever recognize a common humanity. Then, one by one, he held up various documents. Expressing the "testimony of his own soul," borrowing a page from Martin Luther's defiance of canon law and the papal bull, he torched a copy of the Fugitive Slave Law, the commissioner's decision on Burns, and the grand jury's indictment against the Abolitionists. After burning each document, in the African American call-and-response style, Garrison shouted, "And let all the people say 'Amen.'" The assembly applauded, cheered, and shouted a hearty, nearly unanimous "Amen." Finally, Garrison held up a copy of the American Constitution. He lambasted it as "the source and parent of the other atrocities—a covenant with death and an agreement with hell." Setting it afire, he proclaimed, "So perish all compromises with tyranny," and called on the people for a response. A roar of "Amen'" went up to the heavens, along with a few hisses and "wrathful exclamations." This dramatic "pinnacle" and act of defiance toward American political culture highlighted both the despair and renewed determination of the AASS as it entered its second generation of agitation. An "outburst of feeling" prompted Charles L. Remond to speak, despite not being on the program. He echoed the sentiments of other blacks in stating, amid loud applause, that Garrison's actions were especially meaningful because "he did so in the name of three million slaves, with whom he [Remond] was identified by complexion."[32]

After a lunch break, Wendell Phillips introduced Sojourner Truth. Having listened, she took her subject from a preceding speaker, John C. Cluer, a fifty-one-year-old Scot and former Chartist who had been arrested for his role in the courthouse melee, indicted for murder, and brutalized during ten isolating days in jail. "I amaze myself," he had told the audience. He was a confirmed pacifist who now advocated "war, rather than interminable slavery!" Disgusted with government complicity in slavery and proud of his participation in the protest, Cluer drew loud applause when he said that he "got within his breast a little bit of Scotch thistle, which pricked him up to struggle for liberty, and he would do so as long as he lived."[33] This was Sojourner's springboard for making some provocative comparisons and ominous predictions and for signifying, or conjecturing her own meaning from others' comments.

Commanding the "undivided attention of the great audience," she carefully distinguished between "good" and evil whites. But she also reminded whites of their complicity with slavery. While blessings awaited her people, she predicted both earthly punishment and doom in judgment for whites. She identified with John Cluer's treatment during his jail time, saying that since he had "felt" oppression briefly, perhaps he could appreciate something of the sufferings her race endured as a way of life. Cluer's brief encounter with incarceration brutalities paled in comparison to what enslaved folk experienced. Nonetheless, she said, inciting laughter and cheers, "it was good that white folks should sometimes feel the prick," and they would feel more. "God would yet execute his judgments upon the white people for their oppression and cruelty," she prophesied, and against the innocent as well as the guilty. Should God have more mercy on "Anglo-Saxons than on Africans," given what whites had done to blacks? Whites were indeed fortunate that blacks were not more vengeful, and were a "good deal better" than they ought to be or had reason to be. "White people owed the colored race a big debt," she said, and if they tried to pay it all back, "they wouldn't have anything left for seed." The audience laughed, but she was not joking. The debt was so immense, she continued, that whites could only repent and ask forgiveness. Blacks had labored, suffered, and remained un-educated while whites reaped the benefits. But the blood of blacks was not shed in vain, she said, for "the promises of Scripture were all for the black people." In the heavenly life, for all their earthly tribulation, saints would be "washed in the blood of the lamb," said Sojourner the Spiritualist. "You know who that means," she said. Black people would have "peace and joy in the kingdom." In her final remarks, she directly addressed her own disheartened people. "Wait a little longer," she counseled. "And I shall hail you where slaveholders do not come, and where bloodhounds cannot enter." One seldom heard a speech, a reporter commented, that so excelled in "shrewdness, good sense, and genuine soul-eloquence."[34]

Meanwhile, the Kansas-Nebraska Act had inspired the state-by-state birth of the Republican Party, which—although neither avowedly antislavery nor against the Fugitive Slave Law—opposed slavery's territorial extension. No Garrisonians joined the new party, but some softened their opposition to politics and smoothed over internal differences. While Samuel J. May called for political action, pro-Douglass black Abolitionists pledged to work with Garrison. After a fractured 1853, both leaders attended the 1854 annual meeting in New York City and the September convention in Syracuse.[35]

Events of 1854 strengthened veteran Abolitionists and brought new converts. Lydia Maria and David Child resurfaced; Jonathan "Branded Hand" Walker stirred up agitation in his new western home; William Wells Brown returned from Europe after a five-year absence. Now a published novelist and free man, thanks to British Abolitionists, Brown embraced an internationalist perspective on antislavery; rebellion; African contributions to Western culture; and the slave power's expansionist aims abroad. New Yorkers Susan B. Anthony, Lucy Colman, and Aaron Powell joined Sojourner on the Abolitionist circuit, as did Frances Ellen Watkins, a young black poet who attended the Framingham meeting. Even a chastened Elizabeth Greenfield, fresh from European triumphs, gave a benefit concert at Tremont Temple for Leonard Grimes's "Fugitive Church" and Boston's Vigilance Committee.[36]

III

After the Burns tragedy, Sojourner Truth traveled throughout New England, speaking to enthusiastic audiences. She shared the platform with C. C. Burleigh, Henry C. Wright, Hopedale Community founder Adin Ballou, and others on August First, when thousands commemorated the twentieth anniversary of West Indian Emancipation. Later that month, she was the guest of Caleb Stetson, pastor of the Second Unitarian Church in South Scituate, Massachusetts. Although many people knew Sojourner Truth, Stetson wrote to Garrison, she "is not equally well-known to the readers of your paper in this vicinity" and had never been to their town. She addressed a very large audience in the church, Stetson wrote, "twice as large . . . as the usual congregation." She spoke "so modestly, so naturally, and with such a spirit of truth and love" that her "revelations" and descriptions of the "experience of her life" profoundly affected the audience. Apparently not all of Stetson's parishioners approved; the Harvard-trained minister's antislavery preaching later cost him the pulpit. Sojourner spent part of September in the Danvers Park region before heading for the AASS's semiannual meeting in upstate New York. Her Danvers Park sponsor wrote Garrison that "our venerable friend" had held several well-attended meetings. At her Sunday gatherings, "the house was crowded to its utmost capacity," and her rousing messages both "entertained" and "instructed." She spoke as a mother, triumphant follower of Christ, and "efficient laborer in the anti-slavery field." Her power and appeal were "truly wonderful" her friend wrote. She conveyed confidence "in the justice and goodness of her God" and won the "hearts and consciences of the people."[37]

Most audiences had read *Uncle Tom's Cabin* and wanted to hear Sojourner's personal stories of motherhood and spirituality, and she readily obliged. However, she tried to inspire activism, not sentimental sorrow. "Don't pity me," she told audiences, even as she spoke of drinking the "dregs of human misery" as "only a slave mother could." She wanted to transform passive listeners into antislavery activists. She wanted audiences to *feel* the pain she, Mau-mau Bet, and Bomefree had endured; and to move listeners beyond the armchair exercise of weeping over *Uncle Tom's Cabin*. "I go in for agitatin,'" she asserted. And even in the afterlife, she said, people should not expect to stroll around God's throne or spend eternity singing for the Lord. "Why that's all nonsense. . . . De Lord is this very time—getting ready to set you to work." After all, "we be done with our own selves," and could help the secular earthly folk. What was this work? "Hm. I don't know—its mighty big thing to regulate—this here world—I just look at the millions of the stars in de sky—and they all got lots of chores . . .—but this is one thing, the better you are Children—the easier it'll be for yere."[38]

In the fall of 1854, she attended the antislavery meeting in Syracuse, and she probably went to Rochester, where her daughter Sophia had married and settled down with Thomas Schuyler. Frances (Fannie), their first child, Sojourner's only granddaughter, was born in October 1854. But the Sojourner returned home for a momentous event. On November 1, 1854, "Isabella Van Wagenen, also known as 'Sojourner Truth,'" obtained clear title to her Park Street house and lot. Formerly enslaved people considered owning a piece of land more important than other civil liberties. Indeed, land ownership *was* freedom. The Sojourner now had roots and would never be a vagabond or a "wanderer." She had also fulfilled a belated promise of providing a permanent refuge for her children.[39]

That winter, as family matters slowed her movements, her friends offered assistance. Gilbert Haven and his wife became her neighbors, while he was pastor of Northampton's little Methodist chapel. When she was in Ohio, the Havens helped her little family. When they were transferred soon after her return, the

Havens employed Diana as family housekeeper, and Sojourner was a welcome guest. Her friends the Gales in Norfolk County, Massachusetts, hired her twelve-year-old grandson Jimmy as an apprentice. But he was such a handful they asked her to take him back. "I am very sorry Jimmy has troubled you," she told them. "I did hope that he would be a good boy and be a help and not a hindrance." Before she could retrieve him, her daughter Elizabeth returned to Florence very ill and needing care. Sojourner collected Jimmy but quickly returned to her ailing daughter and three-year-old grandson Sammy. It was months before Elizabeth rallied; by the spring of 1855, however, Sojourner was on the road again. She spent May and June in the Boston area and sent a letter to Mary Gale from Bath, Maine: "I leave here for Lewiston, and from there to Dover, NH where I should like to hear from you." She apologized for her long silence; her hands were full that winter with an ill daughter and two active grandsons. She heaped blessings on Methodist friends for the great kindness they had bestowed on her family. May "the giver of all good, the widow's God, and the vindicator of the oppressed," she prayed, "shield you and yours from the ills and evils of this life" and offer "abundant entrance into the land of rest where there is no oppression but freedom through the righteousness of Christ." She headed for Great Falls, Massachusetts, and urged the Gales to write her at the home of "Elder Steers."[40]

Sojourner Truth the Come-outer remained close to progressives within the Methodist denomination. In particular, her enduring friendship with Gilbert Haven outlasted his many reassignments, editorship of the influential *Zion's Herald,* and rise in the Episcopacy as bishop. Although the product of an antislavery family, young Haven had attended reactionary Wesleyan University, where he had supported the Liberty Party, challenged the proslavery faculty and slaveholding president, and been labeled "a ranting, fanatical Abolitionist." He served as head Sabbath-school teacher at Middletown's African Methodist Church. He was Abolitionist enough, he wrote his mother, to harbor blacks, mingle with them, and take as a bride one of the handsome ladies "of all shades," from the color of ink to that of paper, in his Sunday school class. "Stranger things have happened," he added. "They think very much of me and I of them." As a pastor, Haven consistently preached radical abolition from the pulpit. Nonetheless, most Come-outers considered him a compromiser, while ultraconservatives criticized his liberal politics and friendship with blacks. After the notorious Bible convention, the Episcopacy disparaged Haven's relationship with the high-profile Sojourner Truth, whom they labeled an atheist. The New England Conference publicly demanded that Methodist ministers ban her from their churches. The Church could not outlaw Truth, Haven fired back; he insisted that she was not in league with "heretics" such as Andrew Jackson Davis and Garrison.[41]

Haven refused to position Sojourner Truth in company with her unconventional friends; she was a fellow Methodist whose natural preaching gifts and reform commitments he greatly admired, almost envied. This erudite minister preached from a written text, and his sermons, which parishioners called discussions, were "the poorest part of him." Her biblical recall, quick wit, audience rapport, and effortless extemporaneous sermons amazed him; he who dubbed her "Queen" of the platform. Both were vigorous, self-sacrificing humanists of unquestionable piety. In Northampton, he sermonized to vacationing Southerners about racial equality, interracial marriage, and the Fugitive Slave Law. Admitting that he "never had any great influence in the pulpit," he became ambitious for influence within the Church. While she agitated on the platform, he gradually rose in the Episcopacy and used this success to promote abolition. She and the Havens enjoyed social as well as political and spiritual fellowship—exchanging stories, singing hymns, reciting Scripture and poetry, and telling jokes over meals and teas. Their egalitarian relationship puzzled even Haven's closest friends. After he left Northampton, a white male associate called on Haven at the same time the "prophetess—Sojourner Truth, paid him a visit," along with "two other Negroes." The visitor observed Haven, "his wife, and the three colored women sitting socially at table enjoying a cup of tea." Haven, the visitor recalled, "looked at me with a sly smile," as if "to say that the situation was somewhat peculiar, but that everything was all right, and that this was exactly the way it ought to be."[42]

Garrison printed Sojourner's songs as sheet music, which she sold along with her *Narrative*. Her voice "rings like a clarion," Aaron Powell observed in 1855, as she stood singing in the aisle during intermission at an upstate New York antislavery convention: "I'm going straight to Canada-a, where coloured men are free e-e-e!" She "harangued" the Abolitionists good-naturedly, announcing in a "stentorian voice" that her songs cost only 5 cents. "*Ain't that cheap*," she added. "Now friends! Don't be scar't." A female reporter for *Frederick Douglass' Paper* also noted Sojourner's presence. "It is the first time we have had the pleasure of 'laying our eyes on her.'" Yet "we have so often heard that she has such a store of 'mother wit.'" The reporter was anxious to hear Sojourner, who sat on the platform and "made several attempts to speak." The disappointed observer noted that "while we were there she did not get an opportunity." The convention was cantankerous and thoroughly male-dominated. During intermission, Sojourner "did very well with her book for the Abolitionists bought it like fun."[43]

Sojourner was now a key speaker at many meetings, opening sessions as she had in the West. When she was unexpectedly asked to open a meeting in 1853, she greatly delighted the audience by saying that she had come to hear what she had to say. Soon afterward, Wendell Phillips began an address to the Massachusetts Anti-Slavery Society by referring to the "Sojourner" homily: "Mr. Chairman—I listened to a lecture a short time ago, from that very remarkable woman, once a slave SOJOURNER TRUTH. She began by saying,

'My friends, I have come here out of curiosity to hear what I am going to say' (great laughter). And I might almost commence in the same tone." On another occasion, Sojourner preceded Phillips and then introduced him by borrowing from Scripture. The one coming after her was "mightier than I." Phillips, himself a masterful extemporaneous speaker, framed his own address around Sojourner's speech. Wendell Phillips and Parker Pillsbury, arguably the most outstanding white speakers, marveled at Sojourner Truth. According to Phillips, "I once heard her describe the captain of a slave ship going up to judgment, followed by his victims as they gathered from the depths of the sea, in a strain that reminded me of Clearance's dream in Shakespeare, and equaled it. The anecdotes of her ready wit and quick, striking replies are numberless. But the whole together give little idea of the rich, quaint, poetic and often profound speech of a most remarkable person, who used to say to us, 'You read books; God himself talks to me.'"[44]

She said that her greatest apprehension was preceding renowned Theodore Parker. She later recalled her thoughts when she was once told that Parker would follow her on the platform:

> Ah Lord, I said. Help me pore thy spirit in mine. Oh Lord, fill me full—Oh how I prayed—and de Lord helped me. I guess I did try and when I got thru I said, Now Theodore you'll pull all the words to pieces—so I put my chin between my hands & asked de Lord to help me stand it—So there it was—De first words he said was 'Well now, Sojourner Truth say,' and then he went on and told what I said and it sounded most beautiful—and when he took up another something I said and began in the same way . . . then I just couldn't stand it—Sounded so sweet what he said—I just got up and interrupted him and said, 'God de Lord . . . done did what I say.' And so he went on—all he did was use up my talk—every time with just them words, 'Well now, Sojourner say.'[45]

Sojourner's verbal acumen was particularly impressive because she was a non–native English speaker. Her "way" with words had many facets, including her use of colorful interpretations of English as persuasive linguistic instruments. In 1854 she held meetings with Lucy Stone and Stephen Foster in Springfield. The audience objected to Foster's abrasive anticlericism and disunion sentiments. One man who loudly, vigorously, and repeatedly interrupted Foster incited a "mobocratic spirit" among the audience. Concluding his lengthy tirade against Foster, the man shouted, "Your statements are too sweeping." At that moment, Sojourner Truth "sprang to her feet." Lucy Stone recalled that her short, energetic speech "drew a picture which every one present both saw and felt, of what slavery is to its victims, and of the guilt of those who inflict it and of those who uphold it." Such a hush fell on the audience that a whisper could have been heard. "With the tone of one of the old prophets, turning to Mr. Foster, she said: 'Sweep away, Stephen, sweep away.'" Foster finished his address and the meeting "closed without further incident."[46]

In drawing her raw material from the Bible, she was especially clever and adroit, but also vitriolic. She used Scripture to inspire a change of heart, to provoke reflection, to ridicule, and to satirize. She was particularly biting when signifying on ministers. Lydia Maria Child remembered chairing a meeting in which condemnation of the churches greatly aroused a "gentleman in a white neckcloth," with a crimson face "glowing with the excitement of indignation." He asked to exercise his "free speech," and Child invited him to the platform. As "an orthodox minister of the gospel," he began, "I came here this afternoon to hear some of the eloquence and wit which I understood were so abundant at these meetings; but instead . . . I have thus far listened to little save insults heaped upon the clergy." This was the minister's first antislavery meeting, and he vowed it would be his last. Making "vain efforts to choke down his rising wrath," he shouted, "I can find a better use for my leisure hours than attendance upon gatherings where the only speakers are women and jackasses!" He stunned the audience, and the hall was in "dead silence for a moment." Then Sojourner Truth "slowly rose from one of the rear seats" and addressed the chair: "'That gentleman tells us he's a minister of the gospel,' she said, 'and so he probably knows what's in the Scripture. There was another minister, a long time ago, named Balaam. He got mighty mad, too, at an ass that spoke. But, Missus Chairman, I'd like to remind the gentleman that it was the ass and not the minister that saw the angel.'"[47]

The clergyman certainly knew the story. The Moab prince Balaam planned to "smite" the children of Israel on their trek to the Promised Land. Although God had forbidden the destruction of this "blessed" people, Balaam nonetheless "saddled his ass" to ride against the Israelites. An angry Jehovah sent the militant archangel Michael, invisible to Balaam, to stand in the road with a sword and block the path of the ass. The frightened animal turned away from the road repeatedly, while Balaam "smote" the ass for disobedience. Finally God opened Balaam's eyes and he too "saw the angel." Because of Balaam's perversity, God had to work through an ass.[48] Sojourner's metaphor implied that like the ass in the Bible, Abolitionists and women had a second sense and supernatural visionary power, while blind proslavery ministers perverted God's will, as did Balaam.

She and the antislavery apostles always had to deal with operators who tried to prey on them, blacks as well as whites. While she traveled in Maine with William Wells Brown and Stephen Foster, they met a nearly white New York City con artist posing as the son of "John Randolph of Roanoke." This charlatan, Paschal Randolph, had left his family destitute on an upstate New York farm leased on credit from Gerrit Smith. In Maine, Randolph dogged the Abolitionists' trail. At their large City Hall meeting in Portland, he offered to handle the introductions. Brown refused, "not liking the son of a Virginia statesman"; nonetheless, Randolph managed to collect the evening's offerings. Giving the money to Brown in a handkerchief, Randolph quickly left, having "picked out the bills and large silver coins," leaving 3–cent pieces and coppers. At other meetings, Brown again saw the "tall, slim, wiry-walking, empty-headed, thin-faced, cunning-looking colored man" being "very officious with the collections." The "impudent scamp," Brown noted angrily, made off with money intended for Sojourner. "A more daring, barefaced theft was never committed," Brown wrote Garrison. "I need not say that he 'who steals my purse steals trash.' But he who steals from poor Sojourner Truth is even worse than a common thief." Randolph visited every little Maine town fronting as an Abolitionist seeking subscriptions for a book on the life of his "father." The Sojourner was not concerned about his antics, as she believed that God would replenish her purse.[49]

During her 1855 travels, she and her grandson Jimmy stopped in Andover, Massachusetts, and met the famous author Harriet Beecher Stowe. Although Stowe patronized Frederick Douglass, she rebuffed Harriet Jacobs and her near-white daughter. However, Sojourner Truth conformed to Stowe's stereotypical image of enslaved women—dark-skinned, unschooled, homespun, and religious. Stowe immediately incorporated Truth's experiences into *Dred, A Tale of the Dismal Swamp,* published in 1856. Truth, needing another reprinting of her *Narrative*, extracted an endorsement and introduction from Stowe. William Nell, who had the same idea for his new volume on blacks in the military, wrote: "Mrs. Stowe has recently been especially bountiful to Sojourner Truth causing the old woman's heart to feel happy and free."[50]

Stowe's endorsement became a license to appropriate Sojourner Truth's life and voice. The novel *Dred* has been largely forgotten, but Stowe later created an enduring Sojourner myth in "Sojourner Truth, the Libyan Sibyl," an article she wrote based on their 1855 meeting. Sojourner paid a heavy price for being unable to tell her own story. Nonetheless, her influence predated Harriet Beecher Stowe's literary manipulation. Before the two women ever met, Sojourner Truth had made her reputation in the West and returned to the East recognized as a leader. And when Stowe met Truth, during a time of national crises, the Sojourner was a popular radical agitator who could not "read a book," but could "read the people."

I am pleading for the mothers
Who gaze in wild despair,
Upon the hated auction-block
And see their children there.
— SOJOURNER'S HYMN

He that findeth his life shall lose it; and he
that loseth his life for my sake, shall find it.
— MATT. 10:39

CHAPTER 16

Truth Is Powerful

I

After the 1856 conventions, Sojourner Truth held meetings in upstate New York, visited her Rochester family, the Posts, and then went to Ohio. Among friends in Ashtabula County, she had a chance to celebrate J. W. Walker's transition into the spirit world, but also to reflect on the void her friend left in the western movement. Walker had died in Michigan, helping Abolitionists revive their state organization. Although he had left an antislavery legacy "liberally scattered in the cities and towns, the hamlets and cabin settlements of Ohio and Michigan," his excessive labors had ruined his health and caused his premature death. Who, easterners wondered, could replace the "Parker Pillsbury of the West" as "Kansas fever" emerged? Not even Sojourner Truth realized that she would fulfill that mission. After the Kansas-Nebraska Act, slavery was the burning national issue and shifted the center of antislavery action westward. Settlers from both the North and South flooded Kansas territory. Abolitionist poet John Greenleaf Whittier reflected some Northerners' attitudes toward Kansas migration:

We go to rear a wall of men
On freedom's Southern line,
And plant beside the cotton tree
The rugged Northern pine.[1]

Despite such regional chauvinism, armed proslavery Missourians called "border ruffians" greatly outnumbered Northerners. Staking claims in northeastern Kansas (Leavenworth, Atchison, and Easton), Missourians indiscriminately and erroneously considered all Northern settlers "free lovers" and Abolitionists who hid "runaway Niggers." Free Soilers and Emigrant Aid societies furnished boxes of Sharp's repeating rifles to the poorly armed Northern settlers. However, the national government gave Missourians the upper hand. Democratic President Franklin Pierce appointed proslavery territorial governors, who then deputized Southerners into militia units, rigged elections, and winked at lawlessness. Reported outrages included the raping of Free Soil white women, the killing and maiming of free blacks, and putting a bounty on "the scalp of an Abolitionist." One Northern settler was shot and scalped in front of his wife. "A civil war rages on the frontier," Ohio's *Ashtabula Sentinel* bellowed in 1856, under the headline "The Dead Lying in the Streets."[2]

Sojourner Truth and the antislavery apostles vowed to transform the West, so that "no union with slaveholders" reverberated throughout the nation. The August Convention in Salem, Ohio, reflected what Ohioans long hoped for—the Executive Committee's realization that winning the West was the key to abolition. The array of Abolitionists launching the fall campaign was the most impressive ever: Parker Pillsbury, returned after a long European convalescence; Henry C. Wright, now working in Michigan; black Republican John Mercer Langston, teamed with Charles L. Remond and William C. Nell; Sallie Holley and Giles Stebbins, paired with novices Aaron Powell and Susan B. Anthony. For the first time, two black sisters joined Sojourner Truth on the western circuit: Frances Ellen Watkins accompanied the veteran women but also branched off on her own; Sarah Parker Remond traveled with her brother but found the tour too grueling and returned East. Laura Haviland, a petite but powerful preacher, widow, and longtime Michigan Abolitionist, also joined the lecturers.[3]

An attempted escape that ended in tragedy also escalated western activism, dominated speeches, and filled private correspondence. In January 1856, the Garner family had escaped from Kentucky via the frozen Ohio River. While they were waiting at a safe house for underground "president" Levi Coffin, slave catchers surrounded them. As they "fought bravely," but unsuccessfully, Margaret Garner, a young mother, began desperately slashing her sleeping children, determined to "save them all from slavery by death." She cut the throat of her three-year-old daughter and badly injured her other three children. This gruesome event touched every Abolitionist, and women especially debated the complexities of infanticide versus bondage. Lucy Stone visited Margaret Garner in prison and spoke at the trial: "I would tear open my veins and let the earth drink my blood, rather than wear the chains of slavery." But others, including Lucretia Mott and the Forten-Purvis women, opposed Garner's actions and Stone's dramatizations. Mott and her friends lamented that their "advocacy of freedom for the slave" had "led to 'free soil'—'free love,' and now 'free life.'" Certainly Sojourner Truth, slave mother and pacifist, agreed. Garner was acquitted of murder so she could return to bondage. The lecturers retold her tragedy as they fanned out over the West. Slavery seemed more entrenched than ever.[4]

Truth, Colman, Griffing, and Watkins organized antislavery meetings and local conventions throughout northern Ohio and then attended the state's annual Friends of Universal Human Progress Convention, where they met many Michigan Abolitionists. Reformer Henry Willis invited them to the annual Friends' Convention in Battle Creek, offering lodging and hospitality at his beautiful water cure health resort (St. Mary's) outside of town.[5] Battle Creek was a progressive town, rivaling Rochester in "isms"—although Spiritualism, Abolitionism, and Adventism dominated. Indeed, in Battle Creek Sojourner met many former New Yorkers, including kinfolk of the Posts.

Arriving in Michigan, she met the Progressive Friends, who were the nucleus of abolition there; and some of them she knew from national conventions. As in Ohio, in Michigan the antislavery involvement had begun early. Its state society, formed in Ann Arbor in 1836, had embraced politics in 1848 along with the Liberty Party. Some members had joined the Western Anti-Slavery Society, which sent J. W. Walker, Henry C. Wright, and Giles Stebbins into Michigan in 1850. In 1852, Abolitionists reconstituted the Michigan State Anti-Slavery Society as a Garrisonian organization. In 1853, as Sojourner was returning home from Ohio, Walker, the Fosters, Sallie Holley, Marius Robinson, and Garrison himself were holding protracted meetings in Michigan from Adrian to Detroit. Prior to Walker's death, Michigan Abolitionists had convinced that talented general agent to relocate his family to their state. They soon made a similar offer to Sojourner Truth.[6]

She was a huge attraction among the Abolitionist Friends. Her quaint mannerisms, impressive stature, and little book endorsed by Harriet Beecher Stowe gained immediate attention. But it was on the platform that she captivated the assembly. She first impressed them with her original hymn "I'm Pleading for My People," then spoke "with much feeling" about antislavery and other reforms. Her rational insights, sharp intellect, and broad antislavery vision impressed listeners most. She engaged in a long debate over a resolution that damned the word "Christian" and labeled all churches "proslavery." Some of the assembly felt such strong language was counterproductive, and unnecessarily brought already unpopular Abolitionists under further attack as infidels. Henry C. Wright disagreed. "Jesus of Nazareth," he said, would abhor the term "Christian" as contemporary professors of faith abused it. Sojourner was critical generally of churches and ministers and had felt the persecution of so-called Christians, but she refused to categorically condemn them all. Moreover, she told Wright, Jesus taught forgiveness, and Abolitionist leaders should assume a "Christ-like" attitude toward everyone. She agreed with Wright in principle, but reasoned that the *name* "Christian" was unimportant, especially if attacking it alienated the very people Abolitionists hoped to convert. "If we want to lead the people," she added, "we must not get out of dere sight."[7]

Their debate was halted when a "Mrs. Seymour" of Waukegan, Illinois, went "under spiritual influence." This interruption did not disturb Spiritualists Truth, Watkins, Wright, and Griffing but greatly irritated former Spiritualist Lucy Colman. This "trance" indicates how much Spiritualism and abolition went hand in hand among Progressive Friends. It seemingly supported Wright: "'Mene, Mene Tekel Upharsin' is written on all popular churches. Truth will elevate forever—Truth! Let it be free to investigate. The Christian churches have been quarreling about their creeds and dogmas while four millions of their brothers and sisters were in bondage."

Wright and Truth continued debating after the spiritual communiqué. Since Jesus had been an "infidel," Wright said, that name was honorable for Abolitionists. Truth, who had worn that label for years, argued "with good effect" that Abolitionists needed to win over misguided proslavery churches. Wright disagreed strenuously, asserting that he refused "to go down to help others up." Why he demanded, "must I go down and be a democrat in order to help them up? . . . I don't believe it." Sojourner challenged the broader implications of her associate's position with an acute double entendre, which the audience loved. "Suppose I want to learn to read, whose going to learn me? Will friend Wright come down to teach me?" Battle Creek resident Erastus Hussey picked up her point; just as Abolitionists should not forsake churches, the bulwark of American slavery, "we must go down far enough to reach the poor and the weak." In the interest of time, recorder Marius Robinson omitted the remainder of the debate. But Sojourner's logic won over the audience.[8]

According to Robinson, she mesmerized the audience as she spoke in support of an antislavery resolution. She sang one of "her inimitable songs," then "addressed the meeting in a most effective speech." The *Bugle* editor emulated her "Negro Dutch." Naturally, she revisited Isabella—robbed of childhood, motherhood, and her husband:

> As you were speakin this morning of little children, I was lookin round and thinkin it was most beautiful. But I have had children and yet never owned one,

no never owned one; and of such ther's millions—who goes to teach dem? Who goes to teach dem? Who goes to teach dem? You have teachers for your children, but who will teach de poor slave children?

I want to know what has become of the love I ought to have for my children? I did have love for them but what has become of it, I cannot tell you. I have had two husbands, yet I never possessed one of my own. I have had five children and never could take any one of dem up and say "my child," or "my children," unless it was when no one could see me.

I believe in Jesus, and I was forty years a slave, but I did not know how dear to me was my posterity, I was so beclouded and crushed. But how good and wise is God, for if the slaves knowed what thar true condition was, it would be more than de mine could bear. While de race is sold of all dere rights—what is dare on God's footstool to bring dem up? Has not God given to all his creatures all the same rights. How could I trabel and live and speak? If I ha'nt got something to bear me up, when I'se been robbed of all my affection for my husband and for my children.

Some years ago there appeared to me a form (here the speaker gave a very graphic description of a vision she had) den I learned dat I was a human bein. We had been taught dat we was a speshe of monkey, baboon, or rang-o-tang, and we believed it—we'd never seen any dese animals.

In a "simple and unsophisticated style," she movingly explained the futility of her mother's religious instruction in the wake of the cruelties her young enslaved daughter endured. But after she embraced a personal faith, she relinquished hatred. "I believes in de next world," she proclaimed excitedly, reflecting on her tragic personal losses. "When we gets up yonder we shall have all dem rights 'stored to us again—all dat love what I'se lost—all goin to be 'stored to me 'gain. Oh! how good God is." She ended her tearful, emotion-filled sermon with a song, and the audience gave a "liberal contribution."[9]

This attentive, largely New York audience took Sojourner Truth back in time. Erastus Hussey, from Cayuga County, was a Battle Creek merchant, former mayor, newspaperman, and manager of the town's Underground Railroad. Joseph Merritt, the "soul" of Michigan reform, had migrated from Saratoga, New York. He and his wife, Phoebe Hart, had embraced radical abolition through Elias Hicks. The Merritts' commodious home was Battle Creek's main underground depot and Abolitionist hospitality center. Richard Titus, now an ailing miller, had once been a Long Island ship's captain who transported self-emancipated people from the South. His wife, Frances, was also a devout Spiritualist and Abolitionist. Preston Kellogg was an Adventist New York migrant who had moved his family from proslavery Indiana to Michigan. Both of Kellogg's two sons, John H. the physician and health enthusiast and William K. who made a fortune in manufacturing cereal, later became world famous. These listeners were comfortable with Sojourner's "Negro Dutch," as her emotions interfered with careful English. Hudson Valley friends insisted that Sojourner never lost her "peculiar" brogue, which also suggests that she deliberately used her accent and unorthodox English expressions to charm Anglo-Saxon audiences[10] Yet her diverse oral repertoire included polished and formal English, an energized "down-home" style when excited, as well as tropes, signification, and double entendres that informed, inspired, amused, and even ridiculed some listeners. Successful orators fashioned speaking styles around an occasion and an audience. Sojourner's Battle Creek visit seemed truly providential when Reynolds and Dorcas Young Cornell introduced themselves. Dorcas's father, Edward Young, was the person who had alerted the New York Manumission Society about Peter's disappearance and illegal sale and raised the money for Isabella's attorney. Dorcas later married Reynolds Cornell, and they followed the Quaker migration to Michigan. Like most Quaker Abolitionists, the Cornells broke with the Friends' Meeting and joined the Friends of Universal Human Progress. Outside Battle Creek in Bedford Township, the Cornells established a farming commune called Harmonia—"a refuge free from any denominational affiliation, and the contaminating influences of a crowded city." The Cornells helped establish the new state antislavery society, hosted out-of-town reformers, and made Harmonia a key depot on the "Freedom Train" to Canada. The Cornells, Harmonia, Battle Creek activism, and warm offers to remain in Michigan sparked Sojourner's interest.[11]

She was just as imposing at the State Anti-Slavery Convention in Livonia as she had been at the Friends Convention in Battle Creek. The Abolitionists had a grand turnout of people from Adrian, Battle Creek, Detroit, Grand Rapids, Kalamazoo, and elsewhere. Truth and her two companions, Griffing and Colman, occupied the platform for a full day. She was the main attraction, Marius Robinson wrote, speaking of indictments against slavery, revelations of "life-long robberies and sorrows," and rich thoughts about "her confiding faith in truth and her earnest love of humanity." At Livonia, she reconnected with her friend Jonathan "Branded Hand" Walker, and she was again encouraged to relocate as he had.[12]

In July 1857, Sojourner sold her Northampton properties and purchased a lot in the Harmonia commune, which was part of Bedford Township, six miles west of Battle Creek and one mile from the Michigan Central Railroad depot. Her decision to leave the East might seem somewhat puzzling at first glance. Northampton was centrally located between New England and the Middle States, hence convenient for her travels; she had many dear friends there, intricate connections to the Garrisonian leadership, and a mortgage-free home. Indeed, she was financially secure enough to purchase a second adjacent lot in Northampton. But undoubtedly the voice of God gave her rationales for relocating. She may have felt the West offered more opportunities to keep her family together. Her grandson Jimmy entered a blacksmith apprenticeship in Bedford, and Sammy attended Bedford Institute. Diana worked for the Merritt-Chandlers in Battle Creek, and Sophia in Rochester was closer to Michigan than to Massachusetts. Elizabeth apparently remained in the East for some time, working for the Gale family.[13]

In addition, Sojourner still believed in communitarian living. Harmonia promoted peace, progressive social movements, and the "brotherly love" absent in American society. It was an Abolitionist commune, and Henry Cornell was regional agent for the *Anti-Slavery Bugle*. Harmonia Village contained 140 one-acre plots, a Methodist church, trade shops, and a store. Sojourner's lot and cabin were next to the distinguished Cornell Academy, or Bedford Institute. The Cornells' two sons, Hiram and Henry, managed this popular seminary; the modest $10 annual tuition meant that Sammy and other blacks could attend."[14]

Sojourner did not settle at Harmonia because of Spiritualism.[15] Although residents were kindred believers, Spiritualism was not a faith, as she explained when a reporter asked if she had "joined" them. "Why child, there's nothing to join." Spiritualism was an extension of the sacred ethos and mysticism she learned as a child, and a quotidian element of her supernatural telepathy. She believed her "second sight" provided divine protection, otherworldly knowledge, and ability to see and speak with spirits and foretell the future. From a BaKongo perspective, she was a *nganga*, a community leader and channel to the spirit world. She was not alone in asserting a similar divine inspiration after her conversion and sanctification. Biblical antiquity, Greek culture, German mysticism, Dutch Pietism, Wesleyan Methodism, and Swedenborgianism all embraced the *spiritualist* vision. A poltergeist reportedly haunted John Wesley's home in his youth; New Church founder Emanuel Swedenborg's father supposedly spoke with God and the angels; Emanuel claimed to see visions, talk with God, and "in a state of perfect wakefulness converse with the angels and spirits." Spiritualism had given Sojourner inward peace after Bomefree's torturous death and Peter's disappearance at sea; her belief in divine cosmic communication created a soothing unity between human spirits and those beyond the veil. A loved one's spiritual presence added extra harmony, strength, and celestial energy to human life. Physical demise was "a door leading to another room in the 'house not made by hands.'" Nearly all of Sojourner's associates believed fully in the "world of spirits" and practiced channeling through séance circles. Her Spiritualism paralleled both Christianity and Africanity.[16]

Yet her Spiritualism rested on more than attaining "higher altered states of spiritual consciousness" or "dealings with the dead." Her attraction to Spiritualist practitioners was intricately related to her activism, which in turn inspired her move to Michigan; only immediate abolition trumped Spiritualism's re-form agenda. But Abolitionists had to be ever vigilant, because Spiritualists sometimes challenged that order. At Michigan's Friends of Universal Human Progress Convention in 1857, Truth, Pillsbury, and Burleigh forcefully opposed Andrew Jackson Davis's resolution that Spiritualism was "the basis and pervad-ing spirit of all reform and all science." After debates, speeches, and trances, the convention finally recognized abolition as the most comprehensive reform in the "interest of humanity." Spiritualists focused on community and social justice; they valued equality, harmony, and each person's universal spirit.[17]

Harmonia was a biracial community, and Sojourner's neighbors included not only farmers and artisans but educators, newspaper editors, and former statesmen. White males assumed Spiritualism's nominal leadership; however, most mediums were women who attracted thousands to their meetings. Spiri-tualism advanced woman's rights, and more than any other movement became a conduit for female power. In the West, Sojourner Truth articulated her radical trance-visions to thousands during antislavery speeches. Sojourner's alluring, sought-after young associate, trance-speaker Cora Hatch, received antislavery messages from John Quincy Adams and Theodore Parker after his death in 1860. Even non-Spiritualists Parker Pillsbury and Frederick Douglass applauded the movement's value in creating tensions in the larger society and using model communities as springboards for social justice. Spiritualism also offers an-other prism for viewing nineteenth-century bridges across race, gender, and class lines. In New England, African Americans Harriet Jacobs and William C. Nell attended (white) LaRoy Sunderland's séances; blacks also held their own independent "Spiritualist Circles," over their pastors' objections. White women Abolitionists embraced Sojourner's Spiritualist pronouncements and wisdoms over other counsel. And Spiritualism connected free Northern with Southern blacks emerging from slavery.[18]

Thus, Spiritualism certainly brought Sojourner full circle, back to an "an-cient faith" deeper than her American roots. She wanted to come to terms with death through physical conversation with the departed and thereby confirm immortality. Spiritualism also embraced progressive reform, especially antislav-ery. Her choice of Harmonia over Battle Creek reveals the strength of her com-munalism and her understanding, from the New Testament, that materialism and profit brought evil. Commune residences reportedly held weekly "circles," and women wore bloomer attire, now called the American costume. Members had Saturday dances, played cards, and engaged in numerous "amusements." According to one account, "There was more 'free love' going on . . . than you could shake a stick at." Detractors asserted that on a clear day, one could stand on Harmonia Hill "and count thirteen homes which had been broken up by the peculiar social life of the seminary bunch." Even if this was mostly a narrow-minded distortion, enough occurred for Sojourner and others to abandon Harmonia after a few years, after an emerging Millerite group took control. If she and her associates did not oppose eclectic liberalism, they opposed the Millerites' institutionalization of the Second Advent, adoption of strict Sabbath-keeping, and growing fatalism. Sojourner eventually moved, but kept her property. The Cornells left the state.[19] Although the Sojourner's final communitarian experiment came to an end, she remained a Spiritualist and a high-profile reformer who energized the western antislavery movement.

Michigan was the underground's "Grand Terminus," where some the most volatile and aggressive confrontations had occurred, in Calhoun County (Battle Creek) and Wayne County (Detroit), before Sojourner's arrival. Michigan's long border with Canada made the state a natural thoroughfare. Detroit was a freedom seeker's last stop before reaching safety "under the paw of the British lion." Blacks mainly controlled the Detroit underground, but the state antislavery society provided a nucleus of stations stretching across northwest Michigan. Although some local historians believe that the Michigan underground fizzled out by the 1840s, in fact the Bloodhound Bill created new activity. Hinterland conductors and station masters were closely connected to Detroit, where William Lambert was head of the Vigilance Committee and George de Baptiste was "Underground Manager." They collaborated with settled self-emancipated blacks and key members of the state society in Adrian, Harmonia, Battle Creek, Grand Rapids, and elsewhere. It was an "open secret" that Sojourner Truth "associated herself with the Underground Railroad," according to one account, although no direct proof was ever adduced against her. Black expatriates such as Mary Ann Shadd (Cary) and Henry Bibb (who died in 1854) worked with the Detroit contingent, which committing acts of cold-blooded daring, including even rioting, in the name of freedom. They created various schemes, including hiring white gangs to go to the South and "steal" slaves, sell them, and resell them until they arrived in the North. They organized a secret society, complete with initiation and degrees of membership: "African-American Mysteries: order of the Men of Oppression." Using signs, signals, and codes, they trusted no one (black or white) ignorant of these gestures. Underground agents also devised passwords—conversations, handgrips, and other means of solidarity known only to an underground "Friend." Although they were generally suspicious of whites, some, including Jonathan "Branded Hand" Walker and John Brown Sr., knew all the tests. Detroit activists transported thousands across the Detroit River to Windsor, Ontario. Given Sojourner Truth's commitment to activism, the shift in the Abolitionist epicenter from the East to the West certainly influenced her move to Michigan, where she and other agitators struggled to win minds and hearts in the battle against slavery.[20]

She was lecturing in Michigan when John Brown Sr. and his band hacked five proslavery men to death at Pottawatomie, in retaliation for "sacking" the Free Soil town of Lawrence and for the brutal murder of a Northern settler. Whig-Republican and Abolitionist presses condemned the destruction of Lawrence and practically ignored Brown's gruesome revenge. The Browns considered northern Ohio home, and Sojourner's black and white Ashtabula friends wore "black strings" in solidarity with Brown, whom they hid until they could flee to Iowa. With a price on their heads, these "fugitives" returned to Kansas, fought a battle with Missourians at a place called "Black Jack," and routed them. Later, Brown and one hundred men fearlessly battled a thousand Missourians at Osawatomie. Free Soilers and western Abolitionists, feeling vulnerable in the wake of random murders, labeled "Osawatomie Brown" a hero. So did some easterners. "Never before in my life had I been distinctively and unequivocally, outside the world of human law," Thomas Wentworth Higginson wrote from Kansas. As he relied on his Sharp's rifle, revolvers, and "wit," the danger gave Higginson "a delightful sensation." Even the cautious Republican Party convert Abraham Lincoln rhetorically caught the Free Soil excitement. Campaigning for the Illinois senate after Pottawatomie, Lincoln condemned Brown's actions but asserted, "We must highly resolve that Kansas must be free . . . let us draw a cordon so to speak around the slave states, and the hateful institution, like a reptile poisoning itself, will perish by its own infamy."[21]

Some diehard moral suasionists also warmed toward the new party, which was cool toward emancipation. Publicly, Garrison decried the Republican Party's "very incongruous elements" and "revolting" position on black freedom; then he wished candidate John Fremont well in his race against James Buchanan. Mrs. Jesse Benton Fremont's antislavery politics and outspokenness charmed Garrisonian as well as Republican women. Samuel J. May cautiously supported Fremont. Frederick Douglass, now a raging militant, loudly condemned the Republican platform at the newly organized Radical abolition convention; then he joined Fremont's campaign and urged other propertied black men to vote Republican.[22]

Sojourner Truth's web of associations expanded her political thinking. Besides taking counsel with the militant northern Ohio women and working among black freedom seekers, she was joined, along with the Garrisonians, by Republican congressmen Joshua Giddings of Ohio and George W. Julian of Indiana on the Western Anti-Slavery Society platform. She also lectured with black advocates of political agitation—Frances Ellen Watkins, William Watkins, H. Ford Douglass, and Fremont Republicans Charles and John Mercer Langston. The same Ashtabula Abolitionists who hid John Brown Sr. hosted Sojourner

Truth. Black string Charles Griffing, husband of Sojourner's traveling companion, Josephine, was Brown Sr.'s intimate friend. Everyone was caught up in the crisis. Brown Jr., who resided in Ashtabula County, greatly impressed Benjamin Jones and Stephen Foster, who interviewed him for the *Bugle*. Falsely accused of the "Pottawatomie massacre," Brown Jr. and his "Rifles" were arrested for treason, beaten, chained together at the ankles, and marched 50 miles like "a gang of coffle slaves." Before proving his innocence, young Brown spent six weeks in prison. Bitterly recounting his brutal treatment, he insisted he had never been a traitor to the United States Government—and then, with flaming eyes, added, "but so help me God, I will be." If only "a thousand such men could be found in Ohio," the Garrisonian interviewers lamented. As Sojourner noted, more whites began to "feel the prick," and "no union with slaveholders" began to sound less nonresistant. Fremont's defeat by a slim margin portended the Republican Party's promise, but the cost was more Southern muscle-flexing and national upheaval.[23]

Meanwhile, Sojourner Truth continued to uplift audiences with heart-rending, soul-stirring speeches. Her greatest gifts were the ability to combine preaching with teaching; to "read the people" and extract antislavery conversions through lived experience. "It has been our privilege of late to form acquaintance with and listen to the story of . . . Sojourner Truth," correspondent Charles Mickley wrote to Marius Robinson late in 1857. Of all the sufferers "at the hands of tyrants," Mickley believed, "none drink so deep of the cup of sorrow and drain the very dregs of human misery" as Sojourner, whose "swift witness" against slavery often left audiences in tears. The "education of the babbling schoolman" could not compare to her, a graduate of the "high College," whose "teacher sat enthroned upon the universe." Noting the significant genius of her name, Mickley called it "but a fair index of her character." She "leaves a whole volume of truths wherever she labors in her mission of love and mercy drawn from her own eventful life as well as from the open book of nature in which she 'reads as she runs.'" She held six meetings in that neighborhood and always had a full house of attentive listeners. Doubters beware, Mickley wrote, for the evidence of her powers was in the fruit. At her final meeting, a man arose and declared his conversion: "I have always been a Democrat and a persecutor of Abolitionists; in view of that fact I couldn't look this woman in the face, so I took my seat in front of the desk with my back towards her. This woman has spoken the truth, I feel that a great work has commenced in my soul. I like that kind of preaching that 'reaches the heart.'" Mickley urged readers to invite Sojourner to their neighborhoods, listen to her, buy the "little but interesting narrative of her life," and "watch for your transition."[24]

Sojourner Truth read the people much the way other activists used the pen. She especially loved speaking in parables, using fables, metaphors, and humorous anecdotes to unravel or reduce complexities to simple yet serious understanding. Her "weevil in the wheat" was a master parable that contextualized a major issue and revealed her signifying technique. Immediately after James Buchanan's inauguration, the Supreme Court handed down a devastating 7-to-2 decision in *Scott v. Sandford*. Writing the majority opinion, Chief Justice Roger Taney ruled that Congress could not exclude slavery from the territories; people of African descent were not American citizens and were not protected under the Constitution. Whether enslaved or free, blacks "had no rights that white men were bound to respect." Sojourner's Quaker friend Joseph Dugdale remembered her metaphor. The boll weevil had destroyed thousands of acres of wheat in the West; she equated the Supreme Court's ruling with the boll weevil's destruction. "Children, I talks to God and God talks to me," she said. "Dis morning I was walking out, and I got over de fence. I saw de wheat a holding up its head, looking very big." Her powerful deep voice rose as she emphasized VERY BIG, drew up to full height, and pretending to grab a stalk of wheat, she discovered "dere was *no* wheat dare!" She asked God, "What *is* de matter wid *dis* wheat? And he says to me, 'Sojourner, dere is a little weasel [*sic*] in it.'" Likewise, hearing all about the Constitution and rights of man, she said, "I comes up and I takes hold of dis Constitution." It also looks "*mighty big*, and I feels for my rights, but der ain't any dare." She again queried God, "What *ails* dis Constitution?" The Constitution, like the infested wheat, was rotten, and God declared, "'Sojourner dere is a little *weasel* [*sic*] in it.'" Dugdale recalled that "the effect on the multitude was irresistible." This "unlearned African woman" he said, had a deep religious faith burning in her soul like fire, and "a magnetic power over an audience perfectly astounding."[25]

She abhorred divisiveness among fellow reformers, but it seemed unavoidable. Complex differences crystallized in 1857 when general agent Abby Kelley Foster, fresh from witnessing Kansas horrors, overruled the Executive Committee's cancellation of a fall Disunion Convention in Cleveland. Thousands applauded when she blasted the eastern leadership as lax and out of touch. Cautioning the assembly against "man-worship," she insisted that Abolitionists should not let their thinking, like their washing, be done by others. True Abolitionists demanded "the entire destruction of the present National government and Union." The Boston leaders, others said, were dangerously close to foot-dragging Republicans. Pillsbury singled out Ohio governor Salmon Chase for a special tongue-lashing because he had betrayed his promise to protect Margaret Garner. The South would salute Republicans who "surrender the Margaret Garners" and uphold both just and unjust laws. The convention's militancy was clear; they resolved to remove kidnappers and slave catchers from their communities "dead or alive."[26]

Black Abolitionists in Detroit attempted to implement this resolution one year later, while Sojourner Truth and others gathered there for the African

Methodist Church Conference. It became a melee as blacks discovered that one of their own had tricked two self-emancipated Kentuckians into going back to Ohio and "their self-styled owners." Cincinnati blacks inflicted three hundred lashes on the collaborator—a blow for each dollar he had received. Returning to Detroit, this "human bloodhound" publicly threatened to "expose the operations of the Underground Railroad." As an angry crowd grew, black leaders sprang into action. Frances Ellen Watkins gave "one of her very best outbursts of eloquent indignation." Henry Garnet wielded a pair of manacles and a bullwhip before the crowd and demanded to know what black people did with traitors. William C. Nell also led the crowd, which converged on City Hall, just as the police took the turncoat into protective custody. "Kill him! Murder the villain," people roared, and rushed the jail with boulders and brickbats. A "very large, strong woman" joined several male ringleaders in vowing to have the traitor's heart's blood. Several men furiously grabbed at the culprit, but police got him to the jailhouse with drawn pistols. The enormous crowd of mostly black citizens milled around the jail nearly all night.[27]

Sojourner certainly would have participated in the fracas. She lived in a community in which every home (including her own) was a safe haven for the fleeing slave. Threatening and sacrificing the safety of conductors or underground work endangered every Abolitionist and jeopardized this challenge to slavery. Sojourner Truth's closest Michigan lecturing associate, Laura Haviland, was also in Detroit at the time. A longtime activist, Haviland, with her husband, helped organize Michigan's first antislavery society. After his premature death, "Aunty Laura" worked the main junket of the Ohio-Indiana-Michigan underground. Her main Cincinnati contacts were Levi and Catherine Coffin and occasionally Salmon Chase. Laura once drove eleven passengers safely to Detroit. But she sometimes accompanied people to Canada West and remained to teach and write letters to families left behind. The elderly little schoolmarm was bold, tough-minded, and quick-thinking; reportedly, she could "smell" a slave catcher. When Calvin Fairbank was incarcerated after his second arrest, Coffin and Chase, fearing discovery, did not respond to his pleas for supplies and necessities. Aunty Laura "was braver than them all," Fairbank remembered. At great risk, she brought "bedding, money, and courage" to him throughout his twelve years in prison in Kentucky. Southerners offered a reward for Laura Haviland, "dead or alive," as they did for Harriet Tubman.[28] Danger and the uncompromising proslavery times nudged Truth, Haviland, and other Garrisonians further away from unconditional nonresistance.

Sojourner Truth went into Indiana, the Abolitionists' worst western battleground. Most Indianans were Southerners, Abby Kelley Foster observed. They hated black people "with a perfect passion" and despised "professional agitators from the East." In the 1830s, Indianans mobbed Theodore Weld and James Boyle;

in 1840, they hissed, hooted and interrupted Arnold Buffum, the AASS's first lecturer there. In 1843, young Frederick Douglass almost left Wayne County, Indiana, as a martyr. When a Whig leader in a coonskin cap and a shoeless Democratic standard-bearer in "dirty shirt and ragged pantaloons" stormed the antislavery platform, Douglass dared to defend himself. He was beaten unconscious and suffered broken ribs and a broken hand that never fully healed. Only the aid of the whites on the platform saved him from death. He did not return to Indiana for fifteen years—in the year of Sojourner's first Indiana experience. During those years, racism had not abated. Indianans even singled out radical Republican and native son George W. Julian, claiming that he carried around a lock of Frederick Douglass's hair to smell whenever he (Julian) grew faint in his "amalgamation" principles.[29]

In 1858, Sojourner Truth first lectured in Indiana. She had wealthy, well-connected friends in northern Indiana, even though the mood was proslavery, and Republicans strove mightily to prove that, like the "Democracy," they, too, wanted to "keep the nigger down." Nonetheless, Indiana's diverse antislavery advocates (United Brethren in Christ, Universalists, Progressive Friends, utopians, some traditional denominations, and blacks) invited her to speak. Supporters advertised her as a longtime Methodist recommended by Harriet Beecher Stowe. As a countertactic, rumors circulated throughout the region that Sojourner was an impostor—a "man disguised in woman's clothing." She spoke without incident until she arrived in Silver Lake, Kosciusko County, where the crossdressing issue nearly caused a riot. Proslavery mobs followed and heckled her throughout the county. Undaunted, she made the "most powerful and galling speeches amid continued interruption and insult." But in Silver Lake, a drunken, noisy mob milled around the United Brethren meetinghouse where she spoke and afterward challenged her. "Dr. T. W. Strain," a physician and "mouth-piece of the Slave Democracy" shouted "'hold on.'" Sojourner Truth, he announced, was a man hired by the Republicans. "Your voice is not that of a woman; it is the voice of a man," Strain asserted; he wanted proof of her womanhood. "[When] put to vote; a boisterous 'aye' was the result; a negative vote was not called for." The men ordered her to reveal her breasts to the women, who vehemently objected. During this exchange, "a gun or pistol was fired near the door." A scuffle and mayhem ensued as Sojourner's sponsors, apparently, tried to remove her from the meetinghouse. But "the tumult was soon suppressed," Abolitionist William Hayward reported, when Sojourner took command of the situation. She agreed to expose her breasts.[30]

Strain, having bet $40 that she was male, aimed to humiliate her by robbing her of womanly and motherly status and denying her witness as an Abolitionist and her integrity as preacher-teacher. The white men wanted to substantiate the concept of black women as objects—whether free or enslaved—not, as they claimed, determine her gender. Yet Sojourner Truth felt no shame. Her breasts, she told the men, "had suckled many a white babe," and on her milk they had grown to "man's estate." But there was nothing manly about her persecutors, she added. Projecting the disgrace meant for black women on her white male tormentors, she said, "she would show her breasts to the whole congregation," for "it was not to her shame, but to their shame, that she uncovered her breast before them." As she "presented her naked breast" to the audience's gaze, "one of the chivalry" pushed aside his companions "to steal a nearer glance." Sojourner observed him instantly. Placing her hand under her breast "in maternal fashion" and drawing it towards the "prurient young scamp," she asked, "'Chile, do *you* wish to suck?'"[31]

The white patriarchy had long attempted to debase and dehumanize the black race by controlling black women's bodies. At the same time, black women have historically been objects of sexual desire to white men. Demanding that Sojourner Truth disrobe was not only symbolic rape; it represented the auction block—one of slavery's pinnacles of personal humiliation. "Why, it is a *sow*, for I see the teat," said one ogling Democrat, exposing his own curiosity, animalism, and subliminal reflex. Equally revealing in this regard were the "two young men" who volunteered to step up and examine Sojourner Truth's breasts. As novelist Toni Morrison has demonstrated, babies were not the only whites who suckled, fondled, and took milk from enslaved women's breasts.[32]

The *Liberator* published Hayward's account without comment, as did Indiana papers. Even the *Bugle* expressed no opinion as Sojourner Truth and Josephine Griffing continued their fall meetings. Yet their pages heaped praise on Frances Ellen Watkins, almost as if to contrast the only two black women on the lecture circuit. Frances, called a quadroon, was freeborn, had been orphaned, and came from a solidly middle-class Baltimore family. She was educated, literate, ladylike, and eloquently literary. Sojourner Truth carried the baggage of bondage, poverty, and nonliteracy. She possessed the bold, unfettered, hard-bitten coarseness of a true radical; one never knew what she might say. The immediate reaction of most Abolitionists to the breast-baring incident was probably similar to that of the female eyewitnesses—"ashamed and indignant."[33]

As she used her voice, she used her body—her breasts, her missing finger, and her back—to bear witness against slavery. Once at Kalamazoo College, students hissed, "thumped on their seats," and "broke into hilarious laughter" when she appeared on the platform. When the noise subsided, her tall, erect form swayed slightly and gracefully as she addressed the assembly. "Well children, when you go to heaven and God asks you what made you hate the colored people, have you got your answer ready?" After pausing for effect, she spoke. She had an answer ready when God asked, "'Sojourner what made you hate the white people?'" She opened the collar of her dress, pulled it down to the shoulders, turned around showed the audience a "perfect network of scars made by the slave master's lash." The overwhelming effect produced a "baptism of tears" that replaced the hisses and scoffs. Thus, the breast-baring incident was not singular for her. Moreover, any woman who took the public stage "unsexed" herself in the eyes of society, and people questioned her gender. When Josephine Griffing traveled alone in the same Indiana county, a female resident offered hospitality but inquired whether "I was *a woman*," and added, "'They say,' that 'no *woman* ever talked as she talks, and I never knew one to talk at all.'"[34] Griffing was not compelled to show her bosom to her hostess or to detractors. Whites reserved that indignity for Sojourner Truth.

Besides the public stage, Michigan relocation afforded Sojourner a rich private life. She spent time with her family, especially her two grandsons; was active locally; and had long visits with friends. Every spring, when blackberries and strawberries ripened, large growers such as the Chandler-Merritts gave Sojourner all the berries she could sell. The growers printed handbills announcing "Aunt Sojourner's" arrival in Battle Creek with the fruit. Reportedly, she was an unforgettable figure, with a large fruit basket sitting on her head, kept secure by her tall graceful carriage and a carefully wrapped turban. As she swayed through the streets singing and calling out her wares, local housewives flocked to her. They waited gladly for her, because her berries "were the best to be had."[35]

The private Sojourner made the historical figure possible and as public speaking was her form of literacy, so was domesticity—including medicinal knowledge, intuitive mother wit, and superior household skills. Friends said her "healing hands" prolonged life, her spiritual power comforted in death, and she left a blessing in every home she visited. Sojourner's "Dear Friend," Edward Ives of Detroit, wrote to her about family and friends during her absence. His son James, whose health she had once restored, "as you know is a feeble man." But James (later the Currier and Ives lithographer) believed "that if you could have had him under your hands a month or two longer . . . he should been a stronger man today." Eliza Leggett's daughter, Margaret Ives, wrote about Sojourner in the journal she kept for her infant son Percival. "Sojourner caught rain water today," she wrote, and bathed the babies in the household. She "is one of the kindest old ladies that has ever lived" and has a "superior mind and very clear perceptions." Her "abiding faith in God is beautiful." Sojourner talked of God, Margaret added, as familiarly "as your father and I talk to each other." [36]

The knitting needle and yarn, the sewing machine, the spinning wheel were also Sojourner's female props, representing domestic culture and communalism. Among her associates, she analyzed biblical discourse and newspaper articles and discussed reform, families, slavery, war, peace, and death. Like

Sojourner, her non-Quaker friends loved singing. Betsy and Cornelia Cowles, like Abby Hutchinson, had concert voices and often sang at conventions. Josephine Griffing also loved singing; during long cold winters, Sojourner and these Abolitionist women sang hymns and antislavery songs into the night, no doubt as a form of entertainment and solidarity. Even Sojourner's rocking chair and pipe were domestic props, inspiring contemplative thoughts used in her speeches. Just as she and other black women activists bonded with white women reformers through domestic culture, she also later created a deep solidarity with freedwomen. She used domestic culture as a poor woman's "parlor literature"—the old white female institution, which middle-class keepers of the hearth revived: exchanging recipes and letters, writing short stories and personal poetry. Both forms of wisdom and networking connected women to the world beyond the household. Sojourner's refined domesticity symbolized her confident intelligence, born of experience and intuition. Her Detroit friend Eliza Leggett often read newspapers, poetry, novels, and other literature aloud. Once while reading *Leaves of Grass* to her children, Eliza noticed their distraction. "Pay attention," she commanded; and then she heard: "'Who wrote that?'" Turning around, she saw Sojourner's tall form standing in the doorway. "Never mind the man's name," the Sojourner said. He only put it on paper. "It was God who wrote it." Sojourner Truth, Eliza wrote Walt Whitman, greatly enjoyed *Leaves of Grass.* Her "great brain accepts the highest truths" Eliza commented. They often attended cultural events together. At a lecture on Raphael's *School of Athens,* "the presenter discussed Plato, Socrates, and others." Sojourner listened attentively and said, "'How good, how simple.'"[37]

She saw the hand of God in everything good, and her belief in her capacity to know and to understand God was uncompromising. How could anyone observe a locomotive and not see God, she asked Eliza Leggett. "People are all the time wanting to know something about God. . . . Why don't they go and look at a beautiful Lokey Motive. If they can't see God in that, they need not expect ever to see him. Just stand by when ye see a great rushing big engine come roaring like thunder and blazing like the sun with a speed like a whirl wind . . . as though it was that God Almighty himself was a coming—And so he is." God put part of his own wisdom into the man who discovered the engine and made it work. "Didn't he Chile—just think of these things and then remember what Sojourner tell you. . . . If you can't see God in a Lokey Motive, ye'll never see him in this world." Some of Sojourner's learned associates sometimes tried to "set the old lady straight," especially about the Bible. They were thoroughly frustrated, as was Eliza's friend Captain Hunt. "Pshaw Child," she said after Hunt's explanations, "the Bible is a riddle any body can play on." After all, Matthias had "played" her with his biblical interpretation; she would not be fooled again. "Oh Sojourner I can't talk to you," Hunt responded in agitation. "No No Chile," agreed Sojourner, "Better go and learn something. You don't know enough yet."[38]

She was not only a doting grandmother determined that her grandsons be useful in the world, she was a household favorite in reform families. Children called her "Godmother" and "Grandmother" and anxiously awaited her visits. Among them was Minnie Merritt Fay, who loved to sit in her lap, feel "her smooth skin," and hear her tell stories in her "soothing voice." Minnie's baby brother, William, stopped his play and danced whenever Sojourner sang and "clapped juba." Other children competed to be her "talking books." While she sometimes lamented being unable to read and write, she could also be defensive. The world owed most of its problems to people who could read, she once said. "You know children," she said on another occasion, "I don't read such small stuff as letters, . . . I read men and nations. I can see through a millstone, though I can't see through a spelling-book." Children also learned lessons from her wry political comments. "We have read you all the Republicans and the Democrats say," Elizabeth Cady Stanton's children announced after reading tirelessly to her. She said with mock amazement, "Why, children, I can't tell one from the other. The millennium must be here; when one can't tell saints from sinners, Republicans from Democrats." Editors and publishers (or their wives) who knew Sojourner as children kept her in the press throughout her life. One story, which I like to call *off-color,* illustrates childhood innocence, American racism, and Sojourner Truth's magnetic appeal. She was the guest in a home where the little girl supposedly had never seen a black person. For some time, the child would have nothing to do with her. "But by her friendly arts the black woman won the child so that as the elder was leaving the home, the younger, jumping into her lap and looking into her eyes, broke out, 'Aunty, they say you's black, but you ain't.'"[39]

III

In 1859, the eastern antislavery leadership further fragmented, while westerners agitated. Wendell Phillips, the Fosters, Thomas Wentworth Higginson, and Parker Pillsbury worried that Garrison had traded his Come-outer Perfectionism for the "reprehensible" Republican Party. Sparks flew in May at the New England Anti-Slavery Convention, when the Fosters and Pillsbury secured a resolution against the Republican Party. Exasperated communitarian Adin Ballou accused the paralyzed Executive Committee of abandoning "Practical Christian Anti-Slavery" in favor of "excessive individualism." Sojourner Truth traveled from Kansas to Wisconsin, speaking among Abolitionists, Free Soilers,

Republicans, Democrats—virtually anyone who would listen. "Few women of cultivation possess as vigorous an intellect, or as warm a heart," noted a Wisconsin Abolitionist who hoped that Sojourner's "seeds of truth" would "take root in many hearts." Wisconsin Republicans received her graciously her friends noted, but condescendingly called her "an exception to the general rule" of black inferiority.[40]

While some radicals hoped for the new party's transformation and others felt they could "shame" free-state men out of their racism, John Brown Sr. took another course. In the dead of winter, in a stunning act of resistance, he liberated eleven enslaved Missourians who were about to be sold and led them on a publicized, relentless, three-month, eleven-hundred-mile trek through four states. The trek had courageous moments that bolstered Brown's reputation as he successfully challenged federal troops in Kansas and evaded a marshal's posse in Nebraska. In Iowa (except for the Quakers in Tabor), citizens cheered Brown for his rescue, fed and housed the caravan, and escorted them under heavy guard to the rail cars in West Liberty. They were hidden in a boxcar and attached to a train headed for Chicago, where private investigator Allan Pinkerton intercepted them and eventually arranged rail transportation to Detroit. Vigilance committee leaders William Lambert and George De Baptiste arranged ferry transportation across the Detroit River into Windsor, Ontario. The party now numbered twelve; an infant, John Brown Daniels, was born in freedom. At the wharf, as the grateful former slaves and "Old Brown" said an emotional farewell, he quoted one of Sojourner's favorite Scriptures, "Lord, lettest thy servant depart in peace, for my eyes have seen thy salvation." Douglass was speaking in Detroit, and Brown gathered with him and other black leaders, including Lambert, De Baptiste, and Isaac Shadd of the *Provincial Freeman*, and outlined his plans to liberate enslaved Virginians. After seeing his charges safely to Canada, Brown met with Frederick Douglass and other blacks to solicit their participation in his plan to liberate enslaved Virginians. Brown then went East to consult his white backers—the "Secret Six" who were financing his insurrection plan (Thomas Wentworth Higginson, Theodore Parker, George Sterns, Franklin Sanborn, Samuel G. Howe, and Gerrit Smith). "Talk! Talk! Talk!" Brown said of the New England Anti-Slavery May convention. "That will never free the slaves. What is needed is action—action." Thus, on October 16, 1859, he led twenty-one men (sixteen whites and five blacks) in an unsuccessful attack on the federal arsenal in Harpers Ferry, Virginia, hoping to begin a slave revolt. When his carpetbag revealed the names of supporters and correspondents, four frightened Secret Six members made themselves scarce. However, Theodore Parker, dying of tuberculosis in Rome, publicly defended Brown, and Higginson was equally unflappable. Brown's white Ohio Republican supporters—Joshua Giddings and Salmon Chase—denied and denounced him. Although John Brown Jr. was not at Harpers Ferry, he was wanted for "questioning," and hid out in Ashtabula County. "The hounds are braying on my back," he wrote Betsy Cowles, and he had no intention of going to Washington. The Langston brothers, epitomizing the black response to Brown's actions, wrote that he was justified on biblical principles, the Constitution, and the ideals of "all good Abolitionists." Frederick Douglass fled the country when "the thing calling itself the Government of Virginia" charged him with murder, robbery, and inciting servile insurrection.[41]

The white Northern public thought Brown was mad. "No human reasonable man will for a moment sympathize with this effort to incite servile insurrection," wrote the moderately antislavery *National Era* (which had serialized *Uncle Tom's Cabin*). "We deeply regret this outbreak." The *Tribune* wrote that emancipation "lies not through insurrection, civil war and bloodshed, but through peace, discussion, and the quiet diffusion of sentiments of humanity and justice."[42] Naturally, notions of Brown's insanity hinged largely on the belief that whites willing to kill other whites and die for black freedom had to be crazy.

Radical Abolitionists took a different position, even if they were pacifists. Brown's capture, trial, and death sentence elevated him to martyrdom and reunited the antislavery cause. John Brown, Garrison noted, "has told us the time," and however misguided, Brown's intentions were honest, truthful, and brave. Others went further: Brown's "attack on the Philistines" was not the work of a "knave, fool, a crazy man or a coward," the *Practical Christian* declared. In the *Bugle*, Marius Robinson proclaimed Brown a hero for whom no apologies were necessary. The *True American* "always believed slavery would die a violent death. We prefer its extinction by moral argument or political suffrage; but at all costs, we prefer its extinction." Black Americans called John Brown their Joshua. New York black women published a supportive letter to Mary Brown in the *Anglo-African*. Blacks visited Mary Brown in Philadelphia, where she was William Still's guest as she traveled to see her condemned husband. According to newspaper accounts, when he walked to his execution, "a black woman with her little child in arms, stood near his way." With his hands bound, he "stepped down for a moment in his course, stooped over, and with the tenderness of one whose love is as broad as the brotherhood of man, kissed it affectionately." Perhaps Harriet Tubman, who was supposed to accompany him to Harpers Ferry, best sums up contemporary black attitudes toward "Old Brown." "It was not Captain Brown that died at Charlestown," she told editor James Redpath in 1963. "It was Christ."[43]

Radical Abolitionist preachers also championed him. Sojourner Truth, in Wisconsin in fall, 1859, identified with the biblical proportions of Brown's actions, including his prediction that war was inevitable. She agreed with Gilbert Haven that Brown's foiled attempt to create an uprising paled compared to "the violent enslavement of forty hundreds of thousands of our kindred in the flesh and in the Lord." Even the gospel of peace did not always "require of its disciples non-resistance to every form of revolting oppression." In choosing freedom through blood or perpetual slavery, radical preachers said, the enslaved "had an unquestioned right to fight for their freedom." After years of peaceful agitation, Sojourner Truth preached that God would rain down destruction on the unrepentant nation for its sins against her people. God had spoken to her in a vision, she told Joseph Dugdale, and revealed certain Scriptures, which she recited: "None calleth for justice, nor any pleadeth for truth; your hands are defiled with blood, and your fingers with iniquity; they conceive mischief, and bring forth iniquity; they hatch cockatrice's eggs, and weave the spider's web; he that eateth their eggs dieth, and that which is crushed breaketh out into a viper." Dugdale found the passages in the apocalyptic text Isaiah 59. "Now I know it double," she said when she heard the words. Spiritualists hailed Brown as joining Abolitionist "spirits" such as deceased singer Judson Hutchinson, who sent "messages" from beyond the veil. "The evil day has come," Judson foretold through "spirit writing." He had seen "the lone chamber of war and the sobbing sounds of anguish have rent the very air." Hence Brown was fulfilling prophecy. As a sacrificial lamb, forfeiting his life "to give deliverance to the captives and let the oppressed go free," John Brown, Haven insisted, made the "gallows as glorious as the cross."[44]

After Abraham Lincoln's 1860 election to the presidency, the Michigan State Anti-Slavery Society met in Adrian. Sojourner Truth joined Laura Haviland, Josephine Griffing, Parker Pillsbury, Giles Stebbins, the Merritts, Titus, and the Chandlers on the platform. It was their largest meeting ever. Participants unanimously passed impressive and sweeping resolutions that denounced the newly elected president and his administration. Slavery was "perfectly safe in Abraham's bosom," they proclaimed; the Republican platform upheld the right to hold slaves and supported the Dred Scott decision and the Fugitive Slave Law. "Every John Brown or Nat Turner is to be hung, every fugitive is to be returned," and Lincoln would admit to the Union "a State with a slave holding constitution." Lincoln and the Republicans would no more support abolition than would South Carolina, which had just seceded. The defiant Michigan society pledged to "build and run a network of Underground Railroads" under Lincoln's administration and create "AN IRREPRESSIBLE CONFLICT with slavery" to bring about its utter extermination by any means, "even bloody revolution." They cared not for peace or for the Union, but for freedom. Since Lincoln's presidency offered little hope for emancipation, and change in party leaders was meaningless, the Abolitionists vowed to force the contradictions through agitation. There was "power *behind* the throne. THE PEOPLE THEMSELVES." The Michigan society vowed to "test the people. Let them take sides for or against freedom." The Business Committee forwarded its resolutions to the New York *Herald, Tribune,* other presses, and all the state and territorial governors—especially those of the South. "Our well known friend Sojourner Truth" sang and made "occasional principle sparklers," the *Bugle* wrote, but reported no one's specific remarks.[45]

Abolitionists again closed ranks, speaking passionately, eloquently, and with determination during the inaugural interregnum. But the nation wanted compromise. Outgoing President Buchanan encouraged an anti-Abolitionist atmosphere; he urged the North to repeal personal liberty laws, support an amendment to protect slavery everywhere, and obey the Fugitive Slave law to foil the South's "justified" revolutionary resistance to the government. The president-elect pledged to enforce the laws, but offered the South an olive branch, noting that "mystic chords of memory" bound the regions together. The press, local authorities, and both political parties encouraged a "mobocratic revival" against the Abolitionists. In Boston's Tremont Hall, a John Brown commemoration became a noisy, hissing, three-hour mob scene. When Frederick Douglass (now back in the states) rose to speak, pandemonium ensued. The police removed Wendell Phillips roughly, but violently threw Douglass down a staircase. When the Abolitionists adjourned to the black Joy Street Church, rioters waited outside; forty supporters escorted Phillips home. Both he and Douglass began carrying revolvers.[46]

In Michigan, Abolitionists faced even more formidable mobs. In early 1861, a convention in Ann Arbor was "one of the stormiest" and fiercest ever encountered, and authorities left Abolitionists to the "tender mercies" of the mob. Rynders's New York City mob had been larger, Pillsbury wrote, but Ann Arbor rioters were more determined. The university's eight hundred Union men and proslavery Southern students were "a power not easily resisted." The Abolitionists were "severely kicked and beaten in the face." When the mayor closed the hall and the Abolitionists adjourned to a small Progressive Friends meetinghouse, "a most ferocious and savage throng" of "collegians, clerks, drunken Irish boys, lawyers, and pug-uglies" closed down the convention, breaking the seats, smashing window glass, and generally demolishing the house. They moved on to meetings in Indiana, where the "burning of a match wrapped up in a cayenne pepper cartridge" sent the assembly into the winter cold, "coughing and some fainting."[47]

The western movement lost a key source of information in spring 1861 when the *Anti-Slavery Bugle* ceased publication. Reliable activists also left the scene. Frances Ellen Watkins married and settled on a farm in Columbus, Ohio; the Joneses returned to Philadelphia, where Benjamin soon died; the Robinsons returned to New York. Josephine Griffing left her husband, moved to Michigan, and became matron of St. Mary's Lake Water Cure outside Battle Creek. The West still "grows in importance" Josephine wrote, though "long ignored" by the AASS. As the Civil War began in April 1861, the Battle Creek area became a center of western abolition. Sojourner Truth, Josephine Griffing, Henry C. Wright, and Parker Pillsbury traveled through Ohio, Iowa, and Illinois touting a new slogan at rousing conventions: "The War—Its Cause and Cure." Slavery had caused the war; emancipation and arming the enslaved was the cure. Some Republicans, even inside Lincoln's cabinet, and some generals agreed. When major-general John C. Fremont emancipated Missouri blacks enslaved by rebels, Lincoln rescinded the order and relieved Fremont. A year later, Lincoln also struck down General David Hunter's conscription of enslaved men in Union-occupied coastal Georgia and South Carolina. Exasperated Abolitionists watched as the Union army first returned fleeing blacks to slave owners, and later, as scores of thousands of blacks fled behind Union lines, labeled them "contraband" and ruthlessly exploited their labor or merely tolerated their presence as useless victims, while their status—free or enslaved—remained uncertain. Abolitionists continued their agitation.[48]

Northern Indiana Abolitionists invited Sojourner Truth and Josephine Griffing to the region even as the Democrats' rhetoric heightened Negrophobia. Indiana, among the first states to support Abraham Lincoln, had a Republican governor and strong Union sentiments. However, Confederate military victories portended a shifting allegiance, as Southern sympathizers and Kentucky rebels muscled their way into power. Riots erupted, and Union recruiters were murdered. Indiana was Kansas, Griffing believed, in terms of violence and assassinations. Yet even some Republicans who opposed slavery in the territories also opposed black emancipation. Republican banners in northern Indiana blared, "The Constitution As It Is, The Union As It Was," and "We won't fight to free the nigger." Such advertisements did little to assuage proslavery Democrats, called copperheads. Truth and Griffing spoke in the region where Sojourner's breast-baring incident had occurred. The Abolitionist presence was weak, and copperheads harassed the women, taking particular aim at Sojourner Truth.[49]

A war had broken out in Steuben County, in June 1861, Josephine Griffing wrote Garrison. The issue was actually freedom of speech, although the "Democracy" insisted that Sojourner violated the state's Black Laws and the Dred Scott decision. Sojourner Truth, whom Griffing called "a cross between the Indian and African race," spoke at the courthouse in Angola, Indiana. Although accompanied by "the most respectable" local ladies, the fiery Sojourner was both provocative and dramatic. Since the South was using colored people to fight *against* the North, Sojourner declared herself "armed (stretching out her long bony arm) to fight for the North." If she were younger, she added, she would "fly to the battlefield" as nurse and cook for her Massachusetts boys, and in a pinch, she would also "put in a blow now and then." Instantly, a drunken mob surrounded her; she was pushed, cursed, threatened with tar and feathers, rails, and shooting and rendered unable to continue her speech. She was extricated from the melee, and spent the night in the home of Judge Gale, a wealthy and prominent Abolitionist. The pursuing mob threatened to invade the house, but the men were too inebriated to do violence. They threatened to burn down the building if she spoke; she vowed to speak to the ashes. As proslavery elements prepared for her next scheduled appearance at the courthouse, fortunately so did Angola's "Home Guard." A loyal Home Guard captain in a neighboring township revealed a poorly kept "secret"—guns, powder, balls, and cap were deposited at Poland's Grocery (liquor store) for use "in suppressing the meeting of Sojourner Truth in the Court House on Sunday." Antislavery ladies and the captain of the Angola Home Guard asked Sojourner to go to the meeting dressed for the war effort. She agreed on behalf of emancipation and the Union, but looking in the mirror, she "fairly frightened" herself. "They put upon me a red, white, and blue shawl, a sash and apron to match, a cap on my head with a star in front, and a star on each shoulder." But she drew the line at arming herself with a "sword or pistol." God was her protector, she said, keeping her safe even among enemies. "Truth is powerful" she proclaimed, "and will prevail."[50]

She rode to the courthouse in a "large, beautiful carriage" with the Home Guard captain, "other gentlemen," and a procession of armed soldiers following them. "I felt as I was going against the Philistines," she said, and prayed for deliverance "out of their hands." Sure enough, when the copperheads saw the armed force, they dispersed "like a flock of frightened crows," except for a little boy sitting on a fence who yelled "'Nigger, nigger!'" Inside the courthouse, the Union band played "The Star-Spangled Banner." Sojourner said she "sang with all my might" as bayonets flashed and banners waved. "It seems that it takes *my* black face to bring out your black hearts; so it's well I came." They feared her blackness, because it was a "looking glass in which you see yourselves." But the issue was Sojourner's rights as a citizen, and she "advocated free speech with more zeal than ever before."[51]

The two women—black and white—endured constant name-calling, flying missiles, and threats of physical harm. Warrants were issued for Sojourner's arrest, and she was sometimes just a step ahead of rebel sympathizers. Mobs dogged her while Home Guards protected her. She was arrested several times for violating the state's Black Laws. "In my experiences with mobs" Josephine wrote, "I have never seen such determination. No dog was ever hung to a bone as have these hungry hounds to Sojourner, under the cover of law." Fearing for her safety and their own, antislavery women once urged her to hide in the woods. She positively refused, vowing to go to jail first. When the rebel constable came with a warrant, a Union officer followed with a document asserting that she was *his* prisoner. The disgusted copperhead left muttering that he would resign before again bothering his "head with niggers." Soon the Indiana (Union) Legion arrived, and everyone marched back to the courthouse, playing on fife and drum. They gave "loud cheers for Sojourner, Free Speech, and the Union." In this case, the prosecution's trial ended quickly when its "half-drunken lawyers" deserted her case in favor of visiting the tavern. The Abolitionists celebrated with a grand picnic. "In every case we have outwitted and beaten them," Josephine reported. In two cases she defended Sojourner; in two others, "we had two of the most able lawyers in the county"; and in two more, Sojourner's friends were acquitted of harboring her and encouraging her presence.[52]

Sojourner Truth and Josephine remained defiant and triumphant. Their six court appearances drew people from every part of Steuben County, especially women. "I have never labored a month in the cause of human freedom with so much acknowledged results," Josephine wrote. Their meetings were immense, although churches were closed to them, so people "listened in God's great temple." On one day they held two meetings two miles apart, and people were so engrossed that they refused to break for refreshments. A ninety-eight-year-old "Revolutionary soldier" walked three miles to "'get into a war for freedom once more before he died.'" Two nursing mothers remained in meeting for five hours, feeding their infants without nourishing themselves, yet "said they were neither tired nor hungry." Never had these two female Abolitionists felt so empowered, sensing that people were uplifted, engaged, and prepared to comprehend the "critical doctrine." They were told that over the entire three weeks of their meetings, armed men in the audiences "declared that they would blow out our brains." Nonetheless, "the battle of Sojourner Truth is nearly fought; and they know whom they have to dread till the end of this war." Sojourner Truth and Josephine vowed they would seek no rest until "the quiet of the grave."[53]

Despite Lincoln's policies, Abolitionists in the field such as Sojourner Truth knew that the war was about slavery. While Sojourner worked the western lecture circuit, eastern Abolitionists pressured the seat of power. The *Liberator* dramatized the domestic conflict with an imaginary prophetic dialogue between Moses and Pharaoh. Like Egypt, the American nation had been smitten horribly because its leaders would not "let the people go." When Congress finally freed the enslaved population of Washington, D.C., in April 1862, the Abolitionists celebrated grandly, and Lydia Maria Child wrote Lincoln a poignant public letter. In July, Sojourner's "broad-rimmed" associates, the Longwood Progressive Friends, presented a memorial to President Lincoln. On this occasion, reportedly, "the scene was unique." These unworldly Quakers, who represented a diverse cross-section of reformers, addressed a president with cautious political and social vision who hoped to halt a crushing war by holding millions of people in chains as a trump. Women and men sat separately as this "straightest of sects" invoked its moral weight. *Standard* editor Oliver Johnson spoke for the Friends as Pennsylvania congressmen watched. Abraham Lincoln, although awkwardly uncomfortable, "listened with marked nervous attention." As Johnson read the memorial, Lincoln's "great eyebrows seemed to drop, listening, quivering over the deep, comprehensive, melancholy eyes." Playing with his watch chain, he "cast a rapid glance over the small outside audience . . . doubtless to see if there was a suspicious reporter." Running his fingers through his hair, it "rose erect, electric. . . . It might be said without exaggeration, that he stood, 'his mane listening.'" Afterward, Congressman David Wilmot told the president to ignore the small sect, whose moral influence was not "irresistible" because it did not represent a daily demand from all "Christians of the land." One month later, powerful Republican editor Horace Greeley's "Prayer of Twenty Million" suggested a national voice, if not the Friends' moral position. And in September, an interdenominational delegation of influential Chicago Christians presented a memorial urging national emancipation. Lincoln's only answer was that the issue of emancipation preoccupied his mind "more than any other."[54]

I have plead with all the force I had that the day
might come that the colored people might own their
own soul and body. Well the day has come, although
it came through blood. It makes no difference how it
came—it did come. — SOJOURNER TRUTH

And proclaim liberty throughout all the land. . . .
It shall be a jubilee unto you. — LEV. 25:10

CHAPTER 17

Proclaim Liberty
throughout the Land

I

Sojourner Truth had spent twenty years speaking against slavery, and
the last seven lecturing throughout seven western states. Her health, which had
been amazingly good, declined along with her spirits. For all of their successes in
Indiana, emancipation seemed in doubt in 1862. Moreover, she refused to return
to Harmonia and lived in a Battle Creek basement. The stress of the Indiana
campaign also took a heavy physical toll on this sixty-five-year-old messenger of
God. Eventually her health failed completely; Joseph and Phebe Merritt cared
for her with help from her daughter Diana. Sojourner's friend Samuel Rogers
remembered that she was "often extremely excited and anxious about how the
war would end." Lincoln was making plans to colonize her people if he could
not use them to get the South back into the Union. Even when Lincoln appeared
ready to sign the Emancipation Proclamation, the old radical was not assuaged.
Dangerously ill late in 1862, expecting to die before seeing complete liberation,
she asked Rogers to preach her funeral. He agreed but added, "I don't think you
had better die just yet. Don't you want to see all your people free?" He advised,
"The best thing you can do is to get well so that you can live to see this war

ended and the slaves free." They discussed the matter at length, he recalled. As January 1, 1863, drew near, the faithful and steadfast Sojourner sent word that she longed to be with friends and coworkers, "and speak to the people a few more times in this glorious day of emancipation."[1]

Her friends everywhere celebrated "the beginning of the end." The Michigan Central Railroad carried passengers for half fare as black citizens from Detroit, Ypsilanti, Ann Arbor, Albion, and Marshall gathered in Battle Creek on December 31. The Baptist and Methodist churches held "watch meetings" (watching the clock bring emancipation in with the new year) others preferred to "trip the light fantastic toe" to a noted black band, with supper included, for $1. In Boston, white Abolitionists joined the literati for a jubilee concert, and blacks gathered at Tremont Temple. William C. Nell presided; Frederick Douglass and Dr. John Rock headed the speakers' list. When the wires brought word of the Proclamation's signing, Tremont shook with thunderous shouts, applause, foot stomping, jumping, and singing:

"Sound the loud timbre!
O'er Egypt's dark sea
Jehovah hath triumphed,
His people are free.

In New York City, Sojourner's antislavery associates celebrated at Cooper Institute and Shiloh Presbyterian, where Horace Greeley joined pastor Henry Garnet as the audience sang John Brown's favorite hymn, "Blow ye the trumpet, blow." At Brooklyn's Colored Methodist Church, *Independent* editor Theodore Tilton joined William Wells Brown and minister Jeremiah Gloucester in the pulpit. In nearby Williamsburgh, Elizabeth Greenfield and her pupils welcomed everyone to a grand matinee and celebratory concert. In Washington, D.C., Bethel AME Church members listened to Union chaplain Henry M. Turner's sermon. But the scene closest to Sojourner's heart was in the District's contraband camps, where superintendent Dr. Danforth Nichols read off the names of counties included in the Proclamation. The news was joyous to some and disappointing for others; but they all knelt and sang "Go down Moses."[2]

In the midst of these emotional outpourings, the Merritts' daughter, Phebe Stickney, wrote to Longwood Friend Joseph Dugdale about Sojourner's condition. "I write to thee and thine to solicit a little assistance." Their much-esteemed friend Sojourner Truth remained bedridden and "quite feeble." Indeed, Stickney lamented, she was doing so poorly, she "probably won't live long." She had no income to "supply herself with the many little comforts that an aged and feeble person needs." Assistance might help her "live a little longer to praise God."[3]

Friends had not forgotten the Sojourner's mighty antislavery works. When Longwood Quakers publicized her plight, letters, donations, and gifts from friends and strangers alike poured into Battle Creek. Assistance even came from abroad. She was surprised and overwhelmed. "Who ever heard of Sojourner Truth in Ireland?" she marveled. Sojourner Truth, a Battle Creek friend wrote to Gerrit Smith, "sends you many thanks for your donations . . . and kind words which she says have lengthened her days." "Our 'venerable friend and teacher,'" Stickney wrote, "says her heart is full of praises and prayers" for the donations, encouragement, acknowledgments, and recognition of her many years of service. This wellspring of admiration and affection was better than any medicine.[4]

Slowly but steadily, Sojourner loosened the throes of death. In the spring of 1863, Frances Titus wrote that "Sojourner is in better health" and more comfortable than she had been during the winter. She was walking great distances, "staff in hand," to strengthen her limbs. Her forward-looking mind reemerged with her improving health. Since it was doubtful that she would ever travel long distances and hold meetings again, she used her photographs, which the Abolitionists called "shadows," to remain in the public eye. During this time, through the new medium of photography, people began sitting for portraits, which were mounted on small pieces of paperboard generally called carte de visite. Reformers often reproduced the likeness of a gravely ill family member. "We feel it best to secure the shadow before the substance faded," William C. Nell wrote regarding his ailing young niece. Abolitionists sold shadows of noted speakers at their fundraising events. Sojourner had had her first shadow made for her 1850 *Narrative* and her second during the 1862 Indiana campaign. In 1863, financial need and perhaps her anticipated earthly passing prompted her to sell her shadow by mail order.[5]

As soon as she was able, she had herself photographed in Battle Creek. In one photograph, she sits with a photo of a young man (most certainly James, about to go to war) in her lap. In another, she stands, tall and straight but relaxed, wearing traveling clothes, including a large, leather work apron, and her head is wrapped in a turban. Oliver Johnson said these looked more like her than any others. "It is a pity you did not preserve the negative," he wrote. She may also have then posed wearing the red, white, and blue attire from her Indiana tour. In 1864, she spent the fall and winter in Detroit and sat for more genteel photographs at the Randall studio, owned by the family of Eliza Leggett's future son-in-law. Randall put a copyright on the images in Sojourner Truth's name. The poses are all suggestive of middle-class domesticity and culture, especially a well-staged one where she stands regally, leaning against a pillar. She sent them to friends who sent donations. Others were asked to pay. "Please accept, she says, her shadow," she offered to Gerrit Smith. "I enclose you three all in different positions," she informed Mary Gale. She wanted Gale to have the best; Sojourner's Detroit friends thought these images were much better than the Battle Creek ones. "I sell the three for $1. or a single one for 35 cents." Admittedly, it was "a little more than the common price," but she included her costs for paper, envelopes, and stamps. Anyone can see "by my card," she added, "that I sell the shadow to support the substance."[6]

Knowing that she lived in epoch-defining times, she kept remembrances of the deeds done by faithful workers in the vineyard. "She carries with her three small books in which she has inscribed the autographs of nearly all the eminent people in America," a reporter noted. "Don't you want to write your name in de *Book of Life*?" she asked friends and acquaintances.[7] Her *Book of Life* included interesting newspaper clippings; signatures and testimonials from the known and unknown; inscriptions from intimate associates; and published stories about herself. Indeed, her *Narrative*, photographs, songs, and press accounts represent autobiography, biography, and her impact on the times.

Moreover, her compilations represent attempts to have some control over her own representation. She knew that her persona was being appropriated. On more than one occasion, Harriet Beecher Stowe arrogated Sojourner Truth's larger-than-life personality for Stowe's own purposes. After using Truth as a character in her 1856 novel, in 1860 Stowe popularized Sojourner's confrontation with Douglass as a means of venting against president-elect Lincoln. Stowe concocted a scene in "Faneuil Hall" and said she was invoking the words of "an old black slave-woman calling herself 'Sojourner Truth.'" Sojourner, Stowe wrote, "lifted her dark face, working with intense feeling, and said in a low, deep voice which was heard in every corner of the room: 'Frederick, is God dead?'" The meaning of Sojourner's question "rang through," to Douglass, Stowe wrote, and it should "ring through this nation." To anyone condemning agitation and making "a covenant with death, and an agreement with hell, old Africa rises, and raising her poor maimed, scarred hand to heaven, asks us—'IS GOD DEAD?'"[8]

Stowe's most notable distorted appropriation appeared in her 1863 *Atlantic Monthly* article "Sojourner Truth, the Libyan Sibyl." Thinking that Sojourner had "passed away from among us as a wave of the sea," Stowe wrote that in Italy she had entertained American artist William Wetmore Story's breakfast guests with Sojourner stories. Stowe claimed that she suggested the name "African Sibyl" for Story's 1862 prize-winning statue, as a tribute to Sojourner. Whatever she said in Italy, as recounted in the *Atlantic Monthly*, Stowe blemished and fabricated her meeting with Truth to produce a fictionalized female Amazon of "African nature." William Story's artistically idealized *African Sibyl* was oversized, voluptuous, thoughtful, queenly, and elegant; Stowe's literary Truth was an oddity, speaking in a droll, thick, almost incomprehensible dialect, uttering queer homilies and phrases, and expressing herself with gullibility and foolish reciprocity. Stowe also saturated her "Sibyl" with naïve religious faith: "I go 'round a testifying' and 'showin' the people their sins.'"[9]

The comments Stowe attributed to Truth on woman's rights jolted Frances Gage's memory about Akron, after twelve years of silence. According to Stowe, Truth told the women: "'Sisters, I ai'n't clear what you'd be after. Ef women want any rights, more' deys got, why don't dey 'jes take em, an' not be talking' about it?'" Stowe was no woman's rights advocate. Gage was not only an activist but claimed some literary talent. "Many home-circles" throughout the West recalled anecdotes of "the weird, wonderful creature, who was at once a marvel and a mystery," Gage began. While Stowe's version implied that Truth was somewhat foggy and dismissive on woman's rights, Gage remembered that Sojourner was "very clear." Dusting off her creative recall and countering Stowe's version, Gage publicized her rendition of Akron, coining the now famous refrain: "Ar'n't [or 'Ain't'] I a Woman?" As discussed earlier, evidence supports the authenticity of Gage's general recollection, if not her rhetorical metaphor and language.[10] Essentially, both women used Truth to connect themselves with the heady historical times.

No journal was as widely read as the *Atlantic Monthly*, and no female author as popular as Stowe. Hence "Sojourner Truth, the Libyan Sibyl" captured national attention. Garrison read it aloud to guests and his children; other Abolitionists called the article "delightful." Oliver Johnson, an eyewitness to the Truth-Douglass encounter in Salem, Ohio, insisted that Stowe "by no means exaggerated." He quickly pointed out, however, that Sojourner was alive. Abolitionists, always awed by Stowe's literary talents, undoubtedly felt that she had told a simple allegorical tale. Yet Stowe's caricature and misrepresentation was an attempt to burlesque a serious, pensive, bilingual, black American activist. Stowe even reduced Sojourner's complex, ecumenical Perfectionism to the simple Christianity of Uncle Tom and Stowe herself. From that time on, Sojourner Truth, an outspoken champion of human rights, had to struggle against a demeaning racial stereotype created by a woman who never spoke publicly against slavery, never made a single sacrifice for abolition or any reform, and delivered a painful snub to Harriet Jacobs's effort at literary advancement. "Sojourner Truth, the Libyan Sibyl" widened Sojourner Truth's reputation but in ways not altogether positive.[11] Stowe's "Libyan Sibyl" was not only a fiction; it was Sojourner Truth in blackface.

Sojourner said it best: "Mrs. Stowe laid it on thick"—including a crude, offensive depiction of Sojourner's language, which some reporters emulated. Although her Dutchness was always evident, Sojourner was proud of commanding good English. "Her language is not eloquent but it is grammatically correct," wrote one reporter. Another probably exaggerated in saying she spoke "as well as the most learned college professor." Sojourner refused to hear Stowe's article. "Don't read me that old symbol," she said dismissively. Sojourner preferred hearing about the Great War and other stories from the newspapers, especially what the "young sprigs" printed about her. Throughout her life, she would not allow the article to be read to her. And not everyone jumped on Stowe's bandwagon. Battle Creek newspapers did not. Joseph Dugdale noted that Sojourner's life represented preeminent devotion to the cause of liberty and purity; and despite Stowe's "graphic sketch," he insisted that "no pen can give an adequate idea of Sojourner Truth."[12]

The year 1863 was both triumphant and tragic for African Americans; the Emancipation Proclamation angered many Northern whites, who blamed blacks for the war. In March, Detroit authorities arrested a man "reputed to be a Negro" for "committing an outrage upon a white girl, of delicate age." Although he was tried, convicted, and sentenced to life in prison, the *Detroit Free Press*, with its "villainous sentiments in regard to the black man," inflamed the already angry white public. Expecting violence, the authorities called for troops to help escort the prisoner from the courthouse. Thousands followed, throwing stones, brickbats, mud, and other missiles. At first, the soldiers fired a volley of blanks, but the crowd wounded several soldiers, one seriously. The soldiers were then ordered to fire live ammunition, killing one man and wounding several others. The prisoner went safely to jail, and the soldiers back in the barracks. The mob, composed of respectable persons as well as young people of the "street school" crazy with "whisky and prejudice," turned on the black community. They stoned black-occupied homes, tore down fences, and committed other outrages. When one black man shot back, wounding one of the mob, the melee escalated. Random beatings, stabbings, and burning ensued. One young woman's infant was thrown "fifteen feet upon the ground, kicked and beaten, while the mother received similar treatment." The mob also assaulted any whites attempting to reason with them or shield African Americans. The brutality was "harrowing and inhuman." The mob embraced the political slang of the era: "D . . d Abolitionists"; "Shoot the cussed Abolitionists." Boys eight to ten years of age seized bricks and stones and rushed at black men, shouting, "Pray, you d—d nigger, we will kill you." Four companies of the Twenty-seventh Infantry from Ypsilanti arrived by nightfall. Squads of soldiers patrolled the streets all night, although by 11 P.M. all was quiet except the fires. At least thirty buildings, including tenements, were burned, as well as many barns and outhouses; at least forty families were rendered homeless and destitute.[13]

It turned out that the convicted man was not black but a mixture of Spanish and Indian, and a registered Democrat. The *Battle Creek Journal* laid much of the blame on the copperhead *Free Press*, which used every opportunity to increase the already existing prejudice against blacks. "Nigger this and nigger that has been the cry." Prominent citizens used the black man, the *Journal* said, to attack Lincoln's administration, and loaned their influence to the *Free Press* in order to pursue a political course. Outbreaks of passion, violence, and hatred were the result, as instigators knew it would be.[14]

Sojourner Truth soon publicly addressed the issue of racism. Three months after the riots, the State Sabbath School Convention met in Battle Creek. Only one participant, a Mr. Duffield of Adrian, spent time condemning the recent riots and encouraging more outreach to black and non-English-speaking children. On the last afternoon, the Convention held a children's mass meeting at the Methodist Church. "Every foot of standing place" was taken. The long, often complicated speeches could not hold the children's attention. But Sojourner sat near the stairs leading to the platform, listening intently. Toward the end of the session, she interrupted, "Is there an opportunity now that I might say a few words?" Some among this interdenominational gathering of leading male clerical lights knew who she was. The moderator did not, however, and was taken aback. T. W. Jones, a minister from Augusta, rose and announced: "SO-JOURNER TRUTH." According to the reporter, "That was enough; five hundred persons, instantly on their feet, prepared to pay the most earnest and respectful attention." According to the reporter, Henry Ward Beecher, the most famous minister in America, said could not have produced a more "electrical effect on the audience than her name did."[15]

"The Spirit of the Lord," she began using formal English, led her to address the nation's twin evils—slavery and race prejudice, as reflected in the Great War and the recent Detroit riot. Many of the rioters had been no older than these children. She asked the children who gave them white skin, and the answer of course was God. Then she asked: who gave her black skin? The answer was again God, and she pressed them further: Was it not therefore "a reproach upon our Maker to despise a part of his children because he has been pleased to give them a black skin?" Sunday school teachers should tell them that bigotry was sinful, she informed the children. Instead, she chastised, teachers "not only do not teach their pupils that it is a sin, but too often indulge in it themselves." But God loved "colored children as well as white," and the same Savior died for all. Teachers must "root up, if possible, the great sin of prejudice against color from your minds," she insisted. Otherwise, neither racially prejudiced teachers nor children would see salvation, because in heaven "black and white are one in the love of Jesus." She urged the children: "Get rid of your prejudice and learn to love colored children," so everyone could be together in glory. Reportedly, the white audience erupted in applause, and some wept effusively. After she finished, Calvin Clark, a minister from Marshall, emphasized to the children that they had heard "the solemn truth uttered by Sojourner Truth." The *Journal* called it "perhaps the most telling anti-slavery speech that was ever delivered at Battle Creek or in Michigan."[16]

Abolitionists all spoke in one voice—a demand for total irrevocable emancipation. The AASS chose Lydia Maria Child to spearhead the most widespread and successful fundraising campaign in the movement's history to lobby for a constitutional amendment. If Sojourner Truth was queen of the platform, Child was queen of the pen. Taking *Standard* readers on an emotional walk down memory lane, she recalled the Abolitionists' protracted struggles, sacrifices, and differences of opinion. Some had died in service; others had "stopped fatigued by the wayside," but vacancies were always speedily filled. How ironic the contradiction, she mused, that "fanatics of inferior intellectual ability" and "no influence" were now credited with "causing the conclusion."[17]

Yet the job was not finished, and Sojourner had no intention of resting on the glowing laurels Child bestowed. She told the *Standard* in the summer of 1863 that she had "budded out wid the trees," though she might still fall with the autumn leaves. "It is the mind that makes the body," she had always maintained. "New ideas, new thoughts bring a new mind and renew the whole system," preventing the body from becoming "withered up." She had no intention of withering away, and she became "very enthusiastic on the war question." She now viewed Lincoln as God's chosen instrument, but agreed with radical friends that he had to be pushed into checkmating the anti-emancipation Democrats. Like her radical friends, she believed that enlisting black men was the quickest way to end the war. Some states, such as Michigan, greatly opposed black enlistment in 1863. Hence the first Northern black regiment, organized in Massachusetts, drew recruits from all over the North. Her old friends, Lewis Hayden of Boston and Mary Ann Shadd Cary, now living in Detroit, were recruiting in Michigan. "James, my grandson," Sojourner proudly boasted, "has enlisted in the Massachusetts 54th." James was "full of enthusiasm when he heard that colored men were to be received" and was among the first three or four from Battle Creek to join. "'Now is our time Grandmother,'" he told Sojourner, "'to prove that we are men.'" Two sons of Frederick Douglass and one of Martin Delany also joined the regiment, commanded by Robert Gould Shaw. On May 28, 1863, the Fifty-fourth embarked for the South Carolina Sea Islands. Harriet Tubman had arrived there in 1862 and worked as a nurse. By the spring of 1863, she was a pilot, scout, and spy for the military high command. The press, which knew Sojourner Truth, now discovered Harriet Tubman.[18]

National curiosity about African Americans increased as the war to save the Union became a freedom crusade, and black military participation proved essential to the North's victory. Ironically, the *Springfield Republican*, which had once harassed Sojourner Truth and George Thompson, wrote approvingly that Massachusetts governor John Andrew and his secretary had dined at Louis Hayden's home on Thanksgiving Day in 1863, along with twenty-five black guests. "There is no reason why he should not dine with Hayden, or invite him to his own table."[19]

Periodicals sometimes compared the era's two most remarkable black women, Truth and Tubman. James Redpath, the Scottish adventurer and journalist who once promoted John Brown's campaigns, followed "dashing" Harriet in the *Boston Commonwealth*. He also republished Frances Gage's article and reviewed Stowe's *Atlantic Monthly* feature on Sojourner Truth. "We are glad to meet Mrs. Stowe again in a most quaint, characteristic, pathetic story of a character we have long known." Stowe's piece was an "Epic of the Hour," but Redpath sought his own interview with Sojourner Truth.[20]

"I am not personal acquainted with you," Sojourner answered from Battle Creek. "But I know you from reputation. You are a friend who stands for liberty." Therefore, she was glad to be of service. Through Redpath, she refuted Stowe and resumed ownership of her own story. Using wordplay that signified on Stowe in what appeared to be the most unassuming manner, Sojourner said that Stowe's article was "not quite correct." For example, Sojourner had never said she was born in Africa and would "never make use of the word honey," although she might call people "children." Moreover, Sojourner had related a *story* to Stowe, "and she has put it on me." Sojourner added, *"She must have misunderstood me."* If Redpath wanted Sojourner's "correct history," he had only to read her little book, which was "Sojourner herself." She offered to send him six copies at 25 cents apiece. This indicates that, unable to travel and sell her books, she must have been living on her shadow. If Redpath thought he could sell some shadows, she would also send some along. The *Boston Commonwealth*'s extensive excerpts revealed that rather than a humorous fable, Sojourner's *Narrative* was a straightforward, tragic account of slavery and a true-to-life depiction of profound strength and faith.[21]

Tragedy soon struck Sojourner's family. During the first engagement of the Fifty-fourth Massachusetts on James Island, South Carolina, James was wounded and taken prisoner. Since Confederates considered black soldiers fugitives, treated them brutally, sometimes executed them, and always refused prisoner exchanges, he was presumed dead. Sojourner thought he perished during the battle at Fort Wagner, which killed over a thousand men, including Colonel Shaw. Urban rioting throughout the North made news about James more difficult to bear. Detroit rioting looked like a scrimmage compared to the barbarism of her native New York. Elected officials such as Democratic governor Horatio Seymour and mayor Fernando Wood encouraged the draft resistance that led to the riots. A mob of women and men cut off telegraph communication, burned homes of the rich, burned the draft office, and successfully battled the police, marines, regular soldiers, and the National Guard for three days. Whites, among them the editor of the *New York Times,* were beaten and robbed; some soldiers and policemen were beaten to death. But the mob really wanted blacks, and "dreadfully abused" any they encountered, Oliver Johnson wrote Sojourner. None were spared, the *Independent* wrote, whether "ministers, doctors, teachers, men of culture," women, or children. They were stoned, drowned, robbed, beaten, shot, hanged, roasted, and raped, and had limbs cut off. The Colored Orphan Asylum was attacked with axes, amid the children's "shrieks and screams." Teachers carried out children fainting from terror; one child was trampled to death. Twenty blacks were killed on the first day. Despite the bloodbath, Governor Seymour addressed the rampaging mob as "friends." Notorious Isaiah Rynders called for attacks on blacks, newspapers supporting Lincoln's administration, and all "d—d Abolitionists." The *Standard* was saved from destruction, Johnson informed Sojourner, because the mob did not know it was an antislavery paper, but he had to hide their "colored clerk."[22]

Rioting occurred elsewhere in New York. The Williamsburgh church where Sojourner had once spoken was burned to the ground. In Troy, the mob attacked an upscale restaurant and demanded "the negro waiters should be given up to them." Some New York City whites sheltered blacks. Many blacks fled and never returned; some returned well armed, vowing to "make a determined defense of their lives and property." Henry Garnet alone held funeral services for twelve people. Garnet and Redpath echoed Sojourner Truth. Racism, a by-product of slavery, Garnet preached, nurtured hatred. Black men were "dying to save the Union," Redpath wrote, "while Irish mobs, led by Wood . . . and Seymour are murdering their brethren in New York. It was easier to crush rebellion, the *Standard* said, than to cure prejudice.[23]

In the midst of despair, Sojourner Truth helped others gain inspiration from tragedy as she had done. Eliza Leggett, who had recently lost a daughter, collapsed emotionally under the news that her son Percival had been killed in battle. He had come home after being wounded, but returned to his "duty" as soon as he was healed, and almost immediately met his death. Condolence letters poured in, including ones from the Leggetts' old Long Island neighbors Walt Whitman and William Cullen Bryant. But Sojourner, Eliza wrote, "had more power to lift me out of my sorrow when Emma and Percy died—than any other influence." Although Sojourner was dealing with her own grandson's disappearance, she was the "great strength" that helped Eliza's "Spirit" bear the death of her children. "Go to work," Sojourner advised. "You can't help anything that is past." Moreover, she counseled, "Be Oh! So thankful to the good Lord that he lent you these children—do ye spose they are dead? Not at all." Goodness did not die; it lived on. Her children had believed in duty. "Take hold and do what you can just as you think they would do. Don't cry no more—but find work. Oh! Lord there's plenty of it all over."[24]

And work they did, that fall, winter, and spring of 1863–64. With Sammy as her traveling companion, Sojourner was Battle Creek's representative at the Michigan's Ladies Freedmen's Aid Society. She spent much time in Detroit and neighboring towns on behalf of the war effort. She solicited clothing, goods, and other donations; she packed boxes, arranged tables, supervised meals, counted money, and spoke out. There were also heartwarming reunions of radical old friends, who addressed full audiences in black and white churches. Mary Ann Shadd Cary was in Detroit when the war began; Laura Haviland, fresh from Union lines in Mississippi, lectured about her observations, including gruesome accounts of cruelty. Laura displayed neck and leg irons weighing from five to eight pounds that some former slaves reportedly had worn for years as punishment. The "highly intellectual and cultivated" Josephine Griffing also attracted packed houses as she detailed her travels and interviews with freed people. She was in contact with Washington about her findings, and intended to lobby the next session of Congress "to pass a bill establishing a Bureau for the Freedmen." Giles Stebbins also lectured, as did Calvin Fairbanks, newly released from prison. It was a biracial effort. The wives of George De Baptiste and William Lambert topped the list of leaders of the Female Freedman's Aid Society. Times were hard economically, Margaret Leggett Ives wrote in the journal she kept for her baby. Sugar was 40 cents a pound, coffee 60 cents a pound, tea $2 a pound, and molasses over $2 a gallon. Nonetheless, the Abolitionists filled many boxes for Laura to take to the Deep South, and collected significant sums of money. They also participated in the massive three-day bazaar and Freedmen's Fair, held in Chicago, which featured speakers from the East and musical bands and netted $13,000 at the end of the year. Even after Sojourner moved on to Washington, Eliza and her daughter Augusta remained the most stalwart white women in the Michigan relief effort. Eliza's elegant home continued to host Sojourner's western Abolitionist friends, who came to lecture on the plight of the freed people. Young Augusta took their message to the newspapers, and from door to door, even in Detroit's most fashionable neighborhoods. In spite of all they had to contend with "in this Copperhead city," Eliza Leggett wrote a friend, their organization was prospering.[25]

Sojourner Truth's health greatly improved. "I mean to live till I am a hundred years old, if it please God, and see my people all free." When Michigan finally relented and organized a black regiment in November, Sojourner and Eliza were delighted. They took buggy rides out to the barracks to encourage the troops. Sojourner and Sammy went back to Battle Creek, solicited numerous contributions for the soldiers, and transported the supplies back to Camp Ward. Sojourner Truth, wrote the *Detroit Advertiser*, "who carries not only a tongue of fire but a heart of love," drove up to Camp Ward in a carriage laden with boxes and packages containing food, clothing, and "all manner of delicacies for the boys.'" While assisting them in opening boxes and distributing their contents, she offered "motherly conversation." She promised to return and give a proper speech. True to her word, she came the next Sunday. However, "so large a crowd of white citizens" appeared that she devoted her inspirations to them almost exclusively. The "dear old saint" promised the black soldiers a future discourse.

She returned to Camp Ward in midwinter—a testament to her renewed physical fitness. She spoke for over an hour on slavery, the Union, the war, and the meaning of victory for their race. She sang her black battle hymn, "Valiant Soldiers" (set to the melody of "John Brown's Body"), which embraced the war as assurance of black freedom and revealed her understanding of historical and cultural affinities between Northern and Southern blacks. Verses of the long hymn include:

> Look there above the center, where the flag is waving bright;
> We are going out of slavery, we are bound for freedom's light;
> We mean to show Jeff Davis how the Africans can fight,
> As we go marching on.—Cho.
> We are done with hoeing cotton, we are done with hoeing corn;
> We are colored Yankee soldiers as sure as you are born.
> When Massa hears us shouting, he will think 'tis Gabriel's horn,
> As we go marching on—Cho.
> Father Abraham has spoken, and the message has been sent;
> The prison doors have opened, and out the prisoners went
> To join the sable army of African descent,
> As we go marching on—Cho.[26]

"I feel like my old self," Sojourner told Mary Gale that winter of 1864. She and Eliza frequently visited Camp Ward. "Sojourner . . . and Grandma went to the barracks this afternoon and this morning," Margaret Leggett Ives wrote in her infant's journal. Now "they have gone to call upon some of Sojourner's friends." Warm encouragement, said Sojourner, "put me on my feet and filled me with new energy" as well as "new life." Even strangers wanted her photograph, songs, and book. The correspondence of Mrs. Josephine Franklin, a young woman from Brooklyn, New York, demonstrates what blacks thought of Sojourner Truth. "You asked me if I was of your race," began Mrs. Franklin. "I am proud to say I am of the same race that you are, I am colored thank God for that." Franklin gave an eloquent explanation of why she was "thrice proud" of her race, and sent money for Sojourner's photographs on behalf of herself and other women in her family. Only poverty prevented her from purchasing more. "You will accept my love with my husband's [he was in the military] for yourself, and our wishes and prayers for your welfare." Franklin closed her letter to the "Mother of Truth" with an original poem. "Oh if I could but write," Sojourner lamented. "The best that friends can write for me sounds cold compared with the fervent warmth and affection of my heart."[27]

During the war's early stages, refugees from Maryland and Virginia flooded into Washington. Exchanging bondage for quasi freedom, offering knowledge about the Confederacy and critical labor, the refugees also posed a severe problem of human need. Private organizations, religious denominations, and individuals distributed food, clothing, and medicine and set up educational facilities. When Harriet Jacobs of New York City and Julia Wilbur of Rochester arrived in Washington in 1862, four hundred "homeless, penniless people" were living in pitiable conditions under military jurisdiction. By 1863, ten thousand refugees had swelled Washington, while Alexandria, Virginia, had three thousand. The government employed able-bodied men, but single women, children, the ill and elderly languished without medicine, proper food, clothing or blankets. Jacobs wrote candidly about the mistreatment. At first "the sight of the US Uniform . . . inspired them with hope and confidence." Although possessing almost nothing, blacks fed white soldiers from their tables and "lodged them in humble dwellings." In exchange for these kindnesses, they "received insults, even beatings." Deeply aggrieved, Jacobs wrote, "Oh when will the white man learn to know the hearts of my abused and suffering people!" She rejoiced "that the black man is to strike a blow for liberty." Jacobs and Wilbur, though unvaccinated, nursed the people through a ravaging smallpox epidemic. Nearly all of Sojourner's women activist associates were engaged in the war effort.[28]

She also heard of Washington women furthering freedom's cause—including Elizabeth ("Lizzie") Keckley. Born in slavery, Keckley purchased her freedom, moved to Washington, and became Mary Todd Lincoln's dressmaker, fashion adviser, hairstylist, and "soubrette." Keckley organized the Contraband Relief Association among Washington's black middle class in 1862 and, while traveling in the Northeast with Mrs. Lincoln, recruited the wives of Northern black ministers for fundraising. Working-class blacks, for example the waiters at New York's Metropolitan Hotel, also raised large sums of money for Keckley. Mrs. Lincoln and the president quietly contributed to the relief fund. Lizzie Keckley later enlisted Sojourner Truth.[29]

"The Negro prophetess" was doing well, Phebe Iart Merritt wrote the *Boston Commonwealth*. Friends far and near care for her; she "realizes a little by the sale of her photographs," hence wants for nothing. Sojourner enjoyed life as well as ever, taking long daily walks regardless of weather. She had a pleasant smile and kind greeting for everyone, saying it was so good to be alive during "this great and glorious day." Nonetheless, she was wistful. "Oh, if I were only ten years younger I would go down with these soldiers here and be the Mother of the Regiment!" she said after one of her visits to Camp Ward. She reasoned that if she could not ride with the army, she could be useful elsewhere. She also desperately wanted to see the freed people with her own eyes and behold the undoing of the shackles from their limbs. Through the *Standard*, she thanked friends, acquaintances, and strangers for their sustaining prayers and kindness; she wished blessings on them. "I can almost walk without a cane," she said, and asked friends to pray her safely through March, the last winter month. Her improvement and vigor was a sign that God "means me to do what I want to do," anointing her yet again, enlisting her in further service. She planned an eastern sojourn, "to Ohio and New York, to New Jersey and finally to see the freedom of my race, in Washington."[30]

II

Sojourner was putting money aside, Eliza Leggett wrote Wendell Phillips, "for her scheme of visiting Abraham Lincoln and . . . blessing him for what he has done for her race, and then going among the Freedmen to give them encouragement and elevation." But she needed help, and the Harmonia property "gives her no means." Since "a class of Millerites" had taken over the commune, it had become unproductive and cold. She left because she felt "useless and dead." She "wants more than a home," Eliza added, "or rather her home is where her heart is and that is where she thinks Humanity needs her active service." Everyone offered her a home and bread, but she wanted to work, "and we think her work is good." However, Eliza was skeptical about the adequacy of Sojourner's own industry or friends' contributions in sustaining such a long journey. "Sojourner, how *will* you make your way from Detroit to Washington?" Eliza asked. Having taken vows of poverty, Sojourner traveled on faith and charity. "I take no heed of that," she told Eliza. "Child, don't you know that all there is of Sojourner is devoted to the Lord? And do you think he will leave me unprovided with what I need?" God, she said, "will send me where I am needed."[31]

Sojourner and Sammy left Detroit in early July 1864. Traveling slowly, they stopped in Ohio and visited old friends, and Sojourner held meetings. The *Standard* lost track of them until late August, when they reached Rochester. Sallie Holley reported that Sojourner was as vigorous as in her early Ohio days. Now, however, Stowe's imaginary Truth followed Sojourner despite her protests that "Mrs. Stowe got it all mixed up." Holley also capitalized on the fable, writing that the "poet-souled authoress of 'Uncle Tom' with her Hebrew Scripture-taught imagination and feeling" had depicted Sojourner Truth "with captivating power." Sojourner's former Ohio traveling companion now saw her as "unlike anything American." Presenting Sojourner's words in southern dialect, Holley nonetheless insisted that in Rochester, Sojourner "held us by the spell of her rude, native eloquence—full of wit, pathos, pungent common sense, and awing, prophetic cast of thought."[32]

Sojourner Truth and Frederick Douglass once again shared the platform. At sixty-seven, gray-haired, and recently come back from death's door, she reportedly looked well, attired in her new look—a silk and cambric dress and a Quaker-style white kerchief, shawl, and cap. Forty-seven-year-old Douglass was also gray and growing a beard, which Susan B. Anthony said "looks magnifi-cent." Yet Douglass's face showed deep strain from the wear and tear of political factionalism, personal scandal, and the death of his youngest child while he was in England. Twenty years after their first meeting in Northampton, and despite some tactical disagreements, the two former slaves stood together in triumph. Douglass had met Lincoln in 1863 and, like Truth, believed the president was fulfilling prophecy. Both black leaders quoted Isaiah and interpreted the war as a howling jeremiad—a bloodletting fulfillment of divine justice because the nation would not let the oppressed go free. There would be no peace or healing until the nation proclaimed "liberty throughout the land."[33]

The crimes against her race were so foul, Sojourner Truth said, that she "hated to put them into her mouth." She was proud to be black, of a "long suf-fering, patient, inoffensive people," rather than belonging to the guilty, cruel white race. She condemned Northern proslavery churches for communing with Southerners. "'I would sooner eat with de hogs out of de trough dan sit down at the sacrament with dem Southerners—dem devils, dat have ben shippin','burnin,' and huntin,' and tearin' wid bloodhounds, my own brodders and sis-ters for a century.'" Yet in the spirit of the jeremiad, she also prophesied hope. "After the blood and smoke and storm of battle are gone," she said amid loud applause, "this country will be beautiful and justice and freedom." After she finished, the excited crowd called, "Douglass!" "Douglass!" He came forward, greeted Sojourner, and reiterated some of her points. He, too, took pride in his blackness; he would rather be "the most whipped-scarred slave in all the South than the haughtiest slave-master." Reportedly, he spoke grandly in a "rich-toned voice." Then he turned to Sojourner Truth and spoke of their now famous 1852 confrontation: "He remembered when, some years ago, he was saying, in an anti-slavery meeting, he felt that about all had been converted by moral suasion who would be brought to accept anti-slavery truth; and there was no other way than for the slaves with their own right arms to take their freedom in blood, when, Sojourner who was present said, 'Frederick, is God dead?' He asked Sojourner what she thought about it now. Wasn't he right then?"[34] It was a poignant moment for the two soldiers and all Abolitionists present. The press did not record her answer, but she was on her way to Washington to see her people's freedom wrought by war. In a sense, they were both right. And even Douglass recollected Truth's challenge as "Is God dead?"

Through August, she remained in the Rochester vicinity, visiting friends and family. Elizabeth had married William Boyd and joined Sophia in western New York. Sojourner's whereabouts were not widely publicized, but she was in upstate New York until late September and then went briefly to New York City and on to "Copperhead New Jersey." Her hostess was Abby Hutchinson Patton, the former Hutchinson singer, who had married into wealth but remained a reformer and musician and made special appearances. New Jersey was "sullied by complicity with treason," Patton wrote Amy Post; nonetheless, Sojourner campaigned for Lincoln's reelection in Trenton, Newark, and Orange. The mayor of Orange stood in line to shake her hand; she also did a good business in selling her photographs and songs. Her visit was a "triumph for New Jersey," Patton wrote, especially in Orange, where General McClellan (Lincoln's opponent) resided. "He is our neighbor and we hope to keep him here the next four years." Sojourner was "hale and hearty," Patton declared, and continuing on to Washington. She hoped to live "some twenty years or more" and see "every slave emancipated and the colored race being educated and prospered as is becoming to the people of a free republic."[35]

Sojourner Truth, Lucy Colman wrote years later, thought "she could walk right into the White House and have a good chat with the President." The meeting was possible, Colman added, only through Elizabeth Keckley's influence.[36] This seems unlikely. Sojourner Truth was not the first black woman to have an audience with Lincoln, only the most famous. And Sojourner Truth was never naïve about sources of power or introductions; she knew personally Massachusetts Senator Charles Sumner and Indiana congressman George W. Julian; and Jane Swisshelm, Sojourner's nemesis at Akron, hosted her and Sammy during their first weeks in Washington. Swisshelm had become a powerful Republican editor in Minnesota, was called "Mother of the Party," and held a lucrative War Department clerkship. Finally, Sojourner's intimate friend Josephine Griffing was in Washington and working closely with Sumner for a freed people's agency.[37] In fact, Sojourner probably met Lincoln when he conducted one of his "public opinion baths," a sort of open house.

Colman was not a Lincoln supporter. Yet in a widely reprinted 1864 letter, she wrote, "our president received me and the woman whom I went to introduce with real politeness and pleasing cordiality." Lincoln, Colman said, was "the most awkward man in the nation" but deserved praise for his resolute determination. "Whatever may have been the former delinquencies of the President," she wrote, "he has now come to the conclusion to act." As for Sojourner Truth and Abraham Lincoln: "Sojourner delivered to him her thanks for what he had done for her people, saying at the same time, that he was the only President who had done anything for them. Mr. Lincoln rejoined, 'and the only one who ever had such opportunity. Had our friends in the South behaved themselves I could have done nothing whatsoever.' Honest! Was it not! Well, we were shown the Bible which was presented to Mr. Lincoln by the colored people of Baltimore, and altogether the visit was quite satisfactory."[38]

Colman remembered differently twenty-seven years later: the receiving room had been packed; the three-hour wait had been grueling; another woman had joined them; and finally, she and "two of the blackest women I ever saw" had stood before Lincoln. Then they had waited while he finished his story to a delegation. Lincoln "was not himself," Colman wrote. He was unfriendly; called Sojourner "aunty, as he would his washerwoman"; and when Sojourner complimented him as the first anti-slavery president, he was rude. "'I'm not an Abolitionist; I wouldn't free the slaves if I could save the Union in any other way—I'm obliged to do it.'" Deeply offended, Colman stood and addressed Sojourner, "We must not detain the President—are you ready?" When they reached the door, Lincoln called *Colman* back and "earnestly" offered *her* a seat. He needed help with the other black woman, a soldier's wife unable to pay her rent. "'Can't you take her off my hands?'" Lincoln supposedly asked. Colman agreed. He and Colman talked "some minutes," apparently while the two black women stood by the door. Lincoln "was not glad that the war made him the emancipator of four million slaves," Colman surmised, except that by "the logic of events his name would be immortal through the act." Lincoln, said Colman in 1891, believed only "in the white race, not in the colored, and did not want them put on an equality."[39]

In contrast to Colman's 1891 account, Sojourner's version concurs with and correlates to Colman's 1864 account with far greater accuracy. The *Standard* was glad to receive "Sojourner's own account of her visit":

FREEDMAN'S VILLAGE, VA., NOV. 17, 1864. . . .

It was about 8 o'clock, A.M. when I called on the President. Upon entering his reception room, we found about a dozen persons in waiting, among them two colored women. I had quite a pleasant time waiting until he was disengaged, and enjoyed his conversation with others; he showed as much kindness and consideration to the colored persons as to the whites—if there was any difference, more. One case was that of a colored woman who was sick and likely to be turned out of her house on account of her inability to pay her rent. The President listened to her with much attention, and spoke to her with kindness and tenderness. . . .

The President was seated at his desk. Mrs. C. said to him, "This is Sojourner Truth, who has come all the way from Michigan to see you." He then arose, gave me his hand, made a bow, and said, "I am pleased to meet you."

I said to him, "Mr. President, when you first took your seat I feared you would be torn to pieces, for I likened you unto Daniel, who was thrown into the lions' den; and if the lions did not tear you into pieces, I knew that it would be God that had saved you; and I said if He spared me I would see you before the four years expired, and he has done so, and now I am here to see you for myself."

He then congratulated me on my having been spared. Then I said: "I appreciate you for you are the best President who has ever taken the seat." He replied thus: "I expect you have reference to my having emancipated the slaves in my proclamation. But" said he, mentioning the names of several of his predecessors

. . ." they were all just as good, and would have done just as he had done if the time had come. If the people over the river (pointing across the Potomac) had behaved themselves, I could not have done what I have; but they did not, and I was compelled to do these things." I then said, "I thank God that you were the instrument selected by him and the people to do it."

He then showed me the Bible presented to him by the colored people of Baltimore . . . it is beautiful beyond description. After I had looked it over, I said to him: "This is beautiful indeed; the colored people have given this to the Head of the government, and the government once sanctioned laws that would not permit its people to learn enough to enable them to read this Book. And for what? Let them answer who can." . . . I am proud to say, that I never was treated by any one with more kindness and cordiality than was shown to me by that great and good man, Abraham Lincoln, by the grace of God President of the United States for four more years. He took my little book, and with the same hand that signed the death-warrant of slavery, he wrote as follows:

"For Aunty Sojourner Truth,

"Oct. 29, 1864 A. Lincoln."

As I was taking my leave, he arose and took my hand, and said he would be pleased to have me call again. I felt that I was in the presence of a friend, and I now thank God from the bottom of my heart that I always have advocated his cause and done it openly and boldly. I shall feel still more in duty bond to do it in time to come. May God assist me.[40]

Sojourner's letter does not indicate that Lincoln was rude and unfriendly. As for calling Sojourner "Aunty," not everyone used the term as Southern whites did after emancipation—to belittle older black women. Abolitionists used "Aunt" and "Aunty" as an endearment. Levi Coffin's wife Catherine was "Aunt Kate," Laura Haviland was "Aunt Laura," and freed people called Truth "Aunt Sojourner." In 1891, Colman implies that Lincoln displayed arrogance and racism; and one historian believes that Lincoln was "forced into glory." Certainly before the war, he supported the Fugitive Slave Law; his home state practiced black exclusion; he publicly called blacks inferior and would have kept them in bondage. Yet the Gettysburg Address reveals that in asserting leadership over a liberation movement whose time had come, Lincoln embraced his role as the Providential President, destined to implement the Declaration of Independence. Perhaps he even experienced a personal and spiritual transformation that involved a reassessment of his prejudice. He was especially proud of the pulpit-sized gold-plated velvet-bound Bible that had cost Baltimore's blacks an extraordinary $580.75. For the people who walked in bondage for ten generations, the president's philosophical racism was an abstraction (like his philosophical antislavery in the antebellum era). But the Emancipation Proclamation was real, and the Gettysburg Address served notice on the nation that a Thirteenth Amendment was forthcoming.

Perhaps black military service, the war's bloody carnage, and the ghosts of the ancestors began Lincoln's journey to a liberated consciousness. For Sojourner Truth, black freedom was a personal achievement and a collective triumph. Meeting Lincoln, whom she believed God had hewn out of a rock, and having him sign her "Book of Life" was part of her victory. If *Leaves of Grass* impressed her, imagine what she thought of the Gettysburg Address. "'Oh, wait, chile! Have patience!'" she told Detroit friends critical of Lincoln. "'It takes a great while to turn about this great ship of State.'"[41]

Colman's two versions of the Truth-Lincoln meeting raise questions about historical evidence. According to Truth biographer Carleton Mabee, Colman's 1891 account depicts "what really happened, as far as we can tell from the most authentic early sources available," that of "a white, Massachusetts-born Abolitionist." On the other hand, in 1864, Colman wrote under "compulsion to make Lincoln look better." Normally, historians rely on firsthand evidence, and it is surprising that Mabee places so much confidence in Colman's hindsight account. Even in a private letter to her daughter Diana, Sojourner spoke warmly of meeting Lincoln. Had he personally offended her or her people, she would have said so. Perhaps Colman's credibility rather than Truth's needs challenging. Mabee also critiques some writers' suggestions that Sojourner taught Lincoln about slavery and influenced his decisions on emancipation and black participation in the military.[42] However, Sojourner Truth herself made no such claims.

Henry Garnet had left New York to become pastor of Washington's Fifteenth Street Presbyterian Church. He invited Sojourner to hold meetings on behalf of Elizabeth Keckley's Relief Society and Maryland's newly decreed emancipation. Her meetings were very well attended, despite a hefty admission charge of 25 cents per person. She also spoke at the Washington Baptist Church. But neither Washington's Bethel Israel nor Baltimore's Bethel AME churches invited the Methodist woman preacher; both preferred Marylanders Frederick Douglass and Frances Watkins Harper. No doubt Sojourner's lack of education and no-nonsense eloquence influenced such exclusion.[43]

When she arrived in Washington, the black hegira was forty thousand strong, and far beyond the District's capacity. White hostility was so intense, some Southerners attacked blacks on sight. Although the government created quarters and labor stations outside the District as medical and holding facilities, no federal program existed for handling the mass of humanity. Only Northern women and private aid societies followed the armies and aided refugees. But from the war's beginning, reformers called for an agency "to provide for the employment and general welfare for the millions of free and to be made free." Congress bickered over the kind of agency needed. For a full year, Josephine Griffing worked closely with the District Aid Committee, including Garnet, and Senator Sumner's congressional committee on the issue. In 1864, a bill passed the Senate but died in the House. Sojourner Truth was in Washington to help the freed people. The president encouraged her to "see the colored people at Arlington Heights and Mason's Island."[44]

Mason Island, the confiscated estate of the Confederate emissary to Britain, housed families of enslaved Maryland men serving in a military or labor capacity. People there complained bitterly about the government, telling Sojourner Truth they had risked everything, even leaving children, to get behind Union lines and find work. Although slaveholders hunted, jailed, beat, and threatened them, people fled anyway. Now under "Uncle Sam," living in barracks and hired out annually, they suffered terribly. Private employers often refused to pay and the government paid them several months late. "They say they hate this Union," Sojourner informed Diana. "They say they are treated worse or as bad as when they were in slavery." But Sojourner Truth brought the best possible news. On November 1, 1864, Maryland had emancipated everyone. While celebrations had occurred in New York City, Baltimore, and Washington, no one had told the Mason Island people until Sojourner arrived. "I told them they were free" she said, and "one old woman clung around my neck and most choked me she was so glad." She asked superintendent Danforth Nichols to announce it throughout, and she held a great meeting over the news. "I had a good chance to tell the colored people things that they had never heard." Without the shackles of bondage, and despite hardships, she reasoned that they could chart their own destiny.[45]

"I have not language to tell you what rags and wretchedness and hunger and poverty I saw [in the camps]," Sojourner said. Thousands "suffered with cold and hunger until death." Mean, unsympathetic, unabashedly greedy officials refused to give black people a chance. Officials forced them to rent barracks with no bedsteads or blankets, and scolded reformers who interfered. "Mr. G," Julia Wilbur wrote in 1862, "says I am out of my sphere, and he does not like to see a woman wear man's clothes." However, this once timid female learned agitation through the woman's rights movement and eventually stood up to Mr. G. By the time Sojourner encountered him, he was "as meek as man ever was" and a help rather than an obstacle. Sojourner also believed that disorganization was the midwife of chaos; each camp had a different policy over something as basic as clothing distribution. In Alexandria, Jacobs and Wilbur sold clothing to freed people; Sojourner thought this took self-help too far when thousands were nearly naked. People "died like cattle" she said, swept away by deprivation, disease, corruption, racism, and the government's insistence that people with nothing fend for themselves. Whites took the "loaves and fishes," Sojourner observed, while "the freedmen get the scales and crust."[46]

Sojourner settled at Freedman's Village, on land that was part of Robert E. Lee's massive Arlington estate, inherited through his wife Martha Custis, granddaughter of Martha Custis Washington. The Lees' enslaved people expressed "horror and scorn" toward the general. Martha's old nurse, "Aunt Sally," said Lee had sold her nineteen children away. When Arlington folk burnt their hated plantation quarters, the government constructed one hundred one-and-a-half-story houses, facing each other in a circle, designed for two families each, sixteen hundred people in all. Government workers earned $10 monthly, from which $5 went toward constructing the village and $3 for rent. Village workshops employed blacksmiths, carpenters, and wheelwrights. Children, women, and the elderly farmed the land; this produce fed horses, other camps, and hospital patients. The village had a home for displaced people, a hospital, a school, and a chapel controlled by the conservative American Tract Society.[47]

Sojourner's first appearance was a sensation, wrote the new captain of the guard, George Carse. People crowded into the building to hear her. "I never saw it so full before." Nothing gained quicker attention from sympathetic officials or the freed people than the words of one who had suffered from the yoke of bondage. Sojourner spoke plainly and truthfully. "She is one of them—she can call them her people." She immediately assumed a leadership role. "I think I can be useful and will stay." She received an official commission from the father of the martyred colonel of the Fifty-fourth Massachusetts Regiment:

NEW YORK, DEC. 1, 1864

This certifies that The National Freedmen's Relief Association has appointed Sojourner Truth to be a counselor to the freed people at Arlington Heights, Va., and hereby commends her to the favor and confidence of the officers of government, and of all persons who take an interest in relieving the condition of the freedmen, or in promoting their intellectual, moral, and religious instruction.
F. G. Shaw President,
Charles C. Leigh,
Chairman of Home Com.[48]

Heritage, race, gender, and servitude bonded her with her Southern black sisters; yet she observed that they were "instructed in field labor, but not in household duties." Although few of them knew how to knit or how to make a loaf of yeast bread, they wanted to learn, she said. "They all seem to think a great deal of me," she told friends, "and I am listened to with attention and respect." More than being a domestic role model for "the way we do things in the North," she wanted freed people to see what was possible even when one had been born and reared in chattel slavery. Liza Grayson, a widow who had fled when her Virginia owner attempted to sell two of her three children, listened closely to Sojourner's counsel, probably seeing her as the mother she did not have. Captain Carse provided a little house for Sojourner and Sammy. The "colored people like to hear what is going on," Sojourner said, and she asked Oliver Johnson to send the *Standard*. "Sammy, my grandson, reads for them." She personally needed nothing except a few sheets and pillows but welcomed donations in exchange for her shadow and songs. Sojourner and Sammy expected to pass winter at Freedman's Village. "From all things I judge it is the will of both God and the people that I should remain."[49]

Freedman's Village "hardly looks like the same place since Sojourner went among them, so much more order and cleanliness," Lucy Colman noted. "'Be clean, be clean, for cleanliness is a part of godliness,'" Sojourner preached. Sojourner "is a very wonderful person," noted Frances Perkins, whose entourage visited Freedman's Village in 1865. They all sat in Sojourner's house, and listened to her criticize the indifferent "colored people in Washington" and the "fiends and devils" in the government who exploited her people. Her face brightened when Captain Carse entered and joined their discussion. In echoing her sentiments and righteous indignation, "he swore right and left," which did not disturb her in the least. "What an energetic sort of conversation he & Sojourner must carry on together."[50]

Northern friends worried about Sojourner living in a drafty government house containing only beds and "a few benches to sit upon." Why should Sojourner Truth sit on hard, cold benches while "her friends are sitting on cushioned seats at home," pondered Amy Post, writing to Esther Titus. She was "too good and too old to be neglected." Besides linens, Amy said, "I am going to send her some money to get her a rocking chair." She added, "Esther, I wish thee and I could be down there with Sojourner. There is a great deal being done . . . but not near as much as necessary." Yet Sojourner Truth rejoiced in being at Freedman's Village, imparting domestic skills, secular wisdom, and spirituality. Captain Carse gave her a building large enough to accommodate two hundred people. She need ask permission of no one "but go straight on and do what she thinks best." While educated black and white ministers disdained the freed people's visceral worship and devotion, Sojourner Truth's Wesleyan Methodism "warms the heart." She understood her people's spiritual exuberance and ecstasy because, like her, they saw a divine hand in their liberation. At her meetings, freed people could be themselves. "Well and happy" in her employment, and having safely reached her destination, she advised, "you may publish my whereabouts, and anything in this letter you think would interest the friends of Freedom, Justice, and Truth, in the *Standard* and *Anglo-African*, and any other paper you may see fit."[51]

Maryland planters, attempting to implement a neoslavery apprenticeship, terrorized Freedman's Village and raided it for the children. Planters kidnapped children by wagonloads, labeled them vagrants, hired them out, and confiscated their wages. County courts cooperated with kidnappers, refusing to allow parents in court or to hear their claims. Magistrates imprisoned persistent parents while planters resorted to herding adults into barns at gunpoint and setting fire to the structures. When Sojourner confronted and challenged the planters, freed people also fought back. "The truth has never been given as it was," she told an audience after the war. The Arlington Heights freed people had "gone through fire and water," she said. "Our boys would take some of the children, and taking them on their backs, would get them away from the rebels." White Marylanders, Sojourner said, "are the most GROSS, LOW, SAVAGE, UNFEELING SET that ever was given birth, and treated my people worse than beasts."[52]

The true "Jubilee" and birth of a free people began in 1865, as the reelected president firmly took the helm. His persistence narrowly pushed the Thirteenth Amendment through Congress, and blacks cheered from galleries they once could not enter. At Freedman's Village, Sojourner Truth insisted that her people have the chapel for "a love feast in their own way." Lucy Colman and others from Washington witnessed a memorable occasion. In between song after impressive song, freed people eloquently bore witness against slavery. The musical diversity was undoubtedly amazing: African American spirituals familiar to Sojourner through the underground; Isaac Watts's "lined-out" Methodist hymns, popular among blacks everywhere; and Sojourner's own freedom melodies. She was the main speaker, but others also gave praise, testifying of their faith and trials. Congressmen "sat with tears running down their cheeks." The service, they said, was unequaled in "devotion, thankfulness, and trust in God."[53]

Dramatic events continued that winter: John S. Rock of Boston became the first black lawyer admitted to practice in the Supreme Court, which had once declared blacks nonpersons. Henry Garnet, backed by his famous choir and an audience one-third black, was the first minister of his race to preach a Sunday sermon at the Capitol. The government finally passed a watered-down bill establishing a Bureau of Freedmen, Refugees, and Abandoned Lands (known as the Freedmen's Bureau). Congress also chartered the Freedman's Savings Bank, and Lincoln signed a bill abolishing segregation on Washington streetcars. Black soldiers marched in the president's inauguration, as did the Lodges of Colored Odd Fellows and Masons. Thousands of blacks listened as Lincoln quoted Isaiah, the Abolitionists' favorite Old Testament seer. Lincoln's most memorable passage sounded like Truth, Douglass, or Garrison: "Fondly do we hope, fervently do we pray that this mighty scourge of war may soon pass away. Yet, if God wills that it continue until all the wealth piled by the bondman's two hundred and fifty years of unrequited toil shall be sunk, and until every drop of blood drawn with the lash shall be paid by another drawn with the sword, as was said three thousand years ago, so still it must be said, The judgments of the Lord are true and righteous altogether."[54] Yet for African Americans, dark moments foretold another future. It took months to ratify the Thirteenth Amendment in the North. The eminent and very black John Rock was manhandled when leaving Washington and detained as a draft dodger until high officials intervened. Parts of Lincoln's Inaugural Address played to the Confederacy; he moved in that direction by readmitting states to the Union when "ten per cent" of pre-1860 eligible voters pledged loyalty to the government and accepted the Thirteenth Amendment. In Louisiana, the first state to accept these terms, General Nathaniel Banks forced freed people into unfair labor contracts, curtailed their movement, and denied them political rights. Angry Republicans passed a countermeasure (the Wade-Davis Bill) to open a way for black franchise. Lincoln ignored the bill (a pocket veto).[55]

A week before the inauguration, Mrs. Lincoln arranged a public reception, and Captain Carse invited Sojourner. That morning, she distributed clothing in Washington at the Freedmen's Aid Association headquarters. British journalist Fred Tomkins appeared at the office, anxious to meet Sojourner Truth, whose reputation preceded their encounter. "I had never seen her before, but I knew it was 'Sojourner,'" Captain Carse's "very right hand." Tomkins bowed to the "erect tall aged black woman, neatly clad, wearing a pair of gold spectacles." They conversed about the freed people, whom Sojourner called "'gentle as lambs, but they must be brought under rule and regulation.'" Watching her with the freed women, conversing with her and hearing stories from her many Washington friends, Tomkins concluded that she was "the most remarkable woman that I ever met with." She was "full of intelligence, and tenderness" but also "full of faith and the Holy Ghost." She looked forward to congratulating the president and meeting Mrs. Lincoln.[56]

Sojourner Truth's treatment at the reception illustrated that color prejudice would not die with slavery. "The softest Beethoven strains I ever heard filled the reception and drawing-rooms that day," Tomkins recalled. Captain Carse, with Sojourner Truth on one arm and his wife on the other, was stopped at the White House door. "I saw Sojourner refused admission" Tomkins wrote, "and heard the young officer say, 'If she is not good enough to enter, I am not.'" The disgusted captain and "dignified and lady-like" Sojourner Truth left. Carse and Tomkins complained about the rebuff to Lucy Colman, who said nothing could be done. Even Lizzie Keckley "was never permitted to go into the house as a caller." The White House policy, Colman insisted, was no "people of color" at any public receptions. This was not quite true; at the 1864 New Year's Day reception, Lincoln greeted "four colored men of genteel exterior." And the guards who turned away Sojourner Truth admitted Frederick Douglass when a congressman asked Lincoln to intercede. On the morning of the reception, Tompkins wrote, Sojourner was bright, upbeat, commanding, and enthusiastic. That evening, the White House insult left "the good old woman bent with grief." She was "a 'jewel in ebony,'" Tomkins wrote, with every right to enter the White House and attend an *open* reception.[57]

Tomkins had a long interview with Lincoln several evenings later, and expressed "regret that so good and faithful a subject of the Republic should be the only person I saw who had been refused admission." Lincoln apologized, Tomkins wrote, saying "it should not occur again," that he had "often seen her" and would do so again. Tomkins wrote that Lincoln sent for Sojourner a few days later, but no proof of that visit has been found. However, a year after Lincoln's death, the *Standard* published a witty anecdote that does not sound like proud Sojourner Truth but does suggest a second meeting: "Mr. Lincoln, I'm happy to see you and give you my photograph. It's black, but it's got a white back on it. I shall be glad to get yours with a greenback to it."[58]

The freed people's reaction to Lincoln's assassination received little press; they felt deep sadness. The Bible and other gifts blacks presented to him; his triumphant march among Richmond blacks days before his death; blacks presence at his Second Inaugural and their night vigil as he lay dying—these were all testaments of profound esteem. At Freedman's Village, Sojourner Truth and her young teacher friend Emily Howland held a memorial. Like other Spiritualists, they believed that Lincoln had accomplished his earthly mission and was now among other martyrs of the movement. He himself had once told Wendell Phillips that "Moses began the emancipation of the Jews but didn't take Israel to the Promised Land, after all." Sojourner said that she knew Lincoln would not live long. Yet when she saw him in the Capitol lying "cold and still in death," tears fell down her cheeks.[59]

Although she could speak to blacks "as a white person could not," Sojourner encountered some pitfalls at Freedman's Village. She could be harsh. In upbraiding freed people, she called some of their habits disgusting. "You have your liberty," she told women grabbing at donated garments, "but what's your liberty worth without regulation; by your thoughtless eagerness you hinder your friends." These women left children unattended in midwinter and were anxious to return to their "muddy hovels." But crowding would not shorten their wait, she scolded. "I have spoken to some of you before about this foolish haste." Now, she exclaimed, using satire, "I say to you in the words of the fable, that having tried what turf will do, if that fail, the next time I shall try stones.'" Freed people, she said, "must learn to be independent—learn industry and economy," show others they "could be something," and move beyond temporary camps and contributions. When she advised blacks to "learn to love the white people," she meant whites advocating black causes. She herself pungently criticized whites in general. "I often think what John meant when he said—'These are they which came out of great tribulation and have washed their robes and made them white in the blood of the Lamb.'" He meant black people and "the anti-slavery people who suffered for us," she told a white audience. "It can't be you, for you have not passed through great tribulation." At Freedman's Village, she sometimes signified on antebellum ostracism toward white Abolitionists and introduced these reformers as "colored people."[60]

Her position on morality was uncompromising, and this probably led to her leaving Freedman's Village. Prostitution and sexual exploitation existed in all the camps; each one had a cluster of half-white "contraband babies." Julia Wilbur complained that the army had "5 nor 6 soldiers stationed right in the middle of these women & children," supposedly for protection. Instead, these white soldiers seduced or raped women and young girls and committed flagrant acts of violence against the few black men in residence. Putting aside her "fastidiousness and delicacy," Wilbur, a self-described "Old Maid," spoke out. White soldiers constantly "tormented and insulted" black women who refused their advances. These men "seem to think that a colored girl can't be virtuous" and "will not allow that the Negro is a man." Seeing so many "nearly white" freed people, Wilbur wrote, "makes me so sick and disgusted with *white mankind* in general that I despair of ever accomplishing any good here." Black women "have been more sinned against than sinning," she observed. Yet while Wilbur felt ill equipped to counsel freed women on sexuality, Sojourner Truth had no such compunctions. She considered the physical order at Freedman's Village merely cosmetic, because it was the worst "den of iniquity" among the camps, according to reports. She made little headway in attacking morals. "I spent over six months at Arlington Heights," she wrote Amy Post, "as councilor for my people, acceptably to the good." However, "not at all times to those who desired nothing higher than the lowest and the vilest of habits." She was leaving. "For you know I must be faithful Sojourner everywhere."[61]

III

By summer 1865, Sojourner was in Washington alone. After Appomattox, her grandson James Caldwell was released from Confederate prison and mustered out of the Fifty-fourth Massachusetts. When Sojourner saw James in Boston, his condition was heartbreaking. He was deeply traumatized, in debilitating health, and mentally unstable. Her grandson Sammy accompanied his ailing cousin to Rochester, where apparently they remained instead of going to Battle Creek, where James's mother, Diana had married Jacob Corbin. Sojourner continued her work among the freed people as Andrew Johnson took the oath of office. "Whatever Andrew Johnson may be," said Frederick Douglass, who had observed Johnson scowling at him during Lincoln's second inauguration, "he certainly is no friend of our race." Sojourner Truth met Johnson in company with Lucy Colman. In 1891, Colman remembered that unlike Lincoln, Johnson was courtly, standing as long as Sojourner did and calling her "Mrs. Truth." Sojourner understood this condescending ridicule, and like Douglass, had a "poor opinion" of Johnson. He "reminded her of the fig tree that Jesus cursed—there was not much to him."[62]

In Washington, she joined forces with Josephine Griffing and the Freedmen's Bureau, headed by General Oliver Otis Howard. Griffing was appointed assistant to General John Eaton, Howard's deputy commissioner. Eaton immediately appointed Sojourner attendant manager at Freedmen's Hospital; Sojourner's federal appointment lasted longer than her friend Josephine. President Johnson ordered the Bureau to abandon its initial free labor concept of leasing, with purchase rights, 40 acres of deserted and confiscated Southern land to individual freed men. Instead, General Howard was forced to return to Confederate lands and coerce blacks back onto plantations. Thousands refused, and this created a humanitarian crisis. Lambasting the contract labor system and the Bureau's relief policies, Griffing publicly accused Howard of using hunger and nakedness as weapons against freed people. She was fired within six months, but then hired as general agent for the National Freedman's Relief Association in the District of Columbia. She continued to champion the freed people. The Bureau denied her assertion that twenty thousand died in the District region in 1865. But hospital physicians concurred, maintaining that the Quartermaster's Office alone issued "an average of eighty coffins per week," mostly for children. The Bureau allowed thousands to starve, Griffing lamented, and "I pray that I may not be . . . held responsible for the suffering and death of these innocent children, and that of the neglected old people who have claims against this country."[63]

Sojourner and Josephine resided at the Relief Association headquarters, a large house on North Capitol Street in the hub of national politics. The house was a food, fuel, and clothing distribution center; counseling center; employment office; industrial school; and guesthouse. The constant flow of destitute freed people so near Capitol Hill reminded politicians of an unfinished revolution. The house was also a bustling landmark of action for Freedmen's Hospital nurses and doctors, District teachers, radical politicians, ministers, and out-of-town reformers. Sojourner's "trance-speaker" associate Cora Hatch Daniels, a great favorite in black churches, joined the Capitol Street reformers when she was in town. Washington was exactly the place to be, Cora wrote Amy Post. "There are important events transpiring here now."[64]

Sojourner's hospital duties involved nursing people with contagious respiratory diseases, typhoid, smallpox, and cholera. She also attended homeless elderly people who were living out their last years in the hospital and suffering from rheumatism, arthritis, and palsy. Staggering numbers of unwed mothers and ill soldiers increased the hospital's clientele. Chief surgeon Charles Purvis, son of Abolitionists Robert and Harriet Forten Purvis, attributed many ailments to social and economic deprivation—living in poorly constructed alley houses near sewers; crowded sleeping conditions without ventilation; and dirty, germ-infested bedclothes. The freed people's diet was unwholesome and their clothing scanty. "Strong, unreasonable, and unchristian prejudice," Dr. Purvis noted, exacerbated the human misery. The Army quartermaster provided inadequate, sometimes vermin-infested supplies; hospital sanitation was primitive—one washroom per ward where attendants also cleaned medical appliances. Miraculously, Sojourner remained disease free. By the spring of 1866, however, she was ill from exhaustion, and the cold drafts in their home brought on lameness; she could not attend the momentous May anniversary meetings in New York. When she recovered, she was back to work.[65]

The doctors' reliance on her "indefatigable zeal" went beyond hospital rounds. She traveled for supplies, visited the orphanage, nursed shut-ins, and went from house to house, advising her people to seek "'truth, knowledge, and lands.'" As in New York City, she went where other women dared not follow. Added to all of this was public speaking, and teaching a sewing class at the Capitol Street house. Among the voluntary laborers in behalf of District freed people, one Relief Association annual report noted, "perhaps none are more deserving our thanks for cooperation than Sojourner Truth," who labored with "power and success to correct the social evils growing out of the system." Her devotion to the needy "won for her among the colored people the name of 'angel of mercy.'" Out west, Laura Haviland prepared to rejoin Sojourner and Josephine. "Sister Sojourner . . . I have received my commission to return to Washington and Richmond as soon as I can possibly get ready, i.e., collect about $300 more to go with. . . . Oh, how I want to know how you are getting along. . . . Yours for the poor and needy."[66]

Sojourner's practice of jumping aboard streetcars with white passengers angered conductors who were bent on ignoring desegregation laws. But she insisted that as a citizen "from the Empire State of New York," she knew the laws. Successfully boarding the cars delighted her, and she sometimes rode farther than necessary. Once, trying to board with Griffing, she was not quick enough, and the conductor "dragged me a number of yards." Holding onto the rail, she literally ran with the moving car before the conductor stopped. Her shoulder was injured. The two friends had the car number and complained to the railway president, who immediately dismissed the errant conductor. She rode in peace for a while. Once two white women objected to her and her black helper's presence. "'Tis a shame and a disgrace,'" the whites said. "'They ought to have a nigger car on the track.'" Sojourner's timid companion "hung her poor old head nearly down to her lap," but Sojourner said, "ladies and gentlemen" rode carriages, while "poor white and colored folks" rode streetcars. Pointing out of the window, Sojourner suggested that rather than "talk of nigger car," the women take a carriage for "three or four miles for sixpence." As they left, she smirked, "Good by, ladies."[67]

Another confrontation caused a more serious injury. "I had occasion to go for blackberry wine and other necessaries for the patients in the Freedmen's Hospital," she told the *Standard*, and boarded the streetcar with Laura Haviland. The conductor told Sojourner to get off, and she refused. "Then I'll put you off," he shouted. "Take care" she cautioned, concerned about her supplies. "You'll break my basket." She still refused to get off. He pulled on her right arm while Laura grabbed her left to keep her in the car. "Does she belong to you!" the conductor asked angrily. "If she does, take her in out of the way." Sojourner could ride as a servant but not as a citizen. "She *does not* belong to me," Laura replied, "but she belongs to humanity." The conductor vigorously heaved Sojourner past Laura, shouting, "Take her and go." Sojourner warned, "Don't push me over the people." But he threw her onto the platform ground, and whites boarded the cars over her body. She was not fully recovered from the previous bruising. Freedmen's Hospital doctors said she had a dislocated shoulder, and reported the incident. Metropolitan Railway dismissed the conductor, who was arrested when Sojourner charged him with assault and battery. The case went to the grand jury of the United States, she reported triumphantly, and she attended the trial. "Assault on Sojourner Truth" read the *Standard*—a woman "whose name for many years has been as a household word through every northern State of the Union." The old slaveholding spirit dies hard, she told Amy Post, "but die it must." Her "lame and swollen" shoulder got better, she said. "I fear it will trouble me for a long time, if I ever get entirely over it."[68]

Yet she was happy, because the cars "looked like pepper and salt." Over a year later, William Wells Brown visited Washington and noted that "streetcars, omnibuses, carriages, and everything of the kind are open to the colored people. How unlike Philadelphia." Sojourner Truth deserves much credit for challenging Washington's de facto streetcar segregation.[69]

Among the freed people, poverty and illness seemed overwhelming, and able-bodied blacks rarely found employment. In eight months' time, Griffing's agency placed only 254 people out of 2,114 job applicants. Sojourner watched the "Black Maria" (paddy wagon) bulging with freed people driving to police court daily. While she preached against "vice and ignorance," she also knew that personal tragedy nurtured despair, and lack of opportunity destroyed willpower. She encountered a healthy-looking woman sitting in the sun on Capitol Street waiting for rations. "'Why don't you go to work and get out of the Government poor-house?" Sojourner scolded. "See how old and how strong I am *because* I work." Not even Sojourner Truth need tell freed women about labor. "'I reckon you'se alyers been on your own, and had your chillen too; dat's a difference between you and me,'" the woman answered gloomily. "'All my days I'se bin a workin' for nothin'; my chillen's all sole! I haint got no heart to work no how till I finds'um! May be I'll knock around den as you does.'"[70] Such experiences often created psychological lethargy and spiritual breakdown.

During the 1866 winter, tragic scenes plagued the Capitol Street Relief headquarters. When the door opened, Frances Gage observed, shivering freed people rushed in from the piercing wind, like a huge "cloud of darkness, poverty, rags, hunger, cold, and suffering." Some had Bureau tickets, "testifying to their need"; others, equally deprived, had none. "We are needing help for our freed people here in the District," Griffing wrote Amy Post—food, wood, clothes, beds, and bedding. Only private largess could prevent more starvation. While Congress debated over extending the Bureau's existence, entire families perished, "many of them soldiers' wives & children" and single mothers whose few days' work barely paid the rent. Some mothers, Laura Haviland wrote, sat up with their children all night, holding them close in turn to prevent their freezing. "You cannot imagine the destitution in this very severe weather." It could not last, she added. "Some door must be opened." Sojourner was especially frustrated because most black leaders seemed impervious. "Where is Frederick that his voice is not heard in this trying hour?" she wondered. Douglass was in Washington that winter. Whereas Truth considered land ownership the key to independence and mobility, Douglass believed in suffrage. Sojourner and Josephine published a circular asking for help; they especially implored "colored people" to aid the suffering women and children of their race.[71]

Commissioner Howard got behind Senate Bill 60, to enlarge the Bureau, empower it with broad land provisions, and extend its life indefinitely. "Howard is now seeing more light-in the suffering every day wrought," Griffing wrote optimistically. She now believed "he wishes the Black Man well." During the congressional debates, white reformers, including Frances Gage, Laura Haviland, William Lloyd Garrison, and Giles and Catherine Stebbins joined Sojourner Truth, Henry Garnet, Robert Purvis, and other African Americans in the black gallery section. All cheered jubilantly when Senate Bill 60 passed. They shouted angrily when Andrew Johnson's son delivered his veto, which was sustained. "The president's veto of the Bureau," Haviland informed Amy Post, "is causing great sensation here, as it must everywhere among the lovers of *freedom* and *eternal* rights."[72] Legislative defeat grimly reminded blacks that the nation expected them to rise above generations of bondage simply with the stroke of Abraham Lincoln's pen.

"Washington was too thick" with freed people, Sojourner said. She and Griffing spoke in churches in the District, Virginia, and Maryland, promoting a relocation enterprise. In 1866, Griffing and her daughter shepherded at least twelve hundred freed people to New England homes. Sojourner aimed for the West, and a circular under her name went out to farmers advertising the availability of black labor. Freedmen's Hospital physicians followed Sojourner's advice and urged discharged able-bodied patients to relocate. "Dear Friend," surgeon A. W. Tucker wrote her, "the bearer of this note is desirous of going North and taking thence his family, consisting of wife and daughter. I . . . recommend him to your consideration." Payton Grayson recalled that Sojourner convinced his mother, Liza, to relocate, and took several railroad coaches of freed people to Michigan. She left them at certain stops, having prearranged temporary shelter, and she spread people among "colored friends" who themselves arrived "by way of the famous Underground Railway." She also set up employment possibilities. "When we got to Battle Creek," young Grayson recalled, "Aunt Sojourner came to my mother and said, 'You better get off here. This is my home, Battle Creek, and I think you'll find it will make a good home for you.'" A black family sheltered the Graysons, and Sojourner procured employment for Liza with Henry Willis at St. Mary's Lake. Liza later married a man who also came on one of "Sojourner's trains." Liza remained Sojourner's "staunch and close friend." Sojourner Truth wanted "to help us help ourselves," Payton Grayson insisted. "She did a world's wonder of good for the colored people. . . . There was no one like Aunt Sojourner."[73]

Sojourner also transported freed people to the Rochester area between 1866 and 1867. Griffing's correspondence to Sojourner reveals their commitment to the freed people, their close friendship, and their importance in the reform community. Before leaving Washington, for Rochester, Sojourner had leveled a stinging public rebuke at the Bureau and local people, especially for ignoring the deplorable conditions at Freedman's Village. The old and young at Arlington still had the greatest need, Griffing wrote Sojourner, and received no attention unless outside observers appeared. Now, Griffing wrote, local activists sent a circular to the daily papers, "saying just what *you* said when you was here. . . . I think great good will come of it." Yet the superintendent of the village opposed the circular, "just as you and I have been opposed when we have shown where the freed people have been wronged." Politically, "things are as you left them." While Congress seemed finally "awake for duty," General Howard still did not officially support relocation. If Johnson were not impeached, she added, "we are in hot water." Nonetheless, she affirmed, "God has arisen for the rights of the poor," and "justice reigns in spite of presidents." Johnson dared not veto the Fourteenth Amendment or deny black suffrage, she wrongly surmised.

Despite the pitfalls in Washington, she continued, Sojourner's news about relocation efforts in western New York was heartening. "I knew it would be so," Griffing added. She was glad Sojourner was having such a good time, and implored her to remember everything for sharing when she returned. "How much I would love to be with you," she added wistfully. People in the District constantly inquired about Sojourner. Mr. Baldwin "sent his love to you"; Mr. Newton and Dr. Glennan stopped by to tell Sojourner that her old acquaintance

Dr. Ellis, who had tended her dislocated shoulder, had died of typhoid contracted while attending freed people. Sojourner's dentist had also died, after falling on his head. But by the time Sojourner returned, Josephine added, her gums would be healed enough for an impression, and Dr. Howland will "give you permanent teeth." He promised that "the work will be well done." The house residents all sent love to Sojourner, especially her central New York friends Elizabeth Howland and her mother. "I've missed you much," Griffing wrote in closing, but "still feel glad that you went when you did—as it has been very cold in this building and no new stove or any repairs." Nonetheless, District friends eagerly awaited Sojourner's return.[74]

Sojourner's Michigan friends also missed her, and made certain she did not forget where home was. Young Matilda Gardner wrote her—"Dear Grandmother"—from boarding school, discussing family news, her studies, and the "jolly old time" they would have when everyone was together again. "I am very sorry to think that you don't write to me," Matilda said, after all the letters she had written. Edward Ives wondered when they could expect Sojourner back in Michigan. After Sojourner's grandson Sammy shared his letter with newly widowed Phebe Hart Merritt, she wrote Sojourner about how everyone in Battle Creek missed her, especially Merritt's adult children. Although Phebe was convalescing from a cold, a broken elbow, and a lame shoulder, she wrote a moving, barely legible letter, which characterizes another of Sojourner's intimate female friendships. Race and class seem not to interfere with the warm attachment between these two elderly activists. "May we both live to meet here and be able to sit alone and talk all these days over," Merritt wrote. "May we meet once more and lay our heads together side by side in their resting place." She had things to tell Sojourner, which she could not tell anyone else or write, even in good health. Soon, she wrote, they both must sojourn "to our destined home of the well done good and faithful [servant]." Yet before going to the better land, she longed to see Sojourner in earthly life:

> Do come Sojourner as soon as you can, for time is swiftly passing away with you and me; and may we spend our last days together. I should have written more but [for] my broken elbow and feeble health; only a week last night I was very sick and now I am able to ride out today. I often have sick turns—[?] warm weather comes I hope to be better. I want to write many things. Battle Creek is just as pleasant as ever. Here I am seventy-five years old and Sojourner is old, and we shall pass over the other side before long. When you come do if possible come by way of Paynesville [Painesville, Ohio, where Phebe Merritt's daughter lived]. My hand is [?] I can only write with a pencil. I will stop. Phebe Merritt.[75]

Even at seventy, Sojourner Truth was not quite ready to join Phebe Merritt in watching the sunset. Sojourner believed that God sustained her health and strength to work for humanity; she wanted relocation to become a Northern movement. She traveled back and forth in 1867, from Washington to Rochester; she sent from the District bedding, blankets, and other essentials and arranged for construction of temporary barracks for relocated people. "I shall . . . reach Rochester Wednesday or Thursday night next week with ten or twenty freed people—men & women & a few children," she informed Amy Post. "Please put up the Building for us . . . we are working with all our might, Mrs. Griffing & I. Tell Elizabeth to have all things in order." Sojourner helped finance the relocation with money from the sales of her photographs and earnings from aid societies. Once in Rochester, she held meetings to publicize the enterprise and solicit contributions. Commissioner Howard eventually supported relocation, and Sojourner traveled under the Bureau's sanction, if not their economic assistance.[76]

She proceeded optimistically through much of 1867. Prospective employers sometimes had no clue as to her gender, addressing her as "Dear Sir" or "Respected Sir." Other applicants were old friends and acquaintances, sometimes expecting special consideration. One person reminded her that they met in Boston in 1852 at "the Stearns home." Hopeful employers promised the freed people liberal treatment and education. Occasionally a single letter writer represented a group of people willing to provide good homes and employment. Some wanted a mulatto from Sojourner's "agency"; others wanted a contingency plan in case the employee did not work out. But applications poured in, and she tried to screen all the freed people that she and trusted friends recommended. "I am ready to believe that justice will be the rule in any undertaking which bears the signatures of Sojourner Truth and Isaac Post," a farmer in Monroe County wrote. Another in Geneva wrote to Sojourner, "There is such general confidence in you that we should be inclined to depend upon what you say." She worked especially hard to place single women with children. "I would like to know if you can find me good places for women that have children," she asked Amy Post before making a Rochester trip. These were such good women, she added, that they should select from a range of employer options. In 1866 alone, she transported at least 140 women to western New York. Although more women than men relocated, Sojourner and Josephine refused to separate families.[77]

Accusations of mismanagement plagued these two women, which they attributed to resentment and petty jealousy. Commissioner Howard claimed that Griffing had received thousands of unaccounted-for dollars, and the outraged Connecticut Yankee protested to minister George Whipple, an American Missionary Association donor. She had sold her Ohio home and other property, used "every dollar of it in this work," and thus far received no salary or reimbursement. She appealed "to Christians if not to men of the world to protect me against this unholy persecution"—otherwise she would abandon the project. Julia Wilbur gossiped that Sojourner used the freed people to lecture for personal gain. With Sammy as her scribe, Sojourner Truth complained bitterly to Griffing. Sojourner and Sammy had traveled throughout rural New York at her expense. When people donated money, "it is not more than right for me to have it" to pay for the freed people's travel and maintenance. Her people "all know I am not doing it for my benefit or profit." Wherever she went, "people came flocking in" as soon as they read the name Sojourner Truth, and audiences gave willingly. "I think it little enough" she added, given the debt owed to her people. Most blacks and whites believed she was doing a "great work, more than had ever been done before." Yet Wilbur, a "very near sighted woman," reading the copperhead press, had insisted "that I am doing it for speculating." Sojourner echoed the same despair as Josephine: "I sometimes feel sorry that I have published it [the circular]." The huge organizational effort and tiresome travel were easier to bear than accusations from "friends."[78]

Other people also surprised her. Gerrit Smith ignored the freed people and joined Henry Ward Beecher and Horace Greeley in advocating pardons for rebel leaders and money to rebuild their economy. Wendell Phillips seared them as "Three wise men of Gotham" (who went to sea in a bowl), but Sojourner singled out Smith because once she "had appreciated him so highly." His call for union with rebels, she told the *Standard*, "makes all my nerves quiver." Smith wanted Northerners to be "'like Jesus?'" Sojourner said mockingly. Jesus would not only scorn the rebels but take the freed people's case against the North: "I was sick and in prison, and ye visited me not. I was hungry and ye fed me not. I was naked and ye clothed me not. Depart from me, ye workers of iniquity; I know ye not." Sojourner reminded Smith that Jesus was a Come-outer who told the righteous to "come out from among them . . . lest ye be partakers of the plagues." Smith did not think the rebels should repent? They should "repent in sackcloth and ashes," she said. Instead, they murdered blacks and their white supporters. She reminded Smith of Andersonville (the Confederate prison) and Fort Pillow (site of a massacre of unarmed black soldiers). Her grandson had been a war prisoner along with some of Massachusetts's finest sons, and she was "ashamed to put on paper the horrible things they were obliged to submit to under these rebel fiends. Now, Gerrit Smith wants us to forgive them (before they repent), pay them . . . and excuse their taxes and so on." Since Smith was so wealthy and so generous, she suggested, let him "first give them all he has—keep nothing back." Then "I will believe that he means what he says." Had he forgotten that for centuries slaves were "robbed and starved and butchered" and slaveholders attempted to "take away all their senses and make brutes of them?" Working among her people, and seeing "the scars of their cruelty made my heart bleed," she related. "I said, oh God! Was there no mercy? Is there no justice?" Hearing Smith's words was like being on the ship of State, she said, and "one of the best anchor-cables had broken." Hopefully, "the water is shallow," and the anchor "can be got up again." Her words seemed harsh and out of place for her, she said, but she could not help speaking out.[79]

The relocation enterprise faced various problems. First, reformers could not supply half the laborers that Northerners requested. Farmers were losing patience, Josephine wrote Sojourner, but they were also unrealistic. Disregarding family connection, some farmers stipulated "no young children"—a position Griffing found preposterous—as if "black babies were 12 years old when they were born." More significantly, many blacks simply refused to move. Freed people were "wedded to associations," Elizabeth Keckley said, and to their homes and environments, however squalid. "When you destroy these you destroy half of the happiness of their lives." Many freed men refused to relocate, and their wives would not leave without them. For those who moved east, Keckley believed their love and longing for the past was so strong that they found no beauty in the isolated new life.[80] Perhaps this was difficult for Sojourner to understand. Her attachment was not to place, and her deep communitarian sense was broad, flexible, and biracial. Moreover, since her enslavement experience was not community-based, she could not truly identify with the deep cultural bonding nurtured in the slave quarters of the South.

Yet she had a deep love of family. During the war and early Reconstruction years, she kept up correspondence with her family through friends. "I have heard nothing from my children for a long time, neither from my grand children since they left me," she had Haviland write Amy Post, after Sammy left with James, leaving her in Washington. Cora Hatch Daniels also wrote Amy, "Sojourner wishes you to find and see her daughter and to please [ask her] to write to her all about her grand children—one that was in prison [James], and one that she took care of [Sammy]. It would cheer her dear old heart so much to hear from you and the children." Sojourner was also generous toward her family. "What I wish you to find out now is if my daughter has received money that I sent her some time ago. I sent her ten dollars, and . . . I sent Sammy five dollars & I have not heard whether either of them was received." She wondered if someone was taking her letters, "for I don't know how it is that so many letters get lost." Send mail to Dr. Glennan at Freedmen's Hospital, she advised, "without putting on my name." She closed with "Remember me to my children" and "accept my love and best respects for yourself."[81]

The freed people's economic endeavors also needed support from other high-profile black leaders. Sojourner Truth could not do it alone, and traveling back and forth was wearing her down. Late in 1867, she dispersed one final group of Washington freed people to New York, Ohio, and Michigan. She also tried to keep track of them. "How is Aunt Mary and the women I brought you getting along, and the rest of the women?" she asked Amy Post. "I do want so much to know." Aunt Mary, a special friend of Sojourner, had been in the District since the early days of war. Sojourner asked Amy to read her letter to Aunt Mary and explain that since Sojourner had so many letters to answer and depended on others, she could not personally and separately write Aunt Mary. But she asked Amy to write her all about the freed people: did the sickly baby live? Did Aunt Mary's nephew arrive?[82]

Back in Michigan, Sojourner concentrated on building a home. Everyone returned to Battle Creek, including Sophia and her family, who now lived in Sojourner's house at Harmonia. Sojourner had previously purchased a lot in Battle Creek from Phebe's sons, Richard and William Merritt, with money she received from her hospital work. When she returned, the brothers slowly began transforming a barn on the property into a residence. "I think I shall be very comfortable & then I shall want you to come and see me," she informed Amy. Sojourner worked on her house before the harsh Michigan winter set in. She helped dig her cellar and carried out the dirt in her leather apron. She was having a hard time economically, having mortgaged everything to pay for the building of her home, "lacking my body and a few rags." She needed money to finish the house. "I wish you and Miss Griffing and Miss Watkins would get up a contribution so that I can get my house done," she implored Amy. Then, they all could visit her, as long as they brought their own "victuals." The government and the Relief Association owed Sojourner more reimbursement money and salary. "Have you heard anything about the money I paid for those colored people?" she asked Amy. Letters of inquiry availed nothing. Eventually, Sojourner used all of her savings. She received two generous contributions. One came from minister Photius Fiske, the other from a very chastened Gerrit Smith. Requests for her photograph and donations from friends also trickled in.[83]

The winter rest was good, but knitting, sewing, and visiting could not contain Sojourner's active mind and restless spirit. Right now "I am very poor," she told the *Standard*, and could no longer afford a subscription. But she very much wanted to "hear the news that is going on." Would they send the paper free, "for a while?" The new editor, her old friend Aaron Powell, readily complied. Many newsworthy events piqued her interest: freed men were voting in state elections; President Johnson was impeached in February and on trial by April; the universal suffrage movement forged ahead; violence riddled the South; and the freed people remained economically distressed. She anxiously prepared to rejoin the struggles.[84]

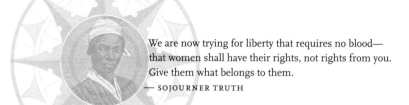

We are now trying for liberty that requires no blood—
that women shall have their rights, not rights from you.
Give them what belongs to them.
— SOJOURNER TRUTH

CHAPTER 18

"Was Woman True?"

SOJOURNER, SUFFRAGE, AND CIVIL RIGHTS

I

Sojourner Truth joined the newly revived woman's movement, which had been quiet during the war in the interest of national solidarity. Indeed, in 1863, women had organized the National Woman's Loyal League to support the Union and collect a million signatures advocating a Thirteenth Amendment abolishing slavery. Funded by the AASS, the league's paid female agents branched throughout the North and West but delivered only four hundred thousand signatures to Congress. Garrison's private comment that the league was more of a woman's rights organization was not far off the mark. League auxiliaries became the nexus for a postwar suffrage movement and propelled Elizabeth Cady Stanton and Susan B. Anthony into national leadership.[1] Sojourner Truth wholeheartedly advocated woman's suffrage. Eventually however, she had to choose between prioritizing race and gender.

"I suppose," she said in 1866, "I am about the only colored woman that goes about to speak for the rights of the colored woman." Although a few other black women activists supported the movement, none rivaled her in consistency and visibility. "My Dear Friend," Susan B. Anthony wrote Sojourner Truth in

January 1866, "I know you will be glad to put your mark to the enclosed petition and get a good many to join it, and send or take it to some member of Congress to present."[2]

This petition, drawn up by Anthony, Stanton, and Lucy Stone—a self-appointed, ad hoc National Woman's Rights Committee—challenged using the word "male" in the proposed amendment to the Constitution. Such wording, Anthony wrote Sojourner, would shut out "all women from voting for president, vice-president, and congressmen, even though they may have the right to vote in the state for state officers." The petition praised pending legislation guaranteeing citizenship to all "persons" born in the United States (except untaxed Indians) and granting them equality before the law. Yet the bill specifically used the words *he, his,* and *him.* "I know Sojourner Truth will say, 'No' to this atrocious exclusion," Anthony wrote. "God bless you, and help you to do the good work before you."[3]

Sojourner did not attend the 1866 annual spring meetings at which the AASS argued heatedly over dissolution. Douglass led virtually all African Americans in adamantly objecting to dissolving the organization. The AASS, Frances Watkins Harper argued, should help blacks create "a level playing field." Most whites agreed. The sensational young newcomer Anna Dickinson thundered against dissolution and the white North's amazing apathy. Abby Kelley Foster, visibly ill but eloquent, spoke about the recent Memphis riots. "When in all the rural districts of the South, men, women, and children are held, worked and treated as slaves, I contend that we have not freedom. When some hundred people, assembled at a hall, were attacked by a gang of white men . . . women killed, and others worse than killed—and nothing done to punish the fearful crimes, who will say the Negro is free?" She vowed that only when black men obtained protection and suffrage would she vote to dissolve. Garrison, now almost a Republican centrist, resigned and dissolved the *Liberator;* Oliver Johnson and Maria Chapman Weston also resigned. But the rank and file voted overwhelmingly to remain active. Wendell Phillips accepted the presidency of the society, and Aaron Powell assumed Johnson's editorship of the *Standard.* Sojourner sent thanks and blessings to friends for "what they have done for me and my people." Yet the nation still owed a big debt to the freed people, who remained in great need.[4]

Abolitionists then attended the National Woman's Rights Convention, which passed a resolution to become the American Equal Rights Association (AERA) and met a few weeks later in Boston. Participants united behind a universal suffrage agenda; several male Abolitionists, including Frederick Douglass, were AERA vice presidents. Sojourner was not there, but the press noted that Frances Watkins Harper was "witty, pathetic, and dramatic—giving fragments of her experience as both a woman and [member] of the proscribed race." Wendell Phillips declared his support for woman's suffrage and protested against all efforts to introduce the word "male" into the proposed amendment to the Constitution.

Nonetheless, he insisted, the black man's peculiar circumstances meant that "*his* claim to this right might fairly be considered to have precedence." White women were split, and Stanton privately chided the Coffin sisters (Lucretia and Martha) for boosting "the negro over our own heads." Once Stanton had managed to convince the sisters, she felt vindicated, and remarked to Martha that Martha's "disease was only skin-deep—a lethargy in your surroundings and not in your soul." Self-preservation, Stanton added, "is the first law of nature." Stanton and Anthony also won over Lucy Stone, who broke with her mentor, Abby Kelley Foster. Amy Post likewise believed that women must "push in by the negro's side." Sojourner's Washington cohorts Laura Haviland and AERA vice president Josephine Griffing agreed. Abby Kelley Foster and Anna Dickinson unequivocally prioritized black male franchise. No one wanted an open quarrel, but both sides stood their ground.[5]

The AERA resolutions applauded the Civil Rights Bill, proposed excluding discrimination based on "color or sex," and criticized antisuffrage women who proclaimed "I have all the rights I want." These women of fashion and wealth, the resolutions said, despised labor and disregarded the toiling female masses who needed the vote. After the Boston meeting, advocates began spreading their suffrage message. At the Longwood Friends Meeting, the universal suffrage issue shared the spotlight with advocacy for the freed people. Frances Watkins Harper lectured for universal suffrage throughout Westchester County, New York. Sojourner joined the campaign briefly late in 1866, speaking at a large convention in Monroe County, New York, along with other high-profile reformers.[6]

"Dear Sojourner," Elizabeth Cady Stanton wrote in March 1867, "Will you try and be present at our coming anniversary and help us bury the woman and the Negro in the citizen and make New York State a genuine republic"?[7] Although busily transporting District area freed people to their new homes, Sojourner attended the AERA anniversary meeting and was Stanton's houseguest. The two women knew each other mostly through mutual friends. Woman's rights allied Stanton with important Abolitionists such as Amy Post and the Coffin sisters, all Seneca Falls delegates. Stanton was Gerrit Smith's cousin and the daughter of a wealthy Democratic judge. Her husband, Henry Stanton, deserted abolition for politics, and Elizabeth did not express antislavery interests until around 1858. During the Civil War, her leadership in the National Woman's Loyal League and Sojourner Truth's stop in New York en route to Washington had renewed their acquaintance. By then, Frances Gage's article had reminded reformers of Truth's stridency on the woman's rights question. At Stanton's elegant home, Sojourner was in the suffragists' hub; women flocked to New York City for the AERA's first anniversary. Stanton made certain that a reporter from the (Democratic) *New York World* was present to write an article.

Elizabeth Cady Stanton and Sojourner Truth had different suffrage goals. For Sojourner, suffrage was an imperative to help poor uneducated black women, like men, become independent. Stanton was born of privilege, from one of New York's oldest families (the Livingstons). She formulated her arguments for women's rights from the perspective of her class and race, as did Sojourner Truth. Stanton chafed at the disfranchisement of educated (white) women. In 1863, she sent a contribution of $5 to the *Standard*'s emancipation fund and enclosed a letter for publication. The letter, which greatly annoyed Lydia Maria Child, reflects Stanton's suffrage position. The black man, Stanton penned, was "still in his babyhood" and only saw objects close to him. He knew "but little the machinery of life, and government and war." An oppressed class, Stanton wrote, neither knew nor understood power, was "always ignorant of their rights," and expected change miraculously. Nonetheless, she complained, the free black man "holds a place the noblest woman has not yet attained." Frederick Douglass could vote in New York because he owned property, and conceivably could become secretary of war or state, or president. Yet compared to women such as herself, she said, the black race was not ready for suffrage. No one who understood the "effect of ignorance, superstition and fear," she wrote, "can expect four million to leap into office a full grown manhood." During the 1867 universal suffrage campaign, Stanton wrote Wendell Phillips that she would rather be enslaved by "an educated white man" than "a degraded, ignorant black one."[8] For Sojourner Truth, suffrage was about humanity and equality, not white privilege.

Sojourner Truth was probably the most popular woman at the 1867 AERA meeting and certainly dominated the platform. The house erupted into loud, sustained cheers when she rose to speak at the first session. After thanking the audience for their enthusiasm, she added, "I don't know how you will feel when I get through." She was fresh from the horrors of Washington. "I come from another field—the country of the slave. They have got their rights—so much good luck, to have slavery partly destroyed; not entirely. I want it root and branch destroyed. Then we will all be free indeed. Now what is to be done about it?" Freed women, she said, needed rights as much as freed men. In her observations, black women and children suffered more than black men. "There is a great stir about colored men getting their rights, but not a word about the colored women, and if colored men get their rights and no colored women get theirs, there will be a bad time about it." Black women did as much, ate as much, and wanted as much as anyone but were paid very little. Poor washer-women often worked when their menfolk were idle, "strutting up and down." When women brought home their meager earnings, men "take it all, and then scold because there is no food." Sojourner applauded the new ruling giving black men voting rights in the District of Columbia. But female suffrage would render black women independent, and they could keep their own money. Like Anthony and Stanton, Sojourner said it was time to push for universal suffrage. "I am for keeping the thing going while things are stirring; because if we wait till it is still, it will take a great while to get it going again."[9]

She was certainly not alone in her concern for freed women. Traveling through the South, Frances Watkins Harper reported that black women complained of physical abuse, infidelity, and desertion. Watkins Harper began "preaching against men ill-treating their wives," and recalled a work song she heard Gullah women of the Sea Islands sing while picking cotton: "Black men beat me / White men cheat me / Won' get my hundud [hundred] all day."[10]

On the convention's second day, black restaurateur George Downing said he was disturbed by Stanton and Mott's rhetoric. Would they oppose black male enfranchisement unless it included woman's suffrage? he asked. Lucretia Mott said nothing. Stanton answered that the black man was too degraded and oppressed himself to be trusted with her rights, and "would be more despotic . . . than even our Saxon rulers." Individual, national, and woman's safety demanded that blacks and women "go into the kingdom [of politics] together." That prompted Downing to offer a resolution: "while we regret that the right sentiment which would secure to women the ballot is not as general as we would have it, nevertheless, we . . . rejoice in the . . . sentiment which favors the enfranchisement of the colored man." Only through universal suffrage, Stanton fired back, could "the virtue, wealth, and education of the women" outweigh the incoming "ignorance, poverty, and vice" of degraded manhood.[11]

Abby Kelley Foster, pale, weak and about to have surgery, took the platform. "Were the Negro and the woman in the same civil, social and religious status today, I should respond yes, with all my heart." However, the black man was still treated as a slave—deprived of wages, family rights, whipped, beaten, and subjected to the most horrible outrages. "Are we not dead to the sentiment of humanity if we wish to postpone his security till woman shall obtain political rights?" Stanton used Sojourner's point about black men oppressing black women, and Charles Remond agreed. Susan B. Anthony denounced everyone who considered it "harvest-time for black men" and "seed-sowing time for women." No one seconded Downing's resolution, because everyone remained adamant in pushing for universal suffrage.[12]

That afternoon, Sojourner combined politics and Scripture in her speech. Recounting the wartime suffering, she insisted that enfranchised women would stop their sons, husbands, and brothers from killing each other for greed. The vote, she said, was a tremendous power that men feared sharing with women. Certainly relinquishing power "cuts like a knife," she said, as the behavior of former slaveholders revealed. But slaveholders could not stop black freedom, and men could not stop women. She recalled that many years ago she had been told that a woman was not fit to rule because she had seven devils in her. "'And do you suppose,'" her scolder had said, "'that a man should put her to rule in the government?'" Now, she realized that seven devils was nothing; behold the man who had a legion, she said, and the devils didn't know where to go. The hall rocked with laughter and applause. Therein lay a bigger problem, she added. The devils had asked if they might go among the swine. Why the swine, she pondered. "Why didn't the devils ask to go among the sheep?" Because they were selfish and greedy, she surmised, "and certainly a man has a little touch of that selfishness that don't want to give the women their rights."[13]

The audience loved it. Jesus' followers were sheep—humble, obedient, and willing. Swine lived in muck and mire, cared only about their appetites, and were basically unclean. "Never mind," Sojourner said teasingly, moving on as the laughter died down. Although she seemed to brush off the issue absent-mindedly, she was on a roll. As she continued with her text, her aplomb and skill in returning to her original counterpoint was memorable—swine versus sheep, power versus humility, sacred versus secular, fickle versus faithful, war versus peace, and of course, man versus woman. She went on to speak of woman's love for Jesus, how she followed, stood, and waited for him. "What a mighty courage," Sojourner marveled. "You cannot find such strength and faith among men." Mary stood and looked for Jesus while the man did not stop long enough to see if he was there or not. "But when the woman stood there (blessed be God, I think I can see her!). She staid until she knew where He was, and said: 'I will carry Him away!' Was woman true?"

Eventually, proclaimed the Sojourner, truth would reign triumphant. "Before I leave here," she said, I want to see equality . . . to see women have their rights." Men always "wanted something more than their own, or to hold something that was not their own." First they had tried to keep the rights of her people; now they wanted all of woman's rights. When colored people and women gained their rights, Sojourner said, that should be the last battle. "Let us finish it up so that there be no more fighting. I have faith in God and there is truth in humanity. Be strong women! Blush not! Tremble not!"

Winning suffrage might take twenty more years of hard struggle, she warned. Men would "brat, brat, brat, brat," saturating the real issue with chatter to get around the "particular thing"—woman's suffrage. But the water was already troubled, she said, using a biblical metaphor in reference to agitation for black male suffrage. "Now is the time to step into the pool." Men were fearful. "They tremble! They dodge! (Laughter.). . . . Men speak great lies, and it has made a great sore, but it will soon heal up." But there were also good men, she added, and women should make a little allowance. She urged women to keep good faith and courage as she would. Her last remarks filled the house with loud laughter and applause: "I am going round to lecture on human rights," she said. "I will shake every place I go in."[14]

While Sojourner emphasized solidarity, Stanton followed with remarks that seemed to feed the divisiveness. A wealthy woman, she lamented, could not vote in New York, while a black man could vote for $250. "The time for doing justice to the negro is past." It was now time to save the republic from degraded manhood. Now Charles Remond was on his feet. Women and black men did not have identical urgency for the franchise, he maintained. Moreover, black men had carried the musket in the late war. In the ensuing discussion, both Stanton and Remond backed off from confrontation by invoking universal suffrage.[15]

Speaking again that evening, Sojourner continued uniting the two causes in a tone of harmony. Removing her hood and depositing "the miraculous bag containing her rations, 'shadows,' and other 'traps,'" she complimented her friends for being of one accord. Never had she attended a meeting, she said, where such politeness and cooperation reigned—"nobody tryin' to hurt anybody's feelin's." But she understood how earnestly people strove to coexist and how dangerously close Stanton came to destroying those efforts. Even though women spoke out passionately, Sojourner said, "talkin' and throwin' arrows—there was nobody gettin' mad, or if they was, they didn't let us know it. [Laughter.]" Sojourner Truth personified the complexities of the suffrage issue: she was black, a woman, a property holder, and an advocate for the dispossessed. Like Stanton and Anthony, Sojourner badly wanted to "go up to the polls" herself, and as a property owner, she had a right. "Every year I got a tax to pay. Taxes you see, be taxes." There was a "road tax, school tax, and all these things." Some Michigan female property owners worked on the road in lieu of paying the tax. They dug up stumps, and "it took 'em a good while," she said amid laughter. But women did it, and "if they can dig up stumps they can vote." She concluded her final appearance with a song and assertion that she would not leave the world until she could vote. She was one of a few blacks who actually paid AERA membership dues. Truth, Thomas Wentworth Higginson, Aaron Powell, Kelley Foster, Remond, and others placed their $1 alongside Gerrit Smith and Abby Hutchinson Patton's $100.[16]

Sojourner returned to Washington believing or hoping that all was well in the suffrage movement. Yet Frederick Douglass and Wendell Phillips's absence caused concern. Lucretia Mott wrote that Phillips's enemies, such as Frances Gage, fed the "jealousy existing with Susan [Anthony] and E. C. Stanton." Others worried about Douglass, who had joined the black men's National Equal Suffrage Association in Washington. It was a "National *Male* Suffrage" not an equal suffrage Association, wrote a *Standard* correspondent, signed "A" (Anthony, no doubt). But Douglass publicly advocated "immediate, complete, and universal enfranchisement." When Radical Republicans suggested that Douglass's presence at the Philadelphia Loyalist Convention would alienate Southern loyalists, he attended anyway, as Rochester's delegate. The convention accepted Douglass without incident, and the Radicals embraced him as their black suffrage poster boy. But the convention prepared to adjourn without a suffrage resolution. So Douglass strode into the crowded hall, arm-in-arm with lovely Anna Dickinson and New York's Theodore Tilton, demanded the floor, warded off an adjournment motion, and spoke "eloquently" for universal suffrage. Despite anger and opposition from the border states, and with surprise backing from Southern loyalists, a universal suffrage resolution passed.[17]

New England Abolitionists pushed their "Negro's hour" agenda amid friction. The rebels, Wendell Phillips said, had only changed their weapons. Vagrancy and apprenticeship laws, the lash, coerced labor, the same ruling oligarchy—all revealed that slavery was not dead. Black suffering remained "almost equal with that endured under the yoke," an AASS resolution declared, and Andrew Johnson was giving the North to the South "bound hand and foot." Congress must guarantee "to the Negro everywhere . . . his political rights, especially the right of suffrage." At the New England Anti-Slavery convention, Parker Pillsbury dismissed Abby Kelley Foster's assertion that the ballot was an antislavery goal and that equal protection under the law would save black men from slavery. "Who," Pillsbury asked, "is going to save the black *woman?*" Kelley Foster answered, "her husband." Pillsbury was astonished. "I say God save her then." The franchise, he added, was a God-given right; to withhold it from anyone was rebellion against God. Wendell Phillips agreed, but the AASS had "special clients of its cause," and Abolitionists should press the demand for black equality above all others. Other Abolitionists cautioned against separating the two goals.[18]

The AERA's acceptance of an invitation to campaign in Kansas created an open breach in the universal suffrage movement. Lucy Stone and her husband, Henry Blackwell, left first and began courting Kansas Democrats. Later Anthony, Stanton, and Olympia Brown joined them. While Sojourner Truth made her last relocation trips in fall 1867 and Douglass stumped for universal suffrage, Anthony and Stanton, smarting over their New York State Constitutional Convention defeat, made Kansas another test case. The suffragists canvassed the entire state, locking horns with black and white Republicans. Stone and Blackwell left Kansas as soon as Stanton, Anthony, and Brown wooed and won a particularly notorious copperhead named George Francis Train. Train devoted energy and money to woman's suffrage and agreed to finance a newspaper, the *Revolution.* Although Stanton called Train a "pure, high-toned man, without a vice," he used women to support his racism, as his political poetry reflects: "Woman votes the black to save, / The black he votes to make woman slave, / Hence when blacks and 'Rads' unite to enslave the whites, / 'Tis time the Democrats championed woman's rights."[19]

Stanton and Parker Pillsbury began publishing the *Revolution* in January 1868. Although it advocated educated suffrage irrespective of sex or color, Train also condemned the Freedmen's Bureau, freed men, and Republicans. The Abolitionists were astonished by the suffragists' alliance with a "crack brained harlequin and semi-lunatic." Black people, Garrison wrote, had no more abusive assailant than Train, "especially when he has an Irish audience before him, to whom he delights to ring the charges upon the 'nigger,' 'nigger,' 'nigger,' ad nauseam. He is as destitute of principle as he is of good sense. . . . He may be of use in drawing an audience, but so would a kangaroo, a gorilla, or a hippopotamus." When Lucretia Mott received the *Revolution*'s first issue gratuitously, she wrote Martha Wright, "I have not the littlest notion of being a subscriber." Likewise, Lydia Maria Child was sorry to see Stanton and Anthony allied with Democrats, and called Train insane.[20]

Meanwhile, Congress implemented Radical Reconstruction, passing the Fourteenth Amendment and moved toward the Fifteenth, guaranteeing complete male enfranchisement. Sojourner Truth was pleased with these advances for her race. Certainly it was half a loaf, but an important half. As a woman, she desired the rest, but was undoubtedly shocked by Anthony and Stanton's behavior. Their rhetoric and strategy played on white fear and hatred of blacks. Suggesting that white women needed protection from lower-class men, the *Revolution* called on "American women of wealth, education virtue and refinement" to beware of the danger in their midst. Otherwise, "the lower orders of Chinese, Africans, Germans and Irish, with their low ideas of womanhood" would "legislate for cultivated white women and their daughters, thereby dictating not only civil but moral codes governing society." Stanton wrote these venomous articles while Southern terrorists were perpetrating sensational and heartbreaking outrages against black and white Unionists.[21]

II

As the *Revolution* prepared to challenge black male suffrage, Sojourner began a lecturing tour in Ohio and New York. She spoke on behalf of the freed people, the Republican presidential candidate Ulysses S. Grant, and universal suffrage. She was a Michigan delegate to the Fifth National Spiritualist Convention in Rochester. Her account of "more than forty years" in the spirit world and her trance experiences greatly impressed the audience. She also used the Spiritualist Convention to speak on behalf of black rights. Frederick Douglass, who attended solely for political reasons, was unanimously invited to the platform. He said he only understood the spirit world as the place where "all good people go" at death. But he understood the humanity and purposes of the convention and that the greatest crimes committed were under the guise of "religious en-thusiasm." The delegates encouraged him to speak about politics. He expressed confidence in Grant and horror at the rise of the Ku Klux Klan, founded by "the murderer and butcher [Nathan Bedford] Forrest." Douglass was grateful that the political actions of 1868 made the victory of 1865 a reality.[22]

Truth and Douglass certainly discussed the suffrage conflict. He had re-cently returned from the 1868 AERA anniversary convention. He could report that no open breach had occurred, he had spoken graciously and favorably of woman's suffrage, and universal suffrage remained on the table. Admitting that some of his race had not taken the "right ground" on the woman question, he himself had advocated "the admission of the vote to the women of the land." Nonetheless, he insisted that white men indirectly represented white women, while "the black wife has no husband who can vote for her." For blacks, suffrage was a matter of life or death. The government loved its white women—"sisters, mothers, wives, and daughters of our rulers; but the negro is loathed." Douglass also chided Stanton, Anthony, and Brown for being dupes of Democrats; Francis Train boasted of defeating blacks and Republicans with women. There was heat but no fire, and Douglass could report to Sojourner that the convention had adjourned cordially. Resolutions had maintained that if Republicans adopted manhood suffrage, their party was no better than "a white man's government," and an aristocracy of sex was no better than one of color. Yet no one's views had shifted, including Sojourner Truth's. That fall, she joined Douglass and other blacks in campaigning for Grant. Lucretia Mott, president of the Philadelphia Female Anti-Slavery Society, joined its members in petitioning for "the right of suffrage for the colored people of this nation." Anthony and Stanton campaigned for Democrat Horatio Seymour, a close friend of the Stantons who had been governor during the murderous New York City draft riots.[23]

After Rochester, Sojourner began an extensive lecturing tour in upstate New York. Phebe Merritt Varney decided to "write a little diary" for the Sojourner. "We met Sojourner at Angola Station," Phebe wrote, and they all stopped at Joseph Linton's for dinner before moving on to Sojourner's old friends the Alonzo Hawleys, where she spent the night. Mrs. Hawley returned Sojourner to the Varneys, and she held a Sunday afternoon service for "an appreciative audience of four hundred people." She held several more meetings early in the week be-fore the Varneys took her to George W. Taylor, who later carried her to Collins (outside Buffalo), home of the region's largest enclave of Progressive Friends and Spiritualists. There her elderly friends Isaac and Lydia Allen extended a hearty welcome to her, and that evening she spoke in nearby Rosenburgh to a large audience. She then spent time with the Cook family, relatives of the Allens, and they all went to Collins Center. She "addressed a large audience in the new Free Church," where "her labors were not in vain." After several days with the

Allens, she journeyed to "Mr. Rosenburgh's who took her to Gowanda where she addressed an "intensely interested audience." Friends were solicitous about her health, making sure she had "quiet time." She rested for several days among the Methodists at Kerr's Corner and then held several engagements, including a large meeting at the Methodist Church. After another several day's rest at the Varneys', she continued speaking to packed audiences in local Methodist churches and schools, where people were "eager to listen to her teachings." After resting again, she accompanied the Varneys to "a political picnic at Hemlock Hall," where thousands heard her. "It is a blessing to be with her and receive her experience from her own lips," Phebe wrote. "We are enjoying a feast which we may never be privileged to enjoy again."[24]

After the Varneys, Isaac Baker and his son-in-law hosted Sojourner for several days, and they all attended a large Republican meeting. Her remarks promoted "such enthusiasm among the people that it opened the way for a very large meeting the next evening." She also held her own meeting at Potters Corner, where "a very large hall was nearly filled with an attentive audience. She spoke for more than an hour in her usually impressive and sarcastic manner, much to the satisfaction of the majority present." She continued holding meetings in little towns and hamlets of western New York throughout September and early October. She spoke "to good satisfaction to those in favor of liberty," one entry said; she spoke at Griffin's Mills "to a good and attentive audience, telling them many truths," said another; she spoke grandly, an observer said, "to the edification of the neighboring people." Toward the end of September, "J. B. C. Eddy went to Harry Abbot's after Sojourner Truth." She remained in that vicinity for two weeks, holding very well-attended meetings. Finally, she moved on to central New York.[25]

Traveling alone on public conveyance was now a handicap for the aging Sojourner. Western New York friends placed her on a train to Syracuse, where she had many associates, including the Jermain Loguen and Samuel May families. "Sojourner Truth came and staid with us until eve. She is a wonderful woman," May wrote in October. She returned the next day for lunch with the Mays. Later that month, she boarded a train for Courtland [sic] and McGrawville, with a note written by May: "The bearer of this note will be Sojourner Truth, a worthy and remarkable woman. She is going to Courtland, to visit Miss Mary E. Mudge and other friends. I shall be obliged to any persons who, on the arrival of the train at the Courtland depot, will help her to find her friend's house." She spent about a week in Courtland County, holding meetings first in the village and then in McGrawville, where she "lectured to a multitude." As the guest of Dr. Goodyear, she received many visitors at his home. Rural New York, once the seat of the Democrats, was fast becoming Republican. Speaking on behalf of Grant, suffrage, and the plight of the freed people, Sojourner attracted crowds wherever she went. People who never before had met her offered hospitality. "We rejoice in the opportunity of becoming partially acquainted with Sojourner Truth."[26]

In Madison County, Gerrit and Ann Smith hosted her in their mansion. The old friends had much to talk about, particularly lamentations over Elizabeth Stanton and Susan Anthony's defection. Smith, a staunch suffragist and Republican, had already written his "Dear Cousin" Stanton that Francis Train was too heavy a load and that her scathing vendettas in the *Revolution* against "great and good" Abolitionists was not helping her cause. Smith described one of Sojourner's inspiring meetings in Peterboro: "The Sabbath was stormy and the snow deep, but in spite of the elements, Sojourner had an interested and attentive audience in the Free Church. She spoke well and truthfully. We shall not soon forget her touching, and at the same time extremely witty, rehearsals of her many experiences in different parts of the county. God bless her and give her health and strength to carry on the good work to which she has given most of her . . . years."[27]

Finally, she returned to Rochester to await the election results. She had spent months campaigning in western and central New York, Amy Post wrote the *Standard*. Her many "long cold rides" had brought back the lameness in her legs. "After the election—and the Presidential candidate (of whom we hope the best things) was elected, she concluded to rest a little" before heading home.[28] It was a victory for her race, if not her sex.

She experienced another triumph that fall. For years, friends had admonished her about tobacco, a habit from her early youth. While always supporting antitobacco resolutions, she had continued to smoke. On her 1868 lecture tour she promised, "I'll quit if I die." Now Sojourner stopped cold, and lived; Amy Post wrote in December that the "inveterate smoker" had "not smoked once for three months." Her admiring associates were jubilant. "It ought to be proclaimed far and wide," wrote her friend Dr. Trask of Fitchburg, Massachusetts. Sojourner's longtime friend Lydia Allen, was elated that "thee is not a slave to the filthy weed." Another admirer wrote, "oh that our young people would do the same.[29]

Sojourner's courageous former cohort, Jonathan "Branded Hand" Walker, was most impressed of all. The memorialized Abolitionist hero, who, like her, lived in Michigan and had been born in 1797, marveled at her energy, "considering the exposure, fatigue, and inconvenience of traveling abroad, and holding public meetings at her advanced age." He invited her to visit him in Muskegon, and stay as long as she liked. She spent so much time traveling, Walker chided, she would "hardly feel at home anywhere until the infirmities of old age compel her to lay by." Applauding her tobacco victory, he recalled his own desperate struggle to "emancipate myself from twenty-five years' slavery to the foul weed." Good people—ministers and other professors of religion—had tried repeatedly and unsuccessfully to abandon tobacco, because of its effect on the nervous system, he wrote. Hence he was amazed that she "achieved so great a victory at your age without a break-down." Her heroic self-sacrificing act was nothing short of a miracle.[30]

In answer to his concerns, she set the record straight. She did not want friends to think she was suffering and panting for her pipe, for she felt no "bodily or mental inconvenience, or depression." Nor was she tempted to smoke. For years, "it was my will and desire to quit smoking," and she longed to give up tobacco. But that alone was not enough. Finally, "I prayed to God that he would make me feel the necessity to give it up, and he did." Since the "Spirit" had spoken, she said, "I have had no taste or appetite" for tobacco. "The dear Lord has filled the part that longed [for tobacco] with his own love and Spirit." She prayed that all smokers could have such an experience. "Sojourner will pray the big prayer of her heart that the love of tobacco may go out of the longing of the people."[31]

III

For six months Sojourner Truth, Susan B. Anthony, and Elizabeth Cady Stanton campaigned in New York for different parties and apparently never crossed paths. At first, the Stanton-Anthony suffragists tried to court both black men and Democrats. At a New York City Union League meeting, Anthony implored black men to adopt a franchise "irrespective of color." The men refused to trust anyone affiliated with Democrats, and called the Republican Party "the least of two evils." One week later, Anthony was a woman's suffrage delegate to the Democratic National Convention, but was not allowed to speak. A man read her letter praising the Democrats as the suffrage party fighting "most valiantly" for "all white men." Continuing to play both sides, Anthony sent a letter in October to the Utica Colored Convention, chaired by Jermain Loguen. "Permit me in behalf of the colored women of the State . . . to urge upon you to extend your demand for the ballot to your wives and daughters—your mothers and sisters." Loguen and a few "friends of woman's suffrage" met bitter opposition when they tried to discuss the letter. The men "almost unanimously" voted to lay the letter on the table.[32] As Sojourner stumped throughout western and central New York for Grant, the freed people, and universal suffrage, by summer's end, Stanton and Anthony had canvassed the state for Seymour.

It has been said that Frederick Douglass considered "woman suffrage agitation itself a betrayal of the ex-slave."[33] While that assessment goes too far, Douglass certainly placed black male suffrage ahead of woman's suffrage in that moment, as did Sojourner Truth, Radical Republicans, and most radical Abolitionists. Nonetheless, after Grant's November victory, many reformers, including a large number of blacks, gathered in Boston to organize for woman's suffrage. While specifically asking Elizabeth Cady Stanton not to attend, the reformers sought endorsement from Mid-Atlantic women. Amy Post and Lucretia Mott refused to go where Elizabeth was unwelcome. Debates were intense. Stone and Blackwell proposed censuring all candidates who were adverse to woman's suffrage. Strongly objecting, Watkins Harper insisted that she "suffered so much in this republic as a Negro," that she could not "fully realize her wrong as a woman." Douglass argued strenuously for black male suffrage, and Senator Henry Wilson insisted that universal suffrage would not pass in Congress. The relentless Abby Kelley Foster, recovering from dangerous surgery, finally won over Lucy Stone. The convention resolved itself into the New England Suffrage Association and endorsed the Republican Party's efforts to obtain black suffrage, even if it placed woman's suffrage on hold. In New York, Stanton and Anthony quickly drafted a petition for a universal suffrage amendment but got few signatures. Stanton angrily wrote her intimate friend and cousin Elizabeth Smith Miller that since her father, Gerrit Smith, had refused to sign the petition, "I am dissecting him in the next *Revolution*."[34]

All blacks, Sojourner Truth included, understood the danger of Stanton and Anthony collaborating with racists, dismissing Southern violence, and putting the political aspirations of middle-class white women ahead of the survival of a people. Few reformers felt the danger of this quagmire more deeply than Josephine Griffing, head of Washington relief efforts for the freed people, but also president of the Washington Woman's Suffrage Association. When Stanton and Anthony called a "National Woman's Suffrage Convention" in Washington in January 1869, Josephine was unsuccessful in soliciting black participants. Douglass spoke for radicals in stating he would deliver no more lectures on woman's suffrage. "I never suspected you of sympathizing with Miss Anthony and Mrs. Stanton in their cause," he wrote Griffing in rebuke. "The conduct of these white women, whose husbands, fathers, and brothers are voters," was selfish: "While the Negro is mobbed, beaten, shot, stabbed, hanged, burnt, and the target of all that is malignant in the North and all that is murderous in the South, his claims may be preferred by me without exposing in any wise myself to the imputation of narrowness or meanness toward the cause of woman. As you very well know, woman has a thousand ways to attach herself to the governing power of the land and already exerts an honorable influence on the cause of legislation."[35] White women were victims of abuse "to be sure," he wrote, but those abuses did not compare with the suffering of his race. The goal of Negro suffrage was not "more sacred" but "more urgent, because it is one of life and death to the long-enslaved people of this country."[36]

Sojourner Truth avoided the contentious New England Suffrage Convention, the Washington Suffrage Convention, and the 1869 anniversary meetings. Wendell Phillips, president of the AASS, refused to attend the AERA's anniversary because Stanton and Anthony had campaigned vigorously in the West against the Fifteenth Amendment. But Douglass refused to give the AERA to the New York suffragists. Although the showdown was steamy, the *Standard* practically ignored it, while the *Revolution* only mentioned that "earnest, eloquent arguments" and "some disagreement" characterized the meeting. But Horace Greeley's *Tribune* covered the proceedings extensively. With Lucretia Mott in bereavement for her husband, Stanton had the chair. She and Anthony moved to transform the AERA into a venue for woman's suffrage, but Douglass argued that the AERA's mission was universal suffrage and equal rights, not woman's rights. Stanton condemned the Fifteenth Amendment and the Republican Party. It was a dark day for the republic, she said, if "our free institutions" were entrusted to every type of male ignorance and vice while the "purifying influences" of the virtuous "educated half of the American people" were ignored. Manhood suffrage "was national suicide, and woman's destruction." Such opposition to black suffrage led Stephen Foster, a member of the Nominating Committee, to oppose Stanton and Anthony as vice presidents.[37]

Tempers flared more the next day as Stanton immediately invoked Train: "God bless him, now and always." Senator Henry Wilson appealed for reason, saying that he, too, advocated woman's suffrage, but it currently was too un-popular among the moderate majority in Congress. The Fifteenth Amendment would facilitate woman's suffrage, he said, and pledged his voice, influence, and vote for a woman's amendment. Douglass proposed a resolution endorsing the Fifteenth Amendment. Stanton, Anthony, and Paulina Wright Davis responded with a wave of racist comments: black men were "exceedingly tyrannical and abusive—much more since they obtained their freedom"; they whipped their wives and robbed them of their young children; black women were much more intelligent than black men because of women's "intimate" relations with white men. All the indignities that Douglass attributed to black men, Stanton and Anthony said, black women suffered as well. Yes, answered Douglass, but black women suffered more because of race than because of womanhood. The meet-ing was in complete chaos. Women should have the right to vote, the *Tribune* said, because they were as disorderly, discourteous, and disorganized as men.[38] For Douglass, it was equivalent to a mobbing.

The convention adjourned without settling anything, and arguments con-tinued the next day at a site in Brooklyn. Douglass, Watkins Harper, and other Fifteenth Amendment advocates attended another meeting that weekend. Un-beknownst to them, after the opposition had left, Stanton and Anthony had noti-fied select people of the Brooklyn meeting that weekend. Stanton and Anthony formed a woman's suffrage organization in the *Revolution* office with about sixty males and females, mostly from the West. The two New Yorkers later called it "national" (National Woman's Suffrage Association); others insisted there was nothing national about it. The *Tribune* always called the group "Miss Anthony's Woman's Suffrage Association."[39]

After the elections, Sojourner Truth returned to Michigan and the Detroit home of Eliza Leggett, where there was much suffrage talk. Sojourner's closest white friends were suffragists, and Susan B. Anthony had recently visited Michigan. Reportedly, Sojourner commented that if white women baited the suffrage hook with a black woman, they would catch a black man. If she said that, she undoubtedly meant that if white suffragists used black women as pawns, black men would suffer. While distancing herself from internal controversy, she publicly campaigned for black male suffrage. In any case, she was roundly welcomed in Detroit and received a host of friends and visitors. One man who read about her "long cold rides" made her a pair of wooden Dutch shoes lined in wool. She was scheduled to speak at the Unitarian Church, and people crowded into the lecture room long before she arrived. "We had to go up into the church & that was soon filled," Eliza Leggett wrote Amy Post. Likewise, Sojourner related happily, "I filled the pulpit for an evening." Reportedly she spoke with "power & gave her testimony with a spirit of wonderful clearness." She discussed the election, her "troubles with the cars," her work among the freed people, and her efforts to advertise "their present conditions as a great tax upon the Government." Sojourner's Detroit visit, Eliza wrote, was "fraught with much comfort" to her family and the community. "She is a Mother in Truth" whose messages to the "children of men" would last, "for they are like apples of gold set in pictures [*sic*] of silver." Sojourner sent Isaac Post $5, which she had borrowed. She asked Amy about a little girl at the train station who had kissed her and given her an orange. Who was she?[40]

While Sojourner was in Detroit, Gerrit Smith sent a correspondence to the Leggett's home labeled "For Sojourner Truth." Years earlier, "the immortal Thomas Clarkson" (the British Abolitionist) had sent Smith a lock of hair to honor his work for the cause of black freedom. Now, in tribute to Sojourner's unflinching commitment, Smith wrote: "Attached to this paper is a single hair from one of those locks." The lock and strand of hair have long since disappeared; the note remains a moving testament of Smith's penitence as a result of her influence and her chastising public letter.[41]

For radical Abolitionists following Perfectionism, the Fifteenth Amendment brought them closer to an earthly peaceable kingdom. Hence, Stanton and Anthony's opposition was a distressing, disheartening moment for woman's suffrage and for long-standing friendships. Whatever motivations one attributes to Stanton and Anthony's behavior, they took a reactionary position on racial equality. In seeking woman's suffrage, they unfortunately became bedfellows with arch racists and condemned black male franchise. The cause of woman,

Lydia Maria Child wrote, "has been wounded in the house of its friends." How could some women want to gain freedom for themselves through "violating the principles of freedom" for others? Sojourner Truth was a woman's rights pioneer with friends in Miss Anthony's Suffrage Association, but her first loyalty was to her oppressed race. She and most radical Abolitionists joined ranks once again, even uniting with Republicans for the sake of "this life and the life to come." In November 1869, while she campaigned in New York, the American Woman's Suffrage Association (AWSA) organized in Cleveland and endorsed the Fifteenth Amendment. Although the impressive delegate roster was made up mostly of a New Englanders, the West and the Mid-Atlantic also sent representatives. Writing apologetically to Amy Post, New Yorker Mary Fenn Davis, wife of the Spiritualist leader, admitted: "My preferences are still strong for the American Suffrage Association."[42]

During Sojourner's fall tour, a rumor circulated that she "was *dying* in Battle Creek." This, Amy Post assured the *Standard*, was *"quite premature in her case."* Sojourner had never been in better health, and her mind was even more "bright and vigorous" than when they had first met in 1851. She was en route to Washington via New York City and New Jersey. She wanted to see the freed people and be on hand for the Fifteenth Amendment's ratification. She also hoped to raise money. Her home was not finished, and she was adrift. "The sum of one thousand dollars will set her free from anxiety and from her mortgage," Amy wrote. "Come friends," she urged, "Let us raise it, remembering her unrequited toil." Most aging Abolitionists had few resources, and the government had not yet paid Josephine Griffing, Laura Haviland, Sojourner Truth, or Harriet Tubman for their work. Unlike Tubman, however, Truth and her white sisters had commissions.[43]

In New York City, *Independent* editor Theodore Tilton and his wife, Elizabeth, hosted Sojourner Truth. She visited with old friends, attended Spiritualist gatherings at the Fox-Underhill home, spoke at Henry Ward Beecher's Plymouth Church, and moved on. "Sojourner Truth is spending a few weeks with friends in Philadelphia," her host, physician Henry Child, wrote in early December. "She is in good health." Friends could write her at his home. Her New Jersey speaking engagements included a talk at the "Plum Street Hall" in the agricultural community of Vineland. Raising her age to "nearly ninety," the *Vineland Weekly* wrote that she had a marvelous "strong and cheerful" voice and a sparkle in her eyes while delivering "a favorite argument or a cutting, withering sarcasm." Speaking on "equality of the races and sexes," she said that before long, her people would be the "salt and pepper" of the country. One day, she prophesied, "black men" would hold prominent political office. Right now, she said, the debt whites owed to her people generated hatred, which was really guilt. It was human nature—"if you owe another anything, it always makes you hate 'em." Merging sacred with secular concerns, she said that God put people on earth and gave them "a living soul" that was able to make the world better. Each person should work for that, especially through agitation, and not depend on others or future generations. She also spoke of her opposition to capital punishment, support for woman's suffrage, and the need for women to speak publicly on their own behalf.[44]

The *Vineland Weekly* attempted to capture her persona. Her "'Truth'-isms," the reporter said, had a funny, homely veneer. "Some of her remarks were the occasion of excessive laughter, because of their quaintness and peculiar originality; her style of delivery." These included "amusing," energetic, and expressive bodily movements and facial contortions. But Sojourner used humor as a critique, especially of white people. Vineland was a progressive commune, but she knew New Jersey—formerly a proslavery, Dutch, copperhead state—was a hard sell on race. She received some of her harshest criticism and rudest treatment in New Jersey. She gave another public lecture at Plum Street Hall the following Sunday morning and then announced a special evening lecture for "the colored people of Vineland." Whites could attend her meeting with blacks if they wished, she said facetiously, as she was "no respecter of color."[45]

That winter, extensive suffrage debates continued, and she certainly joined local meetings in New Jersey, which the pro-Amendment AWSA initiated. She welcomed in the New Year with suffragist friends in New Jersey. "On Saturday, Jan. 1, 1870," suffragist Portia Gage wrote, "our house received a new baptism, through Sojourner Truth. . . . She has been a wonderful teacher to me. I thank my God that I have met Sojourner Truth." State approvals trickled in, and Sojourner waited anxiously in New Jersey for ratification. In Washington, Frederick Douglass and minister Sella Martin had established a newspaper, the *New Era*; Mary Shadd Cary soon joined them as a reporter. Editorials by a "Colored Woman" (certainly Shadd Cary) addressed the split among suffragists and the racism it had unleashed. Black men, said the editorial, had been early woman's rights supporters when "no white man was found with heart large enough." Now, the writer was mortified when Susan B. Anthony spoke "with great bitterness" against black male suffrage. Even white women who once devoted their energies to the oppressed now asked Congress to provide "ways and means for removing the colored people to some place by themselves."[46]

Sojourner was in Washington on March 30, 1870, when secretary of state Hamilton Fish certified the Fifteenth Amendment as ratified. African Americans held a jubilee in every state and territory, giving "thanks to Almighty God and the good people he used as his instruments in bringing about this glorious event." A New York City procession featured portraits of Douglass, Grant, Lincoln, John Brown, and black Senator Hiram Revels. Detroit's "grand celebration" was among the biggest. George De Baptiste publicly resigned as "secretary, treasurer, and general manager of the Underground Railroad." In Baltimore, ten thousand blacks marched in a procession representing African American lodges, firemen, labor groups, cart men, butchers, clubs, soldiers, and the Young Men's Christian Association. Ten thousand more, of "every class and condition," lined the sidewalks. Frederick Douglass, Henry Garnet, John Mercer Langston, Bishop Daniel Payne, and General O. O. Howard rode in carriages as throngs cheered. Washington's black community gathered for a rousing cavalcade of speakers at City Hall. It definitely was the black *man's* hour.[47]

One important lady was "unavoidably left unnoticed," the *New Era* said, because "we were not able to mention all who spoke in front of City Hall in honor of ratification of the Fifteenth Amendment." Therefore, her name "stands at the head of this article" ["Mrs. Sojourner Truth"]. Every informed Northerner or those attending conventions for the last thirty years knew of Sojourner Truth, the reporter noted. But not those south of Mason and Dixon's line. The article mentioned Sojourner's enslavement and long advocacy "in the service of the oppressed." From her "quiet retreat in the town of Battle Creek, Michigan, she has ever and anon issued forth to battle zealously in their behalf." She was as ardent a champion of woman's rights as of abolition, and brought her experience of the former to her activism on the latter. Sympathizing with "this worthy mother in the Israel of reform," the writer hoped that as heaven had permitted her to witness the abolition of slavery, it would prolong her days "to see the removal of sex as a barrier to the enjoyment of political rights." The piece ended by advertising her upcoming lecture.[48]

She remained in Washington, where her time was well spent and her meetings had "quite good attendance." She finally received compensation from General Howard and the bureau and from the relief associations for her twenty-six months' work. Those payments, as well as contributions from friends, enabled her to finish her home and pay off her mortgage. She also met President Grant, who paid $5 for her photograph and wrote his name in her "Book of Life." On one of her visits to the halls of Congress, she received a warm round of applause. Later, numerous legislators, including Hiram Revels (Miss.), "Colored," signed her "Book of Life." Some congressmen added inscriptions indicating the depth and longevity of their friendship with her. The *Battle Creek Weekly Journal* printed an excerpt from a Washington newspaper:

> It was our good fortune to be in the marble room of the Senate chamber, a few days ago, when that old land-mark of the past—the representative of the forever gone age, Sojourner Truth—made her appearance. It was an hour not soon to be forgotten; for it is not often, . . . that we see revered Senators—even him that holds the second chair in the gift of the Republic, vacate their seats in the hall of State, to extend the hand of welcome, ... of praise and substantial blessings. . . . But it was refreshing, as it was strange, to see her who had served in the shackles

ot slavery in the great State of New York for nearly a quarter of a century before a majority of these senators were born, now holding a levee with them in the marble room, where less than a decade ago, she would have been spurned from its outer corridor, by the lowest menial, much less taking the hand of a Senator.[49]

Now she pledged to devote more time to woman's suffrage. "It is her intention to leave here in a few days, as she desires and expects to be in New York City during anniversary week, that she can attend the Woman's Suffrage Meeting, the cause which she is deeply interested in." Stanton and Anthony's new organization was not listed among the anniversary meetings for 1870. Reportedly, Anthony's Woman Suffrage Association was not thriving, and the *Revolution* had folded for lack of subscriptions. But the AWSA's new periodical, the *Woman's Journal*, would have a long successful life and would include news of black women. Anthony, Stanton, and Truth seemingly harbored no ill feelings, despite their differences. To Sojourner's question "Do you want to write your name in de Book of Life?" Elizabeth responded, "I hope, dear Sojourner, that you will be enfranchised before you leave us for the better land. Your true friend, Elizabeth Cady Stanton, New York, May 4, 1870."[50]

The woman's movement changed. Upper-middle-class housewives and financially comfortable women with high professional aspirations replaced the spiritually endowed, selfless, plainly dressed women from the nation's farms and villages. Gay "headgear" with "scarlet feathers" and "forget-me-nots" crowned these women's curled hair; their dresses rustled with layers of taffeta and silk; they wore "dainty thick solid boots," not heavy traveling shoes. Stanton raised eyebrows at the Hartford Woman's Convention in 1869 when she came to the platform attired in a trailing robe of black velvet. Sojourner disapproved of the ornate fashions, and women rigging themselves up in "panniers and Grecian bendbacks and flumineries." Had they forgotten that their sons were "cut off like grass by the war, and the land was covered with their blood." She admitted that she was "awfully hard on dress" and lamented that mothers and "gray-haired grandmothers wear high-heeled shoes and bumps on their heads." Observing the 1870 Woman's Suffrage meeting, she said, "I thought what kind of reformers be you, with goose wings on your head, as if you were going to fly." Lydia Maria Child agreed. Beauty was one thing, and fashion another. Serious women should not go to such "expense and inconvenience" for appearances. No wonder vanity was "universally satirized as a peculiarly female weakness." Nonetheless, Sojourner Truth remained committed to woman's rights. An undated post–Fifteenth Amendment Rochester poster noted, "A free meeting will be held exclusively for women on Tuesday of this week in the City Hall, 4 o'clock. Sojourner Truth and others will speak on subjects of social and pecuniary interests." She also encouraged women to challenge the law. "Dear Sojourner,"

Nanette Gardner wrote from Detroit in 1871, "at your request I record the fact that I succeeded in registering my name in the First Precinct of the Ninth Ward, and on Tuesday, the 4th of April, cast the first vote for a state officer deposited in an American ballot-box by a woman for the last half century." Nanette gave the electors flowers and a poster bearing images similar to those on the old *Liberator* masthead, except the victim was a woman.[51]

After leaving New York City, Sojourner Truth held meetings with Lucretia Mott in New Jersey. "People were very attentive," Lucretia wrote, and thanked them for their talks. "Sojourner did very well. The audience seemed interested in her." After speaking at the Young Men's Christian Union Hall, she went "to labor with the colored people of Jersey."[52] She had a new, more urgent mission in the final decade of her life.

I don't expect I will to live to see it, but when this generation has passed away, there will be a grand change. This colored people is going to be a people. Do you think God has had them robbed and scourged all the days of their lives for nothing? — SOJOURNER TRUTH (1879)

CHAPTER 19

"I Am on My Way to Kansas"

I

Sojourner witnessed the same heart breaking Washington scenes in 1870 she had left in 1867: "able men and women taking dry bread from the government to keep from starving." This, she told a *New York Tribune* reporter, inspired her cause of getting land for her people. They should go out West, "where the land is so plenty," and work for themselves. Back at her former Capitol Street residence, she found Josephine Griffing frail and unwell but hard at work. Freed people still crowded inside to receive cast-off "hats, coats, pants, meat, tea, and coffee, etc," while others waited outside shivering in the cold. At Freedmen's Hospital, Sojourner noted that hundreds of "patients" were actually old, lame, and helpless freed people. The Freedmen's Bureau, before closing down forever, awarded Griffing a final $30,000 appropriation. She purchased daily seven hundred loaves of bread, which barely staved off hunger among the able-bodied while the sick could not consume such coarse rations, and continued to starve. Sojourner joined many reformers who deplored these wretched conditions.[1]

Walking around Washington, she compared the richness of the imposing edifices to the destitute black faces around her. "We helped to pay this cost," she stated. "We have been a source of wealth to this republic." Black people labored in the cotton fields that created the cities, manufactures, and employment for white people. "Beneath the burning southern sun have we toiled . . . earning millions in money. . . . Our nerves and sinews, our tears and blood, have been sacrificed." Freed people, she told an audience, had earned "land enough for white people . . . to be entitled to a small farm apiece themselves."[2]

Land, she said, was her people's entitlement and the key to their economic independence, industry, and mobility. Black Southerners were born and bred to the soil; they loved the land as they loved family connections. Since unpaid black labor was the stepping-stone to white financial success, surely, she said, "some of these dividends must be ours." She was not the only one who thought so. When Republicans first insisted "If we give the Negro a bayonet, why can't we not give him a ballot?" reformers added, "Why can we not first grant him a little place of his own?" Wendell Phillips and Frederick Douglass once advocated land along with the ballot. And in 1867, Radical congressman Thaddeus Stevens had proposed dividing Southern lands into 40-acre plots for purchase by each liberated male or family head, and providing money to build a dwelling. This would not only nourish "the happiness and respectability of the colored race, but their very existence." Homesteads, he added, "to them are far more valuable than the immediate right of suffrage, though both are their due." Congress would not tamper with property rights, but public lands offered another possibility. After Stevens's death, Radical congressman George W. Julian fought successfully to reserve hundreds of thousands of acreage for settler occupation, and black congressman Benjamin Turner proposed establishing a land commission on behalf of landless freed people. Gerrit Smith and three hundred other reformers also sent a petition to the Forty-first Congress supporting the idea. This commission would be made up of disinterested friends of the freed people and would appoint agents to consult with black leaders and associations in the selection and purchase of homestead lands worth $2 million. The commission would retain title until, by installments, the freed people paid back the government.[3]

This idea created a controversy. Powerful Horace Greeley insisted that blacks take advantage of public lands only on their own: "Better tell them at once. . . . Root, hog! Or die!" *Standard* editor Aaron Powell spoke for other reformers in reminding Greeley of rural freed people's unusual circumstances and disabilities. After years of unpaid toil, they had been suddenly emancipated amid a hostile community that cheated them out of their wages and denied them redress. How could freed people travel to public land? Who would pay the "railroad fare and supply their food for the journey—not to mention tools and outfit?" Without a land commission, the disabilities wrought by Andrew Johnson's land policies, the dismantling of the Freedmen's Bureau, and the rise of the Ku-Klux Klan left freed people vulnerable and Reconstruction unfinished. Even personal and political freedom was a cruel mockery instead of a blessing. Powell was amazed that Greeley, "an old-time antislavery man," hastened to give pecuniary aid to Jeff Davis, "the prince of negro-hating rebels" but said coldly to "loyal, brave, landless" black men of the South "'Root hog! Or die!'"[4]

Although black leaders and Radical politicians abandoned the land issue for civil rights, Sojourner Truth stayed the course, speaking about land even as she campaigned for the Fifteenth Amendment. She told District officials and Radical legislators in Washington that blacks had as much right to unoccupied territory as railroads and Indians. Instead of employing people to dole out relief or hiring officials to capture, convict, and punish women and children, why not give them an opportunity for advancement? Men in high places "heard her patiently" but manifested no enthusiasm. She "regretted, now, as ever, that women had no political rights under the government." She noted the contrast between indifferent men with legislative power and the many women working with freed people all over the South. She believed that women would have gladly acquiesced in the land endeavor. She thought of influencing "the head and heart of the government," or rather half of it, since women could not vote. Whatever else was denied to woman, Sojourner said, she always had the right to "stand on praying ground" and to petition; legislators agreed to do whatever "the people" bid them. Hence Sojourner's new calling was a campaign for land for the freed people in the Washington area. "Instead of going home from Washington to take rest," she said, "I am traveling," and taking the issue "before the people."[5]

In early February 1870, she made a brief jaunt to New England. There was no better bully pulpit from which to launch her petition plans than this center of radical reform. Old friends greeted her warmly, and the New England churches that once shunned her now welcomed her. In Providence, she spoke to large and appreciative church audiences. In Fall River, her host was an old friend, prominent Quaker activist and former underground conductor Robert Adams. He arranged speaking engagements at several churches, where she expressed the urgency of relocating Washington-area freed people onto the government's western lands. She also criticized African colonization schemes. Why send American citizens to Africa? she asked. "This colony can just as well be in this country as in Liberia." That, she said, is what "I am contending in my old age." Moving on to her beloved Northampton, she met with old Community and town friends. Samuel Hill, a former teacher and school superintendent, probably wrote her petition, which was first read at a Northampton church meeting:

> To the Senate and House of Representatives, in Congress assembled:—
> "Whereas, From the faithful and earnest representations of Sojourner Truth (who has personally investigated the matter), we believe that the freed colored people in and about Washington, dependent upon government for support, would

be greatly benefited and might become useful citizens by being placed in a position to support themselves: We, the undersigned, therefore earnestly request your honorable body to set apart for them a portion of the public land in the West, and erect buildings thereon for the aged and infirm, and otherwise legislate so as to secure the desired result.[6]

The money spent on handouts, she said, could subsidize an experiment in independence that should include educational facilities; temporary housing; assistance in purchasing tools, livestock, seed, and so on. Freed people could not rise amid Southern white terrorism and political corruption; they needed self-contained communities with their own systems of governance, cooperation, and independent land ownership. Although she rejected expatriation and had lived in integrated settings throughout her years of freedom, she now embraced separatism as the most viable means of black progress in the wake of virulent racism.[7]

She printed fifty petitions with her own money and gave them to trusted friends. After securing signatures, a point person in each state would forward them on to Congress. Throughout 1870, she traveled and preached about her people's plight. When invited to speak to the AWSA in Boston, she interspersed her rousing suffrage speech with calls for land and education for Washington's freed people. Later during the convention, the audience wanted "Sojourner's voice" again. Moderator Paulina Davis acquiesced, but asked her to speak "briefly." This annoyed the veteran activist. Rising and coming forward, she said she "spoke when the spirit moved her—not when the people moved her." And when "limited to a few minutes," the people moved her. Women, she said, needed their rights for the entire world, not just for themselves alone. Woman's rights was part of a human rights struggle, in her eyes. After speaking on behalf of women, she again turned to the question that lay near her heart: "the condition of the poor colored people around Washington." She discussed her petition, asked for signatures, and concluded "that she would stop before she was stopped."[8]

At Boston's Woman's Suffrage Bazaar, she had no platform, but "movings of the spirit" inspired her to speak about her great mission. She stated her case and vowed to "send tons of paper down to Washington for them spouters to chaw on." She lamented that woman could not vote, for she had great faith in women bringing change. For even in biblical times, women had stood for right and truth. Yet she also hailed the great changes had happened in the last few years. "And solacing herself with this reflection, the old heroine retired to admire the beautiful bouquets in the flower department of the Fair."[9]

She also appealed independently to her own "colored people." She met with blacks in Vineland and Orange, New Jersey, and urged them to help. She gave a "thrilling" talk at Leonard Grimes's Twelfth Street Baptist Church in Boston.

Reportedly, her speech was "unique, witty, pathetic, sensible and . . . delivered with a voice that, in volume and tone, was equally remarkable and striking." Afterward, Pastor Grimes reinforced her concerns. In Pennsylvania, she spoke in the Quaker meetings and white Methodist churches. She also tried to "induce the colored people who are in better circumstances, to help further the interests of those less fortunate." Whether speaking to black or white audiences in Pennsylvania, she attracted large attendance and garnered encouraging receptions. "Old Sojourner Truth was here last Thursday night and preached a great sermon in the Methodist Church," one account noted. "A tremendous crowd assembled to hear and see her, and were all pleased with her address and the manner in which it was delivered."[10]

George Scarborough heard Sojourner when she was in Vineland and wrote his sister, Olive Gilbert. Amy Post facilitated a correspondence between Truth and Gilbert. To Olive, Sojourner related her continued reflections about her son Peter. She had accepted his death, and her mind regarding him was finally "set at rest." Sojourner and Olive had been out of touch for many years; two sojourners, Olive said, moving around "as easily as soap bubbles—now here— now there—making our mark, I suppose, everywhere." Her own mark, Olive said, was minute compared to Sojourner's. "I get a glimpse of you often through the papers, which falls upon my spirit like bright rays of the sun," Olive wrote. Even the minister of the little chapel where Gilbert worshipped had, the previous Sunday, invoked something that "'Sojourner Truth said.'" When the two old friends had made that "little book . . . years ago," Olive wrote, neither had suspected that Sojourner Truth was "laying the foundation of such an almost world-wide reputation."[11]

From 1870 to the spring of 1871, Sojourner held meetings and visited friends in the East. Popular orator Anna Dickinson helped her procure more photographs. Selling these and the collections taken at meetings sustained and supported her travels, as she kept the freed people's plight before her audiences. "I found Sojourner Truth at Rockledge for a visitation," Garrison Jr. wrote to his wife, Ellen. She was on a "lecturing and preaching" mission. "She is a remarkable woman, very bright and smart." Helen Garrison had suffered a paralytic stroke in 1863 and was an invalid. The Sojourner's companionship and nursing skills enlivened her old friend's days and relieved the other Garrisons from their round-the-clock nursing duties. In the fall of 1870, she returned to Providence. "The venerable Sojourner Truth . . . is now visiting in this city," the *Providence Journal* reported. "She would be happy to see friends" and "particularly pleased to have an interview with any of the clergy who feel disposed." Returning to the Boston area, she visited old Methodist friends, including the Gale family and soon-to-be bishop Gilbert Haven, who strongly supported her black homeland proposal. Southern whites' "hearts are hardened toward those for whom God has wrought such a great deliverance," Haven preached. So long as the yoke remained around black peoples' necks, the nation remained "cursed with a curse" that prevented black advancement. He publicized Sojourner's campaign in *Zion's Herald* and supervised the collecting of the Massachusetts petitions and their forwarding to Congress. Sojourner spent the Christmas holidays with the Havens, where they had "a big time."[12]

On January 1, 1871, reformers, Republicans, and the curious gathered at Tremont Temple for a celebration of the Emancipation Proclamation's eighth anniversary, sponsored by the National Temperance Association for the Spread of Temperance and Night Schools among the Freed People of the South. Eloquent speeches and inspiring singing filled the program. William Wells Brown, president of the association, ministers R. A. Grimes, J. D. Fulton, and Gilbert Haven, and Sojourner Truth headed the list of speakers. While Fulton spoke, the audience showed more interest in the rustling heard behind him: Sojourner Truth, whom many in the audience had come to see, had entered the hall on the arm of Haven. When Fulton saw her, he said, "Now, Aunty, you take this easy chair," which gave rise to a burst of unexplained laughter that even annoyed Fulton. Sojourner was more displeased with his condescension toward her, which had invited the audience's laughter. "Now Mr. Fulton stop that," she quipped in annoyance. After Fulton finished, Haven spoke. Being on the program after the king and before the queen of the platform, Haven said, he would soon "get out of the way." He briefly addressed the benefits of emancipation and the need for black education and for temperance; he also insisted that the freed people needed homes and land. On that, he said, "I shall let my good friend chiefly dwell." At least one Boston newspaper represented Sojourner's words in barely comprehensible dialect, while another reported her words in Standard English. The duality of this local press coverage reveals the continued caricaturing of Sojourner Truth—encouraging a dismissive attitude toward her appeal and exemplifying the prevalence of Northern racism. However, both accounts related that she received warm applause.[13]

Dual representation followed her. The New Jersey legislature, which, like California's, refused to ratify the Fifteenth Amendment, nonetheless gave her a standing ovation when she visited their chambers. However, the press of Springfield, New Jersey, ridiculed her: "That lively old negro mummy, whose age ranges among the hundreds," had spoken on "copperhead Jersey, hypocrites, freemen, woman's rights, etc." in the Presbyterian church. Many had left while she spoke, the account said; others interrupted and booed her. "She is a crazy, ignorant, repelling negress, and her guardians would do a Christian act to restrict her entirely to private life." This report embarrassed another correspondent. Sadly, he wrote, many people in his "small benighted corner" lacked good breeding, had such "Lilliputian minds," and were "so ignorant a people they knew not they had a great guest," and many "had not even heard of Sojourner Truth." No wonder people stigmatized the state of New Jersey.[14] Yet neither white hostility nor unpopularity deterred the Sojourner.

She received providential encouragement when Battle Creek friends forwarded a letter to her from Byron S. Smith, the land agent in Topeka, Kansas. She had never met Smith, and he knew her only by reputation. But on hearing about her proposal, he had been induced to write. "I venerate and love so your character," he wrote, that he earnestly requested that she "make our town a visit" and make his home her home as long as she liked. He would send her railroad fare and money for her additional expenses. She had been in Kansas many years before. It was a long journey for an elderly missionary in precarious health, and many Abolitionist friends were fast joining the world of spirits. Nonetheless, she surmised that it was God's will that she go. Why else would a man "she had never seen or heard of" invite her to Kansas and pay her expenses? She summoned her grandson Sammy Banks, then in Ohio; he joined her early in 1871.[15]

II

Samuel Hill arranged another round of Northampton talks, after which Sojourner and Sammy went to Rhode Island and then Hopedale and Springfield, Massachusetts. They traveled slowly because of Sojourner's health and because she spoke along the way. They stopped in New York City and reached central New York in mid-March. While lecturing in Syracuse, she contacted Gerrit Smith. She had been in New England, she informed Smith, "and am now on my way to Kansas." She wanted to have a meeting in Peterboro and lodge with the Smiths. She needed no assistance this time, she said. "My grandson is with me." They only needed directions to Smith's home from the depot. "I may never come this way again," the seventy-five-year-old Sojourner concluded.[16] When she did travel that way again, Smith had departed earthly life.

She spoke in Courtland [sic], Peterboro, Elmira, and other small towns. She took the water cure in Elmira, where Mark Twain's wife, Lillian, had a summer home. Perhaps on this visit she secured the famous writer and humorist's signature for her "Book of Life." Moving on to western New York, her Methodist friend minister Daniel Steele of Genesee College blessed her "divine mission." Sojourner Truth, Steele wrote, was a "Mother in Israel" and one of God's anointed whose spiritual power was "greater than that which resides in thrones and scepters." She met with Frederick Douglass in Rochester, but he was not interested in her ideas. Removing blacks from the South would undermine the current Republican political base, and Douglass was now engrossed in the party. He also viewed integration as the only path to black progress, and he anxiously awaited passage of a civil rights bill outlawing segregation throughout the land. Although Truth had always embraced racial integration, the reality of freed Southerners' daily lives pushed her toward separation. Nonetheless, Douglass's entry in her "Book of Life" was a tribute. He applauded her efforts to "lift up the oppressed, and smooth the path of the lowly." But he neither encouraged nor endorsed any type of relocation.[17]

Truth and Douglass were at a true ideological parting of ways. Douglass, a member of the Northern black middle class, wanted his race to reap social and political benefits from Reconstruction. Truth, who had fought for those goals as well, now focused on economic justice for the suffering black poor, and she remained deeply troubled by women's exclusion from the franchise. With her simple and practical yet insightful perspective, she understood that America's race problem was more structural than social and political. In that sense, her vision was wiser, more forward-looking, and collective than that of leaders such as Douglass. She hoped to awaken the North to the plight of at least one segment of the Southern masses. She received more cooperation from whites than from middle-class blacks.

She remained in western New York for two months, talking to people and vowing to "stir 'em up." On one occasion, when she had a thin audience, she reportedly became testy and excited. A Democratic newspaper compared her to "Dinah in 'Uncle Tom's Cabin,'" stating that she wore a handkerchief in the tradition of a Southern mammy. Despite her "extreme age," the account said, her strong voice had no shrillness, and she paced the platform as hale and hearty as a person of half her age. The reporter presented her expressions in dialect, but also captured the pith, spice and sauciness of her language. She walked about with excited energy, gesticulating and rocking back and forth while speaking in a deep and clear but agitated manner. Why, she demanded satirically, were people in the audience asking *her* what do? "Do you want a poor old creeter who do' no how to read to tell educated people what to do? I give you de hint, and you ought to know what do. But if you don't, I kin tell you. De government hab given land to de railroads in de West; can't it do as much for these poor creeters? Let 'em give 'em land and an outset and hab teachers learn 'em to read. Den they can be somebody. Dat's what I want. You owe it to dem, because you took away from dem all dey earned and made 'em what they are. You take no interest in de colored people." Sojourner tweaked her friend Anna Dickinson (insisting she meant no disrespect): if Dickinson came to Rochester to talk about a woman people knew nothing about (Joan of Arc), they would fill the hall. People were willing to "hear nonsense," while Sojourner came "to tell something which you ought to listen to." Whites also eagerly aided people in foreign lands but cared nothing for destitute people in America. Whites had the power to make things right or leave them wrong, she said. She urged them to sign her petitions and for some "good man" to come forward and take them to Washington. "Let de freedmen be emptied out in de West; gib 'em land an' an outset; teach 'em to read, an' den dey will be somebody. Dat's what I want to say."[18]

Not all Rochester papers were condescending. Sojourner, wrote the *Evening Express*, spoke to crowded audiences in Corinthian Hall, Lyceum Hall, and some churches. "An audience that more than filled the Asbury M.E. [Methodist Episcopal] Church gathered last evening to hear that well-known and remarkable colored woman, Sojourner Truth." Daintily dressed ladies with brightly hued bonnets and ribbons filled the church and listened eagerly to "the colored prophetess." She had a great fund of information, especially regarding her race and the conduct of whites toward blacks. She does not rant, the reporter noted, "but is as clear in her statements as though she had been trained in the severest of rhetorical schools." She was shrewd and businesslike, but also had the "imagination of her race, reminding us too sometimes of the old Hebrew seers and prophetesses." She said, in a matter-of-fact manner, that she had seen God. She chided the audience about coming out "to see an old body who has been many years on earth—a slave for years and free forty years." It was singular, she observed, "that white people which brutalized the black people should come out to hear me speak. I have not language to express what I know. . . . I have been robbed of every God-given right." She related her life in slavery and movingly spoke of her spiritual transformation, interspersing her remarks with both pungent criticism of whites and earnest appeals to them on behalf of western homesteads for blacks. Her "natural powers of observation, discrimination, comparison, and intuition," the *Evening Express* wrote, were "only equaled by her straightforward common sense and earnest practical benevolence." She could inspire, sadden, edify, entertain, and even amuse without frivolity. The church pastor was arranging another meeting. All citizens of the community "would do well to be present."[19]

After being away for two years, Michigan's most popular citizen returned in the summer of 1871. In Saginaw she filled the Methodist church and, although she had been ill, gave a powerful talk. She spoke of her confrontations with Maryland slaveholders and how she saw her people "lift up their heads at last when they saw I wasn't afraid." And then, she added, "You never heard such singing as these poor critters did sing." She spoke of how the war had brought out more Northern impostors than the world had ever seen. "Ministers that never preached a sermon in their life, doctors who feel the pulse with gloves on, and never doctored so much as a dog before, but they was good enough to preach to or doctor the contraband, and get $100 a month from the government." Her people had been freed "by blood," and kept lazy by bread handouts from the Bureau and reformers who sent boxes of clothes. Time was out for that, but the government still owed her people, who remained in slavery. The government should set apart a domain for the freed people where they could become useful instead of a burden—"where they could be a people, honored and respected by all the people, and by themselves." Sammy read letters from Kansas residents inviting Sojourner to their state. She closed the meeting by selling her photos and singing her old antebellum hymn "I am pleading for my people."[20]

In Detroit, she used Nanette Gardner's home as her base, where friends and well-wishers came to visit, hear her travel anecdotes, admire the testimonials in her "Book of Life," and listen to her pleadings for the poor. Sojourner, as well as Susan B. Anthony, was a special guest among Detroit suffragists; they gathered to celebrate what reportedly was the first time Michigan women (Gardner in Detroit and Mary Wilson in Battle Creek) had cast a vote. Sojourner held interviews and discussed such topics as the "New Departure" (a political movement), religion, temperance, Horace Greeley, woman suffrage, and the freed people. "She is in most respects a radical," the *Detroit Post* said. The perennial age question arose repeatedly, to her great aggravation. It never went away, and people would not believe she was a mere seventy-five. She sometimes humorously embellished her age but also answered with double entendres. The Unitarian lecture room could not hold her audiences, so she spoke in the church sanctuary. Afterward people crowded around her asking further questions and signing her petitions. Her old friend, Charles Foote, chaplain of the House of Corrections, would collect the petitions and send them to Washington.[21]

III

In August Sojourner and Sammy reached Battle Creek, where the family had all relocated. Sophia and Thomas Schuyler lived at Sojourner's Harmonia property with their children—Wesley, Fannie, Sojourner, and Edward. Diana and Jacob Corbin lived in Battle Creek with their son Jake and Diana's oldest son James, the disabled veteran. Elizabeth and William Boyd, along with their son Willie, lived at Sojourner's College Street home. Although the worldly matriarch's unschooled daughters did not seem to have their mother's enterprising spirit, she gloried in her family, especially her eight grandchildren. Family provided a comfortable retreat after her travels. The College Street house was reportedly a tidy, "cozy little home," with sunny windows and flowers gracing the yard. Grandmother Sojourner always returned with a wealth of stories and fond regards from friends in various regions; she had met another president, been honored in the halls of Congress, and been scoured as well as lauded by the press. The local black community, including many Sojourner had helped to relocate, was also glad to see her.[22] It must have been quite a homecoming.

However, the two travelers took only a short rest. Sojourner's close companions Phebe Merritt and her daughter Phebe Merritt Stickney had both died in 1870. Frances Titus, founder of the Battle Creek Suffrage Association and ardent Stanton follower, became Sojourner's confidant and correspondent; she arranged Sojourner's itinerary and contacted her western network. Sojourner's Kalamazoo friend Mrs. A. Montague organized her talk at the Congregational Church; Laura Haviland and Thomas Chandler arranged lectures in Adrian and Raisin, Michigan. In Monroe, Wisconsin, Sojourner and Sammy were guests of Frances Titus's sister, Mrs. D. H. Morgan, who had known Sojourner since 1851. "Sojourner came to our house on her way to Kansas and held several very excellent meetings in this county," Mrs. Morgan wrote Mary Gale. Don't worry about Sojourner's health and comfort, Mrs. Morgan assured. She was in good hands. "Her grandson is with her and takes the best care of her."[23]

Sojourner and Sammy reached Kansas in late September. In Lawrence, Sojourner had an emotional reunion with the Benson family, and then moved on with Sammy to Topeka as guests of Byron Smith. Throughout the winter, she lectured in the old "bleeding Kansas" territory—Topeka, Lawrence, Wyandotte, and Leavenworth. In spring 1872, she visited the Dugdales, and spoke to her Quaker Abolitionist friends in Mt. Pleasant, Iowa. Before heading North again, she and Sammy made their first trip to the old "border ruffian" center—Kansas City, Missouri. En route back to Michigan that summer, they were hosted in Illinois, where she spoke at the Methodist ministers' Conference. She was also welcomed in Indiana. Sammy returned to Ohio, and she continued on to Battle Creek alone, elated by her reception during her trip and the scrolls of signatures on her petitions.[24]

It was an election year, and she prepared to campaign vigorously. She also arrived home just in time for the joyous thirty-ninth anniversary celebration of West Indian Emancipation. Two of Sojourner's sons-in-law, Jacob Corbin and Thomas Schuyler, were active in Republican Clubs and helped organize local blacks. "Colored people of Battle Creek" gathered at beautiful St. Mary's Lake for recreational activities—singing by Jacob's quartet, a grand picnic, boating, "swinging down the lane,' &c." A local black activist gave the Emancipation oration, "followed by 'Aunt Sojourner Truth' and others." She held forth on her favorite topics—woman's suffrage, Washington politics, and especially the freed people. She brought her audience up to date on her petitions and her plans to present them to Congress. Republicans were blacks' only hope, and she traveled around Michigan urging people to vote for Grant. She was a popular attraction. At the Hillsdale Courthouse, the audience was so immense that only half the people could get seats and "hundreds went away without even gaining admittance." Despite Grant's conservatism and the corruption in his administration, she said, as people "applauded and cheered," the alternative was Horace Greeley, a traitor running as a Democrat. Even more egregious for Sojourner, *Independent* editor Theodore Tilton, once her dear friend, was Greeley's campaign manager. She vowed that if Greeley won, she would move to Canada. She also followed the advice she had given the suffragists and challenged the law by attempting to vote. Going in person to the Battle Creek Board of Registration, she demanded to enter her name on the list. Unlike other Michigan suffragists, she was not only black, she could not write. Nevertheless, she appeared on Election Day and used "many original and quaintly put arguments" in asserting her right to vote. She was politely refused, but she said she learned one thing from the experience. She had always believed that an actual "pole" designated a polling place. In asking bystanders for the "pole's" whereabouts, she was surprised to discover that male voters had not been deceiving her—there was no actual "pole."[25]

She took her petitions everywhere she spoke—in black and white churches and in open-air meetings in Detroit, Grand Rapids, Kalamazoo, Saginaw, Ann Arbor, Adrian, and elsewhere. She had the rare experience of extended time with her family and at her home. Her presidential candidate won, and she rested that winter. But in the spring of 1873, she began her work again. Sojourner earnestly believed in the power of the people. On her short northern Michigan trips, she helped local people in Detroit and Grand Rapids organize the Colored Woman's Christian Temperance Union and the Order of the Eastern Star.[26]

She spent the spring around Detroit, gathering signatures, and often stayed with the Leggetts. One night, after she had spoken with "unusual power," family members gathered around the kitchen stove, enraptured by her presence and stories. During the war, Eliza's daughter, Augusta (Gussie) Leggett Pease, had worked tirelessly with her mother and Sojourner on behalf of the freed people. Sitting around the stove, Gussie could not help but draw the attention of her "Uncle Lew" to Sojourner's image against the light. "Scrupulously tidy & clean," with nothing out of place, Sojourner Truth sat in a "great straight back chair, her elbows resting on her knees and her long arms stretched out with the closed hard knotty hands," revealing one stump of a finger. Gussie thought Sojourner was a painter's vision. The red of her underjacket gave just "a bit of bright color" to her dark waterproof dress with its sleeves turned back from the wrist. "Her head is small," and covered with a white turban, but her "dress about the neck is very like the Quaker dress—the white under handkerchief, the second small silk shawl & the outer casimere . . . always plain . . . generally the gift of some Quaker friend." The long white apron Lucretia Mott had given her completed Sojourner's dress. She talked forcefully about Washington, sometimes digressing but always returning to her original point. "Oh my Lord," Sojourner said, "I wish you could have seen what I saw." Her eyes, Gussie said, "have a keen glitter when she is in earnest, that shine into your intelligence like the light of a soul that can fire up the whole spiritual part of your own." She told the story of one sick old man's plight that captured her soul. He had on a pair of shoes, apparently his first pair ever. "'Oh he said, do let me keep my shoes,'" as he was taken in the ambulance to the hospital. "'Go on said the man. Never mind your shoes.' . . . and the old man tottered into the room. . . . and begged for his shoes." They put him in the tub, Sojourner said, "and he died in the tub. Poor old man actually died in the tub." Sojourner's voice had to be heard, Gussie wrote—from her intense indignant anger to cadences of disgust, and the melting tender pathos in describing the poor man's plea. "One would not believe the voice emanated from the same person." Sojourner thought her plan was so easy—setting aside a few thousand acres, putting up buildings for schools and homes so people could be self-sustaining. She thought it strange that Congress was so reluctant.[27]

Sojourner's pace of life proved unhealthy, and she soon became very ill, which cut off her cash flow. She contacted Amy Post. "Dear Sister," Sojourner pleaded, "I write to you to get a little money. I am hard up. I don't want to mortgage my house because I can't pay it again." If Amy sent money "right off," Sojourner said, she would pay it back directly. The income from her invited lectures, photos, and collections should have made her comfortable, but she was obviously subsidizing her large family. Despite lameness, leg ulcers, and stomach problems, she "did not give up any time to be sick," Frances Titus wrote Mary Gale. By September Sojourner "felt quite like herself again," and walked a mile to see me," Frances wrote. Sojourner prepared to lecture in Wisconsin, republish her *Narrative* and take her petitions to Congress.[28]

In the spring of 1874, Sojourner and Sammy went to Washington. The Bureau was gone, and so was Sojourner's dear collaborator Josephine Griffing. A victim of her commitment to social justice, Griffing had died of tuberculosis in 1872, after a long illness. Sojourner rejoiced that her trusted companion had fought the good fight, hastened the day of Jubilee, and sacrificed her life for the homeless, impoverished, and penniless. There would have been no Freedmen's Bureau without Josephine Griffing, Garrison wrote, and Sojourner hoped to take Griffing's work to another level. Sojourner had corresponded with General Howard, and he had contacted Massachusetts congressman Benjamin F. Butler, who was presenting a proposal to Congress for a disabled soldiers' asylum. "It struck me," Howard wrote Butler, that "an experiment in the direction that Sojourner indicates," could be tied to the asylum project. Otherwise, Howard said, it would be "hard to steer clear of very serious objections" to perceived benevolence. But the "Christian General" admitted that he actually had not given the matter "much thought" or consultation.[29]

In Washington, as Sojourner sat observing court proceedings, a *National Republican* reporter approached and asked if she was Sojourner Truth. When she answered affirmatively, he began peppering her with questions. She interrupted him, pushed her petition in his face, and asked him to read and sign it. That was the price of an interview. She then invited the reporter back to her "pleasant quarters," where she threw off her "odd little bonnet" and offered him a chair. Then, the reporter wrote, began a conversation, "the life and animation of which will defy the honest competition of the best female talker in the city." She began with her life in slavery; then held forth on the topic for which she was so well known in Washington—"angel of mercy" among the freed people. The reporter wanted to know Sojourner's age. "Bless you Chile, I don't tell my age," said the cagey Sojourner. "I'se looking out for a good chance to marry." She told him about meeting "a nice looking old man" during her audition with President Grant. She and the reporter also spoke of Lincoln. It was a most interesting interview, and later the reporter heard her lecture in the Congregational Church. First, she spoke on behalf of the freed people, and her grandson read her petition. Then she spoke on behalf of women. "God grant that it may come to pass in my day, that women will have the same rights as men." In concluding, she thanked the audience and urged them to do as she did: "talk not for this world, but for the life which is to come, and I trust that you will never regret that you heard poor Sojourner Truth."[30]

Benjamin Butler was up for reelection and was House manager of the Civil Rights Bill. Senator Charles Sumner's dying wish had been that it pass. Sojourner Truth sat in galleries crowded with proud black people whose black representatives recounted personal experiences with racism and their people's contributions from antiquity to the present. She continued campaigning, waiting for Butler to bring her petition to the floor. Butler and the Republicans suffered a resounding defeat at the polls in 1874, but passed the Civil Rights Bill in early 1875. That bill "crowded mine out," Sojourner Truth lamented; "it was never heard of after, and did the black man no good." Indeed, one "colored man" told her in 1879, "'That 'ere civil rights bill killed a great many niggers.'"[31]

Sojourner Truth experienced a far worse personal tragedy. Sammy became very ill, and they left for Battle Creek in the fall of 1874 while she was lobbying for her petitions. Sammy's diagnosis was an "aneurism of the sub-clavian artery," which became progressively worse. In December, two noted Battle Creek doctors performed the "difficult and delicate surgery" and waited. Although doctors deemed the operation a "success," Sammy suffered repeated hemorrhages and died on February 24, 1875, at age twenty-three. This popular youth, known for "kindness of heart and pleasant manners," bore his illness with "unexampled patience and fortitude." But his grandmother was devastated, and in the language of David exclaimed "'Would to God I had died for thee.'" She had raised Sammy; his death in the prime of life and the failure of her homeland proposal made the loss even more tragic and mocking. For eight years, she had pleaded, cajoled, and traveled on behalf of the freed people, often with Sammy's assistance. Yet the Washington freed people were no better off. Emotional pain, disappointment, and mourning hastened her physical deterioration. Reports came from Battle Creek that she was very ill and not expected to live. She apparently had a stroke. "I was paralyzed," she said later. "This whole right side, clear up to the top of my head. It closed this eye, and it is rather weak now." Parker Pillsbury was in Battle Creek and wrote that she was "paralyzed with a dreadful ulcer on her leg extending nearly along the whole calf!" Indeed, her ulcerated leg had no flesh and was so gangrened that "two or three women fainted away to see it." But Sojourner was bound to the advice she had once given Eliza Leggett when her son Percy had died—live on and continue the work. Again friends came to Sojourner's rescue. Condolences and contributions poured in. James Boyle, who owned the plates of the *Narrative,* gave them to her. Frances Titus arranged and subsidized its printing, along with one volume of Sojourner's "Book of Life." Such wellsprings of generosity and concern were balms for the aged African Dutch mystic, and she slowly recovered. She had expected to "die while my name was up"; but apparently God was not finished with her.[32]

In January 1876, she contacted William Still, her old friend from abolition and underground days. Her fourteen-year-old grandson Willie wrote for her, and she asked Still to "please excuse" any mistakes. She would be at the Centennial Exhibition in May with a new edition of her book and wanted to lodge with the Stills. Sojourner owed Mrs. Titus for printing the *Narrative*; she had paid all of Sammy's medical and burial expenses and even mortgaged her little house. She could not "travel and browse about" as before and needed to sell books quickly. Moreover, she badly wanted to see Still and other old friends. Since her grandson Willie would accompany her and "do my writing and reading," she would be no bother. In addition, Mrs. Titus was coming, but would "provide a place for herself. She is an excellent woman."[33]

When the time came, Sojourner was too ill to travel. Still wrote a newspaper article entitled "Sojourner Truth. Her Death and Her Strange Career—Some Very Interesting Reminiscences." He referred to the famous Truth-Douglass confrontation, noting that the audience sympathized with the "the poor old ignorant woman" rather than with the "renowned orator." None present, wrote Still (who was not there) would ever forget the occasion. He went on to call Truth "a strangely made creature." But he underscored her influence on the Abolitionist movement and among the freed people and her friendships with "many of the best and purest men" throughout the country. The remainder of his article came directly from her *Narrative* and the long letter she had sent him. "She is now," Still concluded, "beyond the region of earthly wants and is freed from all care."[34]

Capitalizing on this rumor, Lucy Stone also published an obituary in the *Woman's Journal*; Rowland Johnson publicized her death in New Jersey newspapers after supposedly reading about it in "a dozen" others. "It is not true that

I am dead," Sojourner informed him; she supposed that the only way to quell gossip of her dying was to "get out and lecture on my living." In 1877, with her health much improved and Frances as a companion, she began lectures that were as much a book tour as anything else. With a shameless exaggerated version of her later life, published and copyrighted by Frances, she held a flurry of meetings in Kalamazoo, Adrian, Coldwater, Jackson, Ann Arbor, Detroit, and Grand Rapids, Michigan. Then, in 1878, she and Titus visited Ohio before heading to Rochester for the woman's rights convention. They were the guests of the Posts for some time, and Sojourner gave several lectures and visited old friends in central New York. At the Women's Convention she supported women's rights, but also chastised her sisters. Women, Sojourner admonished, "should be something better than toys." The great stumbling blocks among her sisters were "vanity and pride." In the fall of 1878, she and Frances headed for New York City, as guests of Mrs. Daniel Underhill (one of the Fox sisters). One press account noted that Sojourner walked gracefully and nimbly down two flights of stairs; she moved slowly, but was as tall, straight, and erect as ever. The reporter represented her language in Southern dialect but admitted that she spoke in a different way from "southern Negroes." She lectured at the Brooklyn Congregational Church and twice at Cooper Union. She spoke to a "somewhat motley and curious gathering" at St. Mark's (Colored) Episcopal Church. Every Thursday, the wealthy Underhills opened their parlor to her many friends. At one large reception, the audience was entertained by music played by a noted Professor Watson, accompanied by wife and son. The concert was quickened and enlivened by the myriad rare birds in the aviary. The beautiful combination so impressed the Sojourner that as she spoke, "her soul welled out a tide of inspiration seldom heard by erring mortals." New York City friends "prevailed" upon Sojourner to defer her departure and arranged several more speaking engagements.[35]

She and Titus passed again through central and western New York on their way home. She visited the Howland family and other friends before reaching the Posts in Rochester. Besides delivering open lectures in churches and at large halls for an admission fee, she addressed Rochester ladies privately, "for their own special benefit." She no doubt elaborated on a theme she had only mentioned in her earlier talk. Women would get their rights sooner when they became "something better than mere toys." Vanity and pride were the great stumbling blocks.[36]

IV

On her return, she had a little time for summer evening strolls on the arm of her grandson William Boyd; she also expected to make some improvements on her home before going on a brief temperance campaign in Wisconsin. Instead, the Exoduster movement sent her back to Kansas via Chicago. Although she personally had nothing to do with this hegira, she had helped plant the seeds and wanted to encourage the people and Kansas's supportive governor, John St. John. She had prayed for such a movement, she told friends, and equated it with the exodus of the Israelites from Egypt. Black people could never be anything in the South, she insisted, no matter how hard they worked. Physically weak and long past her prime, she was still sharp mentally. One interviewer noted with surprise that her knowledge of current events was greater than that of most Northern whites. Her English, said another reporter, which in all senses is "a foreign tongue," is well spoken. Yet people often exaggerate her expressions, "putting into her mouth the most marked Southern dialect." Sojourner, proud of her command of English, believed this was "taking unfair advantage of her."[37]

Rather than coming from Washington and the Upper South as Sojourner had once envisioned, the Exodusters were toiling sons and daughters of the Gulf States. They came as families, church congregations, and even whole communities. The men were former soldiers and registered voters who wanted emancipation to mean transformation of condition, treatment, status, and opportunity. As Sojourner had said, in the West, "on farms of their own," blacks could rise, getting away from violence, economic and political fraud, intimidation by Southern Democrats, and Republican betrayal. During Reconstruction, blacks in Mississippi, Louisiana, and Texas had organized, tried to vote as an economic block, and formed benevolent associations and cooperative agricultural exchanges—to little avail. These men looked to local ministers as political and spiritual leaders, but were frustrated with leading black Republicans who seemed far removed from poor peoples' circumstances. Sojourner's commitment never wavered, and she remained what Douglass derisively termed in 1879 an "old time Abolitionist."[38]

As Sojourner had noted years earlier, people often got ahead of their leaders. The Exoduster movement began in Louisiana, where common folk organized a small secret council or committee that included a formerly enslaved, politically savvy faith healer named Henry Adams. Men and women from Lower South states met with Adams in New Orleans to assess their condition. Murders, beatings, rapes, financial fraud, imprisonment, and other violence perpetrated on black communities everywhere revealed that political participation, economic advancement, and mobility was hopeless in the South. Some advocated sending petitions to Washington; others suggested migration if the 1876 elections were unfavorable for blacks. The committee, already gathering information about migration, transformed itself into the Colonization Council. At a meeting in Shreveport, Louisiana, the council's representatives concluded that the party of Lincoln "looks coolly on our sufferings and [we] see our rights one by one taken away, one by one . . . and we cry out with a full heart . . . and with a loud voice cry to God, O, how long?" In appealing to the national administration, black Southerners asked for either redress or "some Territory . . . in which we can colonize our race" or "appropriate means so that we can colonize in Liberia."[39]

While Henry Adams favored relocating to Liberia, territorial migration was far more popular. Its spokesperson was a seventy-year-old man from Tennessee named Benjamin "Pap" Singleton. Born in slavery, Singleton had fled briefly to Canada, but then settled in Detroit. There he operated a boardinghouse, which had doubled as an Underground Railroad station.[40] Most likely, he knew Sojourner Truth from those antebellum years. And since he was also in and out of Kansas in 1871 and 1872, he and she probably reconnected there. In any case, while she was advocating a western homeland between 1869 and 1876, he was actually embarking on a "divinely ordained" mission of helping freed people establish such separate communities. In 1875, he organized Baxter Springs in southeastern Kansas, and in 1878 the Dunlap community southwest of Topeka. Another black town, Nicodemus, was organized independently in 1876, and these settlers had the means either to purchase private lands or to take up government lands. Singleton did not lead the Exodusters but encouraged them, as did other black men, including John Mercer Langston and George Downing. Henry Garnet not only praised the Exodusters, but called theirs "one of the most important movements that has ever been undertaken," especially because it was voluntary and without leadership. Only those who were out of touch with common folk opposed relocation, Singleton said. Such leaders were "listening to false prophets" who "got their heads whirlin."[41]

Sojourner Truth and Frances Titus reached the "land of John Brown" in September of 1879. "Such a sight!" Sojourner Truth said of the Exodusters. "I have not language to tell you what rags and wretchedness and hunger and poverty I saw among them." Although Kansas officials had initially encouraged immigration, they had meant whites. Nonetheless, Exodusters received assistance, as Governor St. John, local blacks, and white sympathizers formed the Kansas Freedmen's Relief Association (KFRA). Among liberal white newspapers, the *Chicago Daily Inter-Ocean* and *Topeka Commonwealth* led in publicizing the Exodusters' plight and their persecutions in the South. Among blacks, the *Topeka Colored Citizen* was the clarion. The most destitute Exodusters received temporary living quarters, food, and even their own small hospital. These cultivators of the soil wanted to own their own homesteads in the "land of milk and honey" and refused most offers to work as farm hands. They came by the thousands, via the Mississippi River and the Missouri, Kansas, and Texas Railroad, which the Exodusters shortened to the "Katy." They brought rural dialect, country ways, and ecstatic religion. They also imported a vibrant secular blues culture, born out of not only despair but also hope, labor, love, and life. They camped along the wharves and sang, danced, prayed, and preached.[42]

Sojourner Truth called it "the greatest movement of all time," and the reason for this "stampede" Laura Haviland said, was obvious. In the South, being a Republican and trying to rise were capital crimes. Signed testimonies told of wanton violence committed on all classes, ages, and conditions. "Increasing oppressions" and the most "barbarous murders" were so frequent that people knew not when they would be called out of their beds. "We can do nothing to protect the virtue of our wives and daughters," the men said. Even pregnant women were raped and then murdered. The Senate committee investigating the violence did not call any female witnesses. However, black men testified on women's behalf. One black man said that angry women of New Orleans had organized themselves into a Committee of Five Hundred. They published a statement demanding equal rights and insisted that husbands and brothers "take them where they could live in security and peace and get homes for themselves and education for their children." The women denounced both President Rutherford Hayes and Benjamin Butler. According to one witness, women organized the "emigration society and say they propose to move," with or without their men. Female assertiveness was portrayed in a blues song of the time:

> She caught de KATY, 'n leff me a mule to ride.
> Say she caught de KATY, 'n leff me a mule to ride.
> Well, ma Baby caught de KATY, leff me a mule to ride,
> Dat train pull off, I swung on behind.
> Cause u'm crazy 'bout her,
> Dat hard headed 'oman o' mine.[43]

While Sojourner Truth and her Michigan compatriots labored in Kansas, others, who called the Exodusters' suffering a new "Trail of Tears," also took up the cause. A thousand mostly black folk gathered in New York City's Zion's Church to support the movement. Wendell Phillips and ailing William Lloyd Garrison held a similar meeting in the Cooper Institute. Quakers who worked directly with the KFRA and local blacks were the most constant supporters. Sojourner Truth spent the autumn of 1879 in Topeka among the Exodusters, "giving counsel" to them and "awakening an interest in them among the white people." Haviland and other Michigan reformers had been in Kansas for nearly a year, working with Governor St. John. They had built the first arrivals' accommodations, collected food and clothing, and transported people. Frances Titus wrote Mary Gale that "thousands had been settled in colonies" and had "taken up small tracts of Government lands." However, Haviland said that fifty thousand had fled the oppressive South, and most of them remained displaced.

Sojourner and Frances intended to be in Kansas for one month but stayed longer because they were much needed and Sojourner was greatly inspired. But her health was failing, and she was "very sensitive to the cold." Frances insisted that Sojourner leave while Frances continued the Kansas work. She also asked friends for donations on Sojourner's behalf. "I have taken it upon myself the whole responsibility of her support," Titus wrote. Otherwise, Sojourner "would have been a public charge for the past five years." Above all, Titus added, while Sojourner never sought remuneration, she deserved it for having done good work in Kansas, "and made her mark, which will be long remembered."[44]

One wonders what happened to the proceeds from Sojourner's reissued and expanded book, selling at $1.25 per copy, the collections taken at meetings, and the occasional mail contributions. She apparently received no money from the daughters living in her two homes. As in the past, she probably shared her resources with her family and with the destitute. She welcomed in the new decade in Chicago with Laura Haviland and her daughter, Mrs. C. S. Brownell, who held a reception. As Sojourner sat neatly in a dark alpaca dress, a reporter marveled that "eighty one"-year-old Laura, small, bent, and wrinkled, looked older than Sojourner, who was "over one hundred." Her "hands, like the chin and face generally, were smooth and even plump, but for a few deep lines on the forehead." Black tufts of hair protruded from her Quaker cap; Sojourner insisted that it was not dyed but had grown back black after her last illness. She sat erect in a straight-backed chair, the reporter said, wearing a bemused smile, while her eyes sparkled. Her appearance and demeanor, visitors marveled, was that of someone half her age. She was actually eighty-three, and Laura was seventy-two.[45]

Frances Titus was mainly responsible for adding twenty years to Sojourner's age; Titus apparently calculated that New York's 1817 emancipation law had freed everyone age forty and older immediately. Her error was supported by "white evidence" from Elizabeth Dumont's nephew, Waring Latting. The "last time I thus saw Sojourner," Latting wrote Titus in 1878, "was 1819." She was then twenty-two, but Latting claimed that from "her appearance," she "could not have been less than 44 or 45 years of age." He was "firmly convinced" that as "extraordinary as it may seem," Sojourner Truth was between "103 to 104" years old. People who had known Sojourner better and longer disagreed. "To those who have known her well," Samuel Rogers wrote, "the rapid increase of her years has been amusing." But as Rogers asserted, she had answered Latting herself in her *Narrative*. Nonetheless, Frances published Latting's letter over and over in the newspapers.[46]

Sojourner returned to Michigan in the late winter of 1880, and in the spring, she began a round of talks on temperance and the Exodusters. She spoke to crowded audiences in Michigan towns throughout the year and reportedly obtained a number of abstinence pledges. Elizabeth Cady Stanton was in Michigan at this time, and spoke in Battle Creek. Local newspapers announced but did not report on her address. But even the *New York Times* took note of the aged Sojourner after her visit. "The widely known and extraordinary negress who calls herself Sojourner Truth" was resting in her home, the *Times* wrote in December 1880, although she was still in Chicago. The article, though replete with inaccuracies, noted her association with "intellectual and cultured persons" for many years.[47]

On New Year's Day, 1881, her Battle Creek friends paid a surprise visit to her home with presents and warm wishes. The old Sojourner was definitely slowed down; she gave her last major lecture in June 1881. She spoke before the Michigan state legislature in Lansing against the Wykoff Hanging Bill. Even in old age, she was mentally sharp. "I had thought," she said, "that I lived in the most blessed state in the union," until it became the awful scene of hangings. "When a man kills another man in cold blood, and you hang him, then you murder in cold blood also." She would not sanction any law that upheld murder. "We are the makers of murderers." The Old Testament "eye for an eye" changed when Jesus came and "commissioned us to love one another." Someone ought to write a new Bible, Sojourner said, that discarded all Mosaic law. Moreover, if the legislature wanted to hang something, "make a law that would hang whisky," which, she said, was at the bottom of many crimes.[48]

I'm not dying child. I'm going home like a shooting star. — SOJOURNER TRUTH

Let us run with patience the race that is set before us, looking unto Jesus the author and finisher of our faith. — HEBREWS 12:1–2

Epilogue

WELL DONE, GOOD AND FAITHFUL SERVANT

Sojourner was largely housebound, though not bedridden, by the fall of 1882. Cared for by Diana and Elizabeth, she enjoyed visitors, particularly from newspaper reporters. She still made her own bed, poked the fire, and prepared her own breakfast, but her daughters did the cooking and household chores. Her routine, she said, mainly involved conversing, occasionally singing, and sitting by the wood fire in meditation and prayer. Her leg grew progressively worse, however, and she was ill much of the time during her last year of life. She remained cheerful, patient, and never lost her wry sense of humor. During one of her last illnesses, in 1883, she even had another "shadow" taken. When some teenaged girls asked what she thought of old people falling in love, she answered, "Me? Oh, I wouldn't know." When the famous health reformer Dr. John Harvey Kellogg attended her, he tried to halt the spreading of her gangrene by cutting skin off his arm (after Diana and Elizabeth fled rather than donate skin) and grafting it onto her leg. On one occasion, when Kellogg visited his patient, he asked eighty-six-year-old Sojourner Truth her age. "Why should I tell you my age?" she asked; "It might spoil my chances." She had a "hard summer," Frances Titus wrote Amy Post in 1883. Her leg was much gangrened and intensely painful. "I think she will last only a little time." But she briefly rallied, and her mind seemed "as bright as ever." She hung on through much of the fall, always her healthiest season.[1]

Yet it was not a rumor when Sojourner Truth slipped quietly away and entered "the world of spirits" at 3 A.M.on November 26, 1883. In her last days, weakened by pain and suffering, she lost her ability to communicate. Before that, she likened her final journey to that of "a shooting star." Reportedly and characteristically, her last audible words were to a newspaper correspondent: "Be a follower of Jesus," she whispered. When confirmed word of her death spread, messages came from many quarters. She had outlived most of her associates, but those still alive sent tributes and published memorials. People who had met her only once or twice sent poems and recollections. Flowers, ferns, and floral arrangements poured in. About one thousand friends and onlookers joined her family at the Congregational-Presbyterian Church for the open-casket funeral. The floral arrangement covering the casket represented her spiritual life, earthly labors, and expectations of divine blessing: "a cross, a sheaf of ripened grain, a sickle, and a crown." She was robed in black, with a muslin cap on her head and kerchief around her shoulders. Her Kalamazoo friend Mrs. A. Montague placed a bouquet of "exquisite white flowers" in her maimed right hand. Congregational-ist minister Reed Stuart and Sojourner's longtime friend Giles Stebbins were the main speakers. Afterward, a "concourse of people, composed of all classes and creeds, passed reverently by," taking a farewell look at one "whom in life they had so honored." A long, silent procession—carriages and walkers—followed Sojourner Truth to her resting place in Oak Hill Cemetery. Her family plot was next to that of the cereal magnates Kellogg and Post. Frances Titus gave her age as "one hundred five."[2]

Frances Titus published another edition of Sojourner's *Narrative*, and with the sales proceeds and contributions from a donation list, she commissioned in 1890 a work on a marker for Sojourner's grave. Titus died in 1894. In 1897, the black clubwomen of Battle Creek organized on behalf of "the protection of womanhood," and the Sojourner Truth Memorial Association was formed. In 1929, they replaced the worn-out headstone and erected a "suitable memorial monument to Sojourner Truth," with the inscription "Is God Dead?" Many other tributes, memorials, and dedications from blacks and whites have followed, in-cluding a new monument in 1962, and a highway naming in Calhoun County. Sojourner's descendants, through her daughter Sophia and granddaughter Frances, still gather at Oak Hill cemetery to honor her, along with friends and community folk.[3]

Sojourner Truth certainly heard the very popular poem "Abou Ben Adhem," written by the nineteenth-century radical Leigh Hunt. Observing a spirit writing in a golden book of life names of those "who love the Lord," Abou asked, "is mine one?" When the angel said no, Abou answered, "I pray thee, then, write me as one that loves his fellow men." The angel disappeared, but returned the following night with the golden book. It showed "the names whom Love of God had blest. And Lo! Ben Adhem's name led all the rest." This poem suggests the double entendre behind Sojourner's *Book of Life*. Ostensibly, it represented the transformative historical times, reminding us of the nineteenth century's major struggles, involving thoughtful men, and committed, visionary, mostly forgotten women. "Don't you want to write your name in de *Book of Life*?" Sojourner asked friends, famous figures, and acquaintances. Her *Book of Life* was an autograph journal, compilation of articles, and a summary of sojourns so rich and varied that they seem unbelievable. Yet her *Book of Life* also implies that some of these notable people deserved to be written in the book of everlasting life. And who was more deserving than Sojourner Truth, whose lived experience was itself a "Book of Life"—a testament of her spirituality and service to humanity? Despite the glowing postmortem acknowledgments, Sojourner Truth's most fitting memorials came while she was alive. "The world will long remember her when other names are forgotten," Spiritualist Cora Hatch Daniels wrote in 1866. "You say you wish to leave the world better than you found it," R. B. Taylor, editor of the *Wyandotte (Kansas) Gazette* wrote to Sojourner Truth in 1871. "Posterity will give you credit of having done so."[4]

Battle Creek residents paid many, many tributes to their famous citizen, while she lived and when she died. Perhaps the most fitting of all came from the newspaper, the medium Sojourner called "the last Gospel": "Prominent features of her character," wrote the *Battle Creek Daily Journal*, "and the work which she achieved will be treasured in the hearts of the great body of our people and will have a lasting place on the page of history."[5]

At the Chicago Columbian Exposition in 1893, antilynching activist Ida B. Wells and Frederick Douglass protested the racist depictions of African Americans. This was the nadir for black folk, a very low point in their American history. Perhaps it went unnoticed, but the Michigan Pavilion reportedly displayed a large painting by artist F. C. Courter of Sojourner Truth (from a photograph, but using Diana Corbin's hand) and Abraham Lincoln. Lincoln stands behind a seated Truth, and both admire the Bible given to him by the freed people of Baltimore.[6]

"She was loved by all," wrote the *Chicago Daily Inter-Ocean* on the day after her death, "black and white."[7]

NOTES

INTRODUCTION

1. *CDI*, August 13, 1881; *NSTBL*, 25. In her 1850 *Narrative*, Sojourner's nickname is spelled "Bell." This spelling is used herein.

2. *NASS*, July 4, 1863; "Recollections of Eliza Seaman Leggett," Eliza Seaman Leggett Family Papers, vol. 8, DPL; Parker Pillsbury, *The Acts of the Anti-slavery Apostles* (Concord, N.H., 1883), 486–87.

3. *Battle Creek Daily Journal*, November 28, 1883; F. P. Powell, "The Rise and Decline of the New England Lyceum," *New England Magazine* 17, no. 6 (February 1895): 733–34.

4. *New York World*, May 13, 1867; *NASS*, December 26, 1868; Sojourner Truth to Amy Post, January 18, 1869, Eliza Leggett to Amy Post, n.d. [probably 1869], AIPFP; D. H. Morgan to Mark K. Gale, STC.

5. Pillsbury, *Anti-slavery Apostles*, 137.

CHAPTER I: AFRICAN AND DUTCH RELIGIOUS HERITAGE

1. *ASB*, December 13, 1851; *(Boston) Commonwealth*, July 3, 1863; *NASS*, September 24, 1853; "Diana Corbin," *Battle Creek Moon*, October 25, 1904; Lillie B. Chace Wyman, "Sojourner Truth," *New England Magazine* 24 (1901): 64.

2. *NST*, 3–5; Lewis Hardenbergh, statement against the gains of Johannis Hardenbergh on behalf of "Old Negro James," Hardenbergh file, Ulster County Hall of Records, Kingston, New York; James Pope-Hennessy, *Sins of the Fathers* (London, 1968), 58–59, 99.

3. *ASB*, December 13, 1851; *Liberator*, June 21, 1861; Thomas Donaldson, *Walt Whitman the Man* (New York, 1896), 242, 243.

4. Joyce D. Goodfriend, *Before the Melting Pot: Society and Culture in Colonial New York City, 1664–1730* (Princeton, N.J., 1994), 114–15, 120; James A. Rawley, *The Transatlantic Slave Trade: A History* (New York, 1981), 276–79; David Eltis and David Richardson, "The 'Numbers Game' and Routes to Slavery," *Slavery and Abolition* 18 (April 1997): 6–7; Anne Hilton, *The Kingdom of Kongo* (Oxford, 1985), 210–14; Pope-Hennessy, *Sins of the Fathers*, 183–86; David Richardson, "Slave Exports from West and West-Central Africa, 1700–1810: New Estimates of Volume and Distribution," *Journal of African History* 31 (1989): 11–13, 16–20.

5. Rawley, *Transatlantic Slave Trade*, 334, 386–88; James G. Lydon, "New York and the Slave Trade, 1700–1774," *William and Mary Quarterly*, 3d ser., 35 (1978): 375–81, 384–85, 388–93; Thomas J. Davis, "New York's Long Black Line: A Note on the Growing Slave Population, 1626–1790," *Afro-Americans in New York Life and History* 2 (January 1978): 47–49.

6. Hilton, *Kingdom of Kongo*, 1–7, 33–40, 57, 65–66, 105–7, 165–66; Michael A. Gomez, *Exchanging Our Country Marks: The Transformation of African Identities in the Colonial and Antebellum South* (Chapel Hill, N.C., 1998), 158–67; Rawley, *Transatlantic Slave Trade*, 267–68, 390; David Eltis and Stanley L. Engerman, "Was the Slave Trade Dominated by Men?" *Journal of Interdisciplinary History* 23 (1992): 237–57; and "Fluctuations in Sex and Age Ratios in the Transatlantic Slave Trade, 1663–1864," *Economic History Review* 46 (1993): 308–23; Pope-Hennessy, *Sins of the Fathers*, 78, 88–89, 99, 114, 127–29, 133, 195–203, 228–29.

7. John K. Thornton, "Central African Names and African-American Naming Patterns," *William and Mary Quarterly*, 3d ser., 50 (1993), 727–42; and Thornton, *The Kongolese Saint Anthony: Dona Beatriz Kimpa Vita and the Antonian Movement, 1684–1706* (Cambridge, 1998), 87, 149–50, 152–53.

8. Gomez, *Exchanging Our Country Marks*, 4–5, 8–11, 13–16; Eltis and Richardson, "Numbers Game," 10–11.

9. *NASS*, September 24, 1853; Gomez, *Exchanging Our Country Marks*, 144–46, 151–53; Margaret Washington Creel, *"A Peculiar People": Slave Religion and Community-Culture among the Gullahs* (New York, 1988), 50–52, 286–92, 301–2; Hilton, *Kingdom of Kongo*, 19–31, 89–103, 157–61, 193–96; Thornton, *Dona Beatriz*.

10. Thornton, *Dona Beatriz*, 10, 17–14, 36–58, 82–85, 113–15, 131–48, 153–57, 161–214.

11. *CDI*, August 13, 1879; *Chicago Times*, August 12, 1879.

12. "The Founding of the Nieuw Dorp, or Hurley," *Olde Ulster* 1 (September 1905): 257–64; Van Cleaf Bachman et al., "Het Poelmeisie: An Introduction to the Hudson Valley Dutch Dialect," *New York History* 61 (April 1980): 164–67; Egbert L. Viele, "The Knickerbockers of New York Two Centuries Ago," *Harper's*, December 1876, 33–53; Chase Viele, "The Knickerbockers of Upstate New York," *De Halve Maen* 47 (October 1972): 5–6; and (January 1973): 9–10; 48 (April 1973): 9–10, 16; and (July 1973): 11–12, 14; Goodfriend, *Before the Melting Pot*, 4–8, and "The Dutch Colonial Legacy: 'Not Hasty to Change Old Habits for New,'" *De Halve Maen* 65 (spring 1992): 5–9; Alice P. Kenney, *Stubborn for Liberty: The Dutch in New York* (Syracuse, N.Y., 1975), 93–94, 102, 106–16, 125.

13. Joyce D. Goodfriend, "Black Families in New Netherlands," *Journal of the Afro-American Historical and Genealogical Society* 5 (fall–winter 1984): 95–97; and "Burghers and Blacks: The Evolution of a Slave Society at New Amsterdam," *New York History* 61 (April 1978): 112–44; Davis, "New York's Long Black Line," 40–59.

14. Alf Evers, *The Catskills: From Wilderness to Woodstock* (Garden City, N.Y., 1972), 2–6, 285–91; "Olde Ulster and Washington Irving," *Olde Ulster* 1 (January 1905): 5–11.

15. François-Alexandre-Frédéric, La Rochefoucauld-Liancourt, *Travels through the United States of North America, the Country of the Iroquois, and Upper Canada in the Years 1795, 1796, 1797*, 2 vols. (London, 1799), 2:233; "Olde Ulster and Washington Irving," 6.

16. *NST*, 1–6, xvi–xxii; J. William Hoffman, "An Armory of American Families of Dutch Descent," *NYGBR* 70 (July and October 1939): 255–58, 337–40; "Administration of Lieutenant Jacob Leisler," in E. B. O'Callaghan, ed., *The Documentary History of the State of New York*, ed. 4 vols. (Albany, N.Y., 1850–51), 2:251; "Tax List of the Town of Hurley, 1783," *NYGBR* 16 (January 1985): 1–3; "Reminiscences of Janet Montgomery," in *Yearbook* (Dutchess County Historical Society) 15 (1950): 61–62; "Notes and Queries," *NYGBR* 23 (October 1892): 218; Howard S. F. Randolph, "The Lewis Family of New York and Poughkeepsie," *NYGBR* 60 (April 1929): 131–42; "Family Record of Abraham Hasbrouck," *NYGBR* 71 (1940): 355; "Genealogy of Colonel Jacob Rutsen," *Olde Ulster* 8 (February 1912); 111–18; Historic American

Building Survey Inventory (1966), Huguenot Society, New Paltz, N.Y.; "Schaghticoke Dutch Reformed Church Records, Schaghticoke, Rensselaer County, New York," *NYGBR* 61 (1930): 183–89, 192–89; Viele, "The Knickerbockers," 33–43; Washington Irving, *A History of New York by Diedrich Knickerbocker* (New York, 1809); Evers, *Catskills*, chaps. 9–11, 35; Martin Bruegel, "Unrest: Manorial Society and the Market in the Hudson Valley, 1780–1850," *Journal of American History* 82 (March 1996): 1393–1407.

17. "The Hardenbergh, or 'Great' Patent," *Olde Ulster* 6 (May 1910): 131–36; "The Hardenbergh House at Rosendale," *Olde Ulster* 5 (January 1909): 51–54; Evers, *Catskills*, 25, 251–52; Roswell R. Hoes, ed., *Baptismal and Marriage Registers of the Old Dutch Church of Kingston* (New York, 1891), 183, 215, 236, 272; Mertyle Hardenbergh Miller, *The Hardenbergh Family: A Genealogical Compilation* (New York, 1958), 53–59; "Census of Slaves, 1755," in E. B. O'Callaghan, ed., *Documents Relative to the Colonial History of the State of New York*, 15 vols. (Albany, N.Y., 1853–87), 11:845–51; Sophia Gruys Hinshalwood, "The Dutch Culture Area of the Mid–Hudson Valley" (Ph.D. diss., Rutgers University, 1981), 47, 135–36.

18. *Ecc.Rec.*, 1:508, 548, 689–91, 2:983–90, 995–97, 1041–44, 1131–32, 1243–62, 3:2121, 2197–2200, 2322–2400; Jonathan W. Hasbrouck, "The Coetus and Conferentie Controversy," *Olde Ulster* 1 (January 1905): 37–51; "Secretary Thurloe on the Relations of England and Holland," *English Historical Review* 21 (April 1906): 320; Gerald F. De Jong, *The Dutch Reformed Church in the American Colonies* (Grand Rapids, Mich., 1978), 163–69; James Tanis, *Dutch Calvinistic Pietism in the Middle Colonies: A Study in the Life and Theology of Theodore Jacobus Frelinghuysen* (The Hague, 1967), 48–54; William G. McLoughlin, *Revivals, Awakenings, and Reform: An Essay on Religion and Social Change in America, 1607–1977* (Chicago, 1978), 80–82; Eugene H. Keator, *Historical Discourse: The Two Hundredth Anniversary of the Six Mile Run Reformed Church* (Franklin Park, N.J., 1910), 24, 29; Randall Balmer, *A Perfect Babel of Confusion: Dutch Religion and English Culture in the Middle Colonies* (New York: 1989), 33–50, 55–72, 94–95, 140–46. For scholarly debate over the term "Great Awakening," see Frank Lambert, *Inventing the Great Awakening* (Princeton, N.J., 1999).

19. *Ecc.Rec.*, 3:2180–81, 2201–4, 2348–51, 2381–88, 4:2557, 2587–89, 2745–46, 2901, 2905; *Boel's Complaint against Frelinghuysen*, trans. and ed. Joseph A. Louis Jr. (Rensselaer, N.Y., 1979), 3, 4; Tanis, *Dutch Pietism*, 44–45, 50–67, 74–83, 99–104; Balmer, *Perfect Babel of Confusion*, chap. 3, 119–40; "Ulster County and the Frelinghuysens," *Olde Ulster* 8 (January 1912): 2–3; Keator, *Two Hundredth Anniversary*, 27–30; McLoughlin, *Revivals*, 80–89; J. M. Bumsted and John E. Van de Wetering, *What Must I Do to Be Saved: The Great Awakening in Colonial America* (Hinsdale, Ill., 1976), 46–50; Charles H. Maxon, *The Great Awakening in the Middle Colonies* (Gloucester, Mass., 1958), 11–20.

20. *NST*, 6–7.

21. *Records of the Reformed Church at New Paltz, New York* (New York, 1896), Collections of the Holland Society of New York, New York, 3:74; Johannes Hardenbergh Jr. to Captain Henry Sleight Jr., June 23, 1786 (LM-95) LM2691, and July 14, 1786 (LM 71) LM2691, Ms. Collection, Old Senate House Museum Archives, Kingston, N.Y.; Kenneth Scott, "Ulster County, New York, 1798 Tax List, *NGSQ* 73, no. 2 (June 1985): 123; Theodore W. Welles, "Hardenbergh: Leaves out of Ancestral Tablets, from Colonial Days to the Present," ms., 97–101, Jacob Rutsen Hardenbergh to Johannes Hardenbergh II, December 6, 1777, Richard Varick to Johannes Hardenbergh II, June 20, 1783, all in Johannes Hardenbergh Papers, 1760–1785, Alexander Library, Rutgers University, New Brunswick, N.J.; Thomas Romeyn to Mrs. Harriet Stafford, February 22, 1843, Dutch Reformed Church Archives, Sage Library, New Brunswick, N.J.; *Diary of Dina Van Bergh* (Frelinghuysen-Hardenbergh), trans. Gerard Van Dyke, Occasional Paper Series of the Historical Society of the Reformed Church in America (New Brunswick, N.J., 1993), 1–3, 71, 86, 91, 117–30; "Mrs. Dina Frelinghuysen–Mrs. Dina Hardenbergh," *Olde Ulster* 8 (February 1912): 33–43; "Ulster County and the Fre-

linghuysens," *Olde Ulster* 8 (January 1912): 1–8; "The Washingtons in Kingston," *Olde Ulster* 3 (January-December 1907): 6–17; "Ulster's Fight for Liberty," *Olde Ulster* 1 (February 1905) 33–36; *Ecc.Rec.*, 6:3963–67, 4040, 4060, 4085–86; Peter Studdiford, "A Funeral Sermon on the Death of the Reverend Jacob R. Hardenbergh, D.D., President of Queens College and Pastor of the Dutch Church in New Brunswick," (New Brunswick, N.J., 1791), pamphlet in Alexander Library, Rutgers University, 1–12; "Hardenbergh House," 51–54; O'Callaghan, *Documents Relating to the Colonial History of the State of New York*, 15:301–2; W. W. Abbot and Dorothy Twoling, eds., *The Papers of George Washington: Revolutionary War*, ser. 5 (Charlottesville, Va., 1993), 321–22, 577–78; Joseph Tiedemann, *Reluctant Revolutionaries: New York City and the Road to Independence, 1763–1776* (Ithaca, N.Y., 1997), 21–24, 208; Julian Ursyn Niemcewicz, *Under Their Vine and Fig Tree: Travels through America in 1797–1799, 1805 with some further Accounts of Life in New Jersey,* trans. and ed. Metchie J. E. Budka (Elizabeth, N.J, 1965), 100–103; Talbot W. Chambers, *Memoir of the Life and Character of the Late Hon. Theodore Frelinghuysen, LL.D.* (New York: 1863), 16, 22; Evers, *Catskills*, 133–35, 139–56; Donaldson, *Walt Whitman*, 242; *(Boston) Commonwealth*, July 3, 1863; *CDI*, August 13, 1879, January 1, 1881; *NSTBL*, 273–74. Stories that Sojourner Truth saw Washington were of course untrue. However, her parents probably passed on stories of seeing him. She also knew one of his former slaves in New York.

22. Gayraud S. Wilmore, *Black Religion and Black Radicalism: An Interpretation of the Religious History of African Americans*, 3d rev. enl. ed. (Maryknoll, N.Y., 1998); *NST*, 6–7.

CHAPTER 2: "HOME IS LIKE A GRAVE"

1. *CDI*, August 13, 1879.

2. *Ecc.Rec.*,1:142, 150, 488–89, 508, 2:1609, 1613, 1673, 4:2357; James L. Good, *Origins of the Reformed Church of Germany* (Reading, Pa., 1887), 393–412; Gerald F. De Jong, *The Dutch Reformed Church in the American Colonies* (Grand Rapids, Mich., 1978), 9, and "The Dutch Reformed Church and Negro Slavery in Colonial America," *Church History* 40 (December 1971): 423–36; Robert C. H. Shell, *Children of Bondage: A Social History of the Slave Society at the Cape of Good Hope* (Hanover, N.H., 1994), chap. 11; Alice P. Kenney, *Stubborn for Liberty: The Dutch in New York* (Syracuse, N.Y., 1975), 115–17.

3. Shell, *Children of Bondage*, 330–37; Good, *Origins of the Reformed Church*, 173–76, 196–99, 393–412; Nigel Worden, *Slavery in Dutch South Africa* (Cambridge, 1985), 97–98; Anne Grant, *Memoirs of An American Lady: With Sketches of Manners and Scenes in America* (Albany, N.Y., 1876), 54–55; Jean D. Worden, comp., *The Rochester Reformed Church 1736–1901, Ulster County, New York* (Franklin, Ohio, 1985), 73, 120, 232, 237; *Vital Records of the Low Dutch Church of Klyne Esopus, 1791–1899,* (Ulster Park, N.Y.: 1980), 8, 14; De Jong, *Dutch Reformed Church,* 165–69, and "Dutch Reformed Church," 425–28, 435–36; Allison Blakely, *Blacks in the Dutch World* (Bloomington, Ind., 1993), 205–8; Edward T. Corwin, *History of the Reformed Church; American Church History*, ser. 8 (New York, 1894), 176–79.

4. Will of Johannes Hardenbergh I, in Gustave Anjou, ed., *Ulster County, New York Probate Records*, 2 vols. (New York, 1906), 2:139–40; Robert Livingston's will, written in 1725, proved April 14, 1775, made his wife, Margaret, "sole executrix . . . while she is my widow," and bequeathed everything to her (except that each child could select one enslaved male and female), Will of Robert Livingston of Albany, George W. Schuyler Collection, box 2, folder 1, DRMCCU; Will of Johannes Hardenbergh II, February 19, 1782, printed in Mertyle Hardenbergh Miller, *The Hardenbergh Family: A Genealogical Compilation* (New York, 1958), 56–59; Will of Jacob Rutsen Hardenbergh, March 10, 1790, *New Jersey Index of Wills*, 3 vols., 418–23. In 1792, "Elizabeth Hasbrouck, administrator of estate of Elias Hasbrouck, calls upon all persons whom the deceased is indebted to come forth," *Farmer's Register*, August 10, 1792; Johannes Hardenbergh and Catherine Rutsen Hardenbergh, Deed to Trustees

of Kingston, February 28, 1736 (9925) 2215; Will of Bridget Hardenbergh (signed with *X*), August 10, 1819 (92924) 3023. In 1818 Benjamin and Cornelia Hardenbergh entered into an agreement with Abraham Hasbrouck to relinquish land willed to Cornelia by her father Johannes Hardenbergh. The court "examined the said Cornelia separate and apart from her said husband," to ensure that she "executed the same without any fear or compulsion of or from her said husband." Deed to A. Hasbrouck, January 1, 1822 (2795) 3015, all in Manuscript Collection, Old Senate House Museum Archives, Kingston, N.Y. For a different perspective, see Linda Briggs Briemer, *Women and Property in Colonial New York: The Transition from Dutch to English Law, 1643–1727* (Ann Arbor, Mich., 1983), and, esp. preface, 1–8, 60–76.

5. *NST*, 17, 48–49; Howard Hendricks, "Sojourner Truth: Her Early History in Slavery," *National Magazine* 16 (October 1892): 669; Andrew D. Mellick Jr., The *Story of an Old Farm, or Life in New Jersey in the Eighteenth Century* (Somerville, N.J., 1889), 256–61; Grant, *Memoirs*, 42–47, 178–79; William Henry Steele Demarest, "Dina(h) Van Bergh, the Jufvrouw Hardenbergh," paper presented to the New Brunswick Historical Club, Alexander Library, Rutgers University, October 19, 1939, 6–7; De Jong, *Dutch Reformed Church*, 137, 165; Esther Singleton, *Dutch New York* (New York, 1909), 123; James Tanis, *Dutch Calvinistic Pietism in the Middle Colonies: A Study in the Life and Theology of Theodore Jacobus Frelinghuysen* (The Hague, 1967), 156; Joyce D. Goodfriend, "Recovering the Religious History of Dutch Reformed Women in Colonial New York," *De Halve Maen* 64 (winter 1991): 54, 58.

6. Will of Johannes Hardenbergh, Jr., Record of Wills, bk. C, 164, Ulster County Surrogate's Office, Kingston, N.Y.; Joyce D. Goodfriend, *Before the Melting Pot: Society and Culture in Colonial New York City, 1664–1730* (Princeton, N.J., 1994), 97, 199, 210–11; Randall Balmer, *A Perfect Babel of Confusion: Dutch Religion and English Culture in the Middle Colonies* (New York: 1989), 100–101; De Jong, *Dutch Reformed Church*; 125–27, 164, chap. 12; Grant, *Memoirs*, 42–49, 58.

7. Grant, *Memoirs*, 58; *Diary of Dina Van Bergh* (Frelinghuysen-Hardenbergh), trans. Gerard Van Dyke, Occasional Paper Series of the Historical Society of the Reformed Church in America (New Brunswick, N.J., 1993), 37, 81, 103–7, 114–16; *Ecc.Rec.*, 5:3714; *Records of the Reformed Church at New Paltz, New York* (New York, 1896), Collections of the Holland Society of New York, New York, 3:74; *Genealogical Magazine of New Jersey* 14 (July 1939): 58–70; Edward T. Corwin, *A Manual of the Reformed Church in America, 1628–1878* (New York, 1879), 383–84; Peggy Elmendorph to Miss Blandina Elmendorph, n.d. (during the American Revolution), Manuscript Collection, Old Senate House Museum Archives; Mellick, *Story of an Old Farm*, 256–63; "Mrs. Dina Frelinghuysen–Mrs. Dina Hardenbergh," *Olde Ulster* 8 (February 1912): 33–42; Talbot W. Chambers, *Memoir of the Life and Character of the Late Hon. Theodore Frelinghuysen, LL.D.* (New York: 1863), 19–22; Demarest, "Dina(h) Van Bergh, the Jufvrouw Hardenbergh"; Abraham Messler, *Forty Years at Raritan: Eight Memorial Sermons, with Notes for a History of the Reformed Dutch Churches in Somerset County, N.J.* (New York, 1873), 185, 187–88, 190–94; De Jong, *Dutch Reformed Church*, 137, 165. The feminine quality of Dutch Pietism has been observed in other denominations as well. See, for example, Susan Mack, *Visionary Women, Ecstatic Prophecy in Seventeenth-Century England* (Berkeley, 1992); Susan Juster, "To Slay the Beast: Visionary Women in the Early Republic," in Susan Juster and Lisa MacFarlane, eds., *A Mighty Baptism: Race, Gender, and the Creation of American Protestantism* (Ithaca, N.Y., 1996), 19–37.

8. Grant, *Memoirs*, 58; *Diary of Dina Van Bergh*, 82, 91; *NYT*, September 7, 1853; *NASS*, June 9, 1855; *ASB*, November 8, 1856; *IN* 2:21, 112; Pehr Kalm, *Peter Kalm's Travels in North America*, translated by Adolph B. Benson, 2 vols. (New York, 1937), 2:621–23; Firth Haring Fabend, "Suffer the Little Children: Evangelical Child-Rearing in Reformed Dutch Households, New York and New Jersey, 1826–1876," *De Halve Maen* 68 (summer 1995): 26–29;

Goodfriend, "Recovering the Religious History," 54, 58; Corwin, *History of the Reformed Church*, 159–61; De Jong, *Dutch Reformed Church*, chap. 7; and "The Dutch Reformed Church and Negro Slavery in Colonial America," *Church History* 40 (December 1971): 424–36; Patricia Bonomi, *Under the Cope of Heaven: Religion, Society and Politics in Colonial America* (New York, 1986), 113–15; Alice P. Kenney, "Hudson Valley Dutch Psalmody," *Hymn* 25 (January 1974): 15–26; Howard G. Hageman, *Pulpit and Table: Some Chapters in the History of Worship in the Reformed Churches* (Richmond, Va., 1962), 30–31.

9. Kenney, *Stubborn for Liberty*, 127; Mellick, *Story of an Old Farm*, 265; Alphonso T. Clearwater, *The Old Dutch Church at Shawangunk*, Year Book of the Holland Society (New York, 1928–29); Jean D. Worden, comp., *Wawarsing Reformed Dutch Church, Ulster County, New York, 1745–1883, New Prospect Reformed Dutch Church, Ulster County, New York, 1816–1886, Bloomington Dutch Reformed Church, Ulster County, New York, 1796–1859, Newburgh Circuit, Methodist Episcopal Church, 1789–1834* (Franklin, Ohio, 1987), 14–15; Peter Studdiford, "A Funeral Sermon on the Death of the Reverend Jacob R. Hardenbergh, D.D., President of Queens College and Pastor of the Dutch Church in New Brunswick," (New Brunswick, N.J., 1791), pamphlet in Alexander Library, Rutgers University; De Jong, *Dutch Reformed Church*, 127, 140–41; Royden W. Vosburgh, trans. and comp., *Shaangunk Church* (n.p., n.d.), 13–16; Hageman, *Pulpit and Table*, 30–31, 55; Theodore W. Welles, "Hardenbergh: Leaves out of Ancestral Tablets, from Colonial Days to the Present," Johannes Hardenbergh Papers, 1760–85, Alexander Library, Rutgers University, 97–101.

10. *Diary of Dina Van Bergh*; Kenney, *Stubborn for Liberty*, 88–89; *Boel's Complaint against Frelinghuysen*, trans. and ed. Joseph A. Louis Jr. (Rensselaer, N.Y., 1979), 4–5, 10; De Jong, *Dutch Reformed Church*, chap. 8; Tanis, *Dutch Pietism*, chaps. 3 and 4; Shell, *Children of Bondage*, chap. 10.

11. *Northern Indianan*, October 8, 1858; *NSTBL*, 138; *NST*, 5, 8–9; C. W. Larison, *Sylvia DuBois, A Biografy of the Slav Who Whipt Her Mistres and Gand Her Fredom*, ed. and trans. Jared C. Lobdell (New York, 1988) (originally published 1883), 77; Mellick, *Story of an Old Farm*, 605–6; Will of Capt. Nicholas Schuyler, proved August 27, 1748, George W. Schuyler Collection, box 2, fol. 1, DRMCCU; Will of Johannes Hardenbergh, Jr., 164; Miller, *Hardenbergh Family*, 14, 24–25, 31–33, 53–62, 74–78, 93–94; Inventory of Charles Hardenbergh, written May 12, 1808, filed January 2, 1810, box 17, no. 10, Hall of Records, Ulster County, Kingston, N.Y.; *Diary of Dina Van Bergh*, 120–27, 53–61, 93–94; Caroline J. Otis, "The 'Old Dutch Parsonage' at Somerville," *Somerset County Historical Quarterly* 2 (July 1913): 173–74; Jean D. Worden, comp., *Marbletown Reformed Dutch Church, Ulster County, New York, 1773–1994* (Franklin, Ohio, 1987), 33; and *Bloomington Church*, 252; *Records of the Reformed Church at New Paltz*, 74, 105; Roswell R. Hoes, ed., *Baptismal and Marriage Registers of the Old Dutch Church of Kingston, Ulster County, New York* (New York, 1891), 310; Welles, "Hardenbergh," 97–101; "Ulster and the Frelinghuysens," *Olde Ulster* 8 (January 1912): 1–7; "Mrs. Dina Frelinghuysen–Mrs. Dina Hardenbergh," 37; Kenneth E. Marshall, "Work, Family and Day-to-Day Survival on an Old Farm: Nance Melick, a Rural Late Eighteenth–Early Nineteenth-Century New Jersey Slave Woman," *Slavery and Abolition* 19 (December 1998), 25, 31–32; 26; Firth Fabend, *A Dutch Family in the Middle Colonies* (New Brunswick, N.J., 1991), 35–50, 88–89 (Fabend notes the long space in between the birth of children, but does not mention wet nursing); A. J. Williams-Myers, *Long Hammering: Essays on the Forging of an African American Presence in the Hudson River Valley to the Early Twentieth Century* (Trenton, N.J., 1994), chap. 3; Richard B. Lee, "Lactation, Ovulation, Infanticide and Women's Work: A Study of Hunter-Gather Population Regulation," in Mark Nathan Cohen et al., eds., *Biosocial Mechanisms of Population Control* (New Haven, Conn., 1980), 321–48; Shell, *Children of Bondage*, chaps. 10 and 11 (the term "reproductive exploitation" is borrowed from Shell); Bonomi, *Cope of Heaven*, 115–18; De Jong, *Dutch Reformed Church*,

139–41; Worden, *Slavery in Dutch South Africa*, chap. 7; Simon Schama, *The Embarrassment of Riches: An Interpretation of Dutch Culture in the Golden Age* (Berkeley, 1988), 539–40. This interpretive study of Dutch culture ignores race and colonization.

12. Historic American Buildings Inventory (with photograph), 1966, Huguenot Historical Society, New Paltz, N.Y.; "Notable features" of the Hardenbergh home included "one cellar fireplace in slave quarters (boarded up). One fireplace in living room. . . . Birthplace of famous Negro slave Sojourner Truth in 1775" (birth date obviously an error); *NST*, 5–10, 62–63; U.S. Census Bureau, *Heads of Families at the First Census of the United States in the Year 1790*, State of New York, County of Ulster, Town of Hurley (Washington, D.C., 1908), 171–79; Record of Wills, bk. 1, 486, Ulster County Surrogate's Office; Grant, *Memoirs*, 114; Vivienne L. Kruger, "Born to Run: The Slave Family in Early New York, 1626–1827," 2 vols. (Ph.D. diss., Columbia University, 1985), 1:166–67; Fabend, *Dutch Family*, 36–40, 50–51; David S. Cohen, *The Dutch-American Farm* (New York, 1992), 62, 145; Edgar McManus, *Black Bondage in the North* (Syracuse, N.Y., 1973), 37–39; Roderic H. Blackburn and Ruth Piwonka, *Remembrance of Patria: Dutch Arts and Culture in Colonial America, 1609–1776* (Albany, N.Y., 1988), 117, 120–21; Shell, *Children of Bondage*, 92, 216–27; Worden, *Slavery in Dutch South Africa*, 91. An Anglo-American model that seems close to Dutch American society is found in Kathleen M. Brown, *Good Wives, Nasty Wenches, and Anxious Patriarchs: Gender, Race, and Power in Colonial Virginia* (Chapel Hill, N.C., 1996), 13–17, 87–88, chap. 4, 143–44, 322–24.

13. *NST*, 5–6; Grant, *Memoirs*, 114–16, 178–80; Mellick, *Story of an Old Farm*, 601–12; Will of Johannes Hardenbergh, Jr., 164; Worden, *Rochester Reformed Church*, 193; Kenneth Scott, "Ulster County, New York, 1798 Tax Lists," *NGSQ* 73, no. 2 (June 1985): 123; Fabend, *Dutch Family*, 23–25, 50–51, 80–83; McManus, *Black Bondage*, 7–40; Alice Morse Earle, *Colonial Days in Old New York* (New York, 1896), 5–7, 10–13, 115–53, 162–63, 166–771; Cohen, *Dutch-American Farm*, 61–62, 133–38, 144–45; Singleton, *Dutch New York*, chaps. 2, 4, 6, 7, 11; Schama, *Embarrassment of Riches*, 377–84; Brenda E. Stevenson, *Life in Black and White: Family and Community in the Slave South* (New York, 1996), esp. chap. 6; Dorothy Sterling, ed., *We Are Your Sisters: Black Women in the Nineteenth Century* (New York, 1984), 6–12; Shell, *Children of Bondage*; 290–91, 328–29.

14. Daniel Horsmanden, *The New York Conspiracy*, ed. Thomas J. Davis (Boston, 1971), 202–3; "The Old Court Houses of Ulster County, New York," *New York State Pamphlets* 26 (1918): 5–7; Joseph Tiedemann, *Reluctant Revolutionaries: New York City and the Road to Independence, 1763–1776* (Ithaca, N.Y., 1997), 21–24, 208; "Ulster's Fight for Liberty," *Olde Ulster* 1 (February 1905): 33–36; Alf Evers, *The Catskills, From Wilderness to Woodstock* (Garden City, N.Y., 1972), 133–35; Williams-Myers, *Long Hammering*, 58–59. McManus, *Black Bondage*, 110, 131–39;

15. Grant, *Memoirs*, 52–59; James Fenimore Cooper, *Satanstoe, or The Littlepage Manuscripts: A Tale of the Colony* (New York, 1845), 75–76; Collections of the New-York Historical Society, *Muster Rolls of New York Provincial Troops* (New York, 1891), 93, 219, 485; John C. Dann, ed., *The Revolution Remembered: Eyewitness Accounts of the War for Independence* (Chicago, 1977), 26–28, 390–99; George H. Moore, "Historical Notes on the Employment of Negroes in the American Army of the Revolution," in *The Negro Soldier: A Select Compilation* (New York, 1970); Francis W. Halsey, *The Hudson Valley in the American Revolution* (Albany, N.Y., 1968), 17; David F. Phillips, "Negroes in the American Revolution," *Journal of American History* 5 (1911): 143–46; Benjamin Quarles, *The Negro in the American Revolution* (Chapel Hill, N.C., 1961), 8–9, 56, 70, 97–99, 124; Sidney Kaplan, *The Black Presence in the Era of the American Revolution* (Amherst, Mass., 1989), 44–89; Henry Collins Brown, *Book of Old New-York* (New York, 1913), 347; W. Harrison Bayles, *Old Taverns of New York* (New York, 1915), 198, 202, 308–11.

16. La Rochefoucauld-Liancourt, *Travels through the United States*, 2:233. McManus, *Black Bondage*, 130, 152–58, 171–79; Shane White, *Somewhat More Independent: The End of Slavery in New York City, 1770–1818* (Athens, Ga., 1991).

17. McManus, *Black Bondage*, 177–78.

18. Will of Johannes Hardenbergh, Jr., 164; *Ulster County Gazette*, March 14, 1801, August 13, 1803; *Plebeian*, January 16, 1810; *NST*, 4. Alice Morse Earle, *Stage-Coach and Tavern Days* (n.d.; reprint, New York, 1968), 3–4, 13–16, 20, 39–42, 62–64; Bayles, *Old Taverns*, 58, 80–81; Julian Ursyn Niemcewicz, *Under Their Vine and Fig Tree: Travels through America in 1797–1799, 1805 with Some Further Accounts of Life in New Jersey*, trans. and ed. Metchie J. E. Budka (Elizabeth, N.J., 1965), 235; W. J. Rorabaugh, *The Alcoholic Republic: An American Tradition* (New York, 1979), chaps. 1–2.

19. Dann, *Revolution Remembered*, 341; Bayles, *Old Taverns*, 58–92, 127–28, 174, 308–11, 314–21, 336–43, 345–59; Jonathan W. Hasbrouck, "The Coetus and Conferentie Controversy," *Olde Ulster* 1 (January 1905): 37–51; Rorabaugh, *Alcoholic Republic*, 9–10, 225–29; "The Washingtons in Kingston," *Olde Ulster* 3 (January–December 1907): 6–17; Earle, *Stage-Coach and Tavern Days*, 197–211; Abram W. Hoffman, "The 'Down Rent' War," *Olde Ulster* 10, no. 9 (September 1914): 257–72.

20. Bayles, *Old Taverns*; Singleton, *Dutch New York*, chap. 12; Earle, *Stage-Coach and Tavern Days*, 20, 40.

21. Larison, *Sylvia DuBois*, 78–79; Cohen, *Dutch-American Farm*, 160–68; Kenney, *Stubborn for Liberty*, 87–88; Eckford J. deKay, "Der Colonie Nieu Nederland," *NYFQ* 9 (winter 1953): 245–47; Janet R. MacFarlane, "Recipes: New York Pastry," *NYFQ* 10 (autumn 1954): 218–25.

22. Inventory of Charles Hardenbergh; William Smith to Rev. M. Hulbert, January 29, 1884, in Carl Van Wagenen, ed., *A Genealogy of the Van Wagenen Family* (Interlaken, N.Y., 1994), 75; Miller, *Hardenbergh Family*, ; *IN* 1:10–11.

23. *NST*, 12–14, 16, 59; Grant, *Memoirs*, 51–53, 178–79.

24. *NST*, 4–57; *NYT*, September 5, 1853; *NASS*, September 10, 1853; Grant, *Memoirs*, 72–79; Kruger, "Born to Run," 1:175–76; Wilma King, *Stolen Childhood: Slave Youth in Nineteenth-Century America* (Bloomington, Ind., 1995), 102–8; Singleton, *Dutch New York*, 248–60, 297–301, chap. 13; Tristram Potter Coffin, *The Book of Christmas Folklore* (New York, 1973), 76–79, 81–87; Louise Van Adriaan D. De Groot, *Saint Nicholas, A Psychoanalytic Study of His History and Myth* (The Hague, 1965), 29–35; Nederynen Atteridg, "Dutch Lore in Holland and at Castleton, N.Y.," *NYFQ* 10 (winter 1954): 245–65; Schama, *Embarrassment of Riches*, 184–85. Blakely, *Blacks in the Dutch World*, 39–49, 282, discusses the racial significance of "Zwarte Piet."

25. Blakely, *Blacks in the Dutch World*, 61–64, 282; *NYT*, September 5, 1853; Grant, *Memoirs*, 51; King, *Stolen Childhood*, 59.

26. Absalom Aimwell, *A Pinkster Ode for the Year 1803, Most Respectfully Dedicated to Carolus Africanus Rex. Thus Rendered in English: King Charles, Captain-General and Commander in Chief of the Pinkster Boys* (Albany, N.Y., 1803); Alexander Coventry, "Memoirs of an Emigrant: The Journal of Alexander Coventry, M.D.," typescript, New York State Library, Albany, entries for June 4, 5, 6, 1786, May 27, 1787, June 14, 1791; Cooper, *Satanstoe*, 64–90; *NST*, 48; Mellick, *Story of an Old Farm*, 376–77; Larison, *Sylvia DuBois*, 67–68; A. R. F. F. Michelangelo and Denis De Carli, "A Voyage to Congo, in the Years 1666 and 1667," in John Churchill, ed., *A Collection of Voyages and Travels Some Now First Published in English*, 6 vols., 3d ed. (London, 1774), 1:493–503; Adriaan Cornelis Barnard, "The Feast of Pentecost in the Liturgical Year," trans. Martijna Aarts Briggs (M.A. thesis, Free University, Amsterdam, Holland, 1954); Cohen, *Dutch-American Farm*, 161–63, 190, and "In Search of Carolus Africanus Rex: Afro-Dutch Folklore and Folklife in New York and New Jersey," *Journal of the*

Afro-American Historical and Genealogical Society 5 (1984): 149–62; Schama, *Embarrassment of Riches*, 185; Williams-Myers, *Long Hammering*, chap. 5; Thornton, *Dona Beatriz*, 30–35.

27. Barnard, "Feast of Pentecost," 32–38; *Order of Worship, for the Dutch Reformed Church* (Philadelphia, 1869), esp. 50–55, 83–92, 106–9; Van Wagenen, *Genealogy*, 28, 42, 44, 74, 75.

28. De Jong, *Dutch Reformed Church*, 165–69; Barnard, "Feast of Pentecost," 16–19, 38–41; Hageman, *Pulpit and Table*, 18–23, 27, 33–35, 40, 43–48, 54–55; *Complaint against Frelinghuysen*, 2, 10, 74–77, 96–97, Tanis, *Dutch Pietism*, 111–18; F. Ernest Stoeffler, *The Rise of Evangelical Pietism* (Leiden, 1971), 2–4, 6, 116; F. J. Schrag, "Theodorus Jacopus Frelinghuysen, the Father of American Pietism," *Church History* 14 (September 1945): 205–12; Cooper, *Satanstoe*, 96–97. Gal. 4:6; Rom. 8:26; 1 Cor. 3:16; Heb. 9:8; John 14:15–21; *Order of Worship*, 106–7.

29. *Order of Worship*, 107; Acts 2:1–8 and 11–21; Barnard, "Feast of Pentecost," 45–47; Karl Laman, *Kongo*, 5 vols. (Uppsala, Sweden, 1962), 3:1–6.

30. Nathan O. Hatch, *Democratization of American Christianity* (New Haven, Conn., 1989), 102–13.

31. Coventry, "Memoirs," entry of June 6, 1791; Aimwell, *Pinkster Ode*.

32. *NST*, 5–7.

CHAPTER 3: "BETTER TO ME THAN A MAN"

1. *CDI*, August 13, 1879; *NYT*, September 10, 1853; *NST*, 8–9; Will of Charles Hardenbergh, Record of Wills, bk. D, 196, Ulster County Surrogate's Office, Kingston, N.Y.; Charles Hardenbergh Inventory, written May 12, 1808, filed January 2, 1810, box 17, no. 10, Hall of Records, Ulster County, Kingston, N.Y.; *Plebeian*, July 26, August 2, 9, 23, 30, November 18, 1808, January 16, 1810; *Ulster County Gazette*, August 13, 1803. For a different time-frame assessment, see Carleton Mabee with Susan Mabee Newhouse, *Sojourner Truth, Slave, Prophet, Legend* (New York, 1993), 4–5; Nell Irvin Painter, *Sojourner Truth: A Life, A Symbol* (New York, 1996), 13.

2. *NST*, 14–15; Kenneth Scott, "Ulster County, New York Court Records, 1693–1775," *NGSQ* 61 (March 1973): 60, 61, 62, 64, 206; and "Ulster County Freeholders, 1798–1812," *NGSQ* 53 (March 1965): 10; and "Ulster County, New York, Jury Lists, 1750–1799," *NGSQ* 60 (June 1972): 169–79; *Plebeian*, May 16, 1806.

3. *NST*, 15; *NYT*, September 7, 1853; Sharla Fett, *Healing Works: Healing, Health, and Power on Slave Plantations* (Chapel Hill, N.C., 2002), 57, 128–29.

4. Doreen Asso, *The Real Menstrual Cycle* (New York: 1983), 16; Vern L. Bullough, "Age at Menarche: A Misunderstanding," *Science* 213 (July 1981): 365–66; Rose E. Frisch and Janet W. MacArthur, "Menstrual Cycles: Fatness as a Determinant of Minimum Weight or Height Necessity for Their Maintenance or Onset," *Science* 185 (September 1974): 149–51; Rose E. Frisch, "Critical Weight, a Critical Body Composition, Menarche, and the Maintenance of Menstrual Cycles," in E. S. Watts, F. E. Johnson, and G. W. Lasker, eds., *Biosocial Interrelations in Population Adaptation* (The Hague, 1975), 319–52; Dorothy Sterling, ed., *We Are Your Sisters: Black Women in the Nineteenth Century* (New York, 1984), 18–30; Creel, *"A Peculiar People,"* 46–52, 288–92; David S. Cohen, *The Dutch-American Farm* (New York, 1992), 118–21; Deborah Gray White, *"Ar'n't I a Woman?" Female Slaves in the Plantation South* (New York, 1985), 33; Wilma King, *Stolen Childhood: Slave Youth in Nineteenth-Century America* (Bloomington, Ind., 1995), 91–94; *NST*, 15; *Rochester Evening Express*, April 17, 1871.

5. William Strickland, *Journal of a Tour in the United States of America, 1794–95*, ed. J. E. Strickland (New York, 1971), 74, 163; François-Alexandre-Frédéric, La Rochefoucauld-Liancourt, *Travels through the United States of North America, the Country of the Iroquois,*

and *Upper Canada in the Years 1795, 1796, 1797*, 2 vols. (London, 1799), 2:233; Van Cleaf Bachman, "The Story of the Low Dutch Language II," *De Halve Maen* 52, no. 1 (1982): 11.

6. *NST*, 14–16.

7. Anne Grant, *Memoirs of an American Lady: With Sketches of Manners and Scenes in America* (Albany, N.Y., 1876), 178–80; *NST*, 3–4, 13–14; William Smith to Rev. M. Hulbert, January 29, 1884, in Carl Van Wagenen, ed., *A Genealogy of the Van Wagenen Family* (Interlaken, N.Y., 1994), 75; Alexander Coventry, "Memoirs of an Emigrant: The Journal of Alexander Coventry, M.D.," typescript, New York State Library, Albany, entry for April 9, 1787; Willie F. Page, "From Cuff to Cobust: Alexander Coventry, M.D., and His Slaves, 1789–1827," paper presented at the African American History and Genealogy Conference, Oneonta, N.Y., April 17–19, 1998, 2–3, 5–6; Michael E. Groth, "The African American Struggle against Slavery in the Mid–Hudson Valley, 1787–1827," *Hudson Valley Regional Review* 11 (March 1994): 63–64, 72–73.

8. *NST*, 17; *Vital Records of the Low Dutch Church of Klyne Esopus, 1791–1899*, comp. Arthur Kelly (Ulster Park, N.Y.: 1980), 103; *Records of the Reformed Church at New Paltz, New York* (New York, 1896), Collections of the Holland Society of New York, New York, 3:1–15, 61, 75, 77, 170, 179, 180, 186, 197; "Papers Relating to Ulster and Duchess Counties," in E. B. O'Callaghan, ed., *Documentary History of the State of New York*, 4 vols. (Albany, N.Y., 1850–51), 3:580–61; U.S. Census Bureau, *Heads of Families at the First Census of the United States in the Year 1790*, State of New York, County of Ulster, Town of Hurley (Washington, D.C., 1908), 172; and *Population Schedules of the Second Census of the United States* (1800), State of New York, Town of Kingston, County of Ulster, (Washington, D.C., 1802), 218, 232; and *Third Census* (1810), Town of Kingston, County of Ulster, (Washington, D.C., 1959), 743; Scott, "Ulster County Freeholders," 10; Alphonso T. Clearwater, *The Old Dutch Church at Shawangunk*, Year Book of the Holland Society (New York, 1928–29), 1–4, 12, 17, 33.

9. *NST*, 16–17.

10. *NST*, 17; Howard Hendricks, "Sojourner Truth: Her Early History in Slavery," *National Magazine* 16 (October 1892): 665–71; *NASS*, December 26, 1868; W. J. Rorabaugh, *The Alcoholic Republic: An American Tradition* (New York, 1979), 11–13, 134–35; Simon Schama, *The Embarrassment of Riches: An Interpretation of Dutch Culture in the Golden Age* (Berkeley, 1988), 182–203.

11. *Plebeian*, November 27, 1810. The *Narrative*'s statement that Bell spent a year and a half with the Schryvers seems erroneous, because Charles Hardenbergh's inventory was not filed until 1810, and then his property was liquidated. Since Dumont purchased Bell in 1810, she probably spent about eight months with the Shryvers, and about two with the Neelys. Neither Martimus Schryver nor John Neely listed slaves in the 1810 census, while John I. Dumont Jr. lists three. *NST*, 17, Charles Hardenbergh Inventory; U.S. Census, *Population Schedules for New York* (1810), Town of Kingston, 743, 745, and Town of New Paltz, 713.

12. Dumont genealogy, Harry Clifford Reed Papers, boxes 4 and 5, DRMCCU; *Boel's Complaint against Frelinghuysen*, trans. and ed. Joseph A. Louis Jr. (Rensselaer, N.Y., 1979), 4–7, 23–25, 34–46; *New Paltz Church Records*, 59, 154; Hendricks, "Sojourner Truth," 665–71; Roswell R. Hoes, ed., *Baptismal and Marriage Registers of the Old Dutch Church of Kingston, Ulster County, New York* (New York, 1891), 342, 348, 369, 617, 642, 667; Josephine DuMont, "Sheriff Egbert DuMont," *Olde Ulster* 5 (June 1909): 177–80; and "The Passing of the Dutch Language," *Olde Ulster* 10 (April 1914): 111–14; Bachman, "Story of the Low Dutch Language I," *De Halve Maen* 56, no. 3 (1982): 1, 3, 21, and "Story of the Low Dutch Language II," 10, 13; Timothy Spafford, *Gazetteer of the State of New York, 1824* (reprint, Interlaken, N.Y., 1981), 246–47; "The Dutch Church in Kingston," *Olde Ulster* 5 (October 1909): 304–5, and Jonathan W. Hasbrouck, "The Coetus and Conferentie Controversy," *Olde Ulster* 1 (January 1905): 37–51; David G. Hackett, *The Rude Hand of Innovation: Religion and Social Order in*

Albany, New York, 1652–1836 (New York, 1991), 58–60; Joyce D. Goodfriend, *Before the Melting Pot: Society and Culture in Colonial New York City, 1664–1730* (Princeton, N.J., 1994), chap. 9; Randall Balmer, *A Perfect Babel of Confusion: Dutch Religion and English Culture in the Middle Colonies* (New York: 1989), chap. 7. Today, the Dumont farm site (now in West Park) borders Highway 9W. Dumonts ceased living on the land by the mid-twentieth century.

13. Will of Solomon Waring, Record of Wills, bk. D, 359, Ulster Country Surrogate's Office, Kingston, N.Y. In his will Waring refers to "my two grandchildren, of my youngest daughter, Sally, to wit Getty Dumond and Solomon Waring Dumond" and to daughter "Elizabeth, wife of John I. Dumont." See also "Dumont Family" and "Genealogical Notes on Families Related to DuMonts," Reed Papers, box 5, DRMCCU; *NST*, 19–20.

14. *Poughkeepsie Journal,* March 12, 1797; *NST*, 19–20; Hendricks, "Sojourner Truth," 669; A. J. Williams-Myers, *Long Hammering: Essays on the Forging of an African American Presence in the Hudson River Valley to the Early Twentieth Century* (Trenton, N.J., 1994), 26–28; Adriance Van Brunt, Diary, June 8, 1828–March 20, 1830, n.p., Manuscript Division, New York Public Library; Cohen, *Dutch-American Farm,* chap. 4; Mary Humphreys, *Women of Colonial and Revolutionary Times: Catherine Schuyler* (New York, 1897), 37–38; Alice P. Kenney, *Stubborn for Liberty: The Dutch in New York* (Syracuse, N.Y., 1975), 99–101.

15. Humphreys, *Women of Colonial and Revolutionary Times,* 37–38; Agnes Scott Smith, "The Dutch Had a Word for It," *NYFQ* 2 (August 1946); 165–73; Janet R. MacFarlane, "Recipes: New York Pastry," *NYFQ* 10 (autumn 1954): 218–25; Dorothy V. Bennit, "Albany Preserves Its Dutch Lore," *NYFQ* 11 (winter 1955): 245–55; Hendricks, "Sojourner Truth," 669.

16. *NST*, 18.

17. *NST*, 18–20. Since Getty Dumont was about ten at the time, the event occurred around 1812.

18. Thomas S. Wermuth, "'To Market, to Market': Yeomen Farmers, Merchant Capitalists and the Transition to Capitalism in the Hudson River Valley, Ulster County, 1760–1840" (Ph.D. diss., State University of New York, Binghamton, 1991), iv–v, 104–7, 152–55, 161–70, 184–94; Andrea K. Zimmermann, "Nineteenth-Century Wheat Production in Four New York State Regions: A Comparative Examination," *Hudson Valley Regional Review* 5 (September 1988): 50–53; Cohen, *Dutch-American Farm,* chap. 4.

19. Cohen, *Dutch-American Farm,* 125–26; "Inventors and Inventions of Cayuga County, N.Y.," in *Collections of Cayuga County Historical Society* (Auburn, N.Y., 1882), 2:116–24; Jared Van Wagenen Jr., *The Golden Age of Homespun* (Ithaca, N.Y., 1953), 155; Zimmermann, "Wheat Production," 50–52.

20. Cohen, *Dutch-American Farm,* 111–18, 127–28; Hendricks, "Sojourner Truth," 669; "Inventors and Inventions," 134–38; Van Wagenen, *Golden Age of Homespun,* 225–30; *NST,* 26.

21. Hendricks, "Sojourner Truth," 669; *Proceedings of the First Anniversary of the American Equal Rights Association, May 9 and 10, 1867* (New York, 1867); Van Wagenen, *Golden Age of Homespun,* 229.

22. Van Wagenen, *Golden Age of Homespun,* 227–29; Hendricks, "Sojourner Truth," 669.

23. Van Wagenen, *Golden Age of Homespun,* 263–64; *NST*, 20.

24. Van Wagenen, *Golden Age of Homespun,* 240; *NST*, 3, 7, 25–26; Williams-Myers, *Long Hammering;* Hendricks, "Sojourner Truth," 669; Charles Gehring, "The Survival of the Dutch Language in New York and New Jersey," *De Halve Maen* (winter 1982): 2–3, 21; K. Leroy Irvis, "Negro Tales from Eastern New York, *NYFQ* 11 (autumn 1955): 165–76; David S. Cohen, "In Search of Carolus Africanus Rex: Afro-Dutch Folklore and Folklife in New York and New Jersey," *Journal of the Afro-American Historical and Genealogical Society* 5 (1984): 151–53, 157; Kenneth E. Marshall, "Work, Family and Day-to-Day Survival on an Old Farm:

Nance Melick, a Rural Late Eighteenth–Early Nineteenth–Century New Jersey Slave Woman," *Slavery and Abolition* 19 (December 1998): 27–30; work song quoted in Cohen, "In Search of Carolus Africanus Rex," 157. Mid-Atlantic blacks, rather than displaying "conformity to the dominant European-American culture," as Marshall maintains, created an alternative culture.

25. Catherine Relihan, "Herb Remedies," *NYFQ* 2 (May 1946): 156–58; Audrey Boughton, "Weather Lore," *NYFQ* 1 (May 1945): 123–25, *NYFQ* 1 (August 1945): 188–90, *NYFQ* 1 (November 1945): 251–52; *ASB*, January 3, 1852.

26. *NST*, 20–21.

27. Nonscholarly biographies suggesting a sexual relationship between Isabella and John Dumont include Arthur H. Fauset, *Sojourner Truth: God's Faithful Pilgrim* (Chapel Hill, N.C., 1938), and Hertha Pauli, *Her Name was Sojourner Truth* (New York, 1962). Among scholars, Gerda Lerner, *Female Experience: An American Documentary* (Indianapolis, 1977), 488, wrote: "Her master raped her"; bell hooks, *Ain't I a Woman: Black Women and Feminism,* (Boston, 1981), 160, wrote that Sojourner Truth experienced "persecution, physical abuse, rape, torture"; Mabee, *Sojourner Truth*, 9, wrote "a sexual relationship" . . . "cannot be ruled out."

28. Examples include Anne Grant, *Memoirs of an American Lady: With Sketches of Manners and Scenes in America* (Albany, N.Y., 1876), 55–56; Vivienne L. Kruger, "Born to Run: The Slave Family in Early New York, 1626–1927," 2 vols. (Ph.D. diss., Columbia University, 1985), 342–46; Williams-Myers, *Long Hammering*, 53–54; Harriet Wilson, *Our Nig* (Boston, 1859), chaps. 1 and 2; Sterling, *We Are Your Sisters*, 18–31; Harriet A. Jacobs, *Incidents in the Life of a Slave Girl Written by Herself*, ed. Jean Fagan Yellin (Cambridge, 1987); Melton A. McLaurin, *Celia, a Slave: A True Story of Violence and Retribution in Antebellum Missouri* (Athens, Ga., 1991); Brenda E. Stevenson, *Life in Black and White: Family and Community in the Slave South* (New York, 1996), 41, 137–38, 190–81, 236–41, 245, 259, ; White, *"Ar'n't I a Woman?"* chap. 1.

29. *NST*, 21.

30. *NST*, 9–10; Grant, *Memoirs*, 40–42; Williams-Myers, *Long Hammering*, 49–51; Marshall, "Work, Family and Day-to-Day Survival," 26–29; Lewis Hardenbergh's statement against the gains of Johannis Hardenbergh on behalf of "Old Negro James," Hardenbergh file, Ulster County Hall of Records, Kingston, New York.

31. For an analysis of Sojourner Truth as a white female construction, see Painter, *Sojourner Truth*, 258–87.

32. *IN* 2:126, 1:50, 62–63.

33. For a contrast, see Vale's description of Ann Disbrow Folger, Isabella's white middle-class female coresident (and accuser) in the commune known as the "kingdom of Matthias," where she later lived for a time. *IN* 1:61, 2:21; *Battle Creek Daily Journal*, November 28, 1883.

34. Sylvia Boone, *Radiance from the Waters: Ideals of Feminine Beauty in Mende Art* (New Haven, Conn., 1986), 96–100, 119–20.

35. Boone, *Radiance from the Waters*, 67–78, 87, 91, 117. On nineteenth-century American domesticity, see Kathryn Kish Sklar, *Catharine Beecher: A Study in American Domesticity* (New Haven, Conn., 1973), 8, 87, 151, 158–67, 193–94; Barbara Welter, "The Cult of True Womanhood, 1820–1860," *American Quarterly* 19 (1966): 151–74.

36. "Sojourner Truth" *Battle Creek Daily Journal*, December 6, 1883.

37. Pehr Kalm, *Peter Kalm's Travels in North America*, translated by Adolph B. Benson, 2 vols. (New York, 1937), 611–12; Kenney, *Stubborn for Liberty*, 86–87; Esther Singleton, *Dutch New York* (New York, 1909), 137–42; Schama, *Embarrassment of Riches*, 375–77, 384–93; *NST*, 21.

38. *IN* 1:10–12; Hendricks, "Sojourner Truth," 665–69; *NST*, 17–20, 25; C. W. Larison, *Sylvia DuBois, A Biografy of the Slav Who Whipt Her Mistres and Gand Her Fredom*, ed. and trans. Jared C. Lobdell (1883; reprint, New York, 1988), 55, 63–66; Stevenson, *Life in Black and White*, 196–205, 239–41; Stephanie McCurry, *Masters of Small Worlds: Yeomen Households, Gender Relations, and the Political Culture of the Ante-bellum South Carolina Low Country* (New York, 1995), 72–95.

39. U. P. Hedrick, *A History of Agriculture in the State of New York* (1933; reprint, New York, 1966), 148–59, 224–28; Wermuth, "'To Market, to Market,'" 230–31; Hendrick, "Sojourner Truth," 665–69; Van Wagenen, *Golden Age of Homespun*, 214–16; Andrew D. Mellick Jr., *The Story of an Old Farm, or Life in New Jersey in the Eighteenth Century* (Somerville, N.J., 1889), 613–19; David M. Ellis, *Landlords and Farmers in the Hudson–Mohawk Region, 1790–1850* (Ithaca, N.Y., 1946), 108, 193; Rorabaugh, *Alcoholic Republic*, 11–16, 25–26, 76–78, 83–92, 110–14, 128–27, 134–35.

40. *Plebeian*, September 14, 1803; Mellick, *Story of an Old Farm*, 615–21; Rorabaugh, *Alcoholic Republic*, 76–79, 107, 110–13, 117–18, 149–50, 173–74; Cohen, *Dutch-American Farm*, 153, 165–66; Schama, *Embarrassment of Riches*, 182–203.

41. *NST*, 10–11, 28–37; Van Wagenen, *Golden Age of Homespun*, 262–63; Spafford, *Gazetteer*, 342–44; Ellis, *Landlords and Farmers*, 110–12, 148–49; Wermuth, "'To Market, to Market,'" 207–9.

42. *NST*, 22, 24, 48; Hendricks, "Sojourner Truth," 669; Absalom Aimwell, *A Pinkster Ode for the Year 1803, Most Respectfully Dedicated to Carolus Africanus Rex. Thus Rendered in English: King Charles, Captain-General and Commander in Chief of the Pinkster Boys* (Albany, N.Y., 1803); James Fenimore Cooper, *Satanstoe, or The Littlepage Manuscripts: A Tale of the Colony* (New York, 1845), 56, 70–71, 84–85, 90; Cohen, *Dutch-American Farm*, 160–64; and Cohen, "In Search of Carolus Africanus Rex," 153–57; Williams-Myers, *Long Hammering*, 91–95; Gabriel Furman, *Antiquities of Long Island* (New York, 1874), 265–66; *New York Weekly Journal*, March 7, 14, 21, 28, 1737.

43. Aimwell, *Pinkster Ode*, 165–66; Cooper, *Satanstoe*, 70–71, 76, 90; Furman, *Antiquities of Long Island*, 265–67.

44. *Rising Sun*, June 14, 1898, *American Farmer & Dutchess County Advertiser*, September 3, 1799; *Plebeian*, July 22, 1804, September 15, 1804; *Country Journal and Poughkeepsie Advertiser*, May 30, 1808; *Poughkeepsie Journal*, April 3, 1810; June 5, 1811; Kenneth Scott, ed., "Early Inquests of Ulster County, New York, 1732–1825" *NGSQ* 27 (1969): 57; Complaint of Nillie Koick, January 1766 (7045), 2422, Old Senate House Archives, Kingston, New York; Schama, *Embarrassment of Riches*, 454–80; Faye Dudden, *Serving Women: Household Service in the Nineteenth Century* (New York, 1984), 212–19. On attitudes about sexuality from African American women's perspective, see White, *"Ar'n't I a Woman?"* 29–46; Hazel V. Carby, *Reconstructing Womanhood: The Emergence of the Afro-American Woman Novelist* (New York, 1987), chap. 2. Poem quoted in Allison Blakely, *Blacks in the Dutch World* (Bloomington, Ind., 1993), 172.

45. *NST*, 64.

46. *IN*, 1:3–10, 13–35; and William Leete Stone, *Matthias and His Imposters: Or, The Progress of Fanaticism, Illustrated in the Extraordinary Case of Robert Matthews and Some of His Forerunners and Disciples* (New York, 1835), esp. 166, 179, 193–201, 204–6, 216–21, 231; Nancy Cott, "Passionless: An Interpretation of Victorian Sexual Ideology, 1790–1850," *Signs* 4 (1978): 221–23, 227–28, 234; Sklar, *Catharine Beecher*, 63–87, 90–98, 210–13; Patricia Cline Cohen, "Ministerial Misdeeds: The Onderdonk Trial and Sexual Harassment in the 1840s," in Susan Juster and Lisa MacFarlane, eds., *A Mighty Baptism: Race, Gender, and the Creation of American Protestantism* (Ithaca, N.Y., 1996), 83–84.

47. *NST*, 21; Cott, "Passionless," 234; Cohen, "Ministerial Misdeeds."

1. Arthur Zilversmit, *The First Emancipation: The Abolition of Slavery in the North* (Chicago, 1967), 213–15.

2. Obituary of Diana Corbin and obituary of Sophia Schuyler, in Berenice Lowe Papers, box 1, fols. 4, 7, 9, MHC; U.S. Census Bureau, *Population Schedules of the Fourth Census of the United States* (1820), State of New York, County of Ulster, Town of New Paltz (Washington, D.C., 1821), 71; U.S. Census Bureau, *Population Schedules of the Eighth Census* (1860), State of Michigan, County of Calhoun, Bedford Township (Washington, D.C., 1864); *IN*, 1:15–18; *NST*, 23–25, 30, 63; Howard Hendricks, "Sojourner Truth: Her Early History in Slavery," *National Magazine* 16 (October 1892): 668–69.

3. *NST*, 22–23; *NYT*, September 7, 1853; William Dunlap, *The Diary of William Dunlap*. 3 vols. (New York, 1930), 2:404, 406, 407; and William Dunlap, *History of the Rise and Progress of the Arts of Design in the United States*, 2 vols. (New York, 1965), 3:359–61; *Plebeian*, June 19, 1816, February 8, 22, 1817.

4. *NST*, 18, 22–23; *NYT*, September 7, 1853; U.S. Census Bureau, *Population Schedules for the Third Census* (1810), State of New York, County of Ulster, Town of New Paltz (Washington, D.C., 1859), 713; *Fourth Census* (1820), 71; *Fifth Census* (1830), 203.

5. *Vital Records of the Low Dutch Church of Klyne Esopus, 1791–1899*, comp. Arthur Kelly (Ulster Park, N.Y.: 1980), 8, 14, 29. Obituary of Diana Corbin; Frederick Douglass, *Narrative of the Life of Frederick Douglass an American Slave, Written by Himself* (Boston, 1845), 1; Booker T. Washington, *Up from Slavery* (reprint, 1901; New York, 1986), 2.

6. Gen. 16; Savina J. Teubal, *Hagar the Egyptian: The Lost Tradition of the Matriarchs* (New York, 1990), esp. 20–70; Delores Williams, *Sisters in the Wilderness: The Challenge of Womanist God Talk* (Maryknoll, N.Y., 1993), 2–8, 16–26, 29, 33, 122–30, 136, 139, 148; *NST*, 22–24; Hendricks, "Sojourner Truth," 668; Will of Solomon Waring, Record of wills, book D, 359, Ulster County Surrogate's Court, Kingston, New York.

7. *NST*, 18, 24–26; Deborah Gray White, *"Ar'n't I a Woman?" Female Slaves in the Plantation South* (New York, 1985), 34–39.

8. "Genealogy—Dumont Notes," box 4, Harry Clifford Reed Papers, DRMCCU; *NST*, 21–22, 24–26, 56; *Northern Indianan*, October 8, 1858; *NST*, 56; Janet Golden, *A Social History of Wet Nursing in America: From Breast to Bottle* (New York, 1996), 25–32, 72–75; Margaret Washington Creel, *"A Peculiar People": Slave Religion and Community-Culture among the Gullahs* (New York, 1988), 181–82, 236–39; White, *"Ar'n't I a Woman?"* 39–46.

9. Hendricks, "Sojourner Truth," 668–69; *NST*, 22–27, 64.

10. Lewis Hardenbergh's statement against the gains of Johannis Hardenbergh on behalf of "Old Negro James," November, 1814, Hardenbergh file, Ulster County Hall of Records, Kingston, N.Y.; *NST*, 10–11.

11. *NST*, 11–13; Mertyle Hardenbergh Miller, *The Hardenbergh Family: A Genealogical Compilation* (New York, 1958), 58–60.

12. *NST*, 11–12; *NYT*, September 7, 1853; Miller, *Hardenbergh Family*, 198–99; Vivienne L. Kruger, "Born to Run: The Slave Family in Early New York, 1626–1927," 2 vols. (Ph.D. diss., Columbia University, 1985), 2:546–47; Will of Johannes Hardenbergh, Jr., Record of Wills, bk. C, 164, Ulster County Surrogate's Office, Kingston, N.Y.; Proprietors of the Hardenbergh Patent to Johannes Hardenbergh Jr., July 1785, William Cockburn Collection, box 2, fol. 14, DRMCCU; Nathaniel Bartlett Sylvester, *History of Ulster County, New York*, 2 pts. (Philadelphia, 1880), 2:145, 234; *Order of Worship, for the Dutch Reformed Church* (Philadelphia, 1869), 277.

13. John M. Jansen and Wyatt MacGaffey, *An Anthology of Kongo Religion: Primary Texts from Lower Zaire* (Lawrence, Kans., 1974); Robert Farris Thompson and Joseph Cornet, *The Four Moments of the Sun: Kongo Art in Two Worlds* (Washington, D.C., 1981); *NST*, 13–14;

"Recollections of Eliza Seaman Leggett," Eliza Seaman Leggett Family Papers, vol. 8, DPL; Creel, *"A Peculiar People,"* 308–22.

14. *NYT*, September 7, 1853; NST, 10–13; Kruger, "Born to Run," 1:545–48.

15. *NST*, 26, 64; *IN*, 1:10–11; In the *Narrative*, Gilbert mistakenly states that Bell left Dumont in 1827.

16. *NST*, 28, 44–45.

17. *NST*, 10–14, 25–28; Timothy Spafford, *Gazetteer of the State of New York, 1824* (reprint, Interlaken, N.Y., 1981), 532; *NYT*, September 7, 1853.

18. Barnabas Bates, *Remarks on the Character and Exertions of Elias Hicks, in the Abolition of Slavery: Being an Address Delivered before the African Benevolent Societies for Zion's Chapel, New-York, 1830*, May Pamphlets, vol. 99, no. 4, Anti-slavery Collection, DRMCCU; *Plebeian*, February 8, 1817; Bliss Forbush, *Elias Hicks, Quaker Liberal* (New York, 1956), 30–32, 39–40, 53–54, 64–65, 68–71, 77–79, 121; Zilversmit, *First Emancipation*, 82–83, 146–50, 164–70.

19. U.S. Census Bureau, *Population Schedules for the Fourth Census* (1820), State of New York, County of Ulster, Town of Marbletown (Washington, D.C., 1821), 61; Roe died on October 10, 1826; Federal Writers Project, *Old Gravestones of Ulster County*, Rosendale (N.Y.), 219, Kingston Public Library; *NST*, 28–29; Spafford, *Gazetteer*, 342–44; Shirley V. Anson and Laura M. Jenkins, eds., *Quaker History and Genealogy of the Marlborough Monthly Meeting, Ulster County, New York 1804–1900* (Baltimore, 1980), 3, 9; Forbush, *Elias Hicks*, 36–40, 65, 89, 123–26; Sylvester, *History of Ulster County*, 2:75, 78–79, 94, 170, 177, 263; Alphonso T. Clearwater, *The History of Ulster County* (Kingston, N.Y., 1907), 205–87.

20. *NST*, 29.

21. William Smith to Rev. M. Hulbert, January 29, 1984, in Carl Van Wagenen, ed., *A Genealogy of the Van Wagenen Family* (Interlaken, N.Y., 1884), 75; see also 4, 13, 19, 27, 31, 33, 42, 44, 74; "Tax List of the Town of Hurley, 1783," *NYGBR* 16 (January 1985): 1–3; Jean D. Worden, comp., *Marbletown Reformed Dutch Church, Ulster County, New York*, 1773–1994 (Franklin, Ohio, 1987), 77; and *Wawarsing Reformed Dutch Church, Ulster County, New York, 1745–1883, New Prospect Reformed Dutch Church, Ulster County, New York, 1816–1886, Bloomington Dutch Reformed Church, Ulster County, New York, 1796–1859, Newburgh Circuit, Methodist Episcopal Church, 1789–1834* (Franklin, Ohio, 1987), 252–32, 257, 263, 267, 270, 274; Roswell R. Hoes, ed., *Baptismal and Marriage Registers of the Old Dutch Church of Kingston, Ulster County, New York* (New York, 1891), preface, 320, 324, 336, 358, 393; *IN*, 1:10.

22. Van Wagenen, *Genealogy*, 42, 74–75; U.S. Census Bureau, *Heads of Families at the First Census of the United States in the Year 1790*, State of New York, County of Ulster, Town of Hurley (Washington, D.C., 1908), 170; and *Population Schedules of the Second Census of the United States* (1800), State of New York, County of Ulster, Town of Hurley, (Washington, D.C., 1802); *NST*, 29.

23. *NST*, 29.

24. *NST*, 28–29; *West Chester (PA) Daily Local News*, July 18, 1874.

25. *NST*, 29; *West Chester (PA) Daily Local News*, July 18, 1874.

26. *NST*, 29–30; *Saginaw (MI) Daily Courier*, June 14, 1871.

27. Hulbert letter, in Wagenen, *Genealogy*, 75; *NST*, 30–31; Laws of New York, Passed at the Forty-First Session of the Legislature, articles 4 and 13, November 5, 1816, DRMCCU; Kruger, "Born to Run," 2:852–62; Zilversmit, *First Emancipation*, 199, 213–15.

28. Laws of New York, November 5, 1816, DRMCCU; New York State Legislature Assembly, "Report of the Select Committee on the Petition of Various Citizens to Prevent Kidnapping," Albany, N.Y., 1840, Cornell University Law Library; Kruger, "Born to Run," 2:733–35, 741–51; Wilma King, *Stolen Childhood: Slave Youth in Nineteenth-Century America* (Bloomington, Ind., 1995), 102–3; Carol Wilson, *Freedom at Risk: The Kidnapping of Free Blacks in America, 1780–1865* (Lexington, Ky., 1994), 9–11, 27, 73–74, 84–87, 99–101; Gary B. Nash

and Jean Soderland, *Freedom by Degrees: Emancipation in Pennsylvania and Its Aftermath* (New York, 1991), 114–15, 127, Zilversmit, *First Emancipation*, 208–22; 138, 182, 194; Ann Patton Malone, *Sweet Chariot: Slave Family and Household Structure in Nineteenth-Century Louisiana* (Chapel Hill, N.C., 1992), 74, 92–103, 105, 301 n. 71, 303 n. 103, 304 n. 104.

29. *NST*, 30–31; King, *Stolen Childhood*, 100–107; Wilson, *Freedom at Risk*, 17, 67–68, 71–75, 88–90, 94–97, 110–12; Hendricks, "Sojourner Truth," 669.

30. Joseph Gidney Papers, 1785–1812, Manuscripts Division, New York Public Library; Laws of New York, 1816, DRMCCU; Albert G. Barratt, "The Gidney Family," *HSNBH* 12 (1905): 121–16; *NST*, 30; Kruger, "Born to Run"; Zilversmit, *First Emancipation*, 207–9; Wilson, *Freedom at Risk*, 73–74.

31. "A Record of the Inscriptions in the Town Burying Ground," *HSNBH* 5 (1898): 20, 52–54, 97, 150, 154–55; E. M. Ruttenber, "The King's Highway," *HSNBH* 10 (1903): 28–29; and Barratt, "Gidney Family," 124, 128; "The Gidney Family" and "Gidney-Fowler," box 1, James Irving Clarke Papers, DRMCCU; King, *Stolen Childhood*, 21–23; Wilson, *Freedom at Risk*, 9, 10, 14–15. As early as 1810, the New York Manumission Society reported "the situation of slave children since the year 1799 loudly calls for the intervention of the Society," minutes of the New York Manumission Society, July 19, 1810, 190, reel 1, Papers of the New York Manumission Society, New-York Historical Society. The society continued to intervene in reported cases of kidnapping ("Minutes," July 19, 1810, 16, 142, 160, 165, 167), and some members later joined the (antislavery) Committee of Vigilance. See *Mirror of Liberty*, July 1838, January 1839.

32. *NST*, 31.

33. *NST*, 31.

34. *NST*, 31.

35. Jer. 2:1–7, 5:1–13, 26–31; on the jeremiad in American thought, see Perry Miller, *The New England Mind: The Seventeenth Century* (New York, 1939); Sacvan Bercovitch, *The American Jeremiad* (Madison, Wisc., 1978). On the African American jeremiad, see David Howard-Pitney, *The Afro-American Jeremiad: Appeals for Justice in America* (Philadelphia, 1990), 7–14, 17–25, 86, 112. For discussions on "prophetic salvationism" containing "certain undeniably African features," see Roger Bastide, *African Civilizations in the New World* (New York, 1971), 164–65, 217; Leonard E. Barrett, *Soul Force: African Heritage in Afro-American Religion* (Garden City, N.Y., 1974).

36. *NST*, 31–32.

37. *NST*, 53.

38. Anson and Jenkins, *Quaker History and Genealogy*, 2–4, 210; Delia Hart Stone, "Sojourner Truth," *Woman's Tribune*, November 14, 1903, 124; Hugh Barbour et al., eds., *Quaker Crosscurrents: Three Hundred Years of Friends in the New York Yearly Meetings* (Syracuse, N.Y., 1995), 28–30, 65–71, 116–35; Forbush, *Elias Hicks, Quaker Liberal*, 137–50, 269.

39. *NST*, 33.

40. *Plebeian*, May 14, 1828; Spafford, *Gazetteer*, 269; Kingston Village Minute Book, December 13, 1809, April 22, 1826, New York State Archives Cultural Education Center, Albany; Arthur C. Connelly, *St. James Methodist Church* (Kingston, N.Y., 1923), n.p.; "Kingston in 1828," *Olde Ulster* 10 (June 1914): 180–81; Hoes, *Baptismal and Marriage Registers*, esp. 464–98, 672–83. Stuart M. Blumin, *The Urban Threshold: Growth and Change in a Nineteenth-Century American Community* (Chicago, 1976), 27–30, 50–55, 82.

41. *NST*, 33; Charles H. Burnett, *The Chipp Family in England and America* (Los Angeles, 1933), 33–36.

42. *NST*, 31–35; "Grand Jury Precept to the Sheriff of Ulster County from the Panel of Grand Jurors for the April Circuit Court, 1827," List of Jurors Drawn for the April Circuit, 1829, Huguenot Historical Society, New Paltz, New York; "Family Record of Abraham Hasb-

rouck," *NYGBR* 71 (October 1940): 354–57, and 72 (January 1941): 36–37; General Notations, Charles H. Ruggles Papers, Manuscript Division, New York Public Library; Kingston Village Minute Book, 1805–1830, New York State Archives Cultural Education Center; Sylvester, *History of Ulster County*, 2:99, 100, 200, 203, 259; Frederick E. Westbrook, *The Two Hundredth Anniversary of the Erection of the Building Occupied as the Senate House of the State of New York in 1777* (Kingston, N.Y., 1883), 5–6, 17–19; Miller, *Hardenbergh Family*, 434–39; *Plebeian*, January 24, 1815, March 1, 1816; Will of Solomon Waring, 359–60; "Genealogy (Genealogical Notes on Families related to DuMonts)," "Genealogy—Dumont Notes," and "The Dumont Family," boxes 5 and 6, Reed Papers; "Gidney-Fowler," Family Bible of James Irving Clarke with Records of Births, Marriages & Deaths, box 1, Clarke Papers *DRMCCU*; Westbrook, *Senate House*, 5–6, 19; Barratt, "Gidney Family"; E. M. Ruttenber, "Provincial and Revolutionary Military Organizations," *HSNBH* 2 (1894): 11–12; and "King's Highway," 32; and *History of the County of Orange* (Newburgh, N.Y., 1875), 12–28, 134–38, 209.

43. *NST*, 33–34; *West Chester (PA) Daily Local News*, July 18, 1874.

44. Report of the Standing Committee of the Manumission Society, January 1827, reel 2, Papers of the New York Manumission Society, New York Historical Society, 165.

45. *NST*, 34–35; Stephen Middleton, *The Black Laws in the Old Northwest: A Documentary History* (Westport, Conn., 1993), 159–61, 178–79, 181, 185; Merrily Pierce, "Luke Decker and Slavery: His Cases with Bob and Anthony, 1817–1822," *Indiana Magazine of History* 3 (1989): 31–49.

46. *NST*, 35.

47. *NST*, 36.

48. *NST*, 53.

49. *NST*, 36–37; *IN*, 1:9; Thomas Romeyn to Mrs. Harriet Stafford, February 22, 1843, Sage Library, New Brunswick Theological Seminary, New Brunswick, New Jersey; John Romeyn to Dirck Romeyn, November 22, 1784, J. B. Johnson to Dirck Romeyn, September 20, 1798, in "The Romine Family" (1966), comp. Mildred A. McDonnell, bk. 1, 40, 60, 383–87, 424, Dirk Romeyn Manuscript Collection, Schaffer Library, Union College, Schenectady, New York; Edward T. Corwin, *A Manual of the Reformed Church in America, 1628–1878* (New York, 1879), 383–87, 424; *Plebeian*, December 2, 1820; Notes filed by H. M. Romeyn, November 16, 1821, Huguenot Historical Society; *Records of the Linlithgo Reformed Dutch Church at Livingston, New York*, 3 vols. New York State Library, Albany, vol. 1, pt. 2, 166–67; Miller, *Hardenbergh Family*, 57; Sylvester, *History of Ulster County*, 106.

50. Anne Grant, *Memoirs of an American Lady: With Sketches of Manners and Scenes in America* (Albany, N.Y., 1876), 111–16; Andrew D. Mellick Jr., *The Story of an Old Farm, or Life in New Jersey in the Eighteenth Century* (Somerville, N.J., 1889), 608–11; *NST*, 3–14, 36; *IN*, 1:9–12.

51. Report of the Manumission Society, January 1, 1827, January 15, 1828, reel 2, 165, 169, Papers of the New York Manumission Society, New-York Historical Society; *IN*, 1:10–12; *NST*, 38.

52. *NST*, 37; U.S. Census (1830), Ulster County, 56. Kidnapped victims who asserted their free status were threatened with death. Wilson, *Freedom at Risk*, 27.

53. *NST*, 37–38.

54. *NST*, 53; Report of the Manumission Society, January 15, 1828, reel 2, Papers of the New York Manumission Society, 169, New-York Historical Society.

CHAPTER 5: "A RUSHING MIGHTY WIND"

1. "Isabella Van Wagner . . . experience"; a copy of this note is in the Berenice Bryant Lowe Papers, box 1, fol. 9, MHC; the original has been lost.

2. *Rochester Evening Express*, April 17, 1871; *NST*, 51; Margaret Washington Creel, "A

Peculiar People": Slave Religion and Community-Culture among the Gullahs (New York, 1988), 261–63.

3. Howard Hendricks, "Sojourner Truth: Her Early History in Slavery," *National Magazine* 16 (October 1892): 669; *NST*, 42–47; *Rochester Evening Express*, April 17, 1871.

4. William Smith to Rev. M. Hulbert, January 29, 1884, in Carl Van Wagenen, ed., *A Genealogy of the Van Wagenen Family* (Interlaken, N.Y., 1994), 75; *NST*, 43–47.

5. *NST*, 62; David G. Hackett, *The Rude Hand of Innovation: Religion and Social Order in Albany, New York, 1652–1836* (New York, 1991), 46–48; James R. McGraw, *The John Street Church* (New York, n.d.), 2–5; Robert D. Simpson, ed., *American Methodist Pioneer: The Life and Journals of the Freeborn Garrettson, 1752–1827* (Rutland, Vt., 1984), 9–11, 143, 256–57, 267, 269–71; *The Journal and Letters of Francis Asbury*, ed. Elmer T. Clark et al., 3 vols. (London, 1958), 2:537–38, 700.

6. Simpson, *American Methodist Pioneer*, 271; Warren T. Smith, "Harry Hosier: Black Preacher Extraordinary," *Journal of the Interdenominational Theology Center* 7 no. 2 (spring 1989): 114–17, 119–22; John H. Wigger, *Taking Heaven by Storm: Methodism and the Rise of Popular Christianity in America* (New York, 1998), 135, 139, 145; L. M. Vincent, *Methodism in Poughkeepsie and Vicinity* (Poughkeepsie, N.Y., 1892), 14; Nathan O. Hatch, *Democratization of American Christianity* (New Haven, Conn., 1989), 106; *Journal of Asbury*, 2:198, 537–38.

7. William Smith to Rev. M. Hulbert, January 29, 1884, in Van Wagenen, *Genealogy*, 75; *Journal of Asbury*, 2:537–38, 700; Viv Edwards and Thomas J. Sienkewicz, *Oral Cultures Past and Present: Rappin' and Homer* (New York, 1990), 37–39, 58–74; James Tanis, *Dutch Calvinistic Pietism in the Middle Colonies: A Study in the Life and Theology of Theodore Jacobus Frelinghuysen* (The Hague, 1967), 110–11.

8. Simpson, *American Methodist Pioneer*, 358–59.

9. John Patterson, *Journal of the Travels and Religious Experience of John Patterson* (Harrisburg, Pa., 1817), 11–16; "New-York Conference," *MM* 8, no. 6 (June 1825): 237; *CAJZH*, October 14, 1826, July 29, 1831; Augusta Leslie, "Newburgh, N.Y., Methodist Episcopal Church," *HSNBH* 7 (1901): 7–30; E. M. Ruttenber, "The King's Highway," *HSNBH* 10 (1903): 29; Simpson, *American Methodist Pioneer*, 13, 16, 29, 308, 358–60.

10. Bernard A. Weisburger, *They Gathered at the River: The Story of the Great Revivals and Their Impact upon Religion in America* (Chicago, 1966), 42–49; Jarena Lee, *The Life and Religious Experience of Jarena Lee, A coloured Lady, Giving an Account of Her Call to Preach the Gospel, Revised and Corrected from the Original Manuscript, Written by Herself* (Philadelphia, 1836) 45–48; Zilpha Elaw, *Memoirs of the Life, Religious Experience, Ministerial Travels and Labours of Mrs. Zilpha Elaw, An American Female of Colour; Together with some Account of the Great Religious Revivals in America [Written by Herself]* (London, 1846), 56, 78–83, 103–4, 108–10, 131–35, both in *Sisters of the Spirit: Three Black Women's Autobiographies of the Nineteenth Century*, ed. William L. Andrews (Bloomington, Ind., 1986). "Revival of Religion in Newark, N.J.," *MM* 8, no. 6 (June 1825): 240–41; "Newburgh Camp Meeting," *MM* 8, no. 11 (November 1825): 440–41.

11. Francis Ward, *An Account of Three Camp Meetings Held by the Methodists* (Brooklyn, N.Y., 1806), 9–16; Anon., *Treatise on the Proceedings of a Camp Meeting Held in Bern, N.Y., Albany County* (Albany, N.Y., 1810), 1–6, 8–10.

12. *NST*, 48–49; Richard Cordley, "Sojourner Truth," undated newspaper article, STC; A. J. Williams-Myers, *Long Hammering: Essays on the Forging of an African American Presence in the Hudson River Valley to the Early Twentieth Century* (Trenton, N.J., 1994), chap. 5; Howard G. Hageman, *Pulpit and Table: Some Chapters in the History of Worship in the Reformed Churches* (Richmond, Va., 1962), 40–41.

13. *NST*, 49.

14. *NST*, 48; Exod. 16:2–7.

15. *Hosford's Calendar: On New-York and Vermont. Almanack: For the Year 1827* (Albany, N.Y., 1827), n.p., DRMCCU; *NST*, 48.

16. *NST*, 49.

17. *Rochester Evening Express*, April 17, 1871; Recollection of Eliza Seaman Leggett, Eliza Seaman Leggett Family Papers, vol. 8, DPL; *NST*, 49.

18. *NST*, 49–50.

19. Matt. 3:11; *NST*, 50.

20. *NST*, 50–51.

21. *NST*, 50–51; John 20:22; *Order of Worship, for the Dutch Reformed Church* (Philadelphia, 1869), 107, Adriaan Cornelis Barnard, "The Feast of Pentecost in the Liturgical Year," trans. Martijna Aarts Briggs (M.A. thesis, Free University, Amsterdam, Holland, 1954), 47–48; Acts 2:1–3; "Recollections of Eliza Seaman Leggett," Leggett Papers, vol. 8, DPL.

22. Van Wagenen, *Genealogy*, 75. Freeborn Garrettson, "Union of Fear, Hope, Love, and Joy, in the Believer," *MM* 8, no. 6 (June 1825): 209–10; Elaw, *Memoirs*, 65–67; Barnard, "Feast of Pentecost," 48–50; David Martin, *Tongues of Fire: The Explosion of Protestantism in Latin America* (Cambridge, Mass., 1990); Karl Laman, *Kongo*, 5 vols. (Uppsala, Sweden, 1962), 3:1–6, 216–18.

23. *NST*, 43–55; Elaw, *Memoirs*, 55–56; John Leland Peters, *Christian Perfection and American Methodism* (New York, 1956), 33, 65, 83, 99.

24. *IN*, 2:119; *NST*, 51–55.

25. Jean M. Humez, ed., *Gifts of Power: The Writings of Rebecca Jackson, Black Visionary Shaker Eldress* (Amherst, Mass., 1981), 106–7; Lee, *Life and Religious Experience*, 27–29, Elaw, *Memoirs*, 53–57.

26. *Diary of Dina Van Bergh* (Frelinghuysen-Hardenbergh), trans. Gerard Van Dyke, Occasional Paper Series of the Historical Society of the Reformed Church in America (New Brunswick, N.J., 1993), 37, 71–75, 82–86, 88–89, 106–26; Abraham Messler, *Forty Years at Raritan: Eight Memorial Sermons, with Notes for a History of the Reformed Dutch Churches in Somerset Country, N.J. (New York, 1873)*, 193–94; William Henry Steele Demarest, "Dina(h) Van Bergh, the Jufvrouw Hardenbergh," paper presented to the New Brunswick Historical Club, Rutgers University Library, October 19, 1939; Firth Haring Fabend, "Suffer the Little Children: Evangelical Child-Rearing in Reformed Dutch Households, New York and New Jersey, 1826–1876," *De Halve Maen* 68 (summer 1995): 26–28; Anne Grant, *Memoirs of an American Lady: With Sketches of Manners and Scenes in America* (Albany, N.Y., 1876), 42–47; Gerald F. De Jong, "The Dutch Reformed Church and Negro Slavery in Colonial America," *Church History* 40 (December 1971): 424–36, and *The Dutch Reformed Church in the American Colonies* (Grand Rapids, Mich., 1978), 127, 165–69; E. P. Thompson, *The Making of the English Working Class* (New York, 1963), 42–52; John R. Tyson, ed., *Charles Wesley: A Reader* (New York, 1989), 110–11.

27. Lee, *Life and Religious Experience*, 28–33, Elaw, *Memoirs*, 53–57, 64–66.

28. Lee, *Life and Religious Experience*, 39–40. Kidnapping victims who asserted their free status were beaten and threatened with death. See Carol Wilson, *Freedom at Risk: The Kidnapping of Free Blacks in America, 1780–1865* (Lexington, Ky., 1994), 27; Solomon Northup, *Twelve Years a Slave*, ed. Sue Eakin and Joseph Logsdon (Baton Rouge, La., 1968), 21–27, 37–39.

29. *NST*, 38–39, 42; *NYT*, November 8, 1853. On the fusion of conjuration and Christianity, and Sojourner Truth as "conjure woman," see Theophus H. Smith, *Conjuring Culture: Biblical Formations of Black America* (New York, 1994), 3–15, 39–43, 159–82. On *kindoki* among Gullah Christians, see Creel, *"A Peculiar People,"* 320–21; On *kindoki* among the BaKongo, see Simon Bockie, *Death and the Invisible Powers: The World of Kongo Belief* (Bloomington,

Ind., 1993), 40–57, 66–67. Bockie employs a different meaning for *kindoki* and *ndoki* from other writers, and does not view *kindoki* as witchcraft. For a different perspective, see John M. Jansen and Wyatt MacGaffey, *An Anthology of Kongo Religion: Primary Texts from Lower Zaire* (Lawrence, Kans., 1974), 141, and MacGaffey, *Religion and Society in Central Africa: The BaKongo of Lower Zaire* (Chicago, 1986), 160–65, 170–73.

30. *NST* 41; *NSTBL*, "Memorial Chapter," 23.

31. *NST*, 41–42.

32. *NST*, 42–43.

33. The story of Eliza Gidney Fowler can be traced mainly through her daughter, Mary C. Gearn, and Eliza's brother, Solomon Gidney. See Genealogical Notes, Family Bible of James Irving Clarke, Album of Gloriana Gidney, Poetry of Mary C. Fowler, James Irving Clarke Papers, boxes 1 and 2, and miscellaneous notes, box 2, DRMCCU; Notice to Appear in the Matter of the Will of Solomon Gidney (deceased), in the Surrogate Court, Dutchess Country, New York, by Petition of Julia Ann Fowler, April 17, 1865, file no. 5543, Surrogate's Court, Dutchess Country, New York. Gidney's will is missing from the court records.

34. *Battle Creek Nightly Moon*, June 8, 1880; *Battle Creek Journal*, December 6, 1883; *NST*, 32.

35. *CDI*, August 13, 1879; *NSTBL*, "Memorial Chapter," 6; *NST*, 62; William Smith to Rev. M. Hulbert, January 29, 1884, in Van Wagenen, *Genealogy*, 75.

36. *NST*, 52–53.

CHAPTER 6: SANCTIFICATION AND PERFECTION

1. *NST*, 67; *IN*, 1:11, 18–19; Howard Hendricks, "Sojourner Truth: Her Early History in Slavery," *National Magazine* 16 (October 1892): 668; U.S. Census Bureau, *Population Schedules of the Fifth Census* (1830), State of New York, County of Ulster, Town of New Paltz, (Washington, 1832), 203; NAEI, 4:241, 307, 50, 352; Vivienne L. Kruger, "Born to Run: The Slave Family in Early New York, 1626–1927," 2 vols. (Ph.D. diss., Columbia University, 1985), 2:767–84, 852–65, 887–89, 921–22, 936–41.

2. Laws of the State of New York, Forty-first Session of Legislature, November 5, 1816, article 5; *NST*, 54, 56–64; *Battle Creek Daily Journal*, October 25, 1904. U.S. Census Bureau, *Population Schedules of the Eighth Census* (1860), State of Michigan, County of Calhoun, Bedford Township (Washington, D.C., 1864) (category of "Persons over 20 who cannot read & write"), 90, 91; Sojourner Truth to Mary K. Gale, April 15, 1853, STC; Dorothy Sterling, ed., *We Are Your Sisters: Black Women in the Nineteenth Century* (New York, 1984), 89–93.

3. Carleton Mabee with Susan Mabee Newhouse, *Sojourner Truth, Slave, Prophet, Legend* (New York, 1993), 13–14, 22–23, 31–32, 93; Nell Irvin Painter, *Sojourner Truth: A Life, A Symbol* (New York, 1996), 101–2; Paul Johnson and Sean Wilentz, *The Kingdom of Mathias* (New York, 1994), 116.

4. *Letters of John Pintard to His Daughter Eliza Noel Pintard Davidson, 1816–1833*, ed. Dorothy Barck, 4 vols. (New York, 1937–49), 1:125–26, 137, 145, 181–82, 271–72, 370; 2:271–72, 3:81–82, 282; *NST*, 56; Kruger, "Born to Run," 2:893–96, 921–26; Edwin G. Burrows and Mike Wallace, *Gotham: A History of New York City to 1898* (New York, 1999), 483–85, 855–56; Faye Dudden, *Serving Women: Household Service in the Nineteenth Century* (New York, 1984), 218–19; Larry Whiteaker, *Seduction, Prostitution, and Moral Reform in New York, 1830–1860* (New York, 1997), 23–42; Elizabeth Blackmar, *Manhattan for Rent, 1785–1850* (Ithaca, N.Y., 1989), 114–20.

5. *Freedom's Journal*, June 1, 1827; Kruger, "Born to Run," 2: 926–27; Paul Gilje, *The Road to Mobocracy: Popular Disorder in New York City, 1763–1834* (Chapel Hill, N.C., 1987), 125–32, 138–41, 147–62; Leonard L. Richards, *"Gentlemen of Property and Standing": Anti-abolition Mobs in Jacksonian America* (New York, 1970), 3–10, 21–22, 165–69; Kenneth A. Scherzer, *The Unbounded Community: Neighborhood Life and Social Structure in New York*

City, 1820–1875 (Durham, N.C., 1991), 26–32; Anthony Gronowicz, *Race and Class Politics in New York City before the Civil War* (Boston, 1998), 25–27, 50–52, 57; Burrows and Wallace, *Gotham*, 315–18.

6. Raymond A. Mohl, *Poverty in New York, 1783–1825* (New York, 1971), 21, 93, 176–78, 225–33; Leonard Curry, *The Free Black in Urban America 1800–1850: The Shadow of a Dream* (Chicago, 1981), 8–12, 18–29, 31–36; Mahlon Day, *New York Street Cries in Rhyme* (1825; reprint, New York, 1977), 18, 22; Leslie M. Harris, *In the Shadow of Slavery: African Americans in New York City* (Chicago, 2003), 76–77.

7. *Freedom's Journal*, May 4, June 1, 22, 1827; Kruger, "Born to Run," 926–27; John H. Hewitt, "Mr. Downing and His Oyster House: The Life and Good Works of an African-American Entrepreneur," *New York History* 74 (July 1993): 229–35; Harris, *Shadow of Slavery*, 78–82.

8. Charles G. Sommers, *Memoir of the Reverend John Stanford, D.D., Late Chaplin to the Humane and Criminal Institutions* (New York, 1835), 1–26, 51–54, 62–75, 86–87, 100–115, 153–62, 187, 204–28, 271–81; *Christian Herald and Seaman's Magazine* 9, no. 20 (March 1823): 621–23; *Freedom's Journal*, July 11, 1828; Journals and Notebooks Arthur Tappan, entries of February 26, March 3, 1836, Papers of Arthur Tappan, Manuscript Division, Library of Congress, Washington, D.C.; *Letters of John Pintard*, 3:109, 62, 74–77.

9. *IN* 1:11, 18–19, 2:122, 126; *NST*, 50, 62, *Longworth's American Almanac, New York Register, and City Directory*, 1827, 28, 1828, 29, 1829 39, 1830, 31; Lyman E. La Tourette, "La Tourette Annals in America," Genealogical Records and Files of the La Tourette Family; photostats from the La Tourette Family Bible; Nina La Tourette Romeyn to Loring McMillen, Esq., June 22, 1938, all in La Tourette Family Papers, Staten Island Historical Society, Staten Island, New York; Records of John Street Methodist Church, 413 vols. 237:1, 3, 15, 31, 169, 179, 210, 31, vols. 250, 252, New York Public Library; Will of James La Tourette, June 23, 1841, Surrogate Court, County of New York; Blackmar, *Manhattan for Rent*, 118–20; Dudden, *Serving Women*, 63–65, 177–79, 212–13; Sandra L. Graham, *House and Street: The Domestic World of Servants and Masters in Nineteenth-Century Rio de Janeiro* (Cambridge, 1988), 3–6, 15–19.

10. *IN*, 1:61–63, 2:15–17, *NST*, 68; *NAEI*, vol. 7; Sojourner Truth to Amy Post, January 18, 1869, AIPFP; *NSTBL*, 20–21.

11. *New York Evangelist*, March 26, 1836; *NYT*, July 19, 1854; *Christian Recorder*, May 1861; "Recollections of Eliza Seaman Leggett," Eliza Seaman Leggett Family Papers, vol. 8, DPL; *CDI*, August 13, 1879; George W. Hodges, *Early Negro Church Life in New York* (New York, 1945), 21–23; Carroll Smith-Rosenberg, *Religion and Rise of the American City: The New York City Mission Movement, 1812–1870* (Ithaca, N.Y., 1971), 3, 26, 27, 50, 66.

12. "Memorial Chapter," *NSTBL*, 6; *NYT*, September 7, 1853.

13. *IN*, 1:18–19, 2:21, 112, 115; *Harper's*, August 1892; Adam Clarke, "Christian Perfection," *MM* 11, no. 1 (January 1828): 103–5, 141–46; Gen. 1–11; Joseph J. Foot, "An Enquiry Respecting the Theological Origin of Perfectionism and Its Correlative Branches," *Literary and Theological Review* 9 (March 1836): 7, 10, 15, 29; Robert D. Thomas, *Man Who Would Be Perfect: John Humphrey Noyes and the Utopian Impulse* (Philadelphia, 1977), chap. 3, 70, 72, 77, 82–83, 133–34; Catherine Brekus, *Strangers and Pilgrims: Female Preaching in America 1740–1845* (Chapel Hill, N.C., 1998), 169–70, 294–95; Whitney R. Cross, *The Burned-Over District: The Social and Intellectual History of Enthusiastic Religion in Western New York, 1800–1850* (Ithaca, N.Y., 1950), 177–78, 184, 189–96, 240; John L. Peters, *Christian Perfection and American Methodism* (New York, 1956), 32–39, 64–66, 82–89, 100; Nathan O. Hatch, *Democratization of American Christianity* (New Haven, Conn., 1989), 201–5.

14. Paul K. Conkin, *The Uneasy Center: Reformed Christianity in Antebellum America* (Chapel Hill, N.C., 1995), 121; John Wesley, "Thoughts on Methodism," *MM* 9, no. 6 (June 1826): 225–27.

15. Garth M. Rosell and Richard A. G. DuPuis, eds., *The Memoirs of Charles G. Finney, 1792–1825* (Grand Rapids, Mich., 1989), 74–84, 284–88, 353–55; Charles E. Hambrick-Stowe, *Charles G. Finney and the Spirit of American Evangelicalism* (Grand Rapids, Mich., 1996), chaps. 3–6; Cross, *Burned-Over District*, esp. 6–9, 11–12, 151–84; Gardner Spring, *Personal Reminiscences of the Life and Times of Gardiner Spring* (New York, 1866), 221–28; Paul E. Johnson, *A Shopkeeper's Millennium: Society and Revivals in Rochester, New York, 1815–1837* (New York, 1978), 95–102; William G. McLoughlin, *Revivals, Awakenings, and Reform: An Essay on Religion and Social Change in America, 1607–1977* (Chicago, 1978), 125–28, chap. 10; *Letters of Theodore Dwight Weld and Angelina Grimké Weld, and Sarah Grimké, 1822–1844*, ed. Gilbert H. Barnes and Dwight A. Dumond, 2 vols. (Gloucester, Mass., 1965), 1:9, 10.

16. Edward N. Kirk to Charles Finney, December 24, 1828, R. H. Hurlburt to Charles Finney, February 1, 1831, James Boyle to Charles Finney, April 24, 1827, March 30, November 1, 1832; James and Laura Boyle to Mr. and Mrs. Finney, March 30, 1831, Laura Boyle to Mrs. Lydia Finney, June 11, 1831, FP; Diary of Benjamin, Russell, 1831–41, Benjamin Russell Papers, DRMCCU; David O. Mears, *Life of Edward Norris Kirk* (Boston, 1878), 45–51; Hambrick-Stowe, *Finney*, 38–39, 50–53; Hatch, *Democratization of American Christianity*, 200.

17. L. Brown to Charles Finney, January 6, 1831, Anson Phelps to Charles Finney, January 31, 1831, Lewis Tappan to Charles Finney, February 2, 1831, and March 17, 1831, FP; Spring, *Personal Reminiscences*, 215–28, 231; *MM* 9, no. 1 (August 1826): 309–10; James Boyle, "A Letter to William Lloyd Garrison Respecting the Clerical Appeal, Sectarianism and True Holiness" (Boston, 1838), May Pamphlets, vol. 167, no. 10, Anti-Slavery Collection, DRM-CCU; Thomas, *Man Who Would Be Perfect*, 30–33, chap. 3, 72–74, 83–84, 90, 147–52; Bertram Wyatt-Brown, *Lewis Tappan and the Evangelical War against Slavery* (Baton Rouge, La., 1969), 65–73; McLoughlin, *Revivals*, 122–24; Hatch, *Democratization of American Christianity*, 197–200; Charles C. Cole, "The Free Church Movement in New York City," *New York History* 34, no. 3 (July 1953): 288–93; Cross, *Burned-Over District*, 6–9, 11–12, 151–84, 190–91, 195–96; Smith-Rosenberg, *Religion and the City*, 86–92, 131–34; David G. Hackett, *The Rude Hand of Innovation: Religion and Social Order in Albany, New York, 1652–1836* (New York, 1991), 107–8, 127–3; Johnson, *Shopkeeper's Millennium*, 95–115.

18. Brekus, *Strangers and Pilgrims*, 8, 119–37, 166–71, 183–87; Cross, *Burned-Over District*, 37–38, 177; Jarena Lee, *The Life and Religious Experience of Jarena Lee, A coloured Lady, Giving an Account of Her Call to Preach the Gospel, Revised and Corrected from the Original Manuscript, Written by Herself* (Philadelphia, 1836), 36–38; Zilpha Elaw, *Memoirs of the Life, Religious Experience, Ministerial Travels and Labours of Mrs. Zilpha Elaw, An American Female of Colour; Together with some Account of the Great Religious Revivals in America [Written by Herself]* (London, 1846), 64–66, 75–79, 83–103, and Julia A. J. Foote, *"A Brand Plucked from the Fire": An Autobiographical Sketch* (Cleveland, 1879), 200–211, all in William L. Andrews, ed., *Sisters of the Spirit: Three Black Women's Autobiographies of the Nineteenth Century* (Bloomington, Ind., 1986); James D. Folts, "The Fanatic and the Prophetess: Religious Perfectionism in Western New York, 1835–1839," *New York History* 72, no. 4 (October 1991): 371–72; Lydia Maria Francis Child, *Letters from New York*, 3d ed. (Freeport, N.Y., 1970), 73.

19. Nigel Watson, *The First Epistle of the Corinthians* (London, 1992), 129–32; *IN*, 2:21, 112; *CAJZH*, September 19, 1823, October 14, 1826; October 10, 1828; (Boston) *Commonwealth*, July 2, 1863.

20. Lee, *The Life and Religious Experience*, 27–38, Elaw, *Memoirs*, 53–58, 64–67, 89–129, 131–34; *IN*, 2:21; Harriet Livermore, *Scriptural Evidence in Favor of Female Testimony* (Portsmouth, N.H., 1824).

21. *Christian Advocate and Journal*, October 26, November 23, 1827, February 29, 1828. "The Christian Duty of Christian Women," *Christian Advocate* 4 (January 1826): 1–11 (a

Presbyterian journal not to be confused with the Methodist *Christian Advocate and Journal*); 1 Cor. 14:34, 35, 11:4, 14; Cross, *Burned-Over District*, 177–78; Smith-Rosenberg, *Religion and the City*, 97–124.

22. William T. Hamilton, "A Word for the African," *Freedom's Journal*, October 12, 1827; *Plebeian*, February 1, 8, 18, 1817; Wyatt-Brown, *Lewis Tappan*, 84–86; Julie Winch, *A Gentleman of Color: The Life of James Forten* (New York, 2002), 186–94; Richards, *Gentlemen of Property*, 21–22, 31–34; Harris, *Shadow of Slavery*, 140–42.

23. *IN*, 1:11–13, 18–19, 54–55; *NST*, 67–68; Records of John Street Methodist Church, 237:39, 74, 76, 112, and 238:29, 42, 70, 110, 112; *Freedom's Journal*, March 23, April 6, June 3, 1827; William J. Walls, *The African Methodist Episcopal Zion Church* (Charlotte, N.C., 1974), 26–28, 35–84; Hodges, *Early Negro Church Life in New York*, 5–6, 8–11; J. B. Wakeley, *Lost Chapters Recovered from the Early History of American Methodism* (New York, 1858), 438–44; Gayraud S. Wilmore, *Black Religion and Black Radicalism: An Interpretation of the Religious History of African Americans*, 3d rev. enl. ed. (Maryknoll, N.Y., 1998), 105–15. Howard H. Bell, *A Survey of the Negro Convention Movement, 1830–1861* (New York, 1969), 14–15; William Gravely, "African Methodism and the Rise of Black Denominationalism," in Russell E. Richey and Kenneth Rowee, eds., *Rethinking Methodist History: A Bicentennial Historical Consultation* (Nashville, Tenn., 1985).

24. Walls, *Zion Church*, 48–50, 70–76; "American Colonization Society," *MM* 7, no.1 (January 1824): 27–30; "American Colonization Society," *MM* 9 , no. 1 (January 1826), 31–34 (May 1826), 178–84; *MM* 11 (September 1828): 307; *CAJZH*, May 10, 1833, July 4, July 25, August 15, 1834; Richards, *"Gentlemen of Property,"* 21–22; Hatch, *Democratization of American Christianity*, 201–6.

25. "Minutes and Proceedings of the First Annual Convention of the People of Color, Held by Adjournment in the City of Philadelphia, June 6–11, 1831," in *Minutes of the Proceedings of the National Negro Conventions, 1830–1864*, ed. Howard H. Bell (reprint, New York, 1969); Bella Gross, "The First National Negro Convention," *JNH* 31 (October 1946): 435–43. *NST*, 59, 63.

26. James 1:22, 27, 2: 17–16; *NYT*, September 7, 1853; *Freedom's Journal*, January 25, February 1, February 8, March 7, 1828; *IN* 1:20, 46; Anne M. Boylin, "Benevolence and Antislavery Activity among African American Women in New York and Boston, 1820–1840," in Jean F. Yellin and John C. Van Horne, eds., *The Abolitionist Sisterhood: Women's Political Culture in Antebellum America* (Ithaca, N.Y., 1994), 119–22, 124, 128–33.

27. *NST*, 68; Joshua Leavitt, *Memoir and Select Remains of the Late Reverend John R. M'Dowell, the Martyr of the Seventh Commandment in the Nineteenth Century* (New York, 1838), 97–101, 109–10, 113; *Christian Herald and Seaman's Magazine* 8, no. 6 (August 1821): 183–84; *Freedom's Journal*, July 20, 1827, July 11, 1828; Ladies of the Mission, *The Old Brewery and the Mission House at the Five Points* (New York, 1854), 18–20, 33–37; Daniel Perlman, "Organizations of the Free Negro in New York City, 1800–1860," *JNH* 56, no. 3 (July 1971): 181–85; Scherzer, *Unbounded Community*, 144; Blackmar, *Manhattan for Rent*, 172–77; Smith-Rosenberg, *Religion and the City*, 34–35, 56–57; 205–11; Leslie Harris, "From Abolitionist Amalgamators to Rulers of the Five Points: The Discourse of Interracial Sex and Reform in Antebellum New York City," in Martha Hodes, ed., *Sex, Love, Race: Crossing Boundaries in North American History* (New York, 1999), 191–92, 200; George G. Foster, *New York by Gas-Light, and Other Urban Sketches* (1856), ed. Stuart M. Blumin (Berkeley, 1990), 122–26; Burrows and Wallace, *Gotham*, 101, 122–23, 148, 391, 478–80, 644.

28. Leavitt, *Memoir*, 100, 104, 127, 150, 158–59, 195–96; Foster, *New York by Gas-Light*, 122–23; 36–40; William Leete Stone, *Matthias and His Imposters: Or, The Progress of Fanaticism, Illustrated in the Extraordinary Case of Robert Matthews and Some of His Forerunners and Disciples* (New York, 1935), 59–60; Timothy J. Gilfoyle, *City of Eros: New York City, Prostitu-*

tion, and the Commercialization of Sex, 1790–1920 (New York, 1992), 36–41, 182. Whiteaker, Seduction, 54–56; Graham, House and Street, 45–46.

29. Rev. 17, 18, esp. 17:5, 6, 15; Leavitt, Memoir, 97–107, 112–18, 124–27, 143–45, 158–70.

30. Leavitt, Memoir, 101–7, 112–12, 116–18, 124, 131, 142–44, 166–67, 195–96; CAJZH, July 1, 1831; IN, 1:20; Spring, Personal Reminiscences, 229–30; Stone, Matthias, 62–63, 69; Longworth's City Directory, 1830, 31, 1831, 32; New York Spectator, March 8, 1831; New York Evangelist, July 2, 16, 1831; Lewis Tappan, The Life of Arthur Tappan (New York, 1870), 110–13; Whiteaker, Seduction, 11–12, 51–63.

31. NST, 68; Leavitt, Memoir, 103–9, 110–18, 120–51, 158–59; Freedom's Journal (July 20, 1827, May 2, 1828); Rights of All, October 9, 1829; John J. Zuille, comp., Historical Sketch of the New York African Society for Mutual Relief (New York, 1892), 22, 28, 29; Wilson J. Moses, Alexander Crummell (Amherst, Mass., 1989), 11–13, 18; Hewitt, "Mr. Downing and His Oyster House," 229–35; Blackmar, Manhattan for Rent, 174–75; Gilfoyle, City of Eros, 39–54.

32. Leavitt, Memoir, 101–3, 131–35, 150–51, 164–65; Freedom's Journal, April 18, October 12, 1827, March 21, July 11, 1828; NYT, September 7, 1853; Moses, Alexander Crummell, 16–19; Patricia Hill Collins, Black Feminist Thought: Knowledge, Consciousness and the Politics of Empowerment (New York, 1991), chap. 1.

33. Leavitt, Memoir, 103–7, 124–25, 143–48; New York Spectator, March 8, 1831; NST, 68; Smith-Rosenberg, Religion and the City, 97, 102; Cross, Burned-Over District, 177–79, 241–44.

34. NST, 68; IN, 1:19, 40, 44–50; CAJZH, August 21, December 28, 1832; Sommers, Memoir of Stanford, 153–62, 187, 204–28, 271–81; Stone, Matthias, 49, 51–55, 60–61, 81–82; New York Evangelist, July 16, 1831; Commercial Advertiser, September 26, 1832; James 1:22, 2:5–6; Acts 1:4–5, 2:1–8, 17–21; Leavitt, Memoir, 103–7, 124–15, 143–48; 151; Advocate of Moral Reform, June 1, 1838; Smith-Rosenberg, Religion and the City, 11, 97–105, 118–19; George Wallingford Noyes, Religious Experience of John Humphrey Noyes (New York, 1923), 301–2, 305, 340–42; Thomas, Man Who Would be Perfect, 82–84, 93–96; Cross, Burned-Over District, 248; Johnson and Wilentz, Kingdom of Matthias, 20–27; Scherzer, Unbounded Community, 144–45.

35. James 1:22, 27, 2:17–26, 3:14–15; IN, 1:24–26; Stone, Matthias, 41–69, 90–92; Spring, Personal Reminiscences; Clarke, "Christian Perfection," 103–6; Tappan, Arthur Tappan, 112; Whiteaker, Seduction, 51, 52, 54; Cross, Burned-Over District, 38, 177–78, 84, 189–96, 238–51 (Cross's otherwise excellent study fails to capture the role of women in enthusiastic religious movements); Noyes, Religious Experience, 178–79, 186–87, 192–94; Johnson and Wilentz, Kingdom of Matthias, 21–25, 28–32.

36. 1 Kings 17:1, 18:19–22; 2 Kings 2:1–2, 9–14; Luke 1:17, Matt. 17:1–13; James 5:12–15; Harold H. Rowley, "Elijah on Mount Carmel," Bulletin of the John Rylands Library University of Manchester, 43 (1960): 190–219; Diary of John Stanford, entries for June 8, June 23, June 29, and July 1, July 12, 1830, New-York Historical Society; Stone, Matthias, 67–74; Spring, Personal Reminiscences, 228–29; Johnson and Wilentz, Kingdom of Matthias, 33–35.

37. Stone, Matthias, 61–63, 68–74; IN, 1:7–14, 19, 26–34; Sommers, Memoir of Stanford; Spring, Personal Reminiscences, 229.

38. Stone, Matthias, 52–60, 90–92; IN, 1:23–36; Cross, Burned-Over District, 84, 238–48; 339; John C. Spurlock, Free Love: Marriage and Middle-Class Radicalism in America, 1825–1860 (New York, 1988), 33–35, 39, 73–83.

39. New York Evangelist, January 19, July 2, 9, 16, 1831, February 23, 1833; CAJZH, July 29, 1831; New York Gospel Herald and Universalist Review 2 (December 1831): 402; Stone, Matthias, 79–80; Leavitt, Memoir, 155–59, 178–79, 181–83, 195–98, 252–53, 349, 390–95; 415–18; IN, 1:12, 19; Tappan, Arthur Tappan, 68–70, 88–89, 110–18; Whiteaker, Seduction, 50–55; Johnson and Wilentz, Kingdom of Matthias, 20–22, 25–28, 36.

40. IN, 1:23. 25–27, 41, 43, 2:19–21; New York Evangelist, February 23, 1833.

41. Rev. 21:1–2; exchange of letters between John Humphrey Noyes and James La Tourette, April 2, April 5, 1837, in *Witness*, September 23, 1837, 133–34, 179; Mrs. C. L. Brown to Mrs. Charles G. Finney, June 12, 1834; C. L. Brown to Reverend Charles G. Finney, October 7, 1834; Reverend Charles G. Finney to George Whipple and Henry B. Stanton, January 18, 1835, FP; John 13:1–12; Stone, *Matthias*, 79–82.

42. *IN*, 1:7–10, 50; Stone, *Matthias*, 79–82; John 13:5, 10, 14–16; 1 Thess. 5:26; Gilje, *Road to Mobocracy*, 153–70.

43. "Isabella Van Wagner . . . experience," Berenice Lowe Papers, box 1, fol. 9, MHC; *IN* 2:19; *Battle Creek Nightly Moon*, July 29, 1880.

44. William James, *The Varieties of Religious Experience* (London: 1912), 389–82.

45. *IN*, 1:25, 41–43; John 14:17, 26.

CHAPTER 7: "I WILL CRUSH THEM WITH THE TRUTH"

1. *IN*, 1:19–22.

2. *IN*, 1:19–22.

3. *IN*, 1:19–22, 43.

4. *IN*, 1:19–22, 43.

5. *IN*, 1:40.

6. Acts 1:1–9, 13–15, 22–26; 2:1–2, 4; Rev. 7:4–8; 12:1; 21:12–21; 22:2.

7. *IN*, 1:40.

8. Margaret Matthews, *Matthias, by His Wife* (New York, 1835), 3–7, 12, 14–15, 18–22; Paul Johnson and Sean Wilentz, *The Kingdom of Mathias* (New York, 1994), 52–53, 59–62.

9. Matthews, *Matthias by His Wife*, 8–15, 20; David O. Mears, *Life of Edward Norris Kirk* (Boston, 1878), 5–6, 17–19, 44–51, 76–85.

10. Matthews, *Matthias, by His Wife*, 14–20, 21–28.

11. *IN*, 1:25, 42–43, 45. This chapter relies heavily on Isabella's account in *IN*, because she was the only eyewitness to most of the events.

12. *IN*, 1:43–46.

13. *IN*, 1:43–45; 47, 2;44; William Leete Stone, *Matthias and His Imposters: Or, The Progress of Fanaticism, Illustrated in the Extraordinary Case of Robert Matthews and Some of His Forerunners and Disciples* (New York, 1935), 120–26, 136–38; Johnson and Wilentz, *Kingdom of Matthias*, 98–99.

14. *IN*, 1:43–47.

15. *IN*, 1:46–67; Matt. 13:38, 40; William Green to Charles Finney, August 25, 1832, FP; *Christian Advocate and Journal*, August 24, 1832; Spring, *Personal Reminiscences*, 212–14; Gerard T. Koeppel, *Water for Gotham: A History* (Princeton, N.J., 2000), 3–5, 51–52, 56–69, 111–19, 123–24, 139–40.

16. Koeppel, *Water for Gotham*, 5, 88–101, 123–24, *New York Evangelist*, July 21, August 18, 1832.

17. Koeppel, *Water for Gotham*, 1:21, 47–48, 51; Robin Larsen, ed., *Emanuel Swedenborg: A Continuing Vision* (New York, 1988), 6, 359–60; George Wallingford Noyes, *Religious Experience of John Humphrey Noyes* (New York, 1923), 42–99, 196–202; Whitney R. Cross, *Burned-Over District, The Social and Intellectual History of Enthusiastic Religion in Western New York, 1800–1850* (Ithaca, 1950); 240–49; John C. Spurlock, *Free Love: Marriage and Middle-Class Radicalism in America, 1825–1860* (New York, 1988), 72–81.

18. *IN*, 1:44, 50–51; "The People vs. Robert Matthews," September 24, 1832, District Attorney Indictment Papers, NYCMAR, and Court of General Sessions, December 10, 1832, NYCMAR.

19. *IN*, 1:50–51; John 4:44, 19:6.

20. *IN*, 1:51, 52.

21. *IN*, 1:53–54.

22. *IN*, 1:55; Acts. 4:32.

23. *IN*, 1:63; Acts. 4:32.

24. *IN*, 1:64–65; 2:72–73. *The False Prophet! The Very Interesting and Remarkable Trial of Matthias, the False Prophet* (New York, 1835), 12.

25. *IN*, 1:60–64; 2:17–55, 91–94, 106; Matt. 19:21; *False Prophet*, 13. For an interesting analysis of the importance of the kitchen in domestic economy, see Gilliam Brown, "Getting in the Kitchen with Dinah: Domestic Politics in Uncle Tom's Cabin," *American Quarterly* 36, no. 4 (fall 1984): 503–23; Sandra L. Graham, *House and Street: The Domestic World of Servants and Masters in Nineteenth-Century Rio de Janeiro* (Cambridge, 1988), 115–19.

26. Stone, *Matthias*, 187; *IN*, 1:59, 61–66, 2:44–48, 51–53; Theodore Schroeder, "Matthias the Prophet, 1788–1837," *Journal of Religious Psychology* 6 (1936): 60; *Commercial Advertiser*, April 18, 1835; *False Prophet*, 8–9, 13–15; Matthews, *Matthias, by His Wife*, 39.

27. *False Prophet*, 12–13; *Commercial Advertiser*, September 28, 1834.

28. *IN*, 1:59–63, 2:114; Stone, *Matthias*, 182–83; *False Prophet*, 12.

29. *IN*, 1:61–63, 66–68, 73.

30. *IN*, 1:23–24, 30–32, 61–64, 67; 2:10–12, 21; Stone, *Matthias*, 46–47; Mamaroneck Town Record Book, 1697–1881 and 1756–1878, Westchester County, Mamaroneck, New York, New York State Library, Albany.

31. *IN*, 1:61; *False Prophet*, 7–13.

32. *IN*, 1:53–54, 59; 2:9–11, 16, 108, 114–16.

33. *IN*, 1:69–70, Stone, *Matthias*, 148–51, 170–71; Statement of Benjamin Folger, in *Benjamin Folger v. Robert Matthews, Alias Matthias the Prophet*, September 23, 1834, District Attorney Indictment Papers, NYCMAR.

34. *IN*, 1:64, 71–73; 2:10–11.

35. *IN*, 1:73.

36. Matthews, *Matthias, by His Wife*, 28–30; Stone, *Matthias*, 46–49; *IN*, 1:69–70, 76–79; 2:17, 20–21, 32.

37. Matthews, *Matthias, by His Wife*, 32–35; *IN*, 1:82; 2:14–18, 22–23.

38. Matthews, *Matthias, by His Wife*, 32–33; *IN*, 2:26–29.

39. *IN*, 2:29–31; Matthews, *Matthias, by His Wife*, 33–34.

40. *IN*, 2:17–18, 22–25, 30–39.

41. Matthews, *Matthias by His Wife*, 19–26; *IN*, 1:60, 74; 2:11; *False Prophet*, 7–14; *Folger vs. Matthews*, NYCMAR; Johnson and Wilentz, *Kingdom of Matthias*, chap. 2.

42. *IN*, 2:23, 37–42, 53–54.

43. *IN*, 2:54–55.

44. *IN*, 2:56–59, 61; *Commercial Advertiser*, September 28, 1835.

45. *IN*, 2:61–63, 70, 72, 90–91.

46. *IN* 2:24, 70, 74–76.

47. "Minutes and Proceedings of the First Annual Convention of the People of Color, Held by Adjournment in the City of Philadelphia, June 6–11, 1831," in *Minutes of the Proceedings of the National Negro Conventions, 1830–1864*, ed. Howard H. Bell (reprint, New York, 1969), 5–6, 15, and Howard H. Bell, *A Survey of the Negro Convention Movement, 1830–1861* (New York, 1969), 10–17, 29–33; E. S. Abdy, *Journal of a Residence and Tour in the United States of North America from April 1833, to October 1834*, 2 vols. (London, 1835), 1:121–22, 388–91; William Lloyd Garrison, *Thoughts on Colonization, or An Impartial Exhibition of the Doctrines, Principles and Purposes of the American Colonization Society* (Boston, 1832), in May Pamphlets, vol. 2, no. 13, Anti-Slavery Collection, DRMCCU; Lewis Tappan, *The Life of Arthur Tappan* (New York, 1870), 126–36; Bertram Wyatt-Brown, *Lewis Tappan and the Evangelical War against Slavery* (Baton Rouge, La., 1969), 78–82; Henry Mayer, *All on Fire:*

William Lloyd Garrison and the Abolition of Slavery (New York, 1998), 62–70; Leonard L. Richards, "Gentlemen of Property and Standing": Anti-abolition Mobs in Jacksonian America (New York, 1970), 21–27.

48. Tappan, Arthur Tappan, 167–78; Walter M. Merrill and Louis Ruchames, The Letters of William Lloyd Garrison, 6 vols. (Cambridge, Mass., 1971), 1:203–25, 235–65; Mayer, All on Fire, 27–28, 154–65, 173–77; Fifty-five Communications to Cornelius Lawrence, Mayor of New York City, from Various Communicants, Riots, 1834, misc. file, New York Historical Society; Richards, "Gentlemen of Property," 48–49; Wyatt-Brown, Lewis Tappan, 102–14.

49. Commercial Advertiser, July 7, 8, 10, 11, 1834; CAJZH, July 18, 1834; Albany Argus, July 10, 14, 1834; Liberator, July 12, 19, 1834; New York Courier and Enquirer (from Liberator), October 11, 1834; Richards, "Gentlemen of Property," 122.

50. Tappan, Arthur Tappan, 203–24; Liberator, October 19, 1833, July 19, 26, 1834; New York Times, New York Evening Post (from Albany Argus), July 15, 1834; CAJZH, July 18, 1834; Letters of Theodore Dwight Weld and Angelina Grimké Weld, and Sarah Grimké, 1822–1844, ed. Gilbert H. Barnes and Dwight A. Dumond, 2 vols. (Gloucester, Mass., 1965), 1:153–55; Letters of Garrison, 1:382–83.

51. Liberator, July 19, 1832; BAP, 1:49, Letters of Weld, 1:154; Fifty-five Communications to Cornelius Lawrence, Mayor of New York City, from Various Communicants, Riots, 1834, misc. file, New-York Historical Society.

52. IN, 2:76–77; False Prophet, 8–9.

53. IN, 2:76–80.

54. IN, 2:81–82, 84.

55. IN, 2:64, 86–92.

56. IN, 2:90–92.

57. IN, 2:93–95; Commercial Advertiser, July 11, 1843; CAJZH, July 25, 1834; Richards, "Gentlemen of Property," 114–15; Timothy J. Gilfoyle, City of Eros: New York City, Prostitution, and the Commercialization of Sex, 1790–1920 (New York, 1992), 42, 59–62. Paul Gilje, The Road to Mobocracy: Popular Disorder in New York City, 1763–1834 (Chapel Hill, N.C., 1987), 162–63; Linda K. Kerber, "Abolitionists and Amalgamators: The New York City Race Riots of 1834," New York History 47 (1967): 28–39.

58. IN, 2:107–10; Matthews, Matthias, by His Wife, 46–67; Tappan, Arthur Tappan, 91–94, 217–19, 415–18; Journal of Commerce, September 26, 28, 1834.

59. Statement of Benjamin Folger, in Benjamin Folger v. Robert Matthews, alias Matthias the Prophet, September 23, 1834, and Examination of Robert Matthews, otherwise called Matthias the Prophet, October 1, 1834, District Attorney Indictment Papers, NYCMAR; False Prophet, 3, 8, 13; IN, 1:110; Commercial Advertiser, September 26, October 2, November 8, 11, 1934.

60. Examination of Robert Matthews, October 1, 1834, Folger v. Matthews, District Attorney Indictment Papers, NYCMAR; IN, 2:113–14.

61. Commercial Advertiser, October 2, November 11, 1834.

62. Commercial Advertiser, September 26, October 2, 1834; Stone, Matthias, 63, 316, 317; IN, 2:122; Matthews, Matthias, by His Wife, 46–47.

63. IN, 2:110.

64. M. R. Werner, Barnum (New York, 1923); Richards, "Gentlemen of Property," 40–41, 47–49; Eric Lott, Love and Theft: Blackface Minstrelsy and the American Working Class (New York, 1993), 26–28, 76–77, 111–22, 132–33; Gilfoyle, City of Eros, 41–42, 48, 49, 60–62, 127.

65. NST, 30–38; IN, 1:10–11; 2:110, 112–23. "Hasbrouck Family," 36–37; obituary, A. Bruyn Hasbrouck, February 24, 1879, newspaper file (5740) 2542, Old Senate House Museum Archives, Kingston, New York; "Family Record of Abraham Hasbrouck," NYGBR 71 (October 1940): 354–57 and 72 (January 1941): 36–37.

66. *Longworth's American Almanac, New York Register, and City Directory*, 1827, 1889, 1831, 1833, 1834; *IN*, 1:12; 2:112; Will of James La Tourette, June 14, 1841, New York County Wills, 83:464–65, New York; Wyatt-Brown, *Lewis Tappan*, 157; John B. Jentz, "Artisans, Evangelicals, and the City: A Social History of Abolition and Labor Reform in Jacksonian New York" (Ph.D. diss., City University of New York, 1977), app.

67. Stone, *Matthias*, 68, 179–80, 193–206, 213–21; *IN*, 2:95–96, 112–13.

68. *Commercial Advertiser*, September 28, 1834; *IN*, 2: 16, 114.

69. *Liberator*, October 25, November 29, December 13, 1834, January 3, 1835.

70. *IN*, 2:94–95, 115–16.

71. *IN*, 116–18; Stone, *Matthias*.

72. *IN*, 2:120; *False Prophet*, 3; *Commercial Advertiser*, April 16 and 20, 1835; Stone, *Matthias*, 250.

73. *IN*, 2:120; Stone, *Matthias*, 65, 213–19, 231.

74. *IN*, 1:12, 61–62 and 2:17–18, 123–25.

75. Johnson and Wilentz, *Kingdom of Matthias*, 168.

76. *Cyclopaedia of American Biography* 6 (1899): 225; "Death List of a Day. Mrs. Euphemia Vale Blake," *New York Times*, October 23, 1904; *IN*, 1:3–10, 18–19, 50–54; Mary Wollstonecraft, *A Vindication of the Rights of Women with Strictures on Political and Moral Subjects*, ed. Gilbert Vale (New York, 1845); Gilbert Vale, *A Review of the Awful Disclosures of Maria Monk* (New York, 1836); *The First Annual Report of the New York Committee of Vigilance, for the Year 1837 Together with Important Facts Relative to Their Proceedings* (New York, 1837), May Pamphlets, vol. 2, no. 13, Anti-Slavery Collection, DRMCCU; *Liberator*, July 26, 1834; *Mirror of Liberty*, July 1838; Dorothy Porter, "David Ruggles: An Apostle of Human Rights," *JNH* 28, no. 1 (January 1943): 23–50; Jentz, "Artisans, Evangelicals, and the City," 377, 367, 397.

77. *IN*, 2:3, 121–22; *Commercial Advertiser*, April 16, 20, 1835; "Folger Narrative," in Stone, *Matthias*, 214–26, 245–49; 2 Cor. 6:3–10; Matthews, *Matthias, by His Wife*, 41–42; *New York Herald*, September 4, 1835; Johnson and Wilentz, *Kingdom of Matthias*, 3–7, 175–76.

78. *IN*, 1:61; 2:26–27.

79. *Liberator*, January 7, 1837; Joshua Leavitt, *Memoir and Select Remains of the Late Reverend John R. M'Dowell, the Martyr of the Seventh Commandment in the Nineteenth Century* (New York, 1838), 363–66; Johnson and Wilentz, *Kingdom of Matthias*, 177.

CHAPTER 8: THE ANTISLAVERY VANGUARD, 1833–1843

1. Robert P. Smith, "William Cooper Nell: Crusading Black Abolitionist," *JNH* 55 (July 1970): 183–99; Benjamin Quarles, *Black Abolitionists* (New York, 1969), 16–17, 28; Leon F. Litwack, *North of Slavery: The Negro in the Free States, 1790–1860* (Chicago, 1965), 230–36; Philip S. Foner, *History of Black Americans*, 3 vols., vol. 1, *From Africa to the Emergence of the Cotton Kingdom* (Westport, Conn., 1975), 555–61, 571–72; Kathryn Grover, *The Fugitive's Gibraltar: Escaping Slaves and Abolitionism in New Bedford, Massachusetts* (Amherst, Mass., 2000), 118–19, 138–39.

2. *CA*, March 28, 1840; Edwin Williams, ed., *New York City as It Is, In 1833; And Citizens' Advertising Directory* (New York, 1833), 82–87 (New York: 1840), 114–19; Carol George, "Widening the Circle: The Black Church and the Abolitionist Crusade, 1830–1860," in Lewis Perry and Michael Fellman, eds., *Antislavery Reconsidered: New Perspectives on the Abolitionists* (Baton Rouge, La., 1979), 75–96; Edward D. Smith, *Climbing Jacob's Ladder: The Rise of Black Churches in Eastern American Cities, 1740–1877* (Washington, D.C., 1988), 67.

3. *CA*, March 28, April 18, 1840; Williams, *New York as It Is*, 86–87; William J. Walls, *The African Methodist Episcopal Zion Church* (Charlotte, N.C., 1974), 126–30, 144–45, 169–73, 286.

4. *BAP*, 2:158–60, 168–69, 285–86; *David Ruggles v. James S. Wilson* (battery), August 25, 1838, New York City Police Office Watch Returns, June 19, 1836–October 18, 1840, NY-CMAR; *CA*, January 14, 1837, October 21, 1838, July 8, 1839; June 12, 1841; *Mirror of Liberty*, July 21, 1838; *Liberator*, March 18, April 21, 1837, December 21, 1849; E. S. Abdy, *Journal of a Residence and Tour in the United States of North America from April 1833, to October 1834*, 2 vols. (London, 1835), 2:45–46; Quarles, *Black Abolitionists*, 15, 25, 33–34, 143–52; Dorothy Porter, "David Ruggles: An Apostle of Human Rights," *JNH* 28, no. 1 (January 1943): 23–34; William H. Siebert, *The Underground Railroad from Slavery to Freedom* (New York, 1898), 34–35, 52–53, 126–27; Horatio T. Strother, *The Underground Railroad in Connecticut* (Middletown, Conn., 1962), 57.

5. "An Address Delivered before the Female Branch Society of Zion," April 5, 1837, May Pamphlets, vol. 32, no. 13, Anti-Slavery Collection, DRMCCU; *New York Weekly Advocate*, January 21, February 11, 18, 1837; *CA*, July 21, August 25, 1837, May 23, June 6, 1840; Dorothy Porter, "The Organized Educational Activities of Negro Literary Societies, 1828–1846," *Journal of Negro Education* 5 (October 1936): 564–69; Walls, *Zion Church*, 133–35, 149; Abdy, *Journal*, 2:31–34; Fifty-five Communications to Cornelius Lawrence, Mayor of New York City, from Various Communicants, Riots, 1834, misc. file, New York Historical Society; Dorothy Sterling, ed., *We Are Your Sisters: Black Women in the Nineteenth Century* (New York, 1984), 220–21; Anne M. Boylin, "Benevolence and Antislavery Activity among African American Women in New York and Boston, 1820–1840," in Jean F. Yellin and John C. Van Horne, eds., *The Abolitionist Sisterhood: Women's Political Culture in Antebellum America* (Ithaca, N.Y., 1994), 126–30.

6. *Mirror of Liberty*, July 21, 1838; *CA*, June 30, September 9, 22, 1838, November 3, 17, 1838; Sterling, *We Are Your Sisters*, 220–22.

7. Letter from William Lloyd Garrison, April 4, 1879, in *Maria W. Stewart: America's First Black Woman Political Writer: Essays and Speeches*, ed. Marilyn Richardson (Bloomington, Ind., 1987), 89–90; Sterling, *We Are Your Sisters*, 153–57; *Liberator*, July 13, 1832; Sterling Stuckey, *Slave Culture: Nationalist Theory and the Foundations of Black America* (New York, 1987), 119–20; James O. and Lois E. Horton, *Black Bostonians: Family Life and Community Struggle in the Antebellum North*, rev. ed. (New York, 1999), 69–71; Litwack, *North of Slavery*, 232–34; Foner, *History of Black Americans*, vol. 2, *From the Emergence of the Cotton Kingdom to the Eve of the Compromise of 1850*, 360–67, 402–10.

8. *Liberator*, October 8, 1831; Stewart, "An Address Delivered before the African American Female Intelligence Society of America," spring 1832, 50–55, and "Lecture Delivered at the Franklin Hall," September 21, 1832, 45–40, and "An Address Delivered at the African American Masonic Hall," February 27, 1833, 56–64, *Maria W. Stewart: Essays and Speeches*; Carla Peterson, *"Doers of the Word": African-American Women Speakers and Writers in the North (1830–1880)*, New Brunswick, N.J., 1998), 13–18, 56–72.

9. "Mrs. Stewart's Farewell Address to Her Friends in the City of Boston," *Maria W. Stewart: Essays and Speeches*, 65–74; Horton and Horton, *Black Bostonians*, 70–71.

10. "Statement of Condition of the Pubic Schools for Colored Children, 1838," New York Manumission Society, reel 2, 152–53; *CA*, July 21, September 9, 22, November 3, 1838; *Mirror of Liberty*, July 21, 1838; Wilson J. Moses, *Alexander Crummell* (Amherst, Mass., 1989), 199.

11. *NST*, 87; "Recollections of Eliza Seaman Leggett," Eliza Seaman Leggett Family Papers, vol. 8, DPL.

12. *NST*, 88; *ASB*, June 21, 1851.

13. Carlton Mabee maintains that Isabella was "considerably mired in ignorance" when she left Ulster. Moreover, in consistently referring to Sojourner Truth as ignorant, Mabee uses literacy as the only criteria for intelligence and knowledge. Mabee further believes

that "her ignorance and naiveté had doubtless contributed to her being gullible" in the Matthias experience; however, the educated Folger couple also accepted Matthias's teachings. Mabee's assertion that "for many of Truth's listeners, her lack of literacy *and culture* [my italics] contributed to her fascination" is equally troubling; Carleton Mabee with Susan Mabee Newhouse, *Sojourner Truth, Slave, Prophet, Legend* (New York, 1993), 23, 41–42, 61, 64. It is highly presumptuous to suggest that Sojourner was popular because she could not read and that she lacked culture for the same reason.

14. *Freedom's Journal,* November 30, 1827, February 8, 1828; Sojourner Truth to T. O. Mabbott, December 1, 1876, Oswald Garrison Villard Papers, Houghton Library, Harvard University; *Lansing Republican,* June 7, 1881.

15. Mabee, *Sojourner Truth,* 62–63.

16. Lydia Maria Francis Child, *Letters from New York,* 3d ed. (Freeport, N.Y., 1970), 76.

17. Sterling, *We Are Your Sisters,* 113, 119–20; *BAP,* 3:142–45, 154–67, 201–6; *Liberator,* September 13, 1834; Paul Goodman, *Of One Blood: Abolitionism and the Origins of Racial Equality* (Berkeley, 1998), 26–27, 248; Carolyn L. Karcher, *The First Woman in the Republic: A Cultural Biography of Lydia Maria Child* (Durham, N.C., 1994), 182–83, 215–17; Debra Hansen, *Strained Sisterhood: Gender and Class in the Boston Female Anti-Slavery Society* (Amherst, Mass., 1993), 10–14, 19–20, 64–68; 77–79, 93–102; Amy Swerdlow, "Abolition's Conservative Sisters: The Ladies' New York City Anti-Slavery Societies, 1834–1840," in Yellin and Horne, *Abolitionist Sisterhood,* 35; Horton and Horton, *Black Bostonians.*

18. *The Public Years of Sarah and Angelina Grimké: Selected Writings, 1835–1839,* ed. Larry Ceplair (New York, 1989), 4–6, 23–24; Gerda Lerner, *The Grimké Sisters of South Carolina* (Boston, 1967), 120–21; Katherine DuPre Lumpkin, *The Emancipation of Angelina Grimké* (Chapel Hill, N.C., 1974), 71–72, 95–96.

19. *Letters of Theodore Dwight Weld and Angelina* Grimké Weld, *and Sarah Grimké, 1822–1844,* ed. Gilbert H. Barnes and Dwight A. Dumond, 2 vols. (Gloucester, Mass., 1965), 1:132–33, 441–45, 170–71, 2:673–74; Augustus Wattles to Betsy Cowles, April 9, 1836, Joanna Chester to Betsy Cowles, April 13, 1836, Susan Wattles to Betsy Cowles, June 30, 1838, Mix Cowles Papers, KSU; Luke 9:1–6, 10:1–8; Annual Report of the Ladies New York Anti-Slavery Society (LNYASS), May Pamphlets, vol. 32, no. 8, Anti-Slavery Collection, DRMCCU; Swerdlow, "Abolition's Conservative Sisters," 39–40; Ceplair, *Sarah and Angelina Grimké,* 23–24, 85; Lumpkin, *Angelina Grimké,* 95–96; Lerner, *Grimké Sisters,* 148–56; Bertram Wyatt-Brown, *Lewis Tappan and the Evangelical War against Slavery* (Baton Rouge, La., 1969), 126–32.

20. Third Annual Report, AASS, May 10, 1836, May Pamphlets, vol. 6, no. 10; Annual Report, LNYASS, May 1836, May Pamphlets, vol. 32, no. 8, Anti-Slavery Collection, DRM-CCU; Mrs. C. L. Brown to Mrs. Charles Finney, June 12, 1834, Charles Finney to Arthur Tappan, April 30, 1836, FP; *CA,* October 1837, March 2, 1839; *Letters of Weld,* 1:22–24, 145–57, 176–77; *Liberator,* January 21, 1832, August 16, 1834, May 11, 1837, August 25, 1837; Ceplair, *Sarah and Angelina Grimké,* 125–30; Swerdlow, "Abolition's Conservative Sisters," 32–40.

21. "Proceedings of the Anti-Slavery Convention of American Women, held in the City of New-York, May 9, 10, 11, and 12, 1837," May Pamphlets, vol. 32, no. 9, Anti-Slavery Collection, DRMCCU; Dorothy Sterling, *Ahead of Her Time: Abby Kelley and the Politics of Anti-slavery* (New York, 1991), 40–49, and *We Are Your Sisters,* 113–27, 131; *BAP,* 3:221–25; William Green to Charles Finney, August 28, 1835; September 26, 1836, FP; Swerdlow, "Abolition's Conservative Sisters," 40. "Report of the Trustees of the Schools," November 12, 1833, and "Statement of the Condition of the Public Schools for Colored Children, 1838," Papers of the New York Manumission Society, reel 2, 98, 152–53, New York Historical Society; *CA,* January 25, October 7, 1837; John B. Jentz, "Artisans, Evangelicals, and the City: a Social History of Abolition and Labor Reform in Jacksonian New York" (Ph.D. diss., City University of New York, 1977), app.; Walls, *Zion Church,* 135–37.

22. "Anti-Slavery Convention of Women, 1837"; Angelina Grimké, "An Appeal to the Women of the Nominally Free States," May Pamphlets, vol. 38, no. 19, Anti-Slavery Collection, DRMCCU; Lerner, *Grimké Sisters*, 160–61; Ceplair, *Sarah and Angelina Grimké*, 130–31; Karcher, *First Woman in the Republic*, 183–94, 245–47.

23. "Proceedings of the Anti-Slavery Convention of American Women, 1837"; Karcher, *First Woman in the Republic*, 245–46.

24. *CA*, November 25, 1837; *Liberator*, December 15, 22, 29, 1837, January 5, 1838; *BAP*, 3:445; Quarles, *Black Abolitionists*, 40, 162–63; Sterling, *Ahead of Her Time*, 58; James Brewer Stewart, *Wendell Phillips: Liberty's Hero* (Baton Rouge, La., 1986), 58–66; Louis A. DeCaro Jr., *"Fire from the Midst of You": A Religious Life of John Brown* (New York, 2000), 122.

25. *CA*, September 22, 1838; *Liberator*, April 19, May 17, 1839; Nathaniel Colver to British and Foreign Anti-Slavery Society, November 30, 1840, G. Stuart to J. H. Tredgold, December 28, 1840, Papers of British and Foreign Anti-Slavery Society, Ms. British Empire, 1833–52 (BFASS), Rhodes House, Bodleian Library, Oxford University; *Letters of Weld*, 2:836; *The Letters of William Lloyd Garrison*, ed. Walter M. Merrill and Louis Ruchames, 6 vols. (Cambridge, Mass., 1971–81), 2:486–96; Quarles, *Black Abolitionists*, 40–41; Wyatt-Brown, *Lewis Tappan*, 190–94; George Wallingford Noyes, *Religious Experience of John Humphrey Noyes* (New York, 1923), 24–38, 45; Aileen S. Kraditor, *Means and Ends in American Abolitionism: Garrison and His Critics on Strategy and Tactics, 1834–1850* (New York, 1969), 53–62; Henry Mayer, *All on Fire: William Lloyd Garrison and the Abolition of Slavery* (New York, 1998), 244–48, 262–68, 272–80; Sterling, *Ahead of Her Time*, 60–81, 94–98, 112–13.

26. *Letters of Garrison*, 2:24, 172; *Liberator*, December 15, 1837; Robert D. Thomas, *Man Who Would Be Perfect: John Humphrey Noyes and the Utopian Impulse* (Philadelphia, 1977), 146–51; Kraditor, *Means and Ends*, 57, 78–108, 141–46, 158–63; Wyatt-Brown, *Lewis Tappan*, 109–10; Mayer, *All on Fire*, 222–26, 249–51; Sterling, *Ahead of Her Time*, 58–59.

27. *CA*, May 30, June 6, 1840; *NASS*, June 11, July 23, 1840; *BAP*, 3:329–39; *Letters of Garrison*, 2:535, 3:37; Quarles, *Black Abolitionists*, 42–48; Wyatt-Brown, *Lewis Tappan*, 197–200; Mayer, *All on Fire*, 268–69; Sterling, *Ahead of Her Time*, 101–6.

28. *Letters of Weld*, 1:387; *BAP*, 3:298–301, 333–36, 343; *Letters of Garrison*, 2: 678–79, 3:2, 9; *CA*, June 6, 1840; *Liberator*, June 21, 1839, June 21, 1840; Swerdlow, "Abolition's Conservative Sisters," 31–33, 43–44; Quarles, *Black Abolitionists*, 41–48; Wyatt-Brown, *Lewis Tappan*, 198–200, 249–52; Sterling, *We Are Your Sisters*, 114–15, and *Ahead of Her Time*, 94–101, 395 n. 6; Debra G. Hansen, "The Boston Female Anti-Slavery Society and the Limits of Gender Politics," in Yellin and Van Horne, *Abolitionist Sisterhood*, 53–59. Although Hansen is "convinced" the Ball sisters were "white," Sterling is correct; they were African American.

29. Finney to A. Tappan, April 30, 1836, FP; *Letters of Weld*, 1:270–79; Howard Mumford Jones, *Mutiny on the Amistad: The Saga of a Slave Revolt and Its Impact on American Abolition, Law, and Diplomacy* (New York, 1987), 14–15, 22–29, 35–40, 44–49, 55–58; Wyatt-Brown, *Lewis Tappan*, 178–81, 205–20, 249, 273–81, 292–94, 310–22. (Mende are from Sierra Leone; Wyatt-Brown mistakenly places them in "present-day Nigeria," 207.) Tappan's American Missionary Association was instrumental in black education and the founding of historically black colleges after the Civil War. See Joyce Hollyday, *On the Heels of Freedom: The American Missionary Association's Bold Campaign to Educate Minds, Open Hearts, and Heal the Soul of a Divided Nation* (New York, 2005).

30. *CA*, September 28, October 5, 19, 1839, June 6, 1840; July 24, 1841; *NASS*, December 3, 1841; *BAP*, 3:315, 366, 410; Quarles, *Black Abolitionists*, 76–78; Earl Ofari Hutchinson, *"Let Your Motto Be Resistance,"* in *The Life and Thought of Henry Highland Garnet* (Boston, 1972), 33–45; Wyatt-Brown, *Lewis Tappan*, 205–12.

31. *BAP*, 3:380–84, Jones, *Mutiny on the Amistad*, 192–94; Quarles, *Black Abolitionists*, 225–26; Foner, *History of Black Americans*, 2:159.

32. *NASS*, May 18, 1843; *The Life and Writings of Frederick Douglass*, ed. Philip S. Foner, 4 vols. (New York, 1950); 1:23–27, 46–49, 52–551; Sarah S. Southwick, *Reminiscences of Early Anti-Slavery Days*, (Cambridge, Mass., 1893), 29–30; Parker Pillsbury, *The Acts of the Anti-slavery Apostles* (Concord, N.H., 1883), 326–28; *Letters of Garrison*, 3:156–57; William S. McFeely, *Frederick Douglass* (New York, 1991), 82–90.

33. *NASS*, May 18, 1843; *Letters of Garrison*, 2:607–9; Pillsbury, *Acts of the Anti-Slavery Apostles*, 326–28; *CA*, May 30, 1840; Southwick, *Reminiscences*, 29–30; Wyatt-Brown, *Lewis Tappan*, 180; Earl Ofari Hutchinson, *"Let Your Motto Be Resistance,"* 127–35; Quarles, *Black Abolitionists*, 56–64.

34. Bell, *National Conventions (1843 Minutes)*, 3–7, 10–11; *BAP*, 3:403–12. Quarles, *Black Abolitionists*, 68, 225–27; Stuckey, *Slave Culture*, 127, 154–63; Earl Ofari Hutchinson, *"Let Your Motto Be Resistance,"* 22–26, 33–35.

35. Bell, *National Conventions (1843 Minutes)*, 10, 13–19, 23–24; *BAP*, 4:5–6.

CHAPTER 9: "THE SPIRIT CALLS ME THERE"

1. *NST*, 56–57.

2. Apprentice Register, New York Police Court, May 13, 1836–September 14, 1841, 2 vols., NYCMAR; Theodore S. Wright at the New York State Anti-Slavery Society Meeting, in *CA*, July 8, 1837; Shane White, *Somewhat More Independent: The End of Slavery in New York City, 1770–1818* (Athens, Ga., 1991), 156–66; Paul Gilje and Howard Rock, eds., *Keepers of the Revolution: New Yorkers and Work in the Early Republic* (Ithaca, N.Y., 1992) 209–15, 218–24, 318–24, and Howard Rock, *Artisans of the New Republic: The Tradesmen of New York City in the Age of Jefferson* (New York, 1979), 221–24.

3. *CA*, January 11, April 27, 1837, December 22, 1838; Howard Hendricks, "Sojourner Truth: Her Early History in Slavery," *National Magazine* 16 (October 1892): 669; Paul Gilje, *The Road to Mobocracy: Popular Disorder in New York City, 1763–1834* (Chapel Hill, N.C., 1987), 158–66; George G. Foster, *New York by Gas-Light, and Other Urban Sketches* (1856), ed. Stuart M. Blumin (Berkeley, 1990), 72–76; Eileen Southern, *Music of Black Americans: A History* (New York, 1971), 116–25; Shane White and Graham White, *"Stylin," African American Expressive Culture from Its Beginnings to the Zoot Suit* (Ithaca, N.Y., 1998), 101–4.

4. *NST*, 56–67; District Attorney Indictment Papers, *The People v. George Pine and Peter Williams*, July 15, 1830; *Maria Blossom v. Peter Williams*, July 28, 1830, *The People v. Peter Williams*, September 2, 1830. Court of General Sessions, *The People v. George Pine and Peter Williams*, July 17, 1830; *The People v. Peter Williams*, September 9, 1830, all in NYCMAR.

5. *NST*, 56–57; District Attorney Indictment Papers, *The People v. George Pine and Peter Williams*, September 10, 1830, *The People v. John Jackson als. Oriack, Lewis Van Dyck als. Thomas Johnson, Peter Williams als. Jim Williams*, September 12, 1834, *The People v. William Jackson als. Jesse Thompson and Peter Williams als. Jim Williams*, September 8, 1834; Court of General Sessions, September 12, 1834, September 8, 1834, all in NYCMAR.

6. District Attorney Indictment Papers, *The People v. Peter Williams*, September 8, 1836; *Isaac Conklin v. Peter Williams, Barny Mulligan, Charles Falknor*, January 4, 1839; and Court of General Sessions, September 9, 1836, all in NYCMAR.

7. *NST*, 57–58.

8. *CA*, October 24, 31, 1840, October 31, 1841; *BAP*, 2:224–25, 239; *The Letters of William Lloyd Garrison*, ed. Walter M. Merrill and Louis Ruchames, 6 vols. (Cambridge, Mass., 1971–81), 4:40–41; *Longworth's American Almanac, New York Register, and City Directory* (1838–39), 685, and (1839–40), 711; *NST*, 57, 58; J. B. Wakeley, *Lost Chapters Recovered from the Early History of American Methodism* (New York, 1858), 438–47, 450–53, 460–77; John H. Hewitt, "Peter Williams, Jr., New York's First African American Priest," *New York History* 79 (April

1998): 101–12, 117–23; Wilson J. Moses, *Alexander Crummell* (Amherst, Mass., 1989), 24–33. In the wake of the 1834 riots Onderdonk had pressured Williams into resigning he office at the AASS. But he continued his activism.

9. *BAP*, 1:474–75; *NST*, 56; Margaret S. Creighton, *Rites and Passages: The Experience of American Whaling, 1830–1870* (New York, 1995), 42–45; W. Jeffrey Bolster, *Black Jacks: African American Seamen in the Age of Sail* (Cambridge, Mass., 1997), 185–88, 199, 206, 224–25; *NST*, 58.

10. *Longworth's City Directory* (1838–39), 239; *CA*, July 7, 1839; Martha S. Putney, *Black Sailors: Afro-American Merchant Seamen and Whalemen Prior to the Civil War* (1916; reprint, Westport, Conn., 1987), 30, 49–83, 100–104; Briton C. Busch, *"Whaling Will Never Do for Me": The American Whaleman in the Nineteenth Century* (Lexington, Ky., 1994), 33–36; Julie Winch, *A Gentleman of Color: The Life of James Forten* (New York, 2002), chaps. 1–3; Bolster, *Black Jacks*, 75–80, 160–61, 184–85, 188–89; *Letters of Garrison*, 2:72; Philip S. Foner, "William P. Powell: Militant Champion of Black Seamen," in Philip S. Foner, *Essays in Afro-American History* (Philadelphia, 1978), 88–94.

11. Creighton, *Rites and Passages*, 16–19, 23; *NST*, 59; Foner, "William P. Powell," 89.

12. Ships Papers Collections, "Zone" Ship, reel 72, fol. 205, Nantucket Historical Association; *NST*, 59; in the *Narrative*, Peter's ship is incorrectly named "Done" and the captain "Miller." The late Sidney Kaplan discovered this error. See his "Sojourner Truth's Son Peter," *Negro History Bulletin* 19 (November 1955): 34. See also Federal Writers Project of the Works Progress Administration of Massachusetts, *Whaling Masters Voyages, 1731–1925* (New Bedford, Mass., 1938), 159; *New Bedford Directory*, 1841, 146; Alexander Starbuck, *History of the American Whale Fishery from Its Earliest Inception to the Year 1876*, 2 vols. (New York, 1964), 1:356–57.

13. Consular Records List of American Vessels Calling at Tahiti, National Archives Ships' Papers Collections, "Zone" Ship; *Dennis Wood Abstracts*, 1:538; *NST*, 59–61; Busch, *"Whaling Will Never Do*," 8–9, 19–20, 25; Bolster, *Black Jacks*, 176–79; Foner, "William P. Powell," 94, 101–6.

14. *NST*, 60–61; Ships' Papers Collection, "Zone" Ship; *CDI*, August 12, 1879.

15. *CDI*, August 13, 1879; *NST*, 61, 77–79; Joshua Leavitt, *Memoir and Select Remains of the Late Reverend John R. M'Dowell, the Martyr of the Seventh Commandment in the Nineteenth Century* (New York, 1838), 363–64, *CA*, October 24, 1840; Proof of James La Tourette, County of New-York, Surrogate's Court, June 23, 1841.

16. Logbook of 1838–41, voyage of the ship *Charles Frederick*, log no. 858; Logbook of 1840–44, voyage of the ship *Moss*, log no. 456, Kendall Whaling Museum, New Bedford, Mass.; Logbook of 1840–41(?), voyage of the ship *Almira*, no log no., Martha's Vineyard Historical Society, Edgartown, Massachusetts. My thanks to Mary Beth Norton and Lisa Norling for their insights and research on the probable fate of Peter.

17. Starbuck, *American Whale Fishery*, 1:356–57, 400; Sir Charles Lucas, ed., *The Pitcairn Island Register Book* (London: 1929), 108; Kaplan, "Sojourner Truth's Son," 34; Busch, *"Whaling Will Never Do,"* 9–10; *Dennis Wood Abstracts*, 1:538. The *Zone*'s owners sold the vessel while it was still at sea. Captain Hiller was reassigned to the *Sarah Frances*; he died at sea in 1844, "by the upsetting of a boat while fast to a whale."

18. *CA*, October 24, 1840; *NST*, 60–61.

19. *NASS*, May 11, 1843.

20. *CDI*, August 13, 1879; "Recollections of Eliza Seaman Leggett," Eliza Seaman Leggett Family Papers, vol. 8, DPL; Acts 9: 3–6, 15–16: Luke 10:3–4; *NST*, 80.

21. *NST*, 79–80; *NYT*, November 8, 1853; *ASB*, May 28, 1851; *Battle Creek Nightly Moon*, June 8, 1881; *BAP*, 3:455; Lydia Maria Francis Child, *Letters from New York*, 3d ed. (Freeport, N.Y., 1970), 73–82; Jarena Lee, *The Life and Religious Experience of Jarena Lee, A Coloured Lady, Giving an Account of Her Call to Preach the Gospel, Revised and Corrected from the Origi-*

nal Manuscript, Written by Herself (Philadelphia, 1836), 27–39, 35–38, 42–48; Zilpha Elaw, *Memoirs of the Life, Religious Experience, Ministerial Travels and Labours of Mrs. Zilpha Elaw, An American Female of Colour; Together with Some Account of the Great Religious Revivals in America [Written by Herself]* (London, 1846), 64–66, 80–87, 89–100, 103–110, 83–139, and Julia A. J. Foote, *"A Brand Plucked from the Fire": An Autobiographical Sketch* (Cleveland, 1879), 166, 180, 186–93, 199–226, all in William L. Andrews, ed., *Sisters of the Spirit: Three Black Women's Autobiographies of the Nineteenth Century* (Bloomington, Ind., 1986); William J. Walls, *The African Methodist Episcopal Zion Church* (Charlotte, N.C., 1974), 50, 59, 72–73, 109, 129; Jean M. Humez, ed., *Gifts of Power: The Writings of Rebecca Jackson, Black Visionary Shaker Eldress* (Boston, 1981), 27–31, 200–228; Catherine Brekus, *Strangers and Pilgrims: Female Preaching in America 1740–1845* (Chapel Hill, N.C., 1998), 295–96.

22. *NST*, 80; Gen. 19:13–28.

23. Vivienne L. Kruger, "Born to Run: The Slave Family in Early New York, 1626–1927," 2 vols. (Ph.D. diss., Columbia University, 1985), 1:90–94, 2:742–49, 752–65; David Osborn, "Western Long Island and the Civil War: A Political Chronicle," *Long Island Historical Journal* 7, no. 1 (fall 1994): 86–98; Marc Linder and Lawrence Zacharias, *Of Cabbages and Kings: Agriculture and the Formation of Modern Brooklyn* (Iowa City, 1999), 19, 12–22, 26–31; 52–53, 80–84; Lynda R. Day, *Making a Way to Freedom: A History of African Americans on Long Island* (Interlaken, N.Y., 1997), 65–74.

24. *NST*, 80–82; John C. Smith, *Map of Long Island, with the Environs of New York and the Southern Part of Connecticut* (New York, 1844).

25. *NST*, 81–84.

26. *CA*, January 21, 28, 1837, September 15, 1838; Foote, *"A Brand Plucked from the Fire,"* 167; W. J. Rorabaugh, *The Alcoholic Republic: An American Tradition* (New York, 1979), 189–90, 202–15; *BAP*, 3:17, 4:377–81; *CDI*, August 13, 1879.

27. *NST*, 84; Barnabas Bates, *Remarks on the Character and Exertions of Elias Hicks, in the Abolition of Slavery: Being an Address Delivered before the African Benevolent Societies for Zion's Chapel, New-York, 1830*, May Pamphlets, vol. 99, no. 4, Anti-slavery Collection, DRMCCU; *BAP*, 3:9–15; Day, *Making a Way*, 39–45, 51–52, 54–59, 66–77, 125–27; Smith, *Long Island Map*; Stanley K. Bergersen, "The Quaker School for Negroes, *Nassau County Historical Society Journal* 43 (1988): 29–36; "Christopher Densmore et al., "Slavery and Abolition to 1830," 65–75, and Hugh Barbour et al., "The Orthodox-Hicksite Separation," 116–21, in *Quaker Crosscurrents: Three Hundred Years of Friends in the New York Yearly Meetings*, ed. Hugh Barbour et al. (Syracuse, N.Y., 1995).

28. For characterization of Sojourner's travels as "wanderings," see Carleton Mabee with Susan Mabee Newhouse, *Sojourner Truth, Slave, Prophet, Legend* (New York, 1993), chap. 4, esp. 47.

29. Nathaniel S. Prime, *A History of Long Island, from the First Settlement by Europeans to the Year 1845, with Special Reference to Its Ecclesiastical Concerns*, 2 vols. (New York, 1845), 1:416; *NST*, 84.

30. Bliss Forbush, *Elias Hicks, Quaker Liberal* (New York, 1956), 5, 66–71, 77–79; Arthur Worrall and Hugh Barbour, "Quaker Beginnings in England and New York," in Barbour et al., *Quaker Crosscurrents*, 4–7; Densmore et al., "Slavery and Abolition," 66–75; Barbour et al., "Orthodox-Hicksite Separation," 120–30.

31. *NST*, 79–80, 84; "Recollections of Eliza Seaman Leggett," Leggett Papers, vol. 8, DPL; Eliza Seaman Leggett, "My Book of Life," Memoir, 46, Roslyn Public Library, Roslyn, New York; Eliza Leggett to Amy Post (for Sojourner Truth), February 5, 1864, AIPFP; scrapbook of Nannette Gardiner, MHC; *Blue Rapids (KS) Times*, July 18, 1878; Smith, *Long Island Map*, 94; Barbour et al., "Orthodox-Hicksite Separation," 116–22; Christopher Densmore et al., "After the Separation," in Barbour et al., *Quaker Crosscurrents*, 132–36; Albert J. Wahl, "The

Congregational or Progressive Friends in the Pre–Civil War Reform Movement" (Ph.D. diss., Temple University, 1951); Ann Braude, *Radical Spirits: Spiritualism and Women's Rights in Nineteenth Century America* (Boston, 1989), 10–19, 32–33, 58–59, 65–69.

32. Horatio T. Strother, *The Underground Railroad in Connecticut* (Middletown, Conn., 1962), 38–40, 57–59, 93–94; "Meeting of Anti-Slavery Members of the Methodist Episcopal Church in Middletown, Conn., October 22, 1837," and "Meeting of the State Anti-Slavery Convention, Hartford, Conn., February 28, 1838," Miscellaneous Records of Middlesex country Anti-Slavery Society, Middlesex County Historical Society, Middletown, Conn.; *Liberator*, March 2, December 7, 1838; Susan Strane, *A Whole-Souled Woman: Prudence Crandall and the Education of Black Women* (New York, 1990), 24–65.

33. *NSTBL*, 386; *NST*, 84–85, 88; *Public Ledger and Daily Transcript*, September 11, 1843; *Pittsfield (MA) Sun*, September 28, 1843; Francis D. Nichol, *The Midnight Cry* (Washington, D.C., 1944), 305–11; Florence S. Marcy Crofut, *Guide to the History of the Historic Sites of Connecticut* (New Haven, Conn., 1937), 119, 158, 176–78.

34. Whitney R. Cross, *The Burned-Over District: The Social and Intellectual History of Enthusiastic Religion in Western New York, 1800–1850* (Ithaca, N.Y., 1950), 287–97; *Letters of Garrison*, 2:182, 183; *Public Ledger and Daily Transcript*, September 11, 1843; Nichol, *Midnight Cry*, 126, 135, 136–37, 151; Everett N. Dick, *William Miller and the Advent Crisis* (Berrien Springs, Mich., 1994), 10, 21–22, 59–64, 85–90.

35. Nichol, *Midnight Cry*, 114–22; *Pittsfield (MA) Sun*, September 28, 1843; *Public Ledger and Daily Transcript*, September 11, 1843; Cross, *Burned-Over District*, 297–98; Sylvester Bliss, *Memoirs of William Miller* (Boston, 1853), 233–36; Dick, *William Miller*, 45–56.

36. For a different perspective, see Nell Irvin Painter, *Sojourner Truth: A Life, A Symbol* (New York, 1996), 82–90. Painter links Sojourner's departure from New York City to Millerism, and places her at a hair-raising camp meeting at Stephney, near Bridgeport (Fairfield County), Connecticut, in early September. However, Sojourner arrived in Bridgeport in late July, and then headed northeast, "lecturing some, and working some" until arriving at New Haven, twenty miles away, where she first encountered Millerites. She left Bridgeport weeks before the "fanatical" Stephney gathering. Nor could she have returned to Fairfield County in the time proposed. Since she walked most of the way, and Stephney was on the north side of the Housatonic River, getting back across and then going south to New Haven meant making a complete circle. According to the 1845 map of the state, no bridge existed across the Housatonic near the Stephney Post Office. For an account of the excesses at the meeting near Bridgeport, see *Newark (NJ) Daily Advertiser*, September 14, 1813 (from *New York Journal of Commerce*).

37. *NST*, 88; James Boyle, *Social Reform, Or an Appeal in Behalf of Association, Based upon the Principles of a Pure Christianity* (Northampton, Mass., 1844), 37; J. F. C. Harrison, *The Second Coming: Popular Millenarianism, 1750–1850* (New Brunswick, N.J., 1979), 4–5.

38. *NST*, 88–90; Nichol, *Midnight Cry*, 306–12; Bliss, *Miller Memoirs*, 234–35.

39. Bliss, *Miller Memoirs*, 180–81; Nichol, *Midnight Cry*, 312–13; *NST*, 90; Dan. 3:12–13, 16–18, 19, 23–25.

40. *NST*, 90–92; Rachael Stearns to Maria Weston Chapman, February 4, 1844, Ms.a.9.2.20, 109, BPL.

41. *NST* 91–93; *Bronson Alcott's Fruitlands*, Clara Endicott Sears, comp. (Boston, 1915), 4–5, 21–30, ; Sarah Elbert, *A Hunger for Home: Louisa May Alcott's Place in American Culture* (New Brunswick, N.J., 1987), xvii, 2–4, 7, 10–11, 15, 20, 43–48, 53–73. Annie M. L. Clark, *The Alcotts in Harvard* (Lancaster, Mass., 1901), 10, 12, 14–20, 26; *Letters of Garrison*, 1:395–96; Donald Yacovone, *Samuel Joseph May and the Dilemmas of Liberal Persuasion, 1797–1871* (Philadelphia, 1991), 73–75.

42. *NST*, 88, 91; A. J. Macdonald, "Narrative of Four Months among the Shakers at

Watervliet," 1842, Macdonald Collection, box 3, 689–90, 692, 694–96, 701–2, 707–11, 715, 719–21, and "Extract from Col. Maxwell's Description of the Shaker Community in Enfield, Conn.," Macdonald Collection, box 3, 660, 668–69, Beinecke Rare Book and Manuscript Library, Yale University; Cross, *Burned-Over District*, 31–32; Humez, *Gifts of Power*, 39; Christopher Clark, *Communitarian Moment: the Radical Challenge of the Northampton Association* (Ithaca, N.Y., 1995), 2.

43. Macdonald, "Narrative of Four Months," 704–6, 715–18, *NST*, 91; Lawrence Foster, *Women, Family, and Utopia: Communal Experiments of the Shakers, the Oneida Community, and the Mormons* (Syracuse, N.Y., 1991), 17–38; Humez, *Gifts of Power*, 28–33, 35–41.

44. Joseph Carvel III, *Black Families in Hampden County, Massachusetts, 1650–1855* (Springfield, Mass., 1984), 16; Stearns to Chapman, February 4, 1844, BPL; Louis A. DeCaro Jr., *"Fire from the Midst of You": A Religious Life of John Brown* (New York, 2002), 148–50.

CHAPTER 10: A HOLY CITY

1. Stearns to Chapman, February 4, 1844, Ms. A.9.2.20,109, Weston Sisters Papers, BPL.

2. Lydia Maria Child to Henrietta Sargent, November 18, 1838, Child Correspondence, Anti-Slavery Collection, DRMCCU; Giles Stebbins, *Upward Steps of Seventy Years* (New York, 1890), 54–55; "Mulberry Fever and Silk Enterprise," in Charles A. Sheffield, ed., *History of Florence, Massachusetts, Including a Complete Account of the Northampton Association of Education and Industry* (Florence, Mass., 1895), 63; Christopher Clark, *The Roots of Rural Capitalism: Western Massachusetts, 1780–1860* (Ithaca, N.Y., 1990), 4–6, 82; and *Communitarian Moment: The Radical Challenge of the Northampton Association* (Ithaca, N.Y., 1995), 49–52.

3. *The Letters of William Lloyd Garrison*, ed. Walter M. Merrill and Louis Ruchames, 6 vols. (Cambridge, Mass., 1971–81), 3:171, 174; NAEI, 1:78, 2:68, 154, 158, 175, 3:162, 5:158, 215, 235, 236, 7:75; Stebbins, *Upward Steps*, 15–17, 27–28; *Green Mountain Spring* 1, no. 3 (March 1856): 35–36; *NST*, 91–93, 98; "Northampton Association of Education and Industry," in Sheffield, *History of Florence*, 69; Alice McBee, *From Utopia to Florence: The Story of a Transcendentalist Community in Northampton, Mass., 1830–1852* (reprint, Philadelphia, 1975), 20; Hiram Munger, *The Life and Religious Experience of Hiram Munger* (Boston, 1881), 34–37, 41.

4. *Hampshire Gazette*, August 29, 1843; NAEI, 1:5, 8–9, 35, 97, AAS; Stebbins, *Upward Steps*, 55–56; Hope Hale Davis, "The Northampton Association of Education and Industry," in *The Northampton Book: Chapters from 300 Years in the Life of a New England Town, 1654–1954*, comp. and ed. Tercentenary History Committee (Northampton, Mass., 1954), 110–11; Frances P. Judd, "Reminiscences, 116, and George R. Stetson, "When I Was a Boy," in Sheffield, *History of Florence*, 116, 119–20, 123; McBee, *Utopia to Florence*, 24–32; *Journal of Commerce* (from *Liberator*), October 13, 1843; Clark, *Communitarian Moment*, 49–52, 61, 63; *NST*, 93, 97–98.

5. Frederick Douglass, "What I Found at the Northampton Association," in Sheffield, *History of Florence*, 131–32.

6. NAEI, 2: 3–6, 66–84, AAS; Davis, "Northampton Association," 110–12; *Hampshire Gazette*, August 29, 1843; James Boyle, *Social Reform, Or an Appeal in Behalf of Association, Based upon the Principles of a Pure Christianity* (Northampton, Mass., 1844), 61–63, 68–69, 71; Almira Stetson to James Stetson, May 26, 1844, in *Letters from an American Utopia: The Stetson Family and the Northampton Association, 1843–1846*, ed. Christopher Clark and Kerry W. Buckley (Amherst, Mass., 2004); "Northampton Association," 66–67; McBee, *Utopia to Florence*, 14–33, 50–53; Arthur E. Bestor Jr., "Fourierism in Northampton: A Critical Note," *New England Quarterly* 13, no. 1 (March 1940): 113–19; Carl J. Guarneri, *The Utopian Alterna-*

tive: Fourierism in Nineteenth-Century America (Ithaca, N.Y., 1991), 252–54, 257–58; Clark, *Communitarian Moment*, 42–44, 41, 69, 91–93.

7. Dolly Stetson to James Stetson, April 21, May 23, July 26, October 6, 13, 1844, Almira Stetson, Mary Ann Smith, and Mary Stetson to James Stetson, June 19, 1844, Dolly Stetson to James Stetson, May 4, 1845, all in *Letters from an American Utopia*; Arthur G. Hill, "Anti-Slavery Days in Florence," Lottie Corbin Collection, SSC; Stebbins, *Upward Steps*, 210–11; NAEI, 5:158, 175, 6:45, 75, 132, 196, 206, 209, 212, 213, 219, 228, 238, 248, 256, 258, 259, 262, 331, AAS.

8. Dolly Stetson to James Stetson, May 23, July 26, 1844, March 4, 1845, in *Letters from an American Utopia*; "Northampton Association," 88–95; Boyle, *Social Reform*, 63, 66; Kate de Normandie Wilson, *Dolly Witter Stetson: A Sketch of Her Life* (Brooklyn, Conn., 1907), 30; Judd, "Reminiscences," 116–17, and [Frances B. Judd] [mistakenly written by comp. as "Mrs. Judson], "Memoir," 66–70, A. J. Macdonald Collection, Beinecke Library, Yale University; Clark, *Communitarian Moment*, 116–18, 122–26.

9. NAEI, 2:94–95, 3: 202, 6:23, AAS; *Letters of Garrison*, 3:124–15, 258–60, 558, 572, 597; Judd, "Reminiscences," 116–18; Giles Stebbins, "A Young Man in the Community," in Sheffield, *History of Florence*, 127–28; Stebbins, *Upward Steps*, 56; Journal of Dr. Erasmus D. Hudson, M.D., July 9, 1842, Hudson Family Papers, SSC; McBee, *Utopia to Florence*, 49–50; Clark, *Communitarian Moment*, 120–27.

10. Boyle, *Social Reform*, 66–67; Dolly Stetson to James Stetson, June 16, 1844, in *Letters from an American Utopia*; Stebbins, *Upward Steps*, 56–58; Davis, "Northampton Association," 117; Rev. 18:4; *Letters of Garrison*, 3:24, 26, 101, 172; Robert D. Thomas, *Man Who Would Be Perfect: John Humphrey Noyes and the Utopian Impulse* (Philadelphia, 1977), 147–52, 157–58; John R. McKivigan, "The Antislavery 'Comeouter' Sects: A Neglected Dimension of the Abolitionist Movement," *Civil War History* 26, no. 2 (1980): 145–60.

11. Earnest J. Isaacs, "A History of Nineteenth-Century American Spiritualism as a Religious and Social Movement" (Ph.D. diss., University of Wisconsin, 1975), 26–27, 30–50; Guarneri, *Utopian Alternative*, 348–53; R. Laurence Moore, *In Search of White Crows, Spiritualism, Parapsychology, and American Culture* (New York, 1977), 25, 52–54.

12. *CDI*, August 13, 1879; *Letters of Garrison* 2:442–47, 492, 3:177–78, 258; Stebbins, *Upward Steps*, 52–53; Lillie Buffum Chace Wyman and Arthur Crawford Wyman, *Elizabeth Buffum Chace, 1806–1899: Her Life and Its Environment*, 2 vols. (Boston, 1914), 1:138–39; Hill, "Anti-Slavery Days," Corbin Collection, SSG; Arthur G. Hill, "Samuel Lapham Hill," 205–11, and Seth Hunt, "Charles C. Burleigh," 211–14, in Sheffield, *History of Florence*; Clark, *Communitarian Moment*, 88; Susan Strane, *A Whole-Souled Woman: Prudence Crandall and the Education of Black Women* (New York, 1990), 91–93; Bertram Wyatt-Brown, *Lewis Tappan and the Evangelical War against Slavery* (Baton Rouge, La., 1969), 188–89; McBee, *Utopia to Florence*, 67.

13. Boyle, *Social Reform*, 5–12, 13–16, 21–24, 27–30, 43–56, and *The Funeral Sermon of Dr. James Boyle, with Two Appendixes (Written by Himself)* (Kingsville, Ontario, 1884), app. 2:1–3, and *A Letter to William Lloyd Garrison Respecting the Clerical Appeal, Sectarianism, and True Holiness, etc.* (Boston, 1838), May Pamphlets, Anti-Slavery Collection, DRMCCU; NAEI, 1:6, 2:66, 97, 6:350, 388, 403, AAS; *Excelsior: Journals of the Hutchinson Family Singers, 1842–1846*, ed. Dale Cockrell (Stuyvesant, N.Y., 1989), 268; *Letters of Garrison*, 2:345–47, 444, 446, 3:177–78, 184, 189, 240; Martha Hudson to Erasmus Hudson, April 1849, Hudson Family Papers, SSC; *NSTBL*, 253–64.

14. Dolly Stetson to James Stetson, April 21, 1844, in *Letters from an American Utopia*; Dorothy Sterling, *Ahead of Her Time: Abby Kelley and the Politics of Antislavery* (New York, 1991), 166–67, 172–73, 176, 179; Stebbins, *Upward Steps*, 96–99; Douglass, "What I Found at the Northampton Association," 131–32; Wyman and Wyman 1:139–42; Clark, *Communitarian Moment*, 87–88.

15. *Letters of Garrison*, 3:120–21, 195, 252, 266–67; Almira Stetson et al. to James Stetson, June 19, 1844, in *Letters from an American Utopia*; Parker Pillsbury, *The Acts of the Anti-slavery Apostles* (Concord, N.H., 1883), 10–11, 29; *PF*, March 24, March 27, 1845; Stacey M. Robertson, *Parker Pillsbury: Radical Abolitionist, Male Feminist* (Ithaca, N.Y., 2000), 7, 10–11, 13–25, 85–89, 123–27, 130–46; Sterling, *Ahead of Her Time*, 129–32, 138–42, 193–212.

16. Mary Stetson to James Stetson, June 19, 1844, Dolly Stetson to James Stetson, July 26, 1844, in *Letters from an American Utopia*; Abby Hutchinson Patton to Amy Post, "for Sojourner Truth," September 25, 1864, AIPFP; *Excelsior*, 18, 128, 268–70, 381; McBee, *Utopia to Florence*, 31–32; Sylvester Judd Notebook (no. 3, 1845–46), October 20, 1845, Forbes Library, Northampton, Massachusetts; "Sunday at the Community," *Hampshire Gazette*, November 14, 1843 (from *Massachusetts Whig*); Hill, "Anti-Slavery Days," Corbin Collection, SSC; George R. Stetson, "When I Was a Boy," 121, and "The Traveler's Home," in Sheffield, *History of Florence*, 45–48.

17. Dolly Stetson to James Stetson, June 8, 16, July 26, 1844, May 22, 1845, Giles Stebbins to James Stetson, August 7, 1844, and Christopher Clark, "'We Might Be Happyer Here': Marriage, Education, and Conduct at the Northampton Community," 180–81, all in *Letters from an American Utopia*; *Northampton Free Press*, May 16, 1862; Thomas D. Hamm, *God's Government Begun: The Society for Universal Inquiry and Reform, 1842–46* (Bloomington, Ind., 1995), 108–22.

18. Dolly Stetson to James Stetson, July 26, 1844, February 20, May 4, 1845; Almira and Dolly Stetson to James Stetson, August 4, 1844, in *Letters from an American Utopia*.

19. Dolly Stetson to James Stetson, September 1, October 6, 12, November 19, 1844, May 11, 1845, and Clark, "'We Might Be Happyer Here,'" 182–84, in *Letters from an American Utopia*; Clark, *Communitarian Moment*, 69–71.

20. Dolly Stetson to James Stetson, October 6, November 19, December 5, 1844, March 18, April 3, 13, 1845, in *Letters from an American Utopia*; *Excelsior*, 267–68.

21. Dolly Stetson to James Stetson, October 12, 1844, May 11, 1845, in *Letters from an American Utopia*; Wesley took the name of Sophia's husband (Thomas Schuyler). Wesley died in 1928, at age eighty-five. His birthplace is listed erroneously as Michigan in the newspaper. Certificate of death, Wesley Schuyler, April 19, 1928, liber 7, p. 134, Calhoun County Clerk, Marshall, Michigan; Berenice Lowe, "The Family of Sojourner Truth," *Michigan Heritage* 3, no. 12 (summer 1962): 184.

22. NAEI, 2:66, 3:168, 177, 184, 186, 6:146, 157, 168, 174, 185, 192, 212, 239, 256, 260, 262–67, 294, 307, 394, 403, 411, 419, AAS; U.S. Census Bureau, *Population Schedules for the Seventh Census* (1850), State of Massachusetts, County of Hampshire, Town of Northampton (Washington, D.C., 1853), 108 roll 320; "Northampton Association," 79–89; By a Country Maiden, "When I Was a Girl," in Sheffield, *History of Florence*, 123–26; Stebbins, *Upward Steps*, 58–63, 86–92; Clark, *Communitarian Moment*, 22, 24, 77–81.

23. NAEI, 5:175, 6:45, AAS; *NASS*, August 17, 1843; *Liberator*, December 22, 1843; *PF*, June 19, 1845; Almira Stetson to James Stetson, January 13, 1843, David Ruggles (by amanuensis) to James Stetson, June 20, 1844; Giles Stebbins to James Stetson, August 7, 1844, Mary Stetson to James Stetson, June 19, 1844, August 25, October 13, 1844, Dolly Stetson to James Stetson, n.d. [c. June 8, 1844], October 6, 1844, in *Letters from an American Utopia*; Stetson, "When I Was a Boy," 118–26; Country Maiden, "When I Was a Girl" 123–26; *Letters of Garrison*, 3:215, 222–25; George Thompson Garrison to Henry C. Wright, May 5, 1857, William Lloyd Garrison Jr. to Ellen Wright Garrison, August 6, 1870, Garrison Family Letters, SSC; Stebbins, *Upward Steps*, 56–58, 72–73, 149, 210–13, 221–25; *Battle Creek Journal*, December 5, 1883; Clark, *Communitarian Moment*, 114–17, 132–33.

24. Wyman and Wyman, *ELizabeth Chace*, 1:8; Hill, "Anti-Slavery Days," Corbin Collection, SSC; Dolly Stetson and Mary Stetson to James Stetson, June 3, 1844, in *Letters from an American Utopia*; Stetson, "When I Was a Boy," 121; *CDI*, August 13, 1879.

25. NAEI, 5:234–35, AAS; *Hampshire Gazette,* September 19, 1843; Wyman and Wyman, *Elizabeth Chace,* 1:142; Hill, "Anti-Slavery Days," Corbin Collection, SSC; Munger, *Life and Religious Experiences,* 35–38, 42–47, 78–84, 98–102.

26. *NST,* 93–95; Munger, *Life and Religious Experiences,* 41–43.

27. *NST,* 95–97.

28. Douglass, "What I Found at the Northampton Association," 130–31; *Hampshire Gazette,* April 30, 1844; *NASS,* May 18, 1843; *Liberator,* May 10, 1844; *Letters of Garrison,* 3:157–58; *Excelsior,* 267–69; John Wennersten, "Parke Goodwin, Utopian Socialism and the Politics of Antislavery," *New-York Historical Society Quarterly* 60 (July–October 1976): 113–16, 118–20, 122–25.

29. *Excelsior,* 270; *Liberator* October 13, 1843 (from *Journal of Commerce*).

30. *BAP,* 3:27, 168–80, 285–86; *Liberator,* October 5, 1838, August 20, 1841, August 31, 1844; *Letters of Garrison,* 3:192, 194, 214; *Liberator,* August 31, 1844; David Ruggles to David L. Child, September 4, 1843, Garrison Letters, BPL; *Water Cure Journal and Herald of Reforms* 2 (August, 1846): 189–90, 3 (April–July 1847): 126–27, 224–25, 4 (April 1848): 52–53; *Green Mountain Spring* 1, no. 3 (March 1846): 34–35, no. 4 (May 1846): 70–71, no. 7 (July 1846): 111, and vol. 2, no. 3 (April 1847): 62–63; Dorothy B. Porter, "The Water Cures," in *Northampton Book,* 122–14; and "David Ruggles," *Journal of the National Medical Association* 49, no. 1 (January and March 1957): 69–71, 2 (March 1957): 130–33; Stetson, "When I Was a Boy," 120–22; Country Maiden, "When I Was a Girl," 124.

31. Windham County Anti-Slavery Society Records, CSL; Abby Kelley to Erasmus Hudson, June 1840, April 12, 1841, and George Benson to Erasmus Hudson, May 29, 1840, Hudson Family Papers, SSC; Sterling, *Ahead of Her Time,* 89, 94–96, 107–12; *BAP,* 3:474–76; David E. Swift, *Black Prophets of Justice: Activist Clergy Before the Civil War* (Baton Rouge, La., 1989), 182–87, 189, 192–93, 215–28; William A. Hinds, *American Communities,* 3d ed. (Chicago, 1908), 279; Clark, *Communitarian Moment.*

32. NAEI, 1:163, 2:163, 177, 184, 6: 146, AAS; *Hampshire Herald,* June 3, July 3, 1845; *Liberator,* December 22, 1843; Horatio T. Strother, *The Underground Railroad in Connecticut* (Middletown, Conn., 1962), 163–74; *Letters of Garrison,* 3:193, 194, 4:595–96; R. J. M. Blackett, *Beating against the Barriers: The Lives of Six Nineteenth-Century Afro-Americans* (Ithaca, N.Y., 1989), 290–93; "Northampton Association," 67–68; *Letters of Garrison,* 4:595–96. James Stetson to Dolly Stetson, February 20, 1843, Dolly Stetson to James Stetson, February 20, 1845, in *Letters from an American Utopia.* For a different perspective on the Tappanite-Garrisonian conflict and on African Americans in both the Community and Northampton itself, see Clark, *Communitarian Moment,* 71–75. For a different perspective on the black presence in the Community and Northampton, see Paul Gaffney, "Coloring Utopia," in *Letters from an American Utopia,* 239–278.

33. BAP, 4:3–4; *Letters of Garrison,* 3:169–73, 177–82, 188–89, 191–93; *NASS,* August 17, 1843; *Liberator,* August 9, 31, 1844, September 13, 1844; Sterling, *Ahead of Her Time,* 188–92.

34. *Excelsior,* 268–69; *Liberator,* May 10, 1844, *Hampshire Gazette,* April 30, 1844; Douglass, "What I Found at the Northampton Association," 131–32; John W. Hutchinson, "The Hutchinsons' Visit," in Sheffield, History of Florence, 133–35.

35. *CDI,* August 13, 1879; *Liberator,* June 7, 1844; *Letters of Garrison,* 3:265–66; Munger, *Life and Religious Experience,* 36–37; Hill, "Anti-Slavery Days," Corbin Collection, SSC.

36. *Liberator,* October 10, 1838, August 20, 1841, May 10, 24, June 7, 21, August 31, 1844; *PF,* June 5, 1845; *Letters of Garrison,* 3:265.

37. *Liberator,* May 24, May 31, June 7, June 21, August 31, 1844; *NASS,* September 12, 1844; Dolly Stetson to James Stetson, June 16, 1844; Rush, quoted in Clark, "'We Might Be Happyer Here,'" 166, in *Letters from an American Utopia; Letters of Garrison,* 3:11–12, 23, 254–57, 265, 338; Alvin Oickle, *Jonathan Walker, the Man with the Branded Hand* (Everett,

Mass., 1998), 43–60; Benjamin Quarles, *Black Abolitionists* (New York, 1969), 100, 164–65, Philip S. Foner, *History of Black Americans*, 3 vols., vol. 1, *From Africa to the Emergence of the Cotton Kingdom* (Westport, Conn., 1975), 489, 491–92.

38. *Liberator*, August 31, September 13, 1844; *BAP*, 3:33, 335, 338, 445; *Letters of Garrison*, 3:14, 17, 23, 146; NAEI, 5: 234, 235, 317, AAS.

39. *Hampshire Herald*, July 3, 1845.

40. Jonathan Walker to Amy Post, January 1, 1869, Sojourner Truth to Amy Post, October 1, 1865, February 5, 1869, AIPFP; *Life and Correspondence of Henry Ingersoll Bowditch*, 2 vols., ed. Vincent Y. Bowditch (Boston, 1902), 2:27; *Woman's Journal* 9 (August 1878): 6; *NSTBL*, 305–7; Oickle, *Jonathan Walker*, 12–54, 160–74, 178–80, 192–94, 292, 225–35, 241–49.

41. Dolly Stetson to James Stetson, May 4, 1845, in *Letters from an American Utopia; New York Herald*, May 7, 1845; *Liberator*, May 15, 1845; *NASS*, May 15, 22, 1845.

42. *New York Herald*, May 7, 1845; *NASS*, May 15, 1845; *Liberator*, May 30, 1845; *BAP*, 3:463–67.

43. *NASS*, May 15, 1845; *New York Herald*, May 7, 1845; *CA*, September 8, 1838, November 3, 1838, August 29, 1840; *BAP*, 3:116–18, 201–4; Sarah S. Southwick, *Reminiscences of Early Anti-slavery Days* (Cambridge, Mass., 1893), 29; Stebbins, *Upward Steps*, 84.

44. *NASS*, May 8, 1845.

45. *BAP*, 3:463–64; *Liberator*, May 16, 1845; *NASS*, May 8, May 15, 1845; *PF*, June 5, 19, 1845.

46. U.S. Census Bureau, *Eighth Census* (1860), State of Michigan, County of Calhoun, Bedford Township (Washington, D.C., 1864) Corbin Collection, SSC, 90, 91; Hill, "Anti-Slavery Days"; Harriet Beecher Stowe, "Sojourner Truth, the Libyan Sibyl," *Atlantic Monthly*, April 1863, 474; Berenice Lowe, "The Family of Sojourner Truth," *Michigan Heritage* 3, no. 4 (196162): 182–93.

47. Pillsbury, *Anti-Slavery Apostles*, 326–27; Wyman and Wyman, *Elizabeth Chace*, 1:143–44; Douglass, "What I Found at the Northampton Association," 131–32; *The Life and Writings of Frederick Douglass*, ed. Philip S. Foner, 4 vols. (New York, 1950), 1:47–50; *Excelsior*, 268–69; Dolly Stetson to James Stetson, April 13, 1845, in *Letters from an American Utopia*; *PF*, June 5, 19, 1845; Journal of Percival Pease (Kept by his mother, Augusta Leggett Pease), May 4, 1873, Eliza Seaman Leggett Family Papers, vol. 9, DPL.

48. *PF*, June 5, 1845; NST, 98.

CHAPTER II: THE COLD WATER ARMY, OLIVE GILBERT,
AND SOJOURNER'S *NARRATIVE*

1. David Ruggles to James Stetson, June 20, 1844, Dolly Stetson to James Stetson, August, 4, 1844, in *Letters from an American Utopia: The Stetson Family and the Northampton Association, 1843–1846*, ed. Christopher Clark and Kerry W. Buckley (Amherst, Mass., 2004); Mary R. Cabot, *Annals of Brattleboro, 1681–1895*, 2 vols. (Brattleboro, Vt., 1922), 2:560–65; *Water-Cure Journal* 2 (February 1846): 79; 4 (July 1847): 224; *Green Mountain Spring* 1 (March, 1846): 35–36; 2 (May 1846): 71–72; 3 (March 1847): 42–43; Dorothy Porter, "David Ruggles: An Apostle of Human Rights," *JNH* 28 (January 1943): 68; Harry B. Weiss and Howard R. Kemble, *The Great American Water-Cure Craze: A History of Hydropathy in the United States* (Trenton, N.J., 1967), 130–31, 209–10; Marshall Scott Legan, "Hydropathy in America: A Nineteenth Century Panacea," *Bulletin of the History of Medicine* 45 (May–June 1971): 267–72; William S. Haubrich, *Medical Meanings: A Glossary of Word Origins* (San Diego, 1984), 221, 225; *Dorlands Medical Dictionary*, 27th ed. (Philadelphia, 1988), 1499, 1783.

2. *Green Mountain Spring* 1 (March 1846): 35–36.

3. *Water-Cure Journal* 1 (December 1845): 17–20, changed to *Water-Cure Journal and Herald of Reforms* 7 (January 1849): 3–7; *The Letters of William Lloyd Garrison*, ed. Walter M.

Merrill and Louis Ruchames, 6 vols. (Cambridge, Mass., 1971–81), 3:565–66, 569–72; *Green Mountain Spring* 1 (March 1846): 35–36.

4. Dolly Stetson to James Stetson, February 16, May 19, June 12, 1845, Dolly Sharpe Witter to Dolly and James Stetson, August 28, 1845, in *Letters from an American Utopia; NASS*, March 12, 1846; *Liberator*, January 10, 1849, February 23, 1849; *Green Mountain Spring* 2 (January 1847): 27–28; Porter, "David Ruggles," 68–70, 130–33; Cabot, *Annals of Brattleboro*, 2:567–71.

5. *Green Mountain Spring* 1 (December 1846): 188–90; 2 (February 1847): 17–20; Cabot, *Annals of Brattleboro*, 2:567–68, 573–74, 580–81; Dolly Stetson to James Stetson, March 6, 1845, June 12, in *Letters from an American Utopia*; Susan E. Cayleff, *"Wash and Be Healed": The Water-Cure Movement and Women's Health* (Philadelphia, 1987), 86, 102, 143–44, 148–49; Jane B. Donegan, *"Hydropathic Highway to Health": Women and Water-Cure in Antebellum America* (New York, 1986), 101–2, 140–42, 167–68, 186–95; Louis A. DeCaro Jr., *"Fire from the Midst of You": A Religious Life of John Brown* (New York, 2002), 182–85; Kathryn Kish Sklar, *Catharine Beecher: A Study in American Domesticity* (New Haven, Conn., 1973), 184–87, 205–9; Joan D. Hedrick, *Harriet Beecher Stowe: A Life* (New York, 1994), 173–83; *The Journals of Charlotte Forten Grimké*, ed. Brenda Stevenson (New York, 1988).

6. Dolly Stetson to James Stetson, October 6, 1844, Almira Stetson to James Stetson, June 20, 1845, in *Letters from an American Utopia; Green Mountain Spring* 1 (March 1846): 38–39; 3 (April and November 1848): 52–53, 169–74; *Water-Cure Journal* 2 (November 1846): 189; changed to *Water-Cure Journal and Herald of Reforms* 7 (January 1849): 25, 26, 29, 45; 7 (April 1849): 120; 8 (September 1849): 161–64; David Ruggles to William Lloyd Garrison, December 6, 1847, Ms. A.1.2. vol. 17, 77, BPL; Helen E. Garrison to Elizabeth Pease Nichols, December 14, 1844, Oswald Garrison Villard Letters, Houghton Library, Harvard University; *Letters of Garrison*, 3:510–12; 526–34, 565–99; Cayleff, *"Wash and Be Healed,"* 21–22, 42–45, 110–11, 442–43; Donegan, *"Hydropathic Highway,"* 98–100; Legan, "Hydropathy in America," 275; Richard Shryock, "Sylvester Graham and the Popular Health Movement, 1830–1870," *Mississippi Valley Historical Review* 18 (September 1931): 170–72, 176–77, 179–80; William D. Conklin, comp., *The Jackson Health Resort; As Seen by Those Who Knew It Well* (Dansville, N.Y., 1971), 119–22; Stephen Nissenbaum, *Sex, Diet, and Debility in Jacksonian America: Sylvester Graham and Health Reform* (Westport, Conn., 1980), 38, 53, 79–80, 104–12, 125–27, 140–48.

7. *Letters of Garrison*, 3:597–99; Conklin, *Jackson Health Resort*, 106–7, 139–42, 148–52; Nissenbaum, *Sex, Diet, Debility*, 127; Dorothy Sterling, *Ahead of Her Time: Abby Kelley and the Politics of Antislavery* (New York, 1991), 29–30, 219; Shryock, "Sylvester Graham," 172, 174–75; Cayleff, *Wash and Be Healed*, 109–17; Conklin, *Jackson Health Resort*, 139–41, 154. For a different perspective, linking temperance and reform to expanding industrialism and fundamentalist religion, see W. J. Rorabaugh, *The Alcoholic Republic: An American Tradition* (New York, 1979), 198–222.

8. *Battle Creek Enquirer and News*, June 12, 1932; Conklin, *Jackson Health Resort*, 106–10, 139–42, 148–152; Nissenbaum, *Sex, Diet, and Debility*, 127; Jonathan M. Butler, "The Making of New Order: Millenism and the Origins of Seventh-day Adventism," in Jonathan M. Butler and Ronald L. Numbers, *The Disappointed* (Knoxville, Tenn., 1993), 189–208; R. Laurence Moore, *Religious Outsiders and the Making of Americans* (New York, 1986), 128–33; Sterling, *Ahead of Her Time*, 29–30, 219; Richard W. Schwarz, *John Harvey Kellogg, M.D.* (Nashville, Tenn., 1970), 116–20; Cayleff, *"Wash and Be Healed,"* 115–17. Dr. Kellogg's brother, William K. Kellogg, patented the cereal and made a fortune. Neither invented the cereal. It was first produced by reformer and Abolitionist James C. Jackson, at his Dansville Water Cure Institute, Conklin, *Jackson Health Resort*, 139–41, 147–51.

9. *Battle Creek Citizen*, November 17, 1883; "Sojourner Truth was not a member of the Seventh-day Adventist Church" (letter from James R. Nix, Adventist archivist, to Marlene

Steele, April 3, 1899, in Willard Library, Battle Creek, Michigan). Moore, *Religious Outsiders*, 128–36, maintains that although Adventists were never "political revolutionaries," antebellum reform was embedded in their beliefs. For a different perspective, see Butler, "Adventism," 173–90, and Whitney R. Cross, *The Burned-Over District: The Social and Intellectual History of Enthusiastic Religion in Western New York, 1800–1850* (Ithaca, N.Y., 1950), 311, 318–21.

10. Sources on Millerites as Abolitionists and speaking out on social issues include *Letters of Garrison*, 3:135, 136, 137, 150, 248; *NST*, 88–93; Stearns to Chapman, November 8, 1844, Ms. A.9.2.20.93, BPL; *Letters of Theodore Dwight Weld and Angelina Grimké Weld, and Sarah Grimké, 1822–1844*, ed. Gilbert H. Barnes and Dwight A. Dumond, 2 vols. (Gloucester, Mass., 1965), 2:965–66; Gerda Lerner, *The Grimké Sisters of South Carolina* (Boston, 1967), 306–9; Cayleff, *"Wash and Be Healed*," 94–95; Schwarz, *Kellogg*, 158–73.

11. "Phrenological Character of Sojourner Truth," Berenice Lowe Papers, MHC; Cayleff, *"Wash and Be Healed*," 25–26, 114, 133.

12. *Water-Cure Journal and Herald of Reforms* 7 (January 1849): 15, 29; 7 (February 1849): 45; 7 (April 1849): 113, 120; 8 (December 1849): 161–64; *ASB*, June 21, 1851; Sojourner Truth to Amy Post, January 18, 1869, Lydia Allen to Sojourner Truth, February 1, 1869, AIPFP; "Sojourner Truth" newspaper file, STC.

13. Dolly Stetson to James Stetson, June 16, June 26, October 12, November 19, 1844, Almira Stetson et al. to James Stetson, June 19, December 1, 1844, Giles Stebbins to James Stetson, August 7, 1844, and Christopher Clark, "'We Might Be Happyer Here'": Marriage, Education, and Conduct at the Northampton Community," 169, in *Letters from an American Utopia*; NAEI, 2:94–95, AAS; "Northampton Association," Charles A. Sheffield, ed., *History of Florence, Massachusetts, Including a Complete Account of the Northampton Association of Education and Industry* (Florence, Mass., 1895), 88–90, 94–97; James Boyle, *Social Reform, Or an Appeal in Behalf of Association, Based upon the Principles of a Pure Christianity* (Northampton, Mass., 1844), 62–66, 70; Christopher Clark, *Communitarian Moment: The Radical Challenge of the Northampton Association* (Ithaca, N.Y., 1995), 167–69.

14. Dolly Stetson to James Stetson, 1844, February 16, 1845, March 6, 18, April 3, 13, 15, May 4, 1845, in *Letters from an American Utopia*.

15. Dolly Stetson to James Stetson, June 1, 12, 1845, April 12, 23, May 3, 1846, in *Letters from an American Utopia*; PF, June 5, 1845; NAEI, 3:229, 6: 381.

16. "Frances B. Judd Reminiscences," in Sheffield, *History of Florence*, 116–18; Kate de Normandie Wilson, *Dolly Witter Stetson: A Sketch of Her Life* (Brooklyn, Conn., 1907); *NST*, 98; Alice McBee, *From Utopia to Florence: The Story of a Transcendentalist Community in Northampton, Mass., 1830–1852* (reprint, Philadelphia, 1975), 63–64; "Northampton Association," 99–104; Clark, *Communitarian Moment*, 120–27, 178–82.

17. NSTBL, 269–70; PF, June 5, 1845; *Letters of Garrison*, 3:540–41, 545–47, 577, 585–87, 597–98; Henry Mayer, *All on Fire: William Lloyd Garrison and the Abolition of Slavery* (New York, 1998), 377–78; Clark, *Communitarian Moment*, 203–5.

18. *NST*, 98–99; *Letters of Garrison*, 3:164–65, 597–98; *Green Mountain Spring* 1, no. 12 (December 1846): 188–89; Sojourner Truth to William Lloyd Garrison, April 11, 1864, Garrison Letters, Ms. A, BPL; Hampshire County Record Book, County Court House, Northampton, Mass., vol. 133, Register of Deeds, Northampton, Mass., deed 106, mortgage 124–25; U.S. Census Bureau, *Population Schedules for the Seventh Census* (1850), State of Massachusetts, County of Hampshire, Town of Northampton (Washington, D.C., 1853), 108, 109, 114; McBee, *Utopia to Florence*, 67–71; Clark, *Communitarian Moment*, 188–89.

19. On Gilbert as amanuensis, see Carla Peterson, *"Doers of the Word": African-American Women Speakers and Writers in the North (1830–1880)* (New Brunswick, N.J., 1998), 31–33. On Sojourner's *Narrative* as a secondary source, see Jean Fagan Yellin, *Women and Sisters: The Antislavery Feminists in American Culture* (New Haven, Conn., 1989), 198 n. 3.

20. "Birth, Marriage, and Deaths," Brooklyn, Conn., 6:239, Barbour Collection, CSL; Inventory and Will of Joseph Gilbert, Probate Estate Papers, town of Brooklyn, Plainfield District, Probate Packets, no. 911, August 5, 1802, CSL; Homer W. Brainard and Clarence A. Torrey, *The Gilberts of New England*, 2 pts. (Victoria, B.C., 1959), pt. 2, *Descendants of Matthew Gilbert of New Haven, Humphrey Gilbert of Ipswich, and William Gilbert of Boston*, 119–20, 159; Edmund J. Cleveland and Horace G. Cleveland, *The Genealogy of the Cleveland and Cleaveland Families*, 3 vols. (Hartford, Conn., 1899), 1:82–83, 178–79, 387–88, 895, 2:1782.

21. Original Records of the First Congregational Church, Brooklyn, Conn., 1731–1818, 2 vols., 1:105–6, 127–57, 159, 173, 175, 218, 224; 2:1–32, 46, 49–54, 140–41, 145–46, CSL; William Ellery Channing, "Unitarian Christianity" and "Spiritual Freedom," in *William Ellery Channing Selected Writings*, ed. David Robinson (New York, 1985), 70–102, 194–220; Richard M. Bayles, *History of Windham County* (New York, 1889), 583–91; Ellen D. Larned, *History of Windham County, Connecticut*, 2 vols. (Worcester, Mass., 1880), 2:461–63, 475–78, 480–84; Conrad Wright, *The Unitarian Controversy: Essays on American Unitarian History* (Boston, 1994), 83–110, 137–54; Sarah Elbert, *A Hunger for Home: Louisa May Alcott's Place in American Culture* (New Brunswick, N.J., 1987), xii–xvii; Donald Yacovone, *Samuel Joseph May and the Dilemmas of Liberal Persuasion, 1797–1871* (Philadelphia, 1991), 11–19.

22. Samuel Joseph May, *Memoir of Samuel Joseph May, 1797–1871* (Boston, 1873), 62–63, 76–77, 83–91, 88–91, 103–14, 118–19; Yacovone, *May*, 7–8, 19–27; Susan Strane, *A Whole-Souled Woman: Prudence Crandall and the Education of Black Women* (New York, 1990), 100; *Letters from an American Utopia*, 3–6; Charles C. Forman, "Elected Now by Time": The Unitarian Controversy, 1805–1935," 23–29, and Daniel Walker Howe, "At Morning Blest and Golden Browed," 35–43, 52–59, in *A Stream of Light: A Short History of American Unitarianism*, ed. Conrad Wright (Boston, 1975); and Wright, *Unitarian Controversy*, 37, 54–56.

23. Jean Reville, *Liberal Christianity: Its Origin, Nature, and Mission* (New York, 1903), 1–36, 44–67, 75–80; May, *Memoir*, 88–91, 137–48, 152; William Ellery Channing, "Remarks on the Slavery Question in a Letter to Jonathan Phillips, Esq.," in *The Works of William E. Channing, DD*, 6 vols. (Boston, 1869), 5:16, 74–76, 22–25; Wendell Phillips Garrison and Francis Jackson Garrison, *William Lloyd Garrison, 1805–1879: The Story of His Life, Told by His Children*, 4 vols. (New York, 1885–99), 1:464–67; *Letters of Garrison*, 1:574–75, 577–79, 583–85, 2:14–16, 43–46, 223–24; Original Records of the First Congregational Church, Brooklyn, Conn., 2:169, 186–87, CSL; *Liberator*, December 14, 1833; May, *Memoir*, 152; Wright, *Unitarian Controversy*, 86, 83, 101–2; Forman, "Elected Now by Time," 23–29, and Howe, "At Morning Blest," 40–43, 56–67; Yacovone, *May*, 8, 27–28.

24. *The Benson Family of Newport, Rhode Island* (New York, 1872), 31, 35, 38, 42–47, 51, 54; Garrison and Garrison, *William Lloyd Garrison*, 1:320–21, 338, 425–27; George W. Benson to William Lloyd Garrison, March 5, 1833, Ms. A.1.2, vol. 3, no. 5, and George W. Benson to Samuel J. May, March 19, 1833, Ms. A 1. 2, vol. 3 no. 24, BPL; May, *Memoir*, 113–18; *Letters of Garrison*, 1:277, 280, 286–87, 289–92, 319–21, 562–64, 2:349; Anne Weston to Debra Weston, January 30, 1837, Ms. A.9.2, 9:9, BPL; Lillie Buffum Chace Wyman and Arthur Crawford Wyman, *Elizabeth Buffum Chace, 1806–1899: Her Life and Its Environment*, 2 vols. (Boston, 1914), 1:136, 137;

25. E. S. Abdy, *Journal of a Residence and Tour in the United States of North America from April 1833, to October 1834*, 2 vols. (London, 1835), 1:196–97; George W. Benson to Samuel J. May, March 16, 1833 Ms. A.1.2, vol. 3, no. 23, March 31, 1833 Ms. A.1.2., vol. 3, no. 33, George W. Benson to William Lloyd Garrison, March 30, 1833, Ms. 1.2, vol. 3, no. 34, Prudence Crandall to "Mr. Editor," June 28, 1833, Ms. A.1.2, vol. 3, no. 46, BPL; May, *Memoir*, 148–51; Larned, *Windham County*, 2:431–33; Strane, *Whole-Souled Woman*, 4–8, 23–29, 31–34.

26. Benson to Garrison, March 5, 1833, Ms. A.1.2, vol. 3, no. 18, Prudence Crandall to "Mr. Editor," June 28, 1833, Ms. A.1.2. vol. 3, no. 46, BPL; Garrison and Garrison, *William*

Lloyd Garrison, 1:315–25; Abdy, *Journal*, 1:196–200, 205–7; Samuel J. May, "The Right of Colored People to Education Vindicated; Letters to Andrew Judson, Esq., and Others in Canterbury" (Brooklyn, Conn., 1833), esp. 6–7, 11, 19–21, May Pamphlets, vol. 209, no. 2, Anti-Slavery Collection, DRMCCU; May, *Memoir*, 148–56; Mayer, *All on Fire*, 145–48, 185; Larned, *Windham County*, 2:471, 490–99; Strane, *Whole-Souled Woman*, 31–35, 39, 46–50, 58–61, 94–95, 101–6, 109–12, 145–52, 186; Yacovone, *May*, 48–52; Bertram Wyatt-Brown, *Lewis Tappan and the Evangelical War against Slavery* (Baton Rouge, La., 1969), 90–91.

27. Helen E. Benson to William Lloyd Garrison, February 11, March 3, 1834, Olive Gilbert to William Lloyd Garrison, May 22, 1876, all in Oswald Garrison Villard Letters, Houghton Library, Harvard University; May, *Memoir*, 217; Garrison and Garrison, *William Lloyd Garrison*, 1:425; *Letters of Garrison*, 1:123–24, 138–40, 158–59, 277, 288, 352–54, 434–36, 2:584–89, 2:190, 196–99; Buffum et al., *Elizabeth Chace*, 2:264–69; *Benson Family*, 35, 38, 54; *BAP*, 3:152–53, 318; Abby Kelley to Newbury Darling, June 12, 1840, Abby Kelley Foster Papers, AAS; Horatio T. Strother, *The Underground Railroad in Connecticut* (Middletown, Conn., 1962), 38–39, 119, 132–36; Yacovone, *May*, 73; Strane, *Whole-Souled Woman*, 100; Mayer, *All on Fire*, 147, 148, 149.

28. *Liberator*, August 16, 1834; *Letters of Garrison*, 1:321, 395–9; Records of the Windham County Anti-Slavery Society and Records of the Female Anti-Slavery Society of Brooklyn and Vicinity, 4, CSL, *Constitution and Address of the Female Anti-Slavery Society of Chatham Street Chapel* (New York, 1834). The Plainfield Anti-Slavery Society, organized during the Crandall struggle, may have been the first local crossgender antislavery society.

29. *Liberator*, August 16, 1834; *Letters of Garrison*, 1:360–61, 395–96; Records of the Female Society of Brooklyn, CSL; E. D. Hudson to Abby Kelley, May 29, 1840, Kelley to Darling, June 12, 1840, Abby Kelley Foster Papers, AAS; *Letters of Garrison*, 1:360–61, 364–65, 398–99, Strane, *Whole-Souled Woman*, 144–52, 176–87, 199–210.

30. *Letters of Garrison*, 1:382, 3:167; Records of First Congregational Church of Brooklyn, Conn., 2:185–87, 191, 196, 212, CSL; George W. Benson to Samuel J. May, September 26, 1844, Ms. A.1.2, 14:59, Benson to May, December 23, 1844, Ms. A.1.2, 14:82, BPL; Dolly Stetson to James Stetson, February 20, 1843, October 6, 1844, February 16, 1845, in *Letters from an American Utopia*; Yacovone, *May*, 59, 73–78, 86.

31. NAEI, 3:229, 6:381; *Letters of Garrison*, 3:164–65; *Green Mountain Spring* 1 (December 1846): 188–89; *NST*, 98–99.

32. Record of Deeds, bk. 5, 349, 348–53, bk. 6, 153, bk. 7, 56, bk. 8, 442, 443, Town Hall, Brooklyn, Conn.; Gilbert to Garrison, May 22, 1876, Oswald Garrison Villard Letters, Houghton Library, Harvard University; *Letters of Garrison*, 3:164–65, 4:39–40; U.S. Census Bureau, *Population Schedules for the Seventh Census* (1850), State of Connecticut, County of Windham, Town of Brooklyn (Washington, D.C., 1853), 198; Cleveland and Cleveland, *Cleveland Genealogy*, 387.

33. Olive Gilbert to W. E. Whiting, August 18, 1852, AMA; Gilbert to Garrison, May 22, 1876, Oswald Garrison Villard Letters, Houghton Library, Harvard University; Sklar, *Catharine Beecher*, 60–63; Hedrick, *Stowe*, chap. 13 and 164–68; Carolyn L. Karcher, *The First Woman in the Republic: A Cultural Biography of Lydia Maria Child* (Durham, N.C., 1994), 243–44, 249–51, 264–66, 290–94, 320–23.

34. *NST*, 66–67; *Owensboro Messenger*, November 19, 1905; Lee A. Dew and Aloma W. Dew, *Owensboro: The City on the Yellow Banks* (Bowling Green, Ky., 1988), 38, 42, 46.

35. *Owensboro Messenger*, November 19, 1905; *Letters of Garrison*, 3:164–65, 499, 4:60–61, 38–40; *NST*, 66–67; Dolly Stetson to James Stetson, March 6, 1845, in *Letters from an American Utopia*; Gilbert to Whiting, August 18, 1852, AMA; Cleveland and Cleveland, *Cleveland Genealogies*, 895–96; The U.S. Work Progress Administration Federal Writers Project and Historical Records Survey, comp., "Headstone Inscriptions, South Cemetery

Town of Brooklyn, Conn.," November 8, 1934, CSL; Dew and Dew, *Owensboro*, 36, 42–46; Bayles, *History of Windham County*, 602–5; Randolph P. Runyon, *Delia Webster and the Underground Railroad* (Lexington, Ky., 1996), 11–12, 26–27, 37–39, 89–92, 113–16.

36. *Letters of Garrison*, 3:43–46, 48, 151–54, 164–65, 167, 202–3, 267, 4:40–42; William Lloyd Garrison to George Benson, July 8, 1842, Ms. A.1.1, 3:94, BPL.

37. *PF* June 5, 1845; *ASB*, June 21, 1851; *NSTBL*, 276–78.

38. *NST*, 101–4; Michael Blanchard, "The Politics of Abolition in Northampton," *Historical Journal of Massachusetts* 19 (summer 1991): 184–86; *NSBL*, 277–78, 151–73; (Boston) *Commonwealth*, July 3, 1863; "Dumont Family," box 5, Reed Papers, DRMCCU.

39. *Letters of Garrison*, 3:476–77, 479, 510–16, 518, 526–28, 532–33, 549–52, 618–22, 638–39; *Liberator*, August 31, 1844, October 5, 1849, December 21, 1849; *NASS*, March 12, 1846; *Water-Cure Journal and Herald of Reforms* 9 (February 1850): 54; DeCaro, "*Fire from the Midst of You*," 185.

40. *Letters of Garrison*, 3:510–12; *BAP*, 4:7–15; *North Star*, February 1, 1850; William C. Nell to Amy Post, December 23, 1849, AIPFP.

41. *North Star*, February 1, 1850; *Liberator*, December 21, 1849; Porter, "David Ruggles," 131–33; *BAP*, 3:168–80, 261, 285–86, 415.

42. *Letters of Garrison*, 4:38–40.

43. *NSTBL*, 276–78.

44. *North Star*, October 31, 1850; *Liberator*, February 1, March 29, April 5, 19, 1850; *Letters of Garrison*, 4:43; Frederick Douglass, "What I Found at the Northampton Association," in Sheffield, History of Florence, 131–32.

45. (Boston) *Commonwealth*, July 3, 1863.

CHAPTER 12: THE BLOODHOUND BILL AND INTENSIFIED ACTIVISM

1. *Liberator*, April 16, May 3, 1850.

2. William C. Nell to Amy Post, June 2, December 8, 1850, AIPFP; William C. Cochran, *The Western Reserve and the Fugitive Slave Law: A Prelude to the Civil War* (Cleveland, 1920), 89–98.

3. William Wells Brown to Amy Post, September 20, 1848, AIPFP; Giles Stebbins to William Lloyd Garrison, January 20, 1845, Ms. A.1.2, 15:5, Stebbins to Samuel J. May, May 21, 1855, Ms. A.9.2, 28:48, BPL; John A. Collins to British and Foreign Anti-Slavery Society (BFASS), September 25, 1840, Nathaniel Colver to BFASS, November 30, 1840, BFASS to John A. Collins, January 16, 1841, William Lloyd Garrison to J. H. Tredgold, January 29, 1841, all in Papers of BFASS, Mss. British Empire, Rhodes House Library, Oxford University.

4. *The Letters of William Lloyd Garrison*, ed. Walter M. Merrill and Louis Ruchames, 6 vols. (Cambridge, Mass., 1971–81), 1:44–48, 133–35; Henry Mayer, *All on Fire: William Lloyd Garrison and the Abolition of Slavery* (New York, 1998), 17–19, 22–26, 28–30, 46–55.

5. George Thompson Garrison to Henry C. Wright, May 5, 1857, William Lloyd Garrison Jr. to Ellen Wright Garrison, August 6, 1870, Garrison Family Letters, SSC; William Lloyd Garrison to Wendell Phillips Garrison, August 5, 1874, Ms.A.1.1, vol. 4, no. 56, BPL; Wendell Phillips Garrison and Francis Jackson Garrison, *William Lloyd Garrison, 1805–1879: The Story of His Life, Told by His Children*, 4 vols. (New York, 1885–99), 1:14, 25–27, 2:144–45; *CDI*, August 13, 1879. *BAP*, 3:85–91, 3:298–300, 4:259–65; *Letters of Garrison*, 1:193–97, 465–66; *Liberator*, May 17, 1850 (from *New York Globe*, May 7, 1850); Mayer, *All on Fire*, 137–40, 254–58, 351–52; On romantic racialism, see George M. Fredrickson, *The Black Image in the White Mind: The Debate on Afro-American Character and Destiny, 1817–1914* (reprint, Hanover, N.H., 1987), 118–19, chap. 4.

6. *New York Herald*, May 6, 1850; *PF*, May 16, 1850; *Liberator*, May 17, 1850; *North Star*,

May 16, 1850; *Letters of Garrison,* 4:6; Dorothy Sterling, *Ahead of Her Time: Abby Kelley and the Politics of Antislavery* (New York, 1991), 256.

7. *New York Herald,* May 7, 8, 1850; *New York Globe,* May 7, 1850, quoted in *Liberator,* May 17, 1850; *NYT,* May 8, 1850; *North Star,* May 16, 1850; *Letters of Garrison,* 4:11.

8. *N.Y. Express,* May 9, 1850 (from *Liberator,* May 17, 1850); *NYT,* May 8, 9, 1850; *PF,* May 16, 1850; *North Star,* May 16, 1850.

9. *Liberator,* May 17, 1850; *NASS,* May 16, 1850; *PF,* May 9, 1850, May 16, 1850; *North Star,* June 13, 1850; Sterling, *Ahead of Her Time,* 256–57.

10. *NYT,* May 9, 10, 1850; *Liberator,* May 17, 1850; *NASS,* May 16, May 23, 1850; *PF,* May 9, May 16, 1850.

11. *Letters of Garrison,* 1:87, 3:479–80, 4:271–72; *North Star,* May 16, 1850; *Liberator,* May 17, 1850; *ASB,* June 15, 1850.

12. William Still, *The Underground Rail Road; A Record of Facts, Authentic Narratives, Letters, &c* (Philadelphia, 1872), 67; *BAP,* 3:152–53, 318 and 4:35–36; *Liberator,* July 3, 1846, February 2, 9, April, 20, May 18, June 1, June 8, December 14, 1849, June 7, 1850; *ASB,* June 15, 1850; Nell to Amy Post, June 2, 1850, AIPFP.

13. William C. Nell to Amy Post, July 7, August 5, 1850, AIPFP; *Liberator,* December 14, 1849, March 29, May 3, June 7, July 12, 1850, Isa. 58:6; Jer. 34:17.

14. Frederick Douglass to Amy Post, October 20, 25, 31, 1850, AIPFP; *BAP,* 4:61–80; *Liberator,* October 4, 1850; Jane Rhodes, *Mary Ann Shadd Cary: The Black Press and Protest in the Nineteenth Century* (Bloomington, Ind., 1998), 28–31. Horatio T. Strother, *The Underground Railroad in Connecticut* (Middletown, Conn., 1962), 140–44, 171–74.

15. *Liberator,* October 4, 11, 18, November 1, 1850, April 25, June 20, 1851; *Frederick Douglass' Paper,* August 20, 1852; Benjamin Quarles, *Black Abolitionists* (New York, 1969), 200; Fred Landon, "The Negro Migration to Canada after the Passing of the Fugitive Slave Act," *JNH* 5 (January 1920): 22–36; James O. and Lois E. Horton, *Black Bostonians: Family Life and Community Struggle in the Antebellum North,* rev. ed. (New York, 1999), 49–50, 106–11; William and Aimee Lee Cheek, *John Mercer Langston and the Fight for Black Freedom, 1829–65* (Urbana, Ill., 1989), 170–72.

16. *NASS,* October 10, 1850; *Liberator,* October 4, 18, 1850; *North Star,* October 24, 1850; William H. Siebert, *The Underground Railroad from Slavery to Freedom* (New York, 1898), 10, 38, 75–76, 85; *BAP,* 4:68–72.

17. *PF,* May 26, 1853; *BAP,* 4:31–34, 310–14; Rhodes, *Shadd Cary,* 2–15, 22–24, 27, 32–35, 47–71; Landon, "Negro Migration to Canada," 22–36; Kate Clifford Larson, *Bound for the Promised Land: Harriet Tubman, Portrait of an American Hero* (New York, 2004), 88–94; H. F. Kletzing, *Progress of a Race* (Atlanta, 1897), 460–63.

18. Earl Conrad, *Harriet Tubman* (Washington, D.C., 1943), 32, 35–36, 40–48, 56–62, 106–12; Jean M. Humez, *Harriet Tubman: The Life and the Life Stories* (Madison, Wisc., 2003), 20–23; Catherine Clinton, *Harriet Tubman* (New York, 2004), 34–35; Still, *Underground Rail Road,* 296–97, 755–80; Siebert, *Underground Railroad,* 118, 185–89. Carleton Mabee with Susan Mabee Newhouse, *Sojourner Truth, Slave, Prophet, Legend* (New York, 1993), 104–9. William Still devotes a page and a half to Tubman and twenty-five to his close friend Frances Ellen Watkins Harper, the only other black woman in his account. Still also omitted Douglass because he had accused Still of dishonesty. See Milton C. Sernett, *North Star Country: Upstate New York and the Crusade for African American Freedom* (Syracuse, N.Y., 2002), 180–81.

19. Calvin Fairbank, *During Slavery Times: How He "Fought the Good Fight" to Prepare the Way* (Chicago, 1890), 46, 48, 54–55; Garrison and Garrison, *William Lloyd Garrison,* 3:324; Austin Bense, *Reminiscences of Fugitive Slave Days in Boston* (Boston, 1880), 18; Randolph P. Runyon, *Delia Webster and the Underground Railroad* (Lexington, Ky., 1996), 2–3, 5–7, 9–19, 59–63, 77, 91–94, 104, 106–24, 132; Stanley J. and Anita W. Robboy, "Lewis Hayden:

From Fugitive Slave to Statesman," *New England Quarterly* 46 (December 1973): 599–600; Horton and Horton, *Black Bostonians*, 58–61, 112–14.

20. Garrison and Garrison, *William Lloyd Garrison*, 3:302–3; *Life and Correspondence of Henry Ingersoll Bowditch*, 2 vols., ed. Vincent Y. Bowditch (Boston, 1902), 2:349–54; *Liberator*, October 11, November 1, 1850; William C. Nell to Amy Post, December 8, 1850, AIPFP; Robboy and Robboy, "Fugitive to Statesman," 599–601.

21. Nell to Post, December 8, 1850, AIPFP; *Life and Correspondence of Bowditch*, 2:349–52; Fairbank, *During Slavery Times*, 32, 57, 60–63, 71–75, 77–80; Journal of Percival S. Ives (kept by his mother, Margaret Leggett Ives), August 5, 1864, Eliza Seaman Leggett Family Papers, vol. 6, DPL.

22. *NASS*, November 28, 1850; Fairbank, *During Slavery Times*, 60–62.

23. Nell to Post, June 2, 1850, December 5, 1850, and Douglass to Post, October 31, 1850, AIPFP; Siebert, *Underground Railroad*, 157–58, 251–52; *PF*, November 5, 1844, March 27, 1845; *Liberator*, January 3, 1851; Lillie Buffum Chace Wyman and Arthur Crawford Wyman, *Elizabeth Buffum Chace, 1806–1899: Her Life and Its Environment*, 2 vols. (Boston, 1914), 1:142; Philip S. Foner, *History of Black Americans*, 3 vols., vol. 1, *From Africa to the Emergence of the Cotton Kingdom* (Westport, Conn., 1975), 264, 596–605; *Friends and Sisters: Letters between Lucy Stone and Antoinette Brown Blackwell, 1846–93*, ed. Carol Lasser and Deahl Merrill (Urbana, Ill., 1987), 99–100.

24. *Liberator*, December 14, 1849, February 1, April 5, May 3, July 12, 1850; *ASB*, June 22, July 6, 1850; Andrea M. Kerr, *Lucy Stone: Speaking Out for Equality* (New Brunswick, N.J., 1992), 51–56.

25. *Liberator*, September 6, 1850; *NASS*, October 30, 1850; *New York Herald*, October 25, 25, 1850; *Journals of Charlotte Forten*, ed. Brenda Stevenson (New York, 1988); Kerr, *Lucy Stone*, 62–64.

26. Worcester *Daily Spy*, October 25, 1850; *NYT*, October 25, 1850; *ASB*, January 11, 1851; Philip S. Foner, *Frederick Douglass on Women's Rights* (Greenwood, Conn., 1976), 15–16.

27. *NASS*, October 30, 1850; *New York Herald*, October 25, 1850; *NYT*, October 25, 1850; Sterling, *Ahead of Her Time*, 241–42, 263–68; Kerr, *Lucy Stone*, 59–61.

28. *New York Herald*, October 25, 1850; *PF*, October 31, 1850. For a discussion of the Democratic Party and newspapers' intent to maintain gender hierarchy as a means of social and political power, see Michael D. Pierson, *Free Hearts and Free Homes: Gender and American Antislavery Politics* (Chapel Hill, N.C., 2003), esp. chap. 4.

29. *New York Herald*, October 25, 1850.

30. *New York Herald*, October 25, 1850.

31. *NST*, 88; *NYT*, October 25, 1850; *NASS*, October 30, 1850; Elizabeth Cazden, *Antoinette Brown Blackwell, A Biography* (Old Westbury, N.Y., 1983), 36–56.

32. *NYT*, October 25, 26, 1850; *New York Herald*, October 26, 1850.

33. The "Conscious Whigs" were Whig politicians who opposed slavery and spoke out against it. Their counterparts were the "Cotton Whigs," Northerners who made money off of slavery, and Southern proslavery Whigs.

34. *NYT*, October 26, 1850; *Letters of Garrison*, 4:12–13, 205, 227–28; Suzanne Schulze, *Horace Greeley: A Bio-Bibliography* (New York, 1992), xv–xvi, 1–13, 16–24.

35. *NYT*, October 26, 1850. Cazden, *Blackwell*, 74–82.

36. *NASS*, October 30, 1850; Dorothy Sterling, ed., *We Are Your Sisters: Black Women in the Nineteenth Century* (New York, 1984), 265–66; *NYT*, October 25, 1850.

37. *NYT*, October 25, 1850.

38. Douglass to Post, October 31, 1850, and Nell to Post, December 5, 1850, AIPFP; Sterling, *Ahead of Her Time*, 267–69.

1. Sojourner Truth to William Lloyd Garrison, April 11, 1864, Ms. A.1.2. vol. 33, 406, BPL; *The Letters of William Lloyd Garrison*, ed. Walter M. Merrill and Louis Ruchames, 6 vols. (Cambridge, Mass., 1971–81), 4:45–46, 48–49. William C. Nell to Amy Post, January 19, 1857, Douglass to Post, October 20, 25, 1850, AIPFP; *Springfield (MA) Daily Republican*, February 10, 1851.

2. *BAP*, 2:451, 453, and 3:453; *The Life and Writings of Frederick Douglass*, ed. Philip S. Foner, 4 vols. (New York, 1950), 2:49–50, 86–88; *North Star*, November 24, 1848; *Letters of Garrison*, 3:269, 321; Joseph Carvalho III, *Black Families in Hampden County Massachusetts, 1650–1855* (Westfield, Mass., 1094), 16–20, 27, 32; "John Brown," *Ohio Archaeological and Historical Society Publications* 30 (1921): 229–32; Joseph P. Lynch, "Blacks in Springfield, 1868–1889: A Mobility Study," *Historical Journal of Western Massachusetts* 7, no. 2 (June 1979): 27–29; Louis A. DeCaro Jr., *"Fire from the Midst of You": A Religious Life of John Brown* (New York, 2002), 146–49, 191–94; William Gravely, *Gilbert Haven: Methodist Abolitionist* (Nashville, Tenn., 1973), 128–29; George W. Prentice, *The Life of Gilbert Haven, Bishop of the Methodist Episcopal Church* (New York, 1883), 25–29, 293; 25–29; Stephen B. Oates, *To Purge This Land with Blood: A Biography of John Brown* (Amherst, Mass., 1984), 53–63, 65–69, 72–75.

3. Clare Taylor, ed., *British and American Abolitionists: An Episode in Transatlantic Understanding* (Edinburgh, 1974), 38–52; *Letters of Theodore Dwight Weld and Angelina Grimké Weld, and Sarah Grimké, 1822–1844*, ed. Gilbert H. Barnes and Dwight A. Dumond, 2 vols. (Gloucester, Mass., 1965), 1:268; Wendell Phillips Garrison and Francis Jackson Garrison, *William Lloyd Garrison, 1805–1879: The Story of His Life, Told by His Children*, 4 vols. (New York, 1885–99), 2:18–40; Henry Mayer, *All on Fire: William Lloyd Garrison and the Abolition of Slavery* (New York, 1998), 190–91, 194–99; Paul Goodman, *Of One Blood: Abolitionism and the Origins of Racial Equality* (Berkeley, 1998), 104–5.

4. Douglass to Post, October 20, 1850, Nell to Post, December 8, 1850, AIPFP; Thompson A-S Scrapbook 3, February 17, 1851, REAS; *North Star*, December 5, 1850; *Liberator*, November 29, December 13, 1850, January 17, February 7, March 28, 1851; Truth to Garrison, April 11, 1864, MS. A.I.2. Vol 33, 406, BPL; Taylor, *British and American Abolitionists*, 363.

5. *Springfield (MA) Daily Republican*, February 10, 18, 1851; George Thompson to Abby Kelley Foster, February 17, 1851, Abby Kelley Foster Papers, AAS; Thompson A-S Scrapbook 3, February 17, 1851, REAS; Taylor, *British and American Abolitionists*, 371–72.

6. Thompson to Kelley Foster, February 17, 1851, AAS; *Springfield (MA) Daily Republican*, February 18, 19, 1851.

7. *Springfield (MA) Daily Republican*, February 19, 1851; Thompson to Kelley Foster, February 17, 1851, AAS ; *Letters of Garrison*, 4:48–50, 59–60.

8. *Springfield (MA) Daily Republican*, February 20, 1851; *Liberator*, February 21, 1851; Thompson A-S Scrapbook 3, February 17, 18, 19, 1851 REAS.

9. Thompson to Kelley Foster, Abby Kelley Foster Papers, AAS; *Liberator*, February 21, 1851; Taylor, *British and American Abolitionists*, 363, 371–72.

10. *Gazetteer, of the State of New York* (Syracuse, N.Y., 1860), 558–59, 678, 683; *Liberator*, January 24, 1851; Thompson A-S Scrapbook 3, February 19, 25, n.d., 1851, REAS; Taylor, *British and American Abolitionists*, 263–65.

11. Aaron M. Powell, *Personal Reminiscences* (1899; reprint, Westport, Conn., 1970), 10.

12. Thompson A-S Scrapbook 3, February 22, 1851, REAS; *Liberator*, February 28, 1851.

13. Powell, *Personal Reminiscences*, 8, 11, 15, 16.

14. Thompson A-S Scrapbook 3, February 23, 26, 1851, REAS; *Liberator*, February 28, March 14, 1851; *New York Herald*, October 25, 26, 1850, Taylor, *British and American Abolitionists*, 364, 366.

15. Thompson, A-S Scrapbook 3, February 23, 26, 1851, REAS; *Liberator*, February 28, 1851, Taylor, *British and American Abolitionists,* 364, 366; Thompson Scrapbook, DRMCCU; Judith Wellman, *Grass Roots Reform in the Burned-Over District of Upstate New York* (New York, 2000), chaps. 5, 6; Donald Yacovone, *Samuel Joseph May and the Dilemmas of Liberal Persuasion, 1797–1871* (Philadelphia, 1991), 135, 152–57, 174.

16. Sallie Holley to Abby Kelley Foster, December 27, 1851, Abby Kelley Foster Papers, AAS; W.E. Abbott to Susan Porter, November 29, 1856, box 1, fol. 9, Rochester Ladies Anti-slavery Society Papers, Clements Library, University of Michigan, Ann Arbor. *Ithaca Journal,* November 10, 1936; Alexander Murdoch, "Autobiographical Sketch," n.p., and Sidney Gallwey, "Underground Railroad in Tompkins County," 4–5, 7–13, 15–16, History Center in Tompkins County, Ithaca, New York; Thomas W. Burns, *Initial Ithacans* (Ithaca, N.Y., 1904), 14; Arch Merrill, *Slim Fingers Beckon* (Rochester, N.Y., 1951); Tendai Mutunhu, "Tompkins County: An Underground Railroad Transit in Central New York," *Afro-Americans in New York Life and History* 3 (July 1979): 15–33; Milton C. Sernett, *North Star Country: Upstate New York and the Crusade for African American Freedom* (Syracuse, N.Y., 2002), 162, 164–69, 173–74; Carol M. Hunter, *To Set the Captives Free: Reverend Jermain Wesley Loguen and the Struggle for Freedom in Central New York, 1835–1872* (New York, 1993), 151–69; Wellman, *Grass Roots Reform,* chaps. 5, 6; Howard W. Coles, *The Cradle of Freedom: A History of the Negro in Rochester, Western New York, and Canada* (Rochester, N.Y., 1941), 129–36. My thanks to Mary White for providing me with information on the local underground, which has informed this section.

17. *BAP,* 4:38–41; May Diary, October 8, 9, 1868, DRMCCU; Frederick Douglass to Amy Post, October 28, 1847, AIPFP; *North Star,* April 13, 1851; *PF,* January 20, 27, May 19, 1853; Mutunhu, "Tompkins County Underground Railroad," 15–33; Gallwey, "Underground Railroad in Tompkins County," 11–16; Kathryn Grover, *Make a Way Somehow: African-American Life in a Northern Community, 1790–1865* (Syracuse, N.Y., 1994), 22–30, 111–16, 214–22; Hunter, *To Set the Captives Free,* 55–55; Sernett, *North Star Country,* 162, 164–69, 173–74; Earl Conrad, *Harriet Tubman* (Washington, D.C., 1943), 40–41; 53–61, 71–74.

18. Thompson A-S Scrapbook 3, February 26, 1851, REAS; Taylor, *British and American Abolitionists,* 366–67; "Proceedings of the New York State Anti-Slavery State Society, convened at Utica, October 22, 1835," May Pamphlets, vol. 32, no. 2, and "Gerrit Smith's Reply to Colored Citizens of Albany at Peterboro, March 13, 1846," May Pamphlets, vol. 32, no. 5, Anti-Slavery Collection, DRMCCU; *BAP,* 4:42–44, 271, 274–75, 326, 363; Frederick Douglass to Gerrit Smith, June 10, 1851, box 11, and newspaper clippings, n.d., box 152, both in Gerrit Smith Papers, Syracuse University Library; Gerrit Smith to Sojourner Truth, December 12, 26, 1868, *NASS*; Ann Braude, *Radical Spirits: Spritualism and Women's Rights in Nineteenth-Century America* (Boston, 1989), 28–31; John Stauffer, *The Black Hearts of Men: Radical Abolitionists and the Transformation of Race* (Cambridge, Mass., 2002), 71–76, 92–94, 99–104, 145–44.

19. Frederick Douglass to Amy Post, March 3, 1851, AIPFP; Thompson A-S Scrapbook 3, March 1, 6, 1851, REAS; *Syracuse (NY) Daily Standard,* March 7, 1851.

20. *Liberator,* March 14, 21, 1851; *Syracuse (NY) Daily Standard,* March 7, 1851; William Lloyd Garrison Jr. to Ellen Wright Garrison, August 6, 1870, Garrison Family Letters, Eliza Wright Osborne, "Sketches," 19, Wright Family Papers, both in SSC.

21. *Liberator,* April 4, 1851; *North Star,* March 20, 27, April 3, 1851; William Lloyd Garrison Jr. to Ellen Wright Garrison, August 6, 1870, Osborne, "Sketches," SSC.

22. Newspaper clippings, n.d., box 152, and Frederick Douglass to Gerrit Smith, January 21, 1851, box 11, Smith Papers, Syracuse University Library; *Liberator,* February 28, 1851; Thompson A-S Scrapbook 3, March 13, 1851, REAS; Grover, *Make a Way Somehow,* 216–22.

23. *New York World,* 1864, quoted in Jenny M. Parker, *Rochester: A Story Historical* (Rochester, N.Y., 1884), 245; Eugene E. DuBois, *The City of Frederick Douglass: Rochester's African-American People and Place* (Rochester, N.Y., 1994), 9–16; Musette S. Castle, "A Survey of

the History of African Americans in Rochester, New York; 1800–1860," *Afro-Americans in New York Life and History* 13, no. 2 (July 1989): 9–11; Blake McKelvey, *Rochester on the Genesee: The Growth of a City*, 2nd ed. (Syracuse, N.Y., 1943), 8–14, 24–30, 40–56; and "Lights and Shadows in Local Negro History," *Rochester History* 21, no. 4 (October 1959): 1; Paul E. Johnson, *A Shopkeeper's Millennium: Society and Revivals in Rochester, New York, 1815–1837* (New York, 1978), 15–21, 106–11.

24. Time line of Post family; Frederick Douglass to Amy Post, April 28, 1846, October 28, 1847, September 11, 1849, William Wells Brown to Amy Post, September 20, 1848, Harriet Jacobs to Amy Post, July 16, 1855, William C. Nell to Amy Post, March 11, 1853, January 20, 1854, July 11, 1855, November 10, 1857, AIPFP; Lucy N. Colman, *Reminiscences* (Buffalo, N.Y., 1891), 19–23, 83–85; Giles Stebbins, *Upward Steps of Seventy Years* (New York, 1890), 49, 100–102; Albert Warl, "The Congregational or Progressive Friends in the Pre–Civil War Reform Movement" (Ph.D. diss., Temple University, June 1951), 14–15, 17–22, 39–42, 49–51; Nancy A. Hewitt, *Women's Activism and Social Change in Rochester, New York, 1822–1872* (Ithaca, N.Y., 1984), 93–94, 107–8, 115–16, 130–36, 143; and "Amy Kirby Post," *University of Rochester Library Bulletin* 37 (1984): 8–11; Judith Wellman, *The Road to Seneca Falls: Elizabeth Cady Stanton and the First Woman's Rights Convention* (Urbana, Ill., 2004), 95, 105, 114–19.

25. Benjamin and Elizabeth Jones to Betsy Cowles, October 8, 1847, Betsy Mix Cowles Papers, KSU; Charles L. Remond to Amy Post, October 20, 1850, February 24, 1857, Sarah Parker Remond to Amy Post, March 15, 1857, William Wells Brown to Amy Post, July 16, September 20, 1848, William C. Nell to Jeremiah Sanderson, December 20, 1847, Nell to Amy Post, December 12, 23, 1849, June 2, 1850, July 21, 1853, August 31, December 10, 1853, July 16, 1855, September 22, 1857, May 10, 1868, Frederick Douglass to Amy Post, April 28, 1847, July 17, 1849, October 27, 1859, May 5, 20, 1860, Amy Post to Frederick Douglass, September 11, 1849, August, 24, 25, 1850, February 13, 1860, William Still to Amy Post, October 21, 1859, L. Maria Child to Harriet Jacobs, August 13, 1860, September 27, 1860, Harriet Jacobs to Amy Post, n.d., 1860, AIPFP; *New York Herald*, October 25, 1850. Robert P. Smith, "William Cooper Nell, Crusading Abolitionist," *JNH* 55 (1970): 182–88.

26. Taylor, *British and American Abolitionists*, 372–73; *ASB*, May 10, 1851; Thompson A-S Scrapbook 3, March 27, 1851, REAS; Dorothy Sterling, ed., *We Are Your Sisters: Black Women in the Nineteenth Century* (New York, 1984), 134–37; Coles, *Cradle of Freedom*, 128, 131–36, 156–58; Maria Diedrich, *Love across Color Lines: Ottilie Assing and Frederick Douglass* (New York, 1999), 179–86; William S. McFeely, *Frederick Douglass* (New York, 1991), 163–72.

27. Sojourner Truth to Amy Post, n.d. [probably early June 1851], "Anti–Fugitive Slave Law Meeting of the Colored Citizens of Rochester," October 13, 1851, AIPFP; William H. Siebert, *The Underground Railroad from Slavery to Freedom* (New York, 1898), 414–15; *Syracuse (NY) Daily Standard*, February 27, 1851; *ASB*, January 10, 1857; *Rochester Evening Express*, April 17, 1871; *North Star*, May 26, June 1, July 14, 21, October 6, 1848; *BAP*, 4:39–41; *BAP*, 4:98–101; Abbott to Porter, November 29, 1856, W. J. Watkins to Mrs. Armstrong, December 15, 1856, both in Rochester Ladies Anti-Slavery Society Papers, Clements Library, University of Michigan, Ann Arbor; Coles, *Cradle of Freedom*, 118–26, 128–32, 136, 137; Ruth Naparsteck-Rosenberg, "A Growing Agitation: Rochester before, during, and after the Civil War," *Rochester History* 66, no. 1 (January 1984): 4, 19, and no. 2 (April 1984): 35; DuBois, *City of Frederick Douglass*, 12–19; Castle, "A Survey," 17–24.

28. Castle, "A Survey," 9–11; Coles, *Cradle of Freedom*, 157–58; Grover, *Make a Way Somehow*, 176–81. On historians and Sojourner's nonliteracy, see Carleton Mabee with Susan Mabee Newhouse, *Sojourner Truth, Slave, Prophet, Legend* (New York, 1993), 25–26, 42, 50, 60–66.

29. "The Whole Hog Reformers," *Littell's Living Age* 31 (October 1851): 18; *Liberator*, January 10, 1851; Nell to Post, December 12, 1849, October 1, 1850, August 22, 1851, AIPFP;

Letters of Garrison, 4:449–50; Earnest J. Isaacs, "A History of Nineteenth-Century American Spiritualism as a Religious and Social Movement" (Ph.D. diss., University of Wisconsin, 1975), 23–41, 238–42; Braude, *Radical Spirits*, 56–81.

30. Isaacs, "American Spiritualism," 57–62; Braude, *Radical Spirits*, 10–11, 16–17.

31. *ASB*, May 3, 1851; Taylor, *British and American Abolitionists*, 373–74; *Rochester Daily Democrat*, August 27, 1868; *Rochester Evening Express*, August 26, 27, 28, 29, 1868; *Blue Rapids (KS) Times*, July 18, 1878; *NYT*, December 7, 1878. Stebbins, *Upward Steps*, 101–2; Colman, *Reminiscences*, 25–30.

32. Stebbins, *Upward Steps*, 91–92 Colman, *Reminiscences*, 13–25, 35–36, 61–68; Lucy Colman to Amy Post, March 5, 1857, AIPFP; *Letters of Garrison*, 4:258, 448–40, 518–20, 582–85; Coles, *Cradle of Freedom*, 136–37; Sterling, *Ahead of Her Time*, 164, 166, 167, 285, 306; Kathleen Barry, *Susan B. Anthony: A Biography* (New York, 1988), 40–44, 61, 108–14; Wellman, *The Road to Seneca Falls*, 103, 114, 201.

33. *Syracuse (NY) Daily Standard*, May 12; *ASB*, May 17, 24, 1851.

34. Stebbins, *Upward Steps*, 91–92; *Syracuse (NY) Daily Standard*, May 12, 1851; *ASB*, May 24, 1851; *NYT*, May 13, 1851; *Letters of Garrison*, 4:53, 56–57.

35. *Syracuse (NY) Daily Standard*, May 12, 1851; *Writings of Douglass*, 2:156; *Liberator*, May 16, 1851; *ASB*, May 24, 1851; *Frederick Douglass' Paper*, May 18, 1855; McFeely, *Frederick Douglass*, 168–70.

36. *Liberator*, May 16, 1851, September 2, 16, 1853; *ASB*, May 24, 31, 1851; *NYT*, May 13, 1851; *Syracuse (NY) Daily Standard*, May 12, 1851; Nathaniel Potter to Amy and Isaac Post, April 23, 1852, AIPFP; *Writings of Douglass*, 2:56–59; Mayer, *All on Fire*, 428–30; Yacovone, *May*, 132–40; Hewitt, *Women's Activism*, 150–51, 167, 183–85; Sterling, *Ahead of Her Time*, 271–75.

37. *ASB*, May 24, 1851; B. and E. Jones to Cowles, October 8, 1847, Cowles Papers, *KSU*. The words to the "Bloodhound Song" often vary: "bay, bray, back, track."

38. *NYT*, May 13, 1851; *ASB*, May 10, 17, 24, 31, 1851.

CHAPTER 14: "GOD, YOU DRIVE"

1. Sojourner Truth to Amy Post, 1851, no. 331, AIPFP; Edmund J. Cleveland and Horace G. Cleveland, *The Genealogy of the Cleveland and Cleaveland Families*, 3 vols. (Hartford, Conn., 1899), 23–25, 82–83, 178–79, 387, 895–96.

2. John Malvin, *North to Freedom: The Autobiography of John Malvin, Free Negro, 1795–1880*, ed. Allan Peskin (1879; reprint, Kent, Ohio, 1988), 8–10, 68–74; William C. Cochran, *The Western Reserve and the Fugitive Slave Law: A Prelude to the Civil War* (Cleveland, 1920), 54–64, 72, 78–80; *Letters of Theodore Dwight Weld and Angelina Grimké Weld, and Sarah Grimké, 1822–1844*, ed. Gilbert H. Barnes and Dwight A. Dumond, 2 vols. (Gloucester, Mass., 1965), 1:133–35, 189–93, 211–18, 250–54, 270–74; Frank U. Quillin, *The Color Line in Ohio* (Ann Arbor, Mich., 1913), 15–32, 37–38, 39–41; William and Aimee Lee Cheek, *John Mercer Langston and the Fight for Black Freedom, 1829–65* (Urbana, Ill., 1989), 22, 31–33, 48–57; George W. Knepper, *Ohio and Its People* (Kent, Ohio, 1989), 50–51, 170–75, 179–84, 204–7; Wilbur Zelinsky, "The Population Geography of the Free Negro in Ante-bellum America," *Population Studies* 2 (1949–50): 400.

3. Truth to Post, 1851, AIPFP; *BAP*, 4:73–80; Michael Blanchard, "The Politics of Abolition in Northampton," *Historical Journal of Massachusetts* 19 (summer 1991): 184–92; J. Reuben Sheeler, "The Struggle of the Negro in Ohio for Freedom," *JNH* 31 (April 1946): 215–16; Russell H. Davis, *Black Americans in Cleveland from George Peake to Carl B. Stokes, 1796–1969* (Washington, D.C., 1972), 4–6, 42–52; and *Memorable Negroes in Cleveland's Past* (Cleveland, 1969), 3–5, 18–19; Malvin, *North to Freedom*, 10–20, 64–74; R J. M. Blackett, *Beating against the Barriers: The Lives of Six Nineteenth-Century Afro-Americans* (Ithaca, N.Y.,

1989), 288–301, 310–23, 347; Dorothy Sterling, ed., *We Are Your Sisters: Black Women in the Nineteenth Century* (New York, 1984), 266–67; Ellen N. Lawson, "Lucie Stanton: Life on the Cutting Edge," *Western Reserve Magazine* 10 (1983): 9–10.

4. Truth to Post, 1851, AIPFP; Zelinsky, *Free Negro*, 400; Cochran, *Western Reserve and Fugitive Slave Law*, 79–80; James H. Kennedy, "A History of the City of Cleveland: Its Settlement, Rise and Progress" (Cleveland, 1896), 237–38; William G. Rose, *Cleveland: The Making of a City* (New York, 1950), 211; Malvin, *North to Freedom*, 56–57, 62–67, 75–78.

5. *Pittsburgh Saturday Visitor*, June 21, July 19, 1851; Hannah Tracy Cutler, "Reminiscences," *Woman's Journal*, September 19, 26, 1896.

6. *Liberator*, July 3, 1846, February 9, December 14, 1849; *ASB*, June 7, 21, 1851; Sallie Holley, *A Life for Liberty: Anti-slavery and Other Letters of Sallie Holley*, ed. John W. Chadwick (New York, 1899), 61–66.

7. *ASB*, March 30, June 22, July 6, November 9, 1850, January 11, June 7, 1851; *NYT*, October 26, 1850; *Pittsburgh Saturday Visitor*, February 3, 1849, May 11, 18, November 2, 1850, December 31, 1853; Michael D. Pierson, *Free Hearts and Free Homes: Gender and American Antislavery Politics* (Chapel Hill, N.C., 2003), 57–60, 71–74, 81–90; Peter F. Walker, *Moral Choices, Memory, Desire, and Imagination in Nineteenth-Century American Abolition* (Baton Rouge, La., 1978), 148–56. Pierson is excellent in discussing the difference between moderate antislavery (Free Soil) women and radical women.

8. *ASB*, January 11, February 1, 1851; *Pittsburgh Saturday Visitor*, November 23, 1850.

9. *ASB*, June 21, 1851, *NASS*, May 2, 1863; Carleton Mabee with Susan Mabee Newhouse, *Sojourner Truth, Slave, Prophet, Legend* (New York, 1993), 67–70; Erlene Stetson and Joan David, *Glorying in Tribulation: The Lifework of Sojourner Truth* (East Lansing, Mich., 1994), 111–14; Nell Irvin Painter, *Sojourner Truth: A Life, A Symbol* (New York, 1996), 124–26, 164–78.

10. Mabee, *Sojourner Truth*, 67–73, 75–76; *NASS*, May 2, 1863; *Cleveland True Democrat*, June 6, 1851. The *Cleveland True Democrat*'s lengthy article on the Convention does not mention Sojourner Truth.

11. *NASS*, May 1, 1863; Mabee, *Sojourner Truth*, 67–73, 74–81; Painter basically agrees with Mabee but focuses more on Gage's borrowing from Stowe. Painter emphasizes the role of "symbol" and white "need" for symbol. Painter, *Sojourner Truth*, 129–31, 171–75; Stetson and David (*Glorying in Tribulation*, 118–20) disagree. Mabee's critique (*Sojourner Truth*, 73) of how historians view crossracial gender hostility is based on his reading of Rosalyn Terborg-Penn, *African American Women in the Struggle for the Vote, 1850–1870* (Bloomington, Ind., 1998).

12. Holley, *Life for Liberty*, 61–67.

13. A. A. Guthrie to Betsy Cowles, October 29, 1835, Rachel Babcock to Betsy Cowles, February 10, 1836, George Clark to Betsy Cowles, April 14, 1836, Cowles Papers, KSU; Cutler, "Reminiscences"; *ASB*, July 6, 1850, May 29, June 7, 1851; *NYT*, June 6, 1851.

14. *NST*, 117–18; *Ashtabula Sentinel*, June 14, 1851; *ASB*, June 7, 21, 1851; Cutler, "Reminiscences"; *NYT*, June 6, 1851.

15. *Pittsburgh Saturday Visitor*, June 7, 1851; *NYT*, June 6, 1851; *ASB*, June 21, 1851; Holley, *Life for Liberty*, 57, 65, 126–27; Cutler, "Reminiscences."

16. Lucy Wright to Betsy Cowles, May 20, 1836, Cowles Papers, KSU; Holley, *Life for Liberty*, 57, 65, 126–27; *NST*, 117–18, Cutler, "Reminiscences."

17. *Ashtabula Sentinel*, June 14, 1851; Cutler, "Reminiscences." An account of Swisshelm and "domestic feminism" that does not discuss the Akron Convention, is Pierson, *Free Hearts and Free Homes*, esp. 57–96.

18. *NASS*, May 2, 1863; Nancy A. Hewitt, *Women's Activism and Social Change in Rochester, New York, 1822–1872* (Ithaca, N.Y., 1984), 160; Joan D. Hedrick, Harriet Beecher *Stowe: A Life* (New York, 1994), 249.

19. Mabee, *Sojourner Truth*, 67–82; Pierson, *Free Hearts and Free Homes*, 89–91.

20. *Pittsburgh Saturday Visitor*, June 7, 14, 1851; B. Hudson to Betsy Cowles, March 5, 1846, Cowles Papers, KSU; Holley, *Life for Liberty*, 75–77; Terborg-Penn, *Struggle for the Vote*, 17.

21. *ASB*, June 21, 1851; *NYT*, June 6, 1851; "Too Good to Be Lost—Sojourner Truth," newspaper clipping, Lydia Maria Child Scrapbook, Anti-Slavery Collection, DRMCCU.

22. Preamble and Constitution of the Ashtabula County Female Anti-Slavery Society, 1835, Timothy B. Hudson to Betsy Cowles, March 5, 1846, Cowles Papers, KSU; Truth to Post, 1851, AIPFP; *ASB*, January 11, 1851, May 31, June 7, June 21, 1851; Linda Geary, *Balanced in the Wind: A Biography of Betsy Mix Cowles* (Cranberry, N.J., 1989), 31–34.

23. Truth to Post, 1851, AIPFP; Sojourner Truth to William Lloyd Garrison, August 28, 1851, Ms. A.1.2, vol. 20, 110, BPL; *ASB*, May 31, August 9, 1851; *Cleveland True Democrat*, June 24, 25, 26, 1851, *Ashtabula Sentinel*, July 5, 1851.

24. *ASB*, April 26, May 3, 1851; *Letters of Weld*, 1:178, 182–86, 218–20; Parker Pillsbury, *The Acts of the Anti-slavery Apostles* (Concord, N.H., 1883), 486–87; Wilbur H. Siebert, *The Mysteries of Ohio's Underground Railroads* (Columbus, Ohio, 1951), 214–18; C. B. Galbreath, "Anti-slavery in Columbiana County," *Ohio Archaeological and Historical Society Publications* 30 (1921): 355–75; Russell B. Nye, "Marius Robinson, a Forgotten Abolitionist Leader," *Ohio State Archaeological and Historical Quarterly* 55 (1946): 138–54.

25. Preamble and Constitution of the Ashtabula County Female Anti-Slavery Society, 1835, Rachel A. Babcock to Betsy Cowles, February 10, 1836, Lucy Wright to Betsy Cowles, March 5, 1836, Joanna Chester to Betsy Cowles, April 13, 1836, Susan Wattles to Betsy Cowles, June 30, 1838, Timothy B. Hudson to Betsy Cowles, February 27 and March 5, 1846, Abby Kelley Foster to Betsy Cowles, January 28 and March 15, 1846, Cowles Papers, KSU; Abby Kelley (Foster) to Maria Chapman Weston, July 17, 1845, Ms. 1.9, 2.21, 35, January 14, 1846, Ms. A.9, 2.22, 5, Amelia Kirby to Maria Weston Chapman, July 2, 1845, Ms. A.9, 221, 29, BPL; *PF*, July 17, September 25, 1845; Elizabeth S. Jones to Abby Kelley Foster, April 18, 1848, Abby Kelley Foster Papers, AAS; Giles Stebbins, *Upward Steps of Seventy Years* (New York, 1890), 86–89; Louis Filler, ed., "John Brown in Ohio: An Interview with Charles S. S. Griffing," *Ohio State Archeological and Historical Quarterly* 58 (January 1949): 213–18; Dorothy Sterling, *Ahead of Her Time: Abby Kelley and the Politics of Antislavery* (New York, 1991), 216–26; Louis A. DeCaro Jr., *"Fire from the Midst of You": A Religious Life of John Brown* (New York, 2002), 185–86; Knepper, *Ohio and Its People*, 192–93, 209–14.

26. *Cleveland True Democrat*, August 28, 1851; Douglass A. Gamble, "Joshua Giddings and the Ohio Abolitionists: A Study in Radical Politics," *Ohio History* 88 (winter 1979): 40–48; James Brewer Stewart, *Holy Warriors: The Abolitionists and American Slavery* (New York, 1976), 113–18.

27. *ASB*, August 9, 30, 1851; *PF*, September 4, 1851; *Cleveland True Democrat*, August 28, 1851.

28. Truth to Garrison, August 28, 1851, Garrison Letters, Ms. A.1.2, vol. 20, 110, BPL; *The Letters of William Lloyd Garrison*, ed. Walter M. Merrill and Louis Ruchames, 6 vols. (Cambridge, Mass., 1971–81), 4:203; "Phrenological Character of Sojourner Truth," Berenice Lowe Papers, MHC.

29. *ASB*, August 9, 30, 1851; *PF*, March 18, April 1, 1852; Calvin Fairbank, *During Slavery Times* (Chicago, 1890), 62–63; Pillsbury, *Anti-Slavery Apostles*, 479–503; Holley, *Life for Liberty*, 18, 25–30, 57–72; Galbreath, "Anti-slavery in Columbiana County," 381, 384; Knepper, *Ohio and Its People*, 184–92; Sterling, *Ahead of Her Time*, 214–28, 260–61; Cochran, *Western Reserve and Fugitive Slave Law*, 58–61; Stephen B. Oates, *To Purge This Land with Blood: A Biography of John Brown* (Amherst, Mass., 1984), 47. Ohio had no (white) statewide public school system until 1849 and no (white) public high schools until 1853.

30. *ASB*, September 20, October 4, October 25, 1851, September 22, October 4, 11, 18, 1852; *Liberator*, October 10, 1851.

31. *ASB*, September 15, 1851; *Liberator*, October 17, 1851; Holley, *Life for Liberty*, 61–67.

32. *ASB*, September 22, October 4, 18, 25, 1851.

33. Pillsbury, *Anti-slavery Apostles*, 326; Stebbins, *Upward Steps*, 79; Sterling, *Ahead of Her Time*, 215–18, 275–77, 299, 307–9; William C. Nell to Amy Post, July 19, 1852, September 7, 1852, AIPFP; Lucy N. Colman, *Reminiscences* (Buffalo, N.Y., 1891), 19–22.

34. Pillsbury, *Anti-slavery Apostles*, 85–101; Stebbins, *Upward Steps*, 86.

35. William Lloyd Garrison Jr. to William Lloyd Garrison, January 23, 1857, Garrison Family Letters, SSC; Fairbank, *During Slavery Times*, 62–63; *ASB*, October 25, 1851.

36. *ASB*, October 25, 1851; Sterling, *Ahead of Her Time*, 14–16, 243, 257, 282–83, 297–99.

37. *ASB*, October 25, 1851.

38. *Liberator*, October 17, 1851; *Letters of Garrison*, 3:524; Charles Griffing to Samuel J. May Jr., March 1, 1863, Ms. B. 1.6, 9:87, BPL; Amy Post on "Sojourner Truth" to *NASS*, December 26, 1868; Sojourner Truth to Amy Post, February 5, 1869, AIPFP; *ASB*, April 30, 1853.

39. Pillsbury, *Anti-slavery Apostles*, 353–61; *ASB*, September 15, 20, 1851, October 11, 18, 25, November 1, 1851; Cheek and Cheek, *Langston*, 18, 22, 27–29, 30–33, 40–41, 73, 134; Knepper, *Ohio and Its People*, 172–73, 205–10.

40. *ASB*, November 1, 8, 1851; "Interview with Charles Griffing"; Charles A. Garlick, *Memories of a Runaway Slave* (1902; reprint, Vineland, Ontario, 2005), 3–5, 14, 17, 19, 21–24; "Ex-slaves and Early Black Settlers in Ashtabula Country," newspaper file, Special Collections and Archives, Ashtabula County District Library, Geneva, Ohio; "Joshua Giddings," newspaper clipping, Child Scrapbook, Anti-Slavery Collection, DRMCCU; *Ohio's Underground Railroads*, 285–94; Edwin H. Cady, "William Dean Howells and the Ashtabula Sentinel," *Ohio State Archaeological and Historical Quarterly* 53 (January–March 1944): 39–40.

41. *ASB*, November 1, 8, 1851.

42. *ASB*, November 1, 1851.

43. *ASB*, November 1, 1851.

44. *ASB*, November 1, 8, 1851.

45. *ASB* October 18, 25, November 1, 8, 1851, January 3, 1852.

46. *ASB*, November 22, December 13, 1851; January 31, February 14, 22, March 6, 13, 1852.

47. *ASB*, December 13, 1851, January 31, February 14, 22, March 13, April 3, 1852, Cheek and Cheek, *Langston*, 190–97; *BAP*, 4:126–30; *NSTBL*, 197–99; B. M. Smith to Sojourner Truth, December 31, 1870, STC.

48. Nathaniel Potter to Amy and Isaac Post, April 29, 1852, William C. Nell to Amy Post, July 9, 1849, August 22, 1852, AIPFP; *ASB*, May 8, 29, 1852; Cheek and Cheek, *Langston*, 205–11.

49. Much of the controversy was pure rivalry. However, Douglass criticized black Abolitionist Charles Remond's marriage to a wealthy widow, Matilda Casey (daughter of Peter Williams Jr.), and reminded Robert Purvis that his white father had owned slaves. In turn, Remond and Purvis gossiped that "Jezebel" Julia Griffiths created discord in the Douglass home. White New Englanders privately fueled the flames but publicly called it a "family feud" (between African Americans). Potter to the Posts, April 29, 1852, AIPFP; *ASB*, May 29, 1852; *PF*, May 20, September 4, 1852; Sterling, *We Are Your Sisters*, 274; *BAP*, 3:89–90, 4:180–83.

50. *The Life and Writings of Frederick Douglass*, ed. Philip S. Foner, 4 vols. (New York, 1950), 2:74–77; *ASB*, January 3, 1852.

51. *ASB*, January 3, August 28, 1852; *PF*, August 28, September 4, 1852.

52. *PF*, August 28, September 4, 1852.

53. *ASB*, September 4, 1852; *PF*, August 28, September 4, 1852.

54. *ASB*, August 18, 1852; *PF*, September 4, 1852.

55. *PF*, September 4, 1852.

56. Frederick Douglass to Amy Post, October 25, William C. Nell to Amy Post, December 20, 1853, AIPFP; *PF*, September 4, 1852; Frederick Douglass, *My Bondage and My Freedom* (1855; reprint, New York, 1969), 129–33.

57. *ASB*, November 22, 1851, August 28, 1852; *PF*, September 4, 1852.

58. *ASB*, August 28, 1851, September 4, 1851, *CDI*, December 14, 1893.

59. Heb. 1–4, 10:38, 11:1, 13:3. For a different perspective on the Truth-Douglass encounter, see Mabee, *Sojourner Truth*, 83–92.

60. *Roget's International Thesaurus*, 4th ed., ed. Robert L. Chapman (New York, 1977), 303, 986.

61. Lucretia Mott to John and Rebecca Ketcham, August 30, 1852, in *Selected Letters of Lucretia Coffin Mott*, ed. Beverly W. Palmer (Urbana, Ill., 2002); Margaret Hope Bacon, *Valiant Friend: The Life of Lucretia Mott* (New York, 1980), 140–43. Samuel Joseph May, *Memoir of Samuel Joseph May* (Boston, 1973), 219–22; Carol M. Hunter, *To Set the Captives Free: Reverend Jermain Wesley Loguen and the Struggle for Freedom in Central New York, 1835–1972* (New York, 1993), 122–33; Stanley J. and Anita W. Robboy, "Lewis Hayden: From Fugitive Slave to Statesman," *New England Quarterly* 46 (December 1973): 601–3.

62. *Frederick Douglass' Paper*, October 1, 1852; Cheek and Cheek, *Langston*, 211.

63. *ASB*, September 22, October 4, 11, 18, 1852; Holley, *Life for Liberty*, 74; Colman, *Reminiscences*, 65.

64. Betsy Cowles, "Address to Anti-Slavery Society," n.d., Cowles Papers, KSU; William C. Nell to Amy Post, August 22, 1852, AIPFP; *ASB*, January 3, 1852; *NASS*, July 2, September 24, 1853; *NYT* November 8, 1853.

65. "A Hymn," Sung by James H. [*sic*] Walker at Parting with Sojourner Truth and Others (Kennet Square, Chester County, Pa., February 27, 1853), MHC; *Letters of Garrison*, 4:266; *Liberator*, April 21, 28, 1854.

CHAPTER 15: "I GO IN FOR AGITATIN'"

1. For scholars who view the movement's pinnacle as before 1845, see Louis Ruchames, ed., introduction to *The Abolitionists: A Collection of Their Writing* (New York, 1964); Paul Goodman, *Of One Blood: Abolitionism and the Origins of Racial Equality* (Berkeley, 1998); Aileen S. Kraditor, *Means and Ends in American Abolitionism: Garrison and His Critics on Strategy and Tactics, 1834–1850* (New York, 1969). For emphasis on the 1850s, see Henry Mayer, *All on Fire: William Lloyd Garrison and the Abolition of Slavery* (New York, 1998); Dorothy Sterling, *Ahead of Her Time: Abby Kelley and the Politics of Antislavery* (New York, 1991); William and Aimee Lee Cheek, *John Mercer Langston and the Fight for Black Freedom, 1829–65* (Urbana, Ill., 1989).

2. *PF*, January 20, 27, 1853.

3. *Liberator*, December 31, 1852, *PF*, January 20, 27, March 3, 17, May 12, 19, 26, 1853; David W. Wills, "Womanhood and Domesticity in the A.M.E. Tradition: The Influences of Daniel Alexander Payne," in *Black Apostles at Home and Abroad*, ed. David W. Wills and Richard Newman (Boston, 1982), 135–39, 141–43; Daniel A. Payne, *The Semi-centenary and Retrospection of the African Methodist Episcopal Church* (Freeport, N.Y., 1972), 90–91, 112; *History of the African Methodist Episcopal Church*, ed. Rev. C. S. Smith (Nashville, Tenn., 1891; reprint, New York, 1969), 190; Julie Winch, *Philadelphia's Black Elite: Activism, Accommodation, and the Struggle for Autonomy, 1787–1848* (Philadelphia, 1988), 157–61.

4. *PF*, May 12, 19, 26, 1853; Margaret H. Bacon, *Valiant Friend: The Life of Lucretia Mott* (New York, 1980), 140–43, 146; Jane Rhodes, *Mary Ann Shadd Cary: The Black Press and Protest in the Nineteenth Century* (Bloomington, Ind., 1998), chaps. 1–5.

5. *PF*, November 18, 1852, February 4, 1853; *NYT*, March 4, 1853; Arthur G. Hill, "Anti-Slavery Days in Florence," 3, Lottie Corbin Collection, SSC; Berenice Lowe, "Family of Sojourner Truth," *Michigan Heritage* 3, no. 4 (1961–62): 182–83; Suzanne Schulze, *Horace Greeley: A Bio-Bibliography* (New York, 1992), 17, 23.

6. *PF*, March 17, 1853; *Liberator*, February 4 1853; *NYT*, March 3, 4, 5, 1853.

7. *NYT*, March 12, 13, 14, 16, 17, 1853; Sojourner Truth to Mary K. Gale, April 15, 1853, May 12, 1855, STC; *PF*, May 12, 1853; Bacon, *Valiant Friend* 146.

8. *NYT*, June 3, 1853; *NASS*, June 25, 1853; *PF*, July 2, 1853; Albert Warl, "The Congregational or Progressive Friends in the Pre–Civil War Reform Movement" (Ph.D. diss., Temple University, June 1951), 45, 49–51, 54–60.

9. *Liberator*, August 13, December 17, 1852, June 17, 1853; *NYT*, June 4, 1853; *New York Herald*, September 6, 1853; T. W. Higginson to Theodore Parker, April 18, 1853, Theodore Parker to T. W. Higginson, April 20, 1853, Harriet Beecher Stowe Collection, Huntington Library, San Marino, California; William Gravely, *Gilbert Haven: Methodist Abolitionist* (Nashville, Tenn., 1973), 49; *Memories of Gilbert Haven, Bishop of the Methodist Episcopal Church*, ed. William H. Daniels (Boston, 1880), 47–55.

10. *The Letters of William Lloyd Garrison*, ed. Walter M. Merrill and Louis Ruchames, 6 vols. (Cambridge, Mass., 1971–81), 4:247–52; *NYT*, September 5, 1853; *New York Herald*, September 5, 1853; *PF*, September 8, 1853.

11. *NYT*, September 5, 1853.

12. *Letters of Garrison*, 4:249; *New York Herald*, September 5, 1853; *NYT*, September 5, 1853.

13. "Sojourner at the Second Street Methodist Church," *NYT*, September 6 and 7, 1853; *Directory of the City of New-York, for 1852–1853* (New York, 1852–53), 606, app. 34–38.

14. Sojourner's entire address is taken from *NYT*, September 7, 1853; *Letters of Garrison*, 4:249.

15. *NYT*, September 6, 1853; *New York Herald*, September 8, 1853.

16. *New York Herald*, September 8, 1853; *NYT*, September 7, 1853; *New York Daily Times*, September 8, 1853.

17. *New York Herald*, September 8, 1853.

18. *New York Herald*, September 8, 1853; *NYT*, September 8, 1853; *New York Daily Times*, September 8, 1853; *Liberator*, September 16, 1853; *New York World*, May 13, 1867.

19. *Letters of Garrison*, 4:239; *NASS*, September 24, 1853.

20. *Narrative of Sojourner Truth, A Northern Slave* (New York, 1853); *NSTBL*, 264. Neither the 1850 nor the 1853 editions have introductions. Harriet Beecher Stowe wrote an introduction to the 1855 edition, published in Boston when she and Sojourner met at that time. See *Narrative of Sojourner Truth, A Northern Slave*, with an introduction by Harriet Beecher Stowe (Boston, 1855). The 1853 reprint has been overlooked, and few copies exist. Apparently not even the Library of Congress has one (Letter from Library of Congress to local historian in Michigan.) Originals of the 1850, 1853, and 1855 editions are in DRMCCU. Other scholars believe the Stowe-Truth meeting occurred in 1853.

21. *NYT*, November 8, 1853.

22. *NYT*, November 8, 1853; July 19, 1854; *NASS*, November 5, December 10, 1853; Rhodes, *Shadd Cary*, 53–69; John H. Hewitt Jr., *Protest and Progress: New York's First Black Episcopal Church Fights Racism* (New York, 200), 97–110.

23. *Proceedings of the American Anti-Slavery Society, at Its Second Decade* (Philadelphia, 1854; reprint, Westport, Conn., 1970), 37–43, 73, 76–78, 159; *ASB*, December 17, 1853; *The*

Life and Writings of Frederick Douglass, ed. Philip S. Foner, 4 vols. (New York, 1950), 1:55–58; William C. Nell to Amy Post, August 12, December 20, 1853, AIPFP; *New York Herald*, May 11, 12, 1854; Mayer, *All on Fire*, 432–34.

24. *Proceedings of the American Anti-Slavery Society, Second Decade*, 159–60; William L. Andrews, ed., *Sisters of the Spirit: Three Black Women's Autobiographies of the Nineteenth Century* (Bloomington, Ind., 1986), 6–7; Wills, "Womanhood and Domesticity," 137–40.

25. D. W. Meinig, *The Shaping of America: A Geographical Perspective on Five Hundred Years of History* (New Haven, Conn.: 1993), 2:455–57.

26. *NYT*, January 24, 28, February 4, March 3, May 12, 1854; David Herbert Donald, *Lincoln* (New York, 1995), 167–70, 173.

27. *Letters of Garrison*, 4:246–49, 88; *Liberator*, March 17, April 14, May 12, 26, 1854; *New York Herald*, May 3, 4, 5, 1854; *Provincial Freeman*, May 27, 1854; Stephen B. Oates, *To Purge This Land with Blood: A Biography of John Brown* (Amherst, Mass., 1984), 80–81; Albert J. Von Frank, *The Trials of Anthony Burns: Slavery in Emerson's Boston* (Cambridge, 1998), 13–15; Eric Foner, *Free Labor, Free Men: The Ideology of the Republican Party before the Civil War* (New York, 1970), 92–96; Mayer, *All on Fire*, 434–48.

28. Charles Emery Stevens, *Anthony Burns: A History* (1856; reprint, Williamstown, Mass., 1973), 2, 19–25, 29–42; Thomas Wentworth Higginson, *Cheerful Yesterdays* (Cambridge, Mass., 1898), 147–48, 150–60; *Life and Correspondence of Henry Ingersoll Bowditch*, 2 vols., ed. Vincent Y. Bowditch (Boston, 1902), 1:262–67; *Journals of Charlotte Forten Grimké*, ed. Brenda Stevenson (New York, 1988), 60, 63; *Liberator*, June 2, July 7, 1854; Von Frank, *Trials of Burns*, 21–30, 52–70, 93, 137, 279–80; James O. and Lois E. Horton, *Black Bostonians: Family Life and Community Struggle in the Antebellum North*, rev. ed. (New York, 1999), 115–18.

29. *BAP*, 4:184–85, 229, 397; *Liberator*, June 9, 16, 1854; *Journals of Charlotte Forten Grimké*, 64–67; *Life and Correspondence of Bowditch*, 1:269; Von Frank, *Trials of Burns*, 1–2, 8–13, 23–26, 29–31, 175–76, 204–6, 208–9, 211–12; Horton and Horton, *Black Bostonians*, 120–22.

30. *Liberator*, June 16, July 7, 1854; Von Frank, *Trials of Burns*, 92–96, 137, 168–69, 277, 288, 292–94.

31. William C. Nell to Amy Post, July 31, 1854, AIPFP; *BAP*, 4:153–56, 403–6; *Liberator*, July 7, 14, 1854, September 8, 1854; Mayer, *All on Fire*, 443–44; Sterling, *Ahead of Her Time*, 293–94; Von Frank, *Trials of Burns*, 314–17;

32. *Liberator*, June 7, 14, 1854; Mayer, *All on Fire*, 443–45; Sterling, *Ahead of Her Time*, 293–94.

33. *Liberator*, July 14, 1854.

34. *Liberator*, July 14, 1854.

35. *Liberator*, June 9, 16, 1854; William C. Nell to Amy Post, February 19, December 10, 20, 1853, AIPFP; *New York Herald*, May 11, 12, 1854; *Letters of Garrison*, 4:312–13; Aaron M. Powell, *Personal Reminiscences* (1899; reprint, Westport, Conn., 1970), 64, 68; Sterling, *Ahead of Her Time*, 292–93; Mayer, *All on Fire*, 433–37, 440–42.

36. *Liberator*, September 8, 15, 29, October 6, 20, 1854; *NASS*, December 13, 1856, January 3, 10, 1857; William Still, *The Underground Rail Road; A Record of Facts, Authentic Narratives, Letters, &c* (Philadelphia, 1872), 783–90; Lillie Buffum Chace Wyman and Arthur Crawford Wyman, *Elizabeth Buffum Chace, 1806–1899: Her Life and Its Environment*, 2 vols. (Boston, 1914), 1:141, 142, 196; Powell, *Personal Reminiscences*, 25–31; *Letters of Garrison*, 4:425, 427, 435, 600; *Selected Papers of Elizabeth Cady Stanton and Susan B. Anthony*, ed. Ann D. Gordon, 4 vols. (New Brunswick, N.J., 1997–2006), 1:252–53, 264–67, 327–34, 358, 385–86.

37. *Liberator*, August 11, September 15, October 6, 1854; *Letters of Garrison*, 4:32–33.

38. *NASS*, July 4, 1863; *New York Freeman*, June 11, 1887. *Chautauqua* 7 (October 1886–July 1887): 479; "Recollections of Eliza Seaman Leggett," Eliza Seaman Leggett Family Papers, vol. 8, DPL.

39. Frances McLiechey Certificate of Death, November 2, 1941, Calhoun County Department of Health, file 570, Marshall, Michigan. (Fannie apparently married an Irishman named Frank Liechey and changed her name to McLiechey. Today, this family traces its lineage to Sojourner Truth.) *Battle Creek City Directory*, 1893, 180, 1899–1900, 235; *Battle Creek Daily Journal*, July 27, 1899; *Battle Creek Enquirer and News*, November 26, 1981; Hampshire County Record, vol. 133, Register of Deeds, Northampton, Mass., deed, 106, mortgage, 124–25; George R. Stetson, "When I Was a Boy," in Charles A. Sheffield, ed., *History of Florence, Massachusetts, Including a Complete Account of the Northampton Association of Education and Industry* (Florence, Mass., 1895), 118–19; Petition "To the Senate and House of Representatives, in Congress Assembled," n.d., and S. H. Morgan to Mary K. Gale, September 27, 1871, STC.

40. Sojourner Truth to Mary K. Gale, May 12, July 23, 1855, STC; George W. Prentice, *The Life of Haven*, Bishop of the Methodist Episcopal Church (New York, 1883), 146–67.

41. Gravely, *Gilbert Haven*, 23–26, 34–35, 49–83; Prentice, *Life of Haven*, 146–47; Daniels, *Memorials of Haven*, 46–50; *Zion's Herald*, May 2, 16, 1855.

42. Gravely, *Gilbert Haven*, 11–13, 47–49, 173; Daniels, *Memorials of Haven*, 47–55; NSTBL, 210.

43. *NASS*, May 31, 1855; *Frederick Douglass' Paper*, June 15, 1855.

44. *NASS*, June 25, 1853; Wyman, "Sojourner Truth,"63.

45. "Recollections of Eliza Seaman Leggett," Leggett Papers, vol. 8, DPL.

46. *Springfield (MA) Daily Republican*, September 18, 1848; "Sojourner Truth," undated newspaper clipping, STC.

47. Lydia Maria Francis Child, *Letters from New York*, 3d ed. (Freeport, N.Y., 1970), 81; "Too Good to Be Lost—Sojourner Truth," newspaper clippings, Lydia Maria Child Scrapbook, Anti-Slavery Collection, DRMCCU; *CDI*, April 16, 1881.

48. Num. 22, esp. 5–12, 21–34.

49. Sojourner Truth to Mary K. Gale, July 23, 1855, STC; William C. Nell to Amy Post, August 12, 1855, AIPFP; William Wells Brown to William Lloyd Garrison, August 6, 1855, in *The Mind of the Negro as Reflected in Letters Written during the Crisis, 1800–1860*, ed. Carter G. Woodson (New York, 1926), 327–73.

50. Nell to Post, August 12, 1855, September 22, 1857, Lydia Maria Child to Harriet Jacobs, August 13, 1860, September 27, 1860, AIPFP; Dorothy Sterling, ed., *We Are Your Sisters: Black Women in the Nineteenth Century* (New York, 1984), 76–78; NSTBL 174; Hazel V. Carby, *Reconstructing Womanhood: The Emergence of the Afro-American Woman Novelist* (New York, 1987), 49–50; George M. Fredrickson, *The Black Image in the White Mind: The Debate on Afro-American Character and Destiny, 1817–1914* (reprint, Hanover, N.H., 1987), 110–14, 17–18; Harriet Beecher Stowe, *Dred: A Tale of the Great Dismal Swamp* (1856; reprint, Halifax, England, 1992), 227–44. In her 1855 introduction to Truth's *Narrative*, Stowe erroneously stated that Truth needed money to purchase a home.

CHAPTER 16: TRUTH IS POWERFUL

1. *The Letters of William Lloyd Garrison*, ed. Walter M. Merrill and Louis Ruchames, 6 vols. (Cambridge, Mass., 1971–81), 4:299; *Liberator*, April 21, 29, May 19, 26, 1854; *ASB*, February 18, 23, April 8, 29, 1854, September, 27, 1856, October 31, 1857; *Banner of Light*, May 2, 1863; John Greenleaf Whittier, *Complete Poetical Works of John Greenleaf Whittier* (Boston, 1854), 317.

2. Edwin and Martha Freutz to Lysander Cowles, June 5, 1856, Betsy Mix Cowles Papers, KSU; *Xenia (OH) Torchlight*, March 28, April 18, December 12, 1855; January 30, June 4, June, 11, 1856; *Northern Indianan*, January 10, August 2, 1856; *Ashtabula Sentinel*, May 9, February

14, 1856; *ASB*, June 12, September 4, 13, 18, 27, 1856, October 31, 1857; *Monroe (WI) Sentinel*, April 1, 1857; *Selected Letters of Lucretia Coffin Mott*, ed. Beverly W. Palmer (Urbana, Ill., 2002), 248; C. B. Galbreath, "John Brown," *Ohio Archaeological and Historical Society Publications* 30 (1921): 199–202; Stephen B. Oates, *To Purge This Land with Blood: A Biography of John Brown* (Amherst, Mass., 1984), 82–87, 106–7; Robert R. Dykstra, *Bright Radical Star: Black Freedom and White Supremacy on the Hawkeye Frontier* (Cambridge, Mass., 1993), 136–43, 147–48.

3. Elizabeth S. Jones to Abby Kelley Foster, April 18, 1848, Abby Kelley Foster Papers, AAS; Josephine Griffing to Amy Post, August 23, 1856, AIPFP; *ASB*, September, 27, 1856; October 5, 16, 31, 1857; Lucy N. Colman, *Reminiscences* (Buffalo, N.Y., 1891), 26–30; Edwin Kellogg to N. M. Thomas, September 8, 1841, H. A. Eastland to N. M. Thomas, October 22, 1841, N. M. Thomas Collection, MHC; Laura S. Haviland, *A Woman's Life Work: Including Thirty Years' Service on the Underground Railroad and in the War* (Grand Rapids, Mich., 1881), 40–44, 53–77, 97–121, 139–61; Albert Warl, "The Congregational or Progressive Friends in the Pre–Civil War Reform Movement" (Ph.D. diss., Temple University, June 1951), 165.

4. *ASB*, February 16, 1856, *NASS*, February 16, 1856; *Liberator*, May 14, 1856; Levi Coffin, *Reminiscences of Levi Coffin, the Reputed President of the Underground Railroad* (1876; reprint, Cincinnati, 1880), 37–40; Elizabeth S. Jones to Amy Post, February 4, 1856, AIPFP; *Letters of Mott*, 247; *Annual Report of the American Anti-Slavery Society, May 7, 1856* (New York, 1856), Anti-Slavery Collection, DRMCCU; Steven Weisenburger, *Modern Medea: A Family of Slavery and Child Murder in the Old South* (New York, 1998), 49–53, 62–67, 72–75, 192–94; Andrea M. Kerr, *Lucy Stone: Speaking Out for Equality* (New Brunswick, N.J., 1992), 93, 101; Carolyn L. Karcher, *The First Woman in the Republic: A Cultural Biography of Lydia Maria Child* (Durham, N.C., 1994), 434.

5. *ASB*, September 9, 13, 27, 1856.

6. *Letters of Garrison*, 4:261–66; *Liberator*, April 21, 1854, May 26, 1854, November 15, 1839; "First Michigan State Anti-Slavery Convention, October 16, 1852," and "Second Michigan State Anti-Slavery Convention, October 22, 1853," Blanche Coggan Collection, vol. 455, fol. 5, Archives of Michigan, Lansing; Diary of H. C. Chandler, December 22, 1857, Minnie Merritt Fay Collection, MHC.

7. *ASB*, September 9, 13, 27, 1856, November 8, 1856.

8. *ASB*, November 8, 1856; Griffing to Post, August 23, 1856, AIPFP.

9. ASB, November 8, 1856.

10. *ASB*, March 18, 1854, October 18, November 8, 22, 1856; October 31, November 7, December 5, 1857, February 20, October 2, 23, November 13, 1858, May 14, 21, August 20, 1859, September 29, 1860, October 27, December 8, 1860, January 19, February 2, 1861; *Battle Creek Nightly Moon*, February 13, 1880; Erastus Hussey to Nathan M. Thomas, March 16, 1844, and August 21, 1852, Thomas Collection, MHC; Delia Hart Stone, "Sojourner Truth," *Woman's Tribune*, November 14, 1903, 124; Yvonne Tuchaiski, "Erastus Hussey, Battle Creek Antislavery Activist," *Michigan History* 56 (spring 1972): 3–5; newspaper file, Martich Collection, Willard Public Library, Battle Creek, Michigan.

11. *ASB*, October 16, 1852, January 22, 1853, October 18, 1856; Esther Titus to Amy Post, February 26, 1854, AIPFP; "Recorded Names of Michigan Anti-Slavery Society," Coggin Collection, Archives of Michigan; *Battle Creek News and Enquirer*, October 15, 1916; Martich Collection, 22:12; and *Michigan Quakers: Abstracts of Fifteen Meetings of the Society of Friends, 1831–1960*, comp. Ann and Conrad Burton (Decatur, Mich., 1989), 459, 463–64, both in Willard Public Library.

12. *ASB*, February 18, 23, March 5, 18, 25, April 8, April 29, June 13, 1854, September 9, 13, 27, October 18, 1856; *Liberator*, April 21, May 19, 26, June 3, 1854; Proceedings of the First Anniversary Meeting of the Michigan State Anti-Slavery Society, October 14, 1854, Coggin

Collection, Archives of Michigan; William H. Siebert, *The Underground Railroad from Slavery to Freedom* (New York, 1898), 135, 147; "Aunt Laura Haviland: Early Michigan Quakeress," *Michigan Heritage* 13, no. 1 (1971–72): 4–6.

13. *ASB*, October 18, 1856; Hampshire County Record Book, County Court House, Northampton, Mass., 133:124–25; 175:11–12, 31–32; copy of deed of lot in Harmonia, Martich Collection, Willard Library; Chandler Diary, March 31, April 1, April, 3, 1858, Fay Collection, MHC; U.S. Census Bureau, *Population Schedules of the Eighth Census* (1860) State of Michigan, County of Calhoun, Bedford township (Washington, D.C., 1863), 90, 91; Berenice Lowe, "The Family of Sojourner Truth," *Michigan Heritage* 3, no. 12 (summer 1962): 182.

14. *ASB*, October 31, 1857; *Battle Creek Weekly Journal*, August 27, 1852; *Battle Creek Enquirer and News*, October 5, 1917, November 23, 1917, December 7, 1917, July 10, 1938, June 18, 1944.

15. For a different perspective, see Carleton Mabee with Susan Mabee Newhouse, *Sojourner Truth, Slave, Prophet, Legend* (New York, 1993), 96–103.

16. Betsy Cowles to Louisa Austin, November 20, 1852, Cowles Papers, KSU; Eliza Leggett to Wendell Phillips, April 24, 1864, bMS Am 1953 (810), Blagden Papers, Houghton Library, Harvard University; *Saginaw (MI) Daily Courier*, June 11, 1871; *Blue Rapids (KS) Times*, July 18, 1878; Cora Hatch Daniels to Amy Post, July 22, 1866, AIPFP; Earnest J. Isaacs, "A History of Nineteenth-Century American Spiritualism as a Religious and Social Movement" (Ph.D. diss., University of Wisconsin, 1975), 1–25; Ann Braude, *Radical Spirits: Spritualism and Women's Rights in Nineteenth-Century America* (Boston, 1989), 22–23; Dorothy Sterling, *Ahead of Her Time: Abby Kelley and the Politics of Antislavery* (New York, 1991), 278–79; Henry Mayer, *All on Fire: William Lloyd Garrison and the Abolition of Slavery* (New York, 1998), 465–66, 621–22; Margaret Washington Creel, *"A Peculiar People": Slave Religion and Community-Culture among the Gullahs* (New York, 1988), 52–63, 308–22, 344–50. Lydia Maria Francis Child, *Letters from New York*, 3d ed. (Freeport, N.Y., 1970), 130–36, and Karcher, *First Woman in the Republic*, 403, 585–87; Robin Larsen, ed., *Emanuel Swedenborg: A Continuing Vision* (New York, 1988), 134, 129–36.

17. ASB, October 16, 24, November 7, 1857.

18. *Liberator*, January 10, 1851, February 18, 23, March 3, 1854, May 11, 26, 1854; *ASB*, September 13, 27, November 8, 1856; *Banner of Light*, June 20, 1863; William C. Nell to Amy Post, December 12, 1849, June 2, 1850, January 15, 1851, August 23, 1852, February 19, 1854, September 22, 1857, October 25, 1858, Cora Hatch Daniels to Amy Post, January 2, 1866, February 16, 1867, Phoebe Willis (deceased in 1846) to Isaac Post, July 8, 1867, all in AIPFP; Betsy Cowles to Louisa Austin, November 20, 1852, Cowles Papers, KSU; "Recollections of Eliza Seaman Leggett," Eliza Seaman Leggett Family Papers, vol. 8, DPL; *Letters of Garrison*, 4:421; Giles Stebbins, *Upward Steps of Seventy Years* (New York, 1890), 75–85, 94, 198–218; Warren Chase, *Forty Years on the Spiritual Rostrum* (Boston, 1888), 78–79; Colman, *Reminiscences*, 24–27; Isaacs, "American Spiritualism," 10–11, 16–17, 22–25, 57–89, 102–32, 221–28; 238–43; Braude, *Radical Spirits*, 4–7, 28–29, 59–63, 70–73, 82–116; John Patrick Deveney, *Paschal Beverly Randolph: Black American Spiritualist Rosicrucian and Sex Magician* (Albany, N.Y., 1997), 1, 7–25, 89–119; Sterling, *Ahead of Her Time*, 278–80, 305, 315; Whitney R. Cross, *The Burned-Over District: The Social and Intellectual History of Enthusiastic Religion in Western New York, 1800–1850* (Ithaca, N.Y., 1950), 344–49; Bret E. Carroll, *Spiritualism in Antebellum America* (Bloomington, Ind., 1997), 39–47. Known white Spiritualists included the Posts, Abby Kelley Foster, Lydia Maria Child, Gilbert Haven, Horace Greeley, William Lloyd Garrison, Olive Gilbert, Josephine Griffing, Betsy Cowles, Gerrit Smith, Giles Stebbins, Henry C. Wright, and Mary Todd Lincoln. Known black Spiritualists included Sojourner Truth; William C. Nell and his sister Louisa; Elizabeth Keckley; Harriet Jacobs and her daughter Louisa; the Remonds; and Frances Ellen Watkins. For a different characterization, see Jon Butler, *Awash in a Sea of Faith: Christianizing the American People* (Cambridge, Mass., 1990), 255.

19. *Battle Creek Enquirer and News*, October 5, November 23, 1917, December 7, 1917, July 10, 1938, June 18, 1944; Leggett to Phillips, April 24, 1864, Wendell Phillips Papers, Houghton Library, Harvard University.

20. "Freedom's Railway; Reminiscences of the Brave Old Days of the Famous Underground Line," *Detroit Tribune*, January 17, 1886; Katherine DuPre Lumpkin, "'The General Plan Was Freedom': A Negro Secret Order on the Underground Railroad," *Phylon* 8 (1967): 63, 74–75; *Grand Rapids Press*, February 14, 1982; Haviland, *Woman's Life's Work*, 192–206.

21. *Northern Indianan*, January 10, August 21, 26, 1856; *ASB* May 19, 29, June 12, July 10, 17, September 4, 11, 18, 1856; Thomas Wentworth Higginson, *Cheerful Yesterdays* (Cambridge, Mass., 1898), 199–212; *Letters of Garrison*, 4:584; William and Aimee Lee Cheek, *John Mercer Langston and the Fight for Black Freedom, 1829–65* (Urbana, Ill., 1989), 324–35; Galbreath, "John Brown," 244–45; Oates, *Purge This Land with Blood*, 82–87; 99–100, 126–37.

22. *NASS*, May 17, 1856; *The Life and Writings of Frederick Douglass*, ed. Philip S. Foner, 4 vols. (New York, 1950), 2:81–84; *BAP*, 4:46; (Wisconsin) *Free Democrat*, October 15, 1856; *ASB*, October 31, 1857; Oates, *Purge This Land with Blood*, 99–110, 126–46; Mayer, *All on Fire*, 446–58. Michael D. Pierson, *Free Hearts and Free Homes: Gender and American Antislavery Politics* (Chapel Hill, N.C., 2003), 129–35.

23. Louis Filler, ed., "John Brown in Ohio: An Interview with Charles S. S. Griffing," *Ohio State Archeological and Historical Quarterly* 58 (January 1949): 215; *ASB*, October 31, 1857, 215; Galbreath, "John Brown," 248–50; *ASB*, October 31, 1857; Cheek and Cheek, *Langston*, 320–23; Douglas A. Gamble, "Joshua Giddings and the Ohio Abolitionists: A Study in Radical Politics," *Ohio History* 88 (winter 1979): 40–42, 47–53 Patrick W. Riddleberger, *George Washington Julian, Radical Republican: A Study in Nineteenth-Century Politics and Reform* (Indianapolis, 1966), 38–44, 63, 70–71, 101–15; Jeffrey Rossbach, *Ambivalent Conspirators: John Brown, the Secret Six and a Theory of Violence* (Philadelphia, 1982), 59–60, 69–72.

24. *ASB*, December 27, 1856, September 18, 27, October 5, 16, 1857; *Monroe (WI) Sentinel*, September 16, 1857, January 25, 1860, September 18, 1861, January 8, 1862, Eliza Leggett (for Sojourner Truth) to Amy Post, March 1, March 24, 1858, Frances Titus to Amy Post, October 25, 1868, AIPFP; George Garrison to Henry C. Wright, May 5, 1857, Garrison Family Letters, SSC; Richard N. Current, *The History of Wisconsin: The Civil War Era, 1848–1873*, 2 vols. (Madison, Wisc., 1976), 2:145–46, 200–201, 222–23, 226–27, 264–67; William J. Maher, "The Anti-slavery Movement in Milwaukee and Vicinity, 1842–1860" (M.A. Thesis, University of Wisconsin, Milwaukee, 1954), 3, 21–27, 46–48.

25. *Battle Creek Journal*, October 4–5, 1856; *ASB*, October 31, 1857; *Monroe (WI) Sentinel*, June 15, 1857; *NASS*, February 24, 1861, July 4, 1863; *BAP*, 4:362–65, 3:162; *NSTBL* 146–47; Dykstra, *Bright Radical Star*, 13–22; Cheek and Cheek, *Langston*, 324–25; Mayer, *All on Fire*, 470–73.

26. Nell to Post, August 23, 1857, September 22, 1857, AIPFP; *ASB*, September 17, October 17, November 7, 14, December 5, 1857; *Letters of Garrison*, 4:489–97; Stacey M. Robertson, *Parker Pillsbury: Radical Abolitionist, Male Feminist* (Ithaca, N.Y., 2000), 115–17, 120; Sterling, *Ahead of Her Time*, 310–12; Mayer, *All on Fire*, 489–94.

27. *ASB*, December 5, 1857, February 20, April 17, August 21, October 2, 1858; *NSTBL*, 174.

28. *ASB*, March 18, 1854, September 27, November 8, November 15, 1856; *Northern Indianan*, August 21, 1856; Haviland, *Woman's Life Work*, 28, 32–35, 172–80, 192–204; Calvin Fairbank, *During Slavery Times: How He "Fought the Good Fight" to Prepare the Way* (Chicago, 1890), 86–87.

29. Frederick Douglass, *Life and Times of Frederick Douglass: His Early Life as a Slave, His Escape from Bondage, and His Complete History to the Present Time* (Hartford, Conn., 1881), 215–17; Coffin, *Reminiscences*, 102–5, 172–73; *ASB*, February 20, May 20, August 29, 1854; *Liberator*, May 20, 26, 1854; Colman to Post, May 5, 1857, AIPFP; George W. Julian, *George*

Washington Julian, Political Recollections, 1840–1872 (Chicago, 1884), 71, 64–66; Collins, "Antislavery in Indiana," 32–34, 38–39, 52–54; 57–60, 62–64, 67–73, 76–77, 83–84, 101–5.

30. *Northern Indianan*, October 8, 1858; Marion C. Miller, "The Anti-slavery Movement in Indiana" (Ph.D. diss., Duke University, 1961), 25, 38–40, 52–55, 57–60, 62–64, 67–73, 107–16; William E. Wilson, *Indiana; A History* (Bloomington, Ind., 1966), 88, 102–3; *The Black Laws in the Old Northwest, A Documentary History,* ed. Stephen Middleton (Westport, Conn., 1991), 62–81, 178–79, 181; Emma Lou Thornbrough, *Indiana in the Civil War Era, 1850–1880* (Indianapolis, 1965), 18–28, 69–74, 96–102, and *Negro in Indiana* (Bloomington, Ind., 1966), 107–10; 55–69.

31. *Northern Indianan*, October 8, 1858.

32. *Northern Indianan*, October 8, 1858; Fred Thomkins, *Jewels in Ebony* (London, 1866), 7–8; Winthrop Jordan, *White over Black: American Attitudes toward the Negro, 1550–1812* (Chapel Hill, N.C., 1968), 144–51; Toni Morrison, *Beloved* (New York, 1988), 17.

33. Dorothy Sterling, ed., *We Are Your Sisters: Black Women in the Nineteenth Century* (New York, 1984), 159–62; *ASB*, October 23, 30, 1858; *Northern Indianan*, October 8, 1858.

34. *Liberator*, October 5, 1858, May 3, 1861; *CDI*, December 24, 1883.

35. Newspaper files, Martich Collection, Willard Public Library; Chandler Diary, June 9, 1858, Merritt Papers, Minnie Merritt Fay Collection, Nannette Gardner scrapbook (letters and genealogy), "Gives Close-up of Sojourner," newspaper files, Berenice Lowe Papers, all in MHC; Phoebe Merritt to Sojourner Truth, April 17, 1867, AIPFP.

36. Edward Ives to Sojourner Truth, March 10, 1867, AIPFP; *Battle Creek Daily Journal* (from *Cedar Rapids [IA] Republican*), December 6, 1883; Journal of Percival S. Ives, (kept by his mother, Margaret Legett Ives), Leggett Papers, DPL, vol. 6.

37. Amy Post to Esther Titus, March 28, 1865, Laura Haviland to Amy Post, October 1, 1865; Sojourner Truth to Amy Post, August 25, November 4, 1867, Josephine Griffing to Sojourner Truth, January 7, 1867, AIPFP; Oliver Johnson to Betsy Cowles, March 31, 1857, Cowles Paper, KSU; Thomas Donaldson, *Walt Whitman the Man* (New York, 1996), 244–45; Jennifer Fleischner, *Mrs. Lincoln and Mrs. Keckly: The Remarkable Story of the Friendship between a First Lady and a Former Slave* (New York, 2003), 1–7, 230, 243–44, 271–75; Joan D. Hedrick, *Harriet Beecher Stowe: A Life* (New York, 1994), 76–88.

38. "Recollections of Eliza Seaman Leggett," Eliza Seaman Leggett Family Papers, vol. 8, DPL.

39. Recollections of Minnie Merritt Fay, Community Archives of Heritage Battle Creek, Michigan; *New York World*, May 13, 1867; Harriot Stanton Blatch and Alma Lutz, *The Challenging Years* (New York, 1940); Matilda Gardner to Sojourner Truth, January 30, 1867; Mrs. James Annin to Sojourner Truth, March 15, 1867, Lydia Allen to Sojourner Truth, February 1, 1869, Sojourner Truth to Amy Post, February 5, 1869, AIPFP; Joseph E. Roy, "How to Overcome Race Prejudice," *American Missionary* 53, no. 3 (October 1899): 103.

40. *ASB*, May 21, August 20, October 8, 1859, January 23, 1860; *NASS*, December 3, 1859; *Liberator,* January 27, February 24, 1860; Annin to Truth, March 15, 1867, AIPFP; D. H. Morgan to Mary K. Gale, September 27, 1871, STC; *NSTBL*, 284; Mayer, *All on Fire*, 490–94; Sterling, *Ahead of Her Time*, 315, 318–30.

41. Frederick Douglass to Gerrit Smith, March 22, 1856, box 4, Gerrit Smith Papers, Syracuse University Library; John Brown Jr. to "Dear Friend" (Betsy Cowles). January 21, 1860, Cowles Papers, KSU; Higginson, *Cheerful Yesterdays*, 216–41; "Interview with Charles Griffing," 215–16; Galbreath, "John Brown," 279–83; *Writings of Douglass*, 2:90–92; *BAP*, 4:369; James N. Gloucester to John Brown, February 19, 1858, Jermain Loguen to John Brown, May 6, 1858, Frederick Douglass to *Rochester Democrat*, October 31, 1859, Charles Langston to *Cleveland Plain Dealer*, November, 1859, all in *Blacks on John Brown*, ed. Benjamin Quarles (Urbana, Ill., 1972); Cheek and Cheek, *Langston*, 352–56; Louis A. DeCaro Jr., *"Fire*

from the Midst of You": A Religious Life of John Brown (New York, 2002), 240–50, 253–56, 258; Oates, *Purge This Land with Blood*, 238–51, 282–85, 288, 290–361; David S. Reynolds, *John Brown, Abolitionist* (New York, 2005), 285–87, 291–92, 341–43; Rossbach, *Ambivalent Conspirators*, 111–14, 141–46, 158–66, 170, 199–201, 204–7.

42. *ASB*, October 29, 1859.

43. *ASB*, October 29, November 5, November 15, 1859; *NASS*, December 3, 1859; "Black Women to Mrs. Mary A. Brown," in Quarles, *John Brown*, 16–19, "Sentiments on Martyr Day," in Quarles, *John Brown*, 20–31; (Boston) *Commonwealth*, July 17, 1863; Mayer, *All on Fire*, 500–502; "The Outbreak in Virginia," 1859, an article based on a compilation of daily papers in New York, *Anglo-African* (monthly) *Magazine* (November 1850): 347–60, and (December 1859): 369–53, 398–99. Brown biographer David Reynolds (*John Brown*, 394–95) calls the story of Brown kissing a black child "fabricated." Nonetheless, it is in the aforementioned *Anglo-African* account (p. 398).

44. *Weekly Anglo-African*, November 5, 15, 1859; *NSTBL*, 147–48; Isaac Post to Amy Post (Judson Hutchinson to "'Amy and Leah'"), January 7, 1860, AIPFP; Isaiah 59:4–5; William Gravely, *Gilbert Haven: Methodist Abolitionist* (Nashville, Tenn., 1973), 76; Mayer, *All on Fire*, 499–505; DeCaro, *Fire from the Midst of You*, 245–47, 266–72, 274–77.

45. *ASB*, December 8, 1860.

46. *NASS*, January 19, 26, February 9, 16, 24, 1861; Aaron M. Powell, *Personal Reminiscences* (1899; reprint, Westport, Conn., 1970), 173–77; Sallie Holley to unknown, June 18, 1861, AIPFP; *Writings of Douglass*, 2:98–111; Oscar Sherwin, *Prophet of Liberty: The Life of Wendell Phillips* (New York, 1958), 418–20, 430–38; *ASB*, March 16, May 30, 1861; *Writings of Douglass*, 2:158.

47. *ASB*, February 2, January 19, 1861; *Liberator*, February 8, 15, 1861.

48. *Liberator*, August 31, October 12, November 23, 1860, February 15, March 8, September 27, October 4, 1861; April 26, May 23, August 22, 1862; *Weekly Anglo-African*, June 30, 1860, 1; *ASB*, March 16, May 30, 1861; *Writings of Douglass*, 2:142–65; Thornbrough, *Indiana in the Civil War Era*, 117–23; Sterling, *Ahead of Her Time*, 339.

49. *Liberator*, June 21, 1861; *Steuben (IN) Republican*, May 18, June 15, 1868; Thornbrough, *Indiana in the Civil War Era*, 91–110, 117–13, 145, 180–201.

50. *Liberator*, June 21, 1861; *Steuben (IN) Republican*, June 1, 8, 1861; *NSTBL*, 139–41. In compiling Sojourner's *Book of Life* for publication, Frances Titus erroneously gives the date as 1862. Titus's source was Sojourner, who was eighty-two; Josephine Griffing had died. However, the *NSTBL* account matches others.

51. *Liberator*, June 21, 1861; *NSTBL*, 141.

52. *Liberator*, June 21, 28, 1861; *NSTBL*, 140–42; Thornbrough, *Indiana in the Civil War Era*, 121–23.

53. *Liberator*, June 28, 1861; *NSTBL*, 141–44.

54. *Liberator*, September 27, 1861, July 11, August 22, August 29, 1862; *NASS*, July 5, August 30, 1862; John Hope Franklin, *The Emancipation Proclamation* (reprint, Wheeling, Ill., 1995), 27–28; David Blight, *Frederick Douglass' Civil War: Keeping Faith in Jubilee* (Baton Rouge, La., 1989), 80–82.

CHAPTER 17: PROCLAIM LIBERTY THROUGHOUT THE LAND

1. *Battle Creek Weekly Journal* (from *NYT*), October 3, 10, 1862; *Detroit Advertiser and Tribune*, January 5, 1863; *Battle Creek Weekly Journal*, December 6, 1863; *Battle Creek Daily Journal*, November 28, 1883; Phebe H. M. Stickney to Joseph Dugdale, printed in *NASS*, April 4, 1863; Samuel J. Rogers, "Sojourner Truth," *Christians at Work*, October 12, 1882): 6–7.

2. *Battle Creek Weekly Journal*, December 26, 1862, January 9, 1863; (Boston) *Commonwealth*, January 10, 1863; Frederick Douglass, *Life and Times of Frederick Douglass: His*

Early Life as a Slave, His Escape from Bondage, and His Complete History to the Present Time (Hartford, Conn., 1881), 429; *NASS,* January 10, 1863; John Hope Franklin, *The Emancipation Proclamation* (reprint, Wheeling, Ill., 1995), 84–87; Henry Mayer, *All on Fire: William Lloyd Garrison and the Abolition of Slavery* (New York, 1998), 53–47; Oscar Sherwin, *Prophet of Liberty: The Life of Wendell Phillips* (New York, 1958), 474.

3. *NASS,* April 4, 1863.

4. *NASS,* March 21, 28, April 4, 14, 1863; Sojourner Truth to Gerrit Smith, June 25, 1863, Gerrit Smith Papers, box 37, Syracuse University Library; *Battle Creek Daily Journal,* December 6, 1883.

5. William C. Nell to Amy Post, June 1, 1850, Frances Titus to Esther Titus, May 10, 1863 AIPFP.

6. *NSTBL,* 258; Titus to Titus, May 10, 1863, AIPFP; Truth to Smith, June 25, 1863, Gerrit Smith Papers, box 37, Syracuse Univeristy Library; *NASS,* November 14, 1863; Sojourner Truth to Mary K. Gale, February 23, 1864, STC; Mrs. Josephine Franklin to Sojourner Truth, May 31, 1864, Scrapbook, 4:186, Leggett Papers, DPL. For a full discussion of Sojourner Truth in photographs, see Kathleen Collins, "Shadow and Substance: Sojourner Truth," *History of Photography* 7, no. 3 (July–September 1983): 183–205; see also Nell Irvin Painter, *Sojourner Truth: A Life, A Symbol* (New York, 1996), 185–99.

7. *NSTBL,* 221, 32; *Detroit Advertiser and Tribune,* June 11, 1869.

8. *NASS,* December 29, 1860.

9. Harriet Beecher Stowe, "Sojourner Truth, the Libyan Sibyl," *Atlantic Monthly,* April 1863, *NASS,* November 29, 1862.

10. *NASS,* March 28, May 2, 1863. *Independent,* April 23, 1863. For a fuller discussion, see chapter 14.

11. Diary of H. C. Chandler, April 3, 1858, Minnie Merritt Fay Collection, MHC; *NASS,* April 14, June 27, July 4, 1863; William Lloyd Garrison Jr. to Martha Wright Garrison, August 6, 1870, Garrison Family, SSC. Joan D. Hedrick, *Harriet Beecher Stowe: A Life* (New York, 1994), 233–52, 288–91, 306. On Stowe as an antislavery moderate, see Michael D. Pierson, *Free Hearts and Free Homes: Gender and American Antislavery Politics* (Chapel Hill, N.C., 2003), 48, 61, 72–78, 95–96, 152; on Stowe and racialism, see George M. Fredrickson, *The Black Image in the White Mind: The Debate on Afro-American Character and Destiny, 1817–1914* (reprint, Hanover, N.H., 1987), 110–29.

12. *NASS,* April 14, June 27, July 4, 1863; (Boston) *Commonwealth,* July 3, 1863; *Detroit Advertiser and Tribune,* June 11, 1869; *NSTBL,* 174; Titus to Titus, May 10, 1863, AIPFP; *Rochester Evening Express,* April 17, 1871; newspaper clippings, "Book of Life," Sojourner Truth Collection, Community Archives of Heritage Battle Creek, Michigan; *Chicago Times,* August 12, 1879; Delia Hart Stone, "Sojourner Truth," *Woman's Tribune,* November 14, 1903, 124.

13. *Battle Creek Weekly Journal* (from the *Detroit Tribune and Advertiser*), March 13, 1863.

14. *Battle Creek Weekly Journal,* March 13, 1863.

15. *Battle Creek Weekly Journal,* June 12, 1863; *NASS,* July 4, 11, 1863; Sojourner Truth to Mary K. Gale, February 25, 1864, STC; *CDI,* August 13, 1879; Aaron M. Powell, *Personal Reminiscences* (1899; reprint, Westport, Conn., 1970), 16.

16. *Battle Creek Weekly Journal,* June 12, 1863; *NASS,* July 11, 1863.

17. Titus to Titus, May 10, 1863, AIPFP; *NASS,* February 7, 17, April, 18, May 16, May 30, September 26, October 24, 1863; *The Letters of William Lloyd Garrison,* ed. Walter M. Merrill and Louis Ruchames, 6 vols. (Cambridge, Mass., 1971–81), 5:141–42; Carolyn L. Karcher, *The First Woman in the Republic: A Cultural Biography of Lydia Maria Child* (Durham, N.C., 1994), 418–35, 443–64; Dorothy Sterling, *Ahead of Her Time: Abby Kelley and the Politics of Antislavery* (New York, 1991), 333–37.

18. *NASS*, February 28, March 14, 30, April 18, June 6, July 4, 10, August 1, 1863; *NASS*, July 18, 1863 (from *Wisconsin State Journal*); (Boston) *Commonwealth*, May 15, June 5, 1863; *CDI*, August 13, 1879; Richard Titus to Esther Titus, January 31, 1864, AIPFP; Truth to Gale, February 25, 1864, STC; Powell, *Personal Reminiscences*, 16; David Blight, *Frederick Douglass' Civil War: Keeping Faith with Jubilee* (Baton Rouge, La., 1989), 157–63; Earl Conrad, *Harriet Tubman* (Washington, D.C., 1943), 158–65, 167, 179.

19. *NASS*, January 17, 1864.

20. (Boston) *Commonwealth*, March 27, May 1, 1863; *NASS*, July 18, 1863.

21. (Boston) *Commonwealth*, July 3, 1863.

22. (Boston) *Commonwealth*, January 10, July 31, 1863; *NSTBL*, 258–59; *NASS*, July 18, 25, August 1, September 26, October 17, 1863; *Independent*, July 16, 23, 1863; *New York Evening Post*, July 13, 1863; Iver Bernstein, *The New York City Draft Riots: Their Significance for American Society and Politics in the Age of the Civil War* (New York, 1990), 36–37, 18–31, 48–49, 66.

23. *NASS*, July 25, August 1, September 26, October 17, 1863; Luis F. Emilio, *A Brave Black Regiment: The History of the Fifty-fourth Massachusetts, 1863–1865* (1894; reprint, New York, 1995), 47, 51–68, 72, 355; (Boston) *Commonwealth*, July 31, 1863; Truth to Gale, February 25, 1864, STC.

24. Scrapbook and misc. letters, vol. 2, Journal of Percival S. Ives (kept by his mother, Margaret Leggett Ives), August 5, 1864, vol. 6, "Recollections of Eliza Seaman Leggett," vol. 8, all in Leggett Papers, DPL.

25. Journal of Percival S. Ives, June 24, 25, 27, 28, August 5, 30, November 26, December 20, 1864, vol. 6, Eliza Leggett to Mr. Judd, March 15, 1865, vol. 1, all in Leggett Papers, DPL; Laura S. Haviland, *A Woman's Life Work: Including Thirty Years' Service on the Underground Railroad and in the War* (Grand Rapids, Mich., 1881), 279, 292–94; Nannette Gardner scrapbook, (letters and genealogy), and "Ladies' Michigan State Fair," MHC;

26. *NASS*, September 26, 1863, January 2, February 13, 1864; Truth to Gale, February 25, 1864, STC; Journal of Percival S. Ives, June 28, 1864, Leggett Papers, vol. 6, DPL; *Detroit Advertiser and Tribune*, November 24, December 5, 1863.

27. Truth to Gale, February 25, 1864, STC; Mrs. Josephine Franklin to Sojourner Truth, Scrapbook, 4:186, Leggett Papers, DPL.

28. Dorothy Sterling, ed., *We Are Your Sisters: Black Women in the Nineteenth Century* (New York, 1984), 245–47; (Boston) *Commonwealth*, March 13, April 10, 1863; *NASS*, April 18, June 6, August 1, 1863; Haviland, *Woman's Life's Work*, 242–44, 249–55, 265–71; Adda Dilts, "Aunt Laura Haviland, Early Michigan Quakeress," Michigan Heritage 13, no 1 (1971): 6; William C. Nell to Amy Post, June 10, 1862, Mary Robbins Post to Isaac Post, August 16, 1862, Julia Wilbur to Amy Post, November 5, 1862, January 23, 1863, Julia Wilbur to Esther Titus, February 20, 1863, Amy Post to Isaac Post, December 11, 1863, AIPFP; Julia Wilbur to Mrs. Barnes, January 15, February 23, 1863, Rochester Ladies Anti-Slavery Society Papers, Clements Library, University of Michigan, Ann Arbor; *NASS*, February 28, April 18, 1863; Thomas Holt et al., *A Special Mission: The Story of Freedmen's Hospital, 1862–1962* (Washington, D.C., 1975), 1–3; Barbara J. Fields, *Slavery and Freedom on the Middle Ground: Maryland during the Nineteenth Century* (New Haven, Conn., 1985), 108–11.

29. Elizabeth Keckley, *Behind the Scenes: Thirty Years a Slave and Four Years in the White House* (1868; reprint, New York, 1968), 16–42, 58–62, 65–73, 78–85, 105, 111–16; (Boston) *Commonwealth*, November 15, 1861; *NASS*, May 30, 1863; Sterling, *We Are Your Sisters*, 249–51.

30. *NSTBL*, 126; *NASS*, July 11, 18, 1863, February 13, 1864; (Boston) *Commonwealth*, July 10, 17, December 25, 1863, August 12, 1864.

31. Eliza Leggett to Wendell Phillips, April 24, 1864, Blagden Papers, Houghton Library, Harvard University; *NASS*, August 6, 1864.

32. Journal of Percival S. Ives, June 28, 1864, Leggett Papers, vol. 6, DPL; *NASS*, August 6, September 17, 1864.

33. *NASS*, September 17, 1864; *NSTBL*, 147–48; Speech of Frederick Douglass, n.d. [c. 1864], Papers of Frederick Douglass, reel 18, Manuscript Division, Library of Congress, Washington, D.C.; Lev. 25:10; Blight, *Frederick Douglass' Civil War*, 118–21.

34. *NASS*, September 17, 1864.

35. Truth to Gale, February 25, 1864, STC; Journal of Percival S. Ives, June 30, 1864, Leggett Papers, vol. 6, DPL; Leggett Diary, June 30, 1864, Rosalyn Public Library; Titus to Titus, May 10, 1863, Abby Hutchinson Patton (for Sojourner Truth) to Amy Post, September 25, 1864, AIPFP; *NASS*, October 8, 1864. Some historians believe that Sojourner was in Boston that August, conversing with Harriet Tubman. However, evidence does not support this. Sarah Bradford, in *Scenes from the Life of Harriet Tubman* (1886; reprint, Bedford, Mass., 1993), states that Tubman and Sojourner Truth met but gives no time or date. Earl Conrad (*Harriet Tubman*, 183) cites Bradford but places the meeting in the summer of 1864 in Boston. Carleton Mabee with Susan Mabee Newhouse, *Sojourner Truth, Slave, Prophet, Legend* (New York, 1993), 118, and Painter (*Sojourner Truth*, 202–3) cite Conrad. In the summer of 1864, while Tubman was Dr. John Rock's guest in Boston (Boston) *Commonwealth*, August 12, 1864), Truth was in upstate New York. The two women had other chances to meet besides the summer of 1864.

36. Lucy N. Colman, *Reminiscences* (Buffalo, N.Y., 1891), 66; Keckley, *Behind the Scenes*, 100–105, 113–16, 152–53.

37. *NASS*, November 22, 1862; Josephine Griffing to Gerrit Smith, August 4, 1864, AMA; Giles Stebbins, *Upward Steps of Seventy Years* (New York, 1890), 114–15; Jane Grey Swisshelm, *Half a Century* (1880; reprint, New York, 1970), 162–88, 192–201, 223–39. Keith Melder, "Angel of Mercy in Washington: Josephine Griffing and the Freedmen, 1864–1872," in *Records of the Columbia Historical Society of Washington, D.C., 1963–1965* (Washington, D.C., 1966), 249–50.

38. *NASS*, November 26, 1864.

39. Colman, *Reminiscences*, 66–67.

40. *NASS*, December 17, 1864.

41. *Detroit Advertiser and Tribune*, June 11, 1869; *NSTBL*, 174; Sherwin, *Prophet of Liberty*, 453–54, 457, 460, 464–66, 480; Lerone Bennett, *Forced into Glory: Abraham Lincoln's White Dream* (Chicago, 1999), especially 109–10, 188–214, 286–97, 304–34, 452–65, 480–84, 491–508, 610–11; Franklin, *Emancipation Proclamation*, 14–15, 17, 19, 21–22, 28–33, 80; Gabor S. Boritt, *The Gettysburg Gospel: The Speech That Nobody Knows* (New York, 2006), 116–20, 132–43, 149–62, 194–203; David Herbert Donald, *Lincoln* (New York, 1995), 220–21, 342–44, 429–31, 526–27, 540–41.

42. *NASS*, May 13, 1865; Sojourner Truth to Diana Corbin, November 3, 1864, AIPFP; Mabee, *Sojourner Truth*, 122–23; See also Painter, *Sojourner Truth*, 204–7.

43. *CDI*, August 13, 1879; Truth to Corbin, November 3, 1864, AIPFP; *NASS*, December 3, 10, 1864; *Liberator*, December 9, 1864; Margaret Leech, *Reveille in Washington, 1860–1865* (New York, 1941), 250–52.

44. Henrietta Platt to Amy Post, September 10, 1862, Emily Howland to Amy Post, November 23, 1862, Wilbur to Post, January 23, 1863; Post to Post, December 11, 1863; Truth to Corbin, November 3, 1864, AIPFP; Griffing to Smith, August 2, 4, 1864, and Josephine Griffing to Rev. Mr. Whipple, August 20, 1864, both in AMA; Stebbins, *Upward Steps*, 115–17; *NASS*, December 3, 17, 1864; *Liberator*, December 9, 1864; *CDI*, August 13, 1879; Leech, *Reveille in Washington*, 250–52; Melder, "Angel of Mercy," 253–54; Constance M. Green, *Washington: Village and Capital, 1800–1878* (Princeton, N.J., 1962), 276–77, 283; Holt et al., *Special Mission*, 6–7. Although official records credit the 1863 American Freedmen's Inquiry Commission with the Bureau idea, women advocated it in 1861.

45. (Boston) *Commonwealth*, September 23, 1864; Truth to Corbin, November 3, 1864, AIPFP; *NASS*, December 17, 1864; *Liberator*, January 27, 1865; Felix James, "The Establishment of Freedman's Village in Arlington, Virginia," *Negro History Bulletin* 33, no. 1 (April 1970): 90–91; Fields, *Slavery and Freedom* 117–30.

46. *CDI*, August 13, 1879; Truth to Corbin, November 3, 1864; Wilbur to Post, November 5, 1862, AIPFP; Julia Wilbur to Mrs. Barnes, February 27, 1863, March 10, 1863, Rochester Female Anti-Slavery Society Papers, Clements Library; Sterling, *We Are Your Sisters*, 245–47; Green, *Washington*, 276–78, 301–2.

47. Post to Post, December 11, 1863 AIPFP; *NASS*, December 17, 1864; "Freedman's Village, Arlington Heights, Virginia," *Harpers Weekly*, May 7, 1864, 293, 294; (Boston) *Commonwealth*, September 23, 1864; Frances Perkins to Anna Campbell, January 16, [1865], Helen D. Perkins Collection, Harriet Beecher Stowe Center, Hartford, Connecticut; James, "Freedman's Village," 90–93.

48. Truth to Corbin, November 3, 1864, Post to Post, December 11, 1863, AIPFP; Wilbur to Barnes, March 10, 1863, Rochester Female Anti-Slavery Society Papers, Clements Library; *NASS*, December 17, 1864; Green, *Washington*, 185–86.

49. *NASS*, December 17, 1864; "Recollections of Payton Grayson," from a 1929 newspaper clipping, Berenice Bryant Lowe Papers, MHC; Fields, *Slavery and Freedom*, 24–27, 30–31.

50. *NASS*, December 17, 1864; Post to Titus, March 28, 1865, AIPFP; Perkins to Campbell, January 16, [1865], Helen Perkins Collection, Harriet Beecher Stowe Center.

51. Amy Post to Esther Titus, March 28, 1865, AIPFP; *NASS*, December 17, 1864; March 11, 1865.

52. *Saginaw (MI) Daily Courier*, June 14, 1871; *CDI*, August 13, 1879; Fields, *Slavery and Freedom*, 139–41, 146–55; Holt et al., *Special Mission*, 5–8.

53. Post to Titus, March 28, 1865, AIPFP.

54. *NASS*, December 17, 1864; February 4, 11, 18, March 11, 1865; Douglass, *Life and Times*, 363–64; Mayer, *All on Fire*, 586, 587; Blight, *Frederick Douglass' Civil War*, 114–16, 101–5; Sherwin, *Prophet of Liberty*, 506–10.

55. *NASS*, March 4, 1865; Eric Foner, *Reconstruction: America's Unfinished Revolution 1863–1877* (New York, 1988), 35–37, 48–49, 54–57, 60–61.

56. Fred Tomkins, *Jewels in Ebony*, (London, 1886) 1–5.

57. Tomkins, *Jewels in Ebony*, 1–5; Keckley, *Behind the Scenes*, 152–53, 158; Colman, *Reminiscences*, 51–52; Douglass, *Life and Times*, 356–68; Donald, *Lincoln*, 475. There were two receptions, one on February 25 and one on March 4, Inauguration Day. Frederick Douglass attended both; Sojourner Truth attended neither.

58. *NASS*, April 14, 1866; Tomkins, *Jewels in Ebony*, 2; Keckley, *Behind the Scenes*, 159–60; for a different scenario, see Mabee, *Sojourner Truth*, 123–24; Painter, *Sojourner Truth*, 203–7.

59. *NASS*, May 6, June 10, 1865; *Washington National Republican*, April 21, 1874; Esther Titus to Amy Post, n.d., AIPFP; Sherwin, *Prophet of Liberty*, 476.

60. *NASS*, December 17, 1864; Tomkins, *Jewels in Ebony*, 3–4; Sojourner Truth to Amy Post, October 1, 1865, AIPFP; Perkins to Campbell, January 16, [1865], Perkins Collection, Harriet Beecher Stowe Center; *Rochester Evening Express*, April 17, 1871; Rogers, "Sojourner Truth" 7; "Recollections of Eliza Seaman Leggett," Leggett Papers, vol. 8, DPL.

61. Wilbur to Barnes, February 27, March 10, 1863, Rochester Female Anti-Slavery Society Papers, Clements Library; *NASS*, December 17, 1864, Truth to Corbin, November 3, 1864; Wilbur to Post, November 5, 1862, Truth to Post, October 1, 1865, AIPFP; Perkins to Campbell, January 16, [1865], Perkins Collection, Harriet Beecher Stowe Center.

62. Emilio, *Brave Black Regiment*, 391–97, 400–404, 411–12, 419–20; Truth to Post, October 1865, Cora Hatch Daniels (for Sojourner Truth), January 2, 1866, AIPFP; Sojourner Truth to the *Standard*, *NASS*, April 27, 1867; Colman, *Reminiscences*, 67–68; Douglass, *Life and Times*, 384; *Blue Rapids (KS) Times*, July 18, 1878, in "Book of Life," Sojourner Truth Collection, Community Archives of Heritage Battle Creek; Blight, *Frederick Douglass' Civil War*, 190–91.

63. Griffing to Smith, August 2, 4, 1864, Griffing to Whipple, August 20, 1964, Josephine Griffing to Board of the American Missionary Association, September 4, 25, 1865, AMA; *NASS*, March 11, November 4, 1865; *NSTBL*, 183; Melder, "Angel of Mercy," 254–56, 259–60; Green, *Washington*, 302.

64. *NASS*, February 25, 1865, January 20, 1866; Laura Haviland to Amy Post, February 22, 1866; Hatch Daniels to Post, January 2, 1866, AIPFP; Laura Haviland to Secretary of American Missionary Association (Rev. George Whipple), April 13, June 4, 1868, AMA; Stebbins, *Upward Steps*, 115–16; Melder, "Angel of Mercy," 254–55; Conrad, *Harriet Tubman*, 183–84, 186–87; Rosa Belle Holt, "Heroine in Ebony," *Chautauquan* 23 (July 1896): 462; Jean M. Humez, *Harriet Tubman: The Life and the Life Stories* (Madison, Wisc., 2003), 64–68.

65. Holt et al., *Special Mission*, 19–23; Laura Haviland to Levi Coffin, April 11, 1868, AMA; Annual Report of the National Freedman's Relief Association, 1865–1866, Pamphlet 4: 14, 15, Pamphlet 5: 12, 13, DRMCCU; *Washington National Republican*, April 21, 1874.

66. Annual Report of the National Freedman's Relief Association, 1865–1866, Pamphlet 4: 14, 15, Pamphlet 5: 12, 13, DRMCCU; *Washington National Republican*, April 21, 1874; Truth to Post, October 1, 1865; Hatch Daniels to Post, January 2, 1866, AIPFP; *NSTBL*, 203, 249–50.

67. Truth to Post, October 1, 1865, AIPFP; *NASS*, April 16, 1865; *NSTBL*, 184–86.

68. Truth to Post, October 1, 1865, Haviland to Post, February 22, 1866, AIPFP; *NASS*, October 14, 1865, May 6, 12, 1866; *NSTBL*, 293.

69. *NASS*, March 2, 1867; *NSTBL* 187.

70. *NSTBL*, 194–95; 249–50; Annual Report of the National Freedmen's Relief Association, 1865–1866, Pamphlet 4: 14–16, Pamphlet 5: 12–14, DRMCCU; Keckley, *Behind the Scenes*, 139–40.

71. Hatch Daniels to Post, January 2, 1866, Josephine Griffing to Amy Post, January 10, 1866, Haviland to Post, February 22, 1866, Margaret Connit to Amy Post, January 16, 1866, AIPFP; *NASS*, December 9, 1865, January 20, February 24, 1866; Josephine Griffing to Reverend W. S. Whiting, September 8, 1865, April 18, 1866, AMA; CDI, August 13, 1879; *The Life and Writings of Frederick Douglass*, ed. Philip S. Foner, 4 vols. (New York, 1950), 4:182–91; Green, *Washington*, 301–2.

72. Griffing to Whiting, April 18, 1866, AMA; Griffing to Post, January 10, 1866; Haviland to Post, February 22, 1866, AIPFP; *NASS*, January 20, March 3, 1866; Melder, "Angel of Mercy," 254–56, 259–60; William S. McFeely, *Yankee Stepfather: General O. O. Howard and the Freedmen* (New York, 1968), 199–200, 204–5, 210, 213–19, 226–37, 243–44.

73. Annual Report of the National Freedmen's Relief Association, Pamphlets 4 and 5; Griffing to Whiting, September 8, 1865, April 18, 1866, AMA; *NASS*, April 16, 1865, May 12, September 1, 15, 1866; Sojourner Truth to Amy Post, July 3, 1866, Griffing to Sojourner Truth and Amy Post, March 26, 1867, AIPFP; Melder, "Angel of Mercy," 260–63; Green, *Washington*, 301–2; *NSTBL*, 207, 191–96; Payton Grayson Recollections, Lowe Papers, MHC.

74. Josephine Griffing to Sojourner Truth, January 7, 1867, AIPFP.

75. Matilda Gardner to Sojourner Truth, January 30, 1867, Ives to Truth, March 10, 1867; Edward Phebe Merritt Stickney to Sojourner Truth, April 10, 186[7]; Phebe Hart Merritt to Sojourner Truth, April 17, 1867, AIPFP.

76. Griffing to Sojourner Truth and Amy Post, March 26, 1867, P. Glennan, M.D., to Sojourner Truth, March 25, 1867, Truth to Post, July 3, 1866, April 25, August 25, 1867, AIPFP; *NSTBL*, 191; *NASS*, October 19, 1867.

77. *Rochester Democrat*, February 10, 1867; *NSTBL*, 275; Truth to Post, July 3, 1866; Griffing to Truth and Post, March 26, 1867, J. C. Thayer to Sojourner Truth, March 15, 1867, A. K. Smith to Sojourner Truth, March 16, 1867, B. Manger to Sojourner Truth, March 19, 1867, S. K. Odell to Sojourner Truth, March 19, 1867, Mrs. James Annin to Sojourner Truth, March 15, 1867; G. S. Glen to Sojourner Truth, March 18, 1867, C. Van Epps to Sojourner Truth, March 19, 1867, G. W. Weeks to Sojourner Truth, March 21, 1867, H. F. McVean to Sojourner Truth, March 25, 1867, Ruth Andrews to Sojourner Truth, April 3, 1867, James Milroy to Sojourner Truth, April 10, 1868, Stickney to Truth, April 10, 186[7], Truth to Post, August 25, November 4, 1867, AIPFP; Josephine Griffing to E. A. Lawrence, Esq., September 24, 1868, AMA. For a fuller discussion but a different perspective, see Mabee, *Sojourner Truth*, chap. 13.

78. Josephine Griffing to Rev. George Whipple, March 8, 1867, AMA; Sojourner Truth to Josephine Griffing, March 30, 1867, AIPFP.

79. *NASS*, April 27, June 1, 8, 1867.

80. Griffing to Whipple, March 8, 1867, AMA; *NASS*, June 1, October 19, 1867; Griffing to Truth and Post, March 26, 1867; Glennan to Truth, March 25, 1867, Esther Titus to Amy Post, March 27, 1869, AIPFP; Keckley, *Behind the Scenes*, 139–40.

81. Hatch Daniels to Post, January 2, and July 3, 1866, L. S. H. [Laura Smith Haviland] (for Sojourner Truth) to Amy Post, October 1, 1865, Haviland to Post, February 22, 1866, AIPFP; Sojourner Truth to Gerrit Smith, April 27, 1867, NASS.

82. Sojourner Truth to Amy Post, August 25, November 4, 1867, AIPFP.

83. *NASS*, September 27, 1867; Alonzo E. Newton to Sojourner Truth, April 12, 1867; Truth to Post, August 25, November 4, 1867, AIPFP; *NSTBL*, 259.

84. *NASS*, September 27, 1867; Frances Titus to Amy Post, May 14, 1868, AIPFP; Foner, *Reconstruction*, 281–91, 333–37.

CHAPTER 18: "WAS WOMAN TRUE?"

1. *Proceedings of the Meeting of the Loyal League of Women of the Republic, Held in New York*, May 14, 1863, 2–3, in *The Selected Papers of Elizabeth Cady Stanton and Susan B. Anthony*, ed. Ann D. Gordon (New Brunswick, N.J., 1997), 1:473–74; *The Letters of William Lloyd Garrison*, ed. Walter M. Merrill and Louis Ruchames, 6 vols. (Cambridge, Mass., 1971–81), 5:154; Susan B. Anthony to Amy Post, April, 1866, AIPFP; Dorothy Sterling, *Ahead of Her Time: Abby Kelley and the Politics of Antislavery* (New York, 1991), 333–37.

2. *Proceedings of the First Anniversary of the American Equal Rights Association*, May 9, 10, 1867 (New York, 1867), 20–21; *NASS*, June 1, 1867. Dorothy Sterling, ed., *We Are Your Sisters: Black Women in the Nineteenth Century* (New York, 1984), 176–80; *North Star*, July 14, September 1, 1848; *Frederick Douglass' Paper*, December 15, 1853, November 9, 1855; "Report of the Proceedings of the Colored National Convention, Held at Cleveland, Ohio, on September 6, 1848" (Rochester, N.Y., 1949), 11–12, 17, "Proceedings of the Colored National Convention Held in Philadelphia, October 16, 17, and 18th, 1855) (Salem, N.J., 1856), 7, 10, both in *Minutes of the Proceedings of the National Negro Conventions, 1830–1864*, ed. Howard H. Bell (reprint; New York, 1969). *BAP*, 4:39–41, 295–97, 310; *NSTBL*, 282; Jane Rhodes, *Mary Ann Shadd Cary: The Black Press and Protest in the Nineteenth Century* (Bloomington, Ind., 1998), 109; Rosalyn Terborg-Penn, *African American Women in the Struggle for the Vote, 1850–1870* (Bloomington, Ind., 1998), 16–25.

3. *NASS*, December 30, 1865, January 6, and April 21, 1866; *NSTBL*, 282; Ellen DuBois, *Feminism and Suffrage: The Emergence of an Independent Woman's Movement in America, 1848–1869* (Ithaca, N.Y., 1978), 60–62.

4. *NASS*, May 13, 20, 1865; May 1, 26, June 2, 9, 1866; Sterling, *Ahead of Her Time*, 337–48; Henry Mayer, *All on Fire: William Lloyd Garrison and the Abolition of Slavery* (New York, 1998), 558–71, 577–78, 587.

5. *NASS*, January 6, May 12, 19, 26, June 2, 9, 16, 1866; Haviland to Post, February 22, 1866; Anthony to Post, April, December 2, 12, 1866, AIPFP; *Selected Letters of Lucretia Coffin Mott*, ed. Beverly W. Palmer (Urbana, Ill., 2002), 305, 371; *Elizabeth Cady Stanton as Revealed in Her Letters, Diary and Reminiscences*, Theodore Stanton and Harriot Stanton Blatch, eds. (New York, 1969), 103–4, 108–9, 111–12; Keith Melder, "Angel of Mercy in Washington: Josephine Griffing and the Freedmen, 1864–1972," in *Records of the Columbia Historical Society of Washington, D.C., 1963–1965* (Washington, D.C., 1966), 268–69.

6. *NASS*, June 23, July 14, July 23, 1866; Anthony to Post December, 1866, AIPFP; *Rochester Evening Express*, December 12, 13, 1866; *Rochester Daily Union and Advertiser*, December 13, 1866; Sterling, *Ahead of Her Time*, 346–48.

7. Elizabeth Cady Stanton to Sojourner Truth, March 24, 1867, AIPFP.

8. *Liberator*, May 18, 1860; *NASS*, February 17, 1863; *Stanton Letters*, 110, 119–21; Terborg-Penn, *Struggle for the Vote*, 27; DuBois, *Feminism and Suffrage*, 177–79.

9. *NASS*, June 1, 1867; *AERA Proceedings*, 20–21, New York; May Diary, May 9, 1867, DRMCCU.

10. *NASS*, June 1, 1867; *AERA Proceedings*, 20–21, 26–27, New York; Terborg-Penn, *Struggle for the Vote*, 23; Sterling, *We Are Your Sisters*, 340; DuBois, *Feminism and Suffrage*, 81–83, 87–88, 90–91. For a more critical perspective on Sojourner Truth, see Terborg-Penn, *Struggle for the Vote*, 30–32.

11. *AERA Proceedings*, 52–55, New York; *NASS*, June 1, 1867; Sterling, *Ahead of Her Time*, 348.

12. *AERA Proceedings*, 53–55, 60, 62–63, New York, *NASS*, June 1, 1867; Sterling, *Ahead of Her Time*, 348.

13. *AERA Proceedings*, 63, New York, *NASS*, June 1, 1867.

14. *NASS*, June 1, 1867.

15. *NASS*, June 1, 1867; AERA *Proceedings*, 69, New York.

16. *AERA Proceedings*, 66–68, 79–80, New York.

17. *Letters of Mott*, 384; *NASS*, January 2, September 15, 1866; *The Life and Writings of Frederick Douglass*, ed. Philip S. Foner, 4 vols. (New York, 1950), 4:18–29, 157–64, 166–69.

18. *NASS*, May 19, 1866, June 1, 8, 15, 1867; *Letters of Mott*, 390–91; Oscar Sherwin, *Prophet of Liberty: The Life of Wendell Phillips* (New York, 1958), 540–41.

19. *NASS*, July 29, August 6, 10, September 14, October 5, 12, 19, 1867; *Revolution*, February 5, 1868; *Stanton Letters*, 118–21; *Letters of Mott*, 394–96; DuBois, *Feminism and Suffrage*, 79–97, 100, 177–79; Terborg-Penn, *Struggle for the Vote*, 28–32.

20. *Revolution*, January 8, 15, 22, 29, March 12, 1868; William Lloyd Garrison to Isabella Beecher Hooker, November 12, 1869, Isabella Beecher Hooker Collection, Harriet Beecher Stowe Center, Hartford, Connecticut; *Letters of Mott*, 398–99, 401–44, 419.

21. *NASS*, April 18, August 8, 22, 29, 1868; *Revolution*, January 15, 1868; DuBois, *Feminism and Suffrage*, 175–79 .

22. Frances Titus to Amy Post, March 14, 1868; Ohio Letter: AIPFP; *Rochester Evening Express*, August 27, 1868; *Letters of Mott*, 398–99, 401–44, 419; Carolyn L. Karcher, *The First Woman in the Republic: A Cultural Biography of Lydia Maria Child* (Durham, N.C., 1994), 540–42.

23. *NASS*, June 13, October 10, 1868; *Revolution*; May 21, 1868; *NYT*, May 15, 1868.

24. *NSTBL*, 299–302.

25. *NSTBL*, 299–302.

26. Diary of Samuel J. May, October 8, 9, 1868, DRMCCU; *NSTBL*, 260, 301–2; *NASS*, December 26, 1868.

27. *Revolution*, March 12, 1868; *NASS*, December 18, 1868.

28. *NASS*, December 26, 1868.

29. Lydia Allen to Sojourner Truth, February 1, 1869, AIPFP; *NASS*, December 18, 1868; *NSTBL*, 304–6.

30. Jonathan Walker to Amy Post, January 1, 1869, AIPFP, Jonathan Walker to Sojourner Truth, January 1, 1869, in *NSTBL*, 304–6; *NASS*, December 18, 1869.

31. *NASS*, December 26, 1868; Sojourner Truth to Amy Post, January 18, February 5, 1869, AIPFP.

32. *Revolution* (from the *New York World*), July 2, 1868, July 19, 1868.

33. Quotation from DuBois, *Feminism and Suffrage*, 176–80; Kathleen Barry, *Susan B. Anthony: A Biography* (New York, 1988), 194–200.

34. *Letters of Mott*, 407–8; *Stanton Letters*, 121; Garrison to Hooker, November 12, 1869, Hooker Collection, Harriet Beecher Stowe Center; Sterling, *Ahead of Her Time*, 353–55; DuBois, *Feminism and Suffrage*, 164–72, *Writings of Douglass*, 4:38–41.

35. *Revolution*, January 7, 1869; Frederick Douglass to Josephine Griffing, September 27, 1869, Josephine Sophie White Griffing Papers, Rare Book and Manuscript Library, Columbia University.

36. Douglass to Griffing, September 27, 1869, Griffing Papers, Columbia University.

37. *NASS*, June 13, October 10, 1869; *Revolution*, May 21, 1869; *NYT*, May 13, 1869.

38. *NYT*, May 13, 14, 15, 1869. L. Maria Child, "The Radicals," *Independent*, August 19, 1869, discusses the difference between Radicals and moderates.

39. *NYT*, May 17, October 7, 28, 29, 1869; *Revolution*, May 13, 20, 1869; Garrison to Hooker, November 12, 1869, Hooker Collection, Harriet Beecher Stowe Center; *Letters of Garrison*, 6:137–38; Andrea M. Kerr, *Lucy Stone: Speaking* Out for Equality (New Brunswick, N.J., 1992), 141. In October 1869 Garrison wrote Isabella Hooker that "no national association" existed, though one would be organized in Cleveland. He wrote Helen Garrison that at the Woman's Convention in Hartford, Paulina Davis's reference to the Stanton-Anthony New York organization as national "brought me to my feet, and I went in for Mrs. Livermore's *Agitator* [which became the *Woman's Journal*], as against the *Revolution*—denied there was any national organization, properly speaking." For a different perspective, see Barry, *Susan B. Anthony*, chap. 8.

40. Truth to Post, January 18, February 8, 1869, Eliza Leggett to Amy Post, n.d. [early 1869], AIPFP; *Detroit Advertiser and Tribune*, June 11, 1869.

41. Gerrit Smith to Sojourner Truth, December 5, 1868, Eliza Seaman Leggett Family Papers, misc., DPL.

42. Amy Post to Lucy Stone, November 5, 1869, Mary Fenn Davis to Amy Post, January 16, 1870; AIPFP; *NASS*, December 4, 26, November 6, 1869; *Independent*, October 21, 1869; *Letters of Mott*, 414, 423, 429; Garrison to Hooker, November 12, 1869, Hooker Collection, Harriet Beecher Stowe Center; *Friends and Sisters: Letters between Lucy Stone and Antoinette Brown Blackwell, 1846–93*, ed. Carol Lasser and Deahl Merrill (Urbana, Ill., 1987), 174–77; *Vineland Weekly*, December 25, 1869; Karcher, *First Woman in the Republic*.

43. *NASS*, October 2, 1869; Laura Haviland to Levi Coffin, April 1, 1868, Laura Haviland to Secretary of AMA, AMA.

44. *Vineland Weekly*, December 25, 1869.

45. *Vineland Weekly*, December 25, 1869.

46. *NSTBL*, 290; *NASS*, December 18, 1869, February 12, 1870; *New Era*, January 20, 27, 1870.

47. *NYT,* April 1, 7, 1870; *NASS,* April 2, 1870; Hannah Wright (for Sojourner Truth) to Amy Post, April 26, 1870, AIPFP; *New Era,* April 28, May 26, 1870.

48. *New Era,* April 21, 1870.

49. *Battle Creek Weekly Journal,* June 29, 1870; *NSTBL,* 289, 297–99.

50. Davis to Post, January 16, 1870, Non-correspondence ms., n.d., AIPFP; *NSTBL,* 232, 297.

51. *NYT,* October 7, 28, 29, 30; *Independent,* July 15, 1869; *New Era,* November 17, 1870; Nanette Gardner scrapbook, MHC; newspaper clippings, STC; *NSTBL* 285.

52. Truth (Hannah Wright) to Post, April 26, 1870, AIPFP; *NASS,* March 19, 1870; *NSTBL* 264; *Letters of Mott,* 444–45.

CHAPTER 19: "I AM ON MY WAY TO KANSAS"

1. *NASS,* Feb. 12, 1870; Josephine Griffing to Mayor and Board of Common Council, Washington, D.C., April 8, 1871, Josephine Sophie White Griffing Papers, Rare Book and Manuscript Library, Columbia University; *Saginaw (MI) Daily Courier,* June 24, 1874; *NSTBL,* 192, 197, 239.

2. Rochester Evening Express, April 17, 1871, Journal of Percival Pease (kept by his mother, Augusta Leggett Pease), May 4, 1873, Eliza Seaman Leggett Family Papers, vol. 9, DPL; *NSTBL,* 196–97, 219.

3. *NASS,* March 23, 1867, March 12, 1870; *NSTBL,* 197; Mildred D. Myers, *Miss Emily* (Charlotte Harbor, Fla., 1998), 86; Eric Foner, *Reconstruction: America's Unfinished Revolution 1863–1877* (New York, 1988), 451.

4. *NASS,* December 18, 1869; Hannah Wright (for Sojourner Truth) to Amy Post, April 26, 1870, AIPFP; *NYT,* September 7, 1870; Foner, *Reconstruction,* 451.

5. *NSTBL,* 197–98; 239; Truth (Hannah Wright) to Post, April 26, 1870, AIPFP.

6. William Lloyd Garrison Jr. to Ellen Wright Garrison, August 6, 1870, Garrison Family Letters, SSC; *Providence Daily Journal,* October 20, 1870; Petition of Sojourner Truth, STC; *Battle Creek Weekly Journal,* March 12, 1871; *NSTBL,* 236, 239–40.

7. *Saginaw (MI) Daily Courier,* June 24, 1871.

8. *NSTBL,* 217–18.

9. *NSTBL,* 219–20.

10. *NSTBL,* 220–25.

11. *NSTBL,* 276–78.

12. Garrison Jr. to Garrison, August 6, 1870, Garrison Family Letters, SSC; *Providence Daily Journal,* October 20, 1870; SSC; *Battle Creek Weekly Journal* (from *Zion's Herald*), March 12, 1871; *NSTBL,* 238, 245; 286, 288–89; William Gravely, *Gilbert Haven Methodist Abolitionist,* (Nashville, Tenn.), 172–73.

13. *NSTBL,* 210–13.

14. *Battle Creek Weekly Journal* (from *Orange [NJ] Journal*), June 19, 1870; *NSTBL,* 204–5.

15. B. M. Smith to Sojourner Truth, December 31, 1870, STC; *Battle Creek Weekly Journal,* March 12, 1871; *NSTBL,* 240, 242, 284; genealogy cards, Merritt-Chandler Family, Minnie Merritt Fay Collection, MHC.

16. *Syracuse Journal,* March 20, 1871; *NSTBL,* 229, 240–42, 263; Sojourner Truth to Gerrit Smith, March 23, 1871, box 37, 1863–71, Smith Papers, Syracuse University Library.

17. *NSTBL,* 265; *Battle Creek Daily Journal,* July 24, August 24, 1872 (*Battle Creek Weekly Journal* became a daily in July 1872); Foner, *Reconstruction,* 505, 55–56.

18. *NSTBL,* 226–27.

19. *Rochester Evening Express,* April 17, 18, 1871; *NSTBL,* 227–28.

20. *Saginaw (MI) Daily Courier,* June 24, 1871.

21. Nanette Gardner scrapbook, MHC; newspaper files, Martich Collection, Willard Public Library, Battle Creek, Michigan; *Detroit Post,* July 15, 1871; *NSTBL,* 232–38, 280. The "New Departure" was a wing of the Southern Democrats aimed at convincing the North that the party could put aside issues of Civil War and Reconstruction, ease racial tensions, and focus on fundamental issues.

22. Newspaper files, Martich Collection, Willard Public Library; "Reminiscences of Payton Grayson" in *Battle Creek Moon,* April 16, 1929, Berenice Lowe Papers, MHC; Berenice Lowe, "The Family of Sojourner Truth," *Michigan Heritage* 3, no. 12 (summer 1962): 182, 184. Lowe mistakenly lists 1873 instead of 1844 as the birth date of Sophia Schuyler's son Wesley.

23. *Battle Creek Weekly Journal,* January 18, March 7, May 7, 1870, Mrs. D. H. Morgan to Mary K. Gale, September 27, 1871, STC; *NSTBL,* 268.

24. *Wyandotte (KS) Gazette,* January 25, 1872; *NSTBL,* 245–48, 265–66, 268–71, 284, 291.

25. *Battle Creek Daily Journal,* July 20, 24, 31, 1872, *NSTBL,* 230–33; Journal of Percival Pease, May 4, 1873, Leggett Papers, vol. 9, DPL; Nanette Gardner scrapbook, MHC.

26. Nanette Gardner scrapbook, MHC; "Recollections of Eliza Seaman Leggett," Leggett Papers, vol. 8, DPL; newspaper files, Martich Collection, Willard Public Library.

27. Journal of Percival Pease (Kept by his mother, Augusta Leggett Pease), May 4, 1873, Leggett Papers, vol. 9, DPL.

28. Sojourner Truth to Amy Post, August 26, 1873; Frances Titus to Mary Gale, September 14, 1873, AIPFP; newspaper files, Martich Collection; *NSTBL,* 280, 288, Nanette Gardner Scrapbook, MHC.

29. *NSTBL,* 222, 248, 250–52; *West Chester (PA) Daily Local News,* July 18, 1874; I. M. Hamilton to Josephine Griffing, November 5, 1870, Griffing Papers, Rare Book and Manuscript Library, Columbia University; Giles Stebbins, *Upward Steps of Seventy Years* (New York, 1890), 116–18; Keith Melder, "Angel of Mercy in Washington: Josephine Griffing and the Freedmen, 1864–1972," in *Records of the Columbia Historical Society of Washington, D.C., 1963–1965* (Washington, D.C., 1966), 269.

30. *Washington National Republican,* April 21, 1874.

31. *CDI,* April 16, 1881; Foner, *Reconstruction,* 532–34, 553–56.

32. *Battle Creek Daily Journal,* December 16, 18, 1874, March 10, 1875; Ellen W. Garrison to Maria Mott Davis, January 28, 1875, Garrison Family Letters, SSC; Frances Titus to Mary K. Gale, March 31, 1876, STC; *NSTBL,* 252–52, 276, 279–81, 283; *CDI,* August 13, 1879.

33. Sojourner Truth to William Still, January 4, 1876, Leon Gardiner Collection, Historical Society of Pennsylvania, Philadelphia; *Philadelphia Evening Bulletin,* July 28, 1876.

34. Titus to Gale, March 31, 1876, STC; *Philadelphia Evening Bulletin,* July 28, 1876.

35. *Orange (NJ) Journal,* July 29, 1876; *Coldwater (MI) Republican,* May 4, 8, 1877; *Battle Creek Nightly Moon,* February 6, 1878; "Sojourner Truth," Non-correspondence manuscripts (1878), AIPFP; *Rochester Evening Express,* July 25, 1878; *New York Sun,* November 24, 1878; *NYT,* November 4, December 7, 16, 1878; *New York Times,* February 25, 1879.

36. *Rochester Evening Express,* July 25, 1878; *BAP,* 2:66; "Announcement of Lecture by Sojourner Truth," c. 1879, Non-correspondence manuscripts (1878), AIPFP.

37. *Battle Creek Daily Journal,* July 12, 1879; *Battle Creek Nightly Moon,* May 7, June 25, July 4, August 7, 13, 1879; *CDI,* August 13, 1879; *Kalamazoo Daily Telegraph,* July 8, 1879; *Chicago Times,* August 12, 1879; Rev. Richard Cordley, "Sojourner Truth," article [c. 1879], STC.

38. Nell Irvin Painter, *Exodusters* (New York, 1976), 5–13, 184–231; Robert G. Athearn, *In Search of Canaan: Black Migration to Kansas, 1879–1880* (Lawrence, Kans., 1978), 34.

39. Painter, *Exodusters*, 76–78, 83–88; Athearn, *In Search of Canaan*, 227–39.

40. Painter, *Exodusters*, 109, 115–17.

41. Athearn, *In Search of Canaan*, 75–79, 239; Painter, *Exodusters*, 246.

42. *CDI*, April 16, 1881; *Topeka Commonwealth*, April 19, 1879, May 1, 1879; Athearn, *In Search of Canaan*, 55–60, 87–88, 122–25, 173–74, 186–92, 196–98.

43. Laura S. Haviland, *A Woman's Life Work: Including Thirty Years' Service on the Underground Railroad and in the War* (Grand Rapids, Mich., 1881), 482–90, 493–94, 97, 505–10; Dorothy Sterling, ed., *We Are Your Sisters: Black Women in the Nineteenth Century* (New York, 1984), 372–77; Richard Congress, *Blues Mandolin Man: The Life and Music of Yank Rachell*, American Made Series (Jackson, Miss., 2001), 61. My thanks to Richard Polenberg for helping me to locate the origins of "She Caught de Katy," popularized by Taj Mahal in the 1960s.

44. "Exodus of the Freedmen," *Friends Review* 32, no. 40 (1878–79): 627, *Friends Review* 32, no. 43 (1878–79): 677–78, *Friends Review* 32, no. 50 (1878–79): 794–95, and *Friends Review* 33, no. 21 (1879–80): 330–31, *Friends Review* 33, no. 27 (1879–80): 430–32, *Friends Review* 33, no. 30 (1879–80): 477, *Friends Review* 33, no. 32 (1879–80): 507–8. Most of these reports were probably written by Elizabeth Comstock and Laura Haviland, who through the Society of Friends were instrumental in establishing the Philadelphia-based Kansas Freedmen's Relief Association. *CDI*, August 13, 1879; Haviland, *Woman's Life's Work*, 482–519; *Boston Journal*, December 1879, STC; *Letters of Garrison*, 4:575–83; Athearn, *In Search of Canaan*, 117–18, 121–25.

45. *CDI*, January 2, 1880; *Battle Creek Nightly Moon*, January 3, March 3, 1880; Haviland, *Woman's Life's Work*, 9.

46. *NYT*, January 13, February 25, 1879; Berenice Lowe, "Truth about Sojourner Truth: Her Michigan Days," *Battle Creek Enquirer and News*, July 21, 1856 (reprinted from *Folklore Quarterly*), Lowe Papers, MHC; *Battle Creek Enquirer and News*, August 4, 1881; *CDI*, January 1, 2, 3, 1880, January 3, 1881; April 16, September 24, 1881, November 27, 1883; Samuel J. Rogers, "Sojourner Truth," *Christians at Work*, October 26, 1882, 7.

47. *Battle Creek Nightly Moon*, February 24, 1880, March 3, 6, 9, 10, 1880, June 8, 1881; *New York Times*, December 4, 1880.

48. *Battle Creek Nightly Moon*, January 3, June 8, 1881; *New York Times* (from CDI), January 3, August 4, September 1, 1881.

EPILOGUE

1. *Battle Creek Daily Journal*, January 2, 1882; Frances Titus to Amy Post, July 21, 1883, AIPFP; "Dr. Kellogg Tells of Grafting Skin on Sojourner's Leg," *Battle Creek Enquirer*, June 12, 1932; Berenice Lowe, "Michigan Days," Berenice Lowe Papers, MHC.

2. *CDI*, November 27, 1883; *Battle Creek Citizen*, November 17, 1883, *Detroit Post and Tribune*, November 29, 1883; *Coldwater (MI) Republican*, November 27, 1883; *Battle Creek Nightly Moon*, November 28, 1883; *New York Times*, November 27, 1883; *Cedar Rapids (IA) Republican*, December 6, 1883, newspaper clippings, Lowe Papers, MHC; *NSTBL* (1884 ed.), "A Memorial Chapter."

3. *Battle Creek Daily Journal*, July 13, 1897; April 26, 1929 newspaper clippings, Lowe Papers, MHC; obituaries from newspapers, Martich Collection, Willard Public Library, Battle Creek, Michigan; *Battle Creek Enquirer*, November 27, 2006.

4. Cora Hatch Daniels to Amy Post, January 2, 1866, AIPFP; *NSTBL*, Leigh Hunt, *Abou Ben Adhem* (reprint, Indianapolis, 1920). Many thanks to Sarah Elbert for introducing me to Leigh Hunt and the Abou Ben Adhem poem.

5. *Battle Creek Daily Journal*, November 26, 1883.

6. *CDI*, December 24, 1893.

7. *CDI*, December 24, 1893, November 27, 1883, December 24, 1893.

INDEX

259, 261, 357; Unitarians and, 182. *See also* western emigration

African Dutch. *See* Dutch Americans, slaves of

African emigration, 197, 371–72

African heritage/traditions, 9–12, 39, 70, 96–97; afterlife in, 55, 75; and American Spiritualism, 55, 62, 278, 280; Catholicism and, 11–12, 16–17; divination and, 39, 78, 79, 399n29, 400n29; festivals in, 28, 45; messianism in, 62; oaths in, 65; preachers in, 71; priestesses in, 12, 80, 278; skin color and, 42. *See also* folklore

African Methodist Episcopal Zion Church, 89–90, 92, 130–31, 143, 196, 197; Frederick Douglass and, 139; Matthias and, 100; ST and 89–90, 115, 130, 131, 150–51, 155, 207, 316. *See also* Methodists

afterlife beliefs, 55, 75, 266, 342

Aimwell, Absalom, 388n26

Akan people, 11

Akron Woman's Convention (1851), 222–29. *See also* "Ar'n't I a Woman?" speech

alcohol, 103; production of, 35, 44–45; social uses of, 25–26, 44, 182. *See also* temperance movement

Alcott, Abigail, 154, 184

Alcott, Bronson, 154, 184, 192

Algonquin Indians, 13, 211, 221

Allen, Isaac, 343–44

Allen, Lydia, 343–44, 345

American and Foreign Anti-Slavery Society (AFASS), 137

American Anti-Slavery Society (AASS), 115, 133–34, 136, 182–84; after Civil War, 335, 341; African American women and, 136, 260, 172–74; Frederick Douglass and, 139, 172, 260; Garrison and, 169–70, 206, 260; *Narrative of Sojourner Truth* and, 195; New England chapter of, 115, 151–52, 195, 261–62, 289–90, 341; Jerena Lee at, 260–61; Northampton Community and, 159; publications of, 130; second generation of, 260–61, 264; ST at, 173–74, 189, 260; Thirteen Amendment and, 304, 334; Twentieth Anniversary of, 260–61. *See also* Female Anti-Slavery Society

American Colonization Society (ACS), 88, 115. *See also* African colonization

American Equal Rights Association (AERA), 340, 343; founding of, 335; Kansas campaign and, 341, universal suffrage debates of, 335–42, 348; ST at, 337–40

American Indians, 10, 13, 14, 211, 221, 303; education of, 230; legal issues with, 19; slaves and, 13, 23–24; ST's heritage as, 10, 294; voting rights of, 335

American Missionary Association, 138, 260, 330, 411n29

American Seamen's Protective Union Association, 145

American Tract Society, 318

American Woman's Suffrage Association (AWSA), 350, 351, 353, 358; and Fifteenth Amendment, 350. *See also* woman's rights movement

Amistad court case, 138, 139, 411n29

Andrew, John, 305

Andrews, William L., 398n10

Anglo-African (periodical): on John Brown, 291; ST on, 319

Anjou, Gustave, 384n4

Anthony, Susan B., 217–18, 224, 250, 265, 340, 345, 347; abolition movement and, 265, 273, 312; AERA convention and, 343, 348; anti-capital punishment movement, 137, 172, 216, 351, 375; biography of, 451n33; on black male suffrage, 338, 340, 342; campaign for Seymour, 343, 346; opposition to the Fifteenth Amendment, 343, 346, 347, 348–51; ST and, 334–35, 346, 350, 353, 364; on universal suffrage, 218, 334–35, 341, 343, 346, 347; Train and, 341–42, 343, 353, 364; woman's suffrage and, 348, 349, 350

Anti-Sabbatarianism, 160

Anti-Sabbath Convention, 181

Anti-Slavery Bugle (periodical), 218–20, 224–35, 242, 275, 278, 286, 291; ceases publication, 293

Ararat community, 100

Arminianism, 76

"Ar'n't I a Woman?" speech, 4, 179, 204, 224–25, 228–29, 247, 258, 302

Asbury, Francis, 70–72

Ashanti people, 9–10

Chipp, John, 64–65

cholera, 103, 324

Christmas customs, 27–28

Christiana shootout, 245–46, 250, 262

Christian Recorder (church newspaper): ST and, 249

Churchill, John, 388n26

Cincinnati Ladies Anti-Slavery Sewing Society, 241

Civil Rights Bill, 362, 368,

Clark, Annie M. L., 415n41

Clark, Calvin, 304

Clark, Christopher, 416n2, 416n6, 416n42

Clark, Elmer T., 398n5

Clarkson, Thomas, 349

Clay, Cassius, 251

Clay, Henry, 169, 192, 194, 198, 250

Clearwater, Alphonso T., 386n9

Cleveland, Mary ("Molly"), 181–82

Cleveland, Moses, 221

Clinton, Catherine, 426n18

Cluer, John C., 264

Cochran, William C., 425n1

Coe, Emma, 226, 228, 229

Coffin, Catherine, 284, 315

Coffin, Levi, 230, 251, 284, 439n4, and the Garner family, 273–74

Coffin, Lucretia, 336

Coffin, Martha, 336

Coffin, Tristram Potter, 388n24

Cohen, David S., 387n12

Cohen, Mark Nathan, 386n11

Coke, Thomas, 70, 72

Coles, Howard W., 429n16

Collins, Patricia Hill, 404n32

Colman, Lucy, 217, 265, 274, 275; on Freedman's Village, 319; memoir of, 430n24; on ST-Andrew Johnson meeting, 323–24; on ST-Lincoln meeting, 313–14, 316; on White House race policies, 321

Colonization Council, 371. *See also* African colonization

Colored American (periodical), 130, 131, 135, 136

Colored Congregational Church: ST speech at, 254–55

Colored Conventions, 89, 139–40, 146, 241

Colored Sailors' Home, 131, 144, 194

Colored Women's Temperance Union: ST and, 366

Come-outers and Come-outerism, 159–61, 214–15, 250–51, 267, 289, 331

Committee of Five Hundred, 373

communism, 158, 161, 193

Congo. *See* Kongo

Congregationalists, 15, 182

Congress, Richard, 454n43

Conkin, Paul K., 401n14

Conklin, William D., 421n6

Connelly, Arthur C., 396n40

Conrad, Earl, 426n18

Constitution. *See* U.S. Constitution

Contraband Relief Association, 310

conversion experiences, 69–77, 94, 97, 182

Cooper, James Fenimore, 387n15

copperhead Democrats, 294–95, 303, 308, 312, 331, 351; and woman's suffrage movement, 341–42

Corbin, Diana. *See* Diana (ST's daughter)

Corbin, Jacob (ST's son-in-law), 323, 364, 365

Corbin, Jake. *See* "Jake" (ST's grandson)

Cornell Academy, 278

Cornell, Dorcas Young, 277

Cornell, Henry, 278

Cornell, Reynolds, 277

Cornet, Joseph, 394n13

Corwin, Edward T., 384n3, 385n7

Courter, F. C., 379

Cowles, Betsy Mix, 229–31, 237, 247, 288, 433n22

Cowles, Cornelia, 288

Craft, Ellen, 195, 196, 198, 199

Craft, William, 195, 196, 199

Crandall, Prudence, 183–85, 415n32

Creel, Margaret Washington, 382n9

Creighton, Margaret S., 413n9

Creole mutiny, 138, 237

Crew, Mary, 249

Crofut, Florence S. Marcy, 415n33

Cromwell, Oliver, 15

Cross, Whitney R., 401n13

Crummell, Alexander, 92, 143, 196, 404n31

Cuffe, Paul, 144

cuisine, 151, 177; Dutch American, 26, 36; at Matthias Commune, 102, 103, 107; at Northampton Community, 159, 163, 167, 177; at Temperance Banquet, 254

Curry, Leonard, 401n6

Dumont, Elizabeth Waring, 35–37, 41, 43–46, 53, 61–62, 374

Dumont, Gertrude ("Getty"), 35–39, 44, 45; on ST's children, 51, 60, 81; on ST's marriage, 54

Dumont, Johannes Ignacias, 35

Dumont, John, 35–40, 213; emancipation promise of, 55–56, 59; legal training of, 64; Matthews's trial and, 118, 121, 124; Peter's trial and, 67; punishments by, 43, 44; on slave-owning past, 187–88; ST's relationship with, 37, 40–47, 52–53, 73, 79, 187–88, 213

Dumont, Sarah Waring, 35–36

Dumont, Solomon, 36, 54

Dunlap, William, 394n3

DuPuis, Richard A. G., 402n15

Dutch Americans, 12–23, 121, 161; Anglo-Americans and, 13, 34; cuisine of, 26, 36; families of, 26–28; slaves of, 9–12, 18–26, 57–59, 82, 187; taverns and, 25–26

Dutch language, 20, 25, 35, 39; ST and, 33, 39, 59, 204, 253, 254–55, 270, 275–76, 277, 371

Dutch Reformed Church, 15, 16; Africans and, 19; baptism in, 18–19; family worship and, 20–22, 28; Methodists and, 70, 76; slaves and, 19, 21; women in, 19–20. *See also* Pietists

Duyvel, Flip de, 32

Dykstra, Robert R., 439n2

Earle, Alice Morse, 387n13, 388n18

Easter commemoration, 28–29, 73

Eaton, John, 324

Eddy, J. B. C., 344

Edmondson sisters, 220

education, 133, 139; of African Americans, 183, 184, 216, 221–22, 225, 318, 360; of American Indians, 230; coeducational, 163–64, 186; Samuel J. May on, 182; at Northampton, 163–65; in Ohio, 433n29; suffrage and, 337, 342; trade schools and, 259; of women, 20, 26, 81–82, 216, 226–27. *See also* literacy

Edward (ST's grandson), 364

Edwards, Jonathan, 15, 156

Edwards, Viv, 398n7

Elaw, Zilpha, 77, 78, 87, 398n10

Elbert, Sarah, 415n41, 454n4

Elizabeth (ST's daughter), 56, 81, 162–63, 176, 180, 189, 250, 267, 312, 330; birth of, 51; marriage of, 312; in Michigan, 364, 374, 377

Ellis, David M., 393n39

emancipation, 294, 296; churches support of, 297, Lincoln on, 296–97, 313, 314; in New York, 24, 26, 55–60; in Maryland, 316, 317; Revolutionary War and, 24; ST and, 316, 317; Thirteenth Amendment and, 315; in Virginia, 317–18; of West Indies, 169, 196, 265, 365

Emancipation Proclamation, 298–303, 315, 360, 443n55; celebrations of, 299; eighth anniversary, 360; ST and, 298–99

Emancipator (periodical), 130, 137

Emerson, Ralph Waldo, 172, 199, 200

Emigrant Aid societies, 273

emigration. *See* western emigration

Emilio, Luis F., 445n22

England, 196; and African Americans 196

Episcopalians, 143

Erie Canal, 37

Esopus Indians, 13, 14

ethnicity, 3, 20; African, 9–11, 13; definition of race and, vii; Dutch, 34–35, 45, 67; Huguenot, 13, 35, 83; Irish, 82–83, 141, 157, 258, 341; woman's movement and, 342. *See also* racism

Evers, Alf, 382n14

Exodusters, 371–74, 453n38. *See also* western emigration

Fabend, Firth, 386n11

Fairbank, Calvin, 198, 199, 235, 284, 308, 426n19

Faneuil Hall, 262, 301

Fannie, (ST's granddaughter), 266, 364, 378

fashion trends, 204, 250, 353

fasting, 94, 96

Fauset, Arthur H., 392n27

Fay, Minnie Merritt, 289

Federalist Party, 57, 67, 83, 156

Fellman, Michael, 408n2

Female Anti-Slavery Society: of Ashtabula County, xii, 229, 237–38, 247, 258; of Boston, 133–35, 137; of Brooklyn (Conn.),

184–85; of Cincinnati, 241, of New York, 134–37; of Philadelphia, 133–35, 249–50, 343; of Portage County, 229; of Salem (Mass.), 133; ST and, 249–50. *See also* American Anti-Slavery Society

Female Freedman's Aid Society, 308

Ferguson, Katy, 84

Ferris, Ira, 80

Fett, Sharla, 389n3

Fields, Barbara J., 445n28

Fifteenth Amendment: celebrations of, 351, 352; controversy over, 347–51; New England Suffrage Convention support of, 346–50; non-ratifying states, 360; Republican support for, 347; ST and, 346, 347, 349–52

Fifty-fourth Massachusetts Regiment, 305, 306, 318; and ST's grandson, 305, 306

Filmore, Millard, 196

Finney, Charles Grandison, 85–86, 94, 161, 204, 214, 230, 402n15

Fish, Ann Leah, 217

Fish, Catherine. *See* Stebbins, Catherine

Fish, Hamilton, 351

Fiske, Photius, 333

Folger, Ann, 93, 95; illness of, 122, 123; Robert Matthews and, 105–14, 117–19, 124–26

Folger, Benjamin, 93, 95, 105–7, 109–14, 116–26

Folger, Frances, 93, 95, 114

Folger, Reuben, 93

folklore, 20, 39; afterlife beliefs and, 55, 75, 266, 342; Christmas, 27–28; curses and, 78–80, 106; Easter, 28–29; oral traditions and, 12, 97, 225; Pinkster, 28–30, 45–46, 73–74, 77; witchcraft and, 39, 78, 399n29, 400n29. *See also* African traditions

Foner, Eric, 437n27, 447n55

Foner, Philip S., 408n1, 412n32, 413n10, 428n2

Foord, Sophia, 163

Foote, Charles, 364

Foote, Julia A., 402n18

Forbush, Bliss, 395n18

Forrest, Nathan Bedford, 343

Forten, Charlotte, 262, 421n5

Forten, James, 144, 403n22

Forten, Sarah, 129, 135

Foster, Abby Kelley. *See* Kelley Foster, Abby

Foster, George G., 90–91, 403n27

Foster, Lawrence, 416n43

Foster, Stephen, 161, 172, 177, 203, 209–10; anticlericism of, 172–73, 269–70; black male suffrage and, 348; on use of violence, 262; in Western Reserve, 231; with John Brown, Jr., 282

Fountain, Jonathan, 170

Fourierism, 158, 160, 167, 172, 193

Fowler, Eliza Gidney, 61, 78–80, 400n33

Fowler, John, 61, 78, 79

Fowler, Lorenzo N., 179

Fowler, Lydia, 250

Fowler, Mary Charlotte, 80

Fowler, Orson S., 179

Fox, George, 57

Fox, Kate, 216–17

Fox, Margaret, 216–17

Franklin, John Hope, 443n55

Franklin, Josephine, 309

Frederick Douglass' Paper (periodical), 219, 244–45, 268

Fredrickson, George M., 425n5

Freedman's Aid Society, 308

Freedman's Village, 314; ST and, 317–23, 328

Freedmen's Bureau, 308, 316, 320, 324, 327–31, 342, 367; closing of, 355, 356; proposal for, 308, 316–17, 446n44; ST and, 324, 328,

Freedmen's Hospital, 324–28, 332–33, 355; ST and, 324, 325, 326, 327–28, 332

Freedmen's Relief Association, 318, 324, 327–28, 333

Freedom's Journal (periodical), 83, 88, 130

"free love," 104, 109, 162, 273, 274, 279–80

Free Soil Party, 191–92, 211, 229, 231; John Brown and, 281; emancipation and, 242; Kansas and, 273; racism and, 231; Whigs versus, 192, 231–32, 238

Free Soil settlers, 272–73, 281

Frelinghuysen, Johannes, 77

Frelinghuysen, Theodore, 169–70

Frelinghuysen, Theodorus Jacobus, 15–16

Frelinghuysen family, 66

Fremont, Jesse Benton, 281

Fremont, John C., 281, 282, 294

Friends of Universal Human Progress, 151, 274, 277, 279, 280, 285

Gideon Band for Self-Defense, 245
Gidney, Eleazer, 60–61
Gidney, Elizabeth. *See* Elizabeth (ST's daughter)
Gidney, Eliza, 61, 78–80
Gidney, Jane, 164, 180
Gidney, Jospeph, 64
Gidney, Mary Waring, 62, 79, 80
Gidney, Solomon, 55, 60, 64–67
Gidney, Sophia, 164, 180
Gidney family, 64, 78–81
Gilbert, Joseph, 185
Gilbert, Mary ("Molly"), 181–82
Gilbert, Olive, 36, 46, 52, 62, 157, 166, 181–90; and Sarah Benson, 186–86; Moses Cleveland and, 221; conversion experience of, 182; correspondence with ST by, 175, 189, 359; as Garrisonian, 183–85, 186; hydropathy and, 176–77, 185; on Peter's sale, 62; on ST's conversion, 69–70; on ST's singing, 166–67. See also *Narrative of Sojourner Truth*
Gilfoyle, Timothy J., 403n28
Gilje, Paul, 400n5, 412n2
Gloucester, Elizabeth, 150
Gloucester, James N., 150
Gloucester, Jeremiah, 299
Gold Coast (Ghana), 9–10
Golden, Janet, 394n8
Gomez, Michael A., 382n6
Good, James L., 384n2
Goodfriend, Joyce D., 381n4
Goodman, Paul, 410n17
Gordon, Ann D., 437n36
Gorsuch, Edward, 245, 250
Graham, Isabella, 84
Graham, Sandra L., 406n25
Graham, Sylvester, 132–33, 177, 178. *See also* Grahamism
Grahamism, 158, 177, 178
Grant, Anne, 18–20, 24, 27, 384n3, 392n28
Grant, Ulysses S., 4, 342–46, 365–66; Fifteenth Amendment and, 351; ST meeting, 4, 352, 368; ST campaigns for, 343–46, 365
Gravely, William, 428n2
Grayson, Liza, 318, 328
Grayson, Peyton, 328
Great Awakening, 15, 16, 156
Great Western Revival, 85

Greeley, Horace, 204, 250, 348, 436n5; after Civil War, 331; Emancipation Proclamation and, 299; on opposition to land grants for blacks, 356–57; "Prayer of Twenty Million," 297; presidential candidacy of, 366; ST on, 366
Greenfield, Elizabeth, 249, 265, 299
Grew, Mary, 193, 249
Griffing, Charles, 231; John Brown and, 282; Burleigh and, 233; ST and, 247
Griffing, Josephine, 228–33, 238, 274, 275, 282, 287, 288, 292, 333, 325, 326, 350; during Civil War, 293–94, 308, 316–17; death of, 367; Freedmen's Bureau and, 308, 316, 324, 327, 328, 330, 350, 355, 367; in Indiana, 294–96; relocating freed people and, 327–29, 331, 332; on universal suffrage, 336; on woman's suffrage, 347
Griffiths, Julia, 215, 217, 434n49
Grimes, Leonard, 196, 265, 358–59
Grimes, R. A., 360
Grimké, Angelina, 134–36, 178, 184, 256, 262; biography of, 422n15; letters of, 402n15, writings of, 135
Grimké, Sarah, 134–36, 178, 184, 402n15
griots, 12. *See also* oral traditions
Gronowicz, Anthony, 401n5
Grower, Kathryn, 408n1
Guarneri, Carl J., 416n6
Gullah women, 338

Hackett, David G., 390n12
Hageman, Howard G., 386n8
Haiti, 89
Hale, John, 242
Halsey, Francis W., 387n15
Hambrick-Stowe, Charles E., 402n15
Hamm, Thomas D., 418n17
Hammond, Elisha, 158, 162, 174, 180
Hammond, Eliza, 162, 163, 180–81
Hansen, Debra, 410n17, 411n28
Hardenbergh, Charles, 25, 30, 32, 51
Hardenbergh, Dina Van Bergh Frelinghuysen, 16, 19, 20, 77
Hardenbergh, Elizabeth ("Betsy") (ST's mother), 10, 27, 40, 253; children of, 22, 30, 89–90; chores of, 23, 26; death of, 41; emancipation of, 32; religious beliefs of, 16–17, 21, 69–70

Louis, Joseph A., 383n19
Lovejoy, Elijah P., 136, 138
Lukins, Esther, 217, 218, 220, 229, 240, 246–47
Lundy, Benjamin, 192
Luther, Martin, 85, 235, 263
Lutz, Alma, 442n39
Lyceum speakers' movement, 2–3
lynchings, 379
Lyons, Maritcha, 131

Mabee, Carleton, 224–25, 316, 389n1, 409n13, 432n11
MacFarlane, Lisa, 385n7
MacGaffey, Wyatt, 394n13
Mack, David, 163, 175
Mack, Susan, 385n7
Magdalen Society, 91, 93, 95, 96, 98. *See also* prostitution
Mahan, Asa, 200
Malone, Ann Patton, 396n28
Malvin, John, 222, 431n2
marriage customs: African American, 45, 52–54, 71; Dutch American, 36; at Matthias Commune, 104, 110–13; at Northampton, 162; Shaker, 154
Mars, John, 207
Martin, David, 399n22
Martin, Sella, 351
Massachusetts Anti-Slavery Society, 250, 262
Matthews, George, 105
Matthews, Isabella, 101, 111
Matthews, Margaret, 100, 101, 105, 111, 118–20, 405n8
Matthews, Robert ("Matthias"), 99–126, 131, 132, 137, 148, 149, 152, 164, 178, 204, 288
Matthias Commune, 99–118, 142; communal bathing at, 102, 107, 109–10, 162; court case involving, 118–26
Mau-mau Bet. *See* Hardenbergh, Elizabeth
Maxon, Charles H., 383n19
May, Charles, 163
May, Samuel J., 172, 182–85, 201, 250, 344; biography of, 415n41; Liberty Party and, 219; memoir of, 423n22; Republican Party and, 265, 281; Underground Railroad and, 211–12
Mayer, Henry, 406n47

McBee, Alice, 416n3
McClellan, George, 313
McCurry, Stephanie, 393n38
McDowell, John, 90–92, 95, 115, 126, 408n79
McFeely, William S., 412n32, 448n72
McGraw, James R., 398n5
McKelvey, Blake, 430n23
McLaurin, Melton A., 392n28
McLoughlin, William G., 383n18
McManus, Edgar, 387n12
Mead, Luther, 147
Mears, David O., 402n16
Meinig, D. W., 437n25
Mellick, Andrew D., Jr., 385n5
Memel-Fote, Harris, 42
Merrill, Arch, 429n16
Merrill, Deahl, 427n23
Merrill, Walter M., 411n25
Merritt, John C., 65
Merritt, Joseph, 276, 298
Merritt, Phebe Hart, 276, 298, 310, 329, 333, 365
Merritt, Richard, 333
Merritt, William, 333
mesmerism, 158
Messler, Abraham, 385n7
Methodists, 15, 21, 57, 69–72, 80, 319; antislavery societies and, 200, 238–39, 260; Come-outers and, 267; history of, 70–72; Perfectionism and, 85–86, 88; Pietists and, 71, 76; Primitive, 77, 86, 96; ST and, 69, 71–72, 73–78, 80, 81, 83–88, 90–91, 92–93, 121–22, 238–39, 252, 266–68, 344, 360–63; Spiritualism and, 278; women preachers and, 87–88, 130–31, 147, 148–49, 151, 249, 260–61, 267. *See also* African Methodist Episcopal Zion Church
Mexican-U.S. War, 167, 193, 231
Michael (ST's brother), 89
Michigan Ladies Freedmen's Aid Society, 307–8
Michigan State Anti-Slavery Society, 274, 277, 280, 292–93
Mickley, Charles, 282
Middleton, Stephen, 397n45
Miller, Elizabeth Smith, 201, 212–13, 347
Miller, Mertyle Hardenbergh, 383n17
Miller, Perry, 396n35

New England Methodist Anti-Slavery Convention, 151

New England Suffrage Association, 347

New England Suffrage Convention. *See* New England Suffrage Association

New Light Awakening, 15–16

Newman, Richard, 435n3

New Org Abolitionists, 137, 139, 151–52, 168–71, 181; in Connecticut, 185; Liberty Party and, 187; in Springfield (Mass.), 206

New York Anti-Slavery Society, 115

New York City Union League: Susan B. Anthony and, 346

New York Emancipation, 24, 51, 54, 55; Peter and, 60, 67; ST and, 51, 55–57, 59–60

New York Manumission Society, 24–25, 61, 63–68, 133, 277, 396n31. *See also* American Anti-Slavery Society

New York Negro Plot, 23

nganga (priest/priestess), 12, 80, 278

Nichol, Francis D., 415n33

Nichols, Danforth, 299, 317

Niemcewicz, Julian Ursyn, 384n21

Nissenbaum, Stephen, 421n6

nkisi (sacred medicine), 12

Noah, Mordecai, 100

Non-Resistance, 4, 134, 136, 137, 139–40, 161, 245–46; after John Brown, 291–95; Margaret Garner and, 274; Garnet versus Douglass, 139–40; opposition to, 139–40, 197–199, 200, 213, 241, 245, 246; ST and, 4, 137, 200, 213–14, 242, 246, 257, 274; ST versus Douglass, 242–46

Northampton Community, 156–71, 179–81, 185, 250

North Star (periodical), 188, 215, 219

Northup, Solomon, 399n28

"No Union with Slaveholders" (AASS motto), 169, 191, 231, 283

Noyes, George Wallingford, 404n34

Noyes, John Humphrey, 104, 136–37, 401n13

Nzambi (deity), 12, 17, 31, 70, 76

nzimbu (shell money), 11

Oates, Stephen B., 428n2

Oberlin College, 134, 200, 204, 221, 222, 223, 225, 240

Oberlin Institute, 86

obituaries, for ST, 369–70, 379

O'Callaghan, E. G., 382n16, 383n17

Oickle, Alvin, 419n37

Old Org Abolitionists, 137, 168, 169, 274

Onderdonk, Benjamin, 143, 413n8

Oneida Community, 137, 416n43

oral traditions, 12, 64–65, 87, 97, 225, 277. *See also* literacy

oratory, 3, 9, 21, 62, 154, 234; "Ar'n't I a Woman?" 4, 224–25, 228–29, 258; of Douglass, 139, 243; of Charles Finney, 85–86; of Garrison, 196; parables and, 283, 270, 378–79; "Piquant Speech of a Black Bloomer," 256–57; of ST, 2, 3 87, 147, 152–54, 166–67, 189, 194, 204, 205, 225, 235–37, 242, 248–60, 264–65, 268–70, 275–77, 302, 304, 308–10, 311, 362–64; "Was Woman True?" 338–340. *See also* music

Order of the Eastern Star: ST and, 366

Paas. *See* Easter

Paine, Thomas, 125

Painter, Nell Irvin, 389n1, 415n36, 432n11

Palmer, Beverly W., 435n61

Parker, Jenny M., 429n23

Parker, Mary, 137

Parker, Theodore, 199, 251, 262–63, 269, 279, 290

Parker, William, 245

patriarchal concepts (authority), 5, 16, 19–31, 43, 47, 64, 92, 228, 247, 251–52, 286; biblical, 19, 31, 53, 88, 102, 104, 126, 149, 203, 251–52; holidays and, 27–28; Roman, 22–23; ST and, 17, 31, 40, 74–75, 79, 102, 104, 113–14, 126, 284–86. *See also* gender concepts; woman's rights movement

Patterson, John, 398n9

Patton, Abby. *See* Hutchinson, Abby

Pauli, Hertha, 392n27

Payne, Daniel A., 249, 261, 352, 435n3

Pease, Augusta Leggett: on ST, 308, 366–67

Pelagianism, 85

Pell, Julia, 133

Pennington, J. W. C., 196, 252, 258

Pennsylvania Freeman (periodical), 174, 189, 245, 248

Pentecost, 5, 28–29, 73; ST and, 73–77, 148–49, 204. *See also* Pinkster

Perfectionism, 46–47, 85–88, 90, 109; and black spirituality, 93, 96–97, 100; Come-outers and, 159–60; "doctrine of security" in, 104; Garrison and, 136, 192; Sylvester Graham and, 178; hydropathy and, 178; marriage customs and, 104; Millerites and, 153; Pietists and, 15; Presbyterians and, 100; "saints" of, 93–95; Shaker, 155; slavery and, 86, 96; ST and, 46–47, 78, 85–86, 88, 90, 91, 96, 136, 137, 152, 153, 182, 302; Unitarians and, 182; woman's suffrage and, 349–50

Perkins, Frances, 319

Perry, Lewis, 408n2

Peter (ST's son), 27, 51, 59, 141–47, 277; adolescence of, 141–43; aliases of, 142; court cases involving, 62–68, 78, 142, 145, 277; disappearance at sea of, 146–47, 359, 413n16; education of, 81; Fowler's abuse of, 67, 78–79; illegal sale of, 60–61; as seaman, 143–46

Peter (ST's brother), 28, 30

Peters, John L., 401n13

Peterson, Carla, 409n8

Philadelphia Loyalist Convention, 341

Phillips, Anne, 209

Phillips, Wendell, 136, 161, 172, 194, 199, 208, 322, 331; as AASS president, 335, 348; biographies of, 411n24, 443n46; Anthony Burns and, 262, 263; on black male suffrage, 335–36, 341, 348; on Douglass, 244; on Exodusters, 373; on land grants for freed people, 356; and Stanton, 337, 348; on ST, 268–69; threats against, 293; on universal suffrage, 336, 340, 341; on U.S. Constitution, 194; on woman's rights, 203, 205, 335–37

Phoenix Literary Society, 130

phrenology, 179

Pierce, Franklin, 261, 262, 273

Pierson, Elijah, 90, 91, 93–97, 149, 217; Mrs. Bolton and, 98–99; death of, 116–17, 120; Ann Folger and, 109–11, 114; Charles Laisdell and, 111; Robert Matthews and, 101–3, 105–7, 113

Pierson, Elizabeth, 116

Pierson, Michael D., 427n28

Pierson, Sarah, 93–95, 120

Pietists, 15–16, 31, 170; baptism for, 18–19, 29; Christmas for, 27; family worship by, 20–22; Methodists and, 71, 76; Spiritualism and, 278; visionary, 77, 385n7. *See also* Dutch Reformed Church

Pillsbury, Parker, 2–4, 161, 197, 220, 240, 273; *Acts of the Anti-slavery Apostles,* 412n32; biographies of, 418n15, 441n26; on black male suffrage, 341; during Civil War, 293–94; Douglass and, 242; Free Soil Party and, 232; in Ohio, 233, 234–36, 238–39, 240; on Republican Party, 283, 292; *Revolution* and, 342; speaking style of, 234–35; Spiritualism and, 279; ST and, 2, 3, 236–39; on ST's illness, 369; Walker and, 233–34; on woman's rights, 223–24

Pinkerton, Allan, 290

Pinkster, 28–30, 45–46, 73–75, 77, 204

Piwonka, Ruth, 387n12

Pope-Hennessy, James, 381n2

Portuguese colonies, 10–12

Post, Amy, 173, 205, 214–15, 229, 274, 326, 327, 330, 332, 333, 347, 349, 350; on Freedman's Village, 319; ST and, 214, 215, 217, 221, 272, 313, 345, 349, 350, 359, 367, 370, 378; Spiritualism and, 217; on universal suffrage, 336

Post, Isaac, 214–15, 217, 218, 272, 274, 330; ST and, 3, 349, 370

Powell, Aaron, 210, 265, 268, 273; AERA and, 340; as editor of *National Anti-Slavery Standard,* 333, 335; and support for land grants for freed people, 356–57; memoir of, 428n11

Powell, F. P., 3

Powell, William P., 144, 145, 194

predestination, 85

Prentice, George W., 428n2

Presbyterians, 15, 86, 88, 130; African, 83; Ohioan, 234; Perfectionist, 100

Prigg v. Pennsylvania, 138

Prime, Nathaniel S., 414n29

Principles of Nature, Her Divine Revelations (Davis), 160

Prior, Margaret, 217

Progressive Friends, 151, 209, 251, 274–75, 285, 293, 296, 343

prostitution, 82, 90–92, 98–99, 106, 109,

Stone, William Leete, 88, 98, 102, 111; Benjamin Folger and, 120, 122; Greeley and, 204; *Matthias and His Impostures,* 124, 125, 393n46; racist views of, 115–16, 123

Story, William Wetmore, 301

Stowe, Harriet Beecher, 176, 198, 245; biography of, 421n5; depictions of ST by, 245, 302, 306, 311; *Dred, A Tale of the Dismal Swamp,* 271, 438n50; essay on ST by, 187, 224, 271, 301–3, 306, 444n9; Harriet Jacobs and, 271, 302; *Narrative of Sojourner Truth* and, 271, 274, 285, 311, 436n20, 438n50; *Uncle Tom's Cabin,* 198, 266, 291, 362; ST on, 302, 306; woman's rights and, 302; writing techniques of, 228, 301

Stowell, Martin, 262, 263

St. Phillips Episcopal Church, 115, 130, 132

Strain, T. W., 285; ST and, 284–86

Strane, Susan, 415n32

Strickland, William, 389n5

Strother, Horatio T., 409n4

Stuart, Reed, 378

Stuckey, Sterling, 409n7

Styles, Matthew, 67

suffrage. *See* universal suffrage

Sullivan, George Washington, 165

Sumner, Charles, 199, 250, 313, 316, 368

Sunderland, LaRoy, 279

Swedenborgians, 104, 160, 278, 405n17

Swift, David E., 419n31

Swisshelm, Jane, 223–24, 226–28, 313

Sylvester, Nathaniel Bartlett, 394n12

Tabernacle. *See* Broadway Tabernacle

Taney, Roger, 183, 283

Tanis, James, 383n18

Tappan, Arthur, 83, 86, 88, 137–38, 156; anti-abolition riots and, 115, 116; biography of, 404n30; Magdalen Society and, 91

Tappan, Lewis, 86, 88, 115, 136–38, 156, 168, 192, 241, 260

Taylor, Clare, 428n3

Taylor, George W., 343

Taylor, Zachary, 193, 231

temperance movement, 4, 150–51; William Wells Brown and, 360; hydropathy and, 178; Samuel J. May and, 182; ST's work in, 151, 250–54, 371, 374; woman's rights and, 218, 256. *See also* alcohol

Tennant, Gilbert, 15

Terborg-Penn, Rosalyn, 432n11

Teubal, Savina J., 394n6

Texas, 169, 231

Thayer, Abijah W., 171, 187

Thomas, Robert D., 401n13

Thomas (ST's husband), 45, 51, 54, 56, 71, 82, 276

Thompson, Elizabeth, 112–13

Thompson, E. P., 399n26

Thompson, George, 123, 198–99; on Julia Griffiths, 215; Spiritualism and, 217; Springfield (Mass.) riot and, 207–9; ST and, 206–11; threats against, 207

Thompson, Robert Farris, 394n13

Thoreau, Henry David, 263

Thornbrough, Emma Lou, 442n30

Thornton, John K., 382n7

Tiedemann, Joseph, 384n21

Tilman, Levin, 254

Tilton, Elizabeth, 350

Tilton, Theodore, 299, 341, 350, 366

Titus, Esther, 217, 319

Titus, Frances, 217, 276, and ST, 300, 365, 367, 369, 370, 372–74, 378

Titus, Richard, 276

tobacco, 3, 26, 37, 107, 168, 233, 236; health concerns with, 103, 177; religious concerns with, 107, 154–55; ST's relinquishing of, 171, 179, 345–46

Tomkins, Fred, 321–22, 442n32

Tompkins, Daniel, 57

Torrey, Charles, 170

Totau dance, 45, 46

Train, George Francis, 341–43, 345, 348

transcendentalism, 154, 158

Treat, Joseph, 219–20

Tremont Temple (Hall), 171, 265, 293, 299, 360

trickster stories, 39

Trinity, Holy, 29

Tubman, Harriet, 89, 197–98, 212, 284, 350; biographies of, 426nn17–18, 446n35; on John Brown, 291; during Civil War, 305–6; ST and, 198, 446n35; threats against, 284

Tucker, A. W., 328

Turner, Benjamin, 356

Turner, Henry M., 299

Turner, Nat, 132, 139, 292

Waring, Mary, 64

Waring, Sarah ("Sally"). *See* Dumont, Sarah

Waring, Solomon, 35

Washington, Booker T., 53, 394n5

Washington, George, 14, 16, 24, 25, 84, 225

Washington, Madison, 138, 139

Washington, Martha, 317

Washington, Mary Simpson, 84

Washington Woman's Suffrage Association, 347

"Was Woman True?" speech (1867), 338–40

Water Cure Journal, 175, 188

Watkins, William, 281

Watkins Harper, Frances Ellen, 197, 265, 273, 274, 281, 284, 316; AERA and, 335, 336, 338; background of, 286; black male suffrage and, 347, 348; marriage of, 293; ST and, 273, 274, 275, 277, 281, 286, 316, 333; universal suffrage and, 338

Watson, Nigel, 402n19

Watts, E. S., 389n4

Watts, Isaac, 320

Webb, James Watson, 88, 116, 120

Webb, Thomas, 70

Webster, Daniel, 192, 194, 250

Webster, Delia, 186, 198, 425n35

"weevil in the wheat" (parable), 283

Weiss, Harry B., 420n1

Weld, Angelina. *See* Grimké, Angelina

Weld, Theodore, 134, 136, 178, 230, 284

Wellman, Judith, 429n15, 430n24

Wells, Ida B., 379

Werner, M. R., 407n64

Wesley, John, 77, 85, 278

Wesley (ST's grandson), 164, 250, 364, 418n21, 453n22

Wesleyan Connection, 200

Wesselhoeft, Robert, 175–77

Westbrook, Frederick E., 397n42

Western Anti-Slavery Society, 174, 197, 214, 217, 229, 231–32, 242, 244, 274, 281

western emigration, 241, 259, 272–74, 355–61; division among blacks, 362, Exodusters and, 371–74; ST and, 258–59, 327, 328, 330–33, 341, 355–58, 361–63, 364, 365, 366–68, 373, 374. *See also* African colonization

Western, Henry M., 119, 122–24

West Indian Emancipation, 169, 196; ST and, 265, 365

Weston, Anne, 209, 215

Weston sisters, 134, 137

Whatcoat, Richard, 70

Whig Party, 8, 57, 169–70, 192, 204, 208, 261; Federalists and, 67, 156; Free Soilers and, 192, 231–32, 238; Northampton and, 156; Unitarians and, 82

Whipple, George, 330

White, Deborah Gray, 389n4

White, Ellen, 178

White, Graham, 412n3

White, James, 178

White, Shane, 388n16, 412n3

White, William C., 65

Whiteaker, Larry, 400n4

Whitefield, George, 70

Whiting, Lucy, 105, 122, 126, 147–48, 250

Whiting, Perez, 105, 122, 126, 148, 250

Whitman, Walt, 10, 288, 307, 442n37

Whitsuntide. *See* Pentecost

Whittier, John Greenleaf, 134, 171, 192, 272–73, 273, 438n1

Whole World Temperance Meeting, 252; ST speech at, 252–53

Wigger, John H., 398n6

Wilbur, Julia, 310, 317, 323, 330–31

Wilentz, Sean, 400n3

Wilkins, Frederick ("Shadrach"), 208, 262

Williams, Delores, 394n6

Williams, Edwin, 408n2

Williams, Peter, Jr., 130, 143, 144, 146

Williams, Peter, Sr., 89, 143

Williams-Myers, A. J., 386n11

"Willie" (ST's grandson), 364, 369, 370

Willis, Henry, 274, 328

Williston, John P., 222

Wills, David W., 435n3

Wilmore, Gayraud S., 384n22

Wilmot, David, 297

Wilson, Carol, 395n28

Wilson, Harriet, 392n28

Wilson, Henry, 199, 250; black male suffrage and, 347, 348

Wilson, Kate de Normandie, 417n8

Wilson, Mary, 364

Wilson, William, 169

Wilson, William E., 442n30

Winch, Julie, 403n22

witchcraft, 39, 78, 399n29, 400n29. *See also* folklore

Wollstonecraft, Mary, 125, 408n76

womanist consciousness, vii, 5, 134–35, 159, 180–81,183, 184, 187, 228; ST and, 92, 126, 181, 186–87, 255–57, 259, 319, 325, 326, 328–30, 332–33, 338, 339–40, 353–54, 357–58, 359

Woman's Anti-Slavery Conventions. *See* Woman's National Anti-Slavery, Women's Conventions

Woman's Journal, 353

Woman's Rights Conventions, 201–5, 213, 214, 217, 222–29, 256–58, 261–62, 370, 451n39

woman's rights movement, 4, 334–43, 346–54; Abolitionists and, 132, 136–37, 173, 187, 201–4, 213, 223–24, 258, 334, 345; African American women and, 135, 136, 137, 224–25, 334, 335, 336, 337, 341, 347, 348; black male suffrage versus, 218, 335–42, 346–52; bloomers and, 204, 212, 232, 250, 253, 256; changes in, 353; Douglass and, 201, 203, 205, 336; and exercising the franchise, 353–54; ST and, 201–5, 213, 218, 224, 226–29, 247, 302, 334–42, 347, 353–54, 358, 366, 368, 370; Maria Stewart and, 132; suffrage associations in, 340, 347–50, 353, 358, 365;

temperance and, 218, 256; utopianism and, 185–86. *See also* gender concepts

Woman's Temperance Meeting, 250

Wood, Fernando, 306, 307

Woodson, Carter G., 438n49

Worden, Jean D., 384n3, 386n9, 386n11

Worden, Nigel, 384n3

work songs, 39, 338

World Anti-Slavery Convention, 137

Wright, Conrad, 423n21, 423n22

Wright, David, 213

Wright, Frances, 6, 172

Wright, Henry C., 181, 197, 240, 265, 273, 274, 275, 293–94

Wright, Martha Coffin, 213, 336, 342

Wright, Theodore, 83, 130

Wyatt-Brown, Bertram, 402n17

Wykoff Hanging Bill, 375

Wyman, Lillie Buffum Chace, 417n12

Yacovone, Donald, 415n41

Yellin, Jean F., 403n26, 422n19

Yerrinton, James M., 187, 204, 250

Young, Edward, 63, 65, 277

Zacharias, Lawrence, 414n23

Zilversmit, Arthur, 394n1

Zion Church. *See* African Methodist Episcopal Zion Church

Zion Hill Kingdom. *See* Matthias Commune

Zone (whaling ship), 144–46, 413n12